Facilities Economics

Published by Building Economics Bureau Ltd
Kings House, 32-40 Widmore Road, Bromley, Kent BR1 1RY, UK
Tel: +44 (0) 20 8464 5418 Fax: +44 (0) 20 8313 3363
E-mail: info@beb.co.uk
Website: www.beb.co.uk

Building Economics Bureau Ltd
Kings House
32-40 Widmore Road
Bromley
Kent BR1 1RY
Tel: +44 (0) 20 8464 5418
Fax: +44 (0) 20 8313 3363

Second Edition: 2003

ISBN: 0 904237 39 7

Editor-in-chief Bernard Williams FRICS
Managing Editor Geoff Parsons MSc BSc IRRV MIMgt TEFL
Cover design and typeset by VRB Marketing and John Laker BSc (Hons)
Graphics design and typeset by John Laker BSc (Hons) and Mark Bennett
Transcriber Sue Morton
Printed in the UK by Anthony Rowe Ltd

Acknowledgments
The editors are grateful to the many business colleagues and members of Bernard Williams Associates who have offered helpful advice and constructive criticism during the preparation of this publication.

The Editor

*The editor-in-chief, **Bernard Williams**, wrote the original 'Premises Audits' book in 1986 and was principal author and editor-in-chief of the original UK and EU versions of 'Facilities Economics'. He is an external examiner to the Masters Facilities Management degree course at Sheffield-Hallam University and to the Honours Degree in Facilities Management at the Institute of Technology in Tralee in the Republic of Ireland. He writes and lectures extensively on all aspects of facilities and building economics and is author/co-author of a number of standard reference works including:*

- *An Introduction to Benchmarking Facilities*

- *Cost-effective Facilities*

- *Whole-life Economics of Building Services*

- *Property Development Feasibility Tables*

- *Property Expert's Guide to VAT*

- *Development Grants and Other Assistance*

- *Building and Development Economics in the EU (Financial Times Management reports).*

*He was founder partner in 1969 of **Bernard Williams Associates** – a firm of Chartered Surveyors specialising in Facilities and Building Economics offering comprehensive advice, on an international stage, on all financial and management aspects of providing and using land, buildings and business support services*

BWA now has three divisions each specialising in particular aspects of their work – Facilities Consultancy, Project Services and Building Cost Consultancy and an extensive client base of national and multi-national corporations as well as Central government and Local Authorities; each division boasts a broad range of internationally prestigious commissions and projects.

As well as their mainstream activities BWA have specialists in property and facilities taxation and development grants and assistance and have an ongoing programme of research and development.

In the field of facilities management BWA have what is believed to be Europe's largest independently audited database of facilities costs and data, all analysed in accordance with set rules of classification and measurement.

Bernard retired from the partnership in 2002 but remains as a consultant to the practice with special responsibility for development and marketing of the 'Frisque' suite of facilities decision support programs.

Specialist Contributors

The author is very grateful to the eminent professionals who contributed specialist knowledge and expertise in respect of certain subject areas covered in the text, viz:

Helen Beveridge *MIOSH AMIEMgt is a Senior Environmental Consultant with GIBB Ltd. Helen has a broad range of experience on the environmental issues related to facilities management in Europe. Particular experience of waste management covers domestic, commercial and industrial wastes - from source through management and treatment options to disposal.*

Andrew Boorman *BSc (Hons) Hort. Senior Lecturer in Landscape Management, Writtle College. Course Manager for the College's MSc in Landscape and Amenity Management. Andrew is experienced in commercial and amenity horticulture, including interior landscaping in Europe and Australasia. Currently working on human-plant interactions and benefits of plants outdoors and inside.*

Tony Clarke *MHort. Senior Lecturer in Landscape Management and Industrial Liaison Officer, Writtle College. Active member of the British Association of Landscape Industries (BALI). Main experiences are in landscape and garden construction and garden design. Works closely with the landscape industry in the London area and has extensive contacts across Europe.*

Professor Peter Cooke *is Head of the Centre for Automotive Industries Management at Nottingham Business School in the United Kingdom. Peter spent twenty years in the motor industry. He is the author of eight books on fleet management, and many widely recognised industry studies. His research interests include euro pricing for the automotive industry.*

Julie Corps *MA BSc (Hons) MRICS has worked on this publication and its EU companion volume and is a valuer currently working with Jones Lang LaSalle. Julie has carried out extensive research into valuation methodology and practice in the European context.*

Dr Peter Harris *is Managing Director of Cheriton Technology Management Ltd, an independent research consultant-publisher in the field of energy efficiency and energy management. Peter has more than 25 years experience in energy efficiency in industry and buildings. He is author of four books, has published many articles on energy management technique and has personally delivered training based on these to more than 2,000 people in Europe.*

Alan Kell *MSc BSc is one of Europe's leading public and private sector consultants on the impact of technological, environmental and social change upon the design and use of buildings. Alan is Managing Director of I & I limited and, until recently, the Executive Director of the European Intelligent Building Group. He chairs the new MSc in Intelligent Buildings at the University of Reading.*

John Lane *C Eng MIEE is Director of the Infrastructure Division at Pagoda Consulting Ltd . John specialises in the design and project management of IT infrastructure for new office buildings, call centres, dealing rooms, data centres and web co-location sites.*

Dr Norman Lowe *is a waste water consultant who specialises in realising the best possible value for money spent. He has represented Water UK in European discussions. Prior to setting up as a consultant Norman was Chief Scientist for Welsh Water where he had been for 23 years.*

Cathy Nolan *BSc Grad BIP OH and F Grad Dip Occ Hyg MIOSH MAIOH is Principal Health and Safety Consultant for LAWGIBB and has 12 years experience in health and safety auditing and integrated environmental and health and safety management. Kathy has worked with manufacturing, engineering, chemical, food and beverage industries as well as educational and health care institutions in the UK, Europe and Australasia.*

Geoff Parsons *MSc BSc IRRV MIMgt TEFL is a valuer and estates surveyor by profession and, having spent about 30 years in higher education, is now a freelance author and tutor. He has contributed to several books on property taxation, land policy, development and facilities management. Currently, Geoff is editing a new edition of The Glossary of Property Terms on behalf of The Estates Gazette*

Ian M. Smith *is a consultant in strategic information management: this comprises reprographics, printing, conventional and electronic documentation production, storage and distribution; enterprise output audits and knowledge audits; and processes for the development of a comprehensive strategy for document and knowledge management within an organisation.*

Tony Thomson *MSc FBIFM became aware of the impact of space while working with Hewlett-Packard in the 1970's. Following 10 years as their Property and Facilities Manager Tony joined DEGW where he carries out consulting work for international clients specialising in workplace innovation. Tony is a regular conference presenter on strategic space planning issues.*

Fiona Wishlade *MA LLM is a Senior Research Fellow in the European Policies Research Centre at the University of Strathclyde in Glasgow. She has led and managed a number of research projects on the regional policies of different countries, and on the regional and competition policies of the European Union; Fiona has published widely in these and adjacent policy areas.*

Contents

Contents

Contents

Contents

Introduction

Such has been the pace of change of business and the supporting technologies in the eight years since the First Edition of Facilities Economics was published that this second edition has involved a substantial re-write.

In those eight years the fledgling facilities management industry has continued to get wiser beyond its years. The economic and management principles and techniques it needs to continue its rapid rate of development have had to be thoroughly re-visited and, where necessary, updated by the author. Similarly, there have been many changes to the law, particularly as a result of the developments in EU law - much of this has been indicated within the text by direct reference to EU directives etc or, more substantially, by reference to UK law which embodies EU law.

Also, in this edition the authors have developed the scope of value management in several parts of the text. In doing so they recognise the position that the discipline plays within facilities economics. They are, therefore particularly proud to quote the Institute of Value Management:

> *"The Institute of Value Management is pleased to support this important contribution to Facilities Management, and approves the text insofar as it relates to Value Management. Whilst recognising the breadth of skills required in an effective Facilities Manager it acknowledges the importance of VM in making a critical difference. It explains the concept of VM and the activities involved in a pragmatic and effective way."*

Fortunately facilities management professionals have not been standing still either over this intervening period having extended their knowledge base both in terms of new technologies (many the result of their own research and development activities) and through consulting on a broader international platform.

So, it was a case of 'another dime another dollar' as the author's initial response to considerable demand for a new edition moved quickly and inevitably from minor tinkering into the realms of wholescale re-vamping.

The new members of the audience addressed by this edition may not thus far have been exposed to the author's concept of what 'facilities economics' is all about, so a brief resume of the definition of the term is relevant here.

Adam Smith, in his tome 'The Wealth of Nations', described economics as being about man's efforts to create wealth. The authors of 'Facilities Economics' have linked this viewpoint to the modern concept of facilities in defining 'facilities economics' as 'the study of man's efforts to create wealth through the provision, use and management of facilities'.

This broad description encapsulates the interests of both provider and user and takes a lead from the author's earlier definition of 'building economics': 'the study of man's efforts to create wealth by building'. In that definition, 'building economics' embraces 'all the financial and management aspects of providing and using land and buildings'. As such it is concerned with the wealth created by any or all of developer, builder, financier, consultant, user and investor as a consequence of their involvement with a building at one stage or another in its life-cycle.

'Building economics' is an amalgam of the principal ingredients of the surveying disciplines – ie valuation, cost control, development, investment and property management – and is concerned with their influence on the performance and profitability generated throughout the premises life-cycle from inception to demolition. But 'facilities economics' **embraces** *building economics, supplementing the 'built premises' component with non-premises business support services such as 'security', 'catering', 'office services' and ICT, thereby substantially extending the consideration of the interface between non-core and core business activity.*

The concept of core and non-core activities and the full gamut of services potentially falling within the definition of facilities is discussed at length in the chapters of 'Facilities Economics'. Suffice here to say that 'facilities economics', by the authors' definition, is so widely drawn as to bring into question whether it is reasonable for an individual who has not received a thorough grounding across the whole spectrum of the discipline to take full responsibility for decisions made in the course of its application.

Of course, some individuals holding the post of 'facilities manager' may survive on a knowledge of office services and simple running and maintenance applications and may never have to concern themselves with the wider range of technologies and disciplines discussed in this text.

On the other hand the building industry, with its maintenance and services sub-sets, does have an army of highly trained specialists who yet have absolutely no idea of the contribution made by a building and its operational management to the profitability, efficiency and satisfaction of its occupiers.

And what about investors and their real estate advisors who value portfolios by reference to historic comparables flawed by a misconception of building quality and by the incestuous and ill-informed conventional wisdom prevailing in this market sector?

Just about every one of the players on the 'facilities economics' stage has a unilateral view of its implications whereas 'facilities economics' as a discipline is a concept which desperately needs to be tackled holistically.

The first edition of 'Facilities Economics' sought to achieve just this and this new edition continues and expands on this overriding philosophy.

There is a new adjective (not to be found in any dictionary) culled by the author to describe the approach to the subject adopted in this book: the word is 'pragademic', derived from two words - pragmatic and academic.

The 'pragademic' approach, it is suggested, is one that 'cuts off the corners' to reach a valid solution as quickly and cheaply as possible - but only when the underlying theory of the problem is properly understood, not before.

A pragmatic solution deriving from an academic base is 'pragademic' (it could be 'acedamatic' but that does not roll off the tongue so easily!) and the reader should find this approach pervading every chapter.

This volume provides over sixty Chapters on the economics of facilities divided into six Parts (with each containing one or more of the twelve Sections), namely:

A   Facilities and their Management

            1 Facilities and the corporate plan

            2 Facilities management

B   Premises

            3 Commercial real estate

            4 Space management

            5 Premises operating services

            6 Fitting-out and alterations

C   Support Services

            7 Business support services

            8 Staff support services

D   Relocation and Development

            9 Relocation

            10 The development option

E   Taxation

            11 Taxation considerations

F   The Facilities Audit

            12 Facilities auditing process

*Each Section is divided into its constituent Chapters and the last two Parts give Appendices and Indexes respectively. The latter Part contains the Amplified Contents Index (giving, in effect, **a précis of each chapter**) and the Key Word Index. The penultimate Part contains Tables (Enactments and Standards Guidelines), lists of Professional Associations and Educational and Research Institutions, and explanations of the Abbreviations used in the text.*

The nature of facilities, their management and their interaction with core business is, quite rightly, addressed right at the beginning in Part A. This underwrites the underlying theme in the text that follows i.e. that there is a dynamic admixture of value, cost, time and quality attendant upon every facet of every facilities service. The core of the text, however, is in the work of day-to-day operations, as developed in the two

Parts B and C dealing with Premises and Support Services. Once the organisation needs more, or less, or different space, Part D becomes important, although Part B may feature in the decision-making. Part E, on Taxation, demonstrates how agile facilities managers need to be in almost every aspect of facilities work if optimum economic performance is to be achieved while, Part F explains the importance of constant overview of processes and achievements.

PART A

Facilities and their Management

Section 1

Facilities and the Corporate Plan

1.1   THE SCOPE OF FACILITIES

Introduction

This chapter deals with the meaning and scope of facilities and the critical link between facilities performance and core business efficiency.

The role of the facilities policy in forging this link is explained together with the theoretical distinction between 'core' and 'non-core' business activities.

1.1.1 DEFINITIONS

Facilities

The term 'facilities' in a business context is defined here as 'the premises and services required to accommodate and facilitate business activity'.

Facilities management

Facilities management is defined here as 'the process by which the premises and services required to support core business activities are identified, specified, procured and delivered'.

In its most developed and effective form facilities management in fact has three facets - sponsorship, intelligence and services management (Fig. 1.1.A).

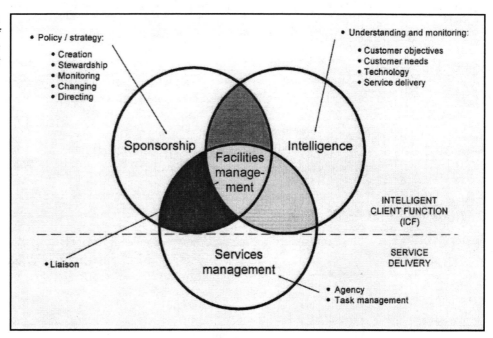

Fig. 1.1.A
Three facets of facilities management

All facilities operations involve all three facets; although services management is capable of being carried out by either contractors or in-house staff - often a mixture of both - the sponsorship and intelligence must always, by definition, belong exclusively in-house.

The Intelligent Client Function (ICF)

The 'sponsorship' and 'intelligence' facets of facilities management together form what is now commonly known as the 'Intelligent (or Informed) Client Function' (ICF).

The ICF is normally an in-house role, one which commonly (but not exclusively) gets separately identified with the advent of the externalisation, or outsourcing, of the directive management of facilities services. The way this role is structured, resourced and empowered will have a massive impact on the value of the services provided in terms of their contribution to core business efficiency. This significant contribution is further discussed in greater detail elsewhere in the text; in particular Chapters 2.1.2 and 2.2.4 both expand on the role of the ICF in the facilities value management process.

Sponsorship

Facilities sponsorship is the essence of the Intelligent/Informed Client Function (ICF); it emerges more clearly as a smaller - but critical - separately identifiable function as responsibility for facilities service management is devolved from in-house to external resources. In the less devolved, hybrid models the sponsorship role is not usually a separate function other than for capital projects where it is well established.

The term sponsorship in respect of facilities implies the ownership of responsibility for the facilities provision, the stewardship of the organisation's policy for the allocation of resources for the accommodation and services required to facilitate corporate objectives.

Intelligence

The 'intelligence' facet is actually both introspective and outward looking: introspective as the eyes and ears of the facilities management function with regard to core business needs and outward-looking in respect of the effectiveness of service delivery (see below) and new techniques and technology available in its support.

Services management

It is most important to understand clearly the distinction between the line management of a particular service or task, such as 'cleaning' or 'distribution', and the overall direction and co-ordination of all the services which is defined here as 'facilities services management'. Both the individual services and the facilities services management contribute to facilities services delivery but the master/servant relationships via which this is effected are many and varied, as are their economic implications. Again, this third and equally important facet of facilities management is discussed at greater length in Chapter 2.1.2.

Liaison/contract management

The responsibility for making the three facets gel together is with the ICF. A critical point of contact is the liaison between the facilities sponsor and the facilities services manager, ie the managing agent or contractor responsible for co-ordinating the work of the task contractors or in-house providers.

This liaison role will usually take the form of 'contract management' but only where the facilities services manager has a contract of service with the sponsor's organisation. Where any of the services tasks are carried out in-house an appropriate term to use in place of 'contract manager' might be 'services liaison manager', although the quasi-contractual nature of in-house task service-level agreements could reasonably accommodate the term 'contract management' in respect of the liaison function.

For the sake of absolute clarity the term 'principal contract management' is used here in connection with the operation of the contract of the managing agent or contractor and the term 'facilities services management' to cover the direction and co-ordination of the services task providers. Another aspect of liaison for the sponsor to address is, of course, that with other internal departments, eg finance.

However, before reviewing further the critical inter-relationships of the three facets of facilities management it is first necessary to consider the scope of facilities services and the way that they relate to corporate objectives and impact upon the bottom line - be that drawn in terms of profit, efficiency or, more likely, both.

1.1.2 SERVICES MANAGEMENT STRUCTURE

There is no absolute consensus as to what activities facilities management should or should not embrace. Even if there were, there would never be universal agreement as to which department, individual or discipline should have the overall responsibility for, and control of, the generic cost centres.

Even old-established functions like personnel, finance, sales and marketing frequently turn up in different titles, regimes and hierarchical structures and facilities management itself, unless - exceptionally - holding down a discrete upper management position, may be found reporting to any of these and other disciplines or a combination thereof. The most broadly drawn facilities management division might be as Fig. 1.1.B which defines scope and cost centres rather than dynamic function.

Fig. 1.1.B
Broadly drawn scope of facilities management

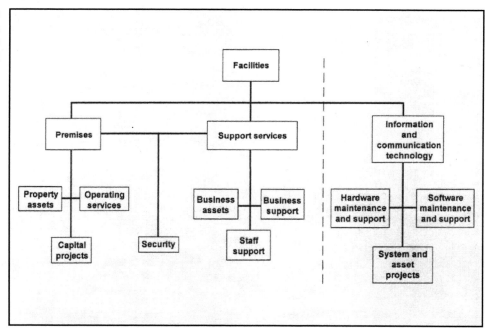

Note that information and communication technology (ICT) is shown as an 'optional' component of the facilities hierarchy.

In practice it is common for the ICT facilities management and general facilities management to co-exist rather than come under one level of middle management. For the purposes of this text, however, ICT has been treated as one of the 'business support services' components of facilities (see Chapter 7.5). Nevertheless such treatment is not in any way to imply that its considerable significance in the scheme of things is other than as depicted in Fig. 1.1.B.

1.1.3 FACILITIES COST CENTRES

Within each of these management divisions costs might be collected under the following cost centres - not an exhaustive list but representing those most commonly found in practice.

Facilities management

- administrative and technical staff, ie 'white collar' workers (both within the Intelligent Client Function and in service delivery)
- facilities management consultants (other than those providing specialist out-source services), eg space planning, maintenance management
- service charge component (see below).

Premises

Property
- rent
- property taxes
- insurance
- depreciation
- service charge component
- projects.

Design
- supervision
- cost control.

Operating costs
- maintenance of fabric
- maintenance of services
- cleaning/housekeeping
- energy
- water and sewerage
- waste disposal
- internal landscaping
- external landscaping
- service charge component (see below).

Support services

Security
- reception
- guarding and security systems.

Staff support
- catering
- sports/social and trade union facilities
- health, safety and welfare.

Business support
- reception/porters/messengers
- storage/archiving
- information and communications systems
- data cabling support
- office furniture
- stationery, printing and reprographics
- motor transport
- disaster recovery.

Information and communication technology (ICT)

Hardware
- equipment
- data cabling
- maintenance and support

Software
- discs

- programs
- maintenance and support
Systems
- projects

Service charges

Service charges, which are described in more detail in Chapter 3.3, occur on leasehold properties and are in respect of facilities and services procured on behalf of tenants by the landlord; in most cases they are normally re-chargeable to the tenant in accordance with the terms of the lease.

Typically service charges will comprise such items as repairs to the fabric, maintenance of common services, cleaning of common areas such as foyer, staircases etc. It is important that costs of these re-chargeable items plus any charges in respect of management, should be analysed into the appropriate facilities cost centres as if they were directly incurred by the tenants on their own behalf. This is to facilitate benchmarking against costs and performance of facilities in owner/occupation regimes.

The significance of a broad scope

The argument in favour of drawing the management of facilities services as (or nearly as) widely as depicted above is that:

- it embraces the whole concept
- it provides a bigger cost-base in support of an appropriate calibre of management.

Against the case is the obviously uneasy mixture of the highly technical aspects of building design and management under Premises and the predominantly administrative character of much of Support Services activity. There is of course no reason why management cannot cope with both aspects but the cultural difficulties which often exist between technical and administrative employees may cause internal rivalries with counter-productive consequences.

Historically, non-technically skilled administrators have tended to rise above professionally qualified specialists on the management ladder particularly in government services. Given the particularly complex and critical inter-relationship between premises and their occupants such a tendency towards favouring the non-technological in any facilities management structure needs to be the subject of careful appraisal in the context of individual personnel, their experience and management capabilities.

1.1.4 THE FACILITIES MISSION

Every department within an organisation should have a mission statement in support of the main business objective. A mission statement should always relate to the corporate goal and describe the intentions of the facilities providers in pursuit of their own supportive contribution. A random example of a facilities mission statement is:

> 'to provide and maintain accommodation and support services to the standards required to facilitate and promote the success of the business with minimum risk to efficiency and personal safety, with pro-active financial control and asset management, and to be constantly prepared for change'.

This is by no means a perfect example, and the reason it has been used is simply to emphasise the fact that because a mission statement, per se, is unenforceable in contract terms, tightness of wording is therefore not of any great consequence.

Whether the mission statement is in the form of a 'charter' within an 'internal market' arrangement as described in Chapter 1.2.3 or whether it is merely internal to the facilities management department is not important. Its very existence in a dedicated group will focus minds and effort on quality of provision, which must be to the good.

1.1.5 FACILITIES AND THE CORPORATE PLAN

The relationship between the activities of facilities management and the business performance requirements is expressed theoretically in Figs.1.1.C and 1.1.F.

Fig. 1.1.C tracks the connection between the premises strand of facilities and the business plan. It emphasises the fact that the way in which the operational requirements are accommodated should be directed by a 'premises policy'.

Fig. 1.1.C
Facilities and the corporate plan - premises policy

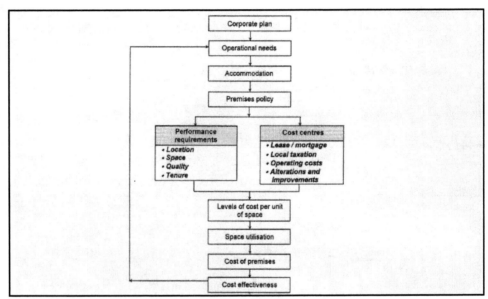

The 'premises policy' should be the outcome of a formal value management process rather than a hit-and-miss compilation of personal prejudices and/or the conventional wisdom. The principles and processes of 'value management', discussed in greater depth in Chapter 2.2, are central to the challenge facing facilities managers when trying to optimise their contribution to business success.

The premises policy

This should determine the objectives for accommodation in terms of:

- location
- quality
- performance
- tenure
- space
- management
- service delivery
- cost
- risk.

The premises policy should be in writing and formally accepted by the Board of Management. It should envisage and state the principal strategy in pursuit of the mission and identify alternative strategies and sub-strategies to deal with changes in business requirements.

For instance, a cornerstone of a company's premises policy might be to come together from several sites into one owner-occupied building in a principal city within, say, seven years. The principal property strategy concerning acquisition and disposal would therefore be to avoid commitments to new long leases whilst rationalising use of existing space to facilitate disposal of the least marketable assets. A sub-strategy in the event of temporary unforeseen reductions in staff numbers might involve 'mothballing' the least efficient space in terms of operating costs - mindful always of the all-important factor of the effects of location and quality on business productivity.

Once part of the corporate business plan the premises policy and its accompanying strategies can be implemented without constant reference back to the Board; reactive decision-making and its dire economic consequences can thus be reduced or eliminated completely.

The various components of the premises policy as listed above are further discussed in detail in their relevant chapters.

Premises economics

The performance of buildings is discussed in more detail in Chapter 1.2.4 Suffice it here to say that the combined effects of location, quality and tenure will determine the price the organisation must pay per unit of space occupied and the risks to which the organisation is exposed as the result of policy. How the organisation uses the space in terms of fitting out and premises management will impact upon the overall performance of the premises; however, the persons and pieces of equipment accommodated will have a very high impact on the premises economics. Provided that the density of space use is not so intense as to have an adverse effect upon the efficiency of the occupants then higher densities will reap economic benefits to the organisation in terms of cost-effective premises.

Increased density will affect operating costs across the board. More people per square metre of available space means more wear-and-tear, greater cooling loads, earlier replacement of components and so on.

However, in nearly all cases the property costs, ie rent/mortgage etc, will be far more significant than the operating costs, eg maintenance, cleaning, energy; so, although the operating costs per capita will increase with greater density of occupation, the reduced cost per capita of the property costs will more than outweigh this cost-penalty (see Fig. 1.1.D).

Fig. 1.1.D
Effect of varying density of space use on premises costs per capita

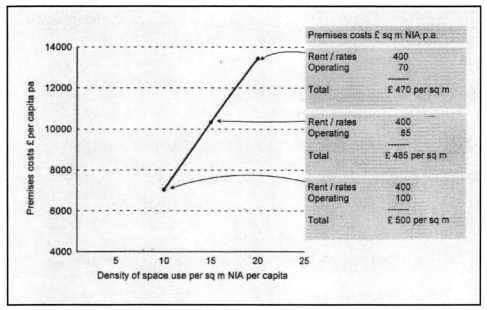

Space use will always be the cost driver in any premises cost equation. However, the performance of the space in terms of the business requirement will be more critical than the cost of providing and maintaining the premises.

Premises costs are rarely more than 5% of turnover (or revenue expenditure in the case of administrative organisations) and usually equate to annual profit levels - see Fig. 1.1.E. Of that 5% the property costs make up the great majority - say 70:30 property:operating costs. The property costs are comparatively fixed - any movement usually being upwards on rent reviews - whereas operating costs are to some extent controllable, if only by further deferral of the inevitable once full economic efficiency has been achieved. Consequently the premises manager must try to minimise the amount of fixed cost space in use, looking out continually for opportunities to get rid of space that is surplus to requirements. The surplus may, of course, be with reference to inadequate quality or performance as well as quantity.

Fig. 1.1.E
Premises costs in the context of turnover and profits

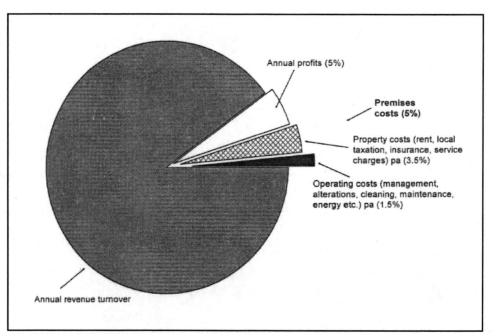

The support services policy

The principles of the support services policy, including the importance of its being derived from a formal process of value management, are similar to those described for the premises policy above.

Fig. 1.1.F shows similarly how the Support Services policy must accommodate the business needs. Space does not generally drive the costs of these services although it can be a significant factor in such cost centres as catering, security and staff facilities. However, the amount of resource consumed by the operation will in most cases drive the costs the hardest; for instance, the amount of stationery consumed per capita, the numbers of vehicles in the transport fleet and average time spent on the telephone are the sort of critical benchmarks against which to target and monitor the effective provision of support services.

The support services policy will link much more obviously with the mainstream business activity and will be more easily understood and readily accepted than its premises counterpart. However, both policies are likely to be equally significant in their overall impact on the bottom-line year-end result.

Fig. 1.1.F
*Facilities and the
corporate plan -
support services
policy*

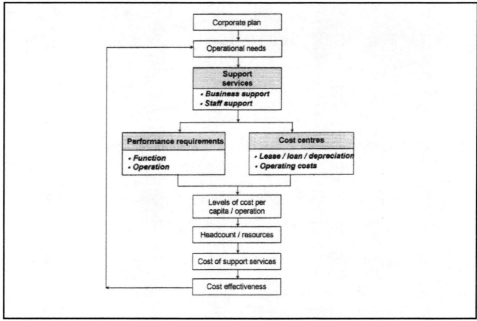

1.1.6 CORE AND NON-CORE ACTIVITIES

The distinction

There is a perception amongst modern business managers - and one which has been extensively encouraged and promoted by external providers - that any activity which does not directly contribute to income (or productive external output) should be considered as 'non-core', ie does not lie at the heart of the raison d'être of the organisation.

Therefore, the solicitor who drafts the conveyancing document has a 'core' function whereas the person who types it has a 'non-core' function; the salesperson closing the deal is 'core' but the person keeping the company's office toilets clean and resistant to spread of disease is not.

This fairly clear distinction between the relative contribution of production and support services is not universally accepted but is still adhered to on most Business Studies courses. If there is a blurring at the edges it occurs most obviously at management level of support services and support level of production services.

For example, the non-core office services manager who has responsibility for ensuring that reports are typed correctly and despatched on time can genuinely feel part of the production process; within the core the sales director's personal assistant - in a secretarial mode - is, at best, no more productive than the office services manager.

However, the inspection of needle-ends to check up on numbers of dancing angels is definitely a non-core activity!

The out-sourced approach

Suffice to say that one of the primary reasons for drawing the 'core' v 'non-core' distinction is to attempt to concentrate the attention of an organisation's management on those activities forming an essential part of the end-product. The corollary of this axiom is that any other activity not involving or requiring the core skills of the business could, and should, be provided and managed by external contractors.

Extreme proponents of this view, such as Drucker[1] would outsource the whole of the word-processing department and its management. Naturally, according to them facilities management goes via the same window.

The Drucker theory is that managers of 'non-core' service functions cannot aspire to top-level management positions in an organisation which is, or should be, dominated by the skills of 'core' activity managers.

The heads of security services will not become managing directors in the conglomerates which employ them so they may lack motivation; however as MD of their own security services contracting companies they can be big fish in smaller ponds and have both status and investment opportunity to spur them on to higher performance and productivity.

Of course, contracting productivity is a two-edged sword: on the one hand competitive bidding can save the customer money while on the other hand the benefits of production efficiencies should go to the service provider - if sound, free-market, economic theory is to prevail. If it does not then providers will cut standards to compete on price, to the customer's detriment.

The logic of outsourcing non-core activity and the benefits thus obtained are clearly not of the black-and-white variety - there are too many examples of good and bad in both in-house and outsource approaches for the arguments to go away completely, or even recede. Insofar as facilities management is the subject of consideration for outsourcing the debate is frequently fuelled by a perceived lack of credibility in the existing facilities personnel and their efficiency; where problems do exist they spring from a pre-1990's legacy of almost universal absence of training and education in the discipline.

In most parts of the Western world the recession of the early 1990's encouraged very many private and public concerns to latch eagerly, possibly desperately, on to the 'non-core' argument in favour of outsourcing. Sometimes this was for genuinely philosophical grounds but too often it was used as an excuse to overcome internal problems of staffing levels and, even worse, to justify the killer blow to end interminable and counter-productive management struggles.

Even where well-respected facilities departments have been externalised, real cost savings have often been identified (in the short-term at least) giving further ammunition to those who just want to get rid of the function regardless of any philosophical arguments to the contrary.

However the core v non-core argument should always be the determining factor unless the organisation's reason is either:

- the existing structure and/or calibre of the facilities organisation is inadequate, and it does not wish to use internal resources or funds to rectify the situation, or

- it simply wishes to reduce payroll staff numbers as a matter of principle.

Impact of professional development

In this context the rapid growth of the competence and status of the 'new breed' of facilities management emerging during the past two decades forms a fascinating back-drop to the developing outsourcing scenario.

There is now a clearly identifiable and highly motivated discipline within facilities management spawning masters degrees and doctorates and demanding a place on the board of management. The distinction between 'core' and 'non-core' within facilities is acknowledged by its own academia; however the aggressive view that the direction

---

[1] Drucker, P. (1992) 'Managing the Future - the 1990's and beyond', Butterworth - Heinemann, USA.

of facilities (as opposed to management of services) constitutes a core function justifying top-level representation within the company is a war that is far from won.

One thing is nevertheless clear: in the course of elevating from Maintenance Manager to Facilities Director the role (and its players) have changed beyond recognition. Just as well too. To use an analogy from another industry, if an aircraft falls out of the sky it may be the fault of the designer, the constructor or the maintenance gang - but in the end it will be sales of flights which will suffer. So with business facilities; if they are badly managed (whether internally or by an outsourced agent) or if their quality does not marry up to the business objectives, the output of the organisation will undoubtedly be adversely affected over time.

Properly implemented proactive facilities management can make a positive contribution to core business efficiency. Yet it must never be forgotten that, on the other hand, badly administered, reactive (or worse, inactive!) facilities management will equally hold back business efficiency while wasting the valuable resources at its disposal.

1.2   THE PERFORMANCE OF FACILITIES

Introduction

The subject of performance is introduced very early on in this work because it is absolutely critical in any consideration of facilities economics.

The chapter explains what performance means in facilities terms, and how it can be specified and measured. The three facets of performance - input, output and financial - are explained in the context of buildings and facilities services together with their importance to facilities managers and users.

Many of the quality management issues raised initially in the chapter are dealt with in greater detail in Chapter 2.4.

1.2.1 THE CONCEPT OF PERFORMANCE

Management and performance

Performance, in business terms, means the manner or quality of functioning.

Modern management theory seeks to target and measure the performance of individuals, work-groups and equipment. This principle is now becoming enshrined in the facilities management culture, with the development and use of performance indicators across the whole range of cost centres.

The facilities management function must expect to be tested like any other aspect of business activity. Among the more important features which need to be assessed in the process of measuring this performance are:

- the extent to which facilities support - or can be adapted to support the changing needs of an organisation

- the contribution that facilities make to organisational effectiveness

- the value added by effective management

- improvements in service and environmental quality

- the risk contained by and associated with using facilities.

The three facets of performance

Fig. 1.2.A
The three facets of performance

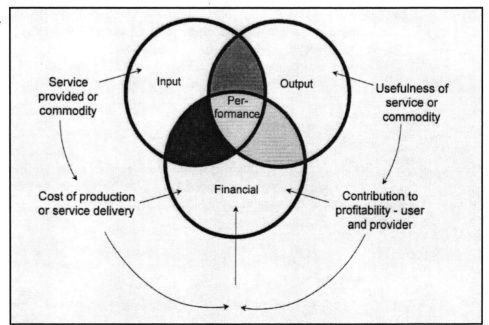

There are three different ways of describing and defining performance, each depending upon the point of view of either the beneficiary or provider of what is delivered.

From the user's perspective the greatest concern is for the output (or effectiveness) of the provision together with the price and the value of the investment. On the other hand, the service provider is concerned with the quality of the input relative to what has been prescribed, the cost of providing it and the profit made out of the price charged. These aspects are clearly inter-related, as depicted in Fig. 1.2.A (previous page).

1.2.2. THE PERFORMANCE OF FACILITIES

Categories of provision

As Fig. 1.2.A implies, performance can relate to commodities, such as a piece of plant or equipment, or to services such as maintenance or mailroom services. However, although in essence the nature of each facet is the same in both commodities and service provision, there are good reasons for considering the application of each category independently in the case of buildings as a commodity.

This chapter therefore deals separately with the 'performance of facilities services' and the 'performance of buildings'.

1.2.3. THE PERFORMANCE OF FACILITIES SERVICES

Facilities services

Facilities services relate to either premises services or support services and in general comprise mainly human resources. However, it is not entirely helpful, when considering facilities economics, to separate the performance of the human resources and the plant/equipment which is associated with the overall facility provided.

So, to look at the performance of maintenance out of context of the building to which it is applied can lead to a failure to understand the 'big picture'. Equally, the cost and quality of the transport fleet and the performance of the bus drivers cannot sensibly be viewed in isolation from each other.

However, in this text the pragmatic approach adopted is to recognize that buildings are an abnormally large component of the cost of premises and to single out the performance of buildings as a 'special' consideration. However, this must not be taken as an encouragement to look at the performance of buildings, as designed and constructed, in isolation from either the services required to keep them operational or the support services which may have some measure of dependence upon them.

Chapter 10.6 on Whole-Life Economics addresses this interdependence and shows how the performance of commodities and services can be appraised in a holistic manner.

For the purposes of this part of the text, the performance of services supporting the operation and occupation of buildings and those concerned with business and staff support are both embraced by the definition of facilities services.

Performance indicators

A performance indicator is a tool used by management to measure the efficiency or effectiveness achieved in the process of carrying out a function.

It comprises a description of the function, the targets to be achieved and the degree of success in meeting them. The targets may relate to time, quality, risk, cost or any combination thereof.

For example, an organisation may run a bus service to remote stores. Its published timetable sets out the targets; the numbers of occasions over a month on which the service is more than (say) five minutes late on leaving from base and arriving at the destination might be described in percentage terms. Thus, in the month of January 87% of departures and 76% of arrivals were within a period of five minutes after schedule, compared with targets of 85% and 80% respectively!

In facilities terms performance indicators are generally applied to service provision, whereas the performance of buildings and components is generally related to 'quality indicators'. It is really the same difference but here we bow to the conventional wisdom and terminology.

The use of performance indicators in quality control is considered in more detail in Chapter 2.4 - 'Quality Management'.

Service level agreements

The publication of the bus timetable and the performance targets discussed above is effectively an offer of service to the customer using that part of the facilities service. If the service is provided by an external contractor the facilities sponsor may wish to make the targets part of the contract and bonus or penalise the contractor according to measured results. Some organisations providing such services in-house now seek to formalise such missions in 'Service Level Agreements' (SLA's) which are quasi-contracts within what is sometimes described as an 'internal market'. This quasi-contract commits the provider to the level of service described in a published document and may, or may not, be accompanied by a cross-charge and/or penalty paid by the provider to the beneficiary of the service ('the customer').

A critical aspect of facilities economics is the identification of the appropriate service level requirement prior to formalising any agreement.

There is sometimes confusion between service level agreements, service level commitments (SLC's) and mission statements. A mission statement is a general statement of intention, such as 'to provide an adequate and reliable bus service'. There is little point in incorporating such a generality in a service level agreement - although it may provide some motivation to the providers if they are reminded of it from time to time when standards obviously fall.

Many organisations moving towards a complete internal market regime stop short of SLA's, relying upon the service level commitment and relevant performance indicators to be established and managed by the provider; individual performance related financial incentives and publication of achievements against target do certainly act as a stimulus to efficiency as long as the commitments and targets are sharply defined and meaningfully measurable. User satisfaction should also be monitored in a formal way, (see Chapter 2.4.3) even though the customer may not be directly charged for the service.

Cross-charging

The important step-up from the service level commitment to the SLA or performance-based contract should be the penultimate stage in completion of a full internal market, ie it should ideally be the prelude to a cross-charging of facilities. In terms of facilities economics the process whereby the costs of services provided have to be borne as an overhead by the internal customer is an optimum arrangement. Such cross-charging should be in the context of an agreement based upon an SLA which is in turn bolstered by an agreed set of key performance indicators (KPI's). The benefits of such an arrangement to the organisation are threefold:

- it can sit neatly within a written facilities policy correctly identifying and costing the relationship between facilities performance and the corporate plan, as described in Chapter 1.1.5

- it encourages purchasers to be more aware of their consumption of the business's resources and so more judicious in their demands as to the extent of the facilities provided

- it makes the facilities provider accountable for the cost and quality of the service which is delivered.

'Back-to-back' agreements

Facilities sponsors who have committed to providing measurable levels of service do not always pass SLA's and KPI's across to external task contractors, although the logic for doing so is overwhelming. For example, an SLA which commits to performance targets in respect of such matters as response time to emergency maintenance and down-time of lifts can easily be written into the external contract - even if the only financial penalty for failure is not to have the contract renewed on expiry.

Often it is the trend towards over-bureaucracy which makes facilities managers hold back from this total commitment to measured performance, and it is essential that any PI regime should be manageable whilst having the desired economic effect. The logic of 'Pareto's principle' which can be adapted to suggest that 80% of the cost, value or resource consumed is contained in 20% of the constituent parts, is always worth following and is a good basis upon which to decide which items to target and measure - and also to decide upon the classification of tolerance bands. It may be better to accept delays of ten rather than five minutes in the bus service if that eases the problem of collecting data thereby reducing the time spent in measurement. There is still nothing to prevent the provider aiming for higher targets, so keeping the customer happy to accept a less stringent 'contract' condition. The right balance is essential if the system is to work to the common good.

Quality of service

Quality management is discussed in detail in Chapter 2.4. Suffice it here to say that if a contractor has a commitment to Quality Assurance to EN ISO 9000, Total Quality Management, or any other formal quality assurance process, there is a good case for the performance indicators and checking processes enshrined in those procedures to be referred to, or fully incorporated in, the external contract or internal SLA.

Implementing the full internal market

Although the culture in many organisations may present resistance to the concept of a full internal market there can be little doubt that the practice will become the norm sooner than the objectors might hope or expect.

There are now some organisations which cross-charge each employee with the facilities they use within the office - if they work from home they do not get charged. It may be that this level of intrusion into employees' routines may prove to be unacceptable in the large majority of organisations. However, home-working (see Chapter 4.1.6) is becoming more and more a feature of business strategy and may itself require some form of performance-related penalties as well as positive incentives in pursuit of premises efficiency.

Benchmarking

A close relative of the performance indicator is the 'benchmark'. Taken from the process of marking datum levels in land surveying, the term 'benchmark', in the context of facilities economics, involves a cross-reference from an organisation's achievements in a particular field of activity to a comparable internal or external peer group source. The concept of benchmarking costs and performance is discussed in Chapter 12.2 - Benchmarking.

1.2.4 THE PERFORMANCE OF BUILDINGS

The significance of building performance

The quickest route to recognition as an intellectual in the world of property and building these days is to drop the word 'performance', in a reasonably relevant manner, into as many sentences as possible.

The concept of performance specification has been fairly familiar to people on the construction side of the fence for many years. Many building materials are specified by their performance characteristics and, indeed, there are a number of institutions specialising in the appraisal of the performance of buildings and materials in use, eg the Building Performance Research Unit subsequently subsumed into the Centre for Facilities Management at the University of Strathclyde (now at the University of Salford) in the UK.

Real estate professionals (being traditionally more conservative) have inevitably been slower to introduce this terminology into their already jargon-filled vocabulary. In fact, since they consider buildings from a very different angle from that of the facilities manager, the performance they are concerned with is more likely to be that of investment market value rather than the functional performance inherent in the design and specification - as if there were in fact no correlation whatsoever between the two.

It is submitted that understanding and acceptance of the concept of performance will be the most critical development in property and building in the next decade and the fact that the term means all things to all people at present is an unfortunate obstacle which has to be overcome in using the concept to help users to achieve the ultimate premises efficiency for which they are all striving.

Of course, it is one thing to understand what is meant by performance and another to be able to measure it. Lord Kelvin is quoted as saying, in the context of measurement generally, 'if you cannot measure it you cannot understand it' and Harrington[1] equally believes that 'if you cannot measure it you cannot improve it'.

What they are both actually arguing for is the need to make sense of complexity, not necessarily by fully calculating costs and benefits but by recognising patterns of relationships.

This text discusses the concept of building performance and its applications in property and building and considers what must be done to facilitate the measurement or other comparative appraisal methodology which clearly is a condition precedent to understanding and improving performance of premises.

Definition of building performance

Building performance is normally associated with building quality. It is a complex issue and difficult to define. It is conventionally considered primarily in terms of physical integrity and durability and the associated capital and revenue costs, but the reality is that it goes infinitely deeper than that.

---

[1] *H. James Harrington et al: 'Business Process Improvement', ASQ Quality Press*

Buildings are simply a means to an end. They are variously concerned with some or all of:

- people
- equipment
- processes
- places
- spaces
- image
- convenience
- comfort
- support systems
- costs
- income
- profitability.

A building's response to accommodating all these requirements represents its performance.

Performance of buildings is therefore defined here as 'the contribution made by a building or estate to the functional and financial requirements of the occupiers and/or owners and the associated physical behaviour of the fabric, services and finishes over time'.

The three facets of building performance

Fig. 1.2.A showed the three facets of performance as 'input, output and financial'. However, input and output in the context of building performance (in fact, any commodity) are specifically related to 'hard' facts about design and construction.

Therefore, for purposes of this chapter, it is suggested that the three components of building performance are: physical, functional and financial (Fig. 1.2.B).

Fig. 1.2.B
The three facets of building performance inter-relationships

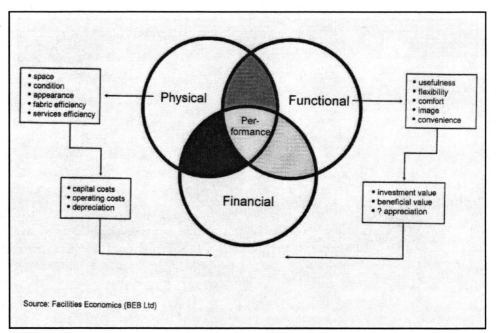

Source: Facilities Economics (BEB Ltd)

Physical performance: relates to the behaviour of the fabric, services and finishes embracing physical properties such as structural integrity, internal environment (heating, lighting, etc) energy efficiency, cleanliness, maintainability, durability and environmental impact.

Functional performance: is the term used to describe the properties afforded by the building to the benefit (or otherwise) of the occupier. Examples are space (quantity and quality), layout, ergonomics, image, ambience, amenity, movement /communications, security, health and safety and flexibility.

Financial performance: is a combination of capital and revenue expenditure, rate of depreciation, investment value and contribution to profitability/efficiency. It springs from the physical and functional performance of the building and the way in which it is used.

These three facets are inextricably linked, although the significance of this relationship is frequently missed by those whose pre-occupation is with one particular facet only, eg property developers, maintenance managers or space planners each pursuing their own particular discipline oblivious to their part in the overall scheme of things.

Techniques exist for evaluation, at design stage, of the likely cost of maintaining a building's physical performance over its life-cycle, although the data presently available upon which to base the necessary forecasts of life, deterioration, maintenance and associated costs is relatively sparse. Nonetheless, life-cycle cost appraisal is an important discipline encouraging designers to justify their decisions to the future occupier.

However, whereas the physical costs (including capital depreciation) over a building's life-cycle are unlikely to be more than about 5% of an organisation's total costs, the benefits of functional performance impacts directly on the efficiency of the organisation's core activities - which can account for some 80 to 90% of its total costs. Consequently it is likely that the benefits of functional performance will have a much greater impact on profitability and efficiency than the more tangible costs attributable only to the physical operation of the premises.

The physical performance of buildings

An inherent function of the performance of the building is its physical performance, ie its rate of deterioration, the operations required to maintain and run it, and the replacement of the components, elements and finally the building over time (see Chapter 10.6.4).

Design teams must be encouraged by clients or their project managers to deliver a life-cycle cost plan at the same time as the capital budget is presented. An example of such a life-cycle cost plan is given in Chapter 10.6.4 (Fig. 10.6.L). In order to produce such a plan the design team must clearly have access to good data on performance and cost-in-use. Such data is not publicly available in any measure of sophistication at present although some consultants and contractors do have reliable databases in respect of some or all building types. However there are a number of publications giving typical life-cycles of the most commonly used components; these include the HAPM manuals[2]. Designers, building owners and occupiers must have access to good historical data on the performance of buildings in use if a meaningful conversation is to take place around the life-cycle cost plan when design proposals are submitted.

Meanwhile statisticians are being kept fully occupied calculating probabilities of life-cycle predictions being fulfilled, especially in some of the larger PFI (Private Finance

---

[2] *HAPM Component Life Manual - E & FN Spon, London*

Initiative) and PPP (Public Private Partnership) projects. Although the results of such statistical analysis may bring some comfort to whole-life funders the risks of premature failure are better controlled by best practice project and construction management. A more technological approach to risk appraisal and containment of component failure is described in detail in Chapter 10.6 (Whole Life Economics).

Whereas the operating, maintenance and replacement costs are not a significant part of the investment appraisal (see Chapter 5.1) they do assume very considerable importance during the life of a building where money has to be found for them. Equally important, of course, is the fact that maintenance and refurbishment costs absorb almost half of the output of the construction industry in the EU in any one year.

This is one of the main anomalies of the PFI- and PPP-type contracts: to the building user the scale of the risk being transferred is minimal whereas to the total premises provider risks such as life-cycle replacement and whole-life maintenance costs are critical to success or failure.

The functional performance of buildings

Most decisions to spend money on buildings in the name of higher quality cannot be formally justified in terms of return on investment because the 'benefit' side cannot be quantified or evaluated. Thus, natural stone facing is perceived as higher quality than the reconstituted variety: we know the cost differential in both capital and life-cycle terms but what value does natural stone add to bottom-line profit (assuming that the options are both permissible)? The same question-mark hangs over investment in faster, bigger lifts, comfort cooling and so on right through the building elements.

Fig. 1.2.C
Zero-based budget - added cost/benefit analysis

Subject:	Partitions	Estimated Costs
Location:	Cellular Offices	
Zero-base specification:	Metal stud and plasterboard	£ 10,000
Proposal:	Proprietary demountable	£ 25,000
Benefits analysis - subjective evaluation		
Effect of proposal on functional performance	Perceived quality	better
	Visual ambience	better
	Comfort	-
	Ergonomics	-
	Flexibility	better
	Safety	-
Effect of proposal on on life-cycle costs	Cleaning	-
	Energy	-
	Maintenance and repairs	better
	Security	-
	Insurance	-
	Replacement	worse
	Management	better
Effect of proposal on on environment	Energy consumption	N/A
	Embodied energy	worse
	Sustainability	better

There are many good anecdotes but good hard data is difficult, if not impossible, to find. There can be little doubt that higher quality in a building can, in many cases, improve the efficiency of the operation going on within it. However there are not too many techniques enabling clients to make decisions on performance. One quite simple pragmatic method involving Functional Analysis which can form a useful part of the formal value management process (see Chapter 2.2.5) is illustrated in Fig. 1.2.C (previous page). In this technique the client and the design team may come together to review some of the more significant items of expenditure and consider the physical, financial and functional implications in a subjective framework without necessarily getting involved in cost/benefit analysis of a complex nature. They test all the key options against an absolute minimum (zero-base) option; the way this technique is operated is described in more detail in Chapter 2.2.5.

That is not to say that the cost/benefit analysis should not be carried out. Indeed, the concept whereby all design decisions are made on the basis of justification of expenditure over and above a zero-base is at the heart of modern thinking on value-management (see Chapter 2.2). The problem here again is one of measurement and valuation: you can measure the payback on energy efficiency measures but how do you value the comfort implications of the sound reduction qualities of double glazing.

An answer to that could, in the first instance, be tested across all the range of probability by the use of sensitivity analysis; over time, the constant use of such calculations and demands for better information by the users will encourage the necessary research to take place in order that the quantification process should become more scientific and valid.

This brings us to the consideration of how the functional efficiency of the building influences the overall productivity of an organisation by the way it accommodates its activities. Chapter 1.1.5 discusses the theory that the level of performance of premises should extend from the business requirement and suggests that the cost of achieving such performance should also be incorporated in the business plan. To achieve such mathematical correlation requires a level of understanding of the concept of the functional value of buildings which is totally missing from current technologies of cost estimating and investment valuation.

The financial performance of buildings - initial and operating costs

As yet there exists no common language between building professionals and their clients whereby the performance required of buildings can be described in terms which are exclusive of specification and design parameters. A cost consultant who recently produced a £10m capital expenditure budget for a new headquarters for a firm of accountants was asked whether the building proposed was equivalent to a Ford Mondeo, BMW or Rolls Royce. They were comforted by a Ford Mondeo analogy, although few around the table realised the potentially dangerous consequences of such immature subjective assessment.

However, if we are to get away from budgeting for new buildings on the basis of what older ones have cost - essential if we are to start to achieve value for money - then we have to invent an alternative language; indeed, not only do we have to invent the language but we have to create a series of cost analyses which accurately reflect the expenditure required to achieve the described performance. Therefore in the formal value management process (see Chapter 2.2.5) costs are allocated to functional performance rather than elements and components.

Performance is of course a key to the ability to value engineer building solutions. In its simplest but most profound definition, Value Management and one of its essential component activities is the 'elimination of redundant performance', ie the avoidance of expenditure on any item of construction which does not add value to the product or which makes the product achieve more than is required (see Chapter 2.2.3).

Although the operating costs must be taken into account in building design and specification, value engineering must look beyond the cost consequences of physical performance if the building design process is to have a real impact on the organisation's efficiency and hence profitability. That means that decisions about cost levels must be related to functional values rather than physical costs.

The financial performance of buildings - investment and functional values

Professional real estate appraisers tend not to understand functional values - or, if they do, they generally disregard their formal consideration in the process of their 'black art' (but see chapter 3.8.2 on 'functional obsolescence').

Real estate developers and investors are guided by these appraisers and their first cousins the real estate agents who purport to know 'what the market demands'.

Generally speaking, as discussed in Chapter 3.5.3, market valuation is made by reference to 'comparative valuation', ie having regard to current transactions involving similar property. There is nothing at all wrong with that, apart from the fact that the computation supporting any transaction underlying the comparable valuation may itself be inaccurate. It may well be a case of the blind leading the blind.

What we therefore need is methods of appraising a property which reflect its performance in terms of the business requirement - one of which features may well be the location; however, in spite of the old assumption, propounded by real estate agents, that the three most important features of a property are 'location, location and location'; this may not be the principal determining factor in terms of value to the user.

The valuation process and valuation methodology are considered in Chapters 3.4 and 3.5 respectively; the facilities manager's role in the valuations which reflect the depreciation of property is discussed in Chapter 3.8.

Measuring building performance

Several methodologies of performance evaluation are already available. For instance the Building Quality Assessment (BQA) procedure, which originated in Australia and New Zealand, has now been validated by the Building Research Establishment for UK and mainland European application. It consists of a sophisticated software program with market weighting for various performance characteristics established by reference to consultants, users and property owners. The output is an Index of Performance which can be used on a comparative basis to assess the relative usefulness of one building to another.

The concept of 'serviceability', developed by Gerald Davis in Canada[3], is also helping users to measure the usefulness of a building's capacity in the context of their own specific needs.

In studies of 'Intelligent Buildings'[4] and 'The Responsible Workplace'[5], Frank Duffy et al have also shown a way forward in understanding the true worth of well-designed premises and facilities and Frank Becker and Robertson Ward Jnr in the USA are among others who are also helping to enlighten the conventional wisdom.

A new system of design quality assessment sponsored by the Department of Trade and Industry is the 'Design Quality Index' (DQI)[6]. This is a toolkit and methodology

---

[3] *Serviceability, tools and methods (STM): Gerald Davis, International Centre for Facilities, Inc*

[4] *Duffy, F., Laing, A., Crisp, V. (1992) 'The Intelligent Building in Europe', DEGW, London, UK.*

[5] *Duffy, F., Laing, A., Crisp, V. (1993) 'The Responsible Workplace: The redesign of work and offices', Butterworth Architecture, Oxford, UK*

[6] *Design Quality Index (DQI) - The Building Research Establishment*

which draws on the BQA system, Serviceability and other earlier work in this field to provide a high level assessment of the functional performance of buildings.

Inevitably, as the necessary data is made available, the appraisal of buildings will have to become more technical, more scientific whether from a construction, valuation or occupation viewpoint. It is crucial that such data covers performance in all its aspects - functional efficiency, physical efficiency and financial efficiency (see Chapter 3.8 - Depreciation of Property).

In quest of better methods of building performance evaluation the inter-action between the building, its occupants and the activities they carry out within it must become a critical area for consideration. Equally importantly, however, the relationships between building-related costs and other expenditure by organisations must be examined to identify the likely scope for added value, or savings in general costs, and the factors that may influence such benefits.

Building performance and the facilities manager

The tools are coming into place: the quality assessment programs emerging from current research will all play their part in making it possible, as never before, to measure and value the performance of buildings.

The growing awareness of the need to operate and manage facilities effectively and an inevitable increase in the involvement of facilities managers in the design process will make a fundamental difference to the way buildings are commissioned, designed, maintained and refurbished. More and more facilities managers and their consultants will become involved in life-cycle cost analysis, projecting their asset plans, and reviewing project proposals in the context of the overall business requirement. Inevitably this will impact upon property rents, yields and hence on values.

Most of all, however, the facilities manager's informed involvement should contribute to the delivery of valuable buildings which exactly meet the business need at exactly the right price.

1.2.5 PERFORMANCE AND VALUE MANAGEMENT

The value tree

The value management process, described in detail in Chapter 2.2, can help users to specify performance by defining 'needs' through the development of a 'value tree'; a value tree describes the business needs and the criteria that need to be satisfied in order to achieve it.

Equally the significance of the required performance can be measured through the 'weighting' of the needs in the value tree.

The value tree should help to avoid the introduction of 'redundant performance'.

Redundant performance

Redundant performance refers to the ability of a commodity, a component or a service to meet needs which are not relevant to the user's requirements. Where that unnecessary capacity has attendant additional costs the value management process requires that it should be replaced with a more appropriate solution, ie minus the unwanted performance and attendant extra costs.

The concept of value engineering, discussed in detail in Chapters 2.2.3 and 6.3.7, embraces 'the elimination of redundant performance and attendant extra costs'. However, that same definition could be applied to the value management process itself, as the same principles apply to the performance of, say, a building as to one of its walls or one of the bricks in it.

An example of redundant performance in a building might be the provision of too much space or the provision of bricks when blocks would do. The theory is that the required performance of a building (P) should be achieved through the sum of the performance of its elements (Σpe) which in turn is achieved through the sum of the performance of the components of the elements (Σpc), ie $P = \Sigma pe = \Sigma pc$

This is a good illustration of the principles underlying the 'balanced scorecard' approach to achieving optimum performance described in Chapter 2.2.6.

In a value management context there is a minimum cost of providing P which can only be achieved if the elements are designed to optimum functional performance using components which also fulfil the optimum criteria. In other words, where redundant performance and attendant extra costs have been eliminated then:

$£P = £\Sigma pe = £\Sigma pc$

Clearly the ability to define the overall performance (P) in functional terms which can be useful to specifiers of facilities is critical to the value management process; equally technical definitions of the performance of elements (pe) are essential if redundant performance is to be identified, measured and eliminated.

Again, the formal value management technique of 'Function Analysis' (see Chapter 2.2.5) should be used in identifying patterns of relationships between functions, eg in a particular scenario a brick wall may have residual and therefore redundant load-bearing, thermal, visual and sound-reduction performance compared to a breeze block wall which fits the specified performance requirements perfectly, and this would be identified by the Function Analysis process.

Research is now taking place which will enable users to assess the performance capabilities of proposed new buildings at the sketch design stage and which will be equally applicable to refurbishment of existing buildings. In due course it should lead to improvements in functional design and evaluation and result in buildings that meet more closely the requirements of the organisations that occupy them. This, in turn, will lead to considerable savings to the industry and its clients. It is, of course, absolutely vital that the investment valuation process is informed by this new level of understanding of building performance and takes it properly into account.

1.3 THE COSTS OF FACILITIES

Introduction

A key feature of 'Facilities Economics' is that, although it is essentially a textbook for practitioners and students alike, it does nevertheless contain hard data on the cost levels of most of the facilities normally found under facilities managers' direction.

This chapter explains the factors which generate and drive costs and how to make cost comparisons both nationally and internationally.

Facilities costs are apt to be the focus of a lot of critical attention by business finance directors. Nevertheless, it must be stressed here that 'value' is the overriding goal of the facilities manager while costs should never be more than the out-turn commitment emanating from a formal value management process (see Chapter 2.2)

1.3.1 COST COMPARISONS - THE PRINCIPLES

Problems with data

The amount of good data about comparative costs of facilities is at a premium; the biggest difficulty by far is the lack of standard protocols for classification and measurement of data between organisations.

Chapter 12.2 on Benchmarking reviews these problems in detail. However, the authors have been able to provide a reliable guide to the normal range of costs of facilities using their own data which is, of course, geared exactly to the protocol for classification and measurement adopted meticulously in the course of their own extensive benchmarking activities.

These protocols are described alongside the cost ranges to which they apply throughout the publication.

Pan-European classification protocol

It may be noted that in September 2000 the Dutch Facilities Management Association introduced a classification protocol for facilities services known as NEN 2748. This system was put forward to the European Commission (EC) as a model for a pan-European classification system to be endorsed by the Commission. The proposal was, however, rejected and the whole issue of a standard system is still in the early stages of consideration within the EU.

On the other hand it is important to recognise that the very extensive database used to support the cost levels in this text is compiled strictly in accordance with the authors' own protocol; because of the way the database has been compiled a re-assembly into the NEN or any other standard classification will therefore be relatively straightforward.

Future revisions of 'Facilities Economics' may well adopt some more widely recognised classification in respect of the cost ranges given in the various sections - giving the added value of an 'instant' high quality database to support a pan-European (or more widespread) classification system.

Cultural differences

Cultural differences between organisations, sites and regions are often cited as being cost drivers. However, insofar as cultural conventions are reflected in the level of output performance, ie the quality achieved, they are not stand-alone drivers of costs **over and above the cost of resources needed to achieve the output.**

The point here is that when comparing cost levels **it is absolutely essential to ignore cultural differences in terms of acceptable output performance** and to concentrate on the 'measured condition' in absolute terms. So, using window cleaning as an exaggerated example it may be that one organisation's culture typically accepts that windows may become - and remain - dirty regardless of the status of the organisation whilst another's may require a pristine or near-pristine state of cleanliness at all times.

When comparing the costs of window cleaning as between the two organisations the latter's costs would probably be much higher on average than the former's. Although this might provide a comparison of the normal costs of window cleaning as between the two organisations it would not be a benchmark (see Chapter 12.2) in terms of relative efficiency: it would merely reflect the culture of the organisations in terms of their perception of the value of having clean windows and the costs would reflect the input, ie the relative frequency and quality of the operation.

Except where specifically stated otherwise the high level typical cost ranges given in this publication therefore reflect straightforward peer group costs for achieving a good but not exceptional level of output performance; any cultural issues relating to output quality can therefore be taken into consideration and the cost range adjusted accordingly when using this data for high level cost comparisons (of course all the other resource drivers have to be taken into account as well on a site-by-site basis).

1.3.2 GENERAL COST COMPARISONS

Interpolation

Having 'dealt with' the important issue of cultural conventions the other factors causing variations in facilities costs between one building and another now need to be addressed.

Inevitably there will be some overlap between this section and the discussion on 'benchmarking' in Chapter 12.2; the factors to be taken into account by readers, when interpolating the operating cost ranges in the text, are the same as needed for eliminating distorting factors when benchmarking peer group operating costs. The cost range for cleaning services given in Chapter 5.3.3 (Fig. 5.3.B) is reproduced here as Fig. 1.3.A.

Fig. 1.3.A
Typical range of cleaning expenditure by sector per unit of floor area

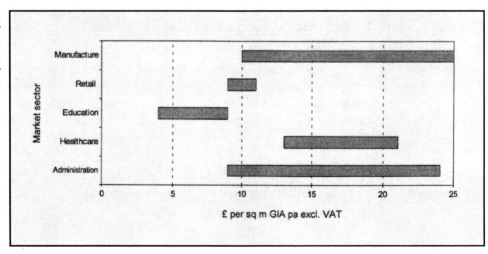

In order to make a high-level interpolation of the cleaning costs in individual buildings from the above ranges (anything other than 'high level' is not feasible from this - or any other - published data) the logic diagram at Fig. 1.3.B needs to be studied.

Fig. 1.3.B
Factors influencing the cost of facilities

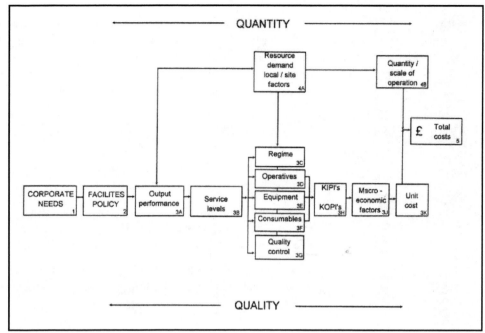

Boxes 1 and 2 reflect the starting point in the value management process as discussed in more detail in Chapter 2.2.4. The facilities policy determines both the output performance and the extent of risk which core business is prepared to accept in respect of the level of support it receives from its facilities.

The output performance (Box 3A) of a new facility, eg cleaning, relates to the quality of the end product whereas the local site features (Box 4A), eg environment and accessibility, impact upon the specification and possibly frequency of the operation.

In the case of cleaning in, say, administration buildings (see Fig. 1.3.A) one of the quantitative resource drivers is the extent of fenestration; when expressing cleaning costs per unit of the floor area (in this case the gross internal area - see Chapter 4.1.2) the ratio of windows to the gross internal area (GIA) is a useful measure of quantity. The use of such ratios for rapid cost estimating is described in Chapter 6.3.3 or 6.3.7. In the 'normal' ranges in Fig. 1.3.A the component of cleaning that relates to the windows will be between say 5 and 15% of the total. Within the range a normal ratio of windows-to-floor area in administration buildings would be about 1:3, ie 1 sq m of windows to 3 sq m GIA.

So, for high level interpolation of the costs in Fig. 1.3.A any building with an abnormally high ratio of windows to floor area would tend towards the top end of that part of the cleaning costs which is in the window cleaning, ie nearer to 15% than 5% of the total, and vice versa. Of course, if the required output performance were considerably above the norm the service levels (Box 3B) would be raised towards the highest level of costs; the combined effects of a large area of windows and a policy of near-immaculate cleanliness would mean that window cleaning costs would almost certainly be at the top of the range.

Almost certainly, but not necessarily. If only it were that easy!

In this example, one application of Box 4A, ie the extent of window cleaning, is driven by one of the local factors - in this case the shape and size of the building. The consequence of this resource driver does not affect the service levels at Boxes 3C to G but is brought into play in Box 4B. However, another local feature might be excessive exposure to pollution in the atmosphere, eg a sea-front location or a site next to the cement works. In this case the frequency of cleaning would need to be greater to achieve a level of cleanliness comparable to that obtainable in an unpolluted location, eg a 'greenfield' site.

The effect here would be to increase the service level regime (Box 3C), ie the frequency and diligence of window cleaning would also increase the unit cost of the operation. So, window cleaning costs of £6,000 pa on a greenfield site where the window/floor ratio was 1:3 would grow to say £30,000 pa (to achieve a similar level of cleanliness) if it were on an exposed site and had a window/floor area ratio of 1:2.

Using the diagram to explain the different effects of these two resource drivers the influence of the increase is a combination of changes in quantitative extent (Box 4B) and qualitative extent (Box 3C) with the latter impact eventually translating into unit cost, ie cost per sq m of window area pa, at Box 3K; the total cost in Box 5 is therefore the product of multiplying the unit cost (Box 3K) by the quantity (Box 4B).

The scale of operation in another cost centre might equally be driven by local business demands (Box 4A). So the volume of mail per capita would drive the costs merely from a quantitative perspective with its impact turning up in Box 4B.

However, an output performance set at high speed of delivery to the workplace following receipt of incoming mail to a building would, again, impact on the 'regime' component of the service level at Box 3C (and probably also in 3D, E, F and G - see below), turning up in Box 3K as an above-normal unit cost.

Service level components

Apart from the 'regime', the other service level components are:

- operatives (Box 3D)
- equipment (Box 3E)
- consumables (Box 3F)
- quality control (Box 3G).

These components are discussed in more detail in Chapter 2.4.3. Here it is only necessary to recognise that the specification of each of the components will impact directly on both service levels and costs.

So, for example, specific technical qualifications for maintenance engineers may raise the rates of pay in pursuit of more reliable output performance achievements. So the Box 3D specification will turn up as an addition to the unit cost in Box 3K.

Going back to the earlier consideration of window cleaning, a site feature at Box 4A might restrict access to the windows for cleaning requiring the use of expansive special equipment (Box 3E), again possibly with extra costs. However, even this will not always be the case for in some circumstances the use of such equipment might be overall cost-efficient. The economic permutations are almost endless, especially when it comes to optimising cost-efficiency, which is where benchmarking can be so helpful to the hard-worked facilities manager struggling to deliver value for money.

Box 3G - Quality control - represents the only facet of facilities management standing in the way of the straightforward conversion of input specification into output achievement. Although the cost of quality control will also work its way through into the unit cost at Box 3K its overriding impact on value cannot be over-emphasised. As discussed in greater detail in Chapter 2.4 (on Quality Management), it is essential to have measurable indicators in terms of input and output quality. Box 3H illustrates the point of application of these measures and their overriding position of control in terms of cost and quality.

Macro-economic factors

In any region, at any one point in time, the cost of providing services will vary depending on the market forces prevailing. The costs of labour, material and equipment will inevitably increase when the economy is buoyant, and far from the increased cost delivering higher quality the problem becomes one of trying to ensure that the quality of the components of the service are maintained at the specified level.

The influence of these factors is indicated at Box 3J.

Total costs

So the total cost of meeting the required output performance (Box 5) can vary enormously depending upon a great number of factors. The reader hoping to use the cost ranges in this text as a shortcut to benchmarking the cost of facilities services (as opposed to understanding the principles) should recognise that useful cost benchmarks do not come out of books. Simple benchmarks such as 'fix-it' times can be of value but, even then, all the factors influencing these results must be brought into account when considering how the key performance criteria were achieved.

In the final event, however, getting value for money by procuring the right thing at the right price is the key objective of both user and provider, and the majority of the remainder of this text is devoted to the achievement of that objective.

Section 2

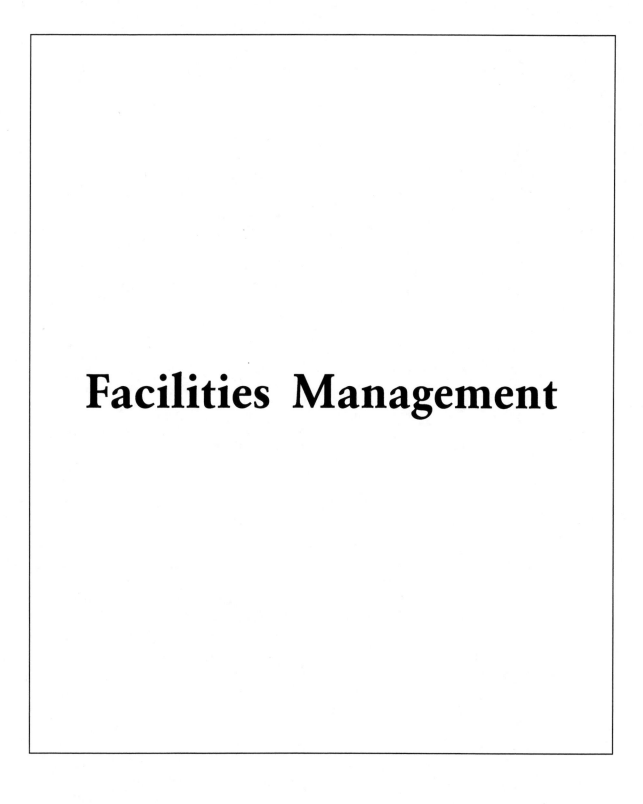

Facilities Management

2.1 FACILITIES MANAGEMENT

Introduction

Facilities management as a discipline is a latter-day phenomenon, having burst upon the business world in most of the developed countries during the 1980's and, in no time at all, having achieved an extraordinarily high level of recognition and status.

This chapter considers the various facets of facilities management and the structures and procurement processes available for its successful performance in support of core business activities.

2.1.1 SCOPE OF FACILITIES MANAGEMENT

The emergence of facilities management

The term 'facilities management' originated in the USA. During the last decade or two the term has gained acceptance throughout the UK being widely adopted by the emerging professional and educational bodies.

In spite of this institutional acceptance of the title the function (or part of it) is still found hidden under a bewildering array of alternative titles, eg

- Facilities and Premises Manager

- Facilities, Premises and Offices Services Manager

- Director of Administration Services

- Head of Services.

The concept of 'services management' was discussed in principle in Chapter 1.1.2. The facilities management role has clearly come a long way from the simple service delivery role of the maintenance manager and office services manager who, quite independently, used to look after 'patches' which few recognised as having any common theme or policy - even where grouped, for administrative convenience, under common line management.

The term 'facilities' used in this work categorically subsumes both 'premises' and 'support services' and includes a level of strategic responsibility patently missing from the earlier patchwork structures. The strategic facets of facilities management ie 'sponsorship' and 'intelligence', were introduced in Chapter 1.1 - 'The scope of Facilities' and are further considered below.

The mission

The facilities department's mission statement (frequently confused with a 'facilities policy' from which it is several thousand light years removed) should embrace property, premises, support services and deal individually and collectively with quality, risk, cost and change. A further example of a mission statement from real-life is shown at Fig. 2.1.A.

Fig. 2.1.A *Facilities* *management* *mission statement*	Quality	Pursue continual improvement of the operating requirements in terms of premises and support services.
	Value	Add or maintain the value of the premises in terms of real estate and contribution to productivity.
	Risk	Control performance (eg safety, efficiency and costs) and be ready for change.

Just like the example given in Chapter 1.1.4 this has its imperfections, eg no mention of risk management, value management restricted to 'premises', but this is not of too much concern; the mission statement is only a flag-waving exercise and it is results that count. Which is not to say that a rallying-call is not a valid contribution in a well-structured management strategy, provided the team members at whom it is directed understand and own the performance level and philosophy that the mission statement is underwriting.

Scope of responsibilities

In its widest definition facilities management embraces the provision and operation of:

- premises

- support services

- ICT (optional).

The management process involves planning, executing and monitoring the performance of its sector. Performance is judged internally with reference to quality, cost, time and risk and externally on its contribution to the organisation's success - by whatever measure that is judged.

The cost centres under the control of this broadly drawn management regime are described in Chapter 1.1.3 (Fig. 1.1.B) and considered individually in detail within parts A and B of this text. The alternative management structures available to handle these responsibilities are discussed below together with the economic implications.

Management functions and skill requirements

The most important attributes of the facilities manager emerging in the New Millennium are leadership and communication skills together with a thorough understanding of value management. The facilities in a large organisation will be able to function efficiently under a non-technical manager provided that there is an appropriate level of technical proficiency reporting to them - whether from an in-house or an outsourced regime.

Facilities management is fairly unique in respect of the range of management disciplines required in order to comply with the overall scope of activities likely to be taking place at one time or another.

There are no hard and fast rules as to which particular management and technical disciplines facilities managers should have as core competencies. However, most educational programmes dealing with facilities management as a core discipline in its own right will introduce students to the management principles underlying each of the facilities services, so the management principles of specialist issues such as space (see Chapter 4.1), security (see Chapter 7.1), health and safety (see Chapter 8.2), and the like are covered within the text for these and other facilities services in Parts B and C.

However there are certain general management disciplines which pervade all aspects of strategic facilities management and so need to be dealt with on their own account. These are:

- value management (Chapter 2.2)

- financial management (Chapter 2.3)

- quality management (Chapter 2.4)

- risk management (Chapter 2.5)

- information management (Chapter 2.6)

- asset management (Chapter 2.7)

- project management (Chapter 2.8)

- change management (Chapter 2.9).

Although facilities managers may not need to be experts in all of these management fields they should have a thorough knowledge of the problems addressed within each one and the skills needed to handle them. As always with wide-ranging disciplines it is more important for the professional to grasp the principles of these various management disciplines than to be masters of all of them; knowing when to import specialist skills and then being in a position to assess the capabilities and performance of such experts is as much a management skill as each of the disciplines considered below.

All the technical skills required in support of facilities management are available externally, if required, either via facilities management contractors or from independent specialist consultants.

An amusing film 'The trick is co-ordination'[1] projects the image of the facilities manager as a juggler - 'juggling with the constraints of facilities management' - and sometimes as a magician pulling a rabbit out of the hat to meet the demands of some unforeseen crisis. The film is virtual reality, particularly when it stresses the wide range of activities over which facilities managers have to preside.

Preside is the operative word here, because it is the leadership and communication skills which are critical to their success. Nevertheless, facilities managers must have sufficient in-depth knowledge of all the activities to know their significance, complexity and their cost drivers; most importantly, they must have the knowledge and ability to present and argue a coherent case for each and every facilities issue at top management level.

2.1.2 MANAGEMENT AND PROCUREMENT STRUCTURES

Facilities management organisation

Dr. Craig Anderson[2] argues that, since organisations are dynamic self-organising systems, charted structures merely indicate the formal lines of communication rather than what the organisation as a whole is there to do or its organic state. His argument that a key function of facilities management is the 'brokerage' of knowledge distributed throughout the organisation as much as resource allocation or service management is endorsed here by the identification of the three facets of facilities management (Fig 1.1.A) of which 'intelligence represents the 'knowledge brokerage' function. Accepting also his argument that this function is not explicit by viewing organisational charts, it is nevertheless interesting to trace the generic patterns of the organisation of facilities management in the post-World War era in the light of developments in technology and management science.

The patterns described below include varying degrees of direct labour employment and outsourcing of task and general management. Before delving into the past, however, it is important to understand that the earlier structures, with little or no recognition of the Intelligent Client Function, were essentially pragmatic in nature. Formal value management was virtually unheard of so any added value was by and large coincidental, although inevitably there were individuals whose ability and

---

[1] (1990) The Responsive Office, Steelcase - Strafor/Polymath, UK.

[2] Anderson, C. (1995) 'A Facilities Evaluation Praxis for Knowledge Generation in Social Systems' - Centre for Facilities Management (CFM), University of Strathclyde (now University of Salford)

personal status enabled them, and the facilities under their direction, to rise above the conventional level of mediocrity.

Direct employment

Looking back, then, to the early days there were many organisations who directly employed all the staff needed to run and maintain premises and business support services. It is possible that one or two examples of 100% in-house operation still exist, but probably not on a large scale. The structure at Fig. 2.1.B relates to a traditional premises management function in which the core premises management comprised engineer/technology - trained personnel in charge of a direct labour force which carried out nearly all the work except really specialist tasks such as lift maintenance.

Fig. 2.1.B
Direct labour organisation - minimal outsourcing

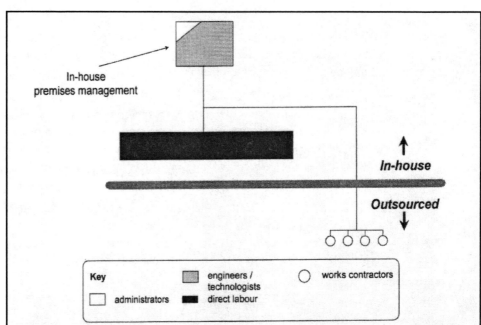

Outsourcing

Over the past two decades there has been a relentless move to outsourcing of one shape or another. The concept of outsourcing was discussed in principle in Chapter 1.1.6; there are two generic versions of the outsourcing approach:

- outsourcing the facilities services management, ie the direction and co-ordination of task contractors/operators

- 'out-tasking' which means contracting-out individual facilities service tasks such as cleaning and security.

The term 'out-tasking' applies whether the facilities services management is in-house or outsourced.

In the premises management arrangement at Fig. 2.1.C (next page) certain of the non-engineering operations such as cleaning and security are out-tasked with tasks such as the maintenance of heating, air-conditioning and electrical services and the repair and maintenance of the 'fabric' being retained as an in-house operation.

Proponents of such an arrangement might perceive the following advantages:

- specialist contractors can do their work without the need for dedicated in-house supervision

- in-house maintenance teams can respond quickly to emergency service requirements

- the core premises management team can shed its 'blue-collar' image by replacing technicians/technologists with non-specialist administrators.

Fig. 2.1C
Outsourcing some of the premises services

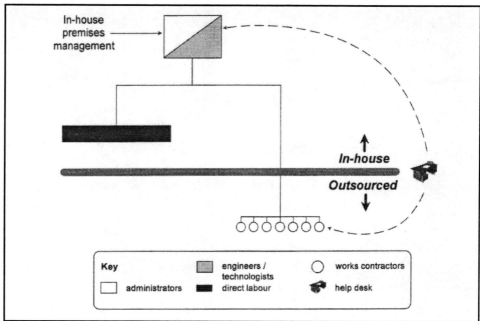

If a help-desk were to be provided in this set-up it would probably only be of the 'first-generation' variety merely helping the maintenance team to manage their operations without any 'added' value user interface benefits.

Sometimes organisations outsource the facilities services management and some of the tasks while retaining the rest of the tasks in-house as discussed above. In these circumstances the facilities sponsor has to decide whether to transfer the direction of the in-house task teams to the facilities services manager or to retain this directive function in-house. The problem with the latter is that it can draw the Intelligent Client Function (ICF) into 'hands-on' management which, as will be discussed later, is likely to mean that the strategic issues fail to get the individual attention they need.

On the other hand the former arrangement whereby in-house teams look to an external directive manager can also raise delicate issues. For instance, who assesses the employees' annual performance ratings and what redress does the external manager have for poor performance? Setting up the service-level agreement as a quasi-contract to mirror, as closely as possible, the conditions of the outsourced tasks will go a long way to reducing the extent of the problem, but in either case this uneasy split of procurement cultures is best avoided wherever possible.

However, most facilities departments in larger organisations now look like the set-up in Fig. 2.1.D (over the page) with just a small handyman gang to sort out 'special' problems, and with all main delivery of accommodation and one or two business support services (like mail/messenger and reprographics) being provided by individual specialist works contractors or small - 'part-bundled' - groups of specialist contractors under a main contractor.

This arrangement sometimes extends to the provision of general and engineering maintenance on site by resident contractors on either a lump sum contract, some form of schedule of measured rates or cost reimbursement. This set up has been accompanied by a shrinking of the core premises management team - both technical and administrative - but with an increase in the calibre of the non-technical staff supporting the interface of the core business and the outsourced service delivery which will also include many non-premises related tasks.

Commercial contracting, ie the provision of predetermined facilities services for a single price per annum, or on a schedule of rates, or both, is depicted at Fig. 2.1.E (over the page). This is the normal arrangement under PFI/ PPP-type contracts but is

Fig. 2.1.D
Outsourcing virtually all premises services on separate or 'bundled' contracts

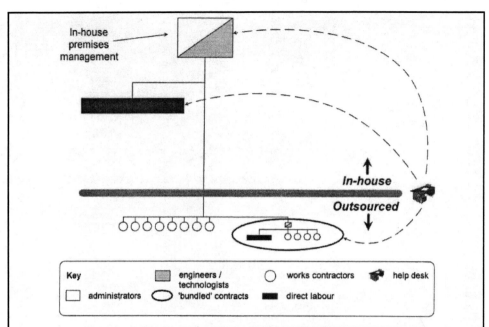

Fig. 2.1.E
Total facilites outsourcing - lump sum contract

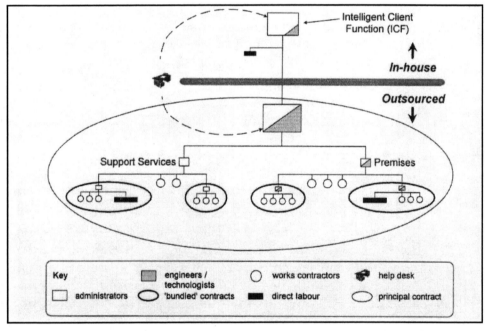

not to be recommended for routine facilities management requirements as it is liable to lead to the employer losing control of the costs and quality of the services provided.

This, together with the inevitable non-scheduled works, contractual claims and conflict of interests normally encountered in any lump sum or cost-reimbursement contract arrangement, explains why the process of individual task-contract management is becoming a more popular alternative.

The process for procuring facilities services is depicted at Fig. 2.1.F is similar to the management contracting and construction management routes applying in construction work and described in more detail in Chapter 6.3.5. Basically, they involve payment of a lump sum or percentage or sliding scale fee to a contractor or management company to organise and manage the tasks to an agreed specification and budget; the employer will sometimes enter into direct contract with the works contractors using a managing agent to co-ordinate the service provision, or the principal management contractor may interpose contractually and as the paying agent. However, in both cases the employer is committed to pay the price charged by the works contractors and is at direct risk of their default, albeit that the managing

Fig. 2.1.F
Total facilties outsourcing - management contract

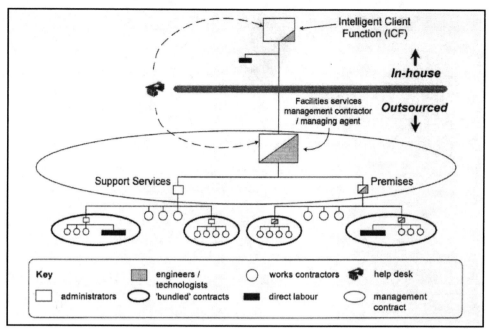

agent or management contractor will work to mitigate problems. Effectively this is the structure of so-called 'partnering' arrangements, the main difference in the latter being that the intention of the parties to work together to mutual benefit is normally expressed in a mission statement, signed by both sides but with little or no contractual significance.

One recent innovation is known as 'bundle-management' in which there is no single external facilities services manager. Instead there are groups of task contractors 'bundled' together under the overall contractual umbrella of one of their number who takes contractual responsibility for their individual and collective performance. Such an arrangement is shown at Fig. 2.1.G. Note that the liaison function between the facilities sponsor and each of the bundle managers becomes partly of a directive nature compared with the single point responsibility of an external facilities services management regime. Getting the balance right in the ICF to ensure that its strategic role is not compromised by too much 'hands-on' activity is make-or-break for such an arrangement.

Fig. 2.1.G
Bundle management contracts

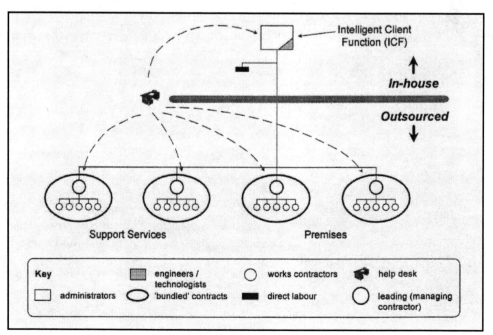

All of these regimes require in-house management teams of varying sizes. However, the 'total management' packages need only a small kernel of core staff to liaise with the outsource partner - and some organisations believe that a simple Board Director/contractor relationship is appropriate, thereby eliminating all non-core facilities personnel. Although this may be appropriate for smaller firms, in general failure to institute a robust 'Intelligent Client Function' (ICF - see below and also Chapter 1.1.1) is a recipe for total disaster.

Structures for in-house management

The on-going protracted debate about the merits and failings of outsourcing has possibly disguised the fact that, for many years, most organisations have had their facilities provided on a part-in/part-out-house basis. Contract services for work such as 'cleaning', 'maintenance', and 'security' have for long been acceptable as an alternative to the payroll and management liability for teams of semi-skilled operatives.

Where the in-house direct labour structure prevails in a substantial form there is a need for well qualified management, both blue-and-white collar, to brief and supervise their work. This can amount to a sizeable overhead, especially if their reimbursement is linked to general salary scales within the organisation which may result in payment at higher-than-open-market levels for their skills. Furthermore, in practice, the contractor's equivalent manager may well find themselves supervising a larger volume of work on different sites; 'Parkinson's Law' (ie that the job will expand to fill the time available) is always a threat to the economic efficiency of in-house regimes.

From the in-house operatives' viewpoint the problem of uncompetitive wage levels also applies, and management may have to deal directly with Trade Union disputes, representations and working practices. A premises audit carried out in a Financial Services organisation a few years back uncovered a building services maintenance cost which was three times the sector norm. Further investigations uncovered plumbing fitters with salaries linked to the organisation's core business scales working a shift system affording them an income of £35,000 per annum; this, together with a complete absence of either stock control or financial management, produced a level of expenditure in line with the worst abuses of the in-house process.

An in-house team set up to provide any services on a 'direct labour' basis should identify that component of staff which could be replaced by contractors and 'market-test', either formally - as with Government, Local Authority and some corporate commercial departments - or by benchmarking using the services of a facilities auditor.

The 'intelligent client'

The outsourcing process usually brings a sea-change to the way facilities are provided and managed. One of the key issues - and one most rarely addressed properly - is the size, structure and remit of the people left behind (or put in) after outsourcing to look after the user's interests and to interface with the outsourced management vehicle.

Too often in recent times this residual client post has been set up as an afterthought by core business managers who do not understand what facilities management is about or how to ensure that the business gets the facilities it needs at the right price. This flawed approach is usually accompanied by an undue measure of haste, wherein organisations have leaped from in-house to outsourced services without considering the intermediate position, ie benchmarking the existing facilities operation and bolstering up where found wanting. Sometimes, simply changing one or two personnel and/or introducing more sophisticated performance management techniques can be just as effective as handing over the whole facilities operation to the first contractor who walks through the door offering to transform the operation at half the cost.

Outsourcing of facilities management is now commonplace world-wide, but there is rather a dearth of spectacular successes. Although failure of the outsourced regime often has to do with inefficiency of client, contractor or both, a frequent contributor to the downfall lies in a thoughtless, unprofessional and precipitate approach to the whole process of decision-making and procurement and the inadequacy of the residual Intelligent Client Function (ICF).

To properly understand the outsourcing issue, it is necessary to revisit the diagram (originally Fig. 1.1.A) showing The three facets of facilities management - sponsorship, intelligence and services management reproduced here in a slightly modified form to illustrate the value and supply chains (Fig. 2.1.H).

Fig. 2.1.H
The value and supply chains of facilities management

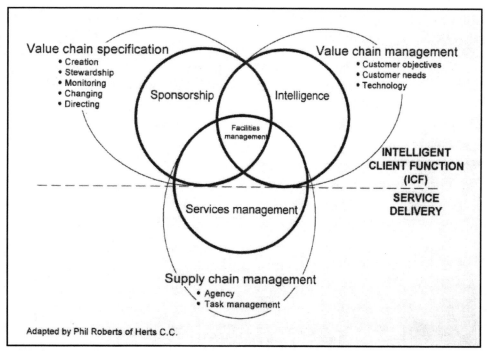

The term sponsorship in respect of facilities implies the ownership of responsibility for the facilities provision ie the stewardship of the organisation's facilities policy for the provision, maintenance and allocation of facilities resources required to support corporate objectives. This policy should stem from the intelligence gathered by the ICF relating to the business needs and the techniques, technology and ability available from the facilities industry to meet them.

The modified version of the 'three facets' diagram illustrates the point that the value chain runs via the 'intelligence' facet spanning the knowledge bases of both the user and the service provider. The supply chain works on the information gleaned in the value chain by development of a facilities policy and a cost-efficient method of services delivery which is, of course, highly dependent upon good communications right along the chain.

Neither the supply chain nor the value chain can operate satisfactorily unless the Intelligent Client Function (ICF) is given a formal identity, totally separated from hands-on service delivery, and is staffed at a meaningful level of experience, ability and numerical strength.

Although normally a by-product of the outsourcing process the creation of the ICF in the form described here is just as applicable - indeed essential - to facilities operated fully or partially in-house.

It is the ICF which draws up the 'balanced scorecard' relating facilities performance to core business requirements (see Chapter 2.2.6) which is part of the value management process spawning and supporting the facilities policy.

Case Studies - the Intelligent Client Function

One public sector department with a portfolio of half-a-dozen buildings totalling some 30,000 sq m outsourced its whole facilities operation a few years ago. The residual client was a full-time senior clerical officer plus 20% of the time of a low-grade executive. Regardless of the individual qualities of these personnel their chances of delivering value for money in their organisation were nil. They would spend all their time dealing with the outsourcing contract (inadequately) and have no time at all (or sufficient authority) to identify and represent the business case for the facilities provided.

A better example is at Fig. 2.1.J where management of another public sector organisation's facilities comprising some 50,000 sq m in ten buildings was outsourced to a managing agent. Although a little top-heavy (the diagram shows the original set-up immediately post-outsourcing) the structure has proved highly cost-effective with sustained levels of improvement in performance and value for money over a five-year period.

Fig. 2.1.J
ICF structure - large headquarters estate

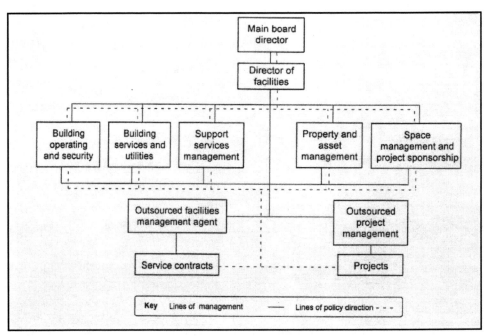

Regardless of the shape of the network it is imperative that strategic responsibility for the overall function lies within the organisation, that the personnel entrusted with sponsoring that responsibility have the appropriate levels of skill and motivation and that they have control over, and have unrestricted access to, all essential information and data (including costs) and systems.

It is extremely important to recognise that, as well as careful management of resources, the strategic role of internal facilities managers equally involves intelligence gathering; they must constantly be aware of the way the business is developing and the consequential effects on the facilities policy and the strategies in place for its delivery.

In a fully devolved outsourced regime the residual 'intelligent client' remains the creator and guardian of the facilities policy, constantly looking inwards to the core activity, picking up signs of change to be accommodated, prompting alternative but efficient changes in procedure which will reduce and/or add value to the facilities overhead.

In a less clearly defined structure, where the internal facilities manager has some 'hands-on' services management activity, this strategic function must be recognised and given its reign (preferably independence) even amidst the hustle and bustle of day-to-day contract administration and man-management.

Ideally, in the larger organisation, the facilities manager should be a Board appointment. It has historically been quite common for 'real estate' to command a Board position, so, if the thesis proposed here, ie that real estate asset management should be a sub-set of facilities rather than a separate entity, and given that some or all of the other facilities support services can be provided in the total facilities management structures being considered, then the level of expenditure and scope of responsibilities being managed within such a regime would clearly justify representation at the highest level of management decision-making.

When facilities have to report through a Director of Finance, Real Estate, Human Resources or any other discipline, there is always the danger that their case may not be properly understood or appreciated.

Certainly many of the older school of Finance Directors still see facilities as a necessary evil, the first port of call at times of adverse cash flow; they can certainly not be relied upon to argue a case to increase facilities budgets to generate increased overall productivity or to contain risk.

Real Estate directors have traditionally put the emphasis on premises as real estate investments rather than admitting their real function which is as an invaluable piece of 'plant' to accommodate the activities envisaged by the corporate plan.

In many respects, if facilities has to get to the Board via another discipline an obvious spokesperson would be the Human Resources Director, given the interaction of facilities with people which is at the heart of the facilities manager's mission. However, as has been stressed several times, it is the calibre of the people that counts, much more than the regime in which they find themselves, always provided that such regime does not physically or philosophically get in the way of delivery of the required facilities performance.

2.1.3 OUTSOURCING

Practical criteria for deciding on an outsourced solution

The theoretical arguments in respect of core v non-core activities have already been developed in Chapter 1.1.6 and the sort of facilities management structures suitable to deal with the outsourcing of large parts of the facilities management activities were described earlier in this chapter. However, in the real world there are many practical issues which need to be taken on board when deciding on whether or not to outsource tasks or services management.

The purpose of outsourcing should not be regarded as predominantly to save money although in many instances, including examples of facilities, this has been a by-product. Generally speaking, facilities management departments have grown organically as the demands made on them by core business have increased. In the process, most have become, to a smaller or greater degree, either uncompetitive, inefficient or both.

As a consequence, specialist firms have found it relatively easy to persuade core management that contracting out of facilities, whether a single task or the whole lot, will bring savings and greater efficiency. Very often they are proved correct.

Some of the better facilities management firms do indeed possess a better calibre of facilities management expertise, qualification and experience than exists in the facilities organisations they are set to replace. They are specialists whereas many of their in-house counterparts are generalists, frequently falling into post by accident or expediency and possibly due to a policy of in-house promotion or redeployment rather than recruitment.

Contractors naturally have a much wider knowledge of the market for services - its strengths, weaknesses and pitfalls - and the service providers operating within it. Many have large purchasing power which can lead to economies of scale and also the use of financial muscle to overcome operating difficulties with individual service providers. On the other hand their culture and philosophy does not always match that of the dedicated in-house facilities manager.

Aside from the philosophical arguments about core/non-core activities there are a number of practical reasons why outsourcing may, in certain cases, work to the core business advantage. These concern:

- cost

- quality

- motivation

- flexibility

- availability of skills.

In theory, there is no reason why a fully resourced in-house team should not carry out its functions as efficiently as any external agent - and save the company the contractor's mark-up for profit and risk (not overheads, however, for they will be common). In practice, however, there are few examples of such efficiency; the advent of benchmarking as a near-standard procedure has shown many in-house set-ups to be uncompetitive in financial and performance terms. Unfortunately for them the general reaction of core business management has been to go straight to an outsourced solution rather than to afford the facilities department an opportunity to re-engineer the existing team structure.

In such cases the objectives often have as much to do with getting rid of internal management problems (such as trades union negotiations and difficult personalities) as with any real belief in the added value promised by the contractors.

Economic issues

The costs of a fully-resourced in-house team, ie one which directly employs all, or substantially all, of the management, technical and operational staff required to carry out the facilities activities, are usually higher - on a like-for-like quality basis - than those emanating from an outsourced solution.

The reasons for this are many and varied, but stem from two main sources:

- the lack of competition

- over-provision.

Lack of competition, as has been discussed earlier, can be addressed by market testing and benchmarking. Nevertheless, there are issues aside from the market place which can cause the in-house regime to be more expensive:

- inefficient size of operation

- 'locking-in' to in-house pay structures

- militant trades union activity

- lack of experience.

Size of operation

Of all these issues it is the size of the operation which is the most critical. An organisation running all its own facilities will need the resources of all the management skills described earlier in the chapter. Even if these were available in-house the likelihood of every one being 'best of breed' or fully gainfully occupied would be remote. A good example of this is considered under 'Health and Safety at Work' in Chapter 8.2.5, here it is seen that, once the project stage of implementing the new legislation is over, the rationale of having a full-time Health and Safety Officer often recedes; 'sharing' becomes a viable option, or specialist consultancy services can take a lot of responsibility off the facilities manager's shoulders. (However, the government may require a director to be nominated for this responsibility.)

The key danger is that the organisation's needs will not exactly fit the optimum resource required to service this. So, a qualified services engineer running the in-house maintenance team may only need to be 70% occupied in that role given the scale and nature of the activity; nevertheless the chances are that they will either:

- work at only 70% efficiency or

- work at 100% efficiency and over-provide services.

'Right sizing', to use the jargon, is the problem here because, in a similar position with a contractor, the engineer would be given responsibility for other sites and thus add to the organisation's bottom line profit.

Pay structures

Linking trades management and operations to in-house pay structures will, in most cases, result in wages and salaries higher than the levels available to the building services and general labour sectors of the external / commercial workforce. Add to this the adverse effects of non-competitive, unbenchmarked management of in-house departments and trades union demands (reasonable or otherwise) in respect of working practices and it is not difficult to see how the in-house effort could cost two, or even three, times the external market norm.

Experience

Another major problem for the in-house team is the rate at which their accumulated experience gets out of date once they are removed from the fertile, competitive, cross-company contracting environment which is so essential to the ability of individuals to retain their market-edge in terms of knowledge and practical application. The mere fact of being separated from day-to-day contact with one's peer group is enough to result in fall-off in ability - including loss of confidence - within a matter of months rather than years. An even worse problem is the prolonged application, by the long-term in-house managers, of increasingly out-dated concepts and solutions to the organisation's changing facilities requirements.

These problems mainly relate to the middle-management tier of facilities, ie the level which can easily be replaced by an external counterpart. At the operational level formal training programmes can improve performance, and at senior management level there should be sufficient daily contact with core management to guarantee keeping abreast of new business management techniques; in any event, technology changes many times faster than management principles.

Some facilities departments have moved over to becoming profit centres in their own right - either externally structured with parent company equity participation or wholly owned in-house. This concept of the facilities group saving costs for the parent organisation - whilst earning a profit in its own right - has its attractions, especially where contracting non-core services to other companies is part of the business plan. Such examples are, however, still in their early years; it remains to be seen, over time, how the core business will fare within such an avant-garde regime as core and non-core interests diverge commercially. A further problem of such an arrangement is that growth of the new business is inevitably accompanied by the gradual replacement of the original senior facilities personnel who take much of the experience and goodwill of the old regime with them.

Quality issues

The trade-off between cost and quality of service is critical and is the most important factor in the outsourcing decision. Well-managed in-house departments frequently run up costs of facilities way above the outsourced norm simply by over-providing quality of service. This feature is particularly common in the more affluent companies where the cost of facilities is not seen as significant and the excuse given for exceeding cost benchmarks is that the higher quality is appropriate to their business needs and status. However, wasted resources are wasted resources wherever they surface and all companies have a moral, if not a business, obligation to make the best use of whatever resources they bring to bear on the operation of their business.

Quality management in facilities is considered in greater detail in Chapter 2.4. Insistence on quality in facilities management has to follow through into any outsourcing arrangement. EN ISO 9000, or a commitment to it, may be relevant to some contracts but much more important is a perceived and proven dedication to:

- customer's satisfaction
- training
- continuous improvement
- flexibility
- systems
- controls
- procedures
- management.

These qualities, together with the supplier's financial status, can easily be checked out by references. Whether quality is delivered will, in the event, be less dependent upon the management regime than the calibre of the people given responsibility for the mission. Nevertheless the people responsible for delivery must be made properly aware of the quality required if under- or over-provision of quality is to be avoided in any of the delivery structures.

Motivation

Examples of the state of inertia which used to prevail in many parts of the public sector and the large corporate commercial organisations have considerably reduced in the past decade or two. The big in-house facilities teams are far better motivated than in the past, partly due to the sense of being part of, and contributing to, the evolution of the new facilities management discipline. Better education in the subject area, an elevation in its perceived importance and an increasingly higher calibre of senior facilities managers have improved motivation enormously across the board. Gone are the sinecures in FM for line managers who failed in their jobs but could not be dismissed; such weak links have been (or soon will be) replaced by dedicated, highly motivated ambitious professionals who may or may not be salaried members of staff.

The employee who joined the firm from school and worked their way up from messenger to head of facilities is now an anachronism, although the few examples of the 'one-firm firm' continue this philosophy to good advantage. Elsewhere, the modern facilities workforce is motivated by prospects of reward and advancement. In the outsourced facilities company both these goals are easier to come by than in the in-house equivalent which is part of a non-core department perceived in the main as being an unproductive overhead rather than a profit-centre.

The evidence arising out of the first serious wave of examples of transfers of in-house staff to contractors indicates that motivation of the transferred employees can often be enhanced by the inevitable change in management style, and working environment.

Flexibility

The well-structured external facilities contract should afford the requisite level of response to emergency change without the employer being unduly exposed to business or financial risk.

The directly employed workforce is, in theory at least, able to be moved from project to project, emergency to emergency, under the direct control of the organisation and without risk of contractual claims, such as for disruption and out-of-sequence working. Where the in-house set up becomes inflexible is where companies need to cut back temporarily on expenditure on facilities provision. In such situations contractors can usually re-deploy spare operatives on other sites, where they are probably operating slightly below projected resource quotas to optimise efficiency. Likewise, the contractor or consultant can usually find the resource required for a special task or project.

However, in-house teams sometimes do not have the authority to take on temporary relief staff as easily as their external counterparts.

The availability of skills

The multiplicity of skills needed in facilities management cannot all be reasonably brought in-house, so some outsourcing is virtually inevitable.

The problem is more exaggerated where the organisation has smaller facilities requirements, in which case full-time appointments of specialists, such as space planners, quantity surveyors, health and safety experts and engineers, is not viable.

In the large organisations, where it may be financially feasible to employ expensive qualified professionals, the costs incurred may be lower than the comparable consultants' fees but this benefit may be offset by:

- difficulty of efficiently matching resource to tasks
- lack of cross-fertilisation of ideas.

The problem of over-resourcing particular functions was discussed earlier in this chapter. Under-resourcing is also a problem where the task outgrows the resource, in which case outsourced assistance is usually needed to complement either numbers, or skills, or both.

A major weakness of the in-house professional appointment is the difficulty of enticing high-flying specialists away from a lucrative consulting or contracting career. Of course, not every post needs a high-flyer but pursuit of excellence demands good quality personnel in all key posts.

Good professionals will look for good ideas as they go about their business. They will then tend to plug them into other regimes where similar functions are being handled less efficiently. Consequently, the biggest problem with lifting consultants or contracting professionals out of their familiar environment and inserting them into cross-disciplined teams is the rapid loss of contact with their peer groups which means that the all-important cross-fertilisation of ideas which the external consultant transfers from one client to another, from one project to another, is lost.

2.1.4 DEVOLVED RESPONSIBILITY

Value management of change

The point has been stressed earlier that no outsourced facilities management solution should be adopted purely on the presumption that the contractor or agent can save the client money. The optimum way to approach the issue is to institute a formal value management process, ideally starting off with an independent 'benchmarking' exercise - not just for the operating costs but also for performance, management systems and structures. If there is any slack in the system it can be identified by the customer: then they can decide how best to tackle it.

Benchmarking is considered in Chapter 12.2 and, in greater detail, in the book 'An Introduction to Benchmarking Facilities'[3]. The process inevitably takes time although the better-organised facilities managers have their costs and performance regularly under review which makes formal benchmarking infinitely quicker.

The benchmarking process, properly executed to cover cost, performance and remedial action should lead seamlessly into function analysis (see Chapter 2.2.5) and the development of a formal facilities policy. This document will identify and specify the levels of performance required in every service together with policies on management of real estate and other assets and the financial implications of all the facilities policy's provisions.

Only when the value management process in respect of the actual policy is complete should attention turn to the issue of service delivery. Now that the organisation knows what it needs and has benchmarked target costs for each task (and the directive management function) it is appropriate to try to understand which service delivery structure will bring best value.

Value management techniques suitable for the above selection processes are described in Chapter 2.2 - Value Management.

Policy control

Maintaining the correct relationship between the provision of facilities and business objectives must always be the responsibility of the ICF (not the services manager). This relationship, and the resulting levels of facilities performance and costs in both the 'premises' and 'support services' wings of the facilities policy, requires constant monitoring in terms of:

- service provision

- cost

- change.

Such monitoring is a key component of the facilities sponsor's activity once the policies are established and agreed. Experience suggests that core business management is rarely likely to be pro-active in its assessment of changes in its facilities requirement. For this reason the 'intelligent' role of the ICF has to take on the responsibility for not only anticipating such changes but also continually examining the way the business operates and prompting changes that will generate the efficiency of facilities without detriment to the core function.

---

[3] *Williams, B (1999) 'An Introduction to Benchmarking Facilities' - BEB Ltd, Bromley, Kent*

Taking independent advice

Many of the organisations who have gone down the outsourcing route have done so on the persuasive advice of one or other of the facilities management contractors or agents operating in the field. Frequently this advice comes from the 'consultancy' side of their business with offers to do an 'independent' review of the facilities -possibly benchmarking costs and performance; usually this shows an opportunity for improvement and, before they know where they are, companies are into some kind of outsourced 'partnering' arrangement with the 'consultant's' parent company.

In many cases this so-called 'consultancy' is simply a marketing ploy to get a foot in the door, with no remit from the parent to come up with anything other than a 'partnering' recommendation.

There is an alternative to this unsatisfactory route. For example, a major government department appointed independent consultants to carry out an independent review of the facilities management in their headquarters estate. They were asked to overview existing arrangements, recommend improvements, identify the most appropriate procurement arrangements, trawl the market for the right players offering the right service with the right experience and help set up and monitor the tendering and selection process.

A key part of the study was to assist in the development of a formal facilities policy (with benchmarked costs and performance written in) and to advise on the structure of the Intelligent Client Function (ICF) which would fulfil the sponsorship and intelligence facets of the facilities management trinity.

The benefits of such an independent approach are clear to see. Not only will the recommended solutions be unbiased (they may even preclude an outsourced solution) but the chances of being properly prepared and established to deal with the outsourced facilities manager are greatly enhanced. Many facilities contractors start out quite happy with a situation where all that is left in the client body is someone to authorise payment of the bills! Unfortunately the inevitable dissatisfaction with service levels and performance usually results in criticism being levied at the contractors through no fault of their own: the real cause of the problem is the lack of an ICF-monitored business-sensitive facilities policy.

Directive management options

The available contract arrangements for directive management of facilities service delivery considered earlier are similar to those in construction contracts ie prime cost (100% in-house), lump sum, fee management, and managing agency (just like construction management when the employer enters into all task contracts and pays the agent a co-ordination fee).

The managing agent role is growing in popularity and is frequently disguised as some form of partnering. However there are questions over the ability and enthusiasm of the larger contractors to carry out what is essentially perceived as being a purely fee-based professional service. The contractor-based facilities managers prefer to contract for the tasks; their buying power may bring cost savings which may, or may not, be passed on to the client, but a key commercial driver is the ability to handle (and invest) the cashflow.

Among the companies who have fared best in the managing agency role are those springing out from professional firms such as surveyors and engineers and the 'management buy-out' firms. Certainly the market is beginning to polarise between these generic groupings and the big firms are by no means getting everything their own way.

A common water-shed in terms of the in/out-source syndrome is the location of the 'budget holder'. Some organisations hand over the budget completely to the outsource agent and only want to know if things are going wrong. Others want to control everything in-house on a 'open-book' basis; some 'profit-sharing', or 'savings over existing levels' deals are carried out on this basis.

Shared savings

The concept of allowing contractors or consultants to share in any savings they make over existing budgets is seriously flawed. It is a route sometimes adopted by facilities managers who have no authority to spend money on consultancy fees; it usually results in the sum given away being many times greater than would have been paid to a consultant to help get the level of existing costs down by application of the three facets of cost control discussed in Chapter 2.3.2 (Fig. 2.3.A).

The partnering approach

However, facilities management is not, or should not be, just about money. In recognition of this, most serious contenders for the innumerable varieties of outsourcing are now praising the virtues of a 'partnering' approach; this longer term relationship again entails the in-house facilities manager in an ICF role, briefing and monitoring the performance of the external manager, being responsible for all strategic decisions and forming an essential interface between the external team and the core-business activity.

In this case, facilities service managers will be seeking long-term partnering agreements whereby both they and their clients can benefit from a continuing improvement of performance in both camps over time.

Supply chain management

Modern approaches to procurement of construction and facilities services frequently embrace the concept of supply chain management. This is the process whereby the end user is able to monitor/control the quality and progress of goods and services from the point of origin right through to delivery and installation/execution.

The process inevitably involves the establishment of lists of 'preferred' suppliers, often tied into some form of 'framework agreement' complying with EU legislation on competitivity, eg pre-bid schedules of rates for call-off of work as required.

These suppliers are usually tied in to the directive management organisation - indeed there already exist some groups offering a package of supply-chain managed services which are, ideally in their eyes, encompassed in some form of 'partnering' arrangement.

The benefits of greater certainty of quality, cost and timeliness have to be weighed against the frailties of a 'closed shop' operation which may not always offer prices in tune with the best available in the open market.

The UK government[4] has experimented with such arrangements on some of its own construction projects and reported substantial savings and improvements in performance.

In the final event quality and reliability are likely to be key criteria in the facilities policy with the benchmarking process being used to ensure that costs and value do not get too far out of alignment.

The devolved risk

Stephen Harrup's[5] lucid illustration of the extent to which core business is potentially

---

[4] *MoD Defence Estates: 'Building Down Barriers'.*

[5] *Harrup, S. (1994) 'The Facilities Manager's Role in Corporate Risk Management', Centre for Facilities Management (CFM), University of Strathclyde, UK.*

at risk through inadequate provision of facilities the further away from 'in-house' the provision of non-core service functions stretches is given at Fig. 2.1.K. The risk portrayed here is, however, not so much price risk as the risk of policy and quality control being devolved to suppliers rather than retained by the ICF.

Fig. 2.1.K
Devolution of services function from the core function - degree of risk exposure

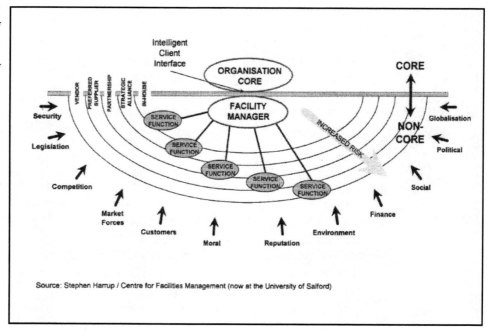

Source: Stephen Harrup / Centre for Facilities Management (now at the University of Salford)

The key features in risk management to be addressed when procuring outsourced service functions are:

- tight, professionally constructed contracts (and that does not necessarily mean by lawyers - many lawyers are very bad at drafting contracts for technologically-based services)

- tight, professionally constructed specifications

- full investigation of potential contractor's financial standing, track record, management and training procedures and control systems

- insistence on full disclosure of all data - to be available on client's premises at all times

- employer's right to choose or reject key personnel

- efficient quality control procedures

- performance levels, indicators, methods of measurement, bonuses and penalties

- efficient mechanisms for dispute resolution.

The 'partnering management contract' approach particularly aims to avoid disputes and undoubtedly, given the right personnel, can elevate the contracting-out process to a much more professionally committed plane.

Familiarisation and due diligence

Where a large in-house direct labour or professional services operation is to be outsourced on a TUPE-type arrangement the process of acclimatisation to the new commercial status is critical. Here again adequate time must be built into the programme to allow this to happen properly. The period should commence well ahead of contractor selection and include adequate re-training opportunities - especially with regard to cultures, objectives, practices and management regimes in the contracting-sector.

For the contractors' part the need to carry out due diligence on the quality and efficiency of the resources (human and physical) they are about to inherit must be recognised. If this process has to be rushed then disaster in the early days of a contract will be inevitable.

Cultural shock is the killer of outsourcing success, not only with regards to the service providers but also in the context of user acceptance of the new regime. When the ICF is formed from residual non-outsourced employees they have to understand that their role is completely non-executive in terms of service delivery: any approaches to the residual personnel by the user concerning work which is now in the domain of the outsourced contractor must be redirected thereby both preserving the integrity of the ICF structure and avoiding confusion as to respective areas of responsibility.

Can outsourcing work?

There is nothing wrong with the outsourcing concept provided it is properly applied and appropriate to the circumstances. Non-confrontational agreements of the management contract/partnering variety generally work better but, in the end, it is not the system or the contract which will make or break it. The calibre and commitment of the people involved - on both sides of the 'contractual wall' - is a key factor and getting good people into place with the right skills and attitude takes time and experience; unfortunately both of these precious assets tend to be missing from most attempts to inflict an outsourcing regime upon a highly vulnerable and dependent user.

The help desk

The days when the premises manager used to pin up notes of telephone requests to deal with problems are long gone. In place of the pin-board it is normal to have either a formal manual register or a computerised help desk system.

Helpdesk systems are becoming the rule rather than the exception, particularly where there is a significant extent of outsourcing. It is however important to emphasise that apart from the obvious need to channel tasks to the relevant service provider, the help desk has three other highly important functions - public relations, performance measurement and customer satisfaction.

One real danger is that the interposition of the helpdesk may distance the ICF from personal contact with their customers. A personalised approach, either by way of a formal physical enquiry point, a dedicated telephone help-line team, or both, can be an invaluable help to the facilities management team to gain the respect and confidence of the users.

Performance targets and achievements should be publicly displayed - this will help the team to a better performance as well - and customer feed-back on the quality of service delivered, both at the helpdesk and the coal-face, actively encouraged.

Whether the help-desk is manned by the in-house or the outsourced team may not be too significant provided that both have access to it for reference. Insofar as it can also function in a performance-monitoring capacity it may usefully form the focal point for any performance-related remuneration for an outsourced service manager or vendor.

The most up-to-date help-desk systems are incorporated into the computer-aided facilities operational and information management systems (CAFOMS and CAFIMS) described in more detail in Chapter 2.6.4 - Facilities Management Systems.

2.1.5 THE COST OF FACILITIES MANAGEMENT

Taking the three facets of facilities management in Fig. 2.1.H and separating the costs of the ICF and the Facilities Services Management role (in whatever form) from the costs of the facilities tasks themselves, we can begin to benchmark the costs of the facilities management function. In a scenario where all of the premises operating services (such as cleaning and maintenance) and most of the support services (such as catering, reprographics and distribution) are out-tasked, a sensible range of costs for the ICF would be from 2.5% - 5% of the annual expenditure (excluding the cost of rent and rates). Services Management (be it fee management, partnering or lump sum) will be from 3% to 10% of these costs depending on the scope of work.

Anything less than these sensible levels will probably lose the organisation money rather than save it. And, depriving the ICF of the necessary resources or status will guarantee that value added by facilities is nil - or less!

Outsourcing can bring a lot of benefits if done with forethought and without a political agenda. However, it is not a panacea, and if it results in the baby being thrown out with the bathwater, ie without leaving behind an effective residual client function, it may well result in disaster.

2.2 VALUE MANAGEMENT

Introduction

The concept of value management has already been introduced in earlier chapters - indeed the decision to delay formal examination of the process until this juncture rather than addressing it in detail from the very start of the text was a close call. In the event, detailed consideration of the concept of value and more formalised approaches to value management have been postponed to this point to enable the principles and practice to be discussed in depth without overshadowing some of the basic issues which needed to be aired up-front in Section 1.

2.2.1 THE CONCEPT OF VALUE

Definitions

Going back to first principles it is important to understand the precise meaning of the word 'value'. The dictionary[1] definition is: 'that which renders anything useful'; so, in facilities terms, a building or piece of equipment or service which is useful to the business can be said to have value.

An appropriate definition of the value of facilities is therefore: 'the usefulness of the facilities provided in the context of the activities they support'. This definition is drawn widely enough to encompass both commercial activities, eg retail, and social activities, eg education.

However, the flexibility of the English Language (and the way it is used) permits many words to have 'shades' of meaning. 'Value' is such a word which is used sometimes to qualify a 'price' or 'cost'; in these circumstances it is usual for adjectives such as 'good' or 'best' to be used in the qualifying process, ie 'good value' or 'best value' which then expresses not only 'usefulness' but also the reasonableness of the price paid - ie: 'value for money'

BS EN 12973:2000: Value Management states that 'the concept of value relies on the relationship between the satisfaction of many differing needs and the resources used in doing so'. So far, so good. However, the BS further goes on to state that 'the fewer resources used or the greater the satisfaction of needs, the greater is the value'. This latter part of the definition needs to be examined carefully in the context of facilities management - and, indeed, with respect to any business case founded upon a calculation of return on investment (ROI) - see below.

2.2.2 VALUE FOR MONEY

Definition

The word 'worth' also means 'value' or 'that quality which renders a thing valuable'. So when, moving on to what the dictionary defines as 'value for money', we read 'something well worth the money spent' it becomes clear that the usefulness of a thing (a facility in this context) has to be set against the price paid for it when determining whether or not value for money has been achieved. In the same way that beauty is said to be in the eye of the beholder so value is discrete to the beneficiary of the offering.

Most people would accept the highest quality available as long as the price paid was little or no greater than the price of meeting actual needs. However, in all but the

---

[1] *Chambers English Dictionary.*

most affluent micro-economic environments people and companies can normally make do perfectly well with simple functioning offerings - needs, not wish-lists, are the order of the day.

As BS EN 12973:2000 says: 'stakeholders, internal and external customers may all hold differing views of what represents value'; therefore providing 'greater satisfaction of needs' may (as the BS also implies) represent value but, on the other hand may not represent optimum value for money - a point which the BS cost/value equation reinforces. The economic law of diminishing returns always comes into play when enhancements to an offering cost more than the added value created; in such cases the return on the investment drops below the optimum level, so although still providing 'value for money' the offering no longer provides 'best value'.

In simple terms, nothing is cheap if it is not what you need. So more quality for proportionately less resources does not necessarily deliver a best value solution; nor does getting more for the budget available

Best Value

The term 'best value' may therefore be defined as: 'the offering which provides the beneficiary with the highest return on investment (ROI)'. Whether that investment and return are measurable in 'hard', ie actual or 'soft', ie estimated terms does not matter provided that in the latter case a diligent and meaningful analysis of costs and benefits is carried out.

In the case of facilities most benefits are 'soft', eg comfort, cleanliness, ergonomic efficiency, whereas the costs of service provision are 'hard'. This means that calculation of a return on the investment may have to rely on financial or social gains assessed through observations, experience or judgements of the beneficial effects of the offering rather than on actual recorded income.

Affordability

Frequently in all walks of life, whether personal or corporate, people realise that they cannot afford to pay for what they would really like - or really need. The ability to afford to buy something relates to having the money or access to funds rather than the willingness to invest.

There are circumstances where people or organisations physically cannot put their hands on more money however much they might need it; if the bank turns down an individual's loan application for the car which is essential for the applicant's self-employed business activities and there is no viable alternative strategy (such as short-term car-hire or reducing other overheads) then that person's business activity will not progress. If, on the other hand, the loan was offered at a rate of interest which was considered unreasonable, ie not a fair price the purchase might be affordable in terms of access to the funds but rejected on principle, or because the same investment in another offering would bring greater rewards: which is where the concept of return on investment has to be set alongside affordability - probably formally, in the case of a business decision, and informally in the case of a personal choice.

An example of a formal calculation of ROI using sensitivity testing is given at Fig 2.2.G below.

Most organisations have what is known as the 'criterion rate of return' on their investments, ie the minimum return they must be sure of if the investment is to be sanctioned. In practice, the rate often varies depending on the object of investment and the risks attached; in times of cash-flow difficulties firms will often seek a far greater return on projects or services involving capital up-front than they will seek where payment can be deferred or provided by others, eg new build owner-occupation as opposed to rental.

Any proposal which does not achieve the criterion ROI is de facto not affordable, regardless of the actual availability of funds because those funds will be reserved for offerings which do meet the required ROI.

In the real world, many organisations have too little funds chasing too many useful resources and so they have to increase the required ROI to enable 'affordable' choices to be made. All of which means that the definition of 'affordable' given above in the context of value still holds good (so long as the ROI has been set at a level which controls affordability) and mere shortage of available cash should not influence 'affordability' in the context of this definition.

2.2.3 VALUE MANAGEMENT PRINCIPLES

Definitions

Referring once more to the BS on Value Management, it describes the process as 'a style of management, particularly dedicated to motivating people, developing skills and promoting synergies and innovation, with the aim of maximising the overall performance of an organisation. It provides a new way to use many existing management methods'.

The BS goes on to discuss what value management is all about, but a more succinct summary from a book about value management of projects[2] describes it as 'a service which maximises the functional value (of a project) by managing its evolution and development from concept to completion, through the comparison and audit of all decisions against a value system determined by the client or customer'.

The term 'value system' here is critical. As the BS states 'Applied at the Corporate level, Value Management relies on a value-based organisational culture taking into account value for stakeholders and customers'. In other words, organisations need to know what is worth investing in and to have established systems and tools to help them in those investment decisions.

Value management of facilities

As facilities can account for up to 20% of an organisation's outgoings they should clearly be part of the overall VM process and not dealt with off-line.

In a facilities management context value management can be described as 'the process whereby facilities which are useful to the business are provided at a price which is both fair and affordable'. A 'fair' price is one which represents a good bargain in the relevant market place; an 'affordable' price is, as discussed above, one that meets the organisation's criteria for return on investment (ROI).

The origins of value management are rooted in the 'value engineering' techniques developed for manufacturing industry in N. America following the Second World War. The distinction between value management and value engineering appears to have been made in Europe where the former term has been adopted by the European Union in its SPRINT programme (Strategic Programme for Innovation and Technology Transfer).

Value management and value engineering

In essence, value management is perceived in Europe as the all-embracing strategic process which incorporates a tactic called 'value engineering' as an essential and integral part of that overall process.

---

[2] *John Kelly and Steven Male - Value Management in Design and Construction, FC&FN Spon.*

Without using these specific terms the BS describes the strategic, high level value management process as one in which: 'objectives shall be specified in terms of value and be clearly established as baselines (enabling) the formulation of detailed objectives at all levels of responsibility'.

These detailed 'objectives' relate to 'a level of satisfaction of needs, a consumption of resources or a combination of both .... the links with the Value objectives that have been defined at strategic levels shall be clear and logical. At each level, agreed measures shall be identified that will make it possible to monitor the evolution of value objectives'.

The technique of value engineering is then brought into play to make sure that the value solution is achieved in the most cost efficient manner.

The author's definition of value engineering, previously referred to in Chapter 1.2.5 in connection with redundant performance is: 'the process whereby products and services are provided to the required performance for the least cost;' the corollary is that value engineering requires 'the elimination of redundant performance and attendant extra costs'.

Whether or not performance is redundant, ie is not required in the context of the functionality sought, is a decision which can only be properly taken within a 'value tree' framework supported by formal systems of 'function analysis' At the same time, however, it should be recognised that the elimination of redundant performance must start at the concept stage if it is to be wholly effective. In other words, determining the overall quality and quantity of space should be subject to a value engineering study just as much as the decision on what grade of carpet (if any) to put on the floors, or how to go about keeping the carpets clean.

If there is one feature which distinguishes value management from value engineering it is the fact that the former involves identifying, promulgating and overseeing the achievement of the organisation's requirements in terms of value, whereas the latter is concerned with the tactical approach to delivery - albeit still at every stage from concept to implementation.

2.2.4 THE VALUE MANAGEMENT PROCESS

A structured approach

The Institute of Value Management (IVM)[3] promotes the concept of a formal value management regime supported by clearly specified procedures involving appropriate tools and techniques. Whilst it may be somewhat premature to insist that facilities managers should always follow these procedures to the letter, they undoubtedly offer the opportunity to link facilities into the formal value management regime (if any) of the core business; at worst, they give facilities managers the opportunity to introduce the concepts in isolation as working models of best practice.

Isolated value engineering exercises may well be beneficial outside of the formal value management framework (eg: space-saving measures) but may well miss the point from time to time and end up in losses instead of benefits. Using the space-saving analogy further, increased densities in buildings may well reduce premises costs per capita but could result in inefficient working conditions; the latter should have been rooted out and eliminated as a possibility in the course of value managing the building use brief. Whoever invented sealed tins for sardines almost certainly had the successful long-term preservation of the contents as part of the original brief - otherwise grease-proof bags might have been selected as the cheapest method of containerisation!

---

[3] *The Institute of Value Management (IVM), 1-3 Birdcage Walk, Westminster, London SW1H 9JJ.*

The three facets of value management

The reader will by now have come to recognise the authors' enthusiasm for interactive trinities and so will not be surprised to learn that there are three inter-related facets of value management: identification/appraisal, implementation and monitoring - see Fig. 2.2.A.

Fig. 2.2.A
The three facets of value management

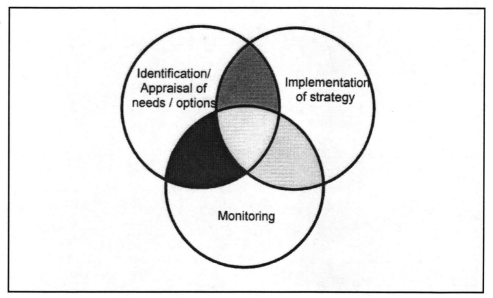

As we saw in another trinity at Fig. 1.1.A (reproduced below in modified form Fig 2.2.B) it is the 'intelligence' facet of facilities management which is responsible primarily for the 'value' chain; in this case, as with risk management, 'intelligence' serves the process of identifying business needs and appraising the value of options available to fulfil them.

Fig. 2.2.B
The three facets of facilities management

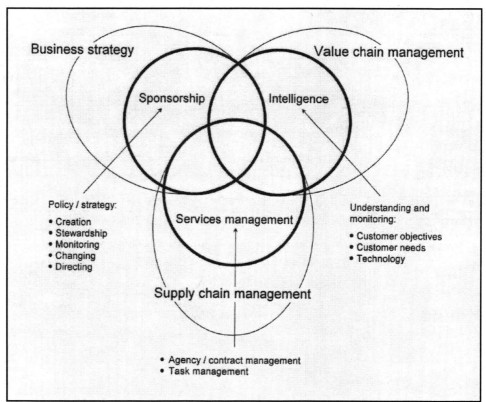

The sponsorship and service management facets control the implementation of the value management strategy. The 'monitoring' facet of value management pervades the whole process since, as we shall be discussing later in Chapter 2.4.3, measurement of both the output and the input performance is critical to success in value management.

Value management in a facilities context

Before considering formal value management procedures it is necessary to understand how they can be applied, and to what, in a facilities management regime.

In essence facilities come in the form of:

- provision of buildings, equipment and supplies

- operation

- maintenance.

Although these are quite different in content and nature the principles to be applied are the same in each case. There will need to be a policy, relating to the business plan as discussed in Chapter 1.1.5, which will itself have been the outcome of a value engineering process testing for any redundant performance in the high level brief. All stages of specification implementation and monitoring will then need to be carried out in tune with the original policy and the value plan it underwrites. However, every industry needs its own particular approach to the application of value management and the facilities industry is no exception.

The approach recommended here involves a detailed consideration of the relationship between risk, quality, cost and value (and time in the case of projects)

Risk, quality, cost and value

The BS definition quoted at the beginning of this chapter referred to value management as providing 'a new way to use many existing management methods'. In particular it embraces risk, quality and financial management all of which need to be considered first, before looking in detail at how they all interact in the value management process.

As discussed later in Chapters 2.4 and 2.5, quality and risk management issues are reciprocal in their application. Briefly, the principal objective of quality management is to establish levels of service which either:

- increase the productive output of the user, or

- contain the risk of failure of support services to a level commensurate with the return expected by the user from the investment in risk containment.

Obviously one is the reciprocal of the other; it is simply a matter of attitude towards investment and appropriate means of expressing the returns.

The financial management principles introduced in Chapter 2.3, correctly applied, will ensure that a fair and affordable price is paid relative to the quality sought.

Then, provided the quality sought contains no 'redundant performance' in the context of the organisation's value plan there will be an optimum value-managed solution.

2.2.5 VALUE MANAGEMENT PROCEDURES

Value management stages

Whether we are considering buildings or facilities services the process of value management is in principle the same. Fig. 2.2.C illustrates the consecutive and cyclical order of the three facets of value management and the activities within each one.

Fig. 2.2.C
The value management process

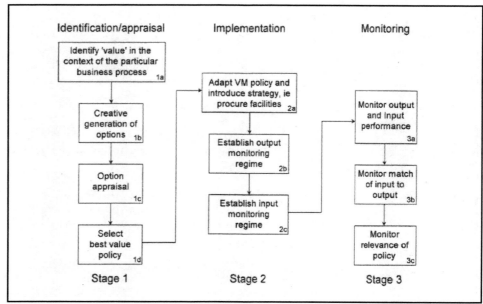

An overview of the whole process

Stage 1 represents the formal process of identifying a facilities requirement and evaluating the optimum level of quality and cost to be adopted in the facilities policy in order to deliver a 'best value' solution.

The policy having been settled, Stage 2 begins with the procurement of the facility which must be accompanied by strategies for measuring input and output performance.

Stage 3 is the measurement process which includes the ongoing requirement to make sure that changed circumstances are always detected and reflected in changed strategies where necessary - thereby completing the cyclical nature of the whole process.

It is beyond the scope of this book to explain either how to deliver a formal VM study or the ways in which it can be adapted to the facilities management regime. Suffice to say that the formal approach to Value Management referred to in Ch. 2.2.4 requires that Stage 1 and Stage 2a should be achieved through the means of a VM study which incorporates VM workshops that adhere to a VM Job Plan. However, this is view of 'best practice' which is rarely formally adopted in facilities management regimes.

Nevertheless, current 'state-of-the-art' facilities management practice would embrace the principles of the more formal approach, albeit laced with a measure of pragmatism, eg informal discussions and negotiations occurring during the 'budget approval round', and at other times when key decisions are taken, may be directed towards the management of value in a way which might otherwise be achieved, rather more reliably, via formal VM workshops.

Stage 1 - identification and appraisal

Obviously it is essential from the outset to have a properly established set of criteria against which the value of the facilities can be established. Activities relating to box 1a in Fig 2.2.C will therefore produce the required return on investment either in money terms or in terms of benefits in kind (the latter usually being converted into a financial return using cost/benefit analysis). Consideration must be given at this stage to:

- establishment, analysis and prioritisation of essential business objectives, eg the importance of cleanliness in a medical environment.

- identification of functional performance criteria if the objectives are to be achieved.

- establishment of constraints, eg physical access, budget levels.

- in a practical fm context these stage 1a considerations will usually be addressed alongside the '**brainstorming**' activities in box 1b although the ROI criteria must always be clearly defined from the outset at 1a.

In many value management scenarios it is necessary to go through a 'pre-briefing' stage wherein a problem, eg staff dissatisfaction with the working environment, is explored in depth to throw up alternative solutions. The process of 'brainstorming' to be adopted at this stage is common to every stage of the value management process. The 'lateral thinking' produced by brainstorming (possibly testing a 'zero-base' scenario as discussed below) occasionally generates best performance solutions from 'outside of the box', ie do not follow the conventional wisdom.

The pre-briefing problem can be addressed formally using what is known as a 'Value Tree'. Using the example above of 'staff dissatisfaction with the working environment' an appropriate value tree might be as portrayed in Fig 2.2.D

Fig. 2.2.D
A value tree

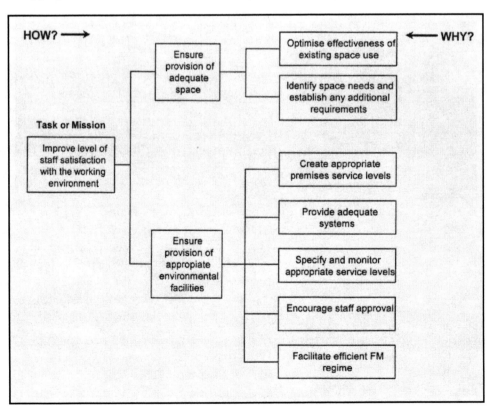

A value tree is a diagram that describes the business driver (mission) for a project or service and the criteria that need to be satisfied in order to achieve it. A value tree should be developed at the earliest stage in order to inform the brief. It should ideally

be carried out by the Intelligent Client Function although, unfortunately, too often key facilities decisions are taken with little or no input from facilities professionals.

The value tree asks the questions how? and why? The answer to the one is the question posed by the other.

Note that this value tree has begun at a point when the client has identified a source of staff dissatisfaction which demands a response from facilities management.

A core business value tree might first have asked the questions: 'why is productivity down?' and/or later: 'why are the staff dissatisfied'. Alternatively, the problem may have been identified in the results of a user satisfaction survey. However, in this example the value tree is a pre-briefing study to determine the most appropriate, ie: best value, solution.

The initial brainstorming might have thrown up alternative solutions such as: move to a new site for a new build or an existing building, either leased or bought; redevelop the existing site; take on additional space, either in a new building or in an existing building (again leasing or buying); or re-configure existing space, perhaps with an extension.

The decision, in this case, to go for a combination of extension and re-planning to the existing building would have taken into account the costs of the various alternative schemes and the value of the benefits derived. In the latter case sensitivity analysis would have been carried out on the relative impact of the solutions on staff satisfaction and hence productivity/avoidance of losses. The one which showed the greatest return on investment - bearing in mind, of course, that there must be a zero-base (or absolute minimum acceptable) achievement level - was the twin strategy shown in the value tree. The scope line for a project begins to the right of the value tree.

Examples of these types of cost/benefit analysis are given in Sections 9 and 10 of Part D - Relocation and Development.

In the case of a facilities service there is normally little option as to whether or not the service needs to be provided, eg you have to keep buildings clean and maintain/repair services so there is little merit in using a value tree to identify the need. In this case the value management process starts with a function analysis.

In formal value management procedures the technique adopted here is known as a Functional Analysis Systems Technique (FAST). The objective of FAST is to produce a complete description of the end purpose of the offering in terms of what it must do.

A FAST diagram includes a 'scope' line on the left of the diagram. The scope line limits the area of the project or service on which attention is being focused. The 'scope' is the portion of the offering that is selected for the value study.

The FAST model displays functions in a logical sequence and tests their dependency. It does not indicate how a function should be performed - ie: it delivers an output specification.

An example of a FAST diagram relative to the determination of a maintenance policy is given at Fig 2.2.E (over the page)

Each of the activities within the scope needs to be put through the value engineering process to ensure that the task is achieved without redundant performance. One way of ensuring that this happens is to set cost targets based on best-performance benchmark costs which are challenging yet demonstrably achievable. This technique is considered in more detail in Chapter 2.3.3.

Fig. 2.2.E
*A FAST diagram -
technical:
maintenance of
cooling systems*

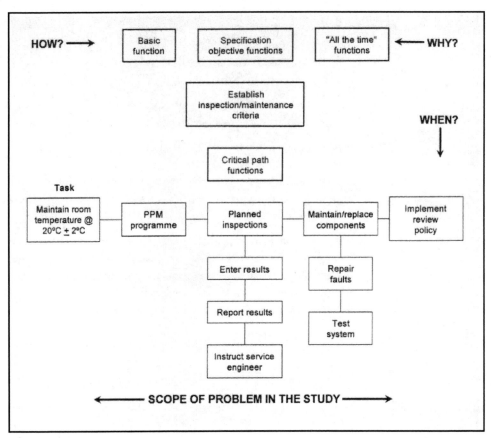

The approach to value engineering facilities recommended here is to start each function analysis (including the original value tree) by considering what might be the implications of a minimal resource solution - known as zero base (see below and Fig 2.2.F, over the page).

As stated above, it is normal for the 'intelligence' facet of the ICF to have already identified the requirement for a particular facility. Having decided therefore that maintenance of the existing cooling systems is required in order to meet temperature range criteria (yet to be determined) stage 1 in Fig 2.2.C will consider issues such as:

- functional requirements of the users

- image

- ergonomics

- legal compliance

- depreciation.

In fact, these are all the criteria headings for risk evaluation described later in Chapter 2.5.1.

Weightings will be allocated to each of these criteria so as to reflect their relative importance in a business context.

At stages 1(b) and 1(c) of Fig 2.2.C the nature of the risks and specific examples of their potential applicability will be identified and tested for probability and significance. So, for example, the impact of bare minimum control of air temperature ranges, and what the organisation might suffer as a result of such a zero-base strategy, are considered in detail so that everyone involved has a clear idea of the issues to be addressed - what 'failure' means in terms of loss of personal comfort and company image and its probable consequences.

Having explored the worst-case scenario and unveiled the nature and significance of the risks entailed the value manager(s) would next consider the impact on the basic risk and consequential losses of increasing the service level above zero-base:

A useful tool of structured evaluation to assist in the processes at 1b and 1c is the proforma shown at Fig 2.2.F which is the same as introduced in the context of capital expenditure in Chapter 1.2.4, Fig. 1.2.C.

Fig. 2.2.F
Zero-base budget - option appraisal

Subject:	Maintenance of cooling system	Estimated Costs
Location:	Generally	
Zero-base specification:	Emergency only	£ 25,000
Proposal:	PPM	£ 200,000
Benefits analysis - subjective evaluation		
Effect of proposal on functional performance	Perceived quality	better
	Visual ambience	N/A
	Comfort	better
	Ergonomics	better
	Flexibility	better
	Safety	better
Effect of proposal on on life-cycle costs	Cleaning	N/A
	Energy	better
	Maintenance and repairs	better
	Security	N/A
	Insurance	N/A
	Replacement	better
	Management	better
Effect of proposal on on environment	Energy consumption	better
	Embodied energy	N/A
	Sustainability	better

This technique permits client and advisors to consider the implications of alternative levels of quality in terms of both functional and physical performance by comparing proposals against a bare minimum - 'zero base' - specification. All they are asked to decide is whether the alternative is better or worse than zero-base for each of the functional, physical and sustainability criteria listed; if the consensus indicates a substantial difference in either direction for any criteria then 'better' or 'worse' may be highlighted in some way.

Sometimes it is helpful to 'weight' the criteria (say out of 100) and then to 'score' the answers out of $\pm$ 10. This will render comparative weighted scores for all the options appraised.

It is not necessary to put costs against physical operations or values against functional benefits.

However, by assessing the potential loss in the context of the additional cost of the risk containment strategy (ie the higher service level) the value and return on investment can be reviewed - either in 'hard' ROI or in terms of a common sense cost/benefit assessment. In most cases the latter will prevail with the former as an option if a formal business case is needed to justify investment in a particular facility and/or service level.

Fig. 2.2.G illustrates how sensitivity analysis can be applied to various ranges of estimated loss to test whether the outcome of the strategy is clear-cut or marginal.

Cost of containment:		Annual return on investment	
Maintenance of hot water (above zero–base)	£ 10,000 pa		
Potential loss avoided			
Sensitivity 1	£ 12,000 pa	$\dfrac{£\ 12{,}000 - 10{,}000}{10{,}000}$ %	= 20%
Sensitivity 2	£ 20,000 pa	$\dfrac{£\ 20{,}000 - 10{,}000}{10{,}000}$ %	= 100%

In the example an additional £10,000 spent on maintenance is estimated to save indirect losses in the range of £12,000 (1) and £20,000 (2). Because the extra £10,000 is spent during the year and is a non-recoverable investment it has to be deducted from the savings to produce a net gain from which the ROI is then calculated.

At this stage the estimated costs of providing the relevant service levels should be drawn from cost benchmarking data to ensure that best performance cost targets form the basis of any decisions to proceed. Programs such as Frisqué (Facilities Risk and Quality Evaluation) can match input and output performance to benchmarked cost targets and also predict the levels of risk exposure attendant upon each point in the range of options.

Going back to the sequence in Fig. 2.2.C above, stage 1(d) determines the policy by reference to value accruing from the options. It will also prompt consideration of the optimum method of implementation normally resulting in some formal procurement process. At this stage the ICF will also determine the output policy performance criteria and the way they will be monitored, all as discussed later in Chapter 2.4.3 - Quality management procedures.

Formal cost targets will be set for the strategy based on the benchmarking data gathered for and adopted in the option appraisal stage (1c).

The necessary material will have been gathered for inclusion in a formal business case (if required) to ensure that the policy and strategies are 'owned' by the business as a whole - not just by the FM department.

Stage 2 - implementation

At 2(a) the service levels and output performance levels selected at Stage 1(d) are translated into bid documents and providers appointed. Such appointments should be the outcome of a risk-based value-managed process addressing the type of service delivery structure and the the short-listing and selection procedures. Providers will be required to put forward and carry out suitable quality control procedures to ensure that good intentions turn into reality and the facilities sponsors must ensure that financial controls protect the planned level of investment.

Stage 2(b) will be concurrent with 2(a) and will determine how the ICF will monitor the key process output performance indicators by which the success of the strategy is to be assessed.

Such measurements might include the use of sophisticated monitoring equipment for issues such as air temperature and dust contamination all as considered in Chapter 2.4.3.

At Stage 2(c) each provider's quality monitoring regime is explored to establish the nature and extent of the ICF's auditing commitment; it is unlikely that any providers, left completely to their own devices, can be expected to keep to the required levels of quality and the ICF needs to hit the right balance of trust and audit having due regard to the providers' abilities.

Stage 3 - monitoring

At Stage 3(a) the service or facility is up and running and the input and output monitoring regimes are active. At 3(b) the ICF is in a position to check if any of the performance targets are not being achieved and, in the case of output targets, whether this is due to inadequate service level specifications or merely faulty service levels.

Alongside this testing process at 3(c) the 'intelligence' facet of the ICF must always be on the alert for changing business needs which may require modifications to the nature, extent and quality of the facilities services being provided; change is a facet of life of which the effects must be treated seriously and continually at all stages in the value management process.

2.2.6 THE 'BALANCED SCORECARD'

A fundamental tenet of facilities economics is that the performance of facilities and the costs of providing them must always be in balance, ie the ends justify the means.

The 'facilities policy' and the Intelligent Client Function introduced in Chapter 1.1.1 are critical to achieving this balance. These concepts together with the focus on justifying the investment in facilities given in the sections of Chapters 2.3, 2.4 and 2.5 dealing with financial, quality and risk management are all testimony to the authors' view of the great significance of this principle.

Today's facilities managers are, quite rightly, very keen to keep up with developments in business management theory and application. Wherever possible they adopt them in their own management activities but, at the very least, they need to have a working knowledge of the management principles and strategies the core business is following.

Fig. 2.2.H
The 'balanced scorecard' as a strategic framework for action

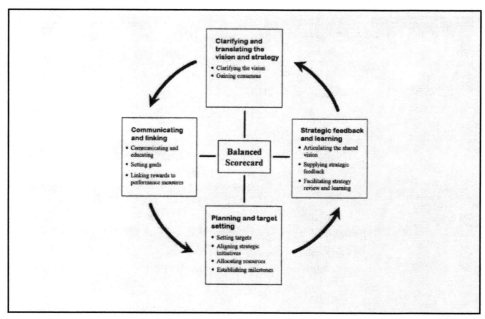

One new approach (or re-definition of an old approach) to value management has been termed the 'Balanced Scorecard'[4]. Just like the authors of this text the originators of the Balanced Scorecard have eschewed the idea that business performance should be dominated by cost control as exercised by traditional financial accounting practice. They want organisations to improve future performance by finding out what really adds value in business terms and then setting strategies in place to develop their application to the best benefit.

Fig. 2.2.H (previous page) illustrates how the process can be used as a framework within which to develop an action plan. Careful study of this figure and the supporting text will reveal that what is being described here is essentially the 'intelligence' and 'sponsorship' roles of the Intelligent Client Function (ICF) described in Chapter 1.1.1.

In its fullest application the balanced scorecard is seen to be a holistic system of value management, linking every effort at quality control within key aspects of an organisation's activities to its overall value plan.

In the same way that the performance of a building was shown in Chapter 1.2.4 to comprise the summation of the performance of its elements/components so the balanced scorecard endeavours to reflect the relationships between the performance of any activity and the overall mission.

The formal approach to a Balanced Scorecard usually relies upon the identification of 'strategic initiatives' ie those actions which will significantly impact on success. Four key action areas are proposed for the typical commercial organisation:

- financial success

- customer satisfaction

- internal management procedures

- learning and growth.

In this context the terms mean:

financial success: the commercial business objective, the return on investment which drives the business strategy (strategy is looked at more closely below) which, in turn, strives to add value to the core business output

customer satisfaction: wider than simply the results of a questionnaire survey. In a corporate sense it is concerned with the end product and its purchasers, identifying the most lucrative outlets for the products (or finding new products to tap into such outlets) and retaining and growing customers and market share

internal procedures: are concerned with quality, response times and costs in the core business production line and new product development

learning and growth: relates to information systems within the organisation and keeping employees keen and effective.

The 'Balanced Scorecard' approach to these issues is to develop a management scenario in which each activity in the business addresses these four issues in the context of their contribution to the overall business strategy - which in turn is focussed at the highest level on the same four components. 'Transparency' is a key word and is used in the sense that every department has a scorecard that can be seen clearly to address the needs of the corporate plan.

---

[4] Kaplan, Robert S., Norton, David P. (1996) 'The Balanced Scorecard: Translating strategy into action', Harvard Business School Press, Boston, Massachusetts USA

Mission and strategy

Picking up on themes addressed in earlier theses by H. Mintzberg 'Crafting Strategy' :Harvard Business Review - July-August 1987) and others, the authors of 'The Balanced Scorecard' stress that 'strategy' must comprise both planning and implementation. An important part of this seamless process is the feedback of information to inform the basic plan and to check on adequacy, logic, efficiency and effectiveness of procedures.

In Chapter 1.1.4 it is propounded that 'Every department should have a mission statement in support of the main business objective.....(which) should always relate to the corporate goal and describe the intentions of the facilities providers in pursuit of their own supportive contribution'. Now, that sounds rather like what Balanced Scorecard means in terms of a holistic, transparent strategy!

However, the chapter goes on to say that a 'mission statement, per se, is unenforceable'; the 'Balanced Scorecard' is also looking to identify a hard-nosed strategy as opposed to jingoistic claims in support of the business' mission. The key is turning the mission into objectives and targets that work right down and across the business.

The Balanced Scorecard in a facilities context

One good thing, from the authors' point of view, about the 'Balanced Scorecard' is that it supports the principles relating facilities policy to the corporate plan first put down on paper in 1984 in 'Premises Audits' and expanded on in this work.

Taking the four generic issues in turn we can see that:

- **financial success** as a corporate goal must be reflected in the cost-efficiency of the services provided and their cost-effectiveness in their contribution to corporate efficiency.

- **customer satisfaction** is a critical part of the facilities management role: identifying user needs and applying the services to match is one aspect of that role and another is helping to provide a good image to the external customers in respect of the buildings and services; the latter is a business market contribution the importance of which is frequently overlooked by facilities and general management alike. The direct effectiveness of the strategy can be measured by user satisfaction surveys and other key output performance indicators (KOPI's) but the indirect effectiveness is a 'soft' component of the profit centre

- **internal procedures** in facilities terms are represented by specifications and service levels, the efficiency of which, in turn, are measured using key input performance indicators (KIPI's). Such procedures have to be relevant to the output sought in support of user efficiency, which is why the creation of specification in isolation from a business case evaluation offends fundamentally against the transparency and holisticity of the Balanced Scorecard approach.

- **learning and growth** are very much the province of the Intelligent Customer whose job it is to find out what facilities and service levels the business needs (intelligence = learning) and to generate (grow), sponsor and monitor the procedures and resources needed to deliver them.

If the procedures described in Fig 2.2.C and the accompanying text are followed in regard to all key facilities then the principles of the 'Balanced Scorecard' will have been fully met including the all-important requirement for strategy and action to be seamless.

The business case for investment in facilities discussed above has to come from the Intelligent Customer by default - few financial directors understand the 'Balanced Scorecard' in a facilities management context. It is unfortunate that financial management is pre-occupied with 'hard' returns which are often produced on paper (artificially but not genuinely) by cutting down on the costs of so-called 'non-core' activities.

In times of recession, pressures to reduce the facilities management budget can be inexorable. The term 'affordability' is frequently bandied about as if quality of support were something to switch on and off according to funds yet with no appreciable impact on the core business. If this were so then the identification/appraisal process at Fig 2.2.C above obviously could not have been implemented.

Valid savings may be sought (and sometimes made) by outsourcing although if this results in the loss of an effective Intelligent Customer Function then the learning and growth facet of the 'Balanced Scorecard' approach will be missing from the facilities operation.

Setting up the Balanced Scorecard

Wherever possible the performance criteria for the individual scorecards should be created by the individual departments and their individual employees. People must identify the critical processes at which they must excel if they are to meet the onus upon them to support the business strategy. They must then set their own targets and means of measurement , ie key performance indicators - and even measure their own results, although inherent human frailties may require some external monitoring of achievements!

Each strategic initiative is associated with a key performance criterion and an appropriate unit of measurement of the outcome. In facilities management parlance we are talking about KPI's - key performance indicators (see below).

So, a strategic initiative with the objective of improving customer satisfaction might have action plans in respect of 'product', 'employees', and 'after-sales'. The early indicator of performance (sometimes called the 'lead indicator' in the Balanced Scoreboard) might be the results of a customer satisfaction survey and a long-term or 'lag' indicator might be market share and/or customer retention. Both these indicators would be seen as 'output' indicators in the context of the following text; however, it would be quite feasible, and sensible, to use key input performance indicators such as quality control records to give an early or 'lead' indication of product improvement (leading to improved customer satisfaction, which is the final output criterion).

Fig. 2.2.J shows how one facilities group is using Balanced Scorecard by having a set of objectives with performance measures for each strategic service unit. Obviously the headings in the strategy boxes are high level only - there is chapter and verse in the back-up documentation to say exactly what is to be achieved, how, when and by whom; it is also quite essential to say who has the responsibility for ensuring the success of the action.

Fig. 2.2.J
Balanced scorecard criteria - mail distribution (2000-2001)

Financial	Year to date	Year end figure	Customer	Year to date	Year end figure
Unit cost per envelope			Customer satisfaction		
Direct costs			Number of complaints		
Savings and cost avoidance			Customer focus and quality (feedback '99)		
Costs per head					

Internal effectiveness	Year to date	Year end figure	People	Year to date	Year end figure
Statement page ratio			Skills – training and development		
SLA performance			Staff satisfaction		
Productivity-DDC (spare capacity)			Staff turnover / retention		
			Manpower – FTE's		
			Manpower – agency		
			Absenteeism / sickness		
			Old to new reward		

Note how all four of the generic issues are addressed using **'Financial'**, **'Customer'**, **'Internal Effectiveness'** and **'People'**; the latter heading is substituted for 'Learning and Growth' but the content certainly meets the requirements for keeping a weather eye on staff skill development, job satisfaction and morale.

The **'learning and growth'** facet of the 'Balanced Scorecard' is the one most likely to suffer in commercial organisations in times of recession when top management is suffering from the combined effects of tighter margins, lower sales volume and constant overheads. Nevertheless, in the same way that companies have learned the benefits of stepping up their marketing in times of recession (and the dramatic results of not doing so), they must also recognise the dangers of downsizing and/or debilitating the facilities management function in the name of 'affordability'. Once the performance of facilities gets out of kilter with the business plan the 'Balanced Scorecard' loses one of its key ingredients and the transparency and holisticity which must underpin it.

Process maps

The development of 'process maps' for key operations has also become an important part of 'state-of-the-art' facilities management culture providing valuable support to the implementation of 'Balanced Scorecard' initiatives. The process map describes how processes are to be carried out, the interfaces between departments, responsibilities for tasks etc. The map is accompanied by notes relating to the special conditions of operation, financial limits, approvals etc.

Fig. 2.2.K is an extract from a process map, in this case describing part of the chain of works preparatory to a move.

Fig. 2.2.K
Extract from a facilities process map

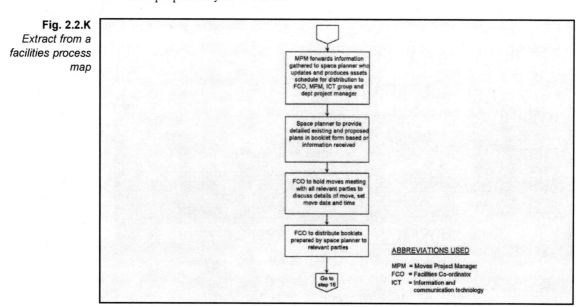

2.2.7 BENCHMARKING - A KEY TOOL OF VALUE MANAGEMENT

Definition of Benchmarking

Reference has already been made to the use of benchmarking in various activities within the value management process.

The concept and practice of benchmarking are considered in detail in Chapter 12.2 (see also 'An Introduction to Benchmarking Facilities' by Bernard Williams (BEB Ltd, Bromley, Kent)), so it is only necessary here to introduce the concept, and briefly explain its operation and its particular relevance to the value management process.

Chapter 12.2.1 defines benchmarking as 'the process of comparing a product, service, process - indeed any activity or object - with other samples from a peer group, with a view to identifying 'best buy' or 'best practice' and targeting oneself to emulate it'.

Best practice

The pursuit of 'best practice' is a cornerstone of the application of benchmarking in a value management context. Having found it, using the best practice approach to any subject area to improve performance is guaranteed to bring rewards - provided always that what is identified as best practice is in fact a requirement which falls out of the 'value tree' in respect of any specific activity.

Benchmark targets

A key use of benchmarking in value management is the opportunity it provides to set cost targets for specific levels of performance which are challenging yet demonstrably achievable. With such data to hand it is possible for the value manager to set targets for the various offerings which demand a value-engineered solution; no need to specify how to achieve the challenging target - just be able to demonstrate it has been achieved by others. The lateral-thinking approach which spawns the creativity on which value management thrives will bring the best out of the teams, and occasionally will generate an original best performance solution.

The peer group data

Benchmarking can be applied to almost any activity or component. The only pre-requisite is that the peer group contains high performance solutions to the problem in question; if the peer group is drawn from a database - especially a costs database - it is imperative that the data should be sound ie: properly collated and analysed. The use of benchmarked cost data derived at second-hand by questionnaires or at first-hand by non-experts cannot be too strongly condemned as a practice. Valid benchmarking data is not available on the cheap - rubbish in, rubbish out is a suitable caveat for would-be DIY benchmarkers. On the other hand, good benchmark data in the hands of people who know what they are about, is an incredibly powerful tool of value management.

In fact it is probably true to say that, without access to good benchmarks, value management, however sophisticated, is likely to prove relatively ineffective.

2.2.8 VALUE MANAGEMENT IN CONTEXT

Although value management is probably the most important facilities management activity it is very much an overseeing and controlling role in respect of the more complex risk, quality and financial management activities.

Adherence to the principles laid down above will be more than adequate to deliver the best value solution; those companies who have introduced these formal value management procedures have shown clearly measurable improvements in across-the-board performance. Nevertheless, this is state-of-the-art facilities management practice and most facilities management set-ups have a long way to go before they can begin to fulfil the requirements of such a demanding regime.

2.3   FINANCIAL MANAGEMENT

Introduction

Financial management is the process of ensuring that the funds available to an organisation for the purposes of running its business are used effectively, readily accessible and properly accounted for.

There are two distinct approaches to financial management which, nevertheless, are both based on the same basic data in respect of income and expenditure. These approaches are:

*   financial accounting

*   financial control

This text is primarily concerned with the latter; nevertheless facilities managers should be familiar with the basics of bookkeeping and presentation of accounts in order to be able to interpret the financial position of their own and other organisations from scrutiny of their trading accounts. The principles and conventions of the reactive accountancy function are discussed later in the chapter.

However the facilities manager must first and foremost understand the pro-active component of financial management, ie 'financial control' which ensures effective use of financial resources and the ready availability of the necessary funds, so this aspect is given priority in the chapter.

2.3.1 DEFINITIONS

Financial accounting

Financial accounting is the process whereby trading transactions and changes in value of assets are recorded in such a way as to enable the financial position of an organisation to be accounted for in a prescribed format at any given time. Bookkeeping entries relate to monies earned and expended and assets bought, sold and depreciated.

Books of accounts are required to be produced for all organisations whether commercial, institutional or charitable. They should show income and expenditure, which is usually in the form of a profit/loss account, and assets and liabilities in the form of a balance sheet.

The requirement to keep and produce accounts will be mainly driven by:

*   The Companies Acts - insofar as they apply to private or public limited liability companies

*   The Charities Commission

*   The Inspector of Taxes

*   Shareholders - with regard to company performance, profits and distribution

*   Internal reporting requirements

Internal reports are usually seen as part of the process of 'management accounting'; management accounts are produced for internal consumption only and may be presented in various formats and protocols to suit the requirements of those seeking specific financial information.

The format of the formal accounts and the conventions adopted may vary depending on the purpose for which they are to be used; eg the Tax Inspector may have different requirements from the shareholders in the way depreciation of assets is to be dealt with for calculation of profit and loss.

Financial control

Control is all about the power of 'direction', so financial control implies a proactive influence on the organisation's financial affairs; compare this to 'bookkeeping' which is a purely reactive (if sometimes creative!) function.

Financial control comprises budgetary control, competitive procurement and value engineering; these activities and their inter-relationships are discussed in detail below.

The term can apply at either macro- or micro-economic level within an organisation. In other words the company's overall financial performance as finally portrayed in the Accounts can be driven proactively in just the same way as a project or a facilities service.

2.3.2 THE PRINCIPLES OF FINANCIAL CONTROL

Cost-effectiveness

Right from the outset it is imperative to distinguish between the word 'effective' as used above in the definition of 'financial management' and 'efficiency'.

'Effectiveness' relates to usefulness and 'efficiency' relates to operability. So, 'cost-effectiveness' means value in terms of benefit delivered for the money and 'cost-efficiency' relates to the reasonableness of the price paid for the service specified. The wrong service procured in a cost-efficient manner will definitely not give value for money, whereas the right service procured inefficiently may well do so.

Although facilities managers cannot control the amount of money a business has available at any one time they can make sure that, for their part, there is enough money available in their sector of the overall budget to meet the commitments emanating from their facilities policy and strategies. So, when they do commit the company to expenditure on facilities, it should be on the basis that it is:

- at the right price

- within budget

- for the right service.

These requirements can only be met with proper application of the principles of financial control, ie with thorough application of competitive procurement, budgetary control and value engineering.

The three facets of financial control

These three facets of financial control are inter-dependent; the absence or misapplication of any one of them will put financial control at risk. Fig. 2.3.A (over the page) illustrates this inter-dependence.

Fig. 2.3.A
Three facets of financial control - inter-relationships

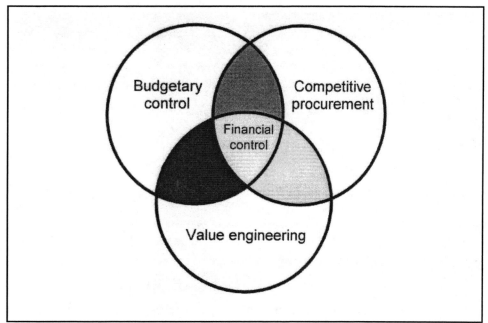

The inclusion of value engineering as a facet of financial control is, at first thought, a contradiction of what has been previously asserted in Chapter 2.2 - Value Management, ie that value engineering is an integral part of the value management process.

However, in practical terms value engineering **must** be an integral part of financial control if the procurement of the wrong offering at the right price is to be avoided at the coalface.

Perhaps a more meaningful expression of the inter-relationship between value management and the three facets of financial control is that suggested in Fig 2.3.B

Fig. 2.3.B
Value management, value engineering and financial control

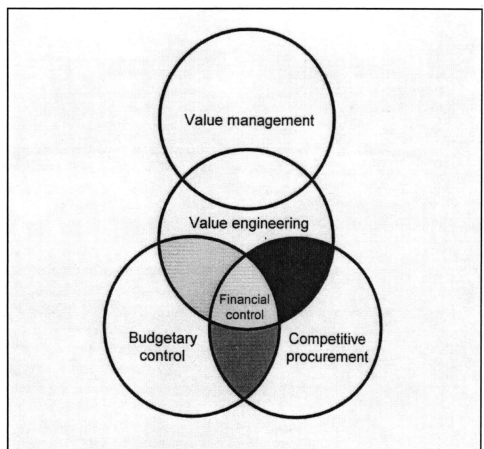

The financial control process is primarily concerned with cost-efficiency; cost-effectiveness is the result of value management which has been discussed, in more detail, in Chapter 2.2. Nevertheless, in the process of delivery of a service or project the facilities manager must recognise the duty to value-engineer solutions within the value management regime albeit as an integral part of the financial control process.

2.3.3 VALUE ENGINEERING

The principles of value engineering were introduced in Chapter 2.2 wherein it was defined as 'the process whereby products and services are provided to the required performance for the least cost'. Value engineering requires the elimination of any 'redundant performance and attendant extra costs', ie should not permit the design or specification of a product or service to generate costs in respect of performance criteria which are not necessary to support the business requirement.

Examples of redundant performance might be:

- cleaning down the internal partitions twice a week when once a month is adequate

- using white envelopes to send out overdue credit reminders when brown manila would do

- designing building floors to carry a superimposed loading of 6KN/sq m when 5KN/sq m is perfectly suitable.

All these examples presume that the excess provision does not add value to the business. It is this process of value analysis which makes value engineering such an important feature of value management and hence facilities economics.

Value engineering and value management

As stated above the 'official' view in the UK and the EU generally is that 'value management' subtends value engineering. The implication is that value management considers overall financial strategies whereas value engineering is only concerned with the use of economic tactics. It will be evident from the examples of redundant performance given above that any consideration of its elimination must be in the context of value to the business. So even at the component or process level choices may well have strategic implications eg will the brown envelopes referred to in the example above really fulfil the business 'image' requirements?

In the USA the term 'value engineering' is applied to more or less the whole of the value management process. However this really is a matter of semantics which should not be allowed to cloud the issues. For purposes of this text the term 'value engineering' is restricted to the process level ie eliminating redundant performance from the process of delivery of a task. So, the best use of resources in keeping the windows clean is the result of value engineering, whereas selecting the 'right' level of cleanliness within the overall business strategy is down to value management albeit that value engineering principles may have been adopted in the course of that selection process.

Setting a challenging budget which is dependent upon value engineering for achievement may be called value management by some, but within this text it is considered to be an essential and integral part of the process of value engineering.

The concept of value

Far more important than terminology is the concept of 'value' discussed in Chapter 2.2.1 which has to be properly understood before the value engineering process can be implemented.

In the context of physical performance value can be assessed in terms of a return on an investment delivering cost reductions. So, investing £10,000 in an energy conservation tool which saves £2500 pa in electricity costs, shows a return on initial investment of 25% pa before tax. If the organisation's criterion rate of return for such an investment is 15% then value has been added; similarly, where £1m spent on refurbishment of the headquarters building results in the asset value being increased by £2m.

However, referring back to an earlier example, if the organisation's public relations image is damaged by the distribution of 'payment overdue' reminders in brown manila envelopes instead of the snappy, crisp embossed parchment enclosing its normal missives then the cost-efficient purchase may well produce a negative return when considered in the context of cost-effectiveness - but can anyone prove it?

This is the real problem with value engineering. Most individual centres of non-core business expenditure are of little significance in terms of overall turnover, yet any modification to the service they are financing, either upwards or downwards, may well have an impact on the business at the point of interaction many times in excess of the money saved or spent - see Fig. 2.3.C.

Fig. 2.3.C
Typical turnover, profit and facilities costs (excluding ICT)

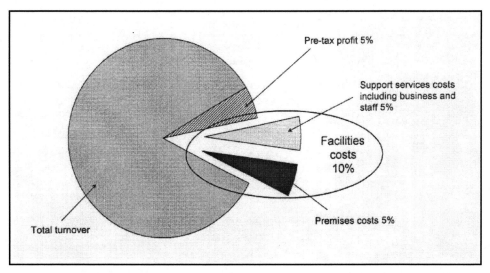

This interaction between facilities and the efficiency of core activity is vastly under-researched and un-documented. Until such time as good data on benefits and disbenefits emanating from facilities decisions is available value engineering appraisal will inevitably be restricted, in the main, to sophisticated objective optimisation of trivial (but quantifiable) issues on the one hand while, on the other hand, the value of many major investments can only be the subject of crude subjective appraisal unsupported by substantive data.

The value management approach described in Chapter 2.2 can go a long way to overcoming these shortcomings by demanding a proper functional analysis with scores and weighting of criteria at every point in the value chain.

2.3.4 COMPETITIVE PROCUREMENT

This term describes the process whereby products are created or purchased at or below the general price level at which similar products may be purchased in the market place.

It does not mean that every project, service or item of office equipment has to be put out to tender; it merely means that the price paid has to be that which is known to be competitive in the market-place.

The facilities manager may be responsible for procurement of a wide range of facilities in widely differing market conditions. In many cases they may delegate the procurement process to specialists, eg to the Purchasing Departments for office stationery, to the quantity surveyor for the fitting-out project. Nevertheless, they must accept overall responsibility for the efficiency of the procurement of facilities and always have a considered and well informed opinion as to the most suitable purchasing procedure and a well referenced list of potential suppliers.

The principles of competitive procurement are well-established and understood. Most facilities managers have responsibility of sorts for procuring the facilities services and the various management routes are considered in depth in Chapter 2.1.

The procurement of fitting-out projects is more complex and is discussed in detail in Chapter 6.3 and the even more complicated process of procurement of new construction is considered in Chapter 10.1.

2.3.5 BUDGETARY CONTROL

Definition

This is the process whereby appropriate budgets are calculated and agreed, and expenditure against them monitored before and after commitment, to ensure that once budgets are set they are neither under-spent nor exceeded other than to meet variations in the performance criteria or market conditions upon which they were based.

Some of the words used in the definition are particularly significant.

'Appropriate budgets' means that they should be suitable for the service to be provided. They must presume that the procurement and value engineering processes will be efficient and not allow any slack which might allow any default in either or both of these inter-dependent facets to go unnoticed.

'Monitored before commitment' implies a pro-active process in which the budget controller assesses the potential impact of a prospective financial event upon the planned cost for that particular cost centre. First of all comes the idea, then the quotation; they can both be tested in the pro-active phase. Any invoice resulting from commitment will be processed in the reactive phase of budgetary control, ie will be recorded so as to evaluate the extent of any under- or over-expenditure. These two distinct phases of budgetary control are illustrated in Fig. 2.3.D (over the page).

Fig. 2.3.D
Pro-active v reactive styles of cost control

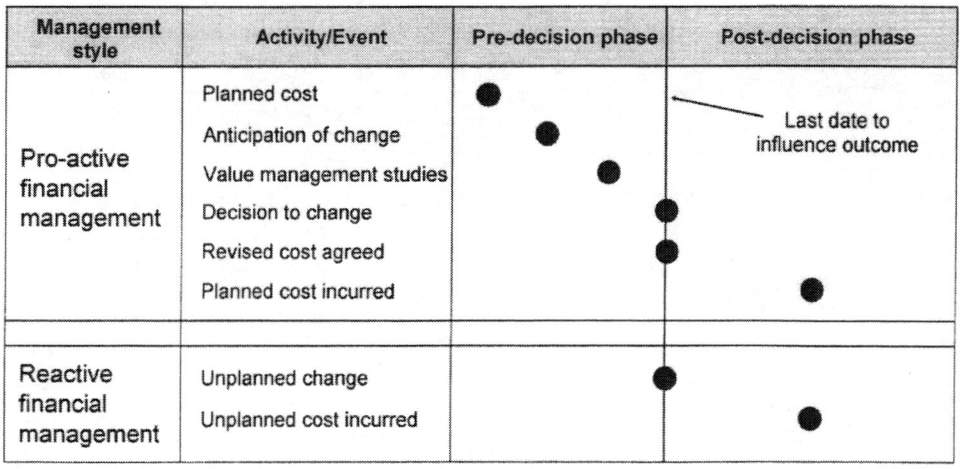

Management style	Activity/Event	Pre-decision phase	Post-decision phase
Pro-active financial management	Planned cost	●	Last date to influence outcome
	Anticipation of change	●	
	Value management studies	●	
	Decision to change	●	
	Revised cost agreed	●	
	Planned cost incurred		●
Reactive financial management	Unplanned change	●	
	Unplanned cost incurred		●

Although most budgetary control systems in facilities and general management are of the reactive variety it is clearly unsatisfactory to have to rely upon a system which tells you how much you have over-spent when it is too late to do other than pay the bill - assuming the money can be found from elsewhere to do so.

Pro-active budgetary control

The first truly pro-active system of budgetary control to be developed in Europe is believed to be the 'Journal System'[1] of cost control of building design and construction; first introduced in 1968, the principles have since been enshrined in the 'premFINANCE' Facilities Financial Control System.[2]

An underlying tenet of both these programs is that, for budgetary control to be effective, the basis of the forecast must be presented in such a way that both financial controller and purchasers can readily identify potential changes; such presentation will also ensure that purchasers accept responsibility for the adequacy of the specifications supporting the budget figures for work under their direction. This 'ownership' of the budget is critical; the financial controller must stand up and be counted for their estimating but must not assume responsibility for reading the minds of those who are actually going to spend the budget.

When the budget is formulated it must be expressed in such a way that potential change for a significant item is obvious. For example, if the stationery budget is based upon a headcount of 850 persons it might be expressed as in Fig. 2.3.E (over the page). Any increase in numbers during the year should be accompanied by a budget review in advance of commitment to increased expenditure. The detail behind this build up is given in Chapter 7.3.3 at Fig. 7.3.D.

---

[1] 'The Journal System of Capital Cost Control', Bernard Williams

[2] 'premFINANCE' Facilities Financial Control System, Bernard Williams Associates

Fig. 2.3.E
*Presentation of
budget proposals-
stationery cost*

Office services budget 2002		
Cost Centre: stationery		
Benchmark data	**Date**	**Quantity**
No. of full time employees	09/01/02	850
No. of executives included	09/01/02	100
No. of wp operators included	09/01/02	20
Budget proposals		
Item		**£**
General office paper products		146,800
Personal desk consumables		48,900
Storage stationery		24,000
Presentation materials		12,000
Administration		4,800
Total		**£ 236,500**
Total per capita ÷ 850		**£ 278**

Where important budgeted items are not shown explicitly in any documentation their existence and identifying features must always be described. For example, in the design stage for a capital project the engineer might have decided that steel sheet piling may be required in part of the foundations.

When the engineers set about their detailed design they will refer to this part of the budget (which they have already 'signed off' in principle) and can therefore inform the cost controller as soon as they can confirm, or otherwise, the real extent of the work provisionally predicted. Failure to observe this procedure could mean that either:

- project tenders containing a far greater amount of sheet piling than originally envisaged will fall way outside of the cost plan (see Chapter 6.3.6) or

- incorporation of desirable design features might be obstructed by the financial controller during the design stage only for the team to find out later that the amount budgeted for sheet steel piling was too great or not needed at all.

Under-spending the budget, possibly as the result of such a default, can have an adverse effect on performance, which may possibly be even more serious than over-expenditure.

Estimates and assumptions

Facilities managers are often heard to claim that calculation of budgets from first principles is pointless given the inevitability of change in this volatile business. The suggestion is that there is no point in making detailed budget provision for specific items of expenditure which may, or may not, be incurred. This argument is, however, self-defeating; going into the forest is one thing, but going in having a map and compass is something else entirely!

'Best estimate' assumptions based upon 'intelligent' predictions are a critical tool of budgetary control. However they do need to be recorded in such a way that the assumptions can be constantly monitored for relevance and accuracy; backs of envelopes may form the platform for calculations needed to produce the report at

Fig. 2.3.F but failure to make the transition from information appraisal to formal presentation is a cast iron guarantee of failure of the whole budgetary control process.

Fig. 2.3.F
Presentation of budget proposals - calculation and expression of assumptions: extract from the 'journal' system

Project: Example						Element: Substructure	
Cost study No.2	Date: March 2001						
Location	Specification	Information source	Quantity	Unit	Rate £	Total £	
Generally	Oversite strip including excavation and transporting topsoil to spoil heaps	Site visit	2,485	sq m	4.80	11,928	
Generally	Excavate to reduce levels and dispose material off site including all necessary working space, earthwork support and compacting bottom of excavation	Site visit	2,400	cubic m	16.00	38,400	
Generally	450mm diameter reinforced driven concrete piling average 10m deep	Engineer 16/10/00	274	No.	320.00	87,680	
N.W Corner	Heavy duty steel sheet piling say 80m girth – provisional allowance	Engineer 25/10/00	Allowance	-	-	16,000	
					Total	463,916	
					Element total to summary	£464,000	

Of course, the examples given here in respect of capital projects are purely illustrative of the principles; few facilities managers would be expected to take responsibility for estimating such specialist works. Nevertheless there are many less technical subjects for which they **do** get given estimating responsibilities. It is therefore important to recognise that estimating is a skilled job, and one in which few facilities managers have adequate training, so they should either seek training to do it scientifically or make sure that they have professional help to hand when predicting the costs of substantial commitments.

2.3.6 INTERDEPENDENCE OF THE THREE FACETS

When proposing a budget for a project or for the annual expenditure on services the facilities manager should be anticipating:

- competitive procurement
- value engineering
- budgetary control.

The value engineering exercise, with its basis in anticipated out-turn benefits and costs, is heavily dependent on the assumption that cost savings (resulting from getting rid of unwanted performance) will turn up in the final analysis - not be frittered away in poor procurement or sloppy estimating/budgetary control.

And what is the point of having the world's most efficient Purchasing Department if they buy the wrong product at the best price available - especially if there was no budget for it in the first place?

In order to get value for money in procurement of any component of facilities all three facets of financial control must be actively pursued and diligently applied within a properly established value management framework. Budgeting at the 'right' level will make some of this happen, but knowing what the 'right' level is will continue to present problems until much more research is carried out on the subject of the interaction between facilities and core business activity.

In the meantime benchmarking costs and performance to the 'best of breed' should guarantee a general trend towards added value.

2.3.7 FINANCIAL APPRAISAL TECHNIQUES

Discounted cash flow

Many facilities, such as premises, last a long time, and it is often necessary to incorporate both initial and future costs in investment appraisal. Equally it is necessary to provide funds to replace an asset at the end of its useful life.

Management accountants use the concept of compound interest on money invested to enable them to carry out various aspects of investment appraisal. However, whereas replacement funds (sinking funds) are calculated by reference to accumulation of compound interest, evaluation of future expenditure is made using the reciprocal of compound interest to discount its value. This technique is known as 'Discounted Cash Flow' (DCF).

DCF works on the principle that in order to aggregate future revenue or capital payments and initial capital investments it is necessary to allow for the fact that, for every pound of deferred payment, an investor has the use of that pound for the period of the deferral and can earn a commercial return on it in the interim.

Therefore, if £1 is invested at 10% pa at the beginning of the year, by the end of one year it will have earned £0.10 interest; if you have to spend £1 in one year's time you can deduct the £0.10 interest earned from the cost, giving a discounted value of £(1 - 0.10) = £0.90.

If the expenditure were deferred for two years £0.21 compound interest would be earned making the future payment worth only £(1 - 0.21) - £0.79.

The principle of this computation is fed into tables of DCF factors per £1 known as the 'Present Value of £1' table. The factors may then be extracted relative to any future years and any rate of interest and applied to the total amount of expenditure in each or any future year. Fig. 2.3.G is an extract from the 'Present Value of £1' tables.

Fig. 2.3.G
The present value of £1

Years	Rate per cent			
	5.5	6	6.5	7
1	0.9478673	0.9433962	0.9389671	0.9345794
2	0.8984524	0.8899964	0.8816593	0.8734387
3	0.8516137	0.8396193	0.8278491	0.8162979
4	0.8072167	0.7920937	0.7773231	0.7628952
5	0.7651344	0.7472582	0.7298808	0.7129862
6	0.7252458	0.7049605	0.6853341	0.6663422
7	0.6874368	0.6650571	0.6435062	0.6227497
8	0.6515989	0.6274124	0.6042312	0.5820091
9	0.6176293	0.5918985	0.5673532	0.5439337
10	0.5854306	0.5583948	0.5327260	0.5083493

Taking a simple example of three equal annual payments of £2,000, the net present value - NPV (ie net of all discount) of those transactions is calculated as shown in Fig. 2.3.H.

Fig. 2.3.H
Calculation of the net present value (NPV) using discount tables

	Year 1	Year 2	Year 3	Years 1 to 3 £
Payment £	2,000	2,000	2,000	(3@) 2,000
Present value of £1 @ 6%	0.9433962	0.8899964	0.8396193	2.6730119 (3 year NPV factor)
Present value for the year	1886.7924	1779.9928	1679.2386	5346.0238 (3 year NPV)
Net present value (NPV) for 3 years	-	-	-	5346.0238

This 'Present Value' table is also the basis of another very important table - the 'Present Value of £1 per Annum'. This gives the accumulation of the net present values of all future annual expenditure (of equal amounts) discounted at the same rate of interest, avoiding the need to calculate an NPV for each year as was shown in Fig. 2.3.H. The same calculation but extracting the appropriate figure from the 'Present Value of £1 per Annum' table at Fig. 2.3.J finds the NPV more simply as shown in Fig. 2.3.K.

Fig. 2.3.J
An extract from 'present value of £1 per annum' tables

Years	Rate per cent			
	5.5	**6**	**6.5**	**7**
1	0.9479	0.9434	0.9390	0.9346
2	1.8463	1.8334	1.8206	1.8080
3	2.6979	2.6730	2.6485	2.6243
4	3.5052	3.4651	3.4258	3.3872
5	4.2703	4.2124	4.1557	4.1002
6	4.9955	4.9173	4.8410	4.7665
7	5.6830	5.5824	5.4845	5.3893
8	6.3346	6.2098	6.0888	5.9713
9	6.9522	6.8017	6.6561	6.5152
10	7.5376	7.3601	7.1888	7.0236

Fig. 2.3.K
Calculation of example at Fig. 2.3.H using 'present value of £1 per annum table'

Annual payment for each of 3yrs £	Present value of £1 per annum @ 6% for 3yrs	Net present value (NPV) cumulative total £
2,000	2.6730	5346*
* The slight difference results from rounding the factors in the previous example to 3 decimal places		

The same calculation will apply to income receivable as well as amounts payable and forms the basis of the 'Years purchase' calculation used by valuers to value income-bearing properties. This process is described in detail in Chapter 3.5.3. The tables, along with those for the sinking fund, mortgage payments and others, all have alternatives calculated for the effect of tax at different rates in the euro - fair enough, because tax is payable on investment returns whether manifesting themselves as interest or profits.

A major application of DCF in facilities is in the appraisal of building investment options, particularly with regard to whole-life costs of alternative designs of buildings and their components. Chapter 10.6.3 considers in depth the application of DCF to such option appraisal and also uses the examples to explain DCF in more detail from first principles.

One further appraisal technique using DCF is known as the Internal Rate of Return - IRR. This is a process used when there is both positive and negative cash flow over time. A calculation is made of the interest rate at which the sum of the discounted present values of both positive and negative cash flows are equal. This rate of interest is then compared with the organisation's criterion rate of return for such investments; if it is better than the criterion rate the project may go ahead, and vice-versa. Computer programs can work these calculations easily (most spreadsheet programs have them built-in) or the figures can be worked by using 'trial and error' interest rates until the figures balance at the IRR percentage. However the system is considered by many mathematicians to be unreliable where amounts of positive and negative cash flow are irregular, so the technique has not been used in any of the examples in this work.

2.3.8 FINANCIAL ACCOUNTING

Financial accounts and the facilities manager

In order to generate, or help to generate, a facilities policy linked to the organisation's business plans it behoves the facilities manager to have a good working knowledge of the company's financial performance. Therefore a good basic understanding of the principles of financial accounting is essential, not least because of the need to converse with Financial Directors and their professional staff in terms which mean something to them in their own technical parlance. Understanding the impact of facilities services costs and assets in the profit and loss and balance sheets of the company is also a pre-requisite to making any proposals which may impact on the bottom line figures.

The role of financial accounts

Whereas the foregoing financial management techniques relate to the way funds are managed strategically in a business, financial accounts are needed to provide a report on a company's financial position at the end of its financial accounting period - normally one year, but sometimes half-yearly or quarterly.

Essentially they summarise overall profits for the year and the assets, liabilities and shareholdings which have evolved in the period.

The report and accounts

The annual report usually contains four accounts namely:

* the profit and loss account
* the balance sheet

- the statement of source and application of funds (cash flow statement)
- reconciliation of movements in shareholder's funds.

The last-mentioned account does not always appear and there are other accounts which are used less frequently, eg statement of total recognised gains and losses.

The report will also contain such items as:

- the chairman's statement
- the chief executive's statement
- a review of performance
- corporate governance
- directors' report
- remuneration report
- auditor's report
- notes on the financial statements
- historical summaries.

The facilities manager who needs to examine the accounts will be best served by reading the various statements, reviews and reports, as well as the notes on the financial statements, in some detail.

If possible the reports for several years should be investigated. This will give a better view of overall financial performance and is likely to reveal trends.

Profit and loss account

A profit and loss account shows the profit or loss performance for the stated period, usually 12 months for the annual report and six months for an interim report. (When comparing several reports, adjustments to the figures may be needed when one (or more) of the reports covers a period which is irregular).

In essence, the profit and loss account shows what has happened to the operating profit or deficit and exceptional items made in the period. Thus it will show dividends paid to shareholders, taxation and retained profit. Fig. 2.3.L (over the page) gives a simple notional profit and loss account for the year.

Balance sheet

A balance sheet shows the state of the organisation's assets and liabilities at a given date, eg for the annual report, the last day of the company's financial year. Fig. 2.3.M (on page A-91) shows a notional balance sheet as at the end of the year.

Cash flow statement

A cash flow statement for the accounting period demonstrates where a company's cash came from and how it has been used.

Statement of total recognised gains and losses

A statement of recognised gains and losses shows capital losses and gains such as might be incurred on sales of plant and machinery, acquisition of new property and the like.

Statutes and standards

The preparation of financial accounts is governed by the Companies Act 1985 and the Financial Reporting Standards. The regime changes from time to time.

Fig. 2.3.L
*Profit and Loss
Account for year to
31 December*

	Year to 31 December (£)
Turnover	34,289,798
Cost of sales	(25,819,319)
Gross profit	8,470,479
Administrative expenses	(7,181,326)
Operating profit	1,289,153
Net interest	(34,954)
Profit before taxation	1,254,199
Tax on profit	(189,250)
Profit after taxation	1,064,949
Minority interests	5,079
Net profit for year (after tax)	1,070,028
Dividends	(222,066)
Retained profit	847,962
Earnings (net profit after tax) per share	£1,070,028 ÷ 53,000* = 20.20 pence
Earnings (dividends paid) per share	£222,066 ÷ 53,000* = 4.20 pence
*Note: Shares issued = 53,000	

Any change in the regime may result in differences of calculation between previous years' accounts and those of the current and later years. The note to the financial statements will usually mention this.

Of course, a change in the regime may also result in changes to company policy which may be reflected in the accounts without specific mention.

Taxation

The amounts payable to the government for taxes are calculated in accordance with the Taxes Act for corporation tax on a company's income; the Taxation of Capital Gains Act 1992 governs capital gains tax. The net amount payable after exemptions, reliefs and concessions will appear in the profit and loss account in due course. It may be noted that the operating profit in the profit and loss account is not the taxable amount: for instance, depreciation used for the financial accounts may not be the same as that required under the Capital Allowance Act 1990 as amended.

Treatment of facilities costs in the accounts

There are published Statements of Standard Accounting Practice (SSAP)[3] laying down the principles under which the financial accounts should be prepared and presented. Nevertheless accounting practices vary quite widely in terms of the description and classification of facilities cost centres, eg 'heating and lighting' may be given as a cost heading whereas the cost of in-house cleaning staff may be lost in a single umbrella heading of 'staff costs'.

---

[3] Accounting standards ( ) Standard Accounting Practice, ASB, London Board

Fig. 2.3.M
Balance sheet at 31 December

	As at 31 December (£)
Fixed assets	
Intangible assets	1,121,568
Tangible assets	680,317
Investments	27,838
	1,829,723
Current assets	
Stocks	616,085
Debtors	7,869,528
Cash	2,288,102
	10,773,715
Creditors: due within one year	(9,097,435)
Net current assets	1,676,280
Total assets less current liabilities	3,506,003
Capital and reserves	
Called-up share capital	268,676
Share premium account	1,198,926
Profit and loss account	2,029,865
Shareholders' funds	3,497,467
Minority interest	8,536
	3,506,003

In practice the accountants' classifications are more or less useless for gleaning even high level information about the costs of facilities services, even though there is now a standard coding system (SAP Code) which should facilitate a greater consistency of analysis as between different companies' expenditure. These codes are too 'raw' to provide meaningful facilities cost data, although it is possible by means of sub-coding to get down to an appropriate level of detail.

Property assets and the accounts

Traditionally, property assets have been accounted for as fixed assets in the balance sheet - at cost. When updating valuations are undertaken the revised values of the property are recorded in the balance sheet replacing the old value of the same fixed assets. Any increase in value is placed in reserves (as a liability the company has to the shareholders).

Such valuations are, or should be, undertaken in accordance with the 'Red Book'[4] of the Royal Institution of Chartered Surveyors.

[4] *Royal Institution of Chartered Surveyors,(2001) RICS Valuation and Appraisal Manual, RICS, London*

Generally, leases have been classified as fixed assets but are treated for depreciation according to their duration. Long leases, ie with over 50 years outstanding, are treated like freeholds - only the values of **buildings** are depreciated. Short leases are depreciated over the duration of the lease outstanding. Of course, leases which have no capital value, eg are held at full rents, are not depreciated.

A draft accounting standard has been introduced which requires obligation under a lease, eg the liability to pay rent in the future, to be treated as a liability in the accounts.

Of course, any repairs, insurance, rent, service charges and other property outgoings are normally treated as business expenses in the profit and loss account. However, certain costs have special treatment and are not treated as business expenses, as such. These include:

- repairs which are incurred shortly after the purchase of property are usually regarded as capital expenditure (for taxation purposes)

- certain payments, eg a premium to a landlord, may result in an annual allowance to the tenant for income taxation purposes

- expenditure on certain buildings, eg industrial buildings, may attract capital allowances (see Chapter 11.2.5).

It may be seen that special treatment of such items as these have an effect on taxable profit but the adjustments do not appear in the profit and loss account.

2.3.9 ANALYSIS OF ACCOUNTS

The analysis and interpretation of a company's report and accounts is undertaken by managers, analysts and investors, among others, to provide a meaningful context for making decisions.

It is beyond the scope of this section to provide a comprehensive look at the analysis of accounts. However, such an examination might include the following:

- a review of external factors affecting continuity of policy and the actual figures

- the wording of the chairman's report and other features of the 'prose' in a report

- auditor's report

- notes to the financial accounts

- ratio analysis of the accounts.

Looking at these in turn:

external factors - the impact that the regulatory regime may have has been mentioned above. Of course, many other external factors have an adverse impact on financial performance, eg the implementation of workers' rights or environmental standards

chairman's report - the words used in the report may carry a particular nuance

auditor's report - generally, the auditor's comments on consistency of the accounts from the previous year to the current year. The auditor also reports on the probity of accounting principles and practices the company has adopted and their compliance with accounting standards. Concerns may arise where the auditors are also the company's accountants - there should be 'Chinese walls' in place. If the auditor is not re-appointed, resigns or is dismissed, the reasons may need to be considered

notes to the financial accounts - these should be read with the accounts as they may give a better insight as to the true interpretation of the results.

ratio analysis - accounting ratios may be calculated from the accounts. They may be used to give measures of success, to show trends over several years to the current year, or compared with those of other companies in the industry. The next section discusses several commonly used accounting ratios.

2.3.10 RATIO ANALYSIS

Ratios derived from published accounts provide a historic perspective of the performance of the company. For some purposes they may, however, be combined with forecasts made by analysts so rendering a future perspective within the overall picture.

It may be noted that, as such, ratio analysis is but one of the analytical methods adopted. Generally, for investment purposes, it is included in a 'fundamentalist' approach, ie a methodology which looks at a company in the context of the overall national economy and the particular industry or sector. Another approach is 'technical analysis'. Here, the analyst uses past performance of a company as evidenced by charts of share price movements against time. A variety of statistical techniques may be used to review performance and to predict future movements of share price.

For facilities managers, ratio analysis, per se, should be of sufficient strength to give insight into the performance of their own company or that of customers, suppliers and contractors with whom their company transacts business. To this end various financial ratios are given below, being related to return on capital, liquidity and performance in general.

The few ratios given in Fig. 2.3.N (over the page) may be extracted from company accounts. Essentially they are balance sheet ratios or profit and loss account ratios. The description given below is basic and may be elaborated on in practice and in specialised texts.

However, a full analysis and interpretation of the ratios depends on full availability of information and on insights into the different ways in which the items in the accounts were originally formulated. Two brief insights are given here but for the facilities manager who wants to be involved in this area, the subject requires more study. For instance, in PFI/PPP companies a change from capitalising costs to entering them as expenses will have an impact on annual profit. The trend in ratios should show the change but what caused the change may not be obvious without reading the notes to the accounts (and perhaps not even then!). Similarly, profits may be increased by non-operating transactions which took place during a company's year. The impact of these transactions is to increase the price/earnings ratio. Anomalies need to be identified, if the trend in ratios is to be appropriately understood.

Profit and loss account ratios

A number of ratios are derived from the profit and loss account and give insights into operational strengths and weaknesses.

Price/earnings ratio: for high level comparison of overall performance with other companies in its business sector the price/earnings ratio is valuable for a company and its shareholders. Of course, price will be determined by the market on a day to day basis (for quoted companies).

Other ratios include profit to sales, sales to stock, turnover to assets, sales to purchases and debtors to creditors. The degree of detail will vary with the extent and availability of financial records.

Profit and Loss Account ratios	Form	Result
Price/Earning Ratio	Market price of the share / Earnings per share	30.5 / 2.02 = 15.1
Profit to sales ratios (margins)	Gross profit / Sales (gross margin) or Net profit / Sales (net margin)	8,470,479 / 34,289,798 = 24.7% or 1,254,199 / 34,289,798 = 3.1%
Sales to stock	Turnover (ie sales) / Stock	34,289,798 / 7,869,528 = 4.357
Turnover to assets	Turnover (ie sales) / Net assets	34,289,798 / 3,506,003 = 9.78
Sales to purchases	Turnover (ie sales) / Purchases*	*Not given in the published accounts
Debtors days	Trade debtors x 365 / Turnover	7,869,528 x 365 / 34,289,798 = 84 days

Balance sheet ratios	Form	Result
Net assets per share	Value of assets after debt / Number of shares issued	3,506,003 / 53,000,000 = £ 0.066
Return on capital	Net income or profit x 100 / Capital or net assets	1,289,153 x 100 / 3,506,003 = 36.8%
Gearing	Loans or debt / Equity	The company has no debt 0%
Liquid ratio	Liquid assets / Current liabilities Current assets - Stock / Current liabilities	10,773,715 – 616,085 / 9,097,435 = 1.165
Current ratio	Current assets / Current liabilities	10,773,715 / 9,097,435 = 1.18

Profit to sales, or **profit margin,** shows how successful the company is in making sales or in reducing costs in the financial year.

Sales to stock (or stock to sales) shows how often the company turns over its stock in the period (or stock as a percentage of sales).

Turnover to assets shows how often the company turns over its assets in the period.

Sales to purchases shows how frequently the purchases need to be renewed in the period in question. A large difference between this figure and that for sales to stock may suggest that inventory is too high or there is dead stock.

Debtors to creditors: gives a measure of efficiency in paying and collecting cash.

Debtor days: indicates how long it is taking to collect cash; an excessive number of days may indicate that 'sales' in the accounts are not necessarily invoiced sales.

Of course, each ratio is best understood in the context of either several years of the company's accounts or by comparing like ratios in the same kind of business for one or more years. Finally, as a caution, the end of year figures used in Fig 2.3.N above may not reflect the whole picture. To take an example the level of stock on the 31 December may be much less or greater than the average level of stock.

Balance sheet ratios

Net asset value per share: this is a useful measure where a company's holding of capital assets, eg an investment trust or a property investment company, or where the value of its fixed assets, eg buildings and land, is high relative to the trading potential of the business carried on. It may be compared at the end of each earlier accounting period, for example, to the market price of the share at the accounting date and to the historic net asset value.

Return on capital: a fundamental perception of investment is the return on capital which the investor expects or does get from putting up money. If that money is mainly borrowed the measure may be related to the cost of borrowing. However, the company's cost of capital is the usual comparison. This ratio is calculated in different ways. For instance, 'capital' or 'net assets' may exclude only current liabilities but not long-term debt. However it may be calculated as return on **shareholder's equity**. The latter measure looks at the return from the shareholder's perspective. Profit may be measured before or after tax; comparisons with published market rates need, therefore, to be careful (tax tends to be included).

Gearing: ie, the ratio of borrowings to income, is a valuable measure where profits (or rental income) are volatile. Thus, where gearing is high a property investment company is vulnerable when rents drop or when interest rates rise. On the other hand, high gearing with fixed interest rates and rising rents result in increased return on equity. It is defined in various ways.

Liquidity: if a vulnerable company needs to mitigate the situation, liquidity becomes important, ie the ability to realise assets to pay off creditors or even meet repayment on long-term loans.

Two liquidity ratios may be cited, ie **liquid ratio** and **current ratio**. However, both relate to assets other than fixed assets so the sums involved may be insufficient to meet obligations.

As a rule of thumb a liquid ratio of 1:1 and a current ratio of 1.5:1 are regarded as norms in meeting obligations in day-to-day business, but what is the norm varies between types of business.

2.4   QUALITY MANAGEMENT

Introduction

Quality is a noun meaning 'basic character or nature'. It is often linked to adjectives such as 'high' or 'low' - to qualify or benchmark levels of achievement; therefore, on its own the noun 'quality' is strictly not a parameter, although in modern times it has come to be used more and more frequently as a modifying word indicating a degree of excellence or superiority, eg 'quality managed facilities'.

The imperfections of syntax in this particular matter can be a source of confusion to those seeking improved efficiency in industry; the term 'performance' is less open to misinterpretation than 'quality' since it is not used as a modifier on its own account. The concept of performance considered in Chapter 1.2.1 could be read as 'quality'. However the terms 'quality control', 'quality assurance' and 'total quality management' are now enshrined in business management jargon and have found their way in recent times into theory and practice of facilities management. As such the terms cannot be expunged from the vocabulary so it is very important that the term 'quality', where used in facilities management, is always in its 'relative' rather than 'absolute' modifying form, thereby discouraging ill-considered pursuit of absolute excellence accompanied by the inevitable accumulation of redundant performance (see Chapter 1.2.5).

Although this distinction between 'performance' and the popular understanding of quality may seem to be pedantic it does serve to highlight the critical significance of the degree of quality sought and achieved in the process of optimising the cost and value of any contribution to productivity.

'Quality', where used in a mission statement to imply the required level of performance, may render that statement inappropriate - possibly harmful - if what is delivered is in excess of the business requirements whilst having incurred greater costs. A typical example is excessive maintenance being provided for the sake of a high standard of engineering performance to the financial detriment of more strategically critical cost centres.

2.4.1   QUALITY AND THE FACILITIES POLICY

The quality of facilities, ie the performance of facilities, should be enshrined in the facilities policy supporting the corporate plan. Chapter 1.1 discusses the relationship between the cost of premises and support services and the business requirement; quality management is the process by which these relationships are forged - hopefully optimised.

'Hopefully', because although management implies the skilful use of resources it does not imply or guarantee success.

Just like financial control and building performance, quality management is dependent upon a trinity of facets - Fig. 2.4.A (over the page).

As with all trinities (religious or otherwise) you cannot expect the whole to be present in the absence of any one of the components.

Fig. 2.4.A
*Three facets of
quality control -
inter-relationships*

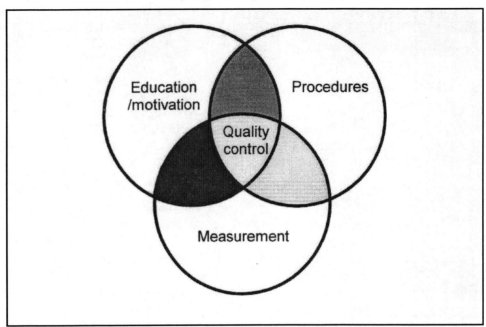

2.4.2 THE BUSINESS CASE

Educational issues

Quality management in facilities is primarily dependent upon a willingness by top management to accept the contribution of appropriate facilities to the productivity of the core business; quality truly does start at the top. However, down the line any facilities manager unable to identify the relationship between their own goals and corporate requirements will be unlikely to make any pro-active contribution even if top management is enlightened enough to be seeking it.

Seeking an improvement in the quality of facilities performance must be accompanied by a two-way educational process - both within the organisation and from within the discipline itself. The core business customer must know what they may expect, and accept or reject it - possibly paying providers against results. On the other hand facilities managers must not only understand the importance of communications between themselves and core business but also have the skills and resources to achieve agreed objectives to time and budget.

Quality management must apply both to the performance of the in-house team, (who should be empowered, well qualified and fully trained), and that of any suppliers whom they engage.

Justifying the strategy

Justification for providing a specific level of quality in facilities can be based on either:

• the conventional wisdom, or

• potential effects on business performance.

The former approach is still the norm in most organisations throughout the UK - and the rest of the world too. Sometimes justification for the adoption or confirmation of a specific level of service is derived from comparisons with peer group organisations - maybe in benchmarking groups - where facilities managers draw confidence (though perhaps not inspiration) from the decisions made by their peers. This is a safe route provided the peers have got it right, but one that will put the facilities manager of the future at risk of being shown to be lacking in pro-active business acumen.

The second route requires development of a far better structured business case which can, if required, be built on options around a 'zero-base' (see Chapter 2.2.5 and Fig. 2.2.F) drawn from normal or minimum peer group conventional practice.

The business impact scenario may be presented in one of two ways. The first, and probably more prevalent, involves predicting the level of benefit to be derived by the business (either in 'hard' or 'soft' terms) from added performance. The 'hard' version is usually impossible to prove conclusively due to a quite universal dearth of good data so must depend on sensitivity analysis of different assumptions with regard to increased benefits.

The other way to express the benefits of increased quality, or the losses through reduction, is to identify and appraise the risks to the organisation of not achieving the appropriate level of support. Clearly this is much the same thing but said in reverse. However, there is one fundamental difference which makes this risk-exposure-based approach more likely to motivate the end user than one promoting the prospect of added value: that is the fact that whereas some people in high places may be sceptical about unsupported presumptions of increased profitability through higher quality facilities most people can accept the existence of a risk - a possibility - of loss through under-provision of quality. Actually quality management and risk management have exactly reciprocal implications.

Fig. 2.4.B
Quality support centres

Quality support centres	Issues for protection
1. Image - externally	a. Sales / margins
2. Image – internally	a. Non-productivity *Absence – sickness* *Absence – malingering* *Absence – strike* *Absence – resignation*
	b. Reduced productivity *Sickness* *'Soldiering'* *Recuperation* *Falling confidence* *Falling morale* *Staff turnover*
	c. Recruitment costs
3. Physical property	a. Loss associated with theft of company property
	b. Loss associated with damage to company property
	c. Loss associated with technical failure
	d. Loss of amenity
4. Intellectual property	a. Theft of information or data
	b. Damage to information or data
5. Persons	a. Loss associated with theft of personal property
	b. Loss associated with damage to personal property
	c. Minor injury
	d. Serious injury
6. Ergonomics	a. Inefficient working conditions
	b. Inefficient equipment
7. Statutory obligations	a. Fine (eg health and safety)
	b. Closure
	c. Non-productivity
	d. Reduced productivity
8. Contract obligations	a. Damages
	b. Forfeiture
	c. Lost control of works
	d. Eviction
9. Asset management plan	a. Excessive depreciation
	b. Premature obsolescence
	c. Excessive remedial costs

Chapter 2.5 deals with aspects of risk management in detail. Here it is necessary to look at the areas of business supported by facilities which are the potential beneficiaries of added quality (see Fig. 2.4.B above): these are, of course, the self-same areas which put the business at risk of loss through failure to provide adequate support.

Of these, in most organisations the impact of facilities on external and internal image is likely to be by far and away the most significant.

Effects on ergonomics and therefore productivity will be fairly important, with the benefits likely to be most achievable at and around the workstation. Frequently it is possible to improve productivity substantially with very little cost other than that incurred by dint of good management, eg disciplined filing and storage, clean desk policies. Meeting legal requirements such as statutory compliance (health and safety) and contract obligations (leasehold commitments) can be a problem when quality falls away but this is predominantly an issue of pure risk management.

Works to the assets which enhance or maintain good image and ergonomics are concerned with quality management in terms of functional performance; however, the process of maintaining the assets at a level which avoids excessive depreciation and/or obsolescence is one for risk management in terms of physical performance. It is not hard to see that the same piece of work could fulfil all these objectives, but the problem is that many property managers (and some facilities managers) are pre-occupied with the physical performance to the detriment of the far more significant functional issues.

The value management process requires that objectives should be weighted (see 'Stage 1 - identification and appraisal' at Chapter 2.2.3

The authors' entirely subjective view as to the relative weightings of these quality management criteria in a **purely commercial scenario** is as follows - on a scale of 1 to 10 with 10 being the highest:

Image	- externally	10
	- internally	5
Physical property		0.5
Intellectual property		5
Persons		2
Ergonomics		2
Legal obligations		0.5
Assets		0.5

The logic of this is that the impact of facilities quality (whether relating to appearance or comfort), on the way visitors, passers-by, customers and staff perceive the organisation will affect business success and productivity to a must greater extent than the effect of any better, or more comfortable or safer working conditions. Loss of intellectual property can be very serious but matters involving fines or penalties are normally insignificant in the context of business turnover.

Although this clinical analysis may not hold good in every business scenario - and may well be considered unacceptable by some on social and moral grounds - facilities managers still need to keep the right balance between philosophical and economic justification of their expenditure.

Recent research[1] has shown that premises issues alone contribute up to 25% of job satisfaction which in turn[2] has been shown to contribute up to 16% of worker productivity. Fig. 2.4.C shows the maximum premises-related contribution of job satisfaction to staff productivity at 4%, ie 25% x 16% contribution of job satisfaction to productivity. Since the normal range of premises costs is between 2.5% and 5% of turnover this means that by raising premises costs from 2.5% to 5% of turnover the full increase of 4% in productivity due to job satisfaction is likely to be achieved.

Fig. 2.4.C
Premises, job satisfaction and profits

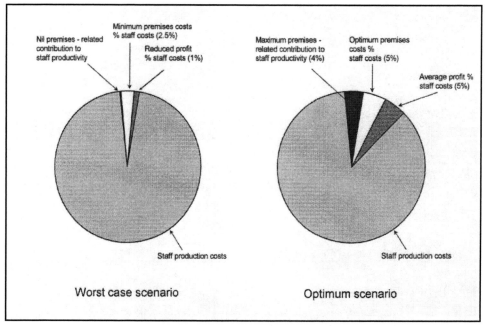

Worst case scenario   Optimum scenario

Although this simple example shows the significant bonus that can accrue through higher quality of premises it must be remembered that it only addresses the issue of staff productivity; the critical contribution of the same expenditure to improved external image is not added into the benefits side of the equation, and the risk containment strategies in respect of legal compliance and asset management are also covered without additional expenditure.

Motivation for good quality in facilities stems mainly from common-sense but, as with the above example, more and more good hard data is coming on stream to help wean decision-making away from the conventional wisdom. Such an example is at Fig. 2.4.D (over the page) which is one of the most fascinating pieces of research which has yet been carried out relating higher premises quality to greater business benefit.

The figure describes the results of a pilot study applying BQA principles (see Chapters 1.2.4 and 9.1.3) to a dozen or so primary schools and shows an extraordinary correlation between building quality and educational achievement. Allowing for the absence of socio-economic groupings and teacher assessments from the statistical analyses the study still points fairly conclusively to the benefits which an ICF could bring to the design process if armed with a solid database of such examples. They would, of course, need to have chapter and verse on the 'benefit drivers' underpinning them plus well-tried and tested quality measurement tools.

But more of quality measurement later. Having developed the motivation for pro-active quality management the procedures need to be put in place to achieve results.

---

[1] *Independent survey conducted by Bernard Williams Associates (BWA).*

[2] *The Sheffield Effectiveness Programme*

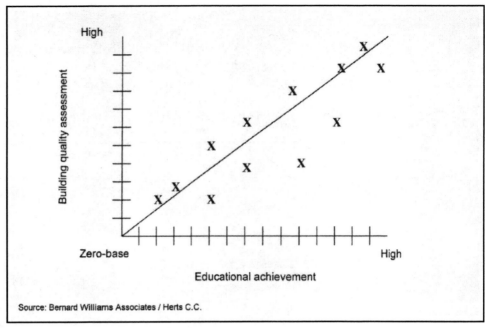

Fig. 2.4.D
*The impact of
building quality on
educational
achievement*

Source: Bernard Williams Associates / Herts C.C.

2.4.3 QUALITY MANAGEMENT PROCEDURES

The processes

The processes by which quality is managed and delivered involve:

- identification of need
- appraisal of options
- specification
- procurement
- monitoring.

This whole process is an essential part of 'value management' which was considered at length in Chapter 2.2. Here we will first consider the structures - formal or informal - which need to be in place to guarantee success of the quality management process (quality assurance). Then the specification process will be examined; monitoring is, of course, the third facet of quality management (see Fig. 2.4.A above) and is also considered separately below.

Quality Assurance

The various Quality Assurance (QA) standards such as EN ISO 9000 can be usefully applied either to part or the whole of the Intelligent Client's work; equally they may insist upon compliance from service providers and suppliers. However, the burden of compliance may be counter-productive for smaller vibrant outfits such as consultancies whose resources may be best directed towards creative problem-solving rather than pushing paper around. Most of such firms engage fully qualified professionals whose basic training affords some guarantee of competence (though rather less than one would hope in many cases). Smaller firms are probably best judged by extensive reference-taking rather than slavish compliance with a standard geared towards the lower common denominators.

The larger firms can afford and may well benefit from EN ISO 9000 compliance though the facilities manager should treat that as an added bonus in support of their own investigations into their standards of quality delivery.

The concept of total quality management (TQM) involving a corporate culture of performance delivery is now becoming increasingly popular in business and its extension to facilities is described by Keith Alexander[3] under the term 'Quality Managed Facilities' (QMF).

QMF describes how a total quality management framework can be used to enable facilities managers to provide services of a quality appropriate to meeting corporate objectives. The approach demands a thorough understanding of the corporate culture and setting up of a framework for managing customers, services and assets at every level from strategic to operational. The difference between such an approach - which is also subjected to performance monitoring - and the simpler QA process is vast and has already been highly successful in a number of major organisations in which it has been instituted.

Specification

No facilities can be provided without someone having stated - formally or informally - what is required. Generally speaking the clearer the instructions the more likely it is that they will result in provision of what is wanted; but asking is one thing and getting is another, and that is where quality management comes into its own.

There are two generic types of specification:

- performance related

- prescriptive.

Performance specification

The concept of output performance was introduced in Chapter 1.2.1 - The performance of facilities; it relates to specification of achievement rather than process. Although, in facilities terms, the output performance always equates to the policy in respect of function of buildings or services, the principles can also apply to the output from the service delivery process when considered in purely process or production terms.

To explain this apparent contradiction let us take as an example the maintenance of the hot water supplies. The physical output from the maintenance operation might be that the thermostat should always cut in at the required point. The beneficial or functional output from a **user's** viewpoint would be a safe and reliable supply of hot water. In the middle of these two outputs is a physical performance output which relates to the minimum and maximum acceptable water temperatures. It is in this middle ground that output and input performance meet, often in a state of considerable confusion.

In order to understand the specification and measurement of performance of facilities it is best to go back to the first principles of the facilities policy (see Chapter 1.1.5).

Key performance indicators (KPIs)

At the highest level the ICF determines the output performance to be included in the facilities policy. Such output may be described in 'mission statement' terminology eg safe, reliable, clean, cool etc and the Key Performance Indicators (KPI's) against which that output would be tested might be the level of user satisfaction, numbers of complaints etc. These policy output criteria - sometimes called 'Critical Success Factors' (CSF's) are not normally suitable as contract performance specifications, and should only reside in the facilities policy and be measured independently by the ICF purely for their own internal purposes.

[3] *The Centre for Facilities Management, University of Salford*

To achieve the policy objectives it is necessary to determine a **strategy,** ie a plan of campaign which will deliver up the working conditions stated in the policy. The strategy describes the output expected from the **tactics** adopted, ie the operational process.

In a facilities context the tactics are the operations in a process specified in a prescriptive form, eg the planned preventative maintenance schedule, the qualifications of the operatives; the output of the process should meet the strategic output requirements, eg the temperature of the hot water and 'down' times.

The strategic output performance specification may be used as the basis for a service level agreement/contract in which the service provider is left with the responsibility of deciding on the input specification to achieve the process output. Whether or not the user chooses to prescribe the process output performance or the service level input criteria is a matter of preference. In either case there will be two further sets of KPI's.

In the case of the process output the KPI's will relate to the strategy, ie the physical performance to be achieved whereas at the tactical level KPI's will relate to strict compliance with the specified input of resources.

Fig. 2.4.E illustrates this concept in hierarchical form.

Fig. 2.4.E
Policy, strategy and tactics - measuring performance

Performance centre	Output	KPI's
Policy	Policy achievement	User satisfaction Complaints Measurable performance (beneficial)
Strategy	Process achievement	Measurable performance (physical)
Tactics	Compliance with input specification	Measurable compliance

Output performance specification

Output performance needs to be measurable, but the extent to which such measurement can be adequate for purposes of contractual performance is critical in any decision to procure services against an output performance specification.

A contract inviting process output performance bids to maintain the hot water services so as to eliminate the risk of too cold or scalding water supplies requires contractors to create, price and monitor their own input service levels (see below). In this case the physical output from the process can be measured in terms of water temperature range and this will be one of the key performance indicators (KPI's) for the measurement of process outputs.

High level policy output specifications loosely invoking terms such as comfort, safety, suitability and availability must not be used for bidding purposes, although there is every reason why these terms - and their definitions/qualifications - should form an integral part of the facilities policy.

One person's physical performance or process output will be another's policy output and sometimes their descriptions will be the same or similar. Nevertheless contracts based on output performance should always look primarily to describe physical, measurable achievements required from service providers.

The use of output performance specification to place responsibility squarely on the shoulders of service providers, ie total risk transfer, may avoid the need for the intelligent customers to monitor service level inputs, but they would do well to insist upon the right to selectively audit the providers' own monitoring of service level input performance.

Prescriptive (input) specification

The works (tactics) required to meet the user's strategic output targets can either be specified in detail by the facilities sponsor (within the ICF) or left to the service provider; in the latter case, as we have already discussed, the provider's own service level and process output targets must be clear and measurable.

The components of a service specification were described in Chapter 1.3 (Fig. 1.3.B - Factors influencing the cost of facilities) under the following headings in boxes 3C-G (inc):

- **regime,** eg the frequency of operations, the time of day at which it is executed, degree of mechanisation, speed of responses

- **resources,** eg staff quality, training, experience, specification of materials, quality and use, specification and maintenance of equipment

- **quality control,** eg informal or formal procedures, penalties and performance bonuses, helpdesk monitoring.

The service level quality of each of these ingredients contributes to the overall performance; where they are considered critical to the achievement of the process output they are flagged up as key performance criteria - KPC's. Thus identified the level of quality to be attained and the means of measuring it must be described and included in the contract specification or Service Level Agreement (SLA).

The *Frisqué* program[4] is able to predict the level of quality needed in respect of each of these components to achieve identifiable levels of process and policy output.

Measuring quality - attitudes

The measurement of quality is only possible where there are parameters: performance indicators are discussed in principle in Chapter 1.2.3. Sometimes such indicators may seem crude relative to the significance or nature of the service being measured, eg the cost of providing and running libraries per book! Nevertheless these indicators, however crude they seem, provide a starting point from which at least some discussion can take place; they can provide a basis on which cross-benchmarking can replace unsupported assertions by those whose power and/or position is threatened by objective assessment or who do not understand the purpose and principles of benchmarking performance achievements.

People who do not **want** to plan will try to destroy the planning process by pointing out the ever-present problems of unforeseen change. In the same mode those averse to performance measurement go to great lengths to identify and highlight the deficiencies of the chosen parameters.

The negative attitude in both cases is wrong even though the arguments may seen persuasive at first hearing; those who do not plan, like those who will not benchmark, have nothing against which their performance may be judged so have only their personal commitment and judgement to support their actions. That may in fact be totally adequate but is totally lacking in accountability, so who can tell?

By way of analogy a business overdraft facility may be afforded against imperfect performance related to the historic profit-and-loss accounts and balance sheet and the

---

[4] *'Facilities Risk and Quality Evaluation' program - BWA Facilities Consultancy*

conduct of the account; the amount of borrowing sought will almost certainly be geared to financial projections by the borrower the basis of which may change significantly over the period. Nevertheless, the imperfect data and process by which both parties make their decisions will lead to a better understanding of the people, the problems and the risks than would be possible in an analytical vacuum.

'It is better to have tried and failed than never to have tried at all' is a paraphrase of a well-known piece of verse which is highly relevant to quality measurement.

Internally imposed benchmarking of quality may be informal or may be the subject of public scrutiny using one of the public standards, eg EN ISO 9000. Internal benchmarking is linked to results whereas external monitoring is often geared to slavish adherence to agreed procedures.

Although the procedures in the standard accreditation processes are agreed in advance by the applicant they are generally geared to avoidance of error rather than enhancement of service. Organisations (or departments) which do not make mistakes in established procedures may provide comfort to their customers but risk the impact of bureaucracy on creativity which is the real source of quality (and risk) control.

In practice the KPI's should always relate to the achievement of operations or status which are essential to the success of the operation at the level being considered.

Measuring process output performance

Using a simple example - the cleanliness of carpets - a process output performance specification might be. 'clean, dry and free of litter, visible dust, loose fragments of material and any removable marks of stains'. The problem with such a specification is that it implies a constant state of such cleanliness whereas, in practice, deterioration will inevitably take place between cleans. Well-meaning attempts to redress this imperfection have resulted in quality levels being defined using process output KPI's like 'no more than 3 pieces of litter per 10 sq m of carpeted area at any one time and then never for more than 1 hour!'

You know what they mean and in practice a menu constructed of such visual images of varying quality levels would be quite a useful private checklist for the 'intelligent client' trying to describe their policy on cleanliness. But ask a contractor to price it? Definitely not - at least, not on a definitive 'best-and-final-offer' basis and not to become the basis of any contract remuneration or penalty.

Technically it is possible to measure the dust content of carpets and set limits beyond which there is a health hazard and in much the same vein one can specify and measure tolerance limits on issues such as air temperature and humidity. The point is that if the intelligent client has good reason for keeping within these tolerances they must be able to specify them and find a sensible way of checking compliance; so, what to specify and how to measure compliance? That is the key issue.

Will the key criteria to meet the ICF's strategy be the visibility of the state of uncleanliness or the amount of dust pollutancy filling the lungs and noses of the unwitting users - or both? Depending on the importance attached to each factor the ICF must make a conscious decision to specify the process output performance criteria in a way that they (the ICF) can check it. If this means carrying out dust content tests and counting up pieces of litter whilst poring over a stop-watch then so be it. In the end, if the ICF cannot justify in economic terms the strategy put in place to match their policy output requirements - and confirm that it is being achieved - then they have no business proposing it in the first place.

A major problem with using process output KPI's as payment or penalty catalysts is the necessarily subjective view of performance achieved in services like cleaning where the output rarely has the possibility of 'hard' measurement. Opportunities for corruption and/or favouritism are clearly there, as is the possibility of uneven interpretation as between different contract managers administering large contracts.

Measuring input performance

At the simplest, prescriptive input level the KPI's will relate to compliance with the terms of the input specification - be it a contract or an internal SLA.

For example, in the case of cleaning carpets, process KPI's for 'Regime' might be:

- frequency of vacuuming
- response time for cleaning up spillages.

For 'Resources' they might be:

- linguistic ability of supervisor
- visual appearance of workforce.

For quality control they might be:

- helpdesk real-time response-time monitoring capability
- speed of identification of critical non-compliance.

Circumstances determine which criteria are key and what effect any non-compliance will have on the overall result, but it is absolutely imperative that nothing gets specified that cannot be measured or which isn't worth the trouble and also that measurement is never requested when to do so is impossible or impractical.

Of course, whatever goes into the contract or service level agreement needs to be checked out for compliance by the contract manager regularly throughout the term of the agreement.

Whereas the service provider will be told how often the carpets are to be cleaned, when, by how many, by whom and with what, the ICF is only concerned with how clean they will look during the working hours and (maybe) the extent of any health hazard. The KPI's in the above example are quite different in their context the former being a measure of physical compliance and the latter relating to a high level success factor.

However it is at this point that the input/output syndrome gets to be most muddled, for the output should not prescribe the number of times a week the carpet is cleaned; equally, the response time for spillage treatment is fairly close to being a process output rather than a regime input. In fact, the process output is not concerned with the 'fix-it' times per se but with the length of time the mess is around and the potential damage it may do if left too long unattended.

This said there is no harm at all, in most cases, in letting the service provider know the policy output criteria and KPI's provided they do not become used as contractual conditions. The latter is the authors' own viewpoint and there are still many people who like to write the policy into the contract/SLA, sometimes even omitting the input criteria completely. However, the problems described above, which often occur in specifying output in sensible measurable terms, are compounded by the difficulty which contractors have in selecting the right level of performance on which to base their bids.

Anyway, having established the KPI's and how to measure them the ICF must also address the service provider's own proposals for quality control, hopefully submitted with their bids.

On the assumption that the provider's quality control proposals are acceptable the ICF must decide the resources of their own needed to audit the contractor's quality control system, the data it is incorporating and the interpretation of results; many imperfectly-established ICF's fail to take account of this need, which is probably less of a commitment when a managing agent, as opposed to a lump sum contract manager, is the directive manager.

Measuring policy output performance - user satisfaction surveys

A useful adjunct to output performance monitoring is the User Satisfaction Survey which can be used either as a policy output KPI or simply as an unofficial method of checking how things are going. However, the exercise can be a minefield ready to cause untold damage to the unwary.

Among the more common problem areas are:

• how the questions are asked

• skewed samples

• suspicion of motives

• over-surveying

• relative expectations

• sympathy for the facilities management team.

The size of the sample is not cited as a problem, which may cause some surprise to those with a statistical bent. The reason is that, whatever the staticians say about the minimum numbers of responses needed to generate a valid conclusion, the authors' experience is that user survey results in the facilities management field show a very high level of consistency across any organisation; in fact in every case the results can be positively indicated from a mere handful of random samples from the batch of questionnaires received.

It is useful to invite the respondents to say how important each service is to them, thereby establishing an order of priority in terms of recovery measures and also to permit a weighted evaluation of the scores.

As stated above the way the questions are posed will have a major impact on the answer. It may be noted that the question mode 'how satisfied are you?' is totally difference in concept from 'are you satisfied with?' and you cannot compare the results of two such dissimilar surveys.

Fig. 2.4.F
Typical questionnaire format

Note: ☺ = 100%   ☹ = 0%

A typical questionnaire format is given at Fig.2.4.F (previous page). It is considered best for the respondents be identifiable by name (optional) grade, location and nature of job and a better volume and quality of responses is usually achieved when the whole process is set up, administered and reported upon externally.

Another advantage of using an external survey agent is the opportunity to compare results on a similar basis where the consultant has a database of responses to similar questions gathered on a similar basis.

An example of a peer group benchmarking study using consultants' data is given at Fig. 2.4.G which also includes the results of a cost benchmarking exercise of the services.

Fig. 2.4.G
Comparing cost and user-satisfaction

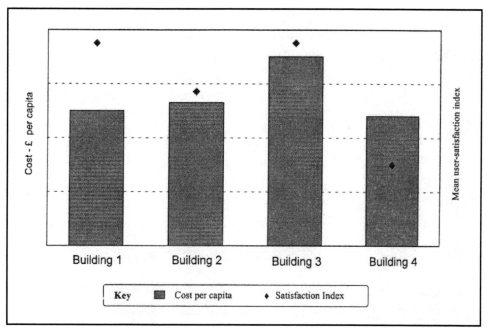

From the figure it appears that:

- expenditure per capita in Building 1 is achieving greater value for money than in Building 3.

- expenditure per capita in Building 4 is similar to that in 1 and 2 but is achieving lower user-satisfaction.

The User Satisfaction Survey also loses its value when questions confuse input with output. Ideally questions should be asked about the output quality, eg 'how satisfied are you with the air temperature?' not 'how satisfied are you with the services maintenance?' The ICF should know whether the HVAC system is capable of delivering the goods if properly maintained and trace any problems back to the service level and/or its provider as appropriate.

When taking smaller samples it is important to avoid skewing by location, grade, sex etc - unless that is a target sector for a specific purpose. Equally, too many surveys - not just from the ICF but often from other departments - can induce survey-fatigue with resulting loss of interest, numbers and reliability of responses.

Some individuals do get suspicious about the motives behind surveys and may give 'political' responses. In the authors' experience this is rarely so predominant as to skew the results; however, a lot can be gleaned from users' comments against particular services in particular the **tone** of complaints when these are a significant feature of the survey.

Sometimes a poor quality of service may get relatively kind results where it is perceived that the FM team are doing their best in difficult circumstances. Usually in such cases, however, this sympathy is expressed in the users' comments rather than in the scores - another very good reason for making sure that users' comments are welcomed.

The mix of grades of staff usually skews the results slightly: generally speaking the lower grades are more concerned with the 'comfort' and 'amenity' facilities whereas the more senior people hold the 'business support' services to be more important. The latter usually find the questionnaires more difficult to complete than the lower grades, presumably because they are concerned to give a fully reasoned answer or, just as likely, they are working out the politics behind both question and potential response.

Some organisations set user satisfaction targets as output performance policy for each service and use the surveys to test compliance half-yearly or yearly.

There are two critical things to remember about interpretation of the results of User Satisfaction Surveys. First the level achievable in each service varies considerably - you cannot expect 90% satisfaction with the air temperature whereas the mail-room may well aspire to such levels. Second, the customer is not always right about relative importance of facilities, and the ICF must know when it is productive to pander to the users' whims and when the business can put the money to better use.

There is a lot of research into the theory underlying user satisfaction surveys, some of which suggests that peoples' expectations vis-à-vis achievements is a significant factor influencing the scores. This may be so and the would-be surveyor of user satisfaction should explore the learned texts to better understand the issues raised above and others which may be relevant to their circumstances.

However, extensive experience of carrying out and analysing the results of surveys across the UK and internationally indicates that there is a very close fit between the scores achieved and the quality delivered regardless of location or nature of the organisation. The key issue in getting realistic comparables appears to be the consistency of the questions and the format of the questionnaires.

Nevertheless wherever possible it is best to use the surveys as a second check on the achievement and suitability of the output performance strategy and only use it as a first measure of assessment when lack of formal monitoring procedures has left no alternative when trying to assess - maybe benchmark - quality achieved.

Complaints

And, finally, some facilities managers use the complaints register as a check on performance; this is common in PFI/PPP output specifications where phrases like '100% complaint-free' are sometimes found. Well, when is a complaint not a complaint? What is reasonable and what not? Again, use of the complaints register as a failsafe against slipping performance is a sensible strategy but as a contract/service level regulator it is too woolly a concept to be relied upon.

In any case, statistically an overwhelming majority of complaints normally come from a tiny minority of users; only where this is not the case should complaints be used as a policy performance measure.

2.4.4 INVESTING IN QUALITY

Quality must be motivated by top management, guided by procedures and measured by results. In facilities management, as in all production processes, the results - good or bad - will find their way, sooner or later, to the bottom line.

As discussed in Chapter 1.2 the delivery of the 'right' performance at the right price is the ultimate economic aim in facilities. The rider is that 'right' performance means exactly what is required by the organisation to achieve its corporate goals; 'right' price is the consequence of a fully cost-controlled operation involving the three facets of which the value-engineering process will have properly identified the level of performance needed within a value management framework.

Although decisions to invest in physical and human resources in pursuit of excellence may well produce the necessary financial return, a change in the culture of an organisation - the way it sees and treats itself and its customers -may well be achieved with no investment other than a shift in management attitude and direction, which may cost nothing more than a few confrontations with the diehards.

Sensible financial investment coupled with application of TQM procedures - both efficiently measured against performance criteria - will bring optimum benefit to an organisation. But one without the other is likely to put the planned improvement process into a low gear - or stall it completely when the going is uphill.

2.5 RISK MANAGEMENT

Introduction

Risk is 'the possibility of incurring misfortune or loss'.[1]

A 'chance' is the possibility of something (good or bad) occurring but is usually used in the more optimistic sense, eg you have a 'chance' of winning the National Lottery but you risk losing your money!

Another word meaning risk is 'hazard', but this is most commonly used to denote a source of danger, eg an icy road presents a hazard to motorists; that same hazard - the source of danger - puts the motorist at risk of having an accident; the seriousness of the consequences of an accident represent a further risk to the motorist who may suffer only minor injuries or be killed. The latter are 'consequential' risks so we can see that risk has three stages:

- the hazard, eg icy road conditions

- the primary risk - an accident may occur

- the consequential risk - the severity of the consequences.

In this chapter the term 'risk' is used to include hazards which are always implied by the risk events described. Consequential risk is addressed by the application of severity weightings in the case study appraisals.

In all three categories there is only a possibility of misfortune or loss occurring; however, in risk identification and appraisal the possibilities at each stage must be separately addressed and evaluated.

2.5.1 THE RISK CENTRES

Another important point about risk in a facilities context is that the act of risk containment, ie the service provided to contain the risk to core business, is itself a source of risk in terms of the execution of the service and its physical and financial consequences. Thus, cleaners may get injured slipping on their own wet floors (as may their customers) and works may overrun their budgets.

However, the facility manager's primary obligation in terms of risk management is to the needs of core business. The areas of risk exposure are exactly the same as those addressed by quality management and first introduced in Chapter 2.4.2, Fig. 2.5.A (see over) reproduces these criteria but this time emphasising the negative slant required in the risk management process.

As was explained in Chapter 2.4.2 risk and quality management have a reciprocal relationship - they are two sides of the same coin. If you raise the quality of maintenance the risk of service failure is reduced, and so on.

The facilities manager is confronted with a wide array of such potential problems in respect of persons, property and money. Some of the risks can be managed internally within the facilities department direct, while risks emanating from third party involvement have to be countered, in part, by extension of obligations to suppliers via their contracts or by insurance, or both.

---

[1] *Collins Concise Dictionary. HarperCollins Publishers, Glasgow, UK.*

Fig. 2.5.A
Risk centres

Possible loss consequences of service failure	
Risk centres	**Potential losses**
1. Image - externally	a. Sales / margins
2. Image – internally	a. Non-productivity *Absence – sickness* *Absence – malingering* *Absence – strike* *Absence – resignation*
	b. Reduced productivity *Sickness* *Soldiering* *Recuperation* *Falling confidence* *Falling morale* *Staff turnover*
	c. Recruitment costs
3. Physical property	a. Loss associated with theft of company property
	b. Loss associated with damage to company property
	c. Loss associated with technical failure
	d. Loss of amenity
4. Intellectual property	a. Theft of information or data
	b. Damage to information or data
5. Persons	a. Loss associated with theft of personal property
	b. Loss associated with damage to personal property
	c. Minor injury
	d. Serious injury
6. Ergonomics	a. Inefficient working conditions
	b. Inefficient equipment
7. Statutory obligations	a. Fine (eg health and safety)
	b. Closure
	c. Non-productivity
	d. Reduced productivity
8. Contract obligations	a. Damages
	b. Forfeiture
	c. Lost control of works
	d. Eviction
9. Asset management plan	a. Excessive depreciation
	b. Premature obsolescence
	c. Excessive remedial costs

Risks to persons for which the facilities manager may have responsibility include:

- health and safety at work

- physical injury or death through disaster

- environmental pollution

- loss of or damage to personal property.

Risks to property can comprise:

- disaster damage

- deterioration

- loss of amenity

- faulty or onerous legal title

- technical failure

- project failure or inefficiency.

Both the above categories have attendant financial risks: direct as in the case of fines, loss of value, cost of reinstatement, and indirect such as loss of productivity, loss of reputation, and loss of confidence - both internally and externally.

Many of these risks in many instances have become more of a burden as the result of legislation emanating originally via the European Union. Health and Safety at Work (Chapter 8.2) and Environmental Management (Chapter 5.8) are just two examples of legislation which have placed the facilities manager (and their employers) at risk of severe penalty for failure to observe and monitor risk to employees, visitors and passers-by.

Perhaps more to the point, this legislation also serves to protect the core business from the inevitable loss or damage emanating from failure to achieve minimum acceptable standards.

Nevertheless, most of the really big threats to business in terms of its facilities support are not covered by legislation. Management of these risks is down to good business practice rather than fear of legal redress.

2.5.2 THE RISK MANAGEMENT PROCESS

The three facets of risk management

The nature and extent of all the risks described above and measures to counter them are fully described in Sections 5 and 8. Here we are concerned with the principles to be observed in risk management, which involve yet another trinity - see Fig. 2.5.B.

Fig. 2.5.B
Three facets of risk management - inter-relationships

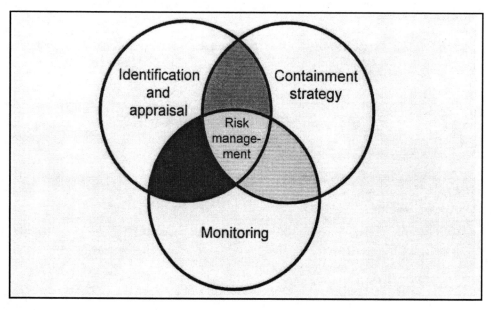

Risk identification

Identification of the centres of risk by reference to Fig. 2.5.A is a condition precedent to identifying the actual risks facing individual organisations going about their core business. As well as identifying specific areas of risk facilities managers must also attempt to assess the level of potential loss and the likelihood of occurrence and put the financial implications alongside the cost of the service level needed to contain the risk to a pre-determined level.

Another look at the 'consequences of failure' in Fig. 2.5.A should quickly reinforce the arguments made above (and in Chapter 2.4.2) concerning the really important risk centres: these are not those areas where the 'hard' values of fines or depreciation can be easily assessed but the ones where potential losses will almost certainly have to be predicted with a high degree of subjectivity. It is also difficult to apportion losses as between those which can be contained by the quality of facilities and those which are at the mercy of the world-at-large.

For example, people who are off work sick or malingering make no contribution whilst those at work who are unfit, stressed or in poor spirits will perform below par. Some business may be lost through the company presenting an image inefficiently while the Company Secretary may have to pay penalties or meet unnecessarily high bills due to someone's earlier failure to follow good practice. Whilst it is true to say that all of those circumstances can be caused by issues other than facilities it is nevertheless clear that some proportion of such core business losses is caused by matters like unhealthy air-conditioning, dirty windows, overheating, breach of covenants and statutes and poorly planned space.

Risk is actually present in all the different aspects of any operation, ie at the policy, strategic and tactical levels discussed in Chapter 2.4.3 (see Fig.2.4.E). For instance, there is a risk of a disadvantageous event occurring at the tactical and strategic levels, such as the lift breaking down. The initial consequence of that event is that some people are stressed, others are annoyed and all will be held up by the event and its subsequent remedy. The more frequently breakdown and unplanned maintenance occur the more likely it is that core business will suffer.

You may or may not be able to prove that business will suffer through these events and their consequences but you can certainly be confident in predicting that it probably will. If core business does suffer, the consequences will in some cases be calculable - as with fines or death through disaster - whereas the loss of productivity due to poor morale may be much harder to assess.

Nevertheless, if you accept the thesis that quality can only be justified on the grounds of risk containment (or increased productivity, if you want to present it the other way) inability to assess and quantify the potential loss (or improvement) is a major obstacle to making and winning a business case.

In these careful times blind adherence to the conventional wisdom is no argument in the face of demands to cut service levels, so we really have to get a better understanding of the risks which our facilities policy is addressing and how much is at stake if services fall below a 'safe' standard; the latter can only be viewed on an organisation-by-organisation basis.

Risk appraisal

One method of measuring the likely extent of damage and the probability of occurrence has been adopted for the risk assessment values in the Frisqué[2] program. The research has centred around:

- the consequences of failure of each of the facilities services

- the probability of the failure leading to a financial loss in one of the above risk centres

- the severity of such a loss should it eventually materialise.

Fig. 2.5.C (over the page) gives an example of the comparative potential loss calculations for failure of a typical facilities service - the maintenance of the cooling system - including the scores and weightings attributed in each case.

---

[2] *Frisque Facilities Risk and Quality Evaluation Program, Bernard Williams Associates*

Fig. 2.5.C
Risk appraisal - loss assessment methodology

Category	Section	Potential process failure event	Possible loss consequence of service failure (see Fig 2.6.A)						
				1a	2a	2b	6a	7a	
Services maintenance	Air cooling / conditioning	Airborne contamination	Probability Ranking 1-5	1	3	5	3	1	
Services maintenance	Air cooling / conditioning	Unacceptable temperatures / humidity	- A -	3	3	5	5	3	
			Consequence ratings indicating severities (L = low, M = medium, H = high)						
Services maintenance	Air cooling / conditioning	Airborne contamination	Consequence rating (on a scale of 0 – 1,000)	237.5 M	118.8 M	118.8 M	2.5 L	0.625 L	
Services maintenance	Air cooling / conditioning	Unacceptable temperatures / humidity	- B -	12.5 L	118.8 M	500 H	200 H	0.625 L	
Weighted units of risk for airborne contamination (A x B) =				237.5	356.4	594	7.5	0.625	= 1,196.03
Weighted units of risk for unacceptable temperature / humidity (A x B) =				37.5	356.4	2,500	1,000	1.875	= 3,895.78
Total weighted units of risk exposure [A x B] for the two failure events									= 5,091.80

Source: © BWA, 2000

It should be noted that the risk ratings on the bottom line are the product of the consideration of the possible loss consequences of failure of the maintenance operation with regards to airborne contamination and unacceptable temperature humidity respectively.

The symbols 1a, 2a etc under the heading of 'Possible loss consequences of service failure' are drawn from Fig. 2.5.A and relate to the risk centre, eg 1= image - externally and the 'potential loss as a consequence of failure occurring', eg 'a' = sales/margins. So 1a is the potential loss of sales/margins as a consequence of an event leading to damage to the company's external image.

The 'consequence ratings' in Fig. 2.5.C are estimated comparatively on a scale of 1-1000 with each unit representing a unit of potential financial loss.

So, the unacceptable temperature/humidity is rated at only 12.5 out of 1,000 for the impact on sales/margins due to internal image (1a) but at 200 out of 1,000 for 6a which assesses the ergonomic performance reduction due to inefficient working conditions.

In the case of temperature/humidity the probability of a '1a' loss occurring is 3 out of 5 and a '6a' is assessed as 5 out of 5, ie certain. The multiplication of the potential losses by the degree of probability in each case gives the total number of units of risk exposure for each possible consequence (1a, 2a etc) and the accumulation of points across the table (from 1a to 7a) is the total for each section.

For the sake of clarity in an example which is, to say the least, complex at first viewing, the following notes may help:

- only the air cooling/conditioning maintenance is being considered

- the two process failure events in the example each give rise to the same categories of possible loss (1a, 2a, etc); this is coincidental and in every event being appraised all the potential losses in risk centre categories 1 to 9 have been reviewed for their relevance to the process failure in question and incorporated or ignored as appropriate

- the total 'weighted units of risk exposure' gives the comparative risk rating for each process failure event; in the case in question these are the only two against air-conditioning/cooling maintenance so the total of 5091.8 units is the total for that section

- although the value of each unit has to be determined in the context of each organisation's financial and business status the ratios between the sections will be consistent in all cases

- the probability weightings are in respect of the knock-on consequences of the service failure and not in respect of the service failure per se; the probability of the latter is dependent upon the service levels, ie the risk containment strategy. In other words, if you keep the tiger in its cage it cannot do any damage. So, before looking further at the consequences of failure and their appraisal it is now necessary to consider the second facet of risk management - risk containment.

Financial risk assessment can be quite an involved process particularly in the case of major projects. An example of appraisal of the risk to an organisation inherent in a range of options for refurbishing its leased headquarters is shown at Fig. 2.5.D.

Fig. 2.5.D
Risk appraisal summary - headquarters refurbishment options

Event		Option A: tenant led project			Option B: landlord led project		
		Quantified		Opportunity costs	Quantified		Opportunity costs
		Time weeks	Cost £'000		Time weeks	Cost £'000	
A. Legal	Delay to lease negotiation	13	480	Add rent £5,712,000*	4	160	Add rent £1,904,000*
	Delay to landlord's approvals	6	240	Add rent £2,856,000*	2	80	Add rent £952,000*
	Blurred definition of base build / fit out	-	-	-	-	160	-
	Incompatibility between base build / fit out	-	-	-	-	800	-
B. Statutory Approvals	Planning permission delay	8	320	Add rent £3,808,000*	2	80	Add rent £952,000*
	Building Regulations delay	-	-	-	-	-	-
	EC Directives	-	-	-	-	-	-
C. Design	Fee levels	-	240	-	-	-	-
	Design period	-	-	-	-	-	-
	Cost control	-	-	-	-	-	-
	Specification	-	-	-	-	240	Add running costs £240,000* pa
D. Construction	Existing structure constrains	-	-	-	-	-	-
	'Unknowns'	2	112	Add rent £952,000*	-	80	-
	Market conditions	-	480	-	-	80	-
	Late instructions	-	160	-	2	320	Add rent £952,000*
	Delay by contractor	-	-	-	-	-	-
	Delay by the design team	-	-	-	-	-	-
	Insured peril	-	-	-	-	-	-
	Programme	-	-	-	4	-	Add rent £1,904,000*
	Commissioning	-	-	-	-	-	-
E. Client	In-house approvals	4	160	Add rent £952,000*	4	160	Add rent £304,000*
	Funding availability	-	-	-	4	160	Add rent £304,000*
	Phasing	-	-	-	8	320	Add rent £304,000*
	Capital allowances	-	-	-	-	-	-
Totals		33◊	2,192~	-	30◊	2,640~	

* Property costs only – loss of productivity due to delay is excluded
◊ Delay not necessarily consecutive
~ Costs not necessarily cumulative

The two options involve:

• Option A - the tenant finances and commissions the work taking advantage of a lengthy and favourable remainder of lease not subject to rent reviews

• Option B - the landlord undertakes and finances the work in exchange for a modern lease.

The back up calculation to one of the risk items - 'delay to lease negotiations' in the landlord-led Option B is shown at Fig. 2.5.E.

Fig. 2.5.E
Risk appraisal - back-up calculation to Option B appraisal of 'delay to lease negotiations'

Event	Risk evaluation			Commentary	Risk control mechanism	Potential effect
	Time	Cost	Quality			
a. Legal 1. Delay to lease negotiations.	/	/	X	Time not of the 'essence' so far as the landlord is concerned.	Agree cut-off dates with landlord but little opportunity to impose penalties if these are not achieved.	Assume landlord proves intransigent – allow for 3 months delay. The majority of buying would take place during a period when tender prices are projected to be increasing at 4% pa (0.33% per month). Additional construction costs would therefor be: £480,000 x 3 months x 0.33% = £48,000,000, whilst additional rent and rates on the tenants existing buildings would amount to : 3 months @ £1,904,000 = £5,712,000.

The extent to which the organisation is exposed to cost and time risk throughout the duration of the project are shown graphically at Fig. 2.5.F and 2.5.G respectively. In both cases the organisation is at greater risk in the landlord-led option (B) except for the time delay exposure (Fig. 2.5.G) for a brief period during the client lead-in phase; this is the consequence of 'delay to lease negotiations' (an item under A in the Risk Appraisal Summary), (Fig. 2.5.D and amplified in Fig. 2.5.E).

Fig. 2.5.F
Risk appraisal - financial loss exposure

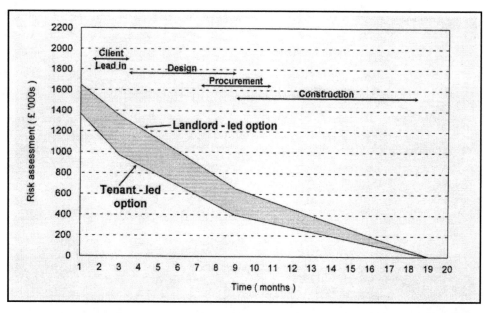

Many risks or benefits do not lend themselves easily to financial evaluation. Cost-benefit analysis involves a lot of risk appraisal and is often criticised as a technique because of the essentially subjective nature of evaluation of human issues such as a poor ambience, excessive noise, loss of life. Nevertheless, following the school of thought which argues that 'if you cannot measure it you cannot understand it!', having a good shot at evaluation will at least enable one to understand the risks and benefits involved and get some sort of feeling as to their relative significance thereby facilitating a fully informed decision-making process.

Fig. 2.5.G
Risk appraisal - time delay exposure

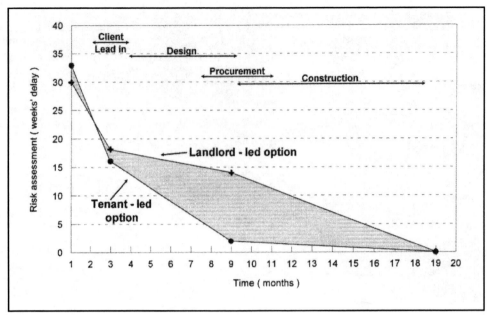

Risk containment

The facilities manager's strategy for containment of the risk will stem from their facilities policy which should spell out the risk management philosophy of the organisation as a whole and the facilities manager's commitment thereto.

In a properly constituted internal market (see Chapter 1.2.3) there should be a service level agreement in support of a policy statement specifically relevant to risk management. The containment strategy for managing the risk will derive from the risk appraisal, eg low risk situations may merely be subjected to a monitoring procedure, whereas high risks such as imminent structural failure may require immediate preventative or, in most cases, corrective action.

Generally speaking facilities managers will have greater discretion in the tactics they adopt for dealing with hazards threatening productive output, than where persons or property are at risk.

Most organisations now have a crisis management strategy which should be in addition to a disaster recovery plan and embrace all three facets described in Fig. 2.5.B

The risk containment strategy in respect of all issues of any consequence ought to be subjected to 'business case' analysis to determine appropriate levels of value for money. The value management process described in Chapter 2.2.4 embraces the principles discussed here. However, it is important to understand the risk appraisal process and the relationships between cause effect, probability and economics as portrayed in Fig. 2.5.H.

Fig. 2.5.H
Cause and effect, probability and economics

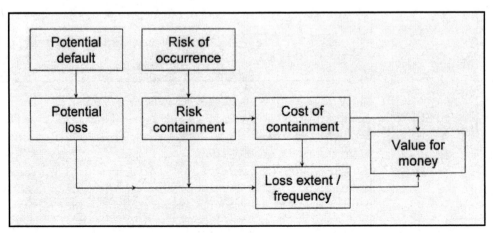

How much is spent on containing the risk relative to the potential quantum of the loss and the probability of it being caused determines whether or not the risk containment strategy is providing value for money.

It is important to note that, whereas the outcome for each such calculation is based on a percentage probability of an event which may or may not materialise, the overall estimated losses to an organisation have been linked back to normal business financial parameters. The actual un-contained loss potentially accepted in one risk centre will undoubtedly turn out to be more or less in the final event. However a risk containment strategy developed along these lines may be expected to hold its relevance in the context of the overall level of loss prevention/acceptance envisaged in the facilities strategy. In plain language it will be expected to even itself out across the whole range of risk and cost centres.

Monitoring

Having identified and appraised the risk and implemented a strategy for containing or eliminating it, the facilities manager must then make sure that the processes they have instituted are monitored regularly - both internally as part of the quality management process and externally by the engagement of facilities auditors. The facilities management audit described in Chapter 12.1 can be extended to cover all management procedures as well as simply financial management, either via one consultant or using independent specialists in areas such as health and safety, environmental pollution and energy consumption.

2.5.3 RISK TRANSFER

In some circumstances the facilities manager can transfer the risk management function, eg some consultants can offer a complete risk management service in specific fields such as the 'Health and Safety at Work' package described in Chapter 8.2.5. This provides a form of preventative insurance which is the only type of insurance a facilities manager must rely upon in matters relating to avoidable misfortune or loss.

Which is not to say that appropriate insurance cover should not be in place to cover the financial consequences of disaster, avoidable or otherwise. So, as shown in Chapter 3.7, insurance contracts will provide for cover against loss or damage to persons and property through fire, negligence and other perils.

Sometimes the term 'transfer of risk' is used in reference to contracting-out facilities services or taking out insurance. This is a misconception for the risk will always remain with facilities managers however widely they are able to 'lay off' responsibility for management or compensation.

Fig. 2.5.J
The cost of managing the risk of fire

Costs	Sprinkler installation	£ pa	Total in £ pa
Capital costs	5,000 sq m at £ 12 per sq m (inc fees and finance) = £60,000		
Annual costs	Amortised cost over 15 years – say	5,000	
	Maintenance – say	1,000	
	Staff / consultants' time – fire risk management	2,000	
	Total costs of fire risk management pa		**8,000**
Insurance cost implications	All-risks insurance – 5,000 sq m at £ 3 per sq m pa	15,000	
	Premium reduction for sprinkler installation – say 10%		**1,500**

Where risks are insurable the cost of risk management can be calculated by costing up the savings on the annual premium against the annual cost of the tactic, eg depreciation and maintenance on a sprinkler installation, plus the staff and consultants' time involved in the risk management process.

An example of such a calculation involving management of the risk of fire is shown at Fig. 2.5.J (previous page). which shows that about 20% of the risk containment strategy (£8,000) can be recovered by savings on the insurance premium (£1,500). However, this is only a part of the story and cost-benefit analysis would need to address:

- costs of alternative strategies

- value of goods/production process at risk

- potential damage due to operation of sprinklers (especially if set off accidentally or when fire is of a minor nature).

2.5.4 FORMAL V INFORMAL APPROACH

The degree of detail used in risk appraisal and decisions about containment strategies will always depend upon the perceived importance of the risk in business (and possibly human) terms and/or the time and trouble people are prepared, or allowed, to take in the process.

That said, all decisions about major risk containment should be based on some formal basis of evaluation, even if that only amounts to a 'brainstorming' session in respect of each risk centre.

Failing that, the conventional wisdom - or the uninformed whim of some individual - will form the basis of the decision. At that point you do not need an Intelligent Customer Function - an ostrich will do very nicely!

2.6   INFORMATION MANAGEMENT

Introduction

The three hardest-to-come-by commodities in the business world are:

- money

- good people

- good information.

In the developing world there will never be enough money for organisations to do everything they would like to do in support of their precious human and equipment assets. However, the fact that good information is at a premium is less a matter of money resources than of good management resources having access to the right tools to dig up the data and information needed to do their job efficiently.

In the brave new world of e-commerce facilities managers' lives will be transformed by the demands and benefits of electronic data assembly, distribution and access. However, data is one thing, information another and knowledge another; so before considering the information needs of facilities management it is important to understand what is meant by data and information - terms often used synonymously but which are, in fact, subtly but distinctly different and the growing significance of knowledge management. The chapter concludes with a brief look at aspects of the legal context for information.

2.6.1   DATA AND INFORMATION

The data processing cycle

Data is the plural of datum which is from the Latin meaning 'given'. Data is therefore defined as 'the ground for inference and deduction', ie the basis of information; information is, in turn, defined as 'intelligence or knowledge derived by perception'.

Just to confuse the issue one person's information is another person's raw or processed data, for this is a cyclical process (see Fig. 2.6.A).

Fig. 2.6.A
The data processing cycle

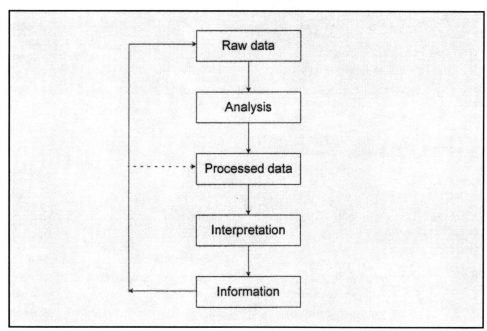

However, this simple cyclical diagram disguises the fact that data use is hierarchical in that there is a continual switching from data to information between the first processing of raw data and the highest level of information.

To take a simple example the raw data emanating from the process of replacing a stop valve could include:

- the time spent

- the cost of labour

- the response time

- the bar-code of the parts

- the age of the component replaced

- the cost-code for the operation

- the supplier(s) of the component(s)

- the name of the service provider.

A good maintenance management program would take most of this data to report on the cost of the job, the performance of the contractor and the status of the job, ie complete. It might possibly also report on stockholdings of components, and post the costs to the customer's account code.

As yet few (if any) of these programs stretch to using such data to modify the asset management plan (although such capacity is probably only necessary for bigger operations than replacing the stop valve in this simple example) but there are some which, via the help-desk, can inform users on the progress in dealing with problems reported.

One thing, however, can be quite certain: the raw labour cost data which was posted to the operational cost centre would be added to all the other similar costs and incorporated into one cost centre. This total cost, the result of processing the data, would become information to the service provider about job costs which could either be invoiced direct or used as information upon which to base an invoice.

The client, upon receipt of the invoice, would have information about the amount being charged and also the data by which to check actual costs against the budget; in the latter case the information received for one purpose ie to authorise payment becomes data to be processed for another purpose, ie to get information on the status of the budget following the replacement of the stop valve.

At some stage the total costs of all the maintenance works would turn up as data in the end-of-year accounts and might then be extracted for benchmarking purposes intended to get information about the service efficiency.

The benchmarker might well have to separate services maintenance from the fabric maintenance ie re-process the data in order to provide the benchmarking data upon which the deductions, eg peer group comparisons, might be made to provide the information required about efficiency.

All the while there are myriad other aspects of the facilities management operation being influenced in some way by this one operation, ie the stop-valve replacement, such as a contractor's bonus/penalty and customer satisfaction with the engineering service in question. The former would probably have linked direct to the maintenance help-desk program but the latter is normally the result of the whole collection of operations. The above is but one small drop in the ocean (or sometimes the last straw, to use another analogy).

Data and information flow

Many organisations consist of organised silos, ie departments and functions up and down which data and information flows. Rarely however, does the data and information get separately identified as 'raw' and 'processed' data and transferred between the silos in a form which can be used for other purposes. Prodgers[1] and Bacon[1] suggest that what is needed is to be able to penetrate the sides of the silo to free up the flow of information across the enterprise where it is required. Fig. 2.6.B illustrates this point.

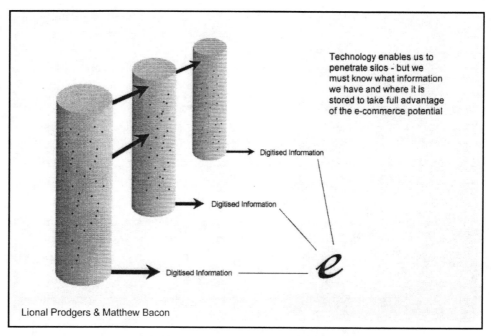

Technology enables us to penetrate silos - but we must know what information we have and where it is stored to take full advantage of the e-commerce potential

Digitised Information

Digitised Information

Digitised Information

Lional Prodgers & Matthew Bacon

The corollary to all of this is that for ICT to help facilities managers to improve their information management they must know what data and information they have, where it is, what they need it for, when and in what format.

2.6.2 KNOWLEDGE

Knowledge is effectively 'applied information; it is an accumulation of lessons, experiences, observations and analyses. It can be described as 'information in action' when used by people who understand how and where to use it appropriately.

In recent years, since the spread of the Internet, it has become accepted that people, rather than processes, are an organisation's most important asset. A company's overall performance depends on the extent to which it can mobilise its intellectual assets. The goal must therefore be to unlock the employee's store of knowledge and creativity.

This knowledge may be contained in the minds of the employees, in their stored files, both conventional and electronic, or in databases, copyrights, patents and corporate management systems.

Knowledge is key to improving an organisation's ability to meet three primary business objectives namely:

• competitive customer service and better customer relationships [Demand]

• better operational performance across the organisation [Process]

---

[1] *Lional Prodgers and Prof M Bacon (Jan 2001) Ark e-management Ltd*

- rapid supply-chain management and increased innovation [Supply]

These three objectives drive IT strategies and will become ever more important success factors in the emerging world of networked business, competitive on-line information and rapidly changing consumer-driven markets.

Each objective demands greater knowledge. Research across 250 European companies by the UK's Cranfield School of Management reveals that the demand for better knowledge will increase significantly in every corporate function in the immediate future - particularly in marketing, planning and R&D.

Sharing the knowledge effectively is rapidly becoming a business imperative. Knowledge sharing harnesses the skills and experience of the people in an organisation and helps them to perform critical business tasks more effectively. It helps to generate and support productivity and innovation within the key processes that underpin the business - from developing new products and services to new ways of serving customers and shareholders.

The crucial factor in determining a company's competitive advantage is its ability to convert **tacit knowledge** (instinctive or intuitive ways of doing things) into **explicit knowledge** (a concept that is readily understood by others).

Sharing knowledge is the key to extracting business value from knowledge resources and creating distinct and sustainable competitive advantage. It can be facilitated by technologies such as electronic document management and corporate intranets but can only take place where there is trust between individuals. People will share their knowledge if there is reciprocity: a knowledge management programme can therefore only work in an atmosphere of community.

According to John Blackwell, of IBM Global Business, businesses must focus on creating enterprise integration through a knowledge-sharing culture, to recognise the value of intellectual capital, and to understand that competition depends not only on the differential possession of physical assets, or even of information, but on the ability to deploy knowledge. Businesses need to stop managing knowledge in a mechanical sense and investigate ways to tap the employees' inherent knowledge. The information held in the computer system cannot be used without the insight and intuition that runs the business.

Knowledge is no longer a nebulous concept: it is seen as a crucial asset that is key to the success of a business. Knowledge management is therefore coming to the fore as a discipline that can enable organisations to operate more productively in a distributed and interconnected world.

2.6.3 THE INTERNET AND INFORMATION MANAGEMENT

A culture change

The Internet offers access to a mine of information of staggering proportions. Nevertheless, still in its infancy, its sprawling unstructured universal mass presents as much opportunity to waste time and money as it does to save it. Yet, can anyone seriously doubt that it will take over all our lives - personal and corporate - on a scale that, by comparison, makes the pervasive influence of TV pale into insignificance.

While this massive culture change is occurring business-at-large is still coming to terms with the effects of the ICT-process revolution of the '80's and '90's and finding that the facility to generate more data more quickly does not always translate into better information. In fact, it is common for people and organisations to go down with 'data-fatigue', unable to provide the quality of information management needed to assimilate good from bad, key from trivial, to help people make the right decisions.

If companies cannot cope with the current output from their own networks what will they be able to make of the vast offerings potentially out there in cyber-space? How can they possibly adapt to the new challenge of so-called e-commerce?

Content Management

Content management is a new discipline focusing on the automated delivery of information from various types of media to Web servers from enterprise repositories. It provides immediate, personalised content delivery to targeted Web users based on a predetermined process and integrated content model. Content management comprises electronic document management (EDM), information retrieval, enterprise intranet portals, Internet infrastructure, electronic publishing and collaborative filtering.

Content management is therefore the most recent strategic ICT application to emerge and has become a prime focus for organisations looking to exploit about 80% of their information that is contained in unstructured form (paper and electronic documents) rather than structured corporate databases. The Internet has enabled the exploitation of such content, in customer service, R&D, supply chain management, intra- and inter-departmental and organisational working and many other areas.

Although most of Content management's functionality was available in other forms before, notably EDM, the key differentiator is that it is acquired and installed as a set of functions bundled together, to serve specific requirements within group of users that have a common value proposition.

Most large organisations are now considering or installing a content management system (CMS). This is driven by the growing recognition that businesses generate huge volumes of information that must be made available to staff, when and where they need it. A content management system also underpins most large corporate websites, which have grown into huge storehouses of information.

Before installing such a system it is important to establish what is to be achieved by installing CMS. The key factors are:

- the information that the business needs, ie what is the system actually for?
- the technology to be used to manage this information.

The fundamental challenge being addressed is 'how to get the right information to the right people, at the right time'.

In planning the content of a CMS organisations should be prepared to rewrite all of their existing documentation - a significant task, but one which will result in significant productivity and process improvements. It is important that experienced professional technical writers and editors are used to write polished, effective content.

The emphasis must be on quality, not quantity, of information. To locate the information that a user needs a search engine may be used. The information or 'content' within a CMS must be structured and easily navigable. Users require consistency and extensive cross-linking. Just as 'content' should be prepared by professional writers its structure should be defined by an information architect and professional indexer.

There should also be a rigorous workflow and review process to ensure quality - bearing in mind that there is legal exposure in every page published. This is comparatively straightforward if there is a dedicated authoring team. The workflow and review processes should be in place before CMS goes live. Just as important, a permanent process should be put in place to ensure the continued accuracy and coverage of the content.

E-commerce

E-commerce is a method of trading in which data and information can be made available electronically within and between businesses to help them to make decisions and to conduct transactions - everything organisations already do, but (so it is said), more efficiently.

Information concentration

Most people would say that the advent of the internet has brought about an information explosion. That may well be true in the sense of a vast amount of hitherto esoteric facts being scattered into cyberspace for potential access by anyone in the world. On the other hand, however, no organisation can hope to take advantage of this bounty without first having organised **its own information** in as concise and holistically integrated manner as is possible. In other words they need an information implosion, ie a collapsing inwards to concentrate at the centre all the data and information scudding aimlessly about amid their own corporate activities.

In order for organisations to harness what the internet has to offer they must first understand how they themselves work. Surprisingly few organisations of any size have process maps tracing the way jobs are done or the inter-dependencies of one job with another; they therefore have no collective idea of what information each part of the business has or what information is needed.

So given a scenario where businesses do not understand how to gather internally the information they need to operate efficiently how will the availability of myriad more nuggets of knowledge via the web help them to improve? The answer has to be that it will not.

Independent v integrated information

Against this background of poor information management at core business level facilities managers have to strive to get their own house in order, probably in isolation although that scenario belongs to the 'silo' syndrome described above. Such an 'isolationist' strategy should only be seen as a stopgap solution pending complete information integration across the business.

2.6.4 WORKFLOW

Workflow may be defined as '**the computerised facilitation or automation of a business process, in whole or part**'. An individual business process may have a life cycle ranging from minutes to days or even months, depending on its complexity and the duration of the various component activities. Workflow is concerned with the automation of procedures where documents, information or tasks progress from one participant to another in accordance with a defined set of rules in order to achieve, or contribute to, a business objective.

Workflow has been closely associated with imaging systems, many of which have workflow capability either built-in or supplied in conjunction with a specific workflow product. Most business procedures involve interaction with paper-based information, which may need to be captured as image data as part of an automation process. Once captured electronically as image data, it is often required to be passed between numerous participants for various purposes within the process, possibly involving interaction with other ICT applications, thereby creating a requirement for workflow functionality.

Workflow Management System

A Workflow Management System provides procedural automation of a business process by managing a logical sequence of work activities utilising appropriate human and/or ICT resources associated with the various activity steps. Such a system defines, manages and executes "workflows" through the execution of software whose order of execution is driven by a computer representation of the workflow logic.

Such systems may be implemented in a variety of ways, use a wide variety of ICT and communications infrastructure and operate in an environment ranging from small local workgroup to inter-enterprise.

Document Management

Document management technology is concerned with managing the lifecycle of electronic documents. Increasingly, this includes facilities for managing document repositories distributed within an organisation as a shared resource with the capability of routing documents to individuals for information access or updating according to their allocated tasks in relation to specific documents. The document may form part of a particular business process that requires access to the document by individual staff undertaking separate activities according to a particular sequence and according to some procedural rules - ie a document-centric form of workflow. [See also 7.2.4 electronic filing]

Email

Email provides powerful facilities for distributing information between individuals within an organisation or between organisations; the use of directory mechanisms not only provides a way of identifying individual participants within an email domain but also potentially recording information about individual user attributes, such as organisational roles or other attributes relating to business procedures. Thus email systems have themselves been progressing towards workflow functionality through the addition of routing commands to define a sequence of recipients for particular types of mail items as part of an identified business procedure.

The workflow market has evolved from requirements across the ICT industry and is likely to continue to do so, with a wide range of products focussed on one or more particular aspects of the overall workflow requirements. Some may be provided in conjunction with other areas of technology, such as image processing or document management, others may be more general purpose. Widespread adoption of web browser technology enables different products to work together and integrate within a consistent overall architecture.

2.6.5 FACILITIES INFORMATION AND APPLICATIONS

Any management task comprises two distinct phases:

- application management
- information management.

So, for example, arranging for the boilers to be serviced is a management application whereas knowing their location, condition and history requires management of information.

Management applications are described elsewhere in their various sections. Here we deal predominantly with the management of facilities information, a process which is fundamental to the success of the dependent application.

Both phases are mutually informative so it is essential that any facilities management system - be it manual or electronic - must be arranged so as to facilitate feedback and feed-forward of data with the minimum of effort and risk of misplacement. Ideally this system should be automatic, so in principle a computerised database system of some description will certainly be warranted in any sizeable facilities management operation.

Chapter 7.5 considers the management of information and communications technology on a business-wide basis; this chapter considers technology for the day-to-day management of facilities.

Fig. 2.6.C illustrates the concept of a 'data-spine' in which all the information emanating from the design of the building to the provision of supplier services and inventories, ie short-term assets - see Chapter 2.7.4, is retained and set up to receive and disseminate information emanating from the various facilities management applications.

Fig. 2.6.C
Facilities management - an integrated approach to information and application management

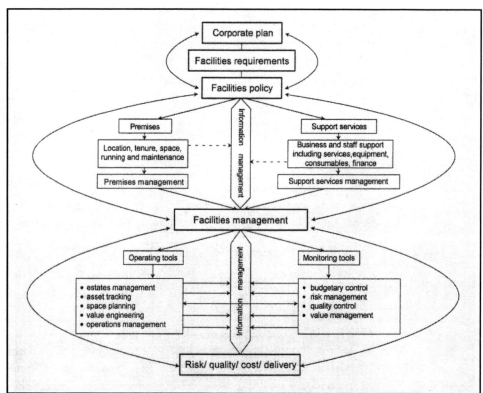

This concept of integrating information and application management via a data-spine has been researched and in some cases developed for individual facets of facilities management. Also there are numerous maintenance management packages which link the information from a condition survey to and from on-going maintenance activity to ensure that application and information work in tandem.

However, maintenance is only a minor component of facilities management in financial terms and a system to handle the arrangement at Fig. 2.6.C has yet to be fully developed in respect of the whole range of facilities management applications.

2.6.6 FACILITIES MANAGEMENT SYSTEMS

CAD-based systems

Computer-aided design/draughting systems are becoming increasingly evident in facilities management for three reasons:

- more and more buildings are being designed, and as-built working drawings produced, on CAD

- space planning lends itself readily to CAD applications

- data-bases linked to CAD have been developed for facilities management applications.

Cafoms

The latter systems are generically referred to as computer-aided facilities management systems (CAFMS) and by the authors as Cafoms - computer-aided facilities operational management systems. They have the advantage over simple data-bases in that they can hold facilities data graphically on a full-sized scalable model. To date development of these systems has been geared to the more common applications, particularly:

- maintenance

- space planning

- security

- energy

- property management

- inventory tracking

- personnel tracking and records

- move management.

More recent packages have addressed the thorny problem of cable management, and some of the more sophisticated CAD systems can provide speedy review of all 'as designed' systems testing at the screen the impact of any proposed modifications on feasibility without corrupting the base schematic data.

The principal disadvantages of the present generation of Cafom systems are:

- they comprise add-on applications to simplify existing facilities management functions rather than addressing applications from first principles and integrating application and information requirements

- the cost of systems and, more importantly the resources (including training) required to operate them and keep the data up-to-date is considerably greater than currently generally available to facilities management departments; justifying the additional costs by reference to increased efficiency is difficult in other than a medium to long-term scenario

- the inflexibility of some systems which will not permit the plotting of a prospective change without the user either making another copy of the database (a recipe for total confusion) or irrevocably changing the database in advance of real-time developments

- time taken to maintain the accuracy of databases can distract resources from day-to-day hands-on management of the facilities.

There are just too many examples of Cafom systems lying around unused -certainly under-utilised - because of inadequate understanding of how Cafom systems might or might not facilitate facilities management activities and the resources required to operate them.

Cafims

The principal objective of computer-aided facilities information management systems (Cafims) is to enable a strategic approach to facilities management by providing a framework integrating data-collection/dissemination with applications in a model similar to that depicted in Fig. 2.6.C above. Pro-active financial management systems have to have access to all information needed by facilities managers to run their activities in a similarly pro-active mode. Such pro-active systems rely for their success on the ability of the facilities manager to identify potential change at a time when it is still possible to influence its implementation and consequence; their introduction will, over time, forge the missing link between all the applications incorporated in Fig. 2.6.C and the pro-active management strategy portrayed in Fig. 2.6.D.

Fig. 2.6.D
Pro-active v reactive management strategy

Management style	Activity/Event	Pre-decision phase	Post-decision phase
Pro-active financial management	Planned cost	●	
	Anticipation of change	●	
	Value management studies	●	Last date to influence outcome
	Decision to change	●	
	Revised cost agreed	●	
	Planned cost incurred		●
Reactive financial management	Unplanned change	●	
	Unplanned cost incurred		●

However, at the present time none of the commercially available Cafom systems has anything approaching a pro-active financial control system so delivery of Cafims deriving from such a concept may be some time coming.

Help desk systems

Help desk systems can be linked to or integrated with CAFIM systems. The helpdesk concept is discussed in more detail in Chapter 2.1.4 - 'Devolved Responsibility'

The economics of computer-aided facilities management systems

The cost of Cafoms will vary considerably depending on the commercial deal available. However, a typical real-life example of the cost of acquiring and running a dedicated networked 4-node system connected into an existing local area network is suggested at Fig. 2.6.E. The cost allocated to 'dedicated operators' is either the time of full-time dedicated staff in larger organisations or a proportion of management time in the smaller set-up.

Fig. 2.6.E
Typical annual equivalent cost of acquiring and operating a dedicated CAFM system

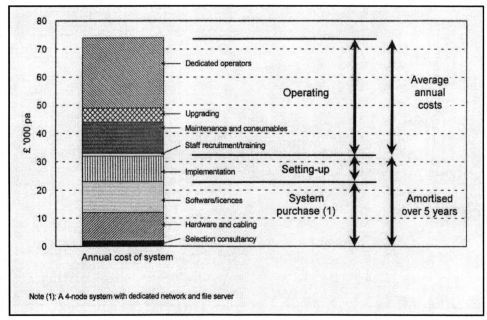

Fig. 2.6.F shows this expenditure in the context of the total cost of full in-house administration of the facilities function; note that as the CAFMS is shared between the ICF and the directive management, the cost is shown as a proportion of the combined function.

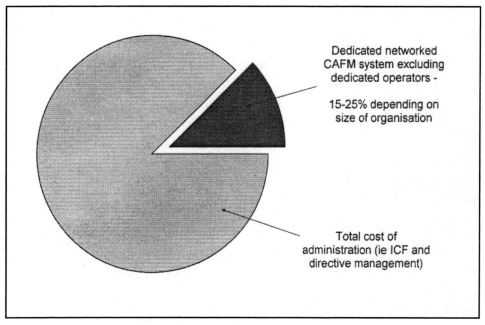

Dedicated networked CAFM system excluding dedicated operators -

15-25% depending on size of organisation

Total cost of administration (ie ICF and directive management)

To consider the cost as additional is a bit unfair since the level of competence and quality achievable using these systems properly is very much enhanced, leading to improvements and savings across many fronts.

A popular feature available from most systems is the cross-charging of space-related costs. However, the CAD component of the package is by no means essential to this important function which the database component or certain specialist financial control programs cope with perfectly adequately.

Facilities management contracting companies are now able to offer these Cafom applications as part of their service. Obviously modern operating systems and hardware can cope with data from many different organisations under management and dedicated trained staff can service a number of organisations more efficiently than an individual organisation can set up and service its own bespoke system.

That is fine, but it is absolutely essential that the internal facilities management team owns, and has in-house access to, all the data concerning their organisation's applications. Losing control of and access to the data in an out-sourced situation is the worst possible scenario which will undoubtedly nullify any other benefits derived from the strategy.

The potential contribution of an effective facilities information management system (FIMS) to decision-making, quality, financial and risk management cannot be over-stated. Until suitable systems become available facilities managers need to be wary of purchasing Cafom tools to facilitate and perpetuate generically inadequate application techniques. The ICT industry must instead be encouraged to develop the integrated Cafom/Cafim systems which are essential for the provision of quality managed facilities (QMF) discussed in Chapter 2.4.3.

2.6.7 E-FM

The Internet and facilities management

The very real problem of information management right across organisations was discussed in Chapter 2.6.2 above along with the increasing significance of the Internet in this context. It is now necessary to pause to reflect on how the internet might change the way that facilities managers do their job - and the way that job itself might be changed.

The definition of facilities management used here is from Chapter 1.1.1

'the process by which the premises and services required to support core business activities are identified, specified, procured and delivered'.

Using this definition we can then look at these four key activities to see how access to the web can influence the processes.

Intelligence gathering

In Chapters 1.1.1 and 2.1.2, we indentified the role played by the ICF in finding out what facilities are needed by core business. It is rare for core business to know what it needs, or can get, by way of facilities support so ICF groups have to make it their business to come up with appropriate suggestions supported by a business case.

A critical part of this process is knowledge of 'state-of-the-art' practice, which can only be established by some form of formal or informal benchmarking of facilities procedures.

Ideally, ICF's should be able to benchmark their facilities to world-best performers and the Internet could easily provide this opportunity. For instance, someone out there may have discovered a casual link between the quality of the internal environment and productivity. That information - including data on temperature, humidity and contamination levels - could be posted on a web-page awaiting universal access. But how can the ICF's in the universe find it, how do they know it is there - and what can they do with the information if they do, by some freak of fortune, get hold of it?

As anyone who has ever searched the Internet knows one can waste hours and hours wading through rubbish in an often vain attempt to get specific information on a topic. However, the whole system is still in its infancy and the fledgling specialist information sites will not take long to get really well organised and established; soon they will be cutting swathes through the cyber-jungle competing hard to be the first to afford fast, universal, selective information capture.

So we can expect that early in the new Millennium a click on key words like 'room temperature' or 'working environment' will give an ICF a complete reference to best performance approaches to the subject area.

However, the ICF accessing the information may not have data in a form to compare with what has been downloaded from the web in which case they will find some excuse not to spend the time and money building up the data from scratch.

On the same issue, information about user satisfaction with the working conditions may rest with the ICF or may just reside in the 'staff-leaving' records in the Human Resources Department. Of course, facilities questionnaire surveys are commonplace these days, but since everyone asks the same questions in a different way none of the answers are comparable thereby making the information virtually useless for external benchmarking.

So, without good data, without good benchmarks, the Internet cannot provide any better information than was available before.

Performance information

Having decided what is good for the organisation the ICF has to go about specifying the buildings and services in terms of quality. Information on performance of products is not generally available in a form that is to be trusted, (ie you can only get it from the manufacturers!), but it will not be too long before portals open up carrying hard information not only on the performance of products in use but also on the performance of service providers.

E-procurement

Expect star-ratings and 'best-value' reports to be accessible on the web. One web-site, (www.i-fm.net) already publishes a guide to the top-20 FM companies in the UK. Another site (www.beb.co.uk) run by Building Economics Bureau (the publishers of 'Facilities Economics') gives a fully researched list of all the leading players in construction and property development across the EU. For the UK it also lists all the main facilities management companies plus the leading service providers across the whole range of premises and business services; it tells you who they are, who owns and directs them, what they do, and who they do it for (see Fig. 2.3.G).

Fig. 2.6.G
Company information (year 2000 entry)

Rentokil Initial Management Services Ltd. (RIMS)
Garland Court Garland Road East Grinstead West Sussex RH19 1DY
Tel: 01342 327171
Fax: 01342 305193
E-mail: sales@ri-ms.com
Web-site: www.rentokil-initial.com
Contact
Mr B Dickinson, Development Director
Classification
National
Directors
Stephen Fretwell, Trevor Davies, Barry Dickinson (Development)
Annual turnover of company
£ 68 million
Major clients (over last 3 years)
Benefits Agency, Ericsson, Esso, MAFF, Marks and Spencer
Other branches
Manchester
Additional company Information
RIMS are a wholly owned subsidiary of Rentokil Initial Plc
Operational mode
Facilities Management Contractor, Facilities Managing Agent
Range of FM services under direction
All facilities management services contained in the following Directory categories, or specifically listed sections: Cleaning and Housekeeping, Maintenance – Services, Building, Grounds, Security and Reception, Utilities, Archiving, Distribution – Mailroom Management, Courier / Postal Services, IT Facilities – CAFM System Suppliers, Printing and Reprographics – Print Room Management, Stationery Store Management, Transport / Fleet Management, Catering – General Catering and Vending
Principal regional activity
United Kingdom (except Northern Ireland)
Business sector preferences
Commercial, Industrial, Retail, Education, Leisure, Central Government, Local Government, PFI Projects
Private/Public sector involvement
Private (80%) / Public (20%)
Parent company
Rentokil Initial Plc
Annual turnover of holding / parent / group company
£ 2.98 billion

Extract from 'Directory of UK Facilities' Service Providers' – www.beb.co.uk

Subscribers to these sites can hyperlink direct to the web-sites of any of the listed companies.

Such information can be the starting point in the e-procurement process. Other sites are set up as fully-structured portals where normally are to be found a limited number of service providers and manufacturers linked or operating closely together to provide complete supply chain information and application management.

The specification and procurement decisions to be made in facilities management are all geared to the end product, which is to support the core business activity. Primarily it is the ICF which has responsibility for key decisions about what, where, when and why and the service provider normally decides on how. The portrayal of these three facets of facilities management at Fig. 2.6.H (adapted from Fig. 1.1.A) shows how the intelligence facet gets the information about user needs and hands it to the sponsor in what is shown as the 'value chain'. The sponsor establishes the facilities business strategy and is primarily in charge of the supply chain which in turn is managed by the service provider(s).

Fig. 2.6.H
Three facets of facilities management

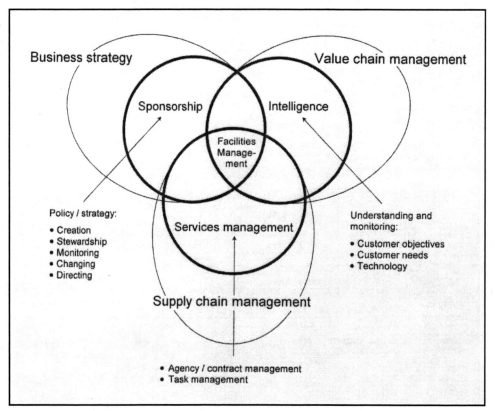

The information about user needs will be gathered internally but decisions about policy and provision of services may well be influenced by external benchmark data concerning peer group activity.

Provided all organisations have their quality and cost data in a form in which it could be automatically benchmarked then the whole process could be conducted via the web with any other organisation prepared to co-operate.

The same information management method can help organisations to procure services and supplies by reference to, and transactions with, providers whose data on costs, quality discounts, performance records, availability, delivery times - everything one needs to know before placing an order - could easily be available in cyber space. Some service providers already include on their web-site all the information normally required for bid pre-qualification, eg policy on health and safety, race relations and sex discrimination.

Not only that, supply chain management can become a web-based reality enabling users to access data about the status of a component with regard to manufacture, delivery, stocks and price changes.

e-Tendering

There are now companies who will arrange for facilities services contracts to be tendered via the internet, allowing an 'auction' to take place as the various bids are delivered and exposed to view to all and sundry.

There are reports of substantial savings being made by this process and no doubt the odd bargain is secured from time to time. However, it must always be remembered that you only get what you pay for, and any supplier undercutting the competition by more than the amount of a reasonable profit margin will either go out of business or under-perform or fight tooth and nail to recover losses via contractual claims. And that is true whatever tendering medium or vehicle is used.

Control of projects and service delivery

Project managers can control progress and quality by accessing and processing data concerning the activities of all participants, and users can monitor at high level the status and performance of all their projects and services by logging in to the project sponsor's master program.

Individual project management programs with internet communications already exist. But the major obstacle to achieving a state-of-the-art process as described above is the ability, or lack thereof, of organisations to recognise the extent of data they possess, to differentiate between raw and processed data and understand how to use both to best effect to get the information needed in an efficient manner.

Management of the supply chain, procurement of components, monitoring of performance are already features of both intranet and internet activity. However the universal take-up of the process is being severely hampered by the inability of clients and providers alike to manage their information in a way that allows them to control - and be monitored - within a seamless, painless, electronic process. Full procurement of services via the web may be a little way off but identification and appraisal of potential bidders via the Internet is bound to be a phenomenal growth area of e-commerce activity in the immediate future.

2.6.8 LEGAL CONTEXT FOR INFORMATION

Legal constraints

The facilities manager may need to develop an awareness of the legal constraints which are imposed on the management of information. Not all the areas of law touched upon briefly below will affect all facilities managers. However it is likely that some will affect many.

The legislation impinges in different ways but may be expected to affect the management of information in areas which include:

- accounts
- computer mis-use
- contempt of court
- copyright and the protection of designs
- data protection
- insider dealing

- market abuse in financial markets
- official secrets
- privacy
- taxation
- tendering.

It is important to develop a strategy for information in each of these areas, if appropriate. Plans arising from the strategy are likely to include:

- monitoring and auditing compliance with the law
- production systems
- retrieval methodology
- disposal and destruction mechanisms
- security and confidentiality practices
- copying and publication
- receipt and dispatch practices
- staff awareness, training and development
- staff access.

Accounts

The accounts of an organisation provide information for use by many 'stakeholders', management, shareholders, suppliers, trade unions and various government bodies.

There are legal requirements for the preparation and submission by registered public and private companies of financial accounts under Section 221 of the Companies Act 1985.

It may be noted that there are certain periods at the time of the publication of the accounts - closed periods - when directors and others may not deal in the shares of their company.

Computers - mis-use

Criminal offences arising from the mis-use of computers are governed by the Computer Mis-use Act 1990. Briefly there are three, namely:

- unauthorised access
- unauthorised use with intent to commit further crimes, eg the 'hackers'
- unauthorised modification of programs or data including the introduction of a virus.

Contempt of Court

Before and during court proceedings it may be held that the destruction of relevant company papers, ie relevant to the hearing as evidence or exhibits, is a contempt of court. Such action may lead to the severest penalties.

Copyright, designs and patents protection

Certain literary, artistic or other kinds of works are protected by legislation, eg the Copyright, Designs and Patents Act 1988. The subject is complex and is outside of the scope of this volume. Suffice to say that any breach of copyright, patent or a protected design may result in an action by the owner of rights in it.

Although perhaps not in the same field in terms of seriousness, it is an offence to photocopy certain items, eg currency notes, passports and share certificates.

Data protection legislation

Whereas the Data Protection Act 1984 applied to electronic data with personal information, the Data Protection Act 1998 requires that, from October 2001, the equivalent paper documentation is safeguarded and managed appropriately.

Such matters as need, setting up, access, security, retention periods and destruction need to be carefully considered and policies established and promoted to staff, eg by training.

The regulatory authority on data protection is the Information Commissioner who has power to act on complaints.

Insider dealing

Insider information is price-sensitive information as yet undisclosed to the market. It is likely to be possessed by or obtained from directors, employees or professional consultants who obtain it in the course of work.

Insider information can give rise to a criminal offence where a person knowingly possessing insider information deals or causes another to deal in such items as quoted shares, gilts and the like. The Criminal Justice Act 1993 provides for a conviction to result in imprisonment or fines.

Market abuse in the financial market

Where information is used in a financial market in an abusive way the Financial Services Authority (FSA) has powers of investigation, determination and discipline under the Financial Services and Markets Act 2000. Generally, this is not a field which will concern many, if any, facilities managers directly.

There is a Code of Market Conduct published by the FSA. Basically, if used properly, information must not give a misleading impression, not distort the market and not be privileged. Market abuse has been highlighted by the FSA in instances of mis-information on internet bulletin boards and use of insider information by journalists.

Official secrets

Contracts on government defence and other projects and programmes may be covered by the Official Secrets Act. Disclosure of information is prohibited unless authorised by the relevant official body in an appropriate way. Unauthorised disclosure may result in the severest of penalties.

Privacy

The right to private life is enshrined the European Convention on Human Rights and is now embodied in the Human Rights Act 1998. Similarly, as discussed above, the Data Protection Acts 1984 and 1998 protect data stored electronically or on hard copy.

For the facilities manager, this means that personal data on employees and others must be kept private and secure, and open only to authorised personnel for operational purposes. Similarly, privacy rights apply to personal data captured on CCTV. However, the Regulation of Investigatory Powers Act 2000 enables the police, on the authority of a senior police officer, to use private CCTV facilities for surveillance purposes. Surveillance by employers of their employees, eg monitoring the use for private purposes of the telephone or e-mail, is also covered by the 1998 Act.

Taxation

The Inland Revenue require the submission by the taxpayer of annual tax returns for self-assessment under the income and corporation taxes legislation. The tax law requires individuals and companies to establish and keep records of various transactions and the Inland Revenue has given advice on the keeping of records for various purposes.

Generally, the facilities manager will not be concerned with the preparation of accounts for taxation but may be required to analyse or categorise information from various cost centres. Such information will then be used by colleagues for computations and, perhaps, claims under taxation.

Tendering

Tendering involves something akin to a secret auction. The bid documents are received in sealed envelopes and must be opened at the stipulated time.

Disclosure of information prior to that time, eg by the premature opening of a sealed bid, is prohibited. Similarly, disclosure after opening the bids so as to enable alterations of a bid is also an offence.

2.7   ASSET MANAGEMENT

Introduction

An asset has been defined an 'anything valuable or useful'.[1]

Fig. 1.1.B in Chapter 1.1.2 showed assets as being subsets of all three main strands of the facilities management function, ie premises, support services and ICT. The property asset is a sub-set of 'premises'.

In some organisations with large property portfolios the management of property assets is sometimes a function which is separate from facilities management; this can - and sometimes does - work well but there is always the danger of real estate dictating the premises policy. Such a scenario is, of course, a recipe for disaster.

As well as managing the premises on behalf of their own users many facilities managers will find themselves presiding over the management of all, or parts of, property assets leased out to their employer's tenants or sub-tenants; a thorough understanding of the principles of property investment management is therefore essential (see Chapter 3.9).

2.7.1 CONFLICTS OF INTEREST

The owner, or prospective owner, of one or more properties who intends to hold the estate for a long period is faced with a number of activities which must be undertaken if the wealth sunk into the property is to be maintained or enhanced. In planning for these activities there may, however, be conflict between what is good long-term management and stewardship of an estate and what is evidence of good short-term performance.

There may also be conflict between national or regional approaches to property management and the need to maintain or project a universally consistent corporate image. Franchisers such as Benetton or MacDonalds would expect their properties to be of the same quality, no matter where they are.

Although facilities management is as much concerned with optimising (facilitating the performance of) human assets as it is with physical assets, the management of human resources falls to the personnel director whereas management of physical assets should be down to the facilities manager.

Should be, but, in practice, not always in their entirety.

2.7.2 CATEGORIES OF ASSETS

The physical assets of an organisation comprise some or all of the following:

* buildings and their services

* fitting out components

* furniture and fittings

* office equipment and consumables

* vehicles

* production plant and machinery

---

[1] *Collins Concise Dictionary. HarperCollins Publishers, Glasgow, UK.*

- work in progress
- raw materials
- finished goods.

A further classification of these assets into property assets and inventories is necessary for a number of reasons, including tax liability, depreciation and management techniques.

Property assets are usually of a long-term nature and may well appreciate in value during the early part of their useful lives - and in some cases for the greater part of their life possibly assisted by inflation, refurbishment or both.

Assets in inventories have short-term life spans - up to say five years, but much shorter in the case of office consumables, raw materials and (hopefully) finished goods. Those that survive in the balance sheet at the year end will either be valued at cost, if they are consumables, or at their depreciated value in the case of equipment and fitting-out components which may be expected to last for a few years - see Chapter 10.6.4 - component life-cycles.

The facilities manager will not normally be concerned with the management of production assets but ought to be concerned with the management of the property, office services and other business support assets.

2.7.3 PROPERTY ASSET MANAGEMENT

Property v premises

As discussed above it is not uncommon for management of property assets to be split into two distinct operations:

- property management
- premises management.

This distinction is highly significant for facilities managers to recognise in that it represents and highlights the dichotomy facing many organisations whose property asset values underpin balance sheets and borrowings. These valuations reflect (or should do) the institutional investors' view of the price obtainable for a property in the open market; this may have no relevance at all to the usefulness of the property as 'premises'[2] - defined as a 'piece of land together with its buildings, especially considered as a place of business'.

Whereas the facilities manager's objective is to ensure that the premises accommodate the requirements of the business plan in a cost-effective manner, a property director working independently of facilities management may have other designs on the asset value of the stock, its disposal and/or replacement.

The significance of property and inventory assets in the context of the balance sheet is shown at Fig. 2.7.A (over the page) which illustrates the situation before and at the end of the severe economic recession of the early 1990's. Property values in the UK dropped by as much as 50% in the period from 1988 to 1993, so the 1990 version of this balance sheet shows how important a good property asset can be in support of business stability. Conversely, the impact of a severe drop in market values on businesses being propped up largely by property assets is only too evident.

Nevertheless, the arguments for the management of property assets to be closely alongside, if not within, facilities management are very strong, especially in the context of the impact of premises on productivity.

---

[2] *Collins Concise Dictionary. HarperCollins Publishers, Glasgow, UK.*

Fig. 2.7.A
Balance sheet assets - 1990 to 2000 transition

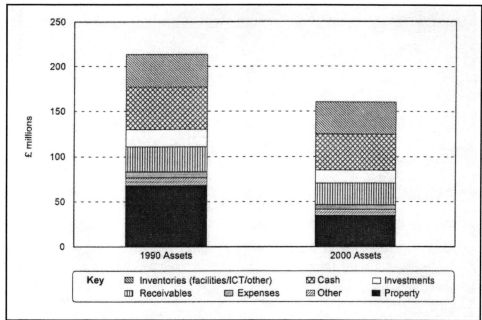

A particularly good example of the close liaison between property and facilities management relates to an organisation in the financial services sector whose facilities management, by successfully creative space planning, managed to reduce its stock of office space from 80,000 sq m to 65,000 sq m over a five-year period.

In most cases the space reductions were timed to coincide with break clauses in leases, and the right balance was struck between retention of useful buildings and disposal of under-performing and/or unnecessarily expensive ones. In this example property management was part of the facilities function, albeit staffed and directed by highly qualified real estate professionals.

Property management functions

Once buildings have been completed and occupied a new phase of their life begins. Property management is required on a planned basis to ensure that they meet occupiers' requirements and maintain their worth to the owner (who may be an investor or the owner-occupier). The management will involve both day-to-day activities and deeper study and action. The latter is sometimes referred to as 'active property management' and requires the estate manager to spot opportunities for, say, redevelopment, major refurbishments, or acquisition of adjoining property, perhaps to realise 'marriage value' - see Chapter 10.1.4.

Generally, investment property management includes:

- assessment of occupational requirements and collection of rent and service charges

- maintenance and repair of buildings, plant and machinery, fixtures, fittings and furniture in 'common areas' of buildings

- insurance against numerous perils affecting buildings, occupiers and other persons, including fire insurance, consequential loss of rent, and employer's compulsory insurance

- assessment of rent on letting, on review or on renewal of leases

- obtaining possession from tenants for the purposes of redevelopment or for other reasons, including the settlement of compensation claims for disturbance and any improvements, if appropriate

- management of vacant property prior to re-letting, or demolition for redevelopment re-letting, or breaking of leases

- evaluations for improvements, redevelopment or disposal

- disposal by sales, assignments, grants of leases, or exchanges by gifts, or by other means

- establishment and maintenance of an environmental management system which enhances aspects of the above

- funding acquisitions, repairs, maintenance, refurbishment and development projects

- planning to avoid or mitigate tax burdens and to take advantage of particular tax incentives

- ensuring compliance with any government requirements such as health and safety or opening hours regulations.

Property management requires a comprehensive property record system to include ready made or bespoke systems which may be either electronic or paper based for the: rent roll, estate terrier, caution system, minor and major works programmes, storage arrangements for deeds, agreements and plans, and a library. Taxation records need to be kept, particularly for service charges. There are a number of excellent estates management programs now available either on a database or linked to computer-aided facilities management systems.

It is not unknown for estates departments to lose track of one or more properties the business owns or manages. The facilities managers responsibility to check that when a property is sold or demolished it is deleted from the estate terrier and when a new building is constructed or acquired it is added to the terrier. Also to make sure that it is deleted from any Computer Aided Design (CAD) systems which are used to calculate floor areas for costs analysis in maintenance and management programs.

Performance appraisal

Estate or portfolio standards are likely to require reappraisal. The property management function requires knowledge of the environment in which the estate exists and needs to have the knowledge and skills to appraise the potential for development and re-development when needs or opportunities arise.

At a different level of conceptualisation, continued investment in the estate by a landlord may be compared with other opportunities to invest, eg in equities or gilts. Similarly, where individual properties in the portfolio are not performing in a way commensurate with the risk involved, rationalisation of the holdings will be affected and new investments sought. In particular, this would appear to be the process undertaken by the financial institutions, eg the pension funds in making any relative shift from property to other investment sectors, or vice versa.

Of course, not all owners have the resources to appraise their estates as fully as may be suggested above, but the function is one which the financial institutions in particular have been concerned to develop and progress. It follows that an owner's criteria for investment should be fully established and appraised.

It should not be forgotten that the poor management of property can significantly alter the valuation of a property portfolio. So it is up to the facilities manager to oversee the tenants or landlords agents, to ensure that effective maintenance is carried out. For further discussion on all valuation issues, see Chapters 3.4 and 3.5.

The condition of the property

The preservation of the condition of the property asset in terms of its market value does not necessarily reflect the business accommodation requirement, and vice-versa, eg a building about to be demolished may invite a property maintenance strategy invoking 'rubber bands and sticking plaster' whereas the potential impact of such a regime on business efficiency might well dictate a modification to, if not abandonment of, this extreme solution in spite of its direct benefits to cash flow.

Maintenance of property assets is considered in detail in Chapter 5.2. It is best considered over a reasonable time-span. The process of forecasting maintenance costs over a medium period - say ten to fifteen years - must not be confused with the forecast accompanying planned/preventative maintenance (PPM), (see Chapter 5.2.2), although the calculations may be identical in outcome. Making a forecast need not (probably should not) generate a commitment to expenditure for it may merely act as an aid to financial and strategic planning. In particular, exposure to major expense in terms of replacement of important components such as boilers, chillers, roof coverings should be tracked ahead so that redundant maintenance may be avoided. Alternatively, maintenance can be slotted into the replacement works programme and/or replacement can be tailored to coincide with works of alteration.

An illustration of this point is the example of a ten-year forecast of maintenance and replacement incorporating a programme of capital works shown at Fig. 2.7.B. (over the page). Extending the replacement of the roof-mounted chillers from year one as originally planned to year three increases 'holding' maintenance and repair but allows the replacement cost to be reduced by a far greater amount - as well as discounting it for the further two-year period. Similarly, roof repairs coincide with major new works.

Whole-life appraisal techniques are discussed fully in Chapter 10.6.3. Whole-life appraisal of asset maintenance and replacement is particularly important at building design stage, and should form the basis of medium term budget projections for purposes of property asset management. However, forecasting the incidence of replacing components for any sort of period ahead is fraught with problems, although there is data available which, used with care and constantly monitored against actual, can be used as a satisfactory working-base.

Fig. 2.7.C (on pages A-147 and A-148) gives typical life-spans for some of the more common materials and components as an example of the conventional wisdom; Chapter 10.6.4 describes sophisticated statistical approaches to assessing component lives (and the hazards influencing them) in a more logical and scientific manner.

The condition of property assets should be recorded early in the life of a new building and immediately on taking occupation of existing premises. The condition survey should concern itself with the major components, leaving minor items to be dealt with on a routine ad hoc basis. Ideally the data in the survey should be entered into a computerised data-base coded up to enable instant retrieval of component data (including maintenance histories); large, beautifully bound, expensive reports growing out-of-date on inaccessible shelves are worse than useless and they are a monument to the failure of the commissioner of such reports to understand what asset management is all about.

From the facilities management perspective the condition of the asset is primarily of concern with regards to image and fitness for purpose. Simple scoring systems by which to assess and, if required, target the maintained condition of the asset are of far greater benefit to the facilities manager than volumes of detailed inspection reports; an example of the use of such a system as part of the quality management process is included in Chapter 2.4.2.

Recent software developments enable the condition survey to be updated using a touch-screen portable computer with the material being downloaded direct to the data-base to update the original condition survey without further keyboard entry.

Fig. 2.7.B *Asset management - maintenance plan incorporating capital works*

	Ten year planned maintenance programme											
	Building B: (all costs as at 1st quarter 2000 and exclusive of VAT)											
Sub-element	Cost per year in £											Total in £
	2000	2001	2002	2003	2004	2005	2006	2007	2008	2009	2010	
Substructure	0	0	0	0	0	0	0	0	0	0	0	0
Superstructure												
Frame	0	748	2,264	352	43,640	319	748	3,683	264	35,009	319	87,346
Upper-floors	0	99	0	0	0	0	0	0	0	0	0	99
Roof	0	45,000	0	0	0	0	0	0	0	0	0	45,000
Stairs	0	0	429	166	0	31,528	0	429	252	0	342,279	67,083
External walls	0	0	0	0	0	0	0	0	0	0	0	0
Services (cont'd)												
Heat source	0	0	0	0	0	0	0	0	0	0	0	0
Space heating and air-treatment	0	3,760	4,880	3,500	0	0	0	30,000	0	0	0	342,140
Ventilating systems	0	0	0	0	0	0	0	0	0	0	0	0
Electrical installations	0	99,137	41,269	40,041	3,016	10,640	0	3,016	0	0	10,516	207,635
Drainage	0	0	0	0	0	0	0	0	0	0	0	0
External services	0	0	0	0	0	0	0	0	0	0	0	0
Capital projects												
Roof works	0	184,500	195,450	0	0	0	0	0	0	0	0	379,950
Toilet area	0	0	49,500	49,500	49,500	0	0	0	0	0	0	148,500
Reception areas	0	0	0	99,000	0	0	0	0	0	0	0	99,000
Replace chillers	0	0	280,000	0	0	0	0	0	0	0	0	280,000
Total in £	0	385,167	745,168	192,769	102,295	58,571	3,5866	192,295	38,776	40,291	170,858	1,962,056

Fig. 2.7.C *Typical economic life of some common components*

Elements from BCIS[3] standard form of cost analysis			Estimated life years	Preventive maintenance
2.C.2	Roof coverings	Slate	30+	Replace damaged or slipped slates as necessary.
		Asphalt	15-30	Recoat with solar paint every 3 years. Replenish chippings as necessary.
		3-layer felt / chippings	10-20	Inspect annually and repair localised damage.
		Clay tiles	30+	Replace damaged tiles if necessary.
		Concrete tiles	20+	Replace damaged tiles as required. Colour may fade.
		Copper	50+	None.
		Aluminium	35+	Annual inspection and maintenance. Regular cleaning with non-alkaline detergent. Renewal of side / end lap seals as necessary.
		UPVC	15-20	Replace damaged sections as required.
2.E	External walls	Stone	50+	Visual inspection every 5 years. If necessary cleaning, repointing and surface repairs.
		Brickwork	50+	If efflorescence occurs salt deposits to be brushed off.
		Concrete blocks	40+	None.
		Reinforced concrete	35+	None.
		Rendering	20-40	Can be washed by water jetting at mains pressure. Cracks and damaged render to be cut out and repaired.
		Timber framing	20-40	None.
		Timber cladding	25-30	Redecorate / stain every 3 years or paint every 5 years. Renew creosote every 3 years.
		Curtain walling	20-40	As manufacturers' instructions
2.F.1	Windows	Softwood	25-40	Stain at 3 years, paint at 5 years. Replace unpainted.
		Hardwood	40-60	Stain at 3 years, paint at 5 years. Replace glazed.
		Galvanised steel	15-35	Redecorate steel after 20 years and every 5 years thereafter. Replacing glazing gaskets, weatherstripping, etc. as required. Replace unpainted ironmongery plated at 10 years or stainless steel at 20 years.
		UPVC	10-25	Clean every 5 months with non-alkaline detergent to maintain appearance. Renew weatherstripping and gaskets every 10 years. Renew hardware every 10 years if plated or 15 years if stainless.
		Aluminium	20-35	If painted, repeat every 5 years. Renew weatherstripping and gaskets every 10 years. Renew hardware every 10 years.
2.F.2	External doors	Softwood	20-30	Redecorate: Stain every 3 years, paint every 5 years. Lubricate ironmongery when required. Replace weatherstripping as required.
		Hardwood	30-50	Redecorate: Stain every 3 years, paint every 5 years. Lubricate ironmongery when required. Replace compounds and seals as required.
		Galvanised steel	15-30	Occasional cleaning with non-abrasive cleaner. Repaint every year.
		UPVC	15-25	Clean every 6 months with non-alkaline detergent. Adjust and lubricate ironmongery as required by manufacturer. Clean track regularly. Replace draught strips and gaskets every 10 years.
		Aluminium	20-30	Clean every 6 months with non-alkaline detergent. Adjust and lubricate ironmongery as required by manufacturer. Clean track regularly. Replace rollers and locking mechanism every 10 years. Replace draught strips and gaskets every 10 years.

[3] Building Cost Information Service, RICS, London

Elements from BCIS[1] standard form of cost analysis			Estimated life years	Preventive maintenance
3.A	Wall finishes	Plaster	35+	None.
		Plasterboard	20-40	None.
3.B	Floor finishes	Vinyl	10-20	None.
		Woodblock	40-70	None.
		Terrazzo	40+	None.
		Quarry tiles	50+	None.
3.C.1	Finishes to ceiling	Mineral tiles	15-40	None.
		Carpets	5-10	Regular cleaning to manufacturers' instructions
5.D.2	Cold water service	Pumps	10-20	Clear pump regularly. Clean strainer regularly. Service pump as recommended by manufacturer.
		Pipework	10-35	None.
		Tanks	15-35	Maintenance of ball valve, checking of overflow pipe, retaining insulation / covers in place.
5.D.3	Hot water service	Pumps	5-20	Visually examine for leaks and if necessary renew gland packing and seals every quarter. Change overdue pumps every quarter.
		Pipework	20-35	None.
		Calorifiers	20-35	Every 2 years inspect scaling to calorifier shell and tubes. Cleaning and descaling when required. Monthly inspection of safety valves and gauges etc.
5.E	Heat source	Steel boilers	10-20	Annual service and maintenance contract.
		Calorifiers	20-35	Every 2 years inspect scaling to calorifier shell and tubes. Cleaning and descaling when required. Monthly inspection of safety valves and gauges etc.
		Tanks	15-35	Maintenance of ball valve, checking of overflow pipe, retaining insulation / covers in place.
		Pipework	20-35	None.
		Control equipment	15-20	Regular inspection / testing
5.F.1	Water / Steam	Steel radiators	15-20	Regular dosing with inhibitor.
		Pipework	10-35	None.
5.F.4	Local heating	Gas burners	15-20	Annual service and maintenance contract
5.F.7	Heating with ventilation (air treated centrally)	Heater batteries	15-20	Annual service and maintenance contract
5.F.8	Heating with cooling air (air treated locally)	Water chillers	15-20	Annual service and maintenance contract
5.F.9	Heating with cooling air (air treated locally)	Cooler batteries	15-20	Annual service and maintenance contract
		Cooling towers	10-25	Water treatment, regular cleaning
5.G	Ventilating system	Air handling systems	8-15	Annual service and maintenance contract
5.H.1	Electric source and mains	Switchgear	15-30	Regular inspection and testing
		Main cables	25-35	Regular inspection and testing
5.H.2	Electric power supplies	Electric motors	20-25	Annual service and maintenance contract
		Main cables	25-35	None.
5.J	Gas installation	Gas burners	15-20	Annual service and maintenance contract
		Pipework	20-35	None.

Ownership and professional advice

Whether property asset management is done in-house, or outsourced through a local agent, or managed in zones, or any combination of the above is dependent upon the type and nature of the portfolio held. (See Chapter 3.4.2 for valuation consultant advice.)

Many large organisations have their own in-house team of property management specialists to perform the oversight function - usually property trained and professionally qualified.

As outsourcing becomes more and more in vogue, both property management and the legal aspects of the investment property management function are likely candidates for the 'non-core' outsourcing route. Some emphasis is now placed on private sector organisations moving towards PFI/PPP-type projects for their accommodation and facilities.

Most of the problems, which occur in property investment management focus around the question of communication. Even if the portfolio manager has the brief to inspect all investments monthly this can be both practically and physically impossible. Day to day management is usually best left to either in-house staff on site or locally based agents.

In order for a property management strategy to be effective, in-house staff/outsourced agents should:

* be capable of making the running of the building as inconspicuous as possible, eg if the lift to the thirteenth floor does not operate, it should be dealt with today and not next week

* have good communications skills

* have technically and professionally competent staff

* have specialist property management knowledge as well as an understanding construction techniques

* be able to focus on the practical management problems of the property from the tenant's perspective as well as the landlord's

* encourage a culture of preventative rather than reactive management

* be flexible and prepared to retrain if necessary.

The cost of property investment management

External management of an estate may cost from 1% to 10% (typically 5%) of income from rents depending upon scale and complexity. Sometimes it is geared to the service charge 10 - 15% is a common figure. Where the income is incidental to the basic business activity some time for the facilities manager liasing and negotiating with tenants and consultant surveyors will have to be added on.

The costs of overseeing a widespread portfolio can be disproportionately high because of the practical problems of inspections and local management as identified above. However, the effort may well be worth it because of the added value that a well managed, diverse portfolio can add to the asset base of the balance sheet.

2.7.4 INVENTORY ASSET MANAGEMENT

The facility manager's role

Unlike property assets the inventory assets are almost invariably in a depreciating mode from the date of acquisition.

As discussed above some or all of such inventories as fitting-out components, (eg partitions, carpets, light fittings, furniture and fittings), office equipment, eg pc's, photocopier, consumables, (such as stationery and reference books), and vehicles may come under a facilities manager's responsibility throughout their limited life-span.

Duties in connection with these assets may involve:

- purchase
- distribution
- installation/placement
- insurance
- inventory
- maintenance
- storage
- disposal.

The facilities manager may also be the budget-holder for these items having responsibility for all three facets of financial control in their respect.

These inventory assets are either semi-fixed, eg suspended ceilings and carpets, or 'loose', such as pc's and motor vehicles. The semi-fixed items demand less resources in terms of asset management than the 'loose' items which are apt to go astray unless their disposition is tightly monitored; they are also likely to suffer from the 'out-of-sight-out-of-mind' syndrome in regard to abuse, lack of maintenance and re-allocation.

Asset registers

The principles of procurement, financial control, maintenance and storage apply equally to loose inventories. Generally, however, it is essential to set up an asset register identifying the following (where applicable) in respect of each component:

- code identification reference
- title
- date of purchase
- name of manufacturer
- model, series, colour, material and manufacturer's reference numbers
- initial (and subsequent) location
- areas served (eg photocopiers)
- internal market ownership
- maintenance periods, servicing contractor and history
- operator's maintenance instructions
- warranty/guarantee data
- condition
- insurance
- other relevant data.

The modern-day asset register must surely be set up on a computerised data-base preferably linked to a CAD program - with inventory assets of all categories (including building and services components) bar-coded to be instantly traceable and their location and records up-dated.

Such systems, discussed earlier in this chapter, do not only enable efficient control of inventories; they also greatly facilitate the process of cross-charging equipment and other items to the beneficial user.

2.7.5 ASSET DEPRECIATION

All company expenditure must either:

- add to the value of the assets in the balance sheet (capitalised), or

- be charged in the profit and loss account (expensed).

Capital expenditure on projects creates assets such as new or improved plant or buildings. The objective is to maintain or increase profits accruing to the business through the use of assets. Due to use, the passage of time and obsolescence these assets lose value in accounting terms, ie depreciate, though, as discussed above, property assets may behave erratically in this respect throughout their life span.

Any amount that can be capitalised will increase profit directly, in the year in which it is incurred, by the amount capitalised - but at the expense of the profits in future years when (increased) capital values will require (increased) depreciation.

The lower the charge for depreciation in a year, the higher the book value of the fixed assets and the higher the profits for that year.

Revenue expenditure includes premises operating costs and business support services costs.

An effective and efficient maintenance strategy will extend the economic life of assets thereby reducing depreciation as an annual expense. It is therefore important for facilities managers to work closely with their accounts departments to ensure that capital expenditure, such as major improvements or adaptations, are recognised as such and not charged as an expense on the profit and loss account instead of being capitalised on the balance sheet.

Further consideration and worked examples of depreciation in respect of property are given in Chapter 3.8, and Chapter 11.2.5 looks at the nature of depreciation of assets for taxation purposes, ie capital allowances.

The application of reserve, contingency and sinking funds to preserve assets, via service charges, is reviewed in Chapter 3.3.1.

2.7.6 ASSET STRIPPING

Some organisations have assets - particularly of the real estate variety - which have a property market value out of proportion to their usefulness to the business they accommodate or which are simply undervalued in the books.

The increase in the status of commercial property as a valuable investment through the '70s and '80s saw a number of shrewd entrepreneurs make their fortunes buying ailing companies at a price reflecting their business performance but not reflecting the underlying property values which the accountants were allowed to include on a 'written-down' basis on the balance sheets. The subsequent break up of the businesses to enable realisation of the real-time property values caused much concern in genuine business circles but also alerted corporate owner-occupiers and their accountants to the dangers of not keeping a regular check on the current market value of their freehold and long-leasehold premises, perhaps using sale and leasebacks or other means to realise the value.

The property value down-turn of the early 1990's lulled many potentially property-rich companies into a false sense of security which made them prey to the stealthy attacks of the asset strippers.

Be aware!

2.8   PROJECT MANAGEMENT

Introduction

Project management in facilities relates to tasks which are, generally speaking, outside of the routine management functions carried out by the department. Such tasks normally involve significant change, but do not necessarily always involve the physical upheaval attendant upon fitting-out, alteration or relocation.

For example, introduction of management regimes to cope with the rigours of new legislation (Health and Safety at Work etc) and introduction of IT processes may be substantially non-physical in their nature whilst still requiring the vision, tenacity and negotiating skills needed to deal with installation projects.

Very often facilities managers will not have the relevant experience to deal with certain types of project. They must recognise and admit this fact and bring on board additional resources with the necessary skills. This may entail adding to the staff complement if a full-time involvement is expected over a long term, but in most cases a better solution will involve the appointment of consultants specialising in management of the particular types of project. Not only does this avoid staff appointments which may turn out to be unwarranted or superfluous, but it also brings access to the resources of a specialist organisation upon which the client may draw for experience and manpower at critical stages of a project.

Management of development projects is considered in technical detail in Chapter 10.1 - The Development Process - which also differentiates between the 'hands-on' project management role and that of the project sponsor. Chapter 6.3 - Procuring the Project - looks in some detail at fitting-out projects particularly with regard to procurement and financial control.

This chapter is predominantly about the tools and techniques available to do the job.

2.8.1 PROJECT RISK EXPOSURE

The project manager's objective is to deliver the project in accordance with the requirements of the brief which should stipulate cost, quality and time. In the process the risk must be managed so as to keep exposure to failure in respect of any of these criteria to an acceptable and pre-agreed level.

Fig. 2.8.A
Project risk exposure

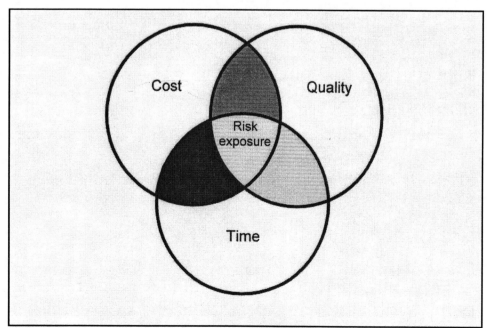

Again, a trinity is present and Fig. 2.8.A (previous page) illustrates how risk management as described above is central to successful avoidance of failure in respect of the three critical facets of any project; it is axiomatic that failure in respect of one facet will aggravate, and most likely render futile, attempts to be successful in the other two. This said, certain projects will have special emphasis on one or two of the facets, eg completion of a critical facility on time may be more important than holding costs in check. Nevertheless, simply diverting resources to the 'time' facet may provide an excuse for discontinuation of even rudimentary controls in the other facets: what often happens in such circumstances is that project managers lose sight of the essential detail of the project - and thence lose control at high level as well.

2.8.2 PROGRAMME MANAGEMENT TOOLS

Principal generic tools

The principles of financial, quality and risk management and various tools to facilitate their application are discussed elsewhere in this section and specifically in respect of fitting-out, construction and development projects in Sections 6 and 10 respectively.

However there are a number of programme management software programs available commercially which are generically applicable to any project, as well as those specifically geared to the more common types of project encountered by construction and development specialists.

Fitting the complexity of the software to the problem in hand is important but there are few projects of consequence facing the facilities manager which would not benefit to some extent from an IT application - even if only on a spreadsheet.

The principal generic types of programming tools are:

- milestone charts
- the Gantt chart
- network analysis (CPM/PERT)
- float analysis
- resource allocation (labour/plant/materials)
- operational schedule
- work breakdown structure (WBS)
- progress analysis and control - 'S' curves
- line of balance.

Milestone chart

This is a simple planning and control tool which is often used as a summary plan.

As Fig. 2.8.B (over the page) demonstrates milestones are specific and readily identifiable points of achievement marking the start and/or completion of stages (either major, minor or intermediate) of a project.

Fig. 2.8.B
A 'milestone' chart

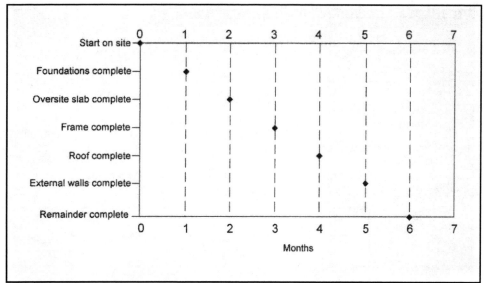

The technique, which was the forerunner of the Gantt chart described below, is still sometimes used to present a report which schedules programmed milestone dates against those actually achieved.

The Gantt chart

This is probably the oldest and most common planning technique in use today. Developed during World War I by Henry Gantt its chief advantages are that it is: easy to understand, easy to construct with little training and can be used to show progress. Like the 'milestone' chart which pre-dated it, the Gantt chart is concerned with beginning and end dates and is particularly suitable for projects where activities are more or less consecutive, each one being dependant upon one logical predecessor. As Fig. 2.8.C illustrates it does not show interrelationships between activities which are not immediately linked; for instance, building regulations and landlord approvals are on the critical path leading to commencement of construction, but this is not obvious from the chart. On large and/or complex projects this can lead to problems in co-ordination of the work.

Fig. 2.8.C
Gantt chart for the fitting-out stage of a relocation project

Ref.	Activity	Duration	May	Jun	Jul	Aug	Sep	Oct	Nov	Dec	Jan	Feb	Mar	Apr
1	Feasibility report	0w												
2	Project board meeting	0w												
3	Further study undertaken	7w												
4	Accommodation selected	0w												
5	Lease negotiations	6w												
6	Develop project brief	2w												
7	Approval to proceed	0w												
8	Detailed design development	4w												
9	Site investigation	4w												
10	Prepare tender documents	2w												
11	Tender period	4w												
12	Tender analysis	1w												
13	Client approvals	1w												
14	Contractor mobilisation	4w												
15	Site enabling works	4w												
16	Construction period	13w												
17	Building regs. Approval	6w												
18	Landlord approvals	8w												

Key ● Event ━ Activity

A compromise on simple projects is the vertical linking of activities by means of a dotted line; however, once this process gets profuse the whole presentation gets more confusing than helpful.

Critical path method (CPM/PERT) - network analysis

The Programme Evaluation and Review Technique (PERT) identifying the 'critical path' through a project was developed in the USA in the late 50's / early 60's to overcome the Gantt chart's deficiency in dealing with interrelationships between activities. Consequently it is used primarily for the more complex projects.

Its method of calculation identifies those activities which are critical to completion of the project and additionally shows the extent to which these activities have spare or 'float' time for their completion.

The process involves identification and numbering of events and activities.

Fig. 2.8.D
Network analysis diagram

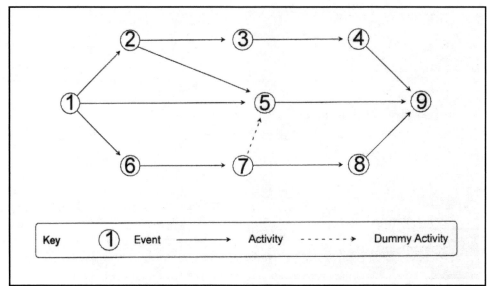

In the diagram of a project network at Fig. 2.8.D the events are numbered 1,2,3 etc; the activities needed for achievement of the events are described by the relationship between two consecutive events, eg 1-2 and 5-9.

In this example the following relationships are important:

- Activities 1-2, 1-5, 1-6 can all start together

- Activities 2-3, 2-5 can start when activity 1-2 is finished

- Activities 2-5, 1-5, 7-5 must all be complete before activity 5-9 can be started

- Activity 7-5 is a dummy activity.

Dummy activities are necessary to indicate a logical relationship - in the example above, activity 5-9 is dependant on activity 6-7, with activity 7-8 being dependant upon activity 6-7 but not on activities 1-5 or 2-5; hence, the need exists for a logical link that does not tie activity 7-8 to event 5.

Whilst a dummy will not usually have a duration it can be of use to control the start of following activities.

The numbering of the activities can be in random sequence, but it makes sensible practice to use ascending numbers, leaving gaps of (say) 10, between event numbers, for the later insertion of extra activities as required.

It is important to note that the length of the activity line does not need to correspond to the duration. When first drawing the network logic, it would be almost impossible to draw it to a timescale - the important thing is to construct a logically correct plan and then analyse this for decision purposes. Most computerised programs offer a feature of plotting the network, with or without a timescale, after analysis, thus obviating the need for formalised drawing of networks.

The critical path through the network traces those events whose late completion will cause delay to start of activities required to achieve another event whose completion date is equally critical to the overall programme time.

Once time is added in to the network it is possible to see the minimum possible programme time for activities leading to critical path events and where there is any 'space' or 'float' time in any of the activities. So, in the example, if events 1, 5 and 9 are on the critical path and activities 1-2, 2-3, 3-4 and 4-9 are estimated to take 20 days, whereas activities 1-6, 6-7, 7-8 and 8-9 are estimated to take only 15 days there is a 'float' time of 5 days in the latter sequence in the network - more if the sum of 1-5 and 5-9 is greater than 20 days.

Float management

Although this 'float' time is spare as a contingency, if the activities in the sequence 1-6, 6-7, 7-8, 8-9 were to slip to, say, 22 days then the critical event No.9 would be two days late, even if the upper and central sequences on the network were delivered within 20 days. Therefore float management deals with the management of the so called 'non-critical' activities to ensure that any slippage that does occur does not delay start of activities on the project's critical path.

Resource allocation

This technique is often allied to network analysis and involves forecasting resource requirements (in terms of labour, materials, plant and finance) from the initial project plan and comparing these requirements with those either available or which can be made available. These factors may impose restraints on the project plan and require it to be modified to take into account, for example:

- resource limitations

- avoidance of undue fluctuations in resource requirements

- the overall resource pattern and its effect on productivity.

Fig. 2.8.E illustrates the resources which are required in terms of operatives per week given either a timely or late build-up of the resources needed to complete the activity to schedule.

Fig. 2.8.E
Resource allocation chart

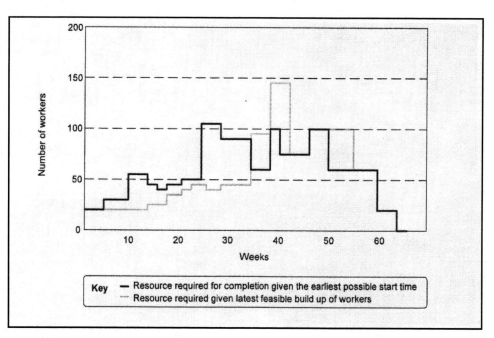

Operational scheduling

Again, this is a step beyond basic network analysis which goes on to designate not only start and finish times for an activity but also who does what and when.

Operational scheduling therefore combines network analysis with resource and time scheduling.

Work breakdown structure (WBS)

WBS is a structured method of identifying the work to be carried out on a project and the procedure involves breaking the work down logically and systematically into its component parts to:

- enable the planning to be done effectively by defining the work required to complete the project and to sub-divide it into manageable tasks that can be planned, controlled and budgeted

- assign responsibility for the completion of those tasks to designated personnel/organisations to integrate the work to be done with the overall organisation structure

- design and integrate the control and information systems with the work to be done and allocation of responsibility for it.

'S' curve progress analysis chart

An 'S' curve is a graph of the cumulative value of operative hours, percentage complete, or cost against time. The graph generally takes the form of an 'S' because most activities (projects) have a slow start followed by a longer period of relatively constant activity and finally a falling off of activity.

Fig. 2.8.F
The 'S' curve used to test project progress

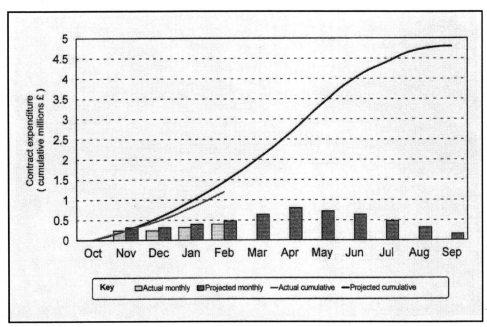

The 'S' curve is a very sensitive tool for the analysis and control of progress. Fig. 2.8.F from a construction project shows how the planned 'S' curve in terms of contract expenditure (on the vertical scale) per month's activity (horizontal scale) was not being achieved when tested against the monthly payment certificates under the contract; consideration of the 'S' curve needed to achieve completion and the resources it would demand would be a good indicator of the possibility of avoiding a delayed completion.

Line of balance (LOB)

This technique developed by the US Navy in the early 50's is a graphical method of scheduling designed to improve the planning and reporting of an on-going production process. It is particularly useful where:

- the project is made up of a number of identical units, eg fitting-out repetitive floors of a multi-storey office block

  or

- the project consists of first the design and then the production of a limited number of units from that design, eg 'customised' toilet pods

  or

- on a one-off project to give a concise presentation of progress against plan.

Fig. 2.8.G presents a 'line-of-balance' analysis of progress on fitting-out repetitive floors in an office building. It shows the actual state of completion of each stage against projections enabling a complete overview of the project to be taken at any point in time.

Fig. 2.8.G
*'Line-of-balance'
chart for completion
of fitting-out
repetitive floors of
an office building*

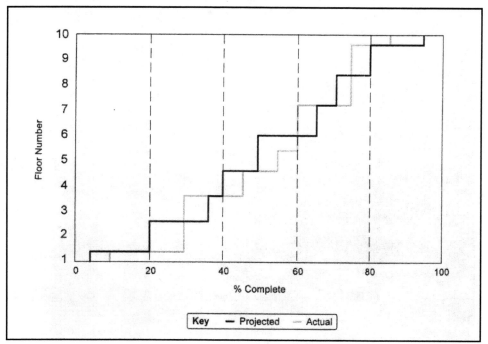

Computerised applications

There are many programme management software packages available, many of which combine some or all of these techniques in one program. Most of these packages are structured on network analysis but can output as Gantt chart, milestones, resource allocation histograms, etc; most spreadsheet programs can produce 'S' curves against a plotted cash flow configuration.

2.8.3 PROJECT MANAGEMENT QUALITIES

'Give us the tools and we'll finish the job' is a famous catch-phrase and the use of the above planning/control tools is critical to successful project management. So is the right project management structure with properly identifiable chains of command, instruction and authorisation procedures and adequate resourcing.

However, as in every other aspect of management, if the personnel deployed to run the show do not have the necessary technical ability and personal qualities (such as leadership and charisma) then no amount of sophisticated software and careful management structuring will produce the goods.

People make projects work, not tools or systems, although the best people generally know which tools and systems to use and how and when to use them.

2.9 CHANGE MANAGEMENT

Introduction

Organisations change constantly, being driven either by their own dynamism or, sometimes reluctantly, by the business environment in which they have to operate.

The extent of pro-active change management needed in pursuit of the corporate plan is more or less predictable, but even then there are many trip-wires along the route lying in wait to obstruct or prevent the smooth transition. Reactive knee-jerk change to accommodate unwelcome external impositions such as new legislation or market forces is always in evidence, even in the most efficient companies, though it is still possible - and highly desirable - also to have a pro-active attitude towards such categories of change driver.

Change management is less a discipline than an attitude; this chapter merely alerts the facilities manager to the need to be ready for change and explains how not to be overtaken by events.

2.9.1 BUSINESS CHANGE

Change should either make the business more profitable, more efficient or a better personal experience - or all three. Profitability, of course, may be viewed in terms of total profits in absolute terms resulting from growth as opposed to a statistical return on investment, which is why efficiency is identified separately here alongside profitability: it is quite common for inherent productivity to reduce with growth thereby reducing the percentage return on investment.

Over the past decade leading into the Millennium most organisations went through at least one major business transformation. Research[1] has shown that the top three change programmes in that period were:

- information and communication technology

- business process re-engineering

- business strategy development.

Unfortunately the research also shows that three-quarters of all change projects fail. Machiavelli put his finger on it when he wrote in 'The Prince':

'There is nothing more difficult to plan, more doubtful of success, nor more dangerous to manage than the creation of a new system. For the initiator has the enmity of all who would profit by the preservation of the old institutions, and merely lukewarm defenders in those who should gain by the new ones'.

2.9.2 MANAGING CHANGE - THE TRADITIONAL APPROACH

For many organisations, a typical change management programme follows a predictable pattern:

- senior management announces a new corporate quality/engineering process improvement programme

- company-wide half-day training workshops are arranged to bring everyone up to speed

---

[1] *Bulletpoint Communications Ltd, Kingsgate House, High Street, Redhill, Surrey RH1 1SL, UK.*

- cross-functional committees are quickly set up to meet and discuss 'the way forward'

- resources are re-allocated, desks duly moved, pc's plugged in at a new abode.

For organisations which manage change skillfully, it can become the driving force that perpetuates success and growth, with every change presenting a new opportunity to increase efficiency or to build the business. But all too often, change fails, as companies fail to rise to the challenges it brings.

2.9.3 CHANGE AND THE FACILITIES MANAGER

The key principles

Most business changes have a significant impact upon the facilities required. Any increase or decrease in quantity, relocation, availability of funds or legislation - whatever the drivers - will change the way space is used and managed and the scope, possibly quality, of the premises and support services provided.

Change therefore calls upon all the facilities management functions - especially value management - and change management is therefore not identified separately as a management discipline. Nevertheless, in pursuit of a holistic value management approach to change in a facilities context, there are some key principles facilities managers must observe if their response to business change requirements is to accommodate the corporate value criteria:

- have a facilities policy which anticipates change and has a ready-made strategy for each possible critical eventuality

- make sure that core business managers understand the implications of their plans in facilities terms - sometimes the knock-on effects in terms of facilities required can be critical to the strategic and financial success of corporate change

- preserve a 'lateral' view of the changes needed to facilities; in other words, do not allow people who do not understand facilities to impose ill-considered facilities solutions on the organisation

- try to maintain flexibility in contract arrangements so as to avoid change 'penalties'; a partnering or managing agency method of controlling service delivery as described in Chapter 2.1.2 will often avoid the problems of contractual claims and unco-operative service providers

- keep your ears close to the ground and keep lines of communication to the top decision-makers as short and fluid as possible - this is the responsibility of the Intelligent Client Function (ICF)

- maintain regular and friendly contact with external agencies of whom you may need to ask a favour, eg local building control authorities, real estate agents and key suppliers/service providers

- always try to find value-engineered solutions to change projects, even when time is at a premium; remember, the extra thought needed in the value-engineering process inevitably brings a better, as well as a more cost-effective, solution

- when change becomes endemic - such as with 'churn' (see Chapter 4.2.2) - plan well ahead for a more efficient solution in the future

- if core business culture (as opposed to needs) brings about an excessive cost of facilities to accommodate it, eg room sizes linked to status, challenge the culture with a well-presented business case: money talks!

- ensure a 'fit' with any needs arising from the Transfer of Undertakings (Protection of Employment) Regulations 1981.

Mergers and takeovers

By far the most serious changes affecting facilities are those involving mergers and takeovers. Many of these strategies fail on account of failure by the instigators to understand the cultural differences between organisations. Many of these cultural differences are critical in human as well as corporate terms, eg the way the space is allocated and presented.

Equally, many merging organisations have a mix of premises which collectively is inappropriate to the needs of the new organisation.

It is imperative that facilities managers introduce and explain these issues to the proponents of the merger/takeover right at the outset of negotiations; the facilities issues may not sway the economics overall but they will very likely have a large impact on the speed at which the re-engineered business processes can achieve the predicted levels of efficiency.

PART B

Premises

Section 3

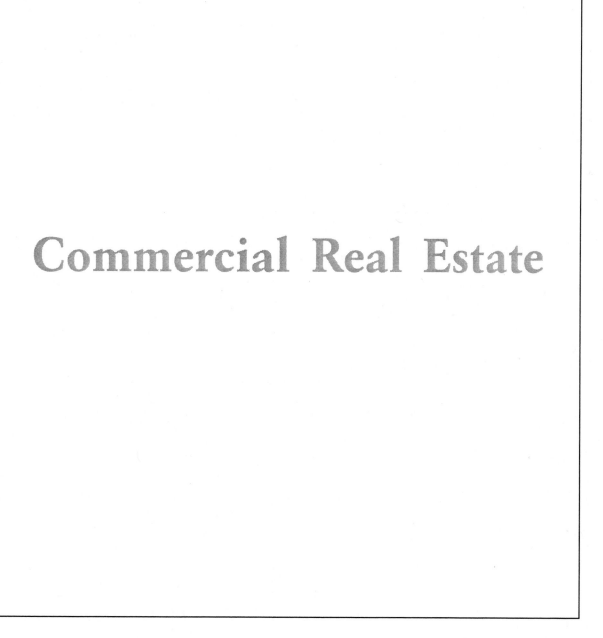

Commercial Real Estate

3.1 INTERESTS IN PROPERTY

Introduction

The facilities manager should have a broad understanding of the legal factors affecting estates and interests in land. The legal estate or interest defines ownership such terms as use and occupation in physical terms and in terms of duration. This section looks, therefore, at legal estates in land, ie freeholds and leaseholds; at licences and restrictive covenants; and at wayleaves and easements. (As described below the law applies to England and Wales since Scotland and Northern Ireland have somewhat different legal systems.)

For business premises, the facilities manager needs to consider how statutes, particularly the Landlord and Tenant Acts, affect tenure.

The Law of Property Act 1925, as amended, established the principles of property ownership in England and Wales. Under that statute it was ordained that there would be but two basic categories of ownership of land and buildings:

- fee simple absolute in possession (freehold)

- leasehold absolute in possession.

3.1.1 FREEHOLD INTERESTS

In theory the owner of freehold property owns it outright and in perpetuity. Deterioration or demolition of any building upon the land in no way changes the perpetual nature of the title. Owners may do anything they wish upon it subject only to any rights others may possess either conferred by the owner or imposed by statute.

In practice, there is little to differentiate between a medium/long lease and a freehold. In most cases there is a mortgagee who is very interested in what happens to the security and the accountants are quick to pounce upon any modification to property having an adverse effect on the balance sheet.

Certain statutes concerning town and country planning, public health, local bye-laws and building regulations may in any case restrict a freeholder's ability to develop or alter property and may impose obligations with regard to matters such as keeping buildings in repair.

A freeholder must respect the 'natural rights' of others such as rights of light or support; there is occupier's liability to occupants and visitors and the land may also be subject to rights or restrictions, to the benefit of others, which are conditions of entitlement to ownership.

A major benefit of owning the freehold is the ability to create lesser interests in all or part of a piece of land. These interests are leaseholds; in certain cases they may take the form of licences to occupy, creating no interest in the land as such. However, the freeholder's common law right to take back physical possession at the expiry of a lease is severely curtailed by statute - in particular, for business tenancies, the Landlord and Tenant Act 1954, as amended.

3.1.2 LEASEHOLD INTERESTS

Types of lease

A leasehold affords the lessee (or leaseholder) exclusive use of the property for a specific period, either a term of years or periodic, eg quarterly, monthly, etc. In return the tenant usually has to pay a rent and accommodate and observe any rights or restrictions incorporated in the legal agreement. The rights in respect of use of the land will usually be quite restricted and specifically laid down in the agreement.

A lease will normally be either a 'building lease' or an 'occupation lease'.

Building leases

These are granted to developers by freeholders who wish to retain ownership in perpetuity while enjoying a rental income from land developed for use by others. The rent paid by the developer (lessee) to the landlord (lessor) is known as a 'ground rent', and relates to the development value of the land but excluding the value of any buildings erected thereon.

Such leases are, for obvious reasons, normally for substantial periods, say 99 years; the buildings revert to the landowner on expiry of the lease subject only to statutory rights of the tenant.

Building Agreement and Agreement for a Lease

An alternative to a building lease is the Building Agreement (or Licence) and Agreement for a Lease. The arrangement affords the freeholder protection that the building is completed satisfactorily before a lease is entered into.

Occupation leases

This type of lease is for exclusive occupation of the tenant for any certain period, but normally not more than 20 years with 'break' clauses (options to the agreement) at specific dates - say after 5 or 10 years. **These break periods must not be confused with the 'rent review' periods discussed below, although they often coincide.**

Sub-leases

Anyone who has a leasehold interest may, subject to the terms of the lease - which usually requires the landlord's consent - sub-let the property at any rent they are able to obtain but only for a period expiring before their own lease period expires. Sub-lessees may enjoy similar protection under statute as their immediate landlord, ie the principal tenant's; the latter will be primarily responsible for any default by the sub-tenant with regard to obligations passed on to the sub-tenant from the main lease.

The landlord and the sub-tenant may however make a joint approach to the courts to restrict the security of tenure provisions of Part II of the Landlord and Tenant Act 1954 as amended. The Example shows three properties occupied in various ways.

Example: Three similar freehold properties (A B & C) are owned by different persons. Each has three floors with a ground floor shop and offices on the upper floors.

A : the freeholder (V Ltd.) occupies the property A

B : in 1995 the freeholder (V Ltd.) granted an occupation lease for 21 years to X Company; they occupy the ground floor shop and two upper offices.

C : in 1995 the freeholder V Ltd granted a lease for 21 years to Y Property Investment Company Ltd.

   : in 1996 Y granted a lease of the ground floor for its remaining term less three days to U Retailers Ltd.

   : in 1997 Y granted a lease of the two upper floors for 10 years to V Ltd.

   : in 1999 V Ltd granted a lease of the top floor for the remainder of its lease less 1 day

Assignments

Subject again to the usual requirement of landlord's consent, a leaseholder may hand over (assign) the remaining portion of the lease to a third party; an assignment can only be at the current passing rent and all existing conditions of the lease will be transferred to the assignee.

Because there is privity of contract between the original parties to a lease an assignor may yet be liable for a default of the assignee. However, the Landlord and Tenant (Covenants) Act 1995, which applies to leases granted after 31 December 1995 (and differently to leases existing at that date), allows a tenant who assigns to be released from the privity of contract obligations unless the landlord obtains an authorised guarantee agreement from him.

3.1.3 LICENCES

The nature of a licence

Whereas a lease, however short, creates an interest in the land a licence does not.

A licence may be either:

*   to occupy land, or

*   to use land

and it may be granted orally or in writing and for any period.

Licences to occupy: Case law on the subject of when a right to occupy is a lease as opposed to a licence is voluminous and beyond the scope of this work. In most cases facilities managers will only consider taking premises under a licence agreement for a short period, eg during refurbishment or relocation of its premises - and then only as a last resort.

The licence agreement should make it clear that no lease or tenancy is to be created, but even explicit wording may yet fail to prevent the courts - or the VAT man - from construing the agreement differently.

The most significant issues about lease v licence are that the latter provides no statutory right of security of tenure, does not breach any covenant against sub-letting and may not give exclusive rights to possession.

Licences to use: These are rights to use land either to carry out some operation or to use specialised facilities, eg storage. Rights over land, eg rights of way, are in effect licences to use; if they are accompanied by consideration then there may be VAT implications.

3.1.4 RESTRICTIVE COVENANTS

It is quite common for the user of both freehold and leasehold property to be subjected to restrictions formally set down in the deeds.

These 'restrictive covenants' emanate from the action of previous owners in attempting to protect their own or others interests from some detrimental use by succeeding users, eg restrictions as to the nature of a manufacturing process to be carried out on the land, or categories of business activity.

In some circumstances vendors or lessors may be merely trying to protect their own enjoyment of adjacent property, whereas in other situations they may be concerned to maintain the general level of values in the adjoining property, eg where substantial investment properties are owned.

Over time these restrictive covenants often mar the value or development potential of the property by restricting what is by then appropriate use of the site.

A breach of a restrictive covenant, that is by ignoring it, may result in legal action by the owner of the property which benefits from it. However, rights to remedy the breach and seek damages to enforce these covenants may be forfeited if the beneficiary has been seen to permit breaches or allowed them to go unchallenged.

Under the Law of Property Act 1925 and Lands Tribunal Act 1976 a freeholder may seek to have restrictive covenants set aside or modified. The Lands Tribunal may grant an order to compensate the beneficiary of any restrictive covenant who would suffer as the result of their adjudication. This may arise in a compulsary purchase situation where no land is taken, ie adjoining land is taken and the benefit of a restructive covenant is lost (see section 10 of the Compulsary Purchase Act 1965).

The Landlord and Tenant Act of 1954 allows similar action where leases of more than 40 years duration have at least 25 years elapsed, ie by amending sub-section (12) of section 84 of the 1925 Act.

Other means of dealing with restrictive covenants include insurance, private treaty negotiation to seek its removal; and acquiring the 'protected' property.

3.1.5 ACCESS

Neighbours' land

From time to time the facilities manager who needs to carry out repair works to a building will find that it cannot be done without access over a neighbour's land. If permission is unobtainable, an application may be made to court for an access order under the Access to Neighbouring Land Act 1992.

Conditions may be applied, eg restriction to a specified location and there may be a requirement to make a payment or compensation or both.

Countryside and rights of way

There is an ancient tradition of access over land in public footpaths and bridleways. More recently, however, the Countryside and Rights of Way Act 2000 provides members of the public access to certain (generally open) land in the countryside. The facilities manager should note that exclusions include:

* aerodromes

* golf courses (except those where public access is permitted)

* mineral workings

* railway land

* development land with planning permission

* parks and gardens

* land covered with buildings

* cultivated land.

Wayleaves and easements

Many bodies have statutory rights to create wayleaves or easements over another's property. Thus gas, electricity, oil and other utility organisations may lay pipes or cables on, under or over property. They usually 'touch' the property but sometimes an electricity cable is an 'oversail' which does not touch the land. The right of entry, eg for repairs and renewal, is included in the right.

Procedures for obtaining such wayleaves and easements vary. Some are negotiated but others involve obtaining powers to compel provision. Of course, rights of objection and compensation exist in most instances. (See Chapter 5.5.8 on water and sewage pipes.)

Landlords

The terms of a lease will provide for the landlord to have right of entry in certain circumstances, see Chapter 3.2.5.

Statutory bodies

Rights of access to land is afforded to officers of bodies possessing statutory powers. These include:

- police officers

- officers of the Valuation Office Agency on rating valuation matters

- Inspectors of Tax and officers of the Customs and Excise.

3.1.6 DUTY OF CARE TO VISITORS AND OTHERS

The occupier of land and buildings has a duty of care to visitors and others, including trespassers who have access to the property. The duty extends to those who do not enter (so this will be covered in this section for completeness).

The Occupiers Liability Acts 1957 and 1984 'codify' aspects of the duty of care towards visitors to the premises. They fall into four groups:

- children

- visitors in general

- workers (other than employees)

- trespassers.

Children: being less thoughtful and more careless than adults they are owed a higher degree of care than others. Facilities managers should ensure that they are safeguarded against 'honeypot' dangers on the premises, ie sources of attraction which present hazards such as ponds, poisonous berries and plants.

Visitors with permission (including implied permission): visitors may expect a reasonable degree of care from the occupier.

Workers: visiting workers may expect, generally, a reasonable degree of care like others but with the knowledge and experience attaching to their expertise should be wiser about the dangers concerning their trade or profession.

Trespassers: those who enter premises without permission (other than children) were not covered by the Occupier's Liability Act 1957. However, the 1984 Act also covers trespassers as well as those with a legitimate presence, eg using a right of way. If the occupier is, or may be expected to be, aware of a danger he or she should take steps to protect visitors, including trespassers, eg with notices, fences or other appropriate means.

In the case of properties which are vacant awaiting demolition or rehabilitation a prudent facilities manager might include one or more of the following safeguards:

- fencing the perimeter and dangerous 'honeypots' within it

- cutting off and sealing services, eg gas, electricity and water

- bricking up or boarding doorways, windows and other apertures

- emptying and cleaning of tanks and other containers of water or other fluids

- removing dangerous contaminants.

The duty of care has been extended to the statutory environment and waste management regime as outlined in Chapter 5.6.8

3.2 LEASEHOLD CONDITIONS

Introduction

Chapter 3.1 draws the distinction between a freehold absolute in possession and a leasehold. In this chapter the construction of a lease is examined in some detail.

The ownership of a lease may arise in one of several ways, namely by:

- the grant of a lease by the freehold owner in the whole or part of a property

- the grant of a sub-lease by a leaseholder - the sub-lease may be for the whole or for part of the leaseholder's property

- the assignment of a lease by an existing leaseholder

- the surrender of an existing lease and the taking of a new lease (broadly on terms of equal value)

- 'sale and leaseback', ie the sale of an existing interest (freehold or leasehold) and the taking back of a new lease (by the original vendor).

This section deals mainly with matters pertaining to the grant of a lease by an absolute owner. For most purposes, the treatment covers the other ways of acquiring a lease; important differences are, however, noted. Also, the three types of transactions - renewal of a lease (or not), surrender and renewal, and sale and leaseback - are touched upon briefly. Generally, parties usually require professional advice prior to the commencement of negotiations.

Service charges are mentioned briefly, but a more thorough discussion of this important financial and legal commitment can be found in Chapter 3.3.

3.2.1 THE CONSTRUCTION OF A LEASE

Despite the lack of standardisation, typical leasehold or sub-lease agreements will contain common specific provisions, in particular with regard to:

- details of the parties to the agreement - including any 'superior' landlord, eg in the case of a sub-lease the sub-lessor's landlord (who may be a leaseholder to the freehold owner) will be named in the sub-lease and their interest in the arrangement defined

- details of the demised areas in, on or under the land, together with, if appropriate, those of access and the common parts;

- details of any landlord's fixtures and fittings and any exclusions, eg in a 'pie-crust' lease for contamination (see Chapter 7.8.)

- the period of the lease and any break points

- the rent, payment details and any rent review provisions

- any covenants, ie obligations, to be observed (see Chapter 3.1)

- permitted uses (or any restrictions on use)

- landlord's obligations and any means of recovering costs from the tenant in their respect, eg service charges, further rent, etc in respect of works to maintain the 'common parts'

- other obligations of the tenant in respect of the premises, eg maintaining in 'good and tenantable repair'

- conditions relating to any alterations or improvements or both, including obtaining landlord's approvals

- alienation, by assignment or subletting

- provisions in respect of national and local taxation as well as value added tax (see Chapters 11.1 to 11.6)

- landlord's rights to enter and inspect and actions they may take in respect of default

- notices

- rights to redevelop or refurbish

- resolution of disputes, eg by arbitration, mediation or other means.

3.2.2 RENT

The nature and payment of rent

Rent is the amount paid by a leaseholder tenant for the use of buildings and/or land (ground rent for land alone). It is usually set at a monthly or an annual figure payable in monthly or quarterly instalments; in periodic tenancies, eg quarterly or monthly, rent is usually paid per period at a time; in all cases rent is conventionally paid in advance.

In Ireland and the UK quarterly rent, where paid, is due on the traditional 'quarter days':

- Lady Day   -   25 March

- Mid-summer Day   -   24 June

- Michaelmas   -   29 September

- Christmas   -   25 December.

A rental level set at, or near, the full market value on given terms and conditions, is known as a 'rack rent'. Where significantly less than the rack rent it may give rise to a valuable interest to an occupation lessee, subject to the timing of the next lease renewal or rent review.

Sometimes, particularly in retail premises, rents are geared to a percentage of turnover. These 'turnover rents' are often applied in new locations, such as new shopping centres, to encourage take-up of leases in advance of proven establishment of a successful trading location. This method of rent collection is becoming increasingly popular but, as it is very difficult to implement on existing developments which have not historically adopted this method of rent collection, it tends to be focused on new sites.

The continued growth in the popularity of its further development is now being challenged by the development of Internet shopping. As traditional profit bases are being eroded developers and retailers are reconsidering this approach to letting; in some instances plans are even afoot to charge an entrance fee to shoppers instead of rents to tenants as one way of meeting the challenge of internet shopping, ie to discourage the practice of viewing goods in the shops and then buying over the web.

Another form of incentive to secure tenants in new locations, but less fashionable in this day and age, is the 'rising' or 'escalating' rent where the levels are pre-set for a number of periods years at a time.

Failure to pay rent, or delay

Most leases permit the landlord to enter and repossess the property if the tenant fails to pay up on the due date, but they must go to court to do so legally. The tenant is obliged to pay the rent, and any 'further rent', even if the landlord is in default in respect of their obligations under the agreement.

Persistent delay in paying the rent may be grounds for the landlord to obtain possession at the end of the lease (Part II Landlord and Tenant Act 1954).

Rent reviews

Modern leases invariably contain provisions for the level of rent to be reviewed at regular intervals and reset to the level prevailing in the current market.

The conventional period is five years although seven and even 14 may be found in older leases. It is interesting to note that just prior to the 1990's recession some landlords were trying to introduce three-yearly reviews because of the high inflation in rents for the limited amount of high quality space then available.

Many of these rent review clauses have wording to ensure that in the event of market levels dropping, eg as happened dramatically in the early 1990's, rents cannot go below the passing level. Such clauses are known as 'upwards only' rent review clauses.

It is important to note that where rents are indexed, rents can go up as well as down and so investors are unlikely to be prepared to invest large sums of money in any but the most prime of properties where they feel they have security. Chapter 3.6.1 contains further discussion of the effect of rents on property investment.

New leases are certainly being negotiated on tough terms for the investors. Investors obviously have to make sure that not only is the future rent guaranteed, but also that the value of the property is not reduced further due to any lack of certainty with regard to 'upwards only' rent reviews.

The timing of the rent review is sometimes set to coincide with dates in the lease at which either party may terminate the agreement. The provisions setting down the rights and obligations of the parties in this respect are commonly known as 'break clauses'. It is quite common for lay people to fall into the trap of thinking that the rent review period is also a potential break-point, which it most often is not.

The facilities manager should note that the outcome of a rent review may be affected by the precise wording of the lease. Numerous court cases have resulted in many seemingly esoteric issues being drawn into the negotiations.

Rent suspension

There may be circumstances where the tenant will want a clause permitting suspension of the obligation to pay rent, eg following a fire or where the landlord has to carry out remedial works for contamination.

Rent on renewals of a lease

When the lease comes to an end, the tenant is afforded security of tenure, subject to the landlord's rights of possession (see 3.2.7 under 'Grounds for possession').

Although the parties may agree different terms, in the event of a dispute, for instance, The Landlord and Tenant Act 1954 provides for the duration of the new lease not to exceed 14 years and for the rent to be the open market rent. However, in fixing the open market rent any value attributable to the following will be disregarded:

* the tenant's occupation of the property
* the goodwill of the tenant's business
* the existence of any licence for licenced premises
* the effect on rent of certain improvements made by the tenant.

The question of improvements is a little complicated but may be summarised as follows: (see also fig. 3.2.A over the page) in arriving at the open market rent

* include any improvements that the tenant contracted to undertake, ie under the terms of the lease

- exclude any 'non-contractual' improvements carried out by the tenant during the term and agreed to by the landlord

- on a second or subsequent renewal, include any 'non-contractual' improvements carried out by the tenant more than 21 years before the renewal.

Fig. 3.2.A
Improvements and rent under a lease

Time scale	Nature of the Lease	ToL*	Term	W*	Improvements	Rent on grant
0	Original (21years)	0		0	I_1 as provided in the lease	Market rent of unimproved property
1						
2						
3				3	I_2 Voluntary improvement	
4						
5						
6						
7						
8						
9						
10						
11						
12						
13						
14						
15						
16						
17						
18				18	I_3 Voluntary improvement	
19						
20						
21		21		21		
22	First renewal (a further 14 years)	0		0		Market rent including I_1 only (I_2 and I_3 : rent attributable is ignored)
23						
24				24	I_4 Voluntary improvement	
25						
26						
27						
28						
29						
30						
31						
32						
33						
34						
35		14		35		
36	Second renewal (a further 14 years)	0		0		Market rent including rent for I_1 and I_2 (Ignore I_3, within 21 years back from year 35; and I_4 within term of first renewal)
37						
38						
39						
40						
41						
42						
43						
45						
46						
47						
48						
49		14		49		

NB: the rent on review will depend on the terms of the lease
* ToL - Terms of Leases (lease period)
* W - Works (years)

An example illustrates these requirements which is shown graphically in Fig. 3.2.A.

Example: Grant of a lease for 21 years with two renewals of 14 years each

Original Lease (21 years)

A freeholder granted a lease for 21 years at the market rent and as a condition of the lease the tenant agreed to extend the building (a contractual improvement - I_1).

In the eighth year the tenant sought and was given permission to further extend the property and did so (voluntary improvement I_2)

Similarly, he further extended the property in the eighteenth year (voluntary improvement I_3)

First renewal of the Lease (a further 14 years)

On renewal the rent will be the open market rent taking into account the contractual improvement (I_1) but ignoring the voluntary improvements (I_2 and I_3).

Second renewal of the Lease (a further 14 years)

On the second renewal the rent will be open market rent taking into account the contractual improvement (I_1) and the first voluntary improvement (I_2) - because it was carried out more than 21 years before the current renewal date. However, the second voluntary improvement (I_3) is disregarded because it was written 21 years of the current date.

3.2.3 REPAIRS, MAINTENANCE AND INSURANCE

Full repairing and insuring lease (FRI)

Under a lease the liabilities of the parties for maintaining, repairing, decorating and insuring the premises will be set down - although historically definitions of terms, rights and obligations have left much to be desired.

Who does what is largely determined by either legislation or the practicality of the situation. So, if the building is let entirely to one leaseholder, then it is likely that the 'fully repairing and insuring' type of lease will apply. In this case the tenant will have full responsibility for upkeep of the property including not only repair and maintenance, redecoration, insurance, all fuel bills and other running costs but also the replacement of defective plant, materials and structure and reinstatement to its original condition on expiration of the lease.

It is common for this liability to be commuted to a payment based on a 'schedule of condition' prepared at the end of the lease. Where a lease is assigned or sub-let during its course a schedule of condition is usually produced at the commencement of the assignment or sub-lease as well as on expiration to enable the assignor's or sub-lessor's compensation to be calculated.

The recent focus on environmental liabilities for past contamination means that a prospective lessee will not want any liability for past contamination and may seek to make the prospective landlord liable. Similarly, the landlord will want access for any remedial works during the course of the lease. Also, the landlord will want to ensure that the tenant has an obligation to remedy the environmental damage caused during the lease, and to have an environmental management strategy.

Multiple occupation leases

Where premises are in multi-occupation the usual arrangement is for the landlord to keep responsibility for repairs, maintenance and insurance of the 'common parts', with the tenants reimbursing them by way of a 'service charge' type of arrangement as discussed below (see Chapter 3.3).

The term 'common parts' usually embraces:

- the external envelope, ie foundations, external walls, windows, doors and roof
- main entrance
- common staircases and lifts
- main services and utilities
- HVAC central plant and distribution
- atria
- external grounds and landscape within the boundaries.

The leaseholder usually has to maintain the 'tenanted area' ie that which they occupy exclusively and pay all the bills specifically relating to their occupation and identifiable as such. So, they will pay their own internal cleaning bills, any metered gas or electricity and internal repairs/redecoration and the like. Whereas the insurance of their own goods and chattels will probably be their own direct contract they will have to pay (via the service charge) their agreed share of insuring the property against fire and other forms of damage.

If the tenant fails to repair and maintain, the landlord has power by virtue of section 146 of the Law of property Act 1925 (as amended) to remedy the situation, eg by forfeiture.

Insurance

Insurance will normally be required in respect of reinstatement of all or part of the building, loss of rent, and loss of service charge. Charges for premiums should be 'dead net', ie after deduction of any discounts. If the landlord or agent acts as the insurance agent they should not include any commission in the insurance charge as this may be in contravention of the Prevention of Corruption Act 1906. (See Chapter 3.7 for a further discussion on insurance.)

Entry

A lease will normally reserve for the landlord a right of entry for various purposes, including:

- inspection and approval of works by the tenant
- carrying out works which the landlord is either obliged to execute or as a result of the tenant's default
- carrying out a schedule of condition or dilapidationsa
- for bailiffs to execute their powers, eg in the event of non-payment of rent.

3.2.4 LANDLORD'S APPROVALS

Alienation

Many leases will require that any proposal by a tenant to transfer ownership of the interest to a third party (alienation) will require the landlord's consent and some may specifically prohibit sub-letting or assignments (see Chapter 3.1.2 above for a further discussion of this issue). Clearly undesirable or unsubstantial tenants are apt to be detrimental to the landlord's interest whether in terms of management, investment value or both. The Landlord and Tenant Act 1988 requires the landlord to act reasonably and promptly with applications and puts the onus on the landlord to prove that he or she has so acted.

Alterations and improvements

Some leases may absolutely prohibit alterations (subject to the Landlord and Tenant Act 1927) or they may be silent on this issue. In the latter case provided the tenant observes the normal national statutory controls and delivers the premises back in good repair there is absolute freedom to make whatever changes are wanted.

Consent to 'improvements' must not be unreasonably withheld even if it has an adverse effect on the value of the property - the landlord may recover compensation and may require reinstatement if that is a reasonable thing to do.

On the other hand, if a business tenant's improvements enhance the value of the property or its 'lettability' they may, having been given notice to quit on expiration of the lease, be able to recover all or part of the costs under the Landlord and Tenant Act 1927 and Part III of the Landlord and Tenant Act 1954. This right of recovery may be lost, for instance, if the improvements are carried out as part of a contractual liability with the landlord in respect of works which are not required to comply with statutory requirements, or if the property is to be demolished.

Correct observation of procedures for applying for consent and securing notice is imperative - starting work in anticipation of approval is a common occurrence with impatient tenants who may not realise the possibility that they may have to pull it all down again if the landlord reasonably refuses consent - even if they had originally been given an informal nod (maybe from a landlord not in possession of all details).

Tenants making improvements with the landlord's consent may come to pay for their trouble when the rent comes to be reviewed under the terms of the lease, unless the terms expressly provide against it or the tenant has received a licence authenticated by the landlord's solicitor. If the lease is renewed under the Landlord and Tenant Act 1954, eg where the tenant agrees to occupy refurbished premises, improvements made voluntarily in the course of the previous agreement, ie not required by a covenant of the lease, and either by the current tenant or completed (by whomever) within the 21 years preceding application for a new tenancy, must be disregarded in computing the new rent.

However, this is an area of property law which contains case law so the safest way for a tenant to go about substantial upgrading may be to do a deal with the landlord on a surrender and a new lease effecting an appropriate compromise of both parties' interests.

If there is a long lease to run at historic rents without rent reviews (many fortunate tenants and unfortunate investors still suffer or enjoy these relics from the past) the tenant should be able to get the best deal by undertaking the improvements with the landlord's approval - and a formal licence of course if required!

A real life example of the financial risk implications of these two options on a city headquarters building is discussed in Chapter 2.5.2 and the financial appraisals of the investment options are illustrated in Fig. 3.2.B (over the page).

In the example the tenants were the beneficiary of a long remainder of an existing lease with no rent review for several years. In spite of the obvious financial advantage to the tenants in undertaking the refurbishment on their account the decision went with the landlord-led option on grounds which were not dictated by pure facilities economics.

Where a tenant has carried out improvements, as part of a deal with the landlord, the wording of the rent review clause may affect the level of rent to be agreed on review; otherwise the provisions given in Fig 3.2.A will apply.

The Disability Discrimination Act 1995 seeks to improve conditions in buildings for disabled persons. It may require a lessee to effect alterations - 'reasonable adjustments' - to the demised property even though the lease may prohibit such works. The Act has precedence and lays down a procedure for the tenant to obtain the landlord's consent, usually within 21 days. The landlord cannot refuse unreasonably but may impose reasonable limitations.

Fig. 3.2.B
Rentalisation v amortisation of refurbishment - financial appraisal of options

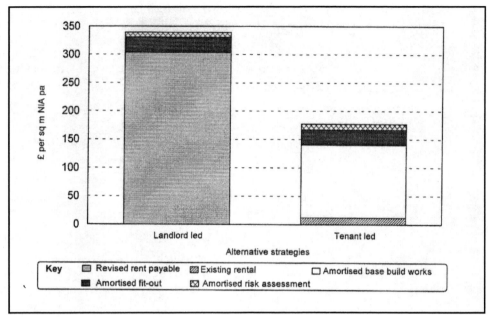

Similarly, restrictive user clauses and other factors may affect the rent achievable on review. Generally, indexation reviews and rent review negotiations require a detailed knowledge of legislation and case law.

3.2.5 SALE AND LEASEBACK

Generally, the sale and leaseback of a building in absolute ownership is a question of negotiation between the parties as to the terms and conditions of the lease taken back. Where a lease is sold and leased back by the existing lessee, the absolute owner would no doubt be involved in the manner described in Chapter 3.5.12.

3.2.6 SURRENDER AND RENEWAL

At some point during the lease a tenant may wish to improve the holding, eg to have a longer term so as to effect improvements to the property (the longer term allows a longer amortisation period).

If approached the landlord may agree to a surrender of the existing lease and the grant of a new lease on different terms. The basic general principle adopted by the parties is the 'before-and-after' approach. In other words, the original holding is compared with the new holding in terms of equal value.

Of course, the viewpoints of both the landlord and the tenant are considered separately and then compared in striking the agreement for the new lease. It may be necessary to take into account other factors, such as any taxation issues which may arise.

3.2.7 LEASE RENEWAL - ISSUES AND OPTIONS

At the end of the lease there may be provisions under the Landlord and Tenant Act 1954 available for its renewal. Assuming that the landlord has no grounds for seeking possession, the lessee has three choices:

- to seek a renewal of the lease under legislation, if applicable

- to seek to negotiate a new lease

- to give up the lease on expiry and leave the premises.

Grounds for possession

Under section 30 (1) of the 1954 Act, the grounds upon which a landlord may seek possession or oppose the tenant's renewal of the lease are, briefly, as follows:

- failure to repair the property

- persistent delay in paying the rent

- breaches of other obligations under the lease

- alternative accommodation is offered on a reasonable basis by the landlord

- where there is a sub-tenancy, a better return could be obtained from the whole property

- the landlord has the intention to demolish the property or re-construct or substantially re-construct it

- occupation by the landlord is intended.

For a renewal of the lease the tenant serves notice under Section 25 of the 1954 Act but the landlord may oppose it with a counter notice. If the landlord wants to initiate the seeking of possession before the tenants service of a Section 25 notice, he or she may serve notice on the tenant under Section 26.

3.2.8 REDEVELOPMENT AND REFURBISHMENT

The landlord may wish to redevelop or refurbish the demised premises. Generally, however, the tenant is protected but the landlord has opportunities subject to certain statutory restrictions. It is important to know when the landlord wants possession for redevelopment. This will be at certain times, namely:

- during the lease

- at the time of a break clause (if any) in the lease

- at the end of the terms of the lease.

If the landlord wants possession during the lease, the tenant is usually protected by the lease and the landlord would normally be obliged to negotiate a voluntary surrender of the lease by the tenant, perhaps buying the tenant out. No doubt the tenant would seek consideration reflecting any gain to the landlord in the 'before-and-after' situation, ie a portion of any 'marriage value' in the transaction.

Where the landlord seeks possession at a break point in the lease or at the end of lease, the statutory procedures would need to be followed. Any compensation would depend upon the grounds used by the landlord to obtain possession. Generally, for redevelopment the tenant may not be entitled to compensation for tenants' improvements made during the lease but may be eligible for compensation for loss of security of tenure.

Again considerable case law underpins the grounds for possession. For instance, for the penultimate demolition, the landlord needs to demonstrate to the court appropriate details of the scheme for re-construction and, perhaps, the financial backing behind it.

3.3 LANDLORD'S ASSET MANAGEMENT AND SERVICE CHARGES

Introduction

One way or another, either as part of the rent or as a formal additional service charge, landlords will always want to control the asset management and to recover from tenants the full cost of managing and maintaining the asset.

Where buildings are leased to more than one tenant it is normally impractical for the tenants themselves to take responsibility for the asset management. In any event, the property investor (the landlord) has a vested interest in ensuring that the asset is maintained at an appropriate level having regard to its current and future value; the landlord will therefore wish to control the specification, timing, cost and delivery of any works or services in connection with the asset. This chapter considers the various ways this control is exercised.

3.3.1 DEALING WITH PHYSICAL DETERIORATION

The problem and its treatment

Physical deterioration is but one of several factors causing 'economic obsolescence' as discussed in detail in Chapter 3.8.2. Deterioration means 'becoming bad or worse'[1] so physical deterioration of a property means a worsening of the condition of the built component of the estate.

During the life of a building physical deterioration will need to be addressed for several reasons, principally:

- to maintain the investment value

- to prevent further, accelerated and more serious deterioration, eg repairing roof leaks

- to keep the premises in good operational order.

The investment value is purely of concern to the landlord.

Timely prevention of greater, though deferred, expenditure is prima facie desirable for the tenants who will probably finish up paying for all the costs incurred; in any case the knock-on implications for business efficiency of a deferral strategy make the latter a false economy.

Although any fall-off in operational efficiency will solely affect the tenants, obvious wear and tear **and** obvious operational deficiencies are a giveaway to the investment valuer so the landlord will normally try to avoid continuation of such deficiencies.

The service charge will not normally apply to 'obsolescence' in the sense of 'going out of use or date', but see further discussion of this term in Chapter 3.8.2.

The lease or agreement covenants both parties to their obligations with regard to dealing with wear and tear; in this connection the substantial increase in the engineering and electronic content of modern buildings has brought increasing difficulties in determining where obsolescence takes over from dilapidation.

More and more the chosen route through this dilemma has been to arrange for a re-structuring of the lease to permit upgrading to be carried out with the mutual consent of the landlord and tenants with the burden of cost thereof being apportioned by negotiation. An example of how this situation may be dealt with is given in Fig. 2.5.F in Chapter 2.5 - Risk Management.

---

[1] *Pearsall J. & Trumble B. (Editors) (1996) The Oxford English Reference Dictionary, Oxford University Press, Oxford, UK*

Equally, when leases incorporate clauses requiring tenants to pay for reinstatement of any physical deterioration at the end of the lease, only the replacement cost is chargeable, not the extra cost of dealing with obsolescence of specified materials, systems or design. In practice the landlord will in these circumstances agree the cost of making good the lease-end physical deterioration (usually known as 'dilapidation') and require the tenant to put this sum towards a refurbishment or re-construction.

Traditionally, the cost of replacement of buildings in their entirety has been considered to be included in the rent, whereas the replacement of part of the fabric has been by way of sinking funds which are vehicles where an amount of money is set aside annually to pay for replacement of fabric or plant and machinery. The problem with sinking funds has been the tax treatment of the monies, the sheer size of the sums set aside and the increasing pressure from accountants to reduce the overheads liability for sinking funds.

Enforcement of the repairing covenants

The ability of the landlord to insist upon repair of buildings is governed by statute, particularly the Leasehold Property Repair Act 1938 and the Landlord and Tenant Act 1927. Current health and safety legislation clearly impinges on the rights and obligations of landlord and tenant in this respect; for example, employers are responsible for ensuring that they have established procedures for risk assessment and health and safety management systems (see Chapter 8.2 for key health and safety legislation). Additionally, the landlord's liability to ensure that the condition of the premises does not fall below defined minimum standards is framed in such legislation as the Defective Premises Act 1957 and the Occupiers' Liability Act 1984.

3.3.2 SERVICE CHARGES

The nature and purpose

The terms under which landlord's works and services will be carried out and paid for are usually specifically stated in the lease. The landlord may carry out the operations in accordance with the terms of the lease and then recover a proportion of the costs from each tenant after submitting an itemised account; this account is called a 'service charge'. It is a distinct cost centre peculiar to leasehold property.

The service charge itself is designed to deal with the annual cost cycle and so address day to day matters, including cleaning and basic repairing (such as the repair of a leaking tap) affecting the common areas, and insurance.

As tenants take shorter and shorter leases there is a growing demand for landlords to take on all building running costs and include them in the rent. The bottom line appears to be that tenants do not want the unknown variables of obsolescence to turn up in service charges or other kinds of payment - they just want to pay one known cost, ie the rent.

When a building is completely let to a sole tenant, eg as in a sale-and-leaseback arrangement - investors sometimes allow the tenant to take responsibility for the asset management; however, they normally keep strict control over what is, and is not, done and maintain rights to intervene and execute the operations themselves in the event of any default by the tenant.

Formal service charges are perhaps the most complex part of leasing arrangements and can present the unwary facilities manager with the greatest risk of mishap. The cost centres within service charges are just as applicable to owner occupiers as they will require similar services, albeit often presented differently in the annual accounts. The future impact of service charges should not be forgotten during a sale-and-leaseback transactions.

What can and cannot be charged through the service charge is determined by both statute and the wording of the legal documentation. The conditions in the legal documentation are often hidden in schedules at the end of the lease. Incorrect apportionment or over-charging is not uncommon and if facilities managers understand what the service charge comprises and apply the same level of vigorous cost analysis as they do to the rest of their cost centres, then savings can potentially be made following approaches to the landlord.

The content of service charges

The service charge will contain the costs of all works carried out by the landlord (including additional expenditure on management, insurances, sinking fund provision and other overheads) in accordance with the terms of the lease.

In some cases the service charge can also incorporate - sometimes by ex-contractual agreement - such items as general office cleaning, lighting and other 'workplace' services, which tenants wish to delegate to the landlords, their agents and contractors.

Without doubt this is the single most complicated cost centre of the premises budget. First, the content of the charge is so significantly variable as to render straight inter-building comparisons virtually meaningless. Second, the level of expenditure is normally outside of the control of the tenant. Third, the legal framework surrounding rights and liabilities of landlord and tenant is a complex of legislation and case law. Fourth, there are some national taxation considerations which mitigate against some aspects of service charges.

Key financial issues

Probably the most significant feature of service charges is the ratio to the rental level. Charges will not vary widely on a cost per sq m basis whereas rental levels are normally much higher in city centres than in provincial locations.

Fig. 3.3.A
Relationship between service charges and rental levels - city centre and provincial office buildings

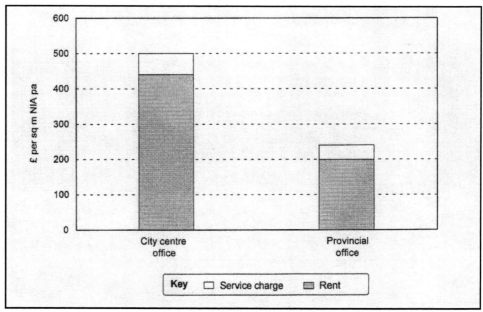

Service charge levels are therefore much more cost-sensitive in low-rental areas than in high-rental areas as indicated in Fig. 3.3.A.

Such is the under-development of the science of premises cost control that few facilities managers have a clear idea of whether they are paying the right price for the services provided by their landlord. It is still common for facilities managers to fail to take account of items of maintenance, cleaning, fuel and the like masked by the title 'service charge' when attempting to compare their cost centres to published data. Equally, they can render such data useless when they do not unscramble service charges from other information they have provided in response to questionnaires.

The facilities manager must pay particular attention to the following issues when addressing the liability to pay a service charge:

- the extent to which the service offered (and performed) safeguards the financial and environmental interests of the tenant

- the total financial implications of the service contract

- the tenant's rights of enforcement in terms of performance and price

- the apportionment of the charge between tenants in a multi-tenanted building

- the relationship of the service charge to the total cost of operating the premises

- taxation on the landlord in respect of sums received from the tenant

- any obligation on the landlord to hold monies in trust for the benefit of the tenants

- following insurance payments for reinstatement after damage, any new works covered by the service charge.

Scope of the service contract

As a general principle, the landlord is only obliged to provide the services specifically stipulated in the lease - and there are nearly as many one-off clauses as there are buildings to let. The lease is normally framed in one of two ways.

The first involves landlords making very wide-ranging covenants including provision and maintenance of future services which are not definitely known to be required - such as, say, the local area network. They are then empowered to levy a service charge in respect of work carried out in performance of the covenants.

The second method is more detailed, listing the likely heads of expenditure against which service charges can be levied. This means that the landlord is only covenanted in respect of the headings listed, although they may be empowered, by a 'landlord's discretion' clause, to do a lot more than the covenant obliges.

The form of words in the lease will have a significant bearing on the rights, duties and liabilities of the parties and this aspect is further discussed below.

The headings under which expenditure is incurred closely follow the cost centres of a tenant's own operating costs - for example, maintenance, alterations, cleaning, security and reception, utilities, general management, insurance and reserve/sinking fund.

The landlord should be able to recover from the tenant, either by way of the service charge or an appropriate level of rent, the reasonable cost of carrying out the landlord's obligations under the lease. There are, however, question marks over certain costs where legal advice is sometimes needed.

Particularly contentious areas are:

- taxation

- interest - on money borrowed to meet expenditure where a shortfall of reserve funds exists

- management fees charged for landlord's personal activities in the field

- replacement, as opposed to repair of components

- where there are replacements, any improvements which may be affected.

As to the question of 'reasonableness', legislation and common law duty of care may impinge upon contractual terms in determining the scope of the service.

3.3.3 COST LEVELS

Perhaps the commonest area of misconception in considering operating cost levels is to assume that the level of the service charge expenditure in any one building - or group of buildings - can be viewed in isolation from the total operating costs of the premises. In making external comparisons of buildings there are also countless variables influencing both the total operating cost level and the proportion of it taken by the service charge:

- scope of the service
- quality of the building
- building design
- operability
- general management costs.

The scope of the service is dictated by the terms of the lease and any independently negotiated extensions or exclusions. This means that, for example, the landlord's cleaning contract may extend to the 'demised areas' or power and/or lighting may or may not be separately metered as between common parts and the individual tenanted areas. The proportion of common areas and the nature of the fabric will also greatly vary the scope of such items as general cleaning, window cleaning, fabric repairs and external decorations.

The quality of the building will also dictate both the amount of services required to operate it and the standards to be achieved in each cost centre. For instance, marble-clad buildings should require less external cleaning than, say, precast concrete panels - but it is also likely to be very important that the marble be kept in peak condition because of the aspirations of tenant and landlord alike. High quality of specification will normally demand high quality of maintenance, regardless of inherently cost-saving characteristics of materials and design.

Design, that somewhat amorphous ingredient of the building's character, embraces quality as well as specification, style, size, shape and 'operability'.

Operability - a piece of jargon coined to cover the inherent capacity of the building to be operated efficiently and economically - for example, are the lift doors wide enough, and the storage areas large enough to facilitate the access of the big, modern, cleaning machines so essential to fast, efficient cleaning operations?

General management costs in the service charge will normally cover the fees paid to managing agents - sometimes embracing the collection of rents - as well as their auditors', accountants' and surveyors' fees. Note that time spent by the landlord in person is not normally recoverable unless it is charged as fees via a separate firm employing their services for the purpose of administration.

The calibre of general management will have a marked effect on the total level of service charge, although variations above and below the norm may each be caused as much by diligence as by neglect. Regular and thoroughly planned maintenance - as opposed to crisis management - may lead to higher charges; but so can irregular maintenance procured in the profligate manner. Landlords have a duty to exercise their obligations to the letter of the lease and may have an implied responsibility to carry out - or have an agent carry out - the necessary functions in a proper and efficient manner. This includes cost control!

Cost levels of service charges are mainly influenced by:

- historic factors
- inflation
- location
- air-conditioning.

Historic factors such as performance by the general manager in looking after the works covered by the service agreement will bear largely on the frequency and cost level of future operating expenditure. Buildings over 20 years old are especially liable to sudden bouts of economic outpouring due to inadequate maintenance or deferred improvements. With new technology such an important feature of the facilities manager's daily problems, even buildings just a few years old can be found wanting in many (expensive) respects - such as flexibility of communications and capacity of services.

Inflation is variable from one cost centre to another. Note that out-sourced contract prices will be more closely geared to the market conditions than direct operations which more closely follow labour-and-material inflation; however, over a period of three years or more any divergencies will be naturally adjusted as, for example, direct labour is 'poached' by contractors in a very active market, forcing up in-house basic rates.

Location impinges on general cost levels in two ways. On the one hand, original cost level and local market conditions vary the base price of certain specific operations from one place to another. At the same time the quality of buildings and the aspirations of the parties to a lease also vary substantially across each country.

Not only are premises operating standards usually higher in, say, the capital cities than in the provincial centres, but also certain cost centres such as 'security' and 'housekeeping' appear as more identifiable cost centres in their own right the more prestigious the building.

Prestige normally goes with location; there are, of course, many out-of-town headquarters buildings, but these are usually owner-occupied and not subject to separate service charges (although the costs are still incurred directly).

Air-conditioning affects the level of service charge in two ways. First, the costs of energy and plant maintenance and replacement are considerably higher than in a non-air-conditioned building. Second, air-conditioned buildings are most usually found in prestigious city centre locations so there tends to be a statistical correlation between air-conditioning and higher quality (and hence more expensive) operating performance and management.

Total service charges analysed during an audit of 100 branch offices of a major financial institution are given at Fig. 3.3.B. The tenancies were mostly between 250 and 500 sq m NIA and there is no distinction in this particular sample between air-conditioned and non-air-conditioned buildings.

However, the figure does show the wide range of costs across the sample, and by showing the service charge in the context of total operating costs in Fig. 3.3.C the danger of looking at service charges in isolation from total operating costs is clearly emphasised.

It is rather easier to forecast the operating costs level, and hence the likely level of service charge, in new buildings, but it must be remembered that the policy for dealing with depreciation and reserve funds will greatly affect whether future service charges grow faster than inflation or start at a higher, most cautious figure which does not catch the tenant out in later years.

Fig. 3.3.B
Service charges - survey of 100 branch offices

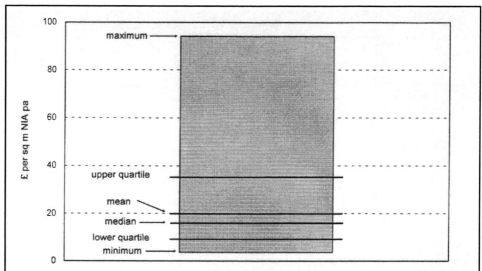

Fig. 3.3.C
Service charges in the context of total operating costs - average of survey of 100 branch offices

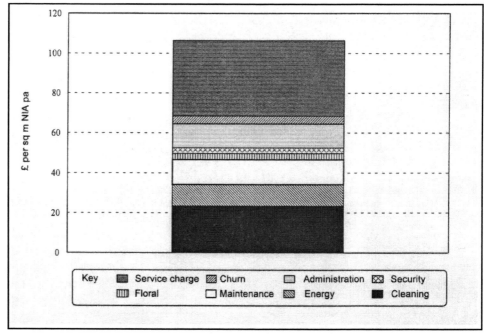

3.3.4 RESERVE FUNDS AND SINKING FUNDS

Although these two funds sound alike, their effect on the level of service charge is markedly different.

The reserve fund is sometimes set up under the lease to make sure there is normally some money available to meet regularly occurring revenue expenditure, such as decorating the common parts, repairs, modernisations. It is normally a regular contribution, so that the service charge in total equalises out occasionally expected but not totally determined future expenditure.

The sinking fund is usually created to pay for the replacement, from time to time, under capital expenditure, of components such as central heating/air-conditioning plant, lifts and roof coverings which may not actually be needed in the timespan of a particular tenant's occupation of the building, or indeed be in their remit to pay for.

Some leases as a variant of the same theme allow the lessor to claim depreciation on their capital expenditure. Tenants (and owner-occupiers) should be wary of sinking funds set to accumulate too rapidly due to a highish (risk-bearing) interest rate or a too short writing-down period. In the latter connection both tenants and owner-occupiers must distinguish clearly between writing-down rates and periods for tax purposes and realistic replacement programmes. It may be prudent to let the premises budget - including the service charge and sinking funds - stand on its own two feet, regardless of the tax regime presently prevailing. Nevertheless, taxation may be an important matter which should be considered and evaluated.

To summarise, the reserve fund is a way of evening out short-term, regular commitments whereas the sinking fund, if it appears in the service charge, may cover eventualities outside of the tenant's probable occupation period - and sometimes at a penal rate.

Whether the funds are held in trust by the landlord for the benefit of the tenants is a most important point of detail. Stated or implied trust status for the fund may help avoid trouble if the landlord becomes bankrupt but it can cause problems with tax avoidance since payment by the tenant into their own trust fund may not be allowable as an expense.

The more usual way of paying reserve funds and sinking funds is as 'further' or 'additional' rent against future expenditure. No real tax problems lurk here for the tenant. However, the landlord may get caught making an extra profit rent as a result of these receipts not being expended until a future accounting year and they may also get taxed on any interest earned on any deposited reserve.

3.3.5 QUALITY AND TYPE OF WORK

There will be no liability for the tenant to pay for any work of a type which is not included specifically in the lease - for example, unless renewal is covered either specifically or implicitly then it cannot be charged. Obviously, if a repair job would be more expensive or otherwise uneconomical then the parties would be well advised to waive any restrictive wording.

On the matter of repair, in the absence of wording to the contrary in the lease, the duty of the landlord to repair extends only to putting the component back into 'good working order; how it is done is discretionary.

Case law remains, as always, fairly inconsistent on issues such as whether landlords have to do the repair in a reasonably cost effective manner where the lease does not specifically so require. Help may be available to the tenant under statute law, eg the Unfair Contract Terms Act 1977 and the Supply of Goods and Services Act 1982. Nevertheless the safest remedy for the tenant is to try to get a 'reasonable care and skill' clause inserted in the lease at the outset. Whether the landlord will agree to this will probably depend on the national standard, how the market is at the time and how badly the tenant is needed.

3.3.6 DISPUTES

Sometimes clauses in a lease relating to the expenditure incurred and charges levied require an annual certification by surveyors, engineers, architects or accountants. Such certificates cannot be binding and conclusive where they involve interpretation of the contract - such as the definition of repair and scope of covenants, which are a matter of law. Arbitration clauses are common and generally desirable although this may limit the right to refer questions of law to only those prescribed in the Arbitration Act 1996.

3.3.7 APPORTIONMENT OF CHARGES

The lease will sometimes be quite specific as to how the service charge should be split between tenants in a multi-tenanted building with possibly a percentage being expressed or calculable in each of the demised areas.

The percentage will usually be related to floor area or taxable values. It is sometimes, however, left as variable by the landlord or agents, eg 'a fair and reasonable proportion' (watch out for this) and sometimes a fixed percentage is payable. Differential percentages relating to certain heads of expenditure are sometimes given as between one tenancy and another in a building - usually where some tenants have an obviously substantially greater or lesser requirement for the service; parts of the building, for example, which are heated but not air-conditioned may have a differential percentage on energy costs and maintenance and repair of plant. As long as such differentials are fair and are clearly expressed then that is fine - but vagueness can lead to all sorts of niggling disputes with neighbouring tenants as well as with the landlord.

It may be noted that the RICS Code of Measuring Practice recommends the use, as appropriate, of either gross internal area (GIA) or net internal area (NIA) for apportionment of service charges in calculating each occupier's liabilities.

3.4 THE VALUATION PROCESS

Introduction

This chapter looks at the interface between the roles of the facilities manager and the valuer/estates surveyor, examining their respective parts in the valuation process. It also looks at which is the most appropriate valuation consultant to appoint and examines the valuation standards of professional institutions and other bodies, terminology of 'value' and the valuation report or certificate. The theory behind various approaches to the value of bare land or land with useable standing buildings is considered in Chapter 3.5.

The objective is to give the facilities manager sufficient knowledge of valuation practice to be able to ask appropriate questions in order to get the right valuation for the right purpose at the right time and at the right price.

Generally, professional valuers work to the standards of the Royal Institution of Chartered Surveyors but a client organisation may specify otherwise, eg to international standards.

3.4.1 THE ROLE OF THE VALUER/ESTATES SURVEYOR

Professional services

The valuer/estates surveyor is the professional who possesses the necessary qualification, ability and experience to execute a valuation.

The services of such a professional are normally required by facilities managers when considering the conduct of any transaction involving land and buildings. This instruction may range from an individual property/plot of land to a large mixed-use portfolio of land and buildings. The valuer may, for example, be asked to advise the facilities managers on:

- the price that should be asked for or paid for property

- levels of rent to be paid for new premises

- a mortgage loan on the security held or available in advance

- real estate implications of take-overs, mergers, receivership and liquidations

- sale and leaseback

- relocation and development

- insurance valuations

- valuations for property taxation and tax planning

- valuations for balance sheet

- compensation due under legislation for compulsory purchase or adverse planning decisions

- plant and machinery replacement.

Notification of the purpose of the valuation is paramount to the valuer as the valuation of an interest in real estate will vary depending upon the purpose of the valuation. For example, the valuation given for fire insurance purposes can be very different from one for market value. This is because in most cases of fire insurance valuation the buildings only are valued and not the land. However, in a market valuation both are included. Building reinstatement costs can be greater than the market value of the property. This is because there is a general assumption that 'like is replaced with like' which can be expensive in the case of period premises. Chapter 3.7.5 discusses alternative money saving approaches to this general assumption.

It is helpful for the valuer to know also the circumstances of the client so that they can advise whether tax issues arise. Chapters 11.1 to 11.6 take a further look at property taxation issues.

The date of valuation is critical for the valuer. Retrospective or forecast valuations may well produce a different result from a valuation done as at today's date, particularly when calculating capital gains tax, for example, or working in a rising or falling market.

The normal fundamental role of the valuer is to estimate the market value, ie the capital sum or annual rental which, at a particular time, on specified terms and subject to legislation, a particular interest in property may be expected to fetch on the open market.

Professional qualifications

Facilities managers may well question the role of the valuer and consider that this role may well be just as easily filled by an accountant or lawyer.

The European Group of Valuers' Associations (TEGoVA, see Chapter 3.4.5 below for further details on this organisation) defines asset valuers as persons of good repute, who can show that they have:

- obtained an appropriate degree or equivalent professional qualification or postgraduate qualification at a recognised establishment of higher education, have at least two years' postgraduate experience and can show that they have maintained and enhanced their professional knowledge through a relevant programme of continuing education

- sufficient local knowledge and experience in valuing fixed or current assets in the location and category of the asset; or having disclosed an insufficiency to the client, before accepting the assignment, have obtained assistance from a competent and knowledgeable person(s)

- where required, membership of a national professional organisation

- met all legal, regulatory, ethical and contractual requirements related to the assignment

- appropriate professional indemnity insurance cover in relation to the responsibilities incurred on each assignment.

In the UK membership of the Royal Institution of Chartered Surveyors and the Institute of Revenues, Rating and Valuation is generally compatible with these requirements.

Why use a recognised asset valuer?

There are nine primary reasons why retaining an asset valuer who is a member of a professional body may be beneficial:

- imperfections in local and national property markets

- the diversity of land and buildings and the interests which exist on them

- legal variations

- different valuation definitions, assumptions and approaches

- professional standards and practices, eg the RICS Appraisal and Valuation Manual

- professional indemnity insurance

- security of money held in client accounts

- requirements for continuing professional development

- monitored ethical standards.

3.4.2 THE VALUATION CONSULTANT

For a one-off individual premises valuation it is probably better to use a well respected local firm. However, an important question which needs to be discussed is whether in valuations for a wide-spread estate it is more appropriate to use several local practices instructed individually in each location or a national valuation/surveying practice.

For a large national portfolio which contains normal or prestige office blocks, then a national practice may be used as they will have the ability to assimilate and process the data more effectively. Yet if the portfolio is particularly specialised and contains large sections of the portfolio away from the capital city a series of local specialist valuation practices may well be more appropriate. The key is to ensure that all the properties in each location are valued on the same assumptions using an agreed methodology and are in line with national, European Valuation Standards (EVS) or other standards.

3.4.3 RICS APPRAISAL AND VALUATION MANUAL

In carrying out their valuations, the RICS requires its members to follow the mandatory requirements of the RICS Appraisal and Valuation Manual. Where some discretion is allowed the valuer is expected to follow the Manual or indicate good reason for not doing so.

The Manual started as a voluntary 'Red Book' in the 1970s and was made mandatory in the early 1990s. It is now being reviewed to bring it in line with the European Valuation Standards (EVS2000)[1] (see 3.4.5 below)

Generally, the Manual, comprising Practice Statements and Guidance Notes, applies to any valuation which is likely to be in the public domain, eg valuations for company accounts. It is not directly concerned with the valuer's methods of appraisal or valuation (see Chapter 3.5 on Valuation Methodology) as such, but with good practice in the process of valuation. The Manual cover such matters as:

- receipt and acknowledgement of instructions
- definitions, eg open market value, existing use value,
- choice of method
- stages in the valuation
- inputs to the valuation
- form of the valuation report and its requirements
- special requirements of certain organisations, eg insurance companies, property funds and pension funds
- special requirements for specified properties, eg mineral properties
- date of valuation.

In some instances, the Manual indicates the valuer's role in relation to those of directors and others in client organisations.

Where the standards do not apply formally, they can still serve as a 'benchmark' for good practice in relevant areas.

Generally, property may be described as owner-occupied, investment and surplus property. The types or bases of valuation required include: open market value;

---

[1] *TEGoVA, (2000), European Valuation Standards 2000, Fourth Edition, The Estates Gazette, London, UK*

existing use value; open market value having regard to trading potential; alternative use value; and, depreciated replacement cost.

Each of these valuations is defined and will have general and special assumptions and imports. Indeed, additional valuations made on other special assumptions may sometimes be required.

3.4.4 CODE OF MEASURING PRACTICE

The RICS Code of Measuring Practice gives the valuer guidance on measuring buildings for valuation and surveying matters, eg service charge apportionments for tenants.

Following the guide, and taking, recording and publishing accurate measurements, should enable the valuer to comply with the Property Misdescriptions Act 1991.

The Code has credence in such fields as land transfers, town and country planning, estate-agency and property management. It recommends the use of metric measurements and distinguishes a different approach to that of BS8888:2000 (on product description) for the treatment of decimal and thousand markers. The Code also refers to the Standard Method of Measurement of Buildings Work (SMM), ie the Code is distinct from SMM.

3.4.5 EUROPEAN VALUATION STANDARDS (EVS 2000)

Global, European and UK standards tend to change, with a general trend towards convergence. International accounting standards are likely to be accepted in USA and Europe and most other developed regions of the world, within a few years. This will 'impose' a common approach for property reporting in company accounts. Thus, the moves towards both international and pan-European accounting standards (encouraged by the increasing number of EU Council Directives) is highlighting the need for 'a benchmark against which consistent and coherent reports can be prepared for clients, compatible with international practice and international accounting and valuation standards, as well as European law.'

During the 1980's it became apparent that there was a need for some consistency in world-wide valuation standards as businesses began to be more global in their perspective. The International Valuation Standards Committee (IVSC) was formed by UK and USA valuation specialists to oversee the establishment of global valuation standards. Those companies who were seeking listing on international stock exchanges could now use a uniform valuation standard world wide.

TEGoVA, mentioned earlier, was formed in 1977 and its members have worked together to produce a series of valuations standards, known as the "Guide Bleu". These standards have now been accepted across Europe and have been published in thirteen languages.

For EVS to be effective they need to be underpinned by regulated standards of professional conduct, ethical codes, compliance requirements and/or state laws.

Valuation bodies' codes and practices set standards of:

- independent, unbiased advice
- minimum acceptable levels of competence
- use of appropriate valuation methods
- accurate and clear reporting

- professional attitude between members
- compliance with national laws.[2]

The EVS 2000 provide the framework which most valuers working Europe-wide adopt, albeit that they are subject to local variations. These standards are designed to cover situations of public record and interest, particularly where publication is involved. As they record good practice they are also recommended for adoption where high standards and consistency are of the essence, in respect of valuations for a variety of purposes outside the public domain. (Currently, the standards are being reviewed with the next revision coming out in 2003.) However, they are not designed to deal with the position as it relates to matters which are extensively covered by national legislation, or jurisprudence. Thus, valuations for fiscal purposes and compulsory acquisition are not the subject matter of EVS 2000. The general principles may however be applied where no other specific guidance exists.[3] Different interpretations may be placed on the date of valuation and definition of market value. Generally, the EVS2000 and the RICS Manual are 'good benchmarks' for practitioners.

Where comparables, ie references to valuations of other, similar premises, are used, adjustments are needed to reflect that, as "transaction prices", they may have been established under different conditions.

3.4.6 SOME NUANCES OF THE TERM 'VALUE'

Generally the value of a property will depend upon the use to which the asset can or has been put. On the market it will have one value whereas in its present or 'existing' use to the owner or occupier it will have another; it may have yet another if it is assumed that the site can be developed with buildings for a different use. Which is the most appropriate definition of value to be used should be determined before formally instructing the valuer who may, however, give preliminary advice as to the advantages and disadvantages of the various approaches in the particular circumstances.

Article 49(2) of the European Council Directive, refers to the 'Market Value definition' (known as the EU definition) as:

> "the price at which land and buildings could be either sold under private contract between a willing seller and an arm's-length buyer on the date of valuation, it being assumed that the property is publicly exposed to the market, that market conditions permit orderly disposal and that a normal period having regard to the nature of the property, is available for the negotiation of the sale."[4]

However, this definition is taken as a starting point and it has been amplified by TEGoVA and the IVSC where many organisations have come together in agreeing the definitions and fundamentals that are attributable to valuation methodology and practice.[5]

The approved IVSC/TEGoVA Market Value definition which is the market norm is:

> "...the estimated amount for which an asset should exchange on the date of valuation between a willing buyer and a willing seller in an arm's-length transaction after proper marketing wherein the parties had each acted knowledgeably, prudently and without compulsion. (Note 'date of valuation' is the date at which the property is deemed to be sold)."

---

[2] *David Mackmin, (1999), "Valuation of Real Estate in Global Markets", Property Management, Vol 17, No 4, MCB University Press, UK*

[3] *Mackmin*

[4] *91/674/EEC*

[5] *IVSC (2000), International Valuation Standards 2000, International Valuation Standards Committee, London, UK*

The approved IVSC/TEGoVA definition for Market Value for Existing Use and market norm is:

*"...the estimated amount for which an asset should exchange on the date of valuation, **based on continuation of its existing use, but assuming the asset is unoccupied**, between a willing buyer and a willing seller in an arm's-length transaction after proper marketing wherein the parties had each acted knowledgeably, prudently and without compulsion."*

The bold wording above identifies the differences in the definitions of 'Market Value' and 'Market Value for Existing Use'.

3.4.7 THE VALUATION CERTIFICATE OR REPORT

The EVS 2000 for certificates is that:

"The valuation certificate by its layout and language must provide clear unequivocal opinion with sufficient detail to ensure all key areas are covered and that no misunderstanding of the real situation of the asset(s) can be misconstrued."

Exactly what is contained in the valuation report or certificate will be determined by the standards to which it relates, ie EU, international or national, and to the location and the nature of the property. However, TEGoVA have established pan-European common practice. It should be noted that the specifics and emphasis will vary between properties and it is important that when facilities managers instruct or read valuation reports or certificates they are very clear about exactly what the instructions were.

For commercial properties valuation reports typically include:

- the instruction, the client, the purpose of the valuation, the date of valuation and any special assumptions and/or restricting conditions

- the basis of the valuation, including type and definition of value

- details of any local firms used to support the organising firm; it may be necessary to provide assurance to the firm that local valuers have complied with the relevant local or international standards

- origin of information such as inspection of official sources, maps, special information from the client, observations from inspection

- property description, owner, tenure, easements and other legal regulations, location, building and development controls in the locality, building descriptions, state of repair, different types of lettable areas, vacancies and valuer's opinions, comments on the location and the property

- details of any plant, machinery and equipment included

- property related economic data, leasing contracts, actual passing rents, rent losses, operating expenses, taxes, assessed value, loans, interests rack or estimated rental value for the property

- cash-flow analysis to illustrate the net operating income before and after debt service over a calculation period and with assumptions concerning inflation, rent and cost of development, vacancies and discount rate

- description of valuation procedure identifying the exact method used and why

- an explanation as to why there has been any deviation from the UK's usual practice and regulatory code and a note of compliance to European Valuation Standards, if relevant

- valuations should be divided, as may be prescribed, into a uniform series of property categories

- a specific reference should be made as to whether any allowance has been made for any taxation legislation

- estimation of market value from direct sales or letting comparables by using defined data in different valuation approaches namely the direct area method (price per sq m), investment method, gross multiplier, related to assessed value, other appropriate methods depending on property

- sensitivity analysis to illustrate uncertainty and risk

- final value estimate including a summary of final value, any rent free periods or vacancies, key figures, limiting factors, appendices, maps, photos, legal data, economic and demographic reports, comparable rental and sales transactions

- any other matters relevant to the valuation.

A more detailed list can be found in GN7.54 EVS 2000.

3.4.8 DISPUTE RESOLUTION

Differences or disputes

Differences arise in many aspects of valuation and estates work, including:

- the level of open market value or rental value for a property

- interpretation of a clause in a lease (or other contract) or a section in an Act

- the estimated cost of works which are actually or notionally (for a valuation) needed.

Such differences are usually settled amicably by the parties in discussion or negotiation between them or their professional advisers. If not, the difference in dispute must be resolved in some other way. Generally, disputes are resolved in one of the following ways:

- if free to do so, the parties (or one of them) may 'walk away', eg in property purchase, private treaty negotiations are unsuccesful

- where a previously agreed means of dispute resolution is provided and it can be invoked, either mutually or unilaterally, eg arbitration is provided under a contract between the parties

- where a statutory means of resolving the dispute is available, eg the Lands Tribunal

- where no means of resolution are specifically provided, the parties agree to avail or submit to a third party resolution

The facilities manager involved in drawing up agreements or contracts with professional advisors, suppliers, landlords and tenants, building contractors and others needs to consider the best form of dispute resolution for the kind of business concerned.

Courts and tribunals may be considered the highest, and perhaps most expensive form of dispute resolution. However, other generic forms include:

- **'official' appointees:** eg ombudsmen for banking, insurance, estate agency

- **self-regulatory professional bodies' procedures:** eg the RICS complaints panel and the Law Society's complaints office

- **other approaches:** eg arbitration, mediation, advocacy and independent professional expert

Criteria for selection

Criteria for selection might include:

- statutory requirements: the law may specify the approach to be adopted
- place of jurisdiction
- availability
- degree of confidentiality
- duration of proceedings from start to finish
- costs and cost limitation procedures
- scope and enforceability of any award.

Disputes on a professional's conduct

Generally, from the client's or other's viewpoint, a valuer's unsatisfactory conduct of valuation matters can be divided into two, namely:

- cases of negligence - leading to actions in law (contract or tort)
- cases of inadequate conduct - leading to complaints procedures

Briefly, in cases of negligence, the professional's conduct must be shown to have been less than that of the competent general practitioner or the competent specialist practitioner (if of that ilk). Also, that the client (or other person) is owed a duty of care and that person has suffered loss.

Briefly, in cases of inadequate conduct, the complainant may need to complain to the valuer's firm, following their complaint procedure. If redress is not obtained, a complaint under the RICS's complaints scheme may be pursued (provided the valuer is a member). The scheme provides for the remission of fees and compensation.

Valuation matters

Disputes between two parties in valuation matters are settled in many different ways. Figure 3.4.A sets those which relate to aspects of property and valuations touched upon in this volume, eg taxation, business rates, landlord and tenant.

Fig. 3.4.A
Some methods of dispute resolution

Type of dispute	Method of resolution
• Compulsory purchase and planning compensation	• Lands Tribunal
• Taxation - valuation	• Lands Tribunal
• Rating • Council tax	• Valuation Tribunal hence Lands Tribunal
• Modification and discharge of restrictive covenants	• Lands Tribunal
• Landlord and tenant 　• Rent reviews 　• Lease renewal	• Independent expert • Professional Arbitration on Court Terms (PACT) • Arbitration • High Court
• Other disputes	Where no method is provided, the parties may agree an approach, eg 　• Mediation 　• Advocacy 　• Independent expert 　• Arbitration
• Complaints by clients	• Firms complaints procedure • Ombudsman for sector (if any) • professional body (if any)

Most disputes are settled by negotiation between the parties. Generally, for statutory valuations the statute provides for the method of dispute resolution in cases where negotiation fails, eg the Lands Tribunal has a wide jurisdiction. Between a landlord and a tenant, the lease normally provides for the method of dispute resolution, eg arbitration.

3.5 VALUATION METHODOLOGY

Introduction

A general understanding of the concepts, theory and techniques behind valuations should enable the facilities manager to be able to assess the validity of valuations presented to them. Should valuations be presented which are either less or more than the value expected then facilities managers should have sufficient understanding of the processes involved to challenge them intelligently.

An overvalued property or portfolio can result in excessive gearing and an undervalued portfolio may leave the company exposed to take-over or merger bids. It is unlikely however that a valuation will be varied by more then 10%, unless the valuers make a technical or calculation error. For example, during one valuation one of the surveyors in a team had a new calculator and was using it incorrectly, so when he came to convert valuations to sterling he significantly altered the valuation of the portfolio. The mistake was not picked up in-house and the client, an oil company, noticed that the valuations were not at the expected level; when checked they were found to be inaccurate and the valuation was changed.

During the course of this chapter the five traditional approaches to valuation will be examined along with valuation reconciliation, methodology for the valuation of leaseholds, premiums, surrenders, reverse premiums and surrenders, sale and leaseback and private finance initiatives.

3.5.1 APPROACHES TO VALUATION

The valuer has a repertoire of five traditional, basic approaches to valuation. The use of an approach will depend upon the type of property and other factors, eg the interest in land.

The approaches are:

- **direct comparison** of capital or rental values with other 'comparable' properties

- **investment method**, used to reflect property investment values

- **residual valuation** used for development situations, actual or assumed

- **'profits' method** to derive rental value, used for unusual trading properties, eg a restaurant or a leisure centre

- **cost basis**, used for unique properties not normally sold on the open market, eg a church or a library. (Also, see Chapter 3.8 for the DRC approach.)

Generally the valuer will use the "RICS Code of measuring practice: A guide for surveyors and valuers" in appraising property.

3.5.2 DIRECT COMPARISON METHOD

The direct comparison method of capital or rental values looks at the existing use of a property and compares it to the prices achieved in other transactions of similar properties in a similar location and of a similar nature. Freeholds are often compared on a price per square metre to enable a realistic comparison to take place. This method of valuation works well where there is a good exchange of data on prices paid for premises sold or let. Valuation by direct comparison can be difficult where there is insufficient reliable data upon which to base valuations; in these instances the valuer's own market knowledge and experience is relied upon. Here it may be appropriate for valuers to check their initial results by the use of other methods.

3.5.3 INVESTMENT METHOD

The investment method of valuation is a derivative of the direct sales comparison approach in that comparisons are made of the two elements - rent and yields - and then further analysis is undertaken.

The rental level

The level of rent is either the passing rent, ie what is currently being paid under a lease (but not necessarily the market level to be reviewed at some point in the future) or a prediction of what a tenant might be prepared to pay at the date of the valuation, for a term of years in occupation of the premises.

The valuer's appraisal of rental comparables will have regard to many critical factors including:

- location - especially 'prime' or 'secondary' status, access to public transport, motorways

- quality of design and construction - including methods of environmental control, special features, improvements made by the tenant

- lease terms - especially indexation provisions, treatment of outgoings, rent review periods, term of years, covenants and break clauses

- current supply and demand for similar property.

Factors affecting yields

The yield is the total return on the capital investment. Therefore, the decision that investors will make regarding the appropriate percentage return from their investment in a rented, (or rentable) absolute in possession property is governed by a highly complex set of factors, such as:

- the length of lease and remaining period

- rental growth forecasts

- the 'covenant' of the tenants (will they be able to pay their rent through time)

- the frequency and conditions of rent reviews/indexation

- comparative impact of inflation on alternative forms of investment

- comparative returns/risks from other forms of investment

- the likelihood of any 'voids' in the income stream, eg rent-free and 'empty' periods

- the quality of the property

- depreciation - current and predicted

- future costs of demolition, refurbishment and replacement

- the liquidity of capital invested

- the amount of capital available and opportunities to invest.

Investment value calculations

The following example explains the arithmetical basis of an investment valuation.

An absolute in possession property let at the market rent of £100,000 per annum net might fetch £1m at auction. Once it has been established that there is no likelihood of additional development value, an analysis of the transaction would show that the purchaser was seeking a 10% initial return (or yield on capital):

$$\frac{£100,000}{£1,000,000} \times \frac{100}{1} = 10\%$$

Analysis of like transactions in similar and other kinds of property would be undertaken to establish a pattern of 'historic' yields. Of course, the valuer will be making judgements about the factors affecting the pattern in the market and may have to make adjustments as part of the overall analysis.

The concept of return on capital of absolute in possession property let at full rent gives

$$\frac{\text{Rent}}{\text{Capital Value}} \quad \text{x} \quad \frac{100}{1} \quad = \quad \text{Yield \%}$$

or

$$\frac{\text{Rent x 100}}{\text{Yield}} \quad = \quad \text{Capital Value}$$

This is usually expressed as 'Rent x Years Purchase (see below) = Capital Value' and is the equation for valuing in freehold investments.

At any time during the course of the lease (or the life of a freehold property) the passing rent and terms may no longer reflect the then current full rental value. The traditional investment method of valuation has therefore developed with techniques which reflect 'term and reversion', ie the length of tenure and the potential for re-letting at the end of the period; this applies to both freeholds and leasehold tenures. Such techniques sometimes reflect 'single' rate or 'dual' rate 'years purchase' (see Figs. 3.5.E/F).

The 'Years Purchase' multiplier

The reciprocal of the initial yield is commonly known as the 'years purchase in perpetuity'. This term is really a misnomer since, although the factor manifests itself as a multiplier of the annual rent (which is where the phrase 'Years Purchase' comes from), it does not in fact derive from a period of time but from the return sought by a real estate investor from their capital invested in an income-producing property (as described above).

In the example above it can be seen that the investor has used a multiplier of ten times the annual rent in deciding what the investment is worth. In other words how much should they to pay for the right to receive that rental income in perpetuity from that tenant under those conditions in that building in that location etc for that length of time. This multiplier is the 'years purchase in perpetuity' and is calculated simply by taking the reciprocal of the investment yield percentage.

So, in the above example:

$$\frac{100}{10} = 10 \text{ YP}$$

If the return were 8% the reciprocal would be:

$$\frac{100}{8} = 12.5 \text{ YP and so on.}$$

Fig. 3.5.A illustrates graphically how the Years Purchase multiplier relates to the initial yield.

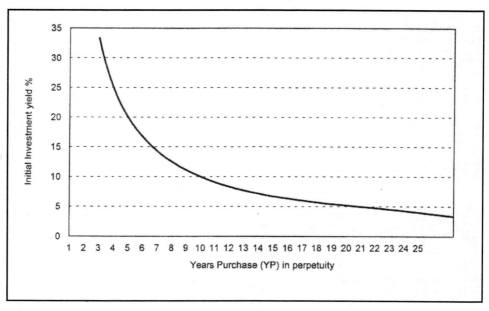

Fig. 3.5.A
Graphic relationship between initial yield and years purchase in perpetuity

Single and dual rate multipliers

Historically valuers adjusted the yield by allowing for a 'sinking fund' to provide for building costs on demolition or refurbishment. The sinking fund (described in more detail in 3.5.8. below) is a theoretical sum of money set aside at regular intervals; at a low (risk-free) interest rate it will accumulate by the end of the period to fund the rebuilding or refurbishment costs. Today however, most investors valuing an absolute in possession interest will apply only the remunerative rate (ie the interest-bearing rate) reflecting the fact that:

- it will not be necessary to replace the capital - as opposed to the purchase of a leasehold

- replacement or refurbishment of any building will be many years hence

- the low risk makes it reasonable to consider that the theoretical sinking fund for such works can be supported out of income at the remunerative rate.

As described the income is assumed to be received in perpetuity. In essence the underlying principle is that of discounting future income at a given or assumed rate of interest. In this instance the income of £100,000 per annum is assumed to be received at the end of every future year for ever, and it is discounted at 10%. In symbols one has

$$\text{YP perpetuity @ R\%} = \frac{1}{(1+i)} + \frac{1}{(1+i)^2} + \frac{1}{(1+i)^3} + ... + \frac{1}{(1+i)^n} + ... + \frac{1}{(1+i)^\infty}$$

$$= \frac{1}{i}$$

Where R = the interest earned by £100 (yield)

and $i = \dfrac{R}{100}$

also $\dfrac{1}{(1+i)^n}$ = the present value of £1 in n years @ R%.

In practice valuers may use discounting which allows for quarterly receipts of rent in advance (rather than one year in arrears). Also, the yield 'R%' is known as the 'all-risk' yield and, in theory at least, reflects obsolescence of the building among many other factors.

An example of the valuation of a freehold using a yield of 6% is demonstrated in Fig. 3.5.B.

Fig. 3.5.B
Valuation of a freehold

Rentable area NIA sq m	Annual rent per sq m NIA £ pa	Annual rent £	Years purchase in perpetuity	Capital value of freehold property £
5,000 x	300* =	1,500,000 x	(1/0.06) 16.667 YP** =	SAY 25,000,000***

*   If required any costs of managing the investment may be deducted at this point
** This figure is available direct from the valuation tables
*** This figure does not include any deduction for purchaser's cost of acquisition (stamp duty, legal and agents fees)

Inflation and the investment yield

The underlying principles of investment in income-bearing property are diametrically opposed to fixed interest investment in gilts/bonds (although significantly influenced by their coupon levels).

Whereas government stocks bear the same rate per annum for the life of the issue - say 15 or 25 years - and are redeemable at cost on expiry of the period. Commercial property will bear a fixed return until the first indexation or rent review (say five years) and a higher (inflated) return for the next period.

Company share values rise and fall with the market but usually increase annually with inflation thereby increasing annually the percentage return on the initial investment. A successful company, like a successful property, will out-perform the market thereby not only 'hedging' against inflation but also generating a capital profit over and above inflation.

Prime shops and offices, like financially stable established companies, command initial yields lower than the average. This is good for their shareholders, not bad, because the initial yield reflects the market-place view of an acceptable return at a moment in time; so the prospective purchaser viewing an ordinary share as a 4% investment (anticipating good future growth) will pay 25 times the earnings per share for the privilege of owning it. In the case of investment property the earnings are the rental income which gets adjusted, usually upward, at the rent reviews. However, commercial company dividends vary (hopefully upwards) annually depending on efficiency and market forces in their line of business.

Gilts or bonds on the other hand, deliver only the investment yield promised on the 'coupon'. Inflation reduces the value of the non-variable income stream and also the value of the capital investment when recovered at the end of the term. When interest rates are high gilts/bonds offer high returns making low initial property and equity yields look poor; the latter then usually rise as capitalisation factors (eg YP) drop causing loss of value (the drop frequently fuelled by the poor economic conditions of which high interest rates are often both a symptom and an applied remedy). However, in good economic times, the growth in property and equities will justify low initial yields, by comparison with high-yielding fixed interest investment, especially when the future income from the latter is discounted to present worth (see Chapter 10.6.3). Discounting of course needs to be applied to future rental increases.

The equated yield

The concept of the 'equated yield' is that the pattern of rent reviews and future growth can be isolated from the other factors influencing the 'all risks' initial yield discussed above. As such the 'equated yield' takes into account assumptions of growth rates and the rent review cycle which triggers the growth, and produces a yield which is directly comparable with fixed interest securities - as well as with other options available for property investment.

Tables of equated yields are available covering a wide range of initial yields, indexation/rent review periods and growth rates and provide an extremely useful tool for investment comparison and also sensitivity analysis on each of the factors.

Refinements of these investment valuation techniques

Sensitivity analysis of investments is where a number of calculations are carried out in respect of a financial appraisal or forecast using one or more variables, eg alternative assumptions for future changes in the yield rates and rack rental levels, to see how they change the result of the investment valuation.

Another modern investment appraisal technique which is frequently used, is discounted cash flow analysis (DCF). This is a technique used in investment and development appraisal whereby future inflows and outflows of cash associated with a particular project are expressed in present-day terms by discounting. The technique is explained in detail in Chapter 10.6.3.

The two most widely used forms of DCF are the internal rate of return (IRR) and the net present value (NPV). This method allows the valuer to discount more precisely calculated cash flows, which include growth of rents, buildings with limited lives, taxation, repair improvements and other real time factors.

3.5.4 THE RESIDUAL METHOD

The residual method of valuation is discussed fully in Chapter 10.3. Its principal application is to determine the value of development land involving either re-development or refurbishment. Generally speaking professional property developers will use this technique alone because it reflects 'affordability' in the context of their own proposals and business criteria.

The residual approach ranges from the basic assessment of the site value based upon a deduction of development costs from the gross development value to a detailed assessment of the cash flow throughout the entire duration of the cash flow. There is no common market practice in this area, but some examples of how this may happen occur in Chapter 10.3.1.

Independent valuations of development land will usually attempt to draw upon comparables using theoretical residual valuations as a safety check - probably showing sensitivity analysis around the value of the many dynamic variables.

3.5.5 THE PROFITS METHOD

The 'profits' method of valuing land and buildings is used where no income stream can be directly attributed to the land or buildings thereon, ie where premises have been particularly designed or adapted for a specific use and it is this speciality which produces or has the potential to produce a business income. Properties in this category are usually so specialised in terms of location and features that the direct comparison method is not appropriate.

The principle is that the valuer, having established the overall profitability of the business, makes deductions from net trading profit, ie for remuneration, risk and the profit share (of the proprietor); this leaves the rental value which is then capitalised at an appropriate YP.

Properties which are usually valued using the profits method are hotels, public houses, cinemas, theatres, bingo clubs, gaming clubs, petrol-filling stations, licensed betting offices and specialised leisure and sporting facilities. Also included in this category are theme parks, holiday complexes and leisure centres. The level of care taken over the preparation of these valuations varies widely from where only an estimated multiplier is placed on the gross income to the more sophisticated detailed examination of accounts.

The basis of the profits method is an estimate of the gross turnover of the business varied to take account of any possible variances which might apply if there were another operator. This estimate is assessed from the actual business accounts and the valuer's expertise in determining how efficiently the business is being operated. The net profits are then assessed and it can be split between a notional rental payment and risk and profit for running the business.

Fig. 3.5.C is an example of a profits valuation of a restaurant which has had an average turnover of approximately £900,000 pa over the last three years and average expenses of £500,000 pa. Taxation, depreciation, owners' drawings, property loan servicing expenses and the like are excluded.

Fig. 3.5.C
Profits-based valuation of a freehold restaurant building

Assessment of rental value	£
Gross turnover (less sales tax and stock adjustment)	900,000
Expenditure (average of say three years, adjusted) (excludes any actual rent)	(500,000)
Net trading profit	400,000
Business share 60%	(240,000)
Rental value 40%	160,000
Assessment of capital values	
Value of goodwill attached to the premises @: say 33.3% ROI = 100/33.3 x £ 160,000* =	480,000
Property value: YP in perpetuity @ say 10% = 100/10 x £ 160,000** =	1,600,000
Total value of assets (ex cluding furniture and fittings)	2,080,000
* business share ** rental value	

The multiplier of three chosen in Fig. 3.5.C reflects the market's interpretation of the 'unique sales contribution' or goodwill that the property adds to the business as distinct from the actual operator or conventional property market considerations. Such contribution would be use-specific and might be attributable to a unique location, or design or both (but note that a 'normal' location and design would be reflected in the 10% property yield).

The apportionment rent:profits in the ratio of approximately 1:1.5 (40% - 60%) in the example is founded on data concerning ratios (1:1) of premises and profits to turnover such as depicted in Fig. 1.1.E in Chapter 1.1.5; remember, of course, that rent is only a part of the total cost of 'premises' (say 3.5% of turnover). The actual ratio is therefore 3.5% to (5 + 3.5)% ie 0.4 which is the same as 1:1.5.

3.5.6 VALUATIONS BASED UPON COST

Sometimes, when open market transactions are not available or are conflicting, valuers will use the 'cost-based' valuation as a double check on the figures they are proposing. The term describes a simple process of building up the total cost of a development on a 'green-field' or 'brown-field' site (as appropriate) as it would stand in the developer's books on completion of the project.

Fig. 3.5.D is an illustration of such a calculation, the detailed principles of which are fully explained in Chapter 10.3.1; the process of 'residual valuation' described in that chapter derives from exactly the same kinds of cost centres and figures as are used here, but leaving either the land, the building cost or the profit to be calculated as a residual within the equation by deduction from the estimated open market value of the building on completion.

Fig. 3.5.D
Valuation based on cost

Item	£
Land price	1,200,000
Land acquisition fees and costs say	60,000
Finance on land etc for 1 year at say 10%	126,000
Building site and development costs: 2,000 sq m GIA at say £ 1,200 per sq m	2,400,000
Fees and finance charges on buildings etc	360,000
Total expenditure	4,146,000
Developers margin for overheads, profit and risk: say 15%	621,900
Cost valuation	4,767,900
SAY	**4,800,000**

There are some properties which are rarely if ever traded in the market place because of their inherent specialised characteristics and do not in themselves make a profit but form part of a larger manufacturing process, or utility which makes a profit or notional profit. In these instances the valuers revert to basing their assessment on the basis of acquiring the land and constructing the buildings separately.

The method can also be used for tax assessments, insurance purposes (see Chapter 3.7.5), reconstruction value, depreciated reconstruction cost, and depreciation for accidents including fires. In the latter cases the cost approach to value is not related to either demand/supply conditions of the market or the situation of the property.

3.5.7 RECONCILIATION

Valuers usually try to use more than one method of property valuation to estimate the value of property. They then stand back from their valuation methodology and ask themselves if this value is appropriate for the property. It is this element which constitutes the true professional valuer's skill and it would be normal for valuers to check their judgement at this stage with colleagues. Once a final reconciliation of all the data is made a valuation of the property is able to be undertaken; this valuation may not always be fully explainable in light of technical correctness, but valuation is, after all, usually considered as being an art rather than a science. Nevertheless, valuers should have addressed all the technical issues to the best of their ability before introducing any element of subjective judgement.

3.5.8 VALUATION OF LEASEHOLDS

The organisation buying a leasehold building for its own occupation will need to establish the market value using the same techniques as an institutional investor would when purchasing the building leased to the organisation for the same period. For instance, as well as setting aside a notional fund to replace the original capital investment (ie a sinking fund) they must also take into account that, should they vacate the premises, there may well be an extensive 'void' period before a new tenant can be found.

Although business judgements may overlay the level of their bid, in a competitive situation the owner/occupier must always have regard to the balance sheet and liquidity implications of turning cash into property or, at least, accepting liability for a commercial mortgage.

Fig. 3.5.E shows how the valuation of the leasehold for 10 years would vary from that involving 40 years occupation at the same single rate of return ie where the remunerative rate and the accumulative rate (sinking fund) are the same percentage.

Note how, at the high rate of 10% in this example, the investment sum required to accumulate to repay the principal over 40 years is of minimal significance.

Fig. 3.5.E
Comparative leasehold valuations - 10 and 40 years terms of occupation

Legal interest	Years purchase	Annual rent	Capital value £ ,000
10 year legal interest: years purchase single rate capitalisation	$\dfrac{1}{(0.1^*+0.0627^{**})}$ x or 6.146 YP***	£ 1,500,000	9,219
40 year legal interest: years purchase single rate capitalisation	$\dfrac{1}{(0.1^*+0.0023^{**})}$ x or 9.775 YP***	£ 1,500,000	14,663
* Remunerative rate at 10%+ ** Accumulative rate (sinking fund) at 10% over the period *** Also available direct from the valuation tables – years purchase single rate			

The sinking fund

A premises headlease of 25 years and upwards can be considered a major investment of a diminishing nature. Consequently, in order to have sufficient funds to replace the premises at the end of a lease a sinking fund (see also Chapters 3.5.3 and 3.5.8 above) may be established. The definition of a sinking fund is:

'a sum of money set aside at regular intervals to earn interest on a compound basis either:

• to be set off against the diminution in value of a wasting asset, eg a lease, or

• to meet some future cash liability'.

In property valuations it is usually assumed that the money will be notionally invested at a 'risk free' rate which is regarded as appropriate according to market conditions. The total amount calculated to accumulate by the sinking fund may be the same as the original investment or liability but possibly with an adjustment to reflect the view taken on future fluctuations in the value of money.

The historic concept of a sinking fund was that it should be invested in absolutely safe and consequently low-yield situations. Consequently there would be a difference between the accumulative rate of the sinking fund and the remunerative rate of the yield percentage. So, rather than take the sinking fund out of the rental income as shown in the Years Purchase multiplier explanation above, the valuation tables treat it as a separate function of the multiplier, effectively reducing it by an amount equivalent to a reduction from the annual rent.

Fig. 3.5.F illustrates how a remunerative rate of 6% and an accumulative rate of 4% are combined by adding the interest at 6% per £ to the annual sinking fund per £ at 4% and then taking the reciprocal to calculate the years purchase multiplier for a leasehold valuation.

Fig. 3.5.F
Calculation of years purchase dual rate from first principles

Years purchase factor calculation in respect of a non-recoverable investment bearing constant income over 20 years	
Sinking fund at 4% pa to redeem £1 capital invested over 20 years:	0.03358
Interest at 6% pa reserved on £1 capital invested in perpetuity 6/100 = :	0.06
Annual equivalent cost (per £1) of purchasing the investment using a finance rate of 6% and a sinking fund of 4%: 0.06 + 0.03358:	0.09358
Years purchase dual rate (6% + 4%) = 1/0.09358	**10.686 YP**

The calculation uses dual rates and reflects the principle that the remunerative rate expresses judgement of the risk whereas the accumulative rate adjusts for the time factor.

The 'annual equivalent cost' referred to in Fig. 3.5.F is not a term used often in connection with real estate. It is, in effect, the annual cost of borrowing on a 100% mortgage and is used extensively in management accounting when capital sums need to be annualised and amortised in investment appraisal.

As discussed below in Chapter 3.8 - 'Depreciation of Property' , the need to make a positive allowance for upgrading buildings on a regular basis must be addressed positively in modern valuations.

Many of the buildings purchased by investors in the late 1970's and early 1980's at low initial yields with no apparent sinking fund provisions were found wanting in the information and communication technology explosion which followed their construction. Consequently, 1990's market revaluations had to take into account the prematurely imminent cost of refurbishment. In some cases extensive voids or substantial rental discounts were overlaid on the sinking fund provision for refurbishment and the higher remunerative yield rates already pulling the valuations down.

The current information and communication technology revolution is beginning to make it possible to reverse this trend. In the next five years ICT is expected to develop economically to a stage where buildings once down-valued for lack of adaptability will once again be economic for occupation. Valuations will have to reflect this. (See Chapter 7.5 ICT for further discussion on this issue.)

3.5.9 PREMIUMS AND SUMS ON ASSIGNMENTS

A 'premium' is a capital sum paid to a landlord by a new tenant. It is appraised in the same manner as capital sums paid to the existing leaseholders or sub-lessee.

A common example is where a leaseholder of a high-performing property wants to move on sometime between indexation/rent reviews and seeks a capital sum from the incoming sub-lessee or assignee who has the benefit of a level of rent well below the market. Similarly, tenants wishing to renew their lease before the natural expiration date may pay a premium to the lessor if the new rent ignores current market increases above that passing under the old lease. (Such transactions may result in taxation - see Chapters 11.2 and 11.3.)

A simple calculation of the former looked at from the point of view of both parties is given at Fig. 3.5.G. Here the landlord is arguing the case on a real estate investment values whereas the tenant is arguing the value to the business in normal commercial terms. This explains the differences between the two yields adopted. In practice, however, the matter will be one for negotiation, and particular business interests are likely to make such a purist approach more difficult.

Valuations such as these do not take liabilities to taxation into account, eg premiums in a landlord's hand are taxed to income taxation and capital gains tax (and the tenant may be eligible for income taxation relief). Capital sums received on the assignment of a lease are liable to capital gains tax in the hands of the assignor. The taxation effect may distort the outcome of such negotiations as may take place in cases like the example shown in Fig 3.5.G. In such instances a Discounted Cash Flow (DCF) may be revealing (see Chapter 10.6.3)

Fig. 3.5.G *Theoretical valuation of a premium from opposing viewpoints*	**Basis of valuation**	**Outgoing tenant's or landlords valuation* £**	**Incoming tenant's valuation* £**
	Estimated rack rental pa	1,500,000	1,350,000
	Passing rent pa	1,000,000	1,000,000
	Estimated profit rental pa over (SAY) 5 years period to lease expiry	500,000	350,000
	Market value of profit rent pa for 5 years at 6%** single rate: x 4.212 YP	2,106,000	
	Business value of profit rent for 5 years at 9%** single rate: x 3.819 YP		1,361,500
	Premium SAY	**2,100,000**	**1,350,000**
	* Excluding tax ** Yields may vary with covenant strength or finance method		

3.5.10 SURRENDERS

Occupiers are sometimes invited to surrender their leasehold interest to their landlord who may have plans for redevelopment or refurbishment putting the premises outside of the existing tenant's financial capacity. In this case the landlord will need to make an offer of compensation to the tenant reflecting:

- the tenant's investment in any improvements

- the 'profit rental' they would otherwise enjoy for the period to the next indexation/rent review (ie the difference between the passing rent and rack rent)

- any inconvenience or incidental loss likely to be suffered.

Typical calculations of the value from both standpoints as a prelude to agreement by negotiation are given at Fig. 3.5.H (over the page).

Basis of valuation	Landlord's valuation £	Occupier's valuation £
Estimated rack rental pa	1,500,000	1,650,000
Passing rent pa	1,000,000	1,000,000
Estimated profit rent pa for the 5 years to next rent review	500,000	650,000
Market value of profit rent pa for 5 years at 7% single rate: 4.098 YP x £ 500,000	2,049,000	
Business value of profit rent for 5 years at 6% single rate: 4.212 YP x £ 650,000		2,737,800
Compensation for improvements	250,000	350,000
Estimated surrender value	**2,299,000**	**3,087,800**
SAY	**2,300,000**	**3,100,000**

3.5.11 REVERSE PREMIUM AND SURRENDER VALUES

Of course, it is possible that there are times when tenants may wish to surrender their leases. So, the organisation taking on a lease where the passing rent is above the current market will be looking for a 'reverse premium', ie a cash sum to be paid to them to offset against the over-valued rental which is to prevail up to the next (presumably stabilising) lease renewal or rent review.

Equally, a leaseholder with no further use for a property which may have little or no prospect of early assignment or sub-lease may persuade the landlord to accept a surrender of the lease together with a compensating and tempting cash sum. Such a deal is rarely acceptable to landlords of substance unless they have reservations about a tenant's covenant.

A desire for an early termination of the lease may have at its root serious business difficulties. It may therefore be in the landlord's best interest to accept surrender especially if a refurbishment or redevelopment opportunity is presented which the leaseholder may not have perceived because of the existing lease structures.

3.5.12 SALE AND LEASEBACK

A sale and leaseback arises where developers or owner occupiers sell their completed projects or existing portfolios to investors and simultaneously take back long leases of the development or business premises at an agreed rent. The agreed rent is calculated on the basis of an appropriate rate of return relative to the purchase price. The developers or owner occupiers then sublet all or part of the projects to occupying tenant(s) (which may be themselves) and may obtain by way of a profit rent the difference between the rent they pay to the institution and that which they receive from their own tenants (or themselves).

Historically, sale and leasebacks were the preserve of developers, however they are now becoming an increasingly used business vehicle for releasing equity from existing owner-occupied portfolios. The usual reasons for entering into a sale and leaseback are to increase a company's return on capital employed, to raise funds for core business development and to reduce gearing. However, not all companies' portfolios are suitable for sale and lease back because they can be too specialised or the business needs to maintain ultimate operational control of the premises. However in PFI/PPP transactions it may be possible that such requirements are accommodated.

An example of the kind of sale and leaseback transaction that can take place is the sale of seven nursing homes by their operator to an investor for £17.6m. The homes were then leased back to the operator at a rent of £1.9m a year, giving an initial yield of 11% pa to the investor and an affordable rent (and useful capital) to the operator.

3.5.13 PRIVATE FINANCE INITIATIVES/PUBLIC PRIVATE PARTNERSHIPS

Private Finance Initiatives (PFI's) and the Public Private Partnership (PPP) are the long term contract for the delivery of facilities and/or services between a public sector authority and a private sector supplier, usually under-pinned by the creation of an asset.

Some PFI/PPP's are a development of the sale and leaseback type of arrangement where government-owned properties are given over to a financial consortium (or developed/refurbished by it) which takes over responsibility for providing premises and some or all facilities services over a given period of time against an output performance specification in return for a 'unitary charge', ie a regular all-inclusive payment from the occupier. The resource usually reverts to government's direct ownership at the end of the agreed term.

For example, if there are three obsolescent public hospitals in an area a consortium may take all three and build a new one on one of the sites. The consortium may then lease back the new site as a fully functioning up-to-date hospital for say 30 years and keep or sell the other two sites. They may even develop them for other uses. At the end of the term the property reverts to the original owner, ie the hospital trust. There is normally, however, an option for the original owner to continue the lease arrangement at expiry of the PFI/PPP period.

The benefit of this to the consortia is that they have a contract from a public sector covenant for the rental income and, frequently, management of the facility until the lease expires. The advantages for the hospital are that they do not have to find the development capital or manage or design the new hospital or pay for it if the specification does not meet the contract requirements. The facilities management of the site may also be outsourced which frees the hospital managers to concentrate simply on running the healthcare functions of the new hospital.

3.6. PREMISES AND PROPERTY 'INVESTMENT'

Introduction

Chapter 1.1.1 suggested that the facilities manager's prime concern must be for the core business; however it is sometimes possible to make money out of the property side without harming the core business and this should be borne in mind when developing and implementing a premises policy.

Rental income levels usually generate an initial return on investment far lower than rates of borrowing or criterion rates of return, therefore the property as an investment is likely to generate a rate of return on the capital sunk in the property which is substantially less than that earned by capital in the business as a whole. The property may, therefore, be used to realise capital by, for instance, a sale and lease back at a rent offering a cost of capital well below the business' criterion rate of return.

It may be noted that Chapter 1.1.5 and Fig. 1.1.C. explained the relationship between the premises policy and the business plan with reference to tenure, costs, values and performance. As well as considering the advantages and disadvantages of owner-occupation as a business strategy, this chapter now looks outwards from the business to consider how property as an investment manifests itself to external investors, who they are and the issues which motivate them and influence their investment decisions. It examines the important aspects of the property market in terms of investment criteria and location, as well as portfolio ownership.

3.6.1 THE NATURE OF PROPERTY AS AN INVESTMENT

Factors influencing value

Chapter 3.5.3 describes the process by which property investment valuations are calculated using rental income and a capital multiplier. In general terms, an external investor in property is looking at six main factors which influence value, namely:

- income stream over time
- appreciation or stability of capital value
- the inherent risk
- liquidity of the asset
- the balance of asset type and geographical location in the portfolio
- ease and costs of management.

Property therefore has much the same considerations as any other income-bearing investment such as stocks and shares, gilt-edged securities and so on.

The principal differences lie in the following factors:

- type of rent or indexation clause
- rent review or indexation intervals
- expected rental growth
- yield impact
- risk factors.

Rent review or indexation intervals

Leases are normally for ten years or more and rent reviews are historically at three, five or seven year intervals and on an upward only basis (see Chapter 3.2). During the 1990's rent reviews have tended to better the rate of inflation; investors have therefore been provided with particularly reliable inflation-proof returns over the term of years.

Expected rental growth

In those sectors where rental growth has been experienced, or where an individual property enhances the market's view of its suitability as a medium for investment, investors will accept a lower initial return on investment (anticipating future growth and stability of value) which in turn pushes up the market price in the manner described in Chapter 3.5.3.

Yield impact

Sometimes a combination of upward increases in rent, be that through indexation or rent review, and the low initial yields (high capitalization factors) have a gearing effect upon values thereby generating high levels of profit for those whose good judgement, or luck, enables them to buy and sell efficiently.

Risk factors

The down-side (apart from the now well established evidence that property is not guaranteed to perform in the foolproof manner suggested above) is that property is not a flexible investment, ie it is bought and sold in very large chunks.

Compare this with the ability to move quickly in and out of stocks and shares – in the proportions deemed appropriate to the optimisation or safeguarding of the portfolio – to understand the property investors' main problem. Taking all these matters into account, general fund managers tend to limit the property investments in their portfolios. Nevertheless there are many types of investment media which are 100% linked to property performance.

3.6.2 OWNERSHIP AND INTERMEDIARIES

Objectives of direct property ownership

Generally, direct property ownership in the private sector falls into five groups: investment, dealing, business occupation, leisure occupation and residential occupation. Any owner may be a developer in the sense that land is acquired and one or more buildings built upon it. Therefore, the objectives of ownership are apparent in:

- holding the property and letting (as an investor)

- selling the property, perhaps after letting (as a dealer);

- or occupying the buildings (for business, residential or leisure purposes).

Moreover, as discussed in Chapter 3.1.1, the occupier may be either the freeholder or a lessee (who holds an equity in the property). Apart from financial or economic targets, such as profit from dealing or return from investment, those holding property may have cultural, ethical, political or social objectives as well.

The business decision to own and occupy will be made on three grounds:

- the opportunity to create a 'bespoke' building tailored to specific user needs (by far the most important consideration)

- the policy of holding potentially appreciating assets to bolster the balance sheet

- the desire to hold property for long term expansion.

The appropriateness of these criteria in different circumstances is considered in more detail in Chapter 9.1.3.

In the public sector, property ownership is 'functional', eg a sewerage works, administration, or 'objective' eg schools, colleges, clinics, hospitals and similar uses. (Of course, schools, hospitals and so on are 'business' property when in the private sector.)

The distinctions made above are also usually important for reasons of taxation.

Status of direct owner

Direct ownership in one of the ways described above ('Objectives of direct property ownership') or perhaps a mix of them may be undertaken by an individual or some other legal 'person', eg a company, a trust or a charity. It is always important to be sure of status since it prescribes what can or cannot be done in respect of property. For instance, in general, charities are unable to deal in property. Also status, among other factors, may be an important matter affecting liability to taxation.

The documentation of 'status', eg the trust deed, will be an important prime source for the facilities manager; it will show the power of acquisition, development, maintenance, fund-raising and so-on. This will, of course, be subject to prevailing law.

Indirect property ownership

Although indirect involvement in property is not an issue for facilities managers an understanding of the process will help to provide a more complete picture of the investment value of property.

Persons with surplus funds may achieve indirect involvement in land and buildings in three general ways, one of which is to use a 'financial intermediary'.

Thus a person may:

- share in the ownership by financial devices - for instance, by investing in the shares of an investment company which buys property or develops land for long term holding

- invest by holding units in a unit trust, by owning property bonds or by holding a pension policy or life insurance policy in a fund which has a proportion of its assets in property: such assets may be either by direct holdings or indirectly in some other vehicle, such as shares in a property company

- lend funds to another by mortgage or other device without the involvement of a financial intermediary, although this use of mortgages is probably not attractive to many investors.

Of course, individuals or companies who are dealers derive their income from the profits obtained from buying and selling property, or from buying land and building and selling on the completed development. Others may share in any profit from such operations by investing in the shares of companies which trade in this way, eg commercial property development companies which are either private companies or quoted on a stock exchange.

Other avenues for indirect investment in the field of property lie in such devices as company debenture stock or preference shares, some of which may be convertible into equities.

Similarly, mortgage bonds (when available), units in property (as they become available) and other devices, or variations of the above, afford opportunities for related investments.

Categories of owner

Owners in the market for commercial land and buildings fall into the following specific categories:

- businesses
- property investment holding companies
- property dealing companies
- pension funds
- insurance companies
- property bonds.

In many cases ownership will be by virtue of the purchase of an existing building. However, those wishing to get involved in property development may do so directly or enter into various forms of 'partnership', such as joint venture companies, straight partnerships, side by side leasing arrangements, forward funding or project management arrangements. Sharing the equity in the project is a prime issue in such ventures. Also, should an owner occupier wish to raise funds some of these property owners may be willing to enter into a sale and leaseback for the property so occupied.

Financial intermediaries

The pension funds and insurance companies together with the building societies, the stock markets, banks and finance houses have, in addition to any direct ownership, another function as 'financial intermediaries', ie they are sources of funds which enable others to purchase existing property, to develop land or to refurbish or improve buildings.

These so-called 'financial intermediaries' have the function of gathering together savings and other funds which are surplus for the time being and allocating some of them to borrowers. (They may, or course, develop land themselves.)

This is not to suggest that financial intermediaries do not create problems. Thus, in property development, their investment criteria for new projects may not entirely suit the needs of users. Similarly, their prudent investment policy may delay or prevent the advent of innovation in the property market.

Again, a general shift of the intermediaries' policy on investment allocations between sectors, say from property to equities, may depress the property market and alter or stifle the route to funds for real estate purposes.

3.6.3 THE MARKET FOR PROPERTY

The 'property market'

The 'property market' comprises property owners (eg as buyers or sellers), users (eg as owners or tenants) and also savers who provide funds for investment in property. The funds are provided either directly or through a complex system of financial intermediaries. As discussed above the financial intermediaries have a role of providing funds but some of them invest in property as well.

The other sense in which 'property market' is used pertains to the type of property in which interest is expressed, eg the office market, the industrial property market, the national and the international markets. It is outside the scope of this work to review the property market (or markets) in detail.

Generally, the 'players' in the market tend to cluster into specific sectors. Thus, developers may specialise in either house-building, developing industrial property, office development, leisure development and so on. On the other hand, investors, eg insurance companies, tend to distribute the holdings in their portfolios into a number of market sectors and geographical locations so as to have a diversity of offices, shops, industrial property etc and spread the risk. Nevertheless some specialise in a specific sector, eg some property unit trusts are 'in' agricultural property or 'in' industrial property.

A dynamic aspect of the property market is spotting trends in one or other of its sectors or geographic locations. These may result from the needs of users, eg hi-tech requirements, or from other factors.

Property investment criteria

The traditional criteria for investment are sufficient to indicate the general range of relative considerations which must be made before selecting a country, field or sector of investment as well as a particular property. Thus, (and in amplification of the main criteria given earlier in this chapter), the investor will have the following in mind:

- the prospect of capital being enhanced or at least maintained in real terms

- the prospect that income will be regularly received and will grow or be maintained in real terms

- management will be relatively inexpensive and the burden of outgoings may be shifted to tenants

- any national or local taxation incentives, exemptions, reliefs, and concessions are enjoyed to the full

- the degree of certainty (recognising that property is relatively illiquid) that the capital may be readily realised within a reasonable time at a reasonable expected cost

- whether opportunities for redevelopment or, at least, improvement will be achievable in due course

- whether the size in capital terms of any single property is suitable for a balanced portfolio

- the potential asset value of the property as security for borrowing

- the duration or lead-time to the effectiveness of decisions – eg development decisions may need several years before fruit is borne, or disposal may take several months before net proceeds are received

- the spread of the investment both geographically and by sector (property or otherwise)

- the availability of short, medium or long-term funds for purchase or for development having regard to the risk and the size of the property

- the degree to which risks can be minimised or shifted to others, eg by taking out insurance policies against the happening of particular perils.

Professional property evaluation and management requires a wide and deep range of knowledge and skills in legal, financial, economic, technical, political and other areas. To the extent that individuals and other persons wish to invest indirectly in property the quality of advice and its application by those who manage the estate are of considerable importance. The national property consultant will have a general knowledge but it may be necessary to refer to the local agent.

Some facilities managers do find themselves in the position of managing (or being responsible for) the management of large estates. This aspect of their work is considered in detail in Chapter 3.9 Commercial Property Management.

Location and property

It is not only the general quality of the property which should be considered by investors, but also the environment or society in which it exists. At an international level, broad issues of a country's stability, eg political, economic and social, require attention. In this context, restraints on ownership of property by foreigners and relative currency fluctuations may be important, but this should not apply to EU companies

Within the UK, location is paramount so that a review must be made and judgement formed on such factors as:

- population: size, socio-economic composition, age structure, mobility, health and morale

- workforce: composition, size, knowledge and skills, availability and mobility

- transport and communications infrastructure, ie road, rail, air and waterways, ports and airports, and various utilities

- planning, fiscal and other 'governmental' policies: structure and local planning policies, scope for implementation, regional selective assistance, and so on

- amenities and attractions: range and quality of housing, shopping, educational and training facilities, leisure and tourist facilities, art, entertainment and other cultural resources

- accommodation: business, cultural, tourist and residential, particularly its composition, quality and quantity

- state of the property market: values (capital and rental), cost of development and the quality of its processes, eg political, planning and financial

- the effect of EU, national, regional and local policies for economic development, planning and other governmental provisions

- the level of recent, past, current and planned capital investment in the area

- any predominance of employment opportunities which may be threatened by long-term structural changes in the economy

- the quality of the image and identity of the area

- the availability of professional consultants, contractors and others able to advise or undertake acquisition, development, construction and disposal as appropriate.

The owner-occupier will, in addition, have due regard to the appropriateness of the location to markets, distributors, distribution routes, competition and so on.

Quality of a property portfolio

The present conventional wisdom does not yet encompass a scientific method of evaluation (or even an appreciation of) the impact of the functional performance of buildings on the user's efficiency and hence on the quality and value of the investment. Various tools, such as the BQA system discussed in Chapter 1.2.4 and 9.1.3 are coming to bear on the issue but in most cases the quality of a property portfolio will still, in the investor's eyes, be reflected in the following:

- the age of its buildings, their condition and cost-in-use, their perceived ability to meet the conventional needs of occupiers and the investment criteria of the owners

- the spread of holdings in different sectors, ie industrial, offices, shops, agricultural, forestry, leisure and others

- the geographical spread

- the pattern of tenures, eg freeholds, long leases and short leases

- the ease of management, eg good security arrangements, indexation or rent reviews and full repairing insuring leases

- the covenants of the tenants, ie their financial stability particularly in terms of their ability to pay the rent and meet their obligations under their leases

- the financial acumen of management and the financial resources in hand or on call to meet immediate needs for repair and maintenance, and in the longer term, for expansion and rationalisation

- the gearing of the portfolio's underlying financial resources, ie as a measure of vulnerability to adverse income or capital changes

- the quality of the operations undertaken by both national and local management and professional advisers to improve the long-term standing of the estate within an achievable plan of operations.

Where the current performance of the portfolio is being measured, short-term considerations may outweigh a longer-term perspective.

The owner-occupier's portfolio

The challenge now facing many owner-occupiers is whether to move away from owning monolithic chunks of space to a more flexible, wider-distributed portfolio on a leasehold basis

As discussed in Chapter 3.5 - Valuation Methodology, the property asset value may have quite a big impact on financial statements. Portfolio diversity in terms of financial flexibility is a key issue with regards to ready asset realisation. A desire for flexibility in space use can encourage organisations to come together from fragmented locations into one large building providing greater efficiency in inter-departmental communications. Examples of the financial case for such a strategy are given in Chapter 9.1.4.

3.7 PROPERTY INSURANCE AND OTHER COVER

Introduction

Insurance is a commercial arrangement whereby an organisation or individual (the insurer) idemnifies another (the insured) against certain specified losses. The insured pays a fee (called a premium) in return for which the indemnifier (the insurer) agrees to reimburse the cost of any losses, or a proportion thereof, incurred within the scope of the insurance agreement (the policy).

Procurement of insurance for damage to or loss of property or injury or death of individuals may feature among the responsibilities of the facilities manager. This chapter is concerned with the insurances that an organisation may need at different times; there is some emphasis on the kinds of cover associated with real property but the chapter also touches upon many aspects of cover in business generally. The chapter examines insurance principles and practices and in particular looks at such matters as:

- the need for cover, including risk management, and various compulsory or quasi-compulsory insurances

- typical perils and consequential damage or injury

- the cover needed when acquiring, procuring and occupying property

- valuations for indemnity

- obtaining insurance cover, premiums and claims.

3.7.1 PRINCIPLES OF INSURANCE

Before looking at the practical application of insurance it is necessary to consider the main principles and definitions which underlie every transaction. The principles and definitions have developed from case law over many years and include:

- **good faith**: the person seeking insurance must always act in good faith, ie be truthful about the risks and hazards with respect to the potential losses to be insured against

- **insurable interest**: the insured should have an insurable interest in what is owned, ie must have an entitlement to be reimbursed for losses incurred

- **indemnity or reinstatement**: the insured may expect to be placed in the same position after the insured event as before

- **subrogation**: if the damage is attributable to a third party, the insured will join the insurer in action to recover the loss

- **average**: where there is under-insurance the insurer may pay out proportionately to the amount of under-insurance (see 3.7.8)

- **betterment**: where the reinstated property is enhanced in value, the incremental increase in value may be set-off against the amount payable by the insurer

- **no-claims**: where the insured has made no claim for a specified period, a reduction in premium payable may be offered or sought

- **contribution policies**: where the insured have two or more policies covering the same risk and suffer a loss they should not receive more from them than their actual loss. In effect each insurer contributes to the amount which will indemnify the insured.

3.7.2 NEED FOR INSURANCE

The need for insurance arises at all stages of the business although not every organisation has a policy of laying-off risks via insurance cover. The facilities manager may, therefore, like to consider insurance requirements and options at different stages of the life-cycle of the organisation. For instance, where an existing building is being acquired and occupied the types of insurance will differ from those required where property is acquired for development or redevelopment prior to occupation by the organisation.

Generally, where insurance is taken the need will have arisen in three situations, namely:

- by compulsion, under legislation, eg for motorists in respect of third party risks

- by contract, ie an obligation to insure is written into the agreement

- by choice.

Of course, as far as the latter is concerned, an organisation may choose **not** to take out an insurance policy; in which case the organisation may be said to "self-insure" against the happening of one or more perils rather than shift the consequences of the risk to another party, the insurer.

Risk management by insurance

In essence, the organisation, through the facilities manager and colleagues, needs to undertake a risk-audit of perils which may have a damaging impact on the organisation. The extent to which the consequences of risks may be transferred to insurers needs to be established and a judgement made of the cost of cover against the prospect of financial damage.

Of course, the risk management strategy will embrace more than insurance, covering risk reduction by such matters as:

- ensuring that staff are well inducted, trained and developed in operational policies and practices so as to eliminate or at least mitigate damage

- procurement of land and buildings which are pollution-free or have been treated to appropriate standard for anticipated uses (and safeguarded under contract, guarantees or warranties)

- careful procurement of buildings and structures which meet, or are better than, current building and planning standards

- careful procurement of resources, eg equipment for appropriate levels of management for storage, and emergencies and accidents

- observance, as appropriate, of codes and standards, eg ISO 14001 for environmental management systems.

Compulsory insurances

Certain types of activity give rise to compulsory insurance, imposed by statute. Examples include third party insurance for road vehicles, marine insurance and aviation insurance (taken by the operator of the business).

To the extent they might be considered a form of insurance, employers contributions to national social security are a business expense in this area. Other types of cover which are compulsory or quasi-compulsory are employer's liability insurance (Employer's Liability (Compulsory Insurance) Act 1969) and professional indemnity insurance, eg the RICS scheme.

Contractual insurance obligations

Many types of contract include provisions for insurance. They include:

- leases of property, where either the landlord or the tenant is obliged to insure; in practice the insured landlord often transfers the cost of the premiums to the tenant, eg by way of service charge

- mortgage and loans contracts, where usually there is an obligation on the part of the borrower to insure any property upon which the loan is secured or to insure the borrower's life - or both

- maintenance and other works contracts, where usually the contractor is required to carry insurance against fire, accidents and third party liabilities.

3.7.3 TYPICAL PERILS AND ALL RISK COVER

Material damage insurance

Whoever is responsible for insurance of property (of all kinds) and personnel will need to obtain cover for indemnity in the wake of such perils as:

- fire
- lightning
- explosion
- aircraft
- riot
- civil commotion
- malicious damage
- earthquake
- storm
- flood
- burst pipes
- impact by road vehicles and other objects
- sprinkler leakage
- landslip, subsidence and heave
- trees
- what might be regarded as 'extra' works (outside of reinstatement) generally known as 'works under the European Community and Public Authorities clause'.

Losses arising from such happenings may be expected to include:

- damage to or destruction of buildings and structures
- damage to or destruction of contents, stock and the like
- loss of business, both temporarily or permanently
- loss of intellectual property, eg records, files and the like
- injury, illness or death of individuals including staff and the third parties.

Getting the right cover

Any organisation occupying business premises should have an appropriate level of insurance cover against risks. It may fall to the facilities manager to ensure that the organisation is adequately covered against all reasonably foreseeable risks and is paying a reasonable insurance premium to obtain such cover with an insurance company of good standing.

Although placing of insurance cover is the role of the insurance broker some companies do not use brokers, preferring to purchase direct (sometimes pocketing the broker's commission). Others have brokers, but the wrong ones, eg those who have their 'favourite' underwriters or who are too lazy to trawl the market for the best deal available.

The cost of insurance vis-a-vis the risk of not having it - or not having enough - must be reasonable. Failure on the part of the facilities manager or broker to get adequate cover at the right price is an inexcusable but frequent occurrence, with definite risk of actionable negligence claims in the event of non-recoverable losses due to inadequate insurance cover. If there should be inadequate cover, either at the commencement or later (perhaps due to a lack of updating), the insurer may invoke 'excess' when any claim is made. The amount paid will then be proportionately reduced.

And how can anyone recognise a good broker? Check first if they are registered under any state or industry scheme. Then take up references. Finally, put the broker into competition with other brokers of comparable status.

It is important that the small print in every policy is very carefully scrutinised. The importance of dealing with the insurance provisions professionally has never been so great.

Consequential loss

In order for an organisation to obtain effective cover against consequential loss it is essential that material damage insurance is in place in respect of the property and the primary risks upon which any consequential loss is dependent. The logic for this apparent imposition is to avoid the consequential loss claim from being expanded to cover business lost while the building lies in ruins awaiting possibly non-existent funds for reinstatement.

The level of cover for the material risk must also match the prospective consequential loss. For example, heavily networked premises may go completely out of action causing a business loss out of all proportion to the cost of reinstatement of what may possibly be only nominal interior damage.

Restricted or denied access due to damage to lifts, stairs or reception may, again, prove consequentially disastrous compared with the material damage. Loss of rent cover for these circumstances is very important. This knock-on effect of partial damage taking out whole areas is also relevant to key business features such as computer rooms, kitchens and critical reference libraries. Loss of rent cover against such parts of a property may be inadequate if the whole area becomes useless within a business context.

3.7.4 ACQUIRING, PROCURING AND HOLDING PROPERTY

Having looked at the general need for cover and how to get it, it may be useful to illustrate how the facilities manager may need to deal with insurances in different ways at different stages as the organisation acquires or develops property and commissions it. Where there is a project of development or redevelopment the stages in the cycle of a property may be identified as 'acquisition', 'clearance of land' (if appropriate), 'construction of works' (if any), 'funding' and 'commissioning' or 'occupation'. (However, insurance and construction are dealt with more fully in Chapters 6.3.5 and 10.1.4)

Acquisition issues

When property is acquired the purchaser should check whether there is a need to insure from the date of contract (rather than the later date of completion of the purchase). Fire and other common perils, eg third party liability, are usually covered but the purchaser should plan the need for other cover, if necessary.

Points which may need to be dealt with include:

- where leased property is acquired, any obligations of the tenants

- where an estate block insurance is operated by the purchaser, the inclusion of the acquired property

- where title to land is seemingly defective, insurance to cover any subsequent challenge to good title, eg where an old and seemingly obsolete restrictive covenant exists

- where remedial works have been undertaken for previous contaminative uses, a note should be made of any vendor's contractual obligations, contractor's guarantees or professional's warranties, ie as to the environmental state of the land (these may affect the environmental insurer's views of the risk)

- where there has been archaeological discovery, a note of any indemnities or warranties, etc in existence.

Where the vendor's insurance is relied upon from a contract obligation, the purchaser's interest should be noted by the vendor's insurer (a similar need arises where a tenant has the obligation to insure).

Funding and insurance

Funding gives rise to insurance obligations. They may include:

- for mortgages and other property secured loans: fire and other perils cover to protect the lender's security

- for a business dependent on individuals: life assurance or 'keyperson' insurance (the latter covers the need for replacement of management capability).

In this context, third party guarantees are often required by banks or other lenders of funds secured by property. Also, the insured may be obliged to carry out works to the insured property, eg execute repairs.

Construction issues

Construction is, obviously, a complex process involving consultant professionals, a main contractor or construction manager, perhaps several sub-contractors and many suppliers of materials and equipment. Facilities managers may need to develop a clear understanding of the way in which their organisations are protected against the defaults of others during and after the construction process. (See Chapters 6.3.5 and 10.1.4.)

Typical problems which arise include:

- the happening of perils during construction, eg fire, the collapse of a crane, injury to a child trespasser

- defects in design or construction which come to light during construction or after completion

- the insolvency of a key professional, the contractor or a sub-contractor
- the failure of materials or equipment.

Remedies

Remedies which are available to the facilities manager's organisation are likely to fall into three kinds, namely:

- an action in law
- a claim against a third party guarantor or surety
- a claim against an insurer.

If the organisation acquired the completed property from the developer **after** completion, a similar but slightly different remedial situation may arise: the principal may take action in law against a professional or a contractor (but not perhaps a sub-contractor or supplier of materials) whose work gives rise to a claim prior to completion. After completion of the works the remedy of taking such action may be for a limited period only. However, where available, latent defects insurance or some other device, eg a bank guarantee, may be a more effective means of recovery.

Although not insurance as such, 'performance bonds' may be used by principal employers under construction contracts. They cover against the risk that a contractor or sub-contractor becomes insolvent or otherwise fails to perform under the contract. The contractor's bank or specialist insurance companies will usually provide the contractor with such a bond after satisfactory completion of appropriate investigations.

Occupation issues

On commissioning a building and occupying it, the facilities manager should ensure that the appropriate insurances are in place, ie in accordance with their original risk assessment. Typically cover will include:

- employer's liability insurance
- public liability insurance
- 'special' contents insurance
- professional indemnity insurance held by any consultants who may be employed form time to time
- all risks insurance (as described below).

Employer's liability insurance

There is now a considerable increase in the cost of employer's liability insurance (ELI) as a result of employee claims. (The problems of repetitive strain injury, eye strain mental stress and the like are all considered in Chapter 8.2.2.)

Although the facilities manager must have a sound risk management programme in place to deal with the avoidance of these problems the size of settlements under the growing number of claims demands that employer's liability insurance cover put in place by the organisation, and by its contractors and sub-contractors, must properly cover the risk.

'Passive smoking' , ie the inadvertent inhalation of another's tobacco fumes, is now well documented as a health hazard and will no doubt produce a defensive response from the underwriter of any insurance policy which does not deal precisely with the issue.

Cynics might say that the move towards controlling or banning smoking in public places is more a response to potential liability for claims in respect of passive smoking rather than a philanthropic attitude of employers and licensors. Anyway, as far back as 1994, the UK's Premises and Facilities Data Service, in its annual report, showed that 95% of its subscribers either banned smoking completely or restricted it severely by location, time or both. Fig. 3.7.A is the relevant extract from the report; it is interesting that the 1993 comparable data had put only 75% in this category (over the page). This is an area where insurance premiums can be saved without taking a risk, although historic risk may still be present.

Fig. 3.7.A
Smoking in offices - sample of company policies

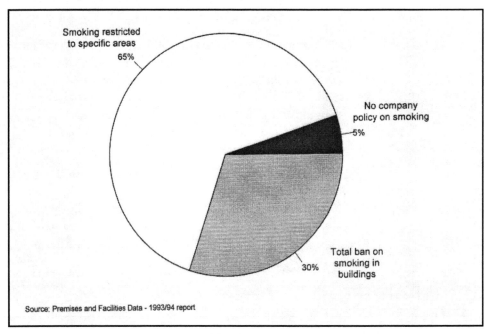

Source: Premises and Facilities Data - 1993/94 report

It should be noted that claims for insidious, ie delayed reaction, injuries or illness are on a 'claims-occurring' basis, ie the insurer covers the risk when the damage is incurred has to underwrite the loss. Contrast this with the 'claims-made' basis of professional indemnity insurance considered below, where the insurer holding the cover when the claim is delivered has to respond.

The problem with the 'claims-occurring' syndrome is that certain personal injury at work may be incremental, resulting in the need to claim on one or a number of previous policies - and who knows where they are or who underwrote them? As further discussed in Chapter 3.7.7 below this may well present a task for the facilities manager, ie to take responsibility for storage and safe-keeping of **all** insurance documents, not just those which are property related. A thoroughly compiled and indexed register of insurance policies is of tremendous value to any organisation (see Chapter 3.7.7 below).

Public liability insurance

Public Liability Insurance (PLI) is not mandatory but the organisation which does not carry appropriate cover (or ensure that its contractors and sub-contractors do) is courting disaster.

PLI relates partly to property and partly to the organisation's business activities so, where possible, a split of the cost should be sought - often a problem with all-risks policies.

Cover is required against injury or death to visitors, passers-by, neighbours (near and far) and property, as the result of some malfunctioning or failure of the services and structure or execution of any construction works; in addition the hazard of pollution of air and water as a result of the way the building is constructed or run, or from its effluent, is now defined as a third party liability and appropriate insurance cover is an important backstop. Importantly, basic cover against such risks only usually applies to one-off incidents; incremental, insidious damage by, for example, pollution needs to be separately insured - and cover is hard to get and expensive.

Contents insurance

It can be argued that contents cover is nothing really to do with 'premises', and the extent of cover needed is as variable as the reinstatement value of the buildings. However, such is the cross-relationship between 'pure' premises management and office services that it is naive to expect that there will always be a clear division of liability.

Most all-risks policies these days tend, in any case, to extend to contents, with an overall sum insured making a split of the costs between premises and contents difficult to establish.

Fig. 3.7.B gives an indication of the typical costs of covering simply the 'contents' risk in office buildings. Figures are relative to a broad range of headquarters and 'back office' buildings.

Fig. 3.7.B
Sample range of contents insurance premiums for office buildings

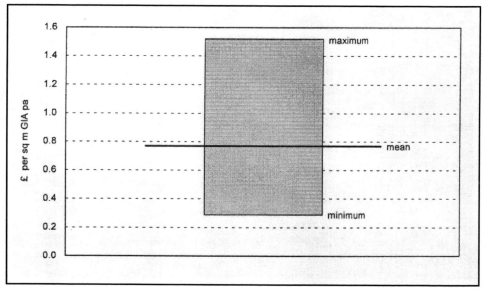

The insured values used to calculate these typical premium charges include demountable partitions (group space layout), furniture and fittings, general office equipment, employees' personal belongings and legal fees in respect of possible disputes on claims.

Excluded are any allowances for business interruption or engineering insurance, which can have a great effect on the amount insured as also allowances for public and employers' liability, for which a minimum of £1 million is recommended, although the nature of the business may cause this to vary significantly.

All risks policy check

The contents all-risks policy should, therefore, be checked for adequacy of cover against:

- loss of general contents
- material damage - including items temporarily removed
- public and employer's liability
- ICT hardware

- ICT software

- cash

- business interruption (see Chapter 3.7.3 - consequential loss)

- directors' and employees' personal effects

- engineering insurance - for high-tec users

- legal expenses - to pay for defence in disputes.

Professional indemnity insurance

The risk of loss of facilities or financial loss through the negligence of a consultant is most commonly encountered in construction or fitting-out projects, although valuation surveyors, large maintenance contractors and others offering specialist advice from time to time are also potential sources of bad advice and consequential loss.

The facilities manager must ensure that each consultant carries an appropriate level of Professional Indemnity Insurance (PII) relevant to any project or service they are carrying out on or in respect of the premises.

Now that out-sourcing is becoming more common companies are realising that many of the functions formerly carried out in-house were highly complex requiring the involvement of experienced and highly responsible managers and technologists. At the same time they could not get insurance against their failure, or fraudulent activities, which they now can if the works are contracted to a third party owing a duty of care. The costs covered will include the legal costs of defending any claim - these may amount to 50% or more of the final payment.

The liability of property occupiers and their agents under Health and Safety legislation for assessing and managing the risks inherent in construction works is now a major risk centre for PII cover.

PII claims are on a claims-made basis as defined above; the consultant's failure to disclose potential liability on any project when applying for cover may well result in the whole policy becoming unenforceable. Consequently anyone relying upon a consultant's PII policy to manage to risk of a project should, in theory, make it their business to ensure that the consultant's application form for insurance cover had been filled in honestly!

Clearly, this is a project manager's recurring nightmare, and proves that there really is no foolproof cover against poorly managed risk.

The alternative approach of the 'decennial' insurance system, where available, is discussed in detail in Chapter 6.3.5.

Loss of rent insurance

In the event of property becoming unusable due to say, fire or flood and a tenant has resorted to a rent suspension clause in the lease, the landlord will suffer a shortfall in income. It is prudent for the landlord, therefore, to have a loss of rent indemnity clause in the insurance policy for the property.

3.7.5 VALUATIONS FOR INSURANCE

Approaches

There are several approaches to the valuation of property for the purpose of insurance, the technical bases of which are described in Chapter 3.5.2 to 3.5.6. The usual approach is the "cost of reinstatement" basis, ie what it would cost to reinstate the building after damage or total loss. However, in certain circumstances, eg where the existing building is essentially obsolete and could not be replaced, the cost of a modern substitute building basis may be agreed with the insurer. The "first loss" basis is generally available for some heritage buildings; here the cost of reinstatement is limited, being up to an agreed proportion of the full reinstatement cost. Finally, there may be instances where the market value of the property is substantially less than the cost of reinstatement. Here the loss is broadly, "market value less the value of the site". In such circumstances a "market value basis" may be agreed.

Reinstatement value

The building owner and any tenants should be concerned to see that the total cost of reinstatement is covered - and that means everything from demolition to reconstruction, professional fees and finance charges. Finance charges are frequently overlooked but can be expensive unless the underwriter agrees (as they should) to meet the payments as they arise ie professional fees when due and the builder's monthly payment on the architect's certificate.

The RICS[1] publishes guidelines for the valuation of work for reinstatement following damage by fire and other perils. A typical calculation for reinstatement of an office building substantially damaged by fire is given at Fig. 3.7.C.

Fig. 3.7.C
Typical calculation for valuation on reinstatement basis

Insurance claim		Amount of claim £
Reinstatement costs	1,000 sq m GIA at £ 960	960,000
Professional fees	10% x £ 960,000	96,000
Alternative accommodation (rent only)*	850 sq m NIA at £ 240 pa for 1.5 yrs	306,000
Removals and charges	At cost	9,600
Betterment	No deduction	
VAT	Fully recoverable	
Total claimed		**1,371,600**

* Local taxes, operating costs/service charge not recoverable as they would otherwise be incurred in the insured building in course of occupation

In building insurance there is always a dilemma as to which index to use for inflation purposes. But there is usually little or no correlation between general inflation (measured by the retail price index), the 'cost of building' indices and 'tender price indices".

It is worth taking time to consider the relative merits of the latter two forms of building costs index:

• the 'general building cost' indices plot the source increases in the costs of labour, plant and materials over time. This method reflects, in theory, the prices which building contractors have to pay for the resources needed to carry out a building project

• the 'tender price index' reflects the charges (including profit) made by building contractors for specified building operations - ie, the market price for building work.

---

[1] *Royal Institution of Chartered Surveyors, Building Cost Information Service Ltd, RICS, London.*

It is not at all uncommon for there to be a startling contrast between cost increases theoretically incurred by builders and the prices charged to their clients.

Periods of recession bringing suppressed demand and hardship can lead to a loss of resources to the building industry which usually catch the industry and its customers unawares in the event of any upturn in the level of demand. This has the effect of reversing the differential pattern of cost increases between tender price and general building cost, pushing tenders higher as builders get overloaded with work and they also build anticipated large cost increases into their bids.

The RICS[1] publishes booklets on insurance reinstatement costs for housing and for flats, but there is no comparable publication for commercial and industrial buildings. Given this volatile situation it would be sensible for building owners to seek the advice of a qualified quantity surveyor or other expert cost advisor on the reinstatement value of their buildings for the coming year; the traditional general escalation clause clearly may leave the owner either unnecessarily exposed to risk of inadequate cover or paying an excessive premium for building insurance.

The tenant, in the conventional fully repairing and insuring lease, may feel that it is the landlord's worry as to whether the reinstatement value is correctly stated to the underwriters. This is a dangerous presumption - what if the landlord is hard hit financially as a consequence of under-insurance? The trading losses suffered by the tenant due to the inevitable delay due to arguing the points and working out the liability for the deficiency will certainly not justify the meagre saving on premiums made prior to the catastrophe.

Modern substitute building

Some buildings, eg a nineteenth century mill, are likely to be obsolete for modern commercial or industrial purposes. In these circumstances a full reinstatement valuation would most likely be inappropriate. The valuer may, therefore, provide a reinstatement valuation for a modern substitute building which will meet occupational requirements and is much cheaper to build. The criteria for justifying such an appraisal include:

- the original building is obsolete for present day usage

- it is not still used for its original purpose

- it is unlikely that planning consent would be obtained to replace the original building.

First loss

In some cases where buildings have suffered very substantial damage but not complete destruction it may make economic sense to reinstate them. The concept of 'first loss' allows, therefore, for partial reinstatement to an agreed proportion of the cost of the original building which has been partially damaged.

Market value approach

Where a building has a market value which is very much less than the cost of total reinstatement, the basis of indemnification would not necessarily be reasonable if reinstatement was effected. Therefore, in such cases the insurer is likely to indemnify on the basis of value rather than cost; the measure being based on the "market value of the property less the value of the site".

3.7.6 INSURANCE PREMIUMS

In the process of auditing premises costs, a quite staggering variation in the annual costs of material damage insurance per capita and per unit of floor area is revealed. The causes of the variations are frequently as much to do with purchasing - whether direct or by brokers - and post-codes as with the risks and values to be insured.

Fig. 3.7.D indicates the typical costs for insuring against these perils in office buildings.

Fig. 3.7.D
Sample range of property (material damage) insurance premiums for office buildings

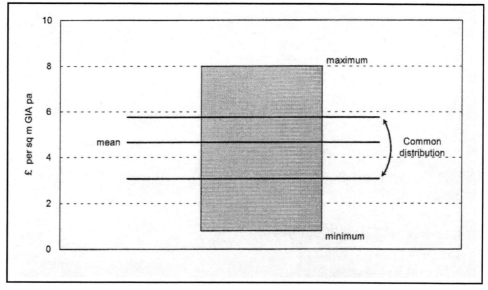

The figures are calculated from a generic sample of office buildings; as such the premiums reflect the full range of building costs across the region.

The insured values used in the formulation of these typical premium charges include demolition, reconstruction, professional fees and short-term finance charges.

Most companies will have to pay the final bill for insuring the building(s) they occupy against fire, and special perils. These days 'all-risk' insurance, to include subsidence and damage caused in the course of criminal activities is generally available on reasonable terms and should be purchased as a matter of course.

Where property is tenanted, it is essential for the cover to include loss of rental during the reinstatement period - normally three years, except in the largest buildings.

Increasing incidents of terrorism in recent times have caused the insurance market to exclude material damage and consequential loss resulting from such action. Substantial premiums can enable lifting of the exclusions, and because fire and explosion are perils against which insurance is obligatory in most leases, many have seen no option but to take out this additional cover; failure to do so may affect a tenant's ability to comply with any liability to repair with potentially disastrous consequences. Of course, adequate formal security and disaster recovery regimes will help to convince the underwriters that the risk is worth taking though they may well charge heavily loaded premiums for sensitive companies and locations.

Premium rating

Premiums for cover of buildings are calculated from schedules of premium rates compiled by the underwriter's actuaries. Typically these will be applied to the reinstatement value and may vary according to such matters as:

• the type of construction of the building

- the age and condition of the buildings, eg the extent to which it meets modern fire protection, escape and security standards
- the use or uses to which it is put
- the number of users and their disposition in the property.

When subletting part or parts of premises, the facilities manager may need to consider, for instance, the impact the new occupiers will have on the insurance rating of the building; the rent obtained from the sub-tenant may be offset in part by increased insurance premiums.

Taxation

It may be noted that a special tax is imposed on insurance premiums. The tax is usually paid by the insurer and may be passed on to the insured.

Generally, insurance premiums may be deducted as a business expense in computing company profits for Corporation Tax.

Also, where a capital sum is received under an insurance policy, any realization of the monies may be liable to capital gains tax, subject to roll-over or other exemption and reliefs (see Chapter 11.3.1).

3.7.7. ADMINISTRATION

Insurance needs to be carefully administered by the facilities manager or specialist insurance managers (with whom the facilities manager will need to liaise).

The practices involved include:

- risk assessment
- procurement of insurance
- claims management
- premiums management
- records administration.

Insurance policies are at the heart of insurance administration. These should be noted in the Register of Insurance Policies and relevant aspects abstracted for operational purposes.

3.7.8 CLAIMS

Planning and preparation

Unless an insurance claim is prepared thoroughly and presented in accordance with the underwriter's requirements it will hold up and possibly prejudice the outcome.

First and foremost it is essential to make sure the premiums are up to date and that the loss claimed is in fact covered by the policy - otherwise everyone's time will be completely wasted. The amount insured must always be kept under review, to make sure that it is in line with the level of financial risk involved. Levels set too high bring no benefits at all.

Proper notes, photographs (if appropriate and humanly possible), and statements should be taken at the time of any incident, not left to the imperfection of the memory.

Frequently, a loss assessor acts for the insured in preparing the claim for submission to the insurance company (who will often be advised by a loss adjuster).

Avoidance of claims

The best way to avoid a claim is to manage the risk properly. Too many claims will push up premiums, apart from which the accident-prone workplace will be de facto less efficient and its occupants less productive - or absent!

Under-insurance and average

The first insurance valuation (see 3.7.5 and Fig. 3.7.C) will cover the first period of insurance cover, normally a year, and also extend through the period during which any reinstatement is being carried out (following damage occurring during the first period) which may go beyond the first period of cover.

Thereafter regular re-valuations (or indexation to buildings costs) are required to ensure an adequate reinstatement value is provided for premium calculation and actual reinstatement should this be necessary.

Problems may arise if the property is destroyed or damaged and it was under-insured at that time, ie the value for reinstatement is inadequate to cover the costs to be incurred. In these circumstances, the insurer may invoke the 'average' rule. This means that the sum actually paid by the insurer with only a proportion of the cost of reinstatement. The proportion paid is the ratio of the reinstatement value to the full cost. For example, a property is insured for £1m but the full reinstatement value is £2m. If damage of £0.5m is caused by a fire, the payment will be £0.5m x 0.5 which is £0.25m

Lease terms

If the landlord is responsible for reinstatement under the lease, the tenant needs to be sure (before taking up the lease) that the insurance reinstatement clause covers the payment of the full cost of reinstatement of the demised premises - the wording needs to be 'watertight'. Also that any rent suspension clause covers the period to the completion of full reinstatement.

3.8 DEPRECIATION OF PROPERTY

Introduction

Organisations 'consume' capital assets in the course of their existence. Briefly, plant and machinery wear out and may be replaced. Similarly, buildings or parts of buildings may be thought to wear out or become uninhabitable and will eventually be abandoned or perhaps replaced.

Accountants, valuers and others need to recognise this phenomenon in financial terms and make one or more allowances for it in the accounts or valuations respectively, The term 'depreciation' is used to describe the way such allowances or adjustments are made. Depreciation is now being officially defined by valuers as linking to five facets: economic, functional, strategic, environmental and the configuration of the holding's buildings and plots. In addition to these five facets, it is apparent that accountants have their own definitions of depreciation. Industry standards are now developing in line with each other but it is taking the market some time to adapt. It may be noted that the collective view of European valuers on the subject is defined in the European Valuation Standards 2000 (EVS 2000).

During the course of this chapter the industry standard definitions of depreciation will be discussed. The five facets will also be defined and explained in relation to land and buildings. The underlying characteristics of premature obsolescence will also be considered and a typical calculation of depreciation demonstrated. The relationship between inflation and depreciation will also be discussed.

Since depreciation affects most assets the chapter begins with a brief account of the meaning and significance of depreciation.

3.8.1 THE MEANING AND SIGNIFICANCE OF DEPRECIATION

Meaning

Starting from a clean sheet of paper, the Oxford Dictionary[1] defines 'depreciation' as 'the amount of wear and tear (of a property etc) for which a reduction may be made in a valuation, an estimate or a balance sheet'.

Both valuers and accountants have taken this basic definition and adapted it to suit their own, different, but equally legitimate, ends.

Traditionally assets are depreciated in a number of ways. Briefly, two commonly used ways are:

- **straight line depreciation** - where a fixed percentage of the original cost or value of an asset is deducted each year to arrive at that year's 'written down value'

- **reducing balance depreciation** - where a fixed percentage of the previous year's value is deducted from it to arrive at the latest year's written down value.

Also a certain asset may have a particular way of depreciation, eg in the UK certain leases are written down in a special manner for capital gains tax purposes.

It may be noted that depreciation is used for particular purposes: namely

- **financial accounting** - the accountant depreciates assets in order to calculate the profits of the organisation

- **taxation accounting** - the government recognises depreciation and provides a statutory basis which provides allowances to set against taxable income (this is not the same as for financial accounting)

---

[1] Pearsall J. & Trumble B. (Editors) (1996) The Oxford English Reference Dictionary (2nd Ed.), Oxford University Press, Oxford, UK

- **management or project accounting** - in devising accounts for operations the appraiser may make specific allowances for depreciation of particular assets

- **project evaluation or investment appraisal** - some appraisal techniques, eg NPV and IRR, provide for 'depreciation' or 'amortisation' in the calculations'

- **in certain valuations** - the valuer will seek to identify the facets given above and allow for any in their valuations.

Broadly, depreciation developed industry by industry but professional practice and, more recently, accounting standards and valuation standards have resulted in common approaches to the depreciation of many assets, with variations according to the industry.

A random selection of four company reports illustrate the 'write-off' periods of typical assets for the sector concerned, ie when used in financial accounts (see Fig. 3.8.A).

Fig. 3.8.A
Depreciation (in years) for four companies (illustrative only)

Asset	Hotel	ICT	Transport	Retail
Freehold buildings	-	50	50	20
Freehold land	-	-	-	-
Plant and equipment	15	5 – 8	-	8 – 10
Furniture	10	5	5 – 10	-
Soft furnishings	5	5	5 – 10	-
Motor vehicles	5	4	3 – 5	-
Computer equipment	5	5	5 – 10	up to 5
Cabling and ducting	-	20	-	-
Leaseholds (long)	-	50	50	20
Airport runways and aprons	-	-	100	-
Public service vehicles	-	-	7 – 16	-
Rolling stock (rail)	-	-	20 – 35	-
Store: fixtures and fittings	-	-	-	8 - 10

Generally Fig. 3.8.A is indicative only. The periods shown are likely to meet the requirements of any relevant accounting standards for the company's activities. Finally, a short lease is usually written-off over its life, as is any asset, in principle.

In reading this chapter it may be borne in mind that the accountant's approach to, and use of, depreciation may be different from that of the valuer. The accountant is usually seeking the calculated figures to put into the financial accounts. However if an asset is disposed of, eg by a sale, any difference between the Sale Price (SP) and the current Written Down Value (WDV) will be used to make adjustments in the accounts. Thus, where the sale price is less than the written down value, the sum (WDV - SP), is treated as a cost in the accounts (and vice-versa): this is the so-called balancing allowance (or charge). It follows that the accountant is less likely to be concerned with valuation since in most instances financial records of costs and the calculations for depreciation will generate the accountant's figures.

For buildings and other similar assets, eg airport runways and aprons, the accountant may use depreciation rates, such as 2% and 1%. However, in some instances there will be no depreciation, eg where the buildings are (as a matter of corporate policy):

- kept in good repair

- well maintained

- regularly improved to modern standards.

The valuer's use and approach to depreciation is not directly concerned with the financial statements. Where one-off or regular valuations are required the valuer's valuation standards require a valuation approach which, in some instances, require forms of depreciation to be taken into account. This is usually in cases where there is no ready market evidence of value. Typical properties include oil refineries, chemical works, steel works, power stations and dock installations. The approach to valuation in these instances is the 'Depreciated Replacement Cost' (DRC).

The accountant sees depreciation as simply 'the measure of the cost or revalued amount of the economic benefits of the tangible fixed asset that have been consumed during the period'[2] The accountants have a pragmatic approach to depreciation. Their definition therefore simply incorporates the combined effects of the five facets mentioned in 'Introduction' above (see also Chapter 3.8.2) each of which the valuer has to address in detail, albeit for somewhat specialised assets, after discussions with the directors and others.

Significance

Apart from allowing in principle for the eventual recovery (or amortisation) of capital in the ways described, depreciation has practical financial effects, namely:

- depreciation for taxation has the effect of reducing the amount of income taxation actually payable in each year until the asset is written off

- depreciation for financial accounting increases the cash retained in the business, since it is treated (in effect) as a notional annual cost against turnover (and hence profits) in each year until the asset is written off.

Practice

The accountant uses depreciation as a negotiable measure of consumption and not as a valuation technique. Fixed assets may be shown to have 'consumed' costs over the accountant's depreciation cycle but the amounts of the deduction must not be confused with measurement of loss of value - at least not until a balancing allowance or charge operates (or a relevant revaluation of an asset operates).

The valuer must first make the distinction between operational and investment properties. If the valuation is for investment purposes (see Chapters 3.4 and 3.5), and not highly specialised, it will be valued on an open market value method. Historically, valuers have taken depreciation into account as a risk factor in the yield applied (unless the asset has a definite limited life).

Some may argue that depreciation is not automatically accompanied by a fall in value, and in many cases over part of an asset's life-time the reverse may in fact be so - for a variety of reasons. The thesis probably turns on the matter of whether value relates to open market or intrinsic productive value.

DRC is a procedure employed to establish existing use value in the absence of market comparables, ie for the types of property identified above. It is usually used as a measure of last resort as a cross-check on the proposed figure.

---

[2] Accounting Standards Board, (1999), Financial Reporting Standard 15, NSB Publications, Central Milton Keynes, UK.

The basic calculation is:

DRC = land price + buildings costs - depreciation.

The resultant figure is conditional upon adequate potential profitability or long-term viability of the enterprise (or public body), compared to the value of the assets employed. DRC is adopted as a proxy for market generated analysis. It is thus unsuitable for use in respect of properties held for investment surplus to the operational requirements of a company as it does not include an element of developer's profit. Therefore if it is to be used in the market place then developer's profit should be included and the equation becomes:

DRC = land price + buildings costs + developer's profit - depreciation.

Before considering further the effects of depreciation on the values of this type of property it is necessary to take a closer look at the factors accompanying, and causing, this phenomenon.

3.8.2 THE FIVE FACETS OF ECONOMIC LIFE OF PROPERTY

The facilities manager together with colleagues may be asked to get involved in discussions with a valuer who is undertaking valuations of corporate fixed assets. In particular the parties to the discussion need to consider five facets germane to the continuance of useful economic use, namely:

- economic obsolescence
- functional obsolescence
- strategic obsolescence
- environmental obsolescence
- configurative obsolescence.

In making the valuation the valuer will make appropriate deductions from the gross replacement cost to reflect any or all of the five facets (see below) as they affect the land, building and plant assets of the property.

Generally depreciation does not apply to land unless it is considered:

- a wasting asset
- planning or other constraints limit its useful economic life.

Economic obsolescence

For buildings economic obsolescence, as defined by the EVS 2000, is mainly geared to the depreciation of the physical performance of buildings that may arise from one or more of the following causes:

- wear and tear
- lack of adequate maintenance and repair
- poor design
- poor construction
- accidental or malicious damage
- dereliction
- demolition (the ultimate in obsolescence!).

In addition it also takes into account:

- construction economics, eg where the cost of refurbishment is greater than the added value thereby created

- development economics, eg where the potential land use has a greater value than the existing investment.

Land as such generally exists in perpetuity and, therefore, its value is less likely than any buildings upon it to be affected by economic obsolescence. Such obsolescence may come about by depreciation of land values due to falling demand which may dictate the use to which land can be put, the price it will fetch in the market, and the time it takes to realise that price. Also planning and fiscal constraints may affect land.

This definition is fairly close to the definition of the term 'physical deterioration' used in Chapter 3.3.1. How economic obsolescence appears in the balance sheet will depend partly on the accountancy conventions adopted. It may be presented as a reserve accumulated to balance the DRC. In the case of property, the current cost accounting practice requires that open market valuation, where there is evidence to support it, should always be reflected in the balance sheet; an open market valuation would take into account depreciation to date. However, under historic accounting practice DRC may be appropriate for relatively new buildings which are clearly provided on partly functional grounds without regard to property investment values. This might apply, for example, to a call-centre, or to a headquarters office building in a poor location uniquely useful to a particular employer.

Functional obsolescence

Generally, functional obsolescence occurs where technological advances or changes in manufacturing practice reduce the usefulness of the asset, relative to its functional performance requirements. As discussed in Chapter 1.2.4 'The performance of buildings', the functional performance of the asset will be intrinsically linked to the physical performance in its as-designed condition; however, the actual physical structure of a building may well have a longer life than the expected life of the assets related to the process that takes place inside it.

In the case of a building it means that it has lost some of its ability to accommodate the business requirement in a manner appropriate to corporate objectives. Causes of this worrying condition can be:

- changes in statutory requirements, eg more stringent fire regulations

- changes in working practices, eg open-plan offices

- introduction of new technologies, eg electronic information technology.

Again, land is less likely to be affected by this kind of obsolescence than the buildings on it. It is related to the ability of a site to continue to accommodate a valuable user. Hindrances to such ability might be:

- changes in the load-bearing capacity of the ground

- access to utility services, eg cabling networks

- reduced vehicular access.

Strategic obsolescence

Strategic obsolescence tends to focus around such matters as:

- corporate policy

- logistics, such as changes in the availability of materials or workforce

- financial constraints

- trading patterns.

It may arise where a change in the corporate plan makes obsolete, at any time, the buildings used to house a specific operation which is no longer needed or which has a much reduced demand. The building could still have a value to another undertaking whether it be a single building, the whole or part of a complex.

Sometimes the buildings may be adapted to other purposes in which case any costs of refurbishment must be addressed in the valuation calculation.

Strategic obsolescence can affect land values because if the owner of a large estate decides to close down in one particular location the change in the value of the land containing the disused buildings, eg old mills, may be very significant.

Environmental obsolescence

Environmental obsolescence is where the existing use and technology adopted may have become outdated in relation to the actual and forseeable local, national or EU policies and controls regarding environmental pollution and waste management.

More particularly for buildings, it may be caused by:

- health and safety regulations
- pollution
- changes to the external environment, such as water levels
- infestation by pests.

For land such obsolescence may arise from the likes of:

- depreciation of local or regional infrastructure
- statutory intervention, eg planning restrictions
- pollution
- ground obstructions (from previous structures)
- encroachment or erosion by the elements, eg the sea.

Configurative obsolescence

As time passes older properties reflect past decisions to develop, extend or adapt buildings and plant. As a result the configuration is not likely to be ideal for modern working situations. Therefore operational problems such as the following may arise:

- unnecessay movement of goods or staff between buildings
- congestion and pinch-points for traffic flows on site
- inadequate areas for open storage, carparking or outside waste handling.

Building performance

From the examples given above the reader will recognise the reasons why few of these examples of obsolescence fit perfectly and exclusively to any one of the three inter-related facets of building performance introduced and discussed in Chapter 1.2.4.

Land

Apart from the points on land made above, interests in land do suffer from the effluxion of time - quite apart from the influence of time on the economic and functional facets of performance. Although land can depreciate, since it exists in perpetuity most depreciation may either disappear or be removed completely without direct intervention by the absolute owner, eg a site with an adverse planning/building restriction attached to it and the restriction is removed. The effects of time on leasehold interests is considered in Chapter 3.5.8.

In the case of property the value to the user may be quite different from the value to the owner (although they may be one and the same). Equally, although both land and buildings will eventually depreciate, the rate - and the reasons therefore will almost certainly be at considerable and continual variance.

There is no doubt that buildings and their fixtures and fittings will lose their usefulness over time; they will either fall into decay and/or become totally redundant and at some stage will get demolished. However, the land, as such, may well appreciate as demolition of an old building makes way for a new development.

3.8.3 PREMATURE OBSOLESCENCE

The invasion of information technology in the 1980's had a dramatic impact upon the functional and physical performance requirements of commercial buildings across the developed world. The 1990's brought the high-speed photocopiers, pcs and printers with attendant power and data cables and excessive heat. Owners and occupiers struggled to find the space and to lose the heat to make the buildings fit for their revised production process and workplace arrangements. This has progressed to a point in the year 2001 where new buildings are constructed to allow natural air flows, minimise energy consumption and storey heights thereby reducing obsolescence in the long term.

The ICT revolution had a dramatic effect since the extensive property development activity at the end of the 1990's had replicated the meanness of nearly all post-war commercial development, ie by providing minimum floor-ceiling heights, inadequate or no air-conditioning and with planning grids related to substantially cellular offices.

A study during the mid-1990's highlighted to the property world the likely impact of this phenomenon on property values. The editor-in chief of Facilities Economics, in his role as building economist to that project, coined the term "premature obsolescence". This term was used to describe the depreciating effect of the cost of the necessary upgrading works, eg raised floors or new floor trunking, new or modified air-conditioning, on the investment value of what were, in many cases, newly-completed buildings.

In some cases the building and engineering technologies of the time had no answer to the lack of adequate height to accommodate either ceiling trunking or false floors. Afflicted buildings were forecast to have a substantial drop in investment values; although these research findings were censored by some of those whose interests were not best served by the bad news, the property market soon got the message and values were adjusted - albeit gradually - over time. The 21st Century is bringing buildings that, hopefully, will have the intelligence and flexibility to avoid the premature obsolescence problems of their predecessors.

3.8.4 CALCULATION OF DEPRECIATION

The approach of deducting from an investment valuation the cost of works to reinstate the level of functional performance is a perfectly valid approach akin to a residual valuation of land, the reversion of a lease, the price of a derelict house or a motor car with a sound body but short of a good engine. Nevertheless, on top of the basic remedial costs is the 'hassle factor', which represents the bargaining discounts a willing buyer of a sub-standard article can negotiate in a buyer's market.

In practice the overall effect of obsolescence - premature or timely - is, as suggested above, usually rolled up by the valuers into the rent and investment yield in such a way that, even if there were a scientific base to the computation, no one would ever know what it was, and would be even less likely to know if it was correct.

The true impact of overall obsolescence is only shown in financial terms when property is sold or transferred. A good comparison of the relationship between investment value and the cost of countering the depreciation caused by obsolescence is given at Fig. 3.8.B.

Fig. 3.8.B
The cost of upgrading to cope with ICT - 'ORBIT' report [3]

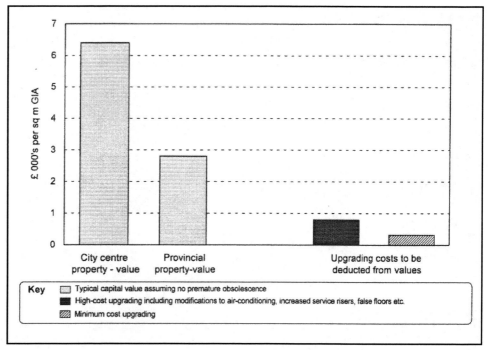

The way that property investment valuation works, with construction-related costs rarely a key ingredient in prime locations, (as shown in Fig. 3.8.C) means that allowances for periodic refurbishment should not have a serious impact; in the example at Fig. 3.8.B the problem was that the buildings afflicted were at a particularly early stage in their economic life at which, if anything, appreciation in value might have been anticipated.

Fig. 3.8.C
The relationship of construction costs to investment values

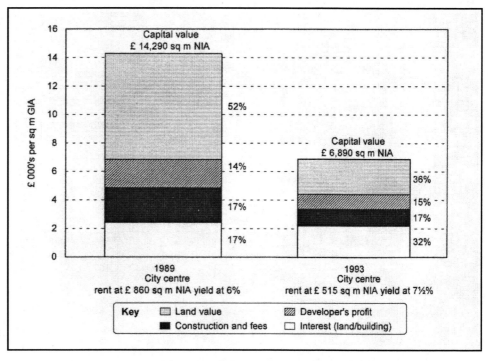

[3] *DEGW / EOSYS, (1984), The impact of information technology on office buildings*

The whole 'premature obsolescence' episode focused the attention of investment fund managers on the need for better asset management and, in particular, for making financial provision in their valuations for timely replacement of major components and more frequent refurbishment.

Getting it exactly right or even close is difficult. For instance, the high-energy pc's and bulky cables of the 1980's are being replaced by low-energy equipment and fibre-optic cables - even wireless networks; the VAV systems can now be replaced by much simpler devices doing much the same job at half the capital and running costs. All at once mean storey heights are acceptable again - even a bonus, for they save on heating and cooling loads - and clever investors are refurbishing them to good advantage, as the example at Fig 7.9.C. in Chapter 7.9 - Disaster Recovery and Prevention, well depicts.

3.8.5 INFLATION AND DEPRECIATION

Inflation may affect property values in three ways:

- supply and demand factors - adverse or favourable depending on whether viewed by tenant or investor - may push up rents

- the 'weight of money' seeking a home in property investments may force initial yields down and hence capitalisation factors up

- high inflation in the economy will raise the rental levels in the short term; however, any consequential economic adversity affecting business generally, and/or the property sector in particular, may well turn the situation on its head - witness the many examples of post-high-inflation slumps in property values.

An important side effect is the propensity for inflation to mask the effects of depreciation of assets in real terms. Strong demand coupled with high inflation may keep the open market value of obsolescent properties at or near that of newish buildings. Conversely, when demand is weak the older building may be vulnerable, unsaleable or, probably, both. The lesson to be learned by investors or owner-occupiers from this scenario is that the troughs will get deeper, as the building ages, even though the peaks may retain some parity. Therefore selling an old building in a peak period would be a sensible strategy - if the peak could be identified as such at the time it materialised!

3.9 PROPERTY MANAGEMENT

Introduction

In Chapter 1.1 'The scope of facilities' – Fig.1.1.B distinguished clearly between the three facets of premises management, ie asset management, capital project management and operating services management. Each of these disciplines is separately addressed in Chapters 2.7 and 2.8, and Section 5 respectively.

Whereas the asset manager within the internal facilities management team is concerned with the physical performance of buildings, a property manager (sometimes called an 'estates surveyor') also has to deal with the legal aspects of property arising out of leases as well as acquisitions and disposals. Where organisations, not being in the core business of property investment, lease or sub-lease part of their premises to another user their asset managers have to take on this property management function; in this case their role is similar to that of estates surveyors or property management companies supplying services to real estate investors.

This short chapter therefore outlines the specific aspects of property management – as opposed to pure asset management – needing to be addressed in the general context of traditional landlord and tenant relationships.

3.9.1 THE TRADITIONAL CONCEPT OF PROPERTY MANAGEMENT

Up to the end of the 1980's, before the full implications of the impact of building performance on core business efficiency became recognised as a facilities management issue, property management was generally thought of as a function independent of facilities management.

To the freehold owner (whether a landlord or an owner/occupier) property management entails four distinct risk centres:

- the income from the asset

- the investment value of the asset

- the operational condition of the asset

- the administration of the services and charge for landlord's asset management (service charge).

The income

Collecting the rent is obviously a critical part of the property manager's role. On a higher plane the job-function includes negotiating rent reviews and new rental terms where tenants wish to extend the term of years in occupation.

Disputes as to the interpretation of conditions of leases will normally be addressed initially by the property manager, although specialist estates surveyors and lawyers usually take over when disputes go to arbitration or to the courts.

The investment value

As well as keeping a watchful eye on the maintained condition in the role of asset manager, the property manager has to have due regard to statutory compliance and also deal with matters of building and development control and local property taxes. In larger property investment companies the strategic property investment planning is normally carried out by specialists (see 3.9.2 below).

The operational condition

In most cases the landlord used to, and still does, carry out the works needed to keep the property in the condition envisaged by the terms of the lease. Usually employing the services of 'managing agents' the landlord looks after the main fabric and building services and charges the costs back to the tenants either directly – by way of service charge – or indirectly within the rent – all as described in detail in Chapters 3.2 and 3.3 above.

Large organisations like local authorities often carry out this function using an in-house team, although the services management is more and more being outsourced.

Landlord's asset management

In buildings with several tenants where the common parts are managed by the landlord's agent and the occupied areas by the tenant's facilities manager there is a growing sense of friction because of the clash of two cultures, ie traditional property management and modern facilities management.

The property manager is likely to be pre-occupied with the condition of the asset with regard to its investment value and, in many cases, tries to keep service levels down so as to make overall property costs look economical. The facilities manager, on the other hand, is the person responsible for managing the risk to the organisation arising from any deficiency in the premises it occupies; and, if a substantial part of these premises is being managed to a different standard by another party whose first allegiance is to the landlord, trouble is bound to arise.

In-house property management

In the case of in-house property management operated independently of the facilities management function there is usually a property director whose concern is primarily with the asset value – how it looks on the balance sheet and its implications for their job; so the situation is just like that in a commercial property investment company (see below).

Outside of the private sector, local authorities and others have responsibility for property management, ie in this case asset management on behalf of the owner, with regard to schools, fire stations and other public buildings. Very often these duties are carried out in a totally separate department from that requiring to use the buildings. The user is therefore at arms-length from both the service provider and the strategic property manager, and often has little say in the level of service provided, meaning that the premises management arm of facilities management is non-existent in practical terms.

The Intelligent Client Function (ICF) should be in charge of premises policy and strategy but where 'arms-length' property management prevails the ICF rarely exists – or, at least, does not have any say in the way the premises are managed.

3.9.2 PROPERTY INVESTMENT MANAGEMENT

This aspect of asset management is usually covered by specialists – either in-house, as with large portfolios, or by consultants where only occasional advice and/or action is required.

It is important to emphasise here the need to avoid letting the tail wag the dog, ie investment values must not lead premises decisions in the same way that they dominate the business case for commercial property investors.

The smart investors are now catching on to this state of cross-purposes and the new millennium is bringing a gradual re-thinking of the traditional property management role and function on the part of the investors. The practice of property investment management requires a professional approach since it is part of the core business of property investors.

Since the commercial property management function is not a facilities management function in its own right this aspect of real estate is not considered in detail here. When facilities managers find themselves responsible for leases and acquisitions/disposals within their organisation's portfolio they are therefore best advised to seek professional assistance – from consultants in the isolated instance or maybe from in-house specialists where it is a normal scenario.

3.9.9 PROPERTY MANAGEMENT RECORDS

Property matters should be dealt with at the right time and in the right place. The records needed to carry out property management efficiently will comprise:

- **estate terrier** - a collection of abstracts for each property's title deeds giving details of tenure, easements, servitudes and rents payable (being ones of a long term nature)

- **rent roll** - a collection of each property's details which would be needed for every day rent collection, repair and maintenance and other rights and obligations of the parties

- **estate accounts** - a set of accounts for every day receipts and payments, dates due and so on

- **revival or caution system** - a calendar of dates and events designed to remind management to do or expect something, eg rent review procedures

- **case files** - a case or file of papers for each property or project -perhaps with annotated property subfiles for topics; these may be subject files, eg contractors, rating, insurance

- **registry of deeds and agreements** - a store for legal documents of each property's deeds and agreements, planning permission and so on - it is important to have a 'sign-in' and 'sign-out' record system

- **library** - a library of regularly used references concerning the estate, eg statutes, orders, regulations, manuals, work instructions and books

- **plan 'chest'** - a store of plans and drawings of each property which may be used for every day requirements

- **insurances register** - a collection of files concerning insurance policies, valuations and the like (see Chapter 3.7.7).

Section 4

Space Management

4.1 SPACE - THE PREMISES COST DRIVER

Introduction

Space has long been central to worldwide facilities thinking. As is clear from all the total cost analyses elsewhere in this book - **space is a great driver of cost**. And yet, despite this centrality to business, space does not often receive appropriate management attention either at the facilities management level or, to an even greater extent, at executive levels in the company. Most often it is treated as something to be minimised in order to reduce costs. Why is this the case? Primarily because many business managers believe all buildings and the spaces within them are just containers for people and, apart from obvious external and location differences, are all much the same and can all house their operations equally well.

The reality is of course quite different. The nature of every building is to place constraints on the way it can be used. It is the degree to which these constraints limit a company's requirement to use a building in a particular way that lies at the heart of how organisational demand is resolved with building supply. The very essence of space planning, space provision and building appraisal is focussed on this demand/supply equation.

The importance of understanding this is brought into sharp focus when relating premises costs to people costs (Fig. 4.1.A). The order of magnitude of the difference is a clear reminder of the importance of the people asset; however what if a link exists between the provision of premises and the way that people perform (workplace productivity)? It is easy to see how poor premises provision could make people less effective, so why is it therefore so hard to accept the corollary. It is in this area of facilities economics that many key decisions will be made and the consequences for the organisation and the achievement of its business objectives could be critical.

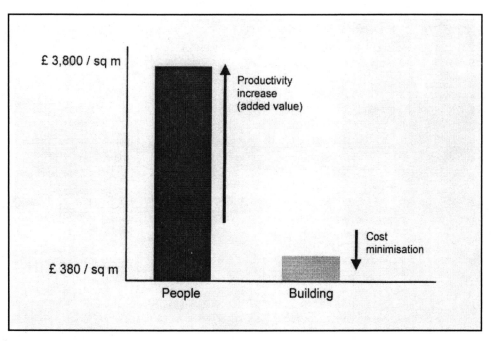

Fig. 4.1.A:
A relationship between premises costs and people costs

Different organisations have different work cultures that influence the way they use their space. At the same time buildings have their own characteristics which impact upon the way they can be used and furniture systems and statutory provisions add a further set of benefits and constraints. Since the late '60s/early '70s the science of space planning has been developed to help building users through one of the most critical issues they have to undertake ie: how best to use the available space with regard to its cost and the productivity of the employees working in it. Since the premises are a non-core overhead there is, and always will be, pressure on organisations to cut down on the costs of space and this is a reasonable challenge for the facilities manager. Nevertheless, the productivity issue should always drive the solution, for the consequences of reduced output will always be greater than any premises cost savings from which it results.

Buildings can kill businesses. Inappropriate leases and rents combined with changes in market conditions can strangle the cash flow. Buildings are slow and stupid, organisations are increasingly fleet of foot. The mismatch can be fatal. As a result the nature of the focus regarding space has been changing and continues to change. New ways of working have challenged the status quo, revolutionising the way that spatial requirements are established and provided. However like so many things in life these changes do not remove the need to understand space and provide an appropriate management regime for its planning and use. In fact, these changes, if anything, make it all the more critical.

Consequently best practice facilities managers must fully understand space and this chapter sets out to provide tools and techniques for measuring, managing and planning space. Finally the chapter will return to the developing trends and organisational change referred to above.

4.1.1 SPACE PLANNING - INTERNATIONAL ISSUES

The key for space planners dealing with premises abroad as well as in the UK is to use sound planning principles as set out in this chapter and elsewhere. If that is done it will be unlikely that they will run foul of legislation; what is far more likely is that they will come head to head with differing user cultures which, despite a common company culture, will be heavily modified by various national cultures or historic customs.

It is impossible to set out all the cultural differences. These cultural differences are particularly emphasised in user reactions to the mix of enclosed offices and open plan. Implementation of new ways of working can become particularly challenging in some cultures. All of this reinforces the need for full user consultation and involvement in the planning process so as to ensure the maximum degree of buy-in.

There are of course legislative differences and the ideal would be to point the reader to a table of these but to the authors' knowledge no such table exists. The range of issues in the area of space planning becomes so wide and with so much being tinged with custom and practice any such table would be unwieldy, if not impossible to produce.

There is also so much overlap with many areas of legislation and the way it is interpreted and applied (health and safety being a prime example), that it is easy to see why there is not absolute harmony.

Space planners operating outside of their own territory may find the following points of general advice helpful:

- check out the net rentable area provision and establish its relationship to the actual building net internal area (as described later)

- check with local furniture suppliers whether there are any particular issues you should be aware of (they will always be helpful, just ensure they are not giving a sales pitch for their particular product)

- check out any previous plans to see where difficulties might arise with changes you want to make (forewarned is forearmed!)

The remainder of this chapter suggests a best practice approach that will in most instances meet all local requirements; as stated earlier the local users will provide the greatest diversity of views and opinions about what conditions they can and cannot work in.

4.1.2 SPACE USE

Buildings are essentially working environments which are wholly or partially enclosed. The area of the environment which is able to be used for productive purposes is what the user pays for; however, included in the cost of providing the usable space are the costs of all the other environments needed to support it eg: space for services plant, stairs, landings and fire escape routes etc.

Whether or not the user is a tenant or the freeholder does not influence this issue; the tenant's rent is usually linked to the lettable floor area - which is not the usable area as is shown below - and the freehold value is usually also geared to the rental value per unit of lettable area.

Both tenant and owner will endeavour to get as much usable space out of the area provided. The main difference in outlook is that the tenant is not concerned with the non-rentable space (although in theory it is being paid for in the building component of the rent) whereas the absolute owner, if also the developer, will be seeking to optimise the proportion of the total built space which is rentable and therefore valuable.

Space use economics from the developer's viewpoint is discussed in Chapter 10.2 so this section is concerned primarily with the tenant's floor space (and the owner-occupier's equivalent thereof) and how it is used.

The building industry is concerned with the building as a container, while the space planner is concerned with the distribution of departments and activities in the most effective way across the usable space within the container. This has resulted in a potentially confused situation particularly with regard to the terminology used by the various parties concerned.

So as to ensure some consistency, the definitions used in this chapter build upon the European Code of Measuring Practice (2000)[1]. In turn the European Code draws heavily upon the Code of Measuring Practice[2] developed and updated as recently as 2001 by the RICS. Useful as these codes are they only provide part of the picture. One of the most important measures, net internal area (NIA), while being defined in the UK Code is replaced in the European Code by Effective Floor Area or Rentable Area. Further to this, NIA is nearly always referred to by professionals in the UK as net lettable area (NLA).

As will be covered later, while NLA or NRA (net rentable area) are important numbers they may not actually be definable measures. No doubt these areas will be based on some agreed method of measurement but in the end the area for which rent is paid often becomes a negotiated figure. In some extreme cases rentable areas have been found to bear little relationship to any agreed code of measurement. For this reason NIA measures, as defined later, should be properly established prior to planning taking place.

The most important measure of all has no definition in any of the codes of measurement. It will however be found in this chapter as net occupiable area (NOA) and it is the real usable area and therefore the actual area being paid for.

From a facilities management or facilities planning perspective the key issue must be consistency of measurement. The approach used in this chapter will ensure that consistency while also ensuring that any definitions can be related to the codes of measurement. This will enable external advisors to be satisfied and aware that the eventual users of the building are well informed about the space they will actually be acquiring.

---

[1] TEGoVA, (2000), European Valuation Standards 2000, Fourth Edition, The Estates Gazette, London.

[2] RICS (2001) Code of measuring practice: A guide for surveyors and valuers, 5th Edition, RICS, London

The definitions that follow are depicted in Fig. 4.1.B.

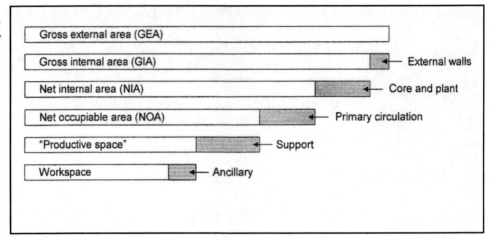

Gross external area (GEA). This is used in some countries for building cost estimation, site coverage plot ratio, planning and zoning. It is the area measured from the outside face of the external walls and projections - that is, the complete footprint on all floors. The measurement should include areas occupied by internal walls, partitions, columns, stairwells, lifts, escalators, toilets, air (or other) vertical ducts, lift motor rooms, central heating or air-conditioning (ventilation) plant rooms, fuel tank rooms, electricity transformer and /or low tension rooms. Open-sided covered areas, ramps, enclosed parking areas, storage rooms and basement archive rooms are also included.

(Definition as per European Code of Measuring Practice 2000)

Gross internal area (GIA). This describes the gross floor area which is the parameter frequently used by quantity surveyors and others estimating building costs at feasibility stage. It is also used by agents when describing industrial, warehouse and shop buildings and by valuers for valuation of industrial units. It is measured between the inside face of the outside walls or to the glassline if at least 50% of the outer building wall is glass. All measurements should be taken at a height of 1.5 metres above the floor.

(Definition as per European Code of Measuring Practice 2000)

Net Internal Area (NIA). This area is best described as GIA less the areas taken up by:

- common lobbies and foyers

- stairs and escalators

- elevators

- toilet areas

- ducts and risers

- enclosed plant on the roof

- mechanical and electrical services plant areas

- internal structure such as columns

- functions with core enclosures

- car parking which was included in gross area.

All the above are often referred to as the core or common areas.

NB The above definition is not part of the European Code of Measuring Practice which refers to Effective Floor Area or Rentable Area. For the space planner the use of rentable areas may be fine but can also be dangerous particularly if the figure is a negotiated one as part of a legal contract. However the definition of the latter is included here for reference and will be seen to be virtually equivalent to NIA in terms of a measurement code:

Effective Floor Area or Rentable Area. This is used for agency, valuation and service charge apportionment. This refers to the usable space within a building, on a floor by floor basis taking into account that each floor should be measured at all levels between the internal surfaces of external building's walls or to the glass line if at least 50% of the outer building is glass. Measurements should be taken at a height of 1.5 metres.

Exclusions from the calculation include internal structural walls and vertical ventilation, wiring or pipe ducts and structural columns (but only if greater than one square metre each), lifts and stairwells, lift motor rooms, tanks (other than those of a process nature), transformer rooms, high and low tension areas, the surface occupied by permanent air-conditioning, heating and cooling apparatus and surface mounted ducting which makes the space unusable having regard to the purpose for which it is said to be used. In addition to the above, to calculate the effective floor area for offices, those areas which are set aside for the provision of services or facilities to the building and not for the exclusive use of the occupiers of the building should be excluded. Areas set aside for public space for thoroughfares and not used exclusively by occupiers of the building are also excluded except that if they have resulted from the subdivision of whole floors to accommodate more than one tenant they are to be included in the calculation. Entrance halls, landings and balconies when and if they are used in common with other occupiers are also excluded from the measurement. In some European countries these may be pro-rated to the various occupiers.

(Definition as per European Code of Measuring Practice 2000)

Net Occupiable Area (NOA). This area can be described as the NIA less the requirements for main corridors or primary circulation (as space planners call it). These circulation routes are required to maintain life safety in emergency situations such as a fire. Across Europe these "fire escape routes" are generally governed by statutory requirements and can be complex in their interpretation covering matters should as their width and maximum distances to fire exits or protected areas. (Note that primary circulation does not include the routes [called secondary circulation] used to access workspaces off the main routes - ie secondary circulation is part of the NOA).

Historically in the EU the term used for NOA has been NUA [Net Usable Area]. However in a global methodology this causes a clash with American terminology where NUA is used nationally but actually refers to space defined earlier as NIA; consequently the term NOA is now generally used instead of NUA in the EU to ensure worldwide consistency.

The component parts of NOA are described in more detail in the following paragraphs (Developing the space budget) but for reference are noted here as: workspace, ancillary and support.

The typical areas of interest across these categories of space are shown in Fig. 4.1.C.

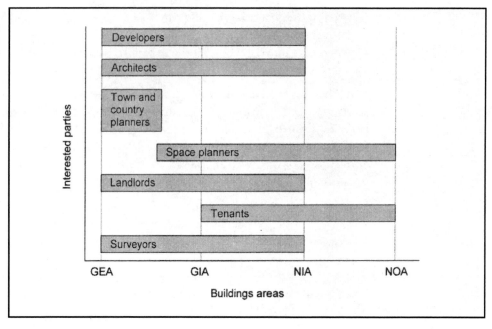

Fig. 4.1.C:
Professional areas of interest in measurement

Developing the space budget

The production of a space budget is the pivotal point of space planning. The process involves taking data from current use, analysing the organisational need and using appropriate space use guidelines to develop a budget for the future space needs of the organisation. It is the numerical representation of the physical demand for space.

The first and most important piece of information to be determined before providing new or reconfigured premises is the amount of space required. The development of a space budget is therefore the first step in the development of a detailed brief or Statement of Requirements (SOR).

A space budget enables organisations to model their need for space based upon a range of options regarding the way it can be used and managed. A spreadsheet model is a typical tool used to establish the space budget. Just like a financial budget, the space budget represents different ways in which space can be "divided" between the many "competing" activities in a building.

In due course the space budget will develop into the full details which are part of a comprehensive SOR. The space budget can also look forward and project the need for space over the next three to five years. The output from the space budget is one figure: the Net Occupiable Area (NOA) required for the facility. NOA is the organisation's need (demand) for space and the intent should be to match this demand with the most appropriate building (supply) available - unfortunately experience suggests that many organisations decide on the building to supply the space before they have accurately established the organisational demand for that commodity!

Fig. 4.1.D (over the page) defines the following components of the space budget:

- workspace

- ancillary (local meeting places, project rooms, storage, etc.)

- support (mail room, reprographics centre, library, network rooms, etc.)

- fit-factor.

The organisational demand expressed as NOA is the sum of these components.

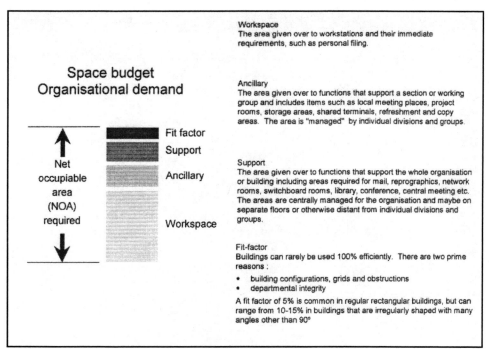

Fig. 4.1.D:
Definitions of some components of the space budget

Spreadsheet models enable different space budgets to be produced for various possible scenarios, including those where sharing of space is to be undertaken. This enables the true space use implications to be measured for each scenario and greatly enhances the decision-making capabilities of the local management or executive team.

Ideally choosing a building should take place once the space budget has been established and not before; however, as observed elsewhere, this is by no means universal practice.

This "wrong way round" approach can lead to a significant mismatch between the organisation and the chosen building often compromising ideal space planning solutions. In the worst case buildings are found to be completely inappropriate or of the wrong size for the intended organisational units.

The space planning process described here follows best practice and has intentionally defined the space budget prior to considering elements of building appraisal.

Building appraisal

Building appraisal is the measurement of buildings in terms of space and performance. It helps evaluate how successfully a building will accommodate an organisational need and to establish the building NOA available for the use of the organisation.

Building appraisal also enables building efficiencies to be measured. These efficiencies are important when considering the performance and value (to a user) of a building.

Floor area per person is freely quoted by users and management alike to justify decisions, defend current practices and argue financial positions. Floor area has become a currency of negotiation and debate; yet just like financial currency, all "areas" around the world are not "equal"; surprisingly, they can vary even in the same country.

Principal areas of difference are:

- the components of area which carry a rental charge

- the ways of measuring floor area

- the ways of describing floor area

- the actual size of buildings compared to the quoted area or negotiated area.

The result is that, when two organisations attempt to compare their space utilisation, it is like comparing apples and oranges.

Any viable real estate strategy must set out definitions of building areas and if the company or comparisons are global the definitions must be capable of being understood and adopted across the required regions. The definitions set out at the beginning of this chapter are now increasingly used as a standard method of building measurement.

The use of "standard" measures may reveal inherent inefficiencies in a particular building which may not otherwise be apparent. The key components of a "standard method of building measurement" are set out in Fig. 4.1.E (over the page) in a simple step by step approach[3]. Both graphical and key issue information is displayed for maximum comprehension. This step-by-step approach represents a way of achieving consistency of measurement on a global scale.

---

[3] *Chilton, James (1998) Unpublished DEGW presentation*

Fig. 4.1.E (a):
Step by step approach to standard method of building measurement. Gross external area

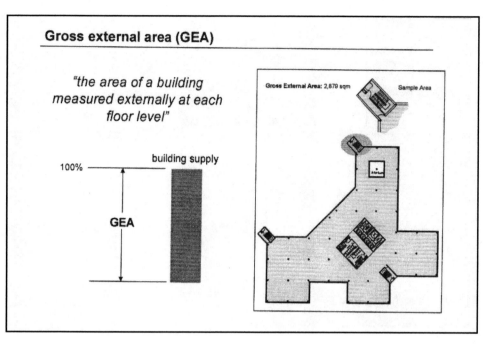

Gross external area (GEA)

"the area of a building measured externally at each floor level"

Fig. 4.1.E (b):
Step by step approach to standard method of building measurement. Gross external area - key points

Gross external area (GEA) - key points

- sometimes called Gross Outside Area (GOA)
- European code of measuring practice term
- measured from outside face of external walls and projections
- complete footprint on all floors
- largest building measurement
- overall area occupied by a building
- applications
    - building cost estimation in some countries
    - Site coverage plot ratio planning and zoning

includes:
- *perimeters wall and projections*
- *internal walls and partitions*
- *columns, stairwells, lifts, escalators, toilets*
- *air or other vertical ducts*
- *lift motor rooms, central heating or air conditioning (ventilation) plant rooms*
- *fuel tank rooms, electricity transformer and/or low tension rooms*
- *open-sided covered areas, ramps, enclosed parking areas*
- *storage rooms and basement archive rooms*

excludes:
- *open balconies*
- *open fire escapes*
- *open vehicle parking areas*

Source: European code of measuring practice

Fig. 4.1.E (c):
Step by step approach to standard method of building measurement. Gross internal area

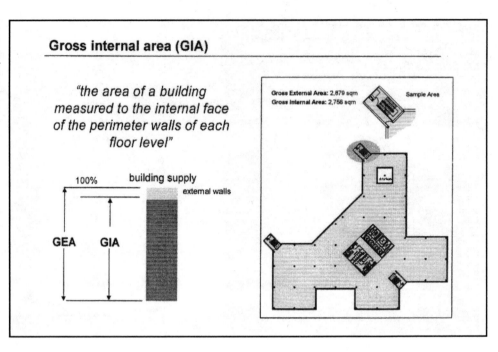

Gross internal area (GIA)

"the area of a building measured to the internal face of the perimeter walls of each floor level"

Gross External Area: 2,879 sqm
Gross Internal Area: 2,758 sqm

Sample Area

100%

building supply
external walls

GEA   GIA

Fig. 4.1.E (d):
Step by step approach to standard method of building measurement. Gross internal area - key points

Gross internal area (GIA) - key points

- sometimes called Gross Floor Area (GFA) or Gross Area
- European code of measuring practice term
- measured between the inside faces of the outside walls
- applications:
    building costs estimations in some countries
    estate agency and valuations
    property management

includes:
- *areas occupied by internal walls and partitions*
- *columns, piers, chimney breasts, stairwells etc*
- *atria with clear height above, measured at base level only**
- *internal open-side balconies**
- *covered rooms*
- *core*
- *loading bays*
- *areas with a headroom of less than 1.5m*

excludes:
- *perimeter wall thickness' and external projections*
- *external open sided balconies, cover ways etc*
- *canopies**

* state separately

Source: European Code of Measuring Practice

Fig. 4.1.E (e):
Step by step approach to standard method of building measurement. Cores

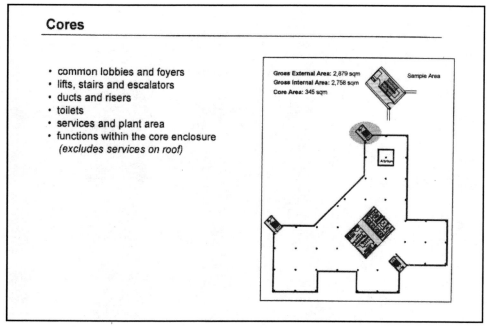

Cores

- common lobbies and foyers
- lifts, stairs and escalators
- ducts and risers
- toilets
- services and plant area
- functions within the core enclosure
  (excludes services on roof)

Gross External Area: 2,879 sqm
Gross Internal Area: 2,758 sqm
Core Area: 345 sqm

Sample Area

Fig. 4.1.E (f):
Step by step approach to standard method of building measurement. Net internal area

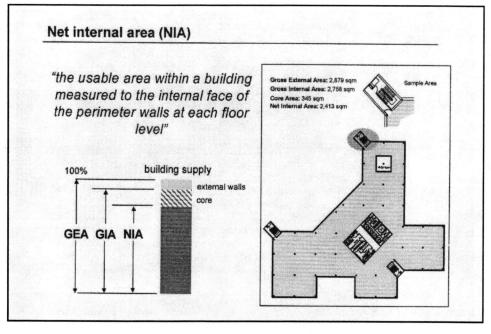

Net internal area (NIA)

"the usable area within a building measured to the internal face of the perimeter walls at each floor level"

Gross External Area: 2,879 sqm
Gross Internal Area: 2,756 sqm
Core Area: 345 sqm
Net Internal Area: 2,413 sqm

Sample Area

100%

building supply

external walls
core

GEA GIA NIA

Fig. 4.1.E (g):
*Step by step
approach to
standard method of
building
measurement.
Net internal area -
key points*

Net internal area (NIA) - key points

- RICS definition
- sum of the GIA less the core area
- also known as net lettable area in the property world (negotiable in law)
- applications
    space planning
    estate agency and valuation
    property management
    cost estimating (fitting-out projects only)

includes:
- *atria with clear height above, measured at base only**
- *entrance halls*
- *notional lift lobbies*
- *kitchens, cleaner cupboards accessed from usable areas*
- *area occupied by skirting and perimeter trunking*

excludes:
- *all core areas*
- *structural elements*

* state separately

Source: RICS Code of Measuring Practice

Fig. 4.1.E (h):
*Step by step
approach to
standard method of
building
measurement.
Primary circulation -
two perspectives*

Primary circulation - two perspectives

PC measurements dependent upon:

(A) building appraisal - Supply
(B) facilities/spatial appraisal - Demand

building appraisal
- the major routes within the NIA that link fire escapes
- must comply with fire regulations
- depth and shape of floor typically dictates minimum amount of primary circulation
- 1500mm width applied typically
- all areas within 7-9m of primary circulation

facilities/spatial appraisal
- driven by client's spatial requirements

Fig. 4.1.E (j):
Step by step approach to standard method of building measurement. Primary circulation

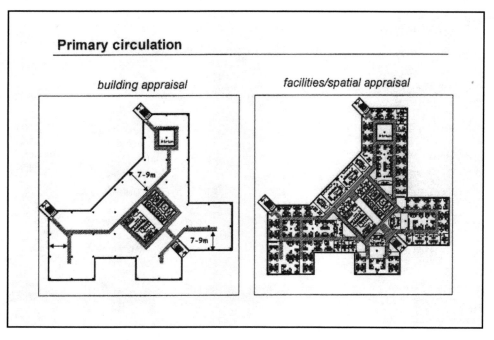

Fig. 4.1.E (k):
Step by step approach to standard method of building measurement. Net occupiable area

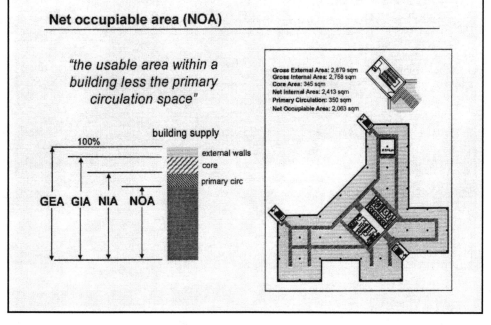

Fig. 4.1.E (l):
*Step by step
approach to
standard method of
building
measurement.
Matching demand
to supply*

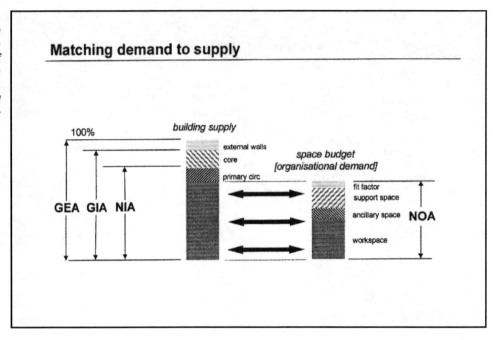

Matching demand to supply

building supply

100%

external walls
core

*space budget
[organisational demand]*

primary circ

GEA GIA NIA

fit factor
support space

ancillary space **NOA**

workspace

Fig. 4.1.E (m):
*Step by step
approach to
standard method of
building
measurement.
Landlord efficiency*

Building efficiencies (typical floor) - landlord efficiency

- net internal area (NIA)
  expressed as a % of GIA

- particular interest of landlord or
  owner

- widely accepted to be 15% of GIA

- high % - low core provision

- low % - high core provision

Efficiency ratings

• excellent: NIA 84% - 87% of GIA

• good: NIA 80% - 83% of GIA

• poor: below 80% and above 87% of GIA

• example:

NIA	2,413	= 87% excellent
GIA	2,758	

Fig. 4.1.E (n):
*Step by step
approach to
standard method of
building
measurement.
Tenant efficiency*

Building efficiencies (typical floor) - tenant efficiency

- net occupiable area expressed as a % of NIA

- particular interest of the tenant

- high NOA:NIA ratio - insufficient primary circulation

- low NOA:NIA ratio - too much circulation

Efficiency ratings

- excellent: 85% NOA or more of NIA

- good: 80% - 84% NOA of NIA

- fair: 75% - 79% NOA of NIA

- poor: less than 75% NOA of NIA

- example:

NOA	2,063	= 85% excellent
NIA	2,413	

Fig. 4.1.E (p):
*Step by step
approach to
standard method of
building
measurement.
Depth of space*

Depth of space

- two critical depths
  perimeter to core
  perimeter to perimeter
- relates to the consideration of aspect measure

- **depth A**
  *area within 6m of external walls or atrium
  [suitable for enclosed offices, open plan
  and ancillary space]*

- **depth B**
  *areas more than 6m and less than 12m
  from external walls or atrium
  [open plan and enclosed offices]*

- **depth C** - *none in adjacent diagram
  areas greater than 12m from external walls
  or atrium [suitable for ancillary and support
  space]*

depth A

depth B

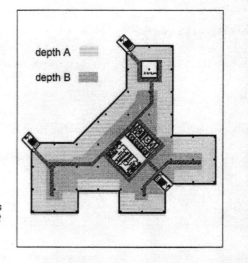

Fig. 4.1.E (q):
*Step by step
approach to
standard method of
building
measurement.
Sub-divisibility*

Sub-divisibility

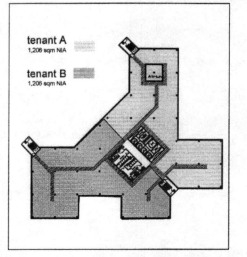

- increases flexibility of space usage
giving:

    *landlords - greater letting option
    tenant - expansion/contraction of space*

- looking for

    *logical/identifiable areas
    minimum common areas
    separate core access/reception*

- expressed as NIA/NLA (either in sq m
or as a percentage)

- tenant A = $\dfrac{1,206 \text{ sq m}}{2,413 \text{ sq m}}$ = 50% NIA

tenant A
1,206 sqm NIA

tenant B
1,206 sqm NIA

Fig. 4.1.E (r):
*Step by step
approach to
standard method of
building
measurement.
Serviceability*

Serviceability

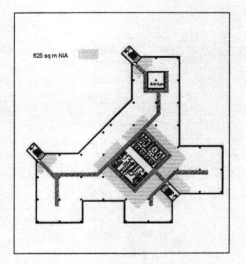

- located adjacent to cores/ducts

- relevant to:

    *kitchens/vending areas
    central support functions
    computer facilities
    additional plant room*

- potential for enclosure

- expressed as percentage of NIA

- within 6m of core

- serviceability = $\dfrac{625 \text{ sq m}}{2,413 \text{ sq m}}$ = 25% NIA

625 sq m NIA

Rentable area vs occupiable area

Although discussed earlier in the chapter the issues surrounding the use of NRA and NOA are again covered here so as to ensure complete clarity with regard to their roles in standard building measurement.

Although NRA is a crucial figure for rent negotiations and legal contracts, it is not a standard measure around the world. Various countries base NRA on different areas. As the real estate market continually battles to maintain a marketing edge many "creative" techniques are used to establish the area that is rented. Rentable area is nearly always negotiable.

Naturally where the real estate is an absolute in possession interest the NRA may not be directly relevant. However as many organisations charge internally for space it may be required to establish a "notional market rent" and in such cases a NRA of some kind will be established ie for the organisations internal market for cross-charging.

The steps of building measurement indicate that NOA is the maximum area available for an organisation to actually use. Also it is the only area that is independent (well almost) of building constraints.

NOA is therefore the most realistic area measurement to use for:

- comparisons between buildings
- benchmarks of space utilisation
- real costs of occupancy.

Hence the aim of any organisation should be to shift to measuring all real estate performance relative to NOA. Examination of the ratio NOA/NIA will ensure that buildings that are particularly inefficient in their provision of "real" occupiable space can be identified before key procurement decisions are made.

Quality of space

Apart from measuring buildings, building appraisal is also concerned with the quality of the space. This is determined by considering such factors as its depth, number of occupiable zones, serviceability (power, drainage, extra building services etc), access and egress, floorplate size and divisibility. A number of these were shown in the steps set out earlier.

In terms of space planning a critical factor of importance is the depth of space; ie the distance from the building perimeter to a central core or perimeter to perimeter. The importance relates to two elements:

- aspect (the ability of occupants to look out on space lit by natural light)
- space planning.

The steps set out depths defined as:

DEPTH A	*Narrow space*	Areas within 6m of external window or atrium wall
DEPTH B	*Medium space*	Areas within 6-12m of external window or atrium wall
DEPTH C	*Deep space*	Areas more than 12m from external window or atrium wall

The relevance of these depths is that certain ones are more appropriate for particular uses than others. The following table (Fig. 4.1.F) summarises this:

Categories of space use				
Type of space	Open plan	Enclosed	Ancillary	Support
Narrow space	+	O	–	–
Medium space	+	+	O	O
Deep space	–	–	+	+

Key   + preferred   O appropriate   – inappropriate

The classification of deep space as "inappropriate" for open plan (ie groups of workspaces which are not separated by walls or partitions) or enclosed workplaces would surprise some office users working for American Companies, who are regularly planned into such spaces in buildings that are designed with deep space.

Finally, depth of space also impacts upon the layout of enclosed offices and open-plan workplaces. This is a question of modularity of components and the way they "fit" together across the depth. Circumstances can arise where the depth of space will cause inefficiencies to be created, such as main corridors that are needlessly wide. These factors can easily be determined by competent space planners.

Choosing the best building

As there is no universally acknowledged prototype of a good building, the following points will help to evaluate possible buildings for an organisation.

Try to avoid buildings which:

- have lots of columns in the floor space (less than 5.5m apart)

- have small floor plates (size of floors less than 920 sq m

- are too narrow (eg: overall depth of office buildings less than 15-18 metres - but depending on usage)

- are irregularly shaped, with lots of angles other than 90°

- are grossly inefficient in terms of their ratio of NOA to NRA.

Optimum efficiency is notoriously difficult to pinpoint, particularly on a worldwide basis. There are many technical circumstances that may cause exceptions to apply, as a result of:

- the building configuration

- the building height (ie number of floors)

- the method of construction and materials used.

In general terms, consideration of building efficiencies by facilities managers should always be for comparative, not absolute, judgements. This is a field where professional advice should be taken from space planning specialists, who are aware of the complexities and dangers involved.

4.1.3 SPACE AUDIT

The need to audit space

Organisations are seldom static. The political, economic and technological climate surrounding them is changing, which affects the technology available to do their job, the markets they work in, the products they deal in and the activities they undertake. The result of this fluidity is a high rate of personnel turnover, shifts in the quality of staff employed, re-organisation of working groups and relationships, and almost certainly an increasing take up of information and communication technology.

Sometimes these changes happen incrementally and are unplanned with the result that in many organisations dramatic changes occur without a clear premises strategy; often such changes are outside the control of the facilities manager resulting from the initiative of individual departments or the information technology function.

The results can be:

* uneven space standards, with gross over-crowding in areas

* a changing distribution of activities within space, as the spatial demands for new activities and equipment are felt

* inefficient usage of space, due to ad hoc planning

* disjointed relationships between departments, and dislocation between buildings as annexes are taken over to meet unpredicted growth, or 'short-term' pressures

* deteriorating visual and climatic environment due to an increase in office automation equipment, with the proliferation of cables, noise and heat

* loss of financial control.

A space audit provides the opportunity to:

* re-visit the opportunities and constraints of the building stock available, and review the 'premises policy'

* review the changing demands of the organisation in the light of the take up of information technology

* test actual space usage against an effective space budget and planning concept

* assess the effectiveness of the facilities management process in planning and managing space and responding to change.

The process of auditing space

The objectives of assessing how space is being used are to:

* relate the amount of space used to norms that may exist for firms in a similar business. These norms, in addition to reflecting net internal, net occupiable and workspace areas per person, may also include a number of different grades, amount and type of enclosure provided, average ancillary space per person, and number of staff per meeting room etc

* assess the way space is being used in practice against organisational guidelines

- identify discrepancies of space provision and usage between departments, grades of staff and working groups. Space planning guidelines formulated by the organisation may bear little relation to changes in patterns of work and the technology used in some groups; the space audit may help to identify these discrepancies.

The quickest way of making an initial assessment of how effectively space is being used is a plan survey. This first study, with the minimum of input, allows an assessment to be made of:

- the proportion of space being used for circulation, support and 'productive work'. This can be compared with company norms and accepted practice

- average workspace area per person in different departments

- size and number of cellular offices.

Using existing floor plans of the building, a 'walk round' survey of the building can be made to note the following information:

- numbers of people (desks) in each room (space)

- numbers of terminals/peripherals (eg printers) in each space

- easily identifiable ancillary activities

- rooms with specialist support functions.

The 'walk round' should be undertaken with the location manager or a representative from each department who can answer questions concerning number of staff per room, designated group boundaries, usage and responsibility for ancillary areas, and who can clarify usage of special space. A review of 5,000 sq m of normal office space should take from three to five hours. From marked up plans an assessment can be made of variations in density and distribution of space usage (Fig. 4.1.G).

Fig. 4.1.G:
Preliminary sketches indicating density and nature of space usage

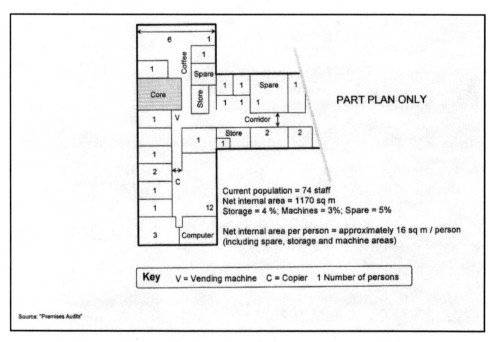

A more accurate analysis of space allocation may be undertaken as a building use survey. Such a survey provides invaluable data before beginning a major replan (Fig. 4.1.H, over the page); it identifies accurately how space is being used in practice, helps in setting future guidelines and maps areas of wastage to be concentrated on in future replans. It may be noted that the area of support and ancillary usage on the single floor in this example may not be typical of the overall pattern. The auditor also identifies areas considered to be redundant or space which is poorly planned.

Fig. 4.1.H:
Building use survey-a more accurate pre-planning analysis

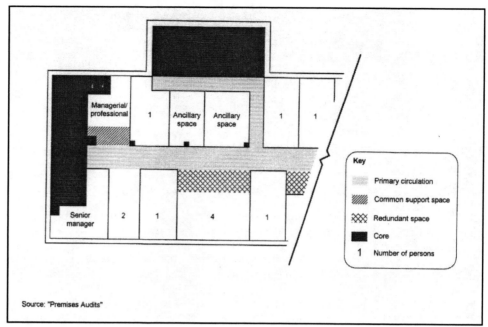

Such a survey is undertaken by drawing in freehand the situation as observed on every floor. In the office, later, more thorough take-offs may be made of space distribution (possibly using CAD). A building use survey of 5,000 sq m of normal office space will take two to three man days.

The final evaluation that may be undertaken is a furniture and equipment survey to ascertain whether there is more or less furniture and equipment being provided than is needed for the job and whether the amount of screening provision or shared furniture - such as meeting tables, filing cabinets and other storage - is compatible with company objectives. Such an assessment may be made by random sampling; first identify areas of varying styles of work and then take an appropriate sample, say 20%. Actual patterns of space usage may vary dramatically from planned standards. In fast-growing organisations the distribution of space and demand may change even as the planning process proceeds!

Reviewing the demands of information and communication technology (ICT)

The impact of technology on the office environment has been dramatic. Its effect is pervasive, influencing:

- the ergonomics of the workplace

- the amount of worksurface required for visual display screens, as well as the additional floor space required to accommodate printers, and servers

- the levels of lighting and the design of light fittings to reduce glare and reflection on screens

- the capacity of the building and furniture to cope with wires and cables

- the need to extract heat from equipment

- the need for acoustic barriers to reduce the noise of machines and equipment

- the pattern of work, and eventually the distribution of space
- the desire for a visual language that can cope with the proliferation of equipment and cables
- the cost of operating the building
- the cost of a new building, refurbishment and fitting-out.

A review of the demands of information technology on the building and space usage should cover:

- desktop and mobile (laptop) computing needs, including future developments such as flat screens and wireless requirements
- a visual survey of typical areas to identify if any unplanned take up of information technology has resulted in a deterioration of the working environment
- impact of telecommunication handsets and any trends to the use of headsets or cordless handsets/headsets
- an assessment of adaptations that have already been made and if possible the expenditure.

Server and central telecommunications installations tend to be budgeted as capital items, but the installations of desk-based systems for word processing and graphics work, are likely to be revenue items, purchased by individual departments, and additional furniture, extra wiring and even a local air handling system may come out of the revenue and maintenance budget; the result is that operating costs appear to increase, which could be the result of a 20 to 30% add-on for adapting to information technology.

To understand trends in ICT take-up, a small group consisting of the ICT manager, telecommunications manager and facilities manager may be brought together to map past experience and predict future trends. This information should act as a basis for predicting changing space needs and a building adaptation policy for dealing with any changes required as a result.

A 'walk round' survey of the building may be used to identify areas where the environment is deteriorating with excessive unplanned technology. Simple indicators are:

- the number and length of trailing wires, which will suggest the need for more outlets
- surface mounted wiring (either along skirtings, or across floors) with a tape covering, reflecting problems of cabling
- fan on desks to take off heat; paper over windows to reduce heat gain and glare on screens
- density of terminals and peripherals which may be measured as floor area per terminal or as a ratio of equipment to staff. These measures may then be used to calculate heat gains, and thresholds for installing mechanical air handling/cooling
- the number of terminals with cardboard hoods or home-made adjusters used to reduce reflection on screens.

Of course, current Health and Safety legislation is addressing many of these issues - See Chapter 8.2.

4.1.4 FACILITY AND SPACE PLANNING

Some would argue that facility planning is the most important facet of facilities management. In terms of space the planning function covers a wide range of activities but at its most fundamental it requires an understanding of the concept, related to demand and supply, that an organisation's needs for facilities will be met by a building as illustrated in Fig. 4.1.J.

Fig. 4.1.J:
Demand-supply-use concept model

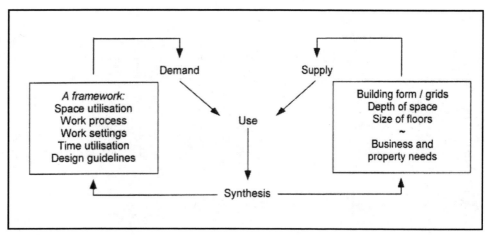

The use of this concept describes the much misunderstood discipline of space planning. Misunderstood primarily because it is undervalued and often thought to only deal with furniture layouts. It is truly more strategic than that, providing an essential management tool for the facilities manager.

Space planning is often considered part of architecture and interior design, but in reality it cannot be said that every architect or interior designer is able to carry out effective and efficient planning. Before employing full time space planners or consultants a facilities manager should make sure that references to successful projects are available in good numbers. Asking the furniture supplier to do it, even for a fee, will almost inevitably lock the organisation into a plan to suit the system or range rather than vice versa.

Space planning can have a fundamental effect on facilities economics and worker productivity and therefore will benefit from high quality professional input rather than being done cheaply by untrained personnel. There is, however, a trend to employ two different groups to provide the total space planning service. First the key professionals provide the initial brief, concept development and even furniture selection advice, then the physical planners (usually CAD literate), who could be from the furniture supplier, provide the layout plans based on the agreed concept.

Space planning stands on its own as a discipline alongside architecture and interior design. It is a process that helps facilities managers manage the space within their accommodation portfolio more effectively. As such it is, or at least should be, inextricably bound up with corporate planning and the development of long range plans that support corporate decisions on real estate.

The key is that space use, like every other aspect of facilities policy, only makes sense when linked to corporate objectives and to the business plan - leading to the following definition of space planning:

> *'the process of achieving appropriate and functional spatial relationships of business functions, and satisfying the needs of the people who perform these functions, in such a way that the resulting physical solutions meet corporate objectives, are cost-effective, can be managed efficiently and, above all, are capable of accommodating change'.*

This definition points out the key factors about the relationship of space planning to the company business plan. It also reminds us of the need to manage space through time. However, the sting is in the tail, for the need to accommodate change is perhaps the trickiest part of all.

Change is all around us and if facilities management has one certainty it is that things will change. Why is it therefore that so many final layouts do the exact opposite providing inflexible and rigid solutions that respond to the past and not to the future needs of changing organisations?

A key aspect of space planning is the process of establishing organisational need and matching it to accommodation provision. The key to effective space planning is the establishment of data for each side of the demand/supply equation and also a clear picture of the way in which previous demand/supply equations have been resolved by analysing the current use (space audit).

Space planning takes the elements of the above equation and by providing a synthesis and feedback loop enables the resolution of demand by appropriate supply to be achieved and the establishment of a new use.

The traditional stages of space planning

The basic stages of space planning are described by the following techniques or processes. In certain projects only one or two of the processes may be utilised, whereas all of them would be required in a project such as a major relocation.

Space auditing

An audit of current space use carried out by visual surveys - counting, measuring and sketching; together with analysis of plans and layouts if they exist. Audit information is most usefully held in a database to enable ease of access and review of existing data to set against new models of organisational need as these are developed (described more fully in 4.1.2).

Organisational brief

Development of the organisational brief (sometimes just called the brief) from a process of interviews: with senior management for the vision, culture and the future direction and with senior department representatives for current working methods and headcount projections. Once produced it should reflect the organisational need.

Space use guidelines

The development of guidelines for the use of space. These guidelines will help the planning of enclosed and open areas and will also encompass ancillary and support areas. Guidelines are not rigid standards, they provide a framework for developing solutions in many circumstances. When a solution is agreed for a given building and organisational function these can be termed the standards (or the guidelines for managing the space in that particular building as described more fully in 4.1.3).

Developing the space budget

The production of a space budget is the pivotal point of space planning. It takes data from current use and the organisational need and, using the space use guidelines, develops a budget for the future space needs of the organisation. It is the numerical representation of the demand for space (described more fully in 4.1.1).

Having established the space use need and matched this with a suitable built facility the process generally continues with the following stages.

Stacking plans

These provide the one-dimensional vertical disposition of an organisation within a building. The plan is driven by company politics, policies and functional adjacency requirements. The stacking plan produces the first output in which users of space within the organisation are likely to take any interest. Stacking plans are usually approved by project executive committees.

Planning concepts

These are physical representations of key structured layout principles utilised to ensure both efficient and effective use of space. The concepts draw together the demand issues and deal with them in two dimensions across the building floorplates. Development of the planning concepts is the next stage working from space guidelines and the space budget (which are one-dimensional). The process lays down the ground rules for space management. Planning concepts will indicate where furniture, ancillary and support areas are to be set out within the space. It will also distinguish the most appropriate zones (established during building appraisal) for enclosed offices, areas requiring special servicing, meeting rooms and open plan areas.

Blocking plans

The stacking plan and the concepts together with the detailed information about departments encapsulated within the space budget drive the production of blocking plans which are the two-dimensional representation of departments and groups within the organisation on each floor of the building. Simple plans only show total departmental use; more detailed ones will show the degrees of cellularisation and positions of ancillary areas.

Block plans only contain department names; further detail is discouraged. Block plans generally require two or more passes through the project committees. Sometimes designers do not distinguish between stacking and blocking plans although distinguishing between them is quite critical to the process of getting an orderly, non-political approach by clients to the issues.

Initial layouts

The first layouts will show all the furniture set out on the floorplate. Generic layouts will not have names against the workstations; more detailed initial layouts will have names and other important departmental information annotated on them. These layouts generally require two or more passes through the project committees. Drawings are generally done on a CAD system.

At this stage contact between the space planners and the end users will increase dramatically.

Final layouts

The 'first pass' layouts as agreed should form the basis for the final layouts. Under the two stage approach these plans are often done by furniture suppliers particularly where new furniture is involved. These drawings will contain all the information required to locate staff and their furniture when the move has to take place. The drawings are generally done on a CAD system and can, with advantage, be linked to a database so that a facility manager can establish schedules of staff, location, furniture and components, extension numbers, communication outlets and the like.

Integration with the furniture process

The selection of new, or use of existing, furniture has a major impact on the space planning process. Use of existing furniture for example greatly extends the time and hence cost of the process. There is a general misconception that the use of existing furniture is a "no cost option" but nothing could be further from the truth. Unfortunately the cost of new furniture is often so large that the cost of time involved in the much more complex process of rationalising the status quo does not hold the same weight in decision making. Of course, the real cost issue is that of efficiency of people working in the reconfigured space, but that argument is rarely articulated - and when it is it is often defeated by scepticism.

The way in which the two processes relating to space and furniture run in parallel can be clearly seen in Fig. 4.1.K.

Fig. 4.1.K:
The complete space and furniture planning process

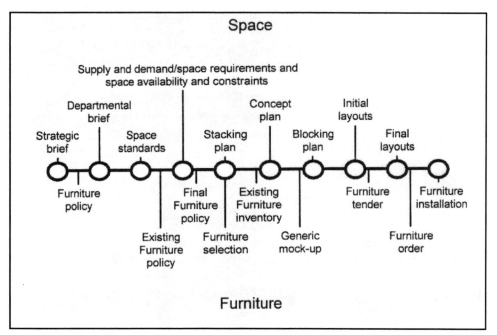

Space standards

Space standards (and their counterparts space or facility guidelines) have always been an essential foundation stone of space planning. In a technical sense they still are, but they need to be applied carefully so as not to cause resistance to their use by employees - particularly at senior levels.

Over time space standards have become guidelines and developed far beyond just specifying the size of a workstation. An understanding of the relevance of standards and guidelines is important.

What are guidelines?

The nature of guidelines can be somewhat elusive - everyone seems to know what they want and yet no one can quite describe the end product. The following brief history of the evolution of space standards into space guidelines is informative and particularly relevant to placing the concept of guidelines in true perspective.

Space standards in the '70s

Corporate standards for the procurement, development and occupation of buildings began as natural extensions of company policy. Developed where repetition of workstations occurred, they defined from past experience the best ways of achieving a given goal, endeavouring to ensure conformity of space use across the company. Their purpose was predominantly to save time and money. The 1970's were the peak of success for space standards, which were used as corporations slowly spread their presence around the world. Organisations were strongly hierarchical and beset with employee grades relating to status; the predominant management style was autocratic. This environment was a perfect match for space standards and, when properly implemented, they were generally successful.

Guidelines in the '80s

However in the 1980's standards came under increasing pressure. Growth was the order of the day, and whilst big was still beautiful the management style was becoming more democratic and the hierarchies were flattening and consequently grades structures followed suit.

Standards and democracy are not comfortable bedfellows. A science of cultural difference developed, which at the time was often seen to be an excuse for ignoring standards developed in another country. Experience of space planning professionals also indicated that standards were often too rigid and that the creation of guidance that provided a realistic framework with a degree of choice was distinctly more appropriate. Rather than 'standards' the new ground rules were called 'guidelines'.

The development of corporate space guidelines progressed through the 80's and by the beginning of the 90's were recognised as the most realistic way of supporting the business goals of international companies. However space guidelines had varying degrees of success in organisations, some working quite well while others never really achieved the results they should have done. This caused some space planning professionals to consider the background to see if they could determine any reasons for the variable effects.

Their research established a number of trends which could be related to the complexity of the guidelines. Simple space guidelines were generally quite successful providing they were produced sensitively and avoided direct prescription. On the other hand wide ranging design guidelines were only successful in organisations such as retailers where identity had to be absolute and precise. Design guides in entrepreneurial organisations were often complete failures, although practitioners were generally reluctant to admit it. Undoubtedly the success rate of more complex guidelines was questionable. This led to the hypothesis that the most important factor was who the guidelines were written for not what they contained!

Who are guidelines written for?

Most design guidelines are developed to control the excesses of external designers, engineers and planners and written either directly for them or to be transmitted through an internal project manager to them. Frequently the nature of these "technical" guidelines are either too prescriptive or patronising and from the standpoint of the chosen design professionals immediately places them in a "box" that minimises their creativity. Interestingly design guides are nearly always written by designers themselves being either part of the in-house property team or a valued consultant designer who "knows and understands" the company. Perhaps these designers have worked too hard at describing the design solution rather than the key information which is required to constitute one!

It is hardly surprising that many designers balk at this state of affairs, initially sounding compliant (during the selection process!) but quickly becoming frustrated by information that they consider inappropriate for the project they have undertaken and probably feeling their role is trivialised. In the case of design guides for some retail companies their apparent success can also be attributed to the fact that no major designer is involved and that design-and- install is employed directly with a contractor or shop fitter.

On an international scale significant differences of approach and application can develop for each project causing conflicts between custom and practice and local cultural values. Before long the lead designer convinces the local office of the problems and suddenly everyone is fighting against the corporate centre. The local office will talk about the centre being out of touch, unprofessional, not aware of the real business issues or any other factor that may help to disguise their lack of enthusiasm for the subservient role. In the environment of such debate the real issues are quickly forgotten and the inherent usefulness of the guideline information is debased and finally ignored. The key question is what can be done to minimise this effect and turn guidelines into the real added value product that they should be.

A more successful approach is to focus upon who guidelines should be written for and to endeavor to extend the initiative beyond that of Real Estate or Facilities alone. An effective way of achieving the ideal is to develop information for the key decision maker.

Influencing key decision makers

The most difficult principle for any corporation's central service functions to accept is that there is more than likely someone important at a local office who will make the key decisions and not them. In fact the first rule of successful guidelines is that the decisions cannot be made by the central service function - at least not in the traditional sense. The ultimate role of the centre is vital to the success of guidelines as we shall describe later.

It can sometimes be tricky sorting out who the real decision makers are, but it is important to make absolutely sure that the right ones have been identified. For example at a local office it may well be simply the office manager, however in some organisations the real power and decision base may be with the regional sales manager based at a local office and not the local office manager.

Guidelines for the turn of the century

The development of guidelines in the current environment owes as much to PR and communications as it does understanding the content. There are likely to be a number of parts to the guideline package the first being an overview for the decision maker. Having established who the decision maker is the guidelines should be produced to directly influence them. The overview will certainly be different from the format of technical guidelines. This overview must:

- talk the language of the decision maker

- be in a format which they will utilise (brochure, video etc)

- identify how the guidelines can help them achieve their goals in both the short and long term

- indicate the important links between organisations and facilities

- set out some key performance indicators which will become highly visible across the corporation

- describe the few critical areas that they need to influence to ensure the optimum solution.

The presentation of such material needs to be quite different from conventional guidelines and should be much more concise enabling a busy person to absorb the key points quickly. More than anything else they must explain why certain decisions that they make will affect their "bottom line". The challenge is to capture their imagination and to provide a mechanism for influencing change.

Whatever happened to space standards?

The foregoing has moved a long way from simple space standards and yet they still form an essential part of space planning. Space budgets cannot be produced without them and as has been shown this is an essential part of the planning process. The key is to understand that every guideline will turn into a standard in a particular building. Once all the various grids and floorplates and depths have been examined the company guidelines turn into building standards. What has happened is that space planners still use standards to do their work, but the strategic thinking is done using guidelines.

Hopefully the importance of guidelines is now clear. **They must stem from the business plan and will ultimately determine the total cost of premises. For this reason they constitute the most critical decision an organisation has to make in connection with premises economics apart from location.**

There is also a golden rule; **guidelines must stem from the functional needs of occupiers rather than from an individual's grade or status within the organisation.** That is not to say that a person in a senior position does not have an appropriate worksetting; just that the decision as to what they have should be based upon what they do rather than what they feel they want or historically have had.

Figs. 4.1.L (a), (b) (over the page) shows two space guidelines ((a) for an enclosed setting and (b) for an open plan worksetting) and clearly shows the level to which guidelines rise above a mere space standard. It should be noted that the open workstation carries elements of secondary circulation within the final standard whereas for the enclosed office the secondary circulation is essentially non existent.

Fig. 4.1.L (a):
Space guideline example: Multi-task activity setting-enclosed

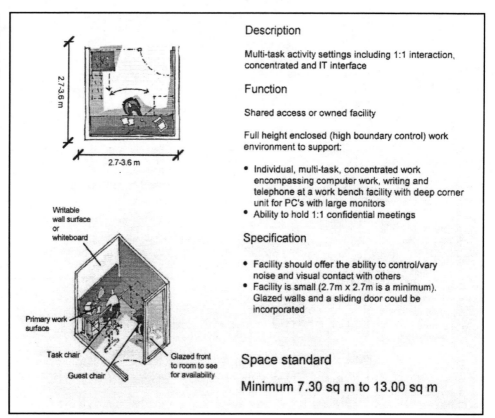

Description

Multi-task activity settings including 1:1 interaction, concentrated and IT interface

Function

Shared access or owned facility

Full height enclosed (high boundary control) work environment to support:

- Individual, multi-task, concentrated work encompassing computer work, writing and telephone at a work bench facility with deep corner unit for PC's with large monitors
- Ability to hold 1:1 confidential meetings

Specification

- Facility should offer the ability to control/vary noise and visual contact with others
- Facility is small (2.7m x 2.7m is a minimum). Glazed walls and a sliding door could be incorporated

Space standard

Minimum 7.30 sq m to 13.00 sq m

(figure labels: 2.7-3.6 m; 2.7-3.6 m; Writable wall surface or whiteboard; Primary work surface; Task chair; Guest chair; Glazed front to room to see for availability)

Planning efficiency

A large number of buildings seem to be designed for the benefit of the passer-by, the investor, the builder - anyone but the occupier, the user of the space.

The building design features which most influence the ability to use the space effectively are:

- window mullions, ceiling grids and structural bays, which influence
  where partitions can be located and the size of enclosed offices that can
  provided. An organisation that has a high demand for enclosed offices
  moving into a building with an inflexible planning grid may find itself with

Fig. 4.1.L (b):
Space guideline example: Professional support activity - open plan

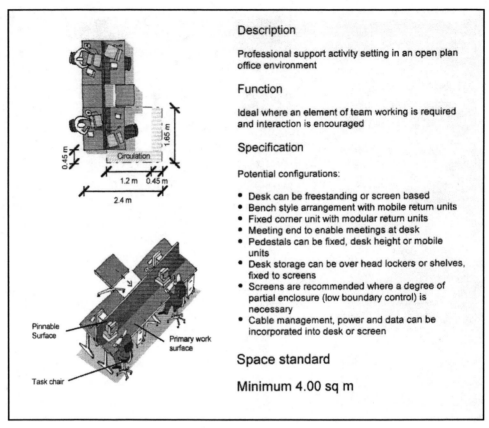

Description

Professional support activity setting in an open plan office environment

Function

Ideal where an element of team working is required and interaction is encouraged

Specification

Potential configurations:

- Desk can be freestanding or screen based
- Bench style arrangement with mobile return units
- Fixed corner unit with modular return units
- Meeting end to enable meetings at desk
- Pedestals can be fixed, desk height or mobile units
- Desk storage can be over head lockers or shelves, fixed to screens
- Screens are recommended where a degree of partial enclosure (low boundary control) is necessary
- Cable management, power and data can be incorporated into desk or screen

Space standard

Minimum 4.00 sq m

larger offices than required creating a major wastage of space. Fig 4.1.M shows the effect of some traditional planning grids on space allocation, and maximum space utilisation (modern office buildings are most often designed to a 1.5 sq m grid which is not dictated by the fenestration modules).

Fig. 4.1.M:
The effect of planning grids on cellular office space efficiency

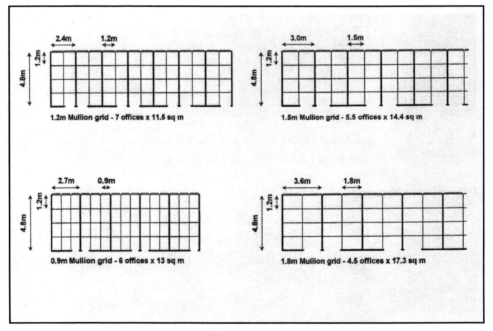

- depth of building, dimension from wall to wall, location of cores and configuration of floor plan, influence how efficiently the space may be utilised. The width of a building may be too great to provide for offices either side of a central corridor, or too narrow to accommodate enclosed offices, a workplace and a primary circulation route.

- the location of columns and service elements (HVAC units) may hamper efficient planning and reduce the effective space available

- the frequency and location of power and data outlets may also restrict planning flexibility.

In addition to the assessment of planning flexibility, the capacity of building shells should also be assessed against such criteria as:

- potential to accommodate enclosed offices

- adaptability to be planned for different styles of layout and size of working groups

- capacity to accommodate cables

- flexibility of air-conditioning to adapt to varying heat loads.

4.1.5 THE COST OF SPACE

Total premises costs in the context of turnover

In Chapter 5.1 the relationship between premises and the total costs of an organisation are considered. Fig 4.1.N is a reminder that premises represent possibly one-third of the total cost of facilities - 5% or so of the total outgoings.

Fig. 4.1.N:
Typical turnover, profit, facilities and ICT costs

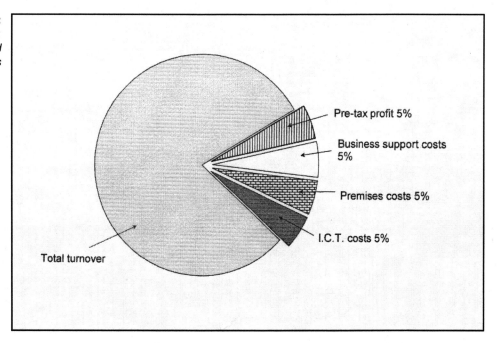

However the whole of the premises costs figure is geared to the amount of space occupied.

Factors influencing the cost of space per unit of area include:

- location

- quality/performance (but see Chapters 2.4 and 2.1 respectively)

- tenure

- operating requirements

- fitting out.

However, because the largest cost component in the premises cost equation is the rent (or mortgage equivalent) the location is generally regarded to be the major influential factor. It may be noted that in the owner-occupier model location is still a key factor as it influences the land price and also, to a certain extent, quality of design and specification and hence construction costs.

UK variations

Even in a tight little enclave like the UK, costs in the various locations vary greatly, and it is not the building costs, nor the operating costs, which rule the day but the residual value of the land derived from the perceived market value of the investment.

The development land values are highest in the high rental, low investment yield areas. It is in these high rental value areas that top-management pressure can be brought to bear on space use - but only in those organisations whose economic performance has got out of-sync with the premises cost regime of the location into which they find themselves hooked.

As discussed elsewhere in this text the operating costs, though sometimes varying a little unaccountably between location, do not impact greatly, or at all, on the overall costs of premises which, at the time of going to press, ranged from £250-350 per sq.m NIA p.a. in the provincial cities and upto £900 per sq.m NIA p.a. in the prime parts of London.

Effects of varying density

The 'knee-jerk' solution to mitigating the high cost of premises is to decrease the space being used by the employees. This is generally done by one or two means, namely:

- changing the layout to provide more workstations per unit of space (squeezing the space standards)

- planning the space and its management to permit multiple use of 'non-territorial' workstations (sometimes called 'dynamic' space use).

In practice these means provide polarised solutions that only work successfully in a few business examples. The solutions also carry with them forgotten consequences. In the case of increased physical density the cost of operating the space must increase. Doors will open and close more frequently, carpets will get more wear, cooling loads will demand more maintenance and consume more energy, security will become more of a problem and furniture costs may increase and so on. With non-territorial space solutions there will be similar extra costs of managing the space to keep it comparable with fully dedicated space use and so these extra costs will reduce any savings from pure space efficiency.

Nevertheless dynamic space use can have a dramatic impact on space use per capita. Fig. 4.1.P (over the page) clearly indicates that when ideal conditions prevail the net office area per capita can be reduced to some 20% of space used in the traditional 'one person per desk' fashion.

Great care is required in interpreting such graphs. Although there is a clear overall reduction in the amount of space per person the distribution of the different elements within each 'mini' space budget is quite different. In fact the distribution will vary depending upon the nature of the work being carried out as this has the greatest impact on the requirements for ancillary and support.

Fig. 4.1.Q (over the page) looks at the cost per capita of dynamic strategies in the context of contrasting economic locations.

It is presumably the prospect of savings of the kind evidenced in these figures that persuades financial directors to direct facilities managers to implement them in less than ideal circumstances! Too often facilities managers give in to these instructions in circumstances when they are likely to be a false economy.

In office buildings non-territorial strategies have worked with varying degrees of success. Some bold experiments of the early 1990's have been softened somewhat;

Fig. 4.1.P:
Dynamic space use-per capita analysis

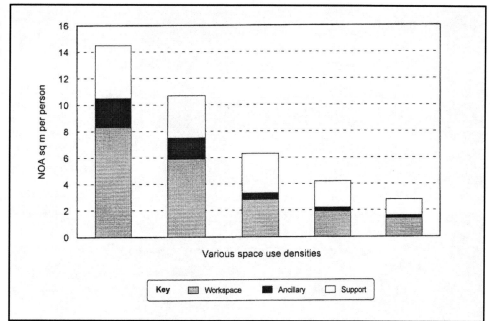

Fig. 4.1.Q:
Dynamic space use-per capita premises costs

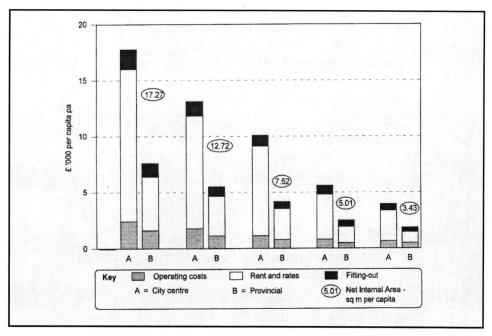

however in examples of companies or departments with highly peripatetic staff like auditors, salesmen and consultants the use of shared workplaces has considerably reduced vast areas of under utilised (over time) floor areas. Whereas dynamic space use is a relatively new concept open plan usage is not. However there are lessons to learn from the wide abuse of the open plan concept in the name of premises economics.

To put it bluntly; when the concept of open plan offices (bürolandschaft) was first introduced in the 1970's many managers who should have known better 'forced' employees to function in workplace environments that did not properly support their day-to-day activities. The end result was poor value for money; being at least an irritant to company employees who worked under even greater pressure as a consequence and at worst resulting in severely impaired company productivity.

The key issue relates to the impact that any proposed workplace strategies have on the productivity of the workforce. Appropriate strategies, be they non-territorial or otherwise, have the very real potential to add value as well as minimising cost. However this added value will only be successfully achieved if the appropriate degree of thought and concentration goes into the creation of such strategies. The involvement of users in thinking about what space they need and how they use it is now fundamentally important if solutions are to be successful and sustainable. The following section sets out many of the various factors that must be considered if 'new ways of working' solutions are to be contemplated.

4.1.6 FUTURE TRENDS IN SPACE USE[4]

New influences

The introduction and continuing advances of ICT have revolutionised the way business is undertaken and the nature of office work. It has taken away routine process work, freeing up employees to add value in better ways. Interaction and the exchange of information and knowledge are now key. Employees are much more empowered about how and even where and when they do their jobs.

Changing social attitudes of people are also influencing the increase in the informality and flexibility of office working practices. Often referred to as new ways of working. All of these developments can be regarded as workplace **dynamics**.

However, despite these developments, most office workplaces are still strongly based, in terms of style and layout, around the original early clerical factories. And not just in old buildings, but often even in brand new buildings too.

The diversity of office work

Studies of the utilisation of office work space can be extremely revealing. A typical study would regularly check a range of desks, offices or other workspaces (such as meeting areas), perhaps every half hour, every day for two or three weeks. This allows a reasonable realistic sample of office life to be captured. The study would not just note whether the workspace is used or empty, but also exactly what activity is being performed there when in use.

A simple study exercise of this nature could typically show (Fig. 4.1.R over the page) that:

- workspace is heavily under-utilised - reflecting the dynamics of office work (meetings, informal interaction, working away from the office and so on); and

- a wide range of, often conflicting and combined, activities are undertaken - reflecting the diversity of office work (reading, typing, writing, PC work, telephone, meetings, reflection and so on).

All workspace costs money, so empty space is a waste. Employees' time costs money, so inappropriate or ineffective worksettings can be a waste too. Such findings need to be interpreted with care, but they do provide some powerful pointers to clear opportunities for change and improvement.

Such studies also need to be set up properly, not least to ensure that the motives of the study are understood by staff. It is the use of space and not the work of the individual that is being studied. They are also best undertaken professionally by specialists, which will also add to the credibility of the findings with staff and management.

---

[4] *Bell, Adryan. (2000) Transforming your workplace, Institute of Personnel and Development, Management Shapers Series (modified version of Chapters 1 and 2)*

Fig. 4.1.R:
*Workplace
utilisation*

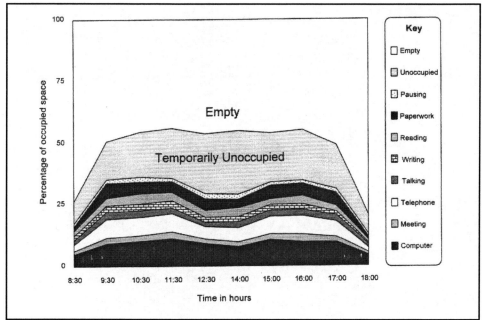

New role of the workplace

Organisations are now realising that, alongside technology, the workplace is one of, if not the most, significant tools to its staff in terms of business effectiveness; if you get it right, it can work wonders but get it wrong, and it can stifle business activities and hinder development and progress.

And getting it wrong probably includes doing nothing.

It is worth noting that despite the increasing flexibility in working practices, including degrees of home and remote working, the office workplace is still very much at the heart of most organisations. It may be used in different ways, it may even be smaller in the future - but it will continue to play a vital role in the life of an organisation and its people.

Increasingly, the workplace will be used for specific reasons and not just out of habit or routine. It will be used as one of a number of working options and be the place where people go, in particular, to interact and obtain and exchange information and knowledge. And these will be the most important and valuable aspects of people's jobs.

But to fulfil this new role effectively, most workplaces will need to change and evolve appropriately.

Efficiency vs effectiveness

The temptation always is to focus on efficiency when looking to transform your workplace. This is partly due to the inevitable pressures to justify the cost (or savings) involved in what you want to do. There is no doubt that efficiencies can be made - notably through the sharing of workspace, where appropriate.

Such efficiencies and savings can be realised reasonably easily - but they should not be the sole focus of your approach. This will arouse suspicion with staff on the motives of the changes. It will provide immediate benefits. But too much emphasis on efficiency only will not bring long term, sustainable benefits.

The more substantial benefits are those based around effectiveness. But such benefits are indirect, less obvious, harder to quantify and take longer to realise. They are typically expressed by 'soft' measures - based on perceptions and feelings. Productivity, creativity, motivation, stimulation, knowledge exchange, staff retention and attraction are all examples of such benefits. But they are extremely important.

New concepts

The drivers of office dynamism and diversity point towards the need for a wider, more appropriate and efficient range of office worksettings. It also suggests the need for increased effectiveness, adaptability, sharing and comfort in the workplace. And even perhaps some excitement.

This implies a clear move away from the clerical factory. A move away from just providing staff with a desk and a chair. And a move away from the traditional planning and thinking of what an office looks like and how it is used. A way of dealing with these new concepts from a space planning perspective has been through the development of a workplace strategy which can be enshrined in the corporate guidelines.

A successful workplace strategy will provide a simple balance of worksettings, that provide the key element for transforming and improving the workplace. These can be viewed essentially as a menu - where you can pick out the best configuration of options to match your organisation and its needs.

Some typical menu options that could form part of such a strategy are described in the following table.

When reading these options, do not get too concerned about how and when such concepts might be implemented. Focus on understanding the concepts and how they can better support working practices.

All these worksettings, of course, need to have appropriate technology and telephony to support the work activities undertaken at them. Technology is a key element of the new workplace and a key enabler of much of the flexibility and mobility required.

Typical options from a workplace strategy

Owned desk

A homebase workstation for staff based in the office at a desk most of the time - ideally allocated on the basis of business need, not status.

Owned office

A homebase office for staff who are office-based most of the time - and regularly need the facilities provided by an office, in terms of privacy, confidentiality and concentration - ideally allocated on the basis of business need, not status.

Shared (hot) desk

A desk used by a number of staff, who use it for only part of their time as they are often at meetings or away from the office - can be used to encourage mixing and cross-fertilisation of staff, although also sometimes arranged in zones to keep teams together and provide identity.

Shared (hot) office

Operating on the same basis as a hot desk, but additionally supporting the need for occasional privacy, confidentiality or concentration.

Touchdown

Workbenches to support short-stay, drop-in style working, often designed for standing up only - useful for visitors - and often placed near entrances or circulation - see Fig. 4.1.S.1 (a): Touchdown (over the page).

Study booth / carrel

Semi-open or enclosed shared / hot desk, located in quieter areas to support concentration - see Fig. 4.1.S.1 (b): Study booths.

Fig. 4.1.S.1:
(a) *Touchdown*
(b) *Study booths*

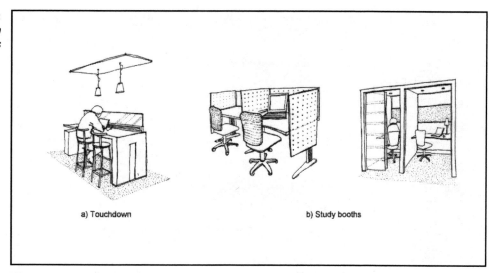

a) Touchdown   b) Study booths

Formal meeting rooms

Enclosed meeting room, on the lines of a traditional meeting room, with formal table and chairs - the room would be typically well equipped in terms of technology support, enabling conference calls, presentations, video conferencing etc. - furniture might also be very adaptable, to allow different styles of meetings to be held.

Informal meeting area

Open, semi-open or even enclosed meeting space - with a more informal feel, often with softer furniture - and situated near main circulation and coffee points - see Fig. 4.1.S.2 (c): Informal meeting.

Quiet area / room

Dedicated areas designed to provide a contrast to the interactive nature of the office - to support reflection and concentration - see Fig. 4.1.S.2 (d): Quiet area / room.

Fig. 4.1.S.2:
(c) *Informal meeting*
(d) *Quiet area/room*

c) Informal meeting   d) Quiet area / room

Project space

Open or enclosed space, designed and dedicated specifically for project and team working activities - typically be set up to support interaction, as well as individual work and its furniture and fittings may be mobile and flexible to accommodate this; whiteboards and pinboards would feature to assist the development of ideas and sharing of knowledge - such space may be allocated to a team or project to 'own' for a particular period of time - see Fig. 4.1.S.3 (e): project/breakout space.

Fig. 4.1.S.3:
(e) *Project/breakout*
space

e) Project / breakout space

Service area

Dedicated area for photocopying, printing, post etc. - normally centrally located and partly enclosed to reduce noise transfer to other areas.

It can be seen that these worksettings are not necessarily as radical in themselves as might have first been thought; often they do not even require new furniture or fittings. Some of them may already exist in the workplace. Also some new worksettings can simply be adapted from existing ones. Some can even fulfil a number of roles. The essential part of any new ways of working concept is the way that these settings are combined and set out within the workspace.

While the actual provision of the work setting should not present any major problems the concepts behind them do require a change in how people use and think about their workplace. As stated earlier the way they are put together and planned is a very important consideration and for this reason alone space planning and space management have not become redundant activities. In fact they are as crucial as ever but now need to operate even more closely with other disciplines such as Information/Communication Technology and Human Resources.

New protocols

Many of these new worksettings may be shared. This requires new disciplines, protocols and behaviours from people. In particular:

- adjusting workspace to meet individual needs, as appropriate

- leaving workspace as found for others to use afterwards, including clearing away of personal items and papers

- booking use of the workspace in advance, where appropriate.

This leads to new ways of managing workspace, particularly in terms of booking systems and filing and storage policies. And also the introduction of clear desk policies. Staff need preparation and guidance to assist in the transition to these concepts. These needs have led to the development of a new service called workplace change management which is geared to preparing people for their new workplace, rather than the traditional way of just preparing the workplace for the people.

In terms of sharing and booking space, it is important to recognise that office work can be both planned and spontaneous. Therefore, it will be important to have some shared workspace that can be booked and secured in advance, as well other shared workspace that is used on a non-bookable, first-come, first served basis. Getting this balance right will be important - but it is something that can be adjusted easily through experience.

New ways of working does not necessarily require that all worksettings are shared. In fact there are a number of examples of these new concepts where every employee has a dedicated workplace (a "homebase" as part of a community or neighbourhood). Where this is the case it is usual to find these bases providing a small but adequate worksetting for each individual enabling other space within the space budget to be made available for group and interactive settings (such as project/breakout space - see Fig. 4.1.S.3 (e) (previous page) that support the work processes of the community.

Where real innovation takes place, up to 50% of new workspace might typically be given over to shared, interactive non-desk space. This is in sharp contrast to most existing offices. Increasingly such new ways of managing workspace are delivered and co-ordinated by an almost hotel-style of operation - complete with a concierge as a new style of office manager.

Non-territorial space planning

The 'just-in-time' non-territorial approach to space planning has now been established in a number of major organisations worldwide including IBM and Ernest & Young. Otherwise known as: hot desking, free address, virtual workplace sharing, and hoteling, the principle of non-territorial space allocation involves giving up the right to a personally designated workspace for other than a short period. The concept reflects the fact that in some occupancy patterns workplaces are unoccupied for up to 70% of the time. So the 'non-territorial approach' plans undesignated workplaces which may be booked as required (or just used as available) and are able to service the occupant, one way or another, with his or her own computer and telephone connection, filing and access to a local meeting area/refreshment centre.

The IFMP[3] has documented a number of these studies, and the details of the projects and the post-occupancy appraisals make fascinating reading. For present purposes, above indicates the premises costs savings possible for the JIT approach; note that the lowest option involves partner/directors offices being used (by arrangement) when empty, which is a feature proving difficult to introduce in many of the projects initiated to date.

Most of the feedback from these projects is positive in terms of staff approval - which implies some impact on productivity, or at least no adverse effects - except in one or two cases where the changes were made without transferring 'ownership' of the concept to the users or consulting with them sufficiently throughout the piece. The latter approach not only alienates the user but also risks a failure properly to understand the way the group or department actually works.

Within non-territorial space planning, working-from (or at) home and serviced suites may be considered as options by the facilities manager. (Also, for non-workspace planning, self-storage may be an option to increase the available space, see Chapter 7.2.3.)

Space reduction for cost's sake is an incredibly damaging strategy. Implementing it without proper consideration of, or consultation with, the users will merely exacerbate the economic folly.

---

[3] *International Facility Management Program - Cornell University*

Outsourced Work Space

The concept of outsourced work space embraces every aspect of facilities economics so the matter of where to include it within this text is a major editorial problem.

In essence outsourced workplace, as the name implies, comprises workstations and supporting facilities and services which are provided by external agencies for an all-inclusive remuneration. In principle it is very close to the concept of the PFI/PPP type of arrangement for externalising provision of accommodation; however, whereas the latter is normally provided for the medium/long term and 'bespoke' to the client organisation's specific needs, the 'serviced office' variant of the concept is normally for short-term 'bridging' of space requirements.

The facility comes in many different formats, from the hiring out of workspace ancillary to an organisations requirements, to fully-fledged commercial operation by companies dedicated to the provision of serviced space on a grand scale.

The demand for outsourced workspace is normally driven by one or more of the following criteria:

- shortage of space in an area

- uncertainty over length of time or amount of space needed in a location - start-up, expansion plans

- 'bridging' in relocation or start-up situations

- additional flexibility, eg use of meeting rooms and workstations by transient personnel.

The process can be viewed as either an exercise in risk transfer or as a means of providing quality/quantity of space needed in a quick and convenient manner - or both. The downside is the cost, which usually translates back into costs per sq.m or per capita which are substantially greater - often by a very large multiplier in the case of short-term occupancy - than that which could be achieved by an in-house solution. However, the reasons for this are rarely to do with profiteering; the outsourced providers take a big risk with the occupancy rates they need in order to recoup start-up and ongoing overheads and also have to bear the additional cost of marketing, sales and contract administration.

In some cases the lack of a single non-property related covenant to support leases results in higher investment yields leading to higher rents to be passed on to the space-hirers.

On the plus side, most outsourced workspace providers have facilities management as a core discipline and use the best practices in setting up and managing the facilities. Furthermore, hiring agreements are normally only a couple of pages long and hirers can buy into and get out of the space they need at relatively short notice.

There will always be a place for outsourced workspaces. However, the problems associated with providing a multiplicity of short-term occupancies are not to be under-estimated. Some highly - publicised financial problems of companies in this field are testament to the need for charges to carry a realistic cover for the risk exposure and overhead costs.

Chapter 7.2.3 deals with Self-storage.

4.2 'CHURN'

Introduction

'Churn' is the facilities manager's jargon for the movement of personnel, groups and departments as a direct result of changed operational requirements.

At its worst incidence it involves wholesale reconfiguration or even new construction but in a highly controlled state may be restricted simply to the movement of people.

The 'churn rate' is the ratio between the number of workstation moves made in a year to the number of personnel working in the premises. The rapid growth and change of the last two decades of the twentieth century caused 'churn' to get out of control in some organisations, both in terms of frequency and the cost of implementation. The lack of any previous experience of the phenomenon - or at least within the context of highly technologically-serviced workspace - caught many firms by surprise and 'churn' rates as high as 2:1, ie an average of two moves per person pa - were reported.

Facilities management is now older and much wiser with regard to the cause and cure of this nasty ailment, but it still needs very careful attention. This chapter serves as a reminder of what can go wrong and why, what it can and should cost to cope with it, and how to avoid unnecessarily incurring the problem. (Aspects of moves resulting from disaster recovery are considered in Chapter 7.9. Also, Chapter 9.3 considers removal in detail.)

4.2.1 THE COST

An analysis of churn in a number of medium and large organisations has indicated a cost per capita (excluding loss productivity) of between £60 and £900 pa. The cost per sq m of NIA ranged from £2.40 to £54 pa and averaged £22. As such it was in many cases higher than any of the other operating cost centres - see Fig. 4.2.A.

Fig. 4.2.A
Average cost of 'churn' within a typical premises operating budget

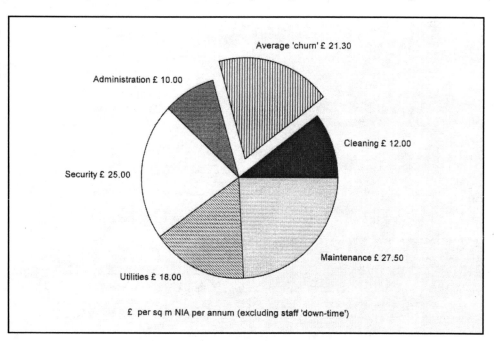

Average 'churn' £ 21.30

Administration £ 10.00

Cleaning £ 12.00

Security £ 25.00

Maintenance £ 27.50

Utilities £ 18.00

£ per sq m NIA per annum (excluding staff 'down-time')

The cost drivers

The cost of churn is driven by the following factors:

- the rate of churn

- the preparation of the new workstation and its facilities

- the preparation of the vacated workstation and its facilities

- the time taken to move the employee's equipment, papers and personal effects

- the time at which the move is carried out

- the grade of personnel affected by the move.

The down-time of employees as a result of the move is not usually counted into the cost, although it can be a significant component, eg a churn rate of 2:1 (two moves per capita pa) can result in a 5% loss of productivity per employee pa.

Many reports are of costs higher than the above sample. Fig. 4.2.B suggests how the cost components of 'churn' might range in a wider sample from £60 to £1,700 per move.

Fig. 4.2.B
Analysis of range of costs of 'churn' per move

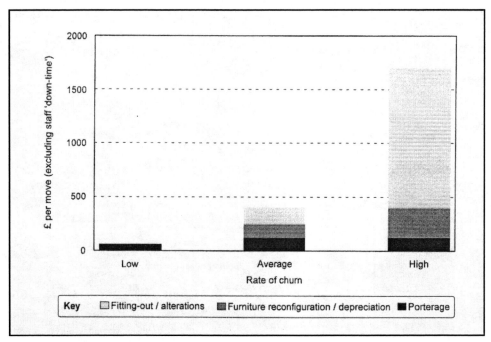

Note, however, that the cost of 'churn' per capita (as opposed to 'per move') is a function of the 'churn rate' referred to earlier and further discussed below.

4.2.2 THE RATE OF CHURN

While in many cases churn cannot be avoided it is certainly possible, by good planning, to minimise its incidence.

Churn is caused by some or all of the following factors:

- business restructuring, including acquisitions and mergers

- staff increases

- staff reductions

- bad space planning

- management whim.

Whereas the facilities manager cannot influence the incidence of the first three of these factors (unless they are catered for in the premises policy), they certainly can - and should - be able to impact on the latter two. It may be noted that where takeovers occur the Transfer of Undertakings (Protection of Employment) Regulations 1981 may apply.

4.2.3 MANAGEMENT AND CONTROL

Control mechanisms

Chapter 4.1.4 describes the space planning function, so here it is only necessary to consider two key aspects of that science relevant to churn - keeping records and planning flexibility.

It is vitally important to keep account of the number of moves - in other words to track the rate of churn. Not for the first time in this work the theories that 'if you can't measure it you can't understand it' and 'if you can't measure it you can't improve it' are used to make a point.

Many of the worst churn rates in recent years crept up on facilities managers by surprise; once they identified the scale of the problem, and began to plan avoidance, the rate dropped back to manageable levels.

In the example, at Fig. 4.2.C a financial services company was experiencing a steep increase in churn compared to its growth in staff numbers. A space planning initiative introduced in Year 2 brought the rate of churn down from 1.5 to below one move per person pa in Year 5. At the same time they reduced the costs per move in stages from £600 to £70 per person moved. The higher costs included departmental time, crates and modifications to electrical services, data, telecommunications, furniture and decor. The low-cost moves involved only the actual moving cost and an absolute minimum of local adjustment/replanning.

The provision of new furniture systems giving the key to the savings was planned to coincide with natural obsolescence of the older variegated and less flexible units and did not introduce a cost penalty. As shown in Fig. 4.2.C the saving worked out to £780 per person pa (ie £840 to £60) for the 2,500 staff -a massive £2m and over £80 per sq m of the lettable floor area pa.

Fig. 4.2.C
Reduction in annual cost of 'churn' through analysis and improved planning

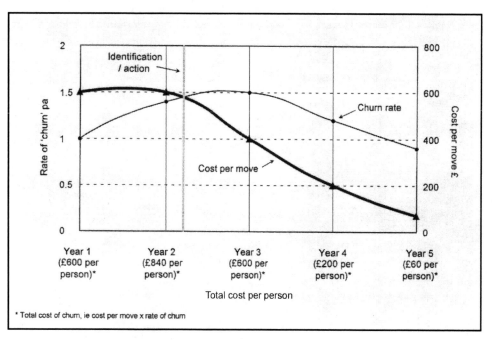

Recording moves is obviously much easier on an electronic database - CAD can be helpful too, especially when it comes to testing re-configuration. Computerised inventories of personnel, their location, job requirements and equipment will also help the fight against churn.

Standardisation of workstations, easily re-configured furniture, good cable management all serve to reduce or avoid the need to carry out alterations in support of a move. Well thought out stacking plans with overflow space built in for expansion will also help to keep the worst scenario - the complete departmental change - around - at bay; a total refit can cost up to £10,000 per capita (or more in high quality areas) and protection must be provided against premature exposure to this risk albeit at the cost of a little slack in the space allocations within the system.

4.2.4 MANAGING THE MOVE

In the ideal situation all that will be necessary will be a team of porters coming in at the weekend to move the employees' personal belongings and equipment to a new location and just plug in. This gives the £70 move - porters are cheap, even at weekend/overtime rates. However one suspects that many facilities managers are around to help at these times and that their unpaid extra hours are not costed into the data provided.

The more expensive moves often involve the transportation of the employees' furniture (usually the result of non-standardisation or variations in quality) and, in the worst cases, substantial re-configuration of the old and new workstations and accompanying alterations, eg to decor, cables, services. It must always be borne in mind that in most cases one move equals two, ie the place vacated will be filled (probably in a modified form) at some time in the future.

4.2.5 MANAGEMENT POLICIES

Finally, the issue of management whim. One organisation used to reward its sales force by up-grading them as they achieved financial milestones. In the good times some of the better salesmen got upgraded twice in a year. The only bad thing was that the management's policy was to match accommodation space and quality to grade with the potential consequence of a really high fitting-out cost penalty on each upgrade, especially when the individual's work place entitlement grew from open plan to cellular office. There are better and more cost-effective ways of rewarding staff than taking £5,000 or so out of profits every time they do particularly well - and giving it to a building contractor!

Section 5

Premises Operating Services

5.1   PREMISES OPERATING COSTS IN CONTEXT

Introduction

In Chapter 1.1.2 (Fig 1.1.B) the cost of 'premises' was shown as breaking down into three distinct sub-categories - property, ie rent and local taxes; capital projects; and, operating costs. This chapter considers the latter.

'Premises operating costs' is a term relating to the cost of the physical activities required in running and maintaining the building and its services; at one time the terms 'running costs' or 'running and maintenance costs' were in conventional use but their lack of precision led to confusion. The authors have therefore adopted this more generic term - 'premises operating costs'.

5.1.1 OPERATING COST CENTRES

The cost centres under this heading are:

- maintenance (see Chapter 5.2)

- cleaning (see Chapter 5.3)

- energy (see Chapter 5.4)

- water and sewerage services (see Chapter 5.5)

- waste management (see Chapter 5.6)

- interior landscaping and décor (see Chapter 5.7).

In addition to these conventional services discussed in this section premises operating costs may sometimes include:

- security (see Chapter 7.1)

- environmental management (see Chapter 5.8)

- 'churn' and alterations (see Chapters 4.2 and 6.1)

- landlord's service charges (see Chapter 3.3)

The authors' own rules of classification of the contents of each of these cost centres, developed over 30 years and used in the detailed benchmarking of over 10,000 buildings, are given in the respective chapters. However, as discussed in Chapter 1.3 (The costs of facilities) and Chapter 12.2 (Benchmarking) although these rules are well tried and tested there is no obligation on anyone else to follow them. The important thing is to know what you mean by, for example, maintenance and cleaning, when you come to make comparisons with other organisations; naturally, you need to know what **they** mean by them as well!

5.1.2 OPERATING COSTS AND PERFORMANCE

Like all supposedly non-core expenditure the operating costs are constantly under pressure from those responsible for overall financial management. They are perceived as an overhead which can be turned on and off like a tap without undue adverse implications for the overall service provision.

Sometimes the financial managers are right in this supposition. Too often facilities managers defend their quarter using warnings of failure which will inevitably result from deprivation or deferral of funds and which turn out to be unsubstantiated; like the boy in the old fable who kept crying 'wolf' in the night, facilities managers who make their case badly by exaggeration put the business at risk of real harm when the rubber band really does break.

Chapter 2.5.4 on risk management contained a strong argument in favour of formal or informal risk approaches appraisal leading to development of a logical business case for the facilities service levels. Certainly defence of one's budget is made much easier if the premises policy and the strategies supporting them are formally accepted as part of the business plan as propounded in Chapter 1.1.5. This relationship is considered again in Fig. 5.1.A which illustrates also that although the costs of operating the premises are predominantly linked to the physical performance of the buildings the latter is itself influenced by the functional demands of the business plan and influences the success, or otherwise, of its execution.

Fig. 5.1.A
Operating costs in the context of the corporate plan

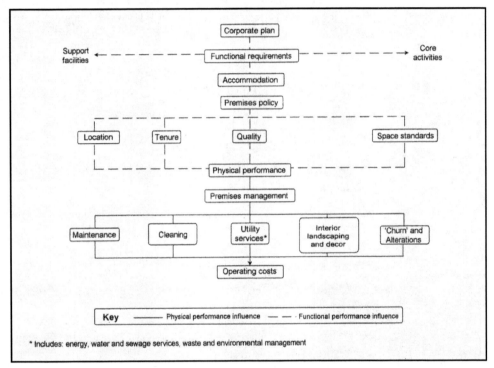

For example, the figure indicates that 'quality' and 'space standards' are established by functional requirements thereby influencing the costs of operating the premises which stem from the resulting physical performance.

One of the biggest problems facing facilities managers is an almost complete lack of hard evidence as to the true consequences of failure in any of the components of physical performance. If the lifts in a seven-storey building are out of action for two days the occupants might complain bitterly - unless they are training for a marathon, trying to slim or are away from the premises on productive business. But proving conclusively that the failure would result in loss of productivity is very difficult.

Reports of personal experiences are in plentiful supply but hard facts are scarce.

Such evidence as exists supports the view that a 'caring' facilities management regime funding less than perfect premises on a small budget will foster a bigger contribution to the bottom line profit realisation than a disinterested set-up running better premises badly with more funds available. Possibly it is the 'pulling together' team spirit syndrome which has the biggest influence on user satisfaction.

Nevertheless, the building which stops supporting vital business is a nightmare situation which few core business managers would contemplate if they were reliably and credibly informed of its imminence.

Designers sometimes tempt providence in this respect. A bespoke building housing a computer installation servicing over 500 organisations has a three-layer felt roof. It should have been asphalt but the architect spent too much of the budget on the external elevations! Water penetration through this cheap and notoriously unreliable material is as inevitable as the consequences will be catastrophic. Funds to prevent such a disaster are an essential business provision and must be made available whatever other cost centres the business may have to plunder.

The facilities manager's role in identifying such performance characteristics when the premises policy and strategies are being created is absolutely critical. The whole issue of justifying the investment in facilities is discussed in more detail in the book/CD Rom 'Justifying the investment in Facilities'[1].

5.1.3 OPERATING COSTS AND TOTAL REVENUE EXPENDITURE

Operating costs as defined above are unlikely to represent more than about 1to1.5% of an organisation's total annual revenue expenditure (see Fig. 5.1.B).

Fig. 5.1.B
Operating costs in the context of turnover

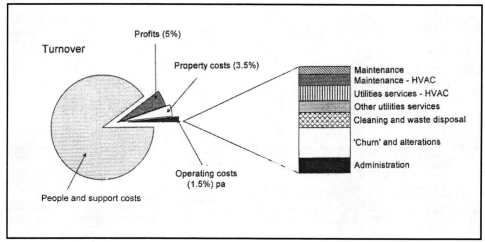

If they do the chances are that they are over-provided and are in need of re-appraisal unless the core activity is unusually low cost eg mainly low-grade clerical.

Even in the latter case, the level of premises performance and costs would normally be graduated downwards with a decrease in the operating costs per capita more than compensating for the increase in operating costs per unit of floor area (see Fig. 5.1.C).

Fig. 5.1.C
Effect of density on premises operating costs per unit area and per capita

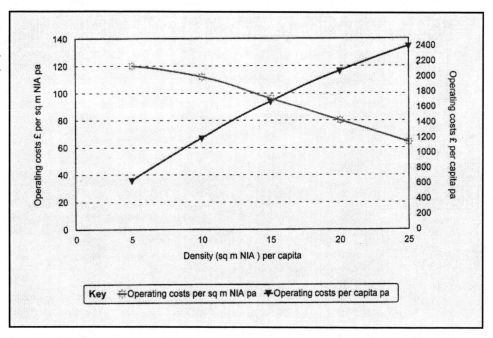

---

[1] *Bernard Williams (2000) 'Justifying the Investment in Facilities' Building Economics Bureau Ltd, London, UK.*

Fig. 5.1.D shows even more vividly how the savings in property costs brought about by increased intensity of usage far outweigh any consequential impact on the premises operating costs.

Fig. 5.1.D
Effect of density on premises operating and property costs per capita

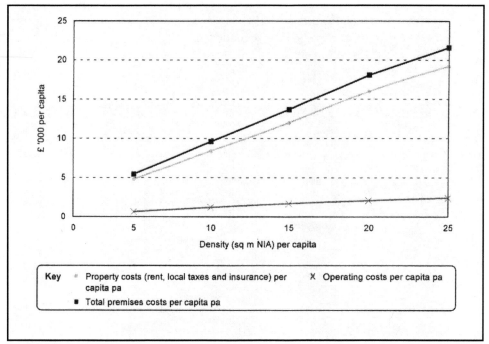

There is a dichotomy between the relative insignificance of the operating cost expenditure (in the context of both investment option appraisal and proportion of total annual expenditure) and the potential risk to vital business from long-term under-provision of funding for these essential tasks.

Yet a further anomaly is the fact that Discounted Cash Flow (DCF) analyses of future expenditure (see Chapter 2.3.7) quickly minimises the significance of future expenditure on facilities; however, down the years the company which does not make sufficient funds available as required for adequate facilities may well find itself in danger of malfunctioning in its core business activity.

To overcome the worst consequences of inadequate funding facilities managers should develop a coded warning procedure linking control of funds for priority operating expenditure to potential harm to vital business. Financial control programs such as premFINANCE incorporate such a feature (see Fig. 5.1.E).

Fig. 5.1.E
Effects of operating costs decisions on core business efficiency - premFINANCE warning codes

Priority status	• Not applicable. • Statutory requirements. • Essential business requirements. • Recommended business requirements. • Nice to have – if affordable.
Consequence of deferral	• Not applicable. • Actual harm to core business. • Actual harm to business profile. • Actual harm to non-business activities. • Risk – could be detrimental to core business. • Risk – could be detrimental to business profile. • Risk – could be detrimental to non-business activities. • Insignificant risk – no detrimental consequence likely.

5.2   MAINTENANCE

Introduction

Maintenance has been defined as: 'the combination of all technical and associated administrative actions intended to retain an item in, or restore it to, a state in which it can perform its required function'.

A car may continue to work without servicing but its performance will deteriorate through two phases: first it will begin to consume more resources, such as fuel and minor repairs, accompanied by failing efficiency, and then it will require major repair and/or replacement of components in response to imminent or actual breakdown.

The impact of inadequate maintenance of buildings will be felt in due course in both the profit and loss account and the balance sheet. Business efficiency will reduce and output fall as a result of inadequate facilities (such as poor air quality or lifts out of order) not to mention down-time and disruption during repairs. Then there are the psychological consequences of an apparent lack of care or pride on the part of top management (however hard the facilities manager may try to minimise the damage); resultant hostility may cause abnormal absence through sickness, and genuine illhealth may also be a direct result of inadequate maintenance especially with regard to the mechanical and electrical services. Legionnaires Disease is living testimony to such failure and the so-called 'Sick Building Syndrome' is also frequently blamed (although this consequence is not yet proven) upon inadequate design and maintenance of the environmental systems (see Chapter 8.2.2).

On the balance sheet building values will be down-graded as the asset depreciates physically at an accelerating rate through lack of expenditure on its preservation.

This chapter gives the facilities manager an insight into the principles and practice of the maintenance of buildings, building services and grounds and the life-cycles of buildings.

5.2.1   MAINTENANCE AND BUILDING PERFORMANCE

The components of maintenance

Maintenance is required in respect of three main aspects of premises:

- the fabric
- the services
- the grounds.

Modern buildings are more likely to suffer early deterioration of the fabric than the hardier and simpler masonry structures prevalent up to the mid-point of the 20th Century. Nevertheless, the problems - mainly the result of a greater dependence on the use of materials and components having no historic performance records - do not normally manifest themselves until sometime into the building's life-cycle.

In any event, maintenance of the fabric is normally a smaller component of the maintenance cost centre. In a modern air-conditioned office building the annual expenditure on maintenance of all categories including replacement of minor components, is typically as illustrated in Fig. 5.2.A. (see over)

Fig. 5.2.A
*Typical distribution
of maintenance
expenditure in a
modern air-
conditioned office
building*

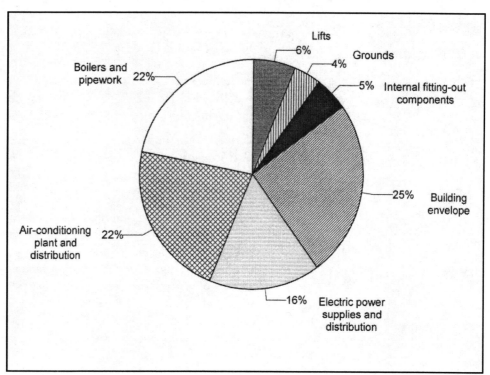

Fig. 5.2.A
Typical distribution of maintenance expenditure in a modern air-conditioned office building

It may be noted that the protocol and costs for maintenance of the fabric, services and grounds are dealt with individually in 5.2.3 to 5.2.5 (below).

5.2.2 MAINTENANCE MANAGEMENT

In-house v out-sourcing

Because of its technical complexities the use of contractors to carry out maintenance of services in air-conditioned buildings was commonplace long before the core v non-core arguments considered in Chapter 2.1.3 had surfaced across the whole sphere of facilities.

With respect to the building fabric 'term' maintenance contracts nowadays often replace the in-house direct labour operation.

Frequently the facilities manager will have professional in-house surveyors and engineers to specify, procure and monitor maintenance contract services and sometimes the professional function will itself be out-sourced either as advisory in support of a technically qualified manager or seconded full-time in an in-house capacity working to a non-technical facilities manager.

The concept of the direct labour organisation looking after maintenance is fast disappearing as the specialist contractors sharpen their act - and their pencils - and benchmark comparisons generally tend to show the direct labour operations to be a less cost-efficient solution.

In theory there is no reason why a well-run direct labour operation should not be as cost-efficient as the out-sourced alternative; in fact, the 'best of breed' in the authors' extensive facilities cost data base is an internally managed almost totally direct labour regime. However an attitude of complacency frequently exists in direct labour operations and is hard to eliminate in the short-term so the tide of opinion of core business management is fairly heavily balanced in favour of the out-sourced option for this supposedly non-core activity; this is particularly the case in the larger, more industrialised countries.

Maintenance policy and strategies

Maintenance strategies have been described as follows:[1]

- planned maintenance - the maintenance organised and carried out with forethought, control and the use of records to a pre-determined plan

- preventative maintenance - the maintenance carried out at pre-determined intervals or corresponding to prescribed criteria and intended to reduce the probability of failure or the performance degradation of an item

- scheduled maintenance - the preventative maintenance carried out to a pre-determined interval of time, number of operations and other factors

- condition-based maintenance - the preventative maintenance initiated as a result of knowledge of the condition of an item from routine or continuous monitoring

- corrective maintenance - the maintenance carried out after a failure has occurred and intended to restore an item to a state in which it can perform its required function

- emergency maintenance - the maintenance which it is necessary to put in hand immediately to avoid serious consequences

- unplanned maintenance - the maintenance carried out to no pre-determined plan.

These strategies may be required in total or in part. Their presence and implementation should be encapsulated in a maintenance policy forming an integral part of the operating costs component of the Premises Policy (see Fig. 5.1.A). The policy and its strategies should take account of potential changes to the stock of buildings - especially incorporation of improvements within major capital projects and have regard to the stage attained in the life-cycle of each property. It should also highlight areas where neglect or failure could be positively harmful to vital business.

The object of a maintenance policy is to ensure that the physical performance of the premises is kept as close as possible to the original designed performance having regard to the core business needs and obligation at any point in time, together with cost-effective procurement and affordability.

Although some facilities managers might take issue with the order of priorities in this statement it does cover all the main issues. Planned preventative maintenance is a strategy which sets out to control performance in terms of day-to-day function, health and safety, longevity and investment value. In the harsh economic climate of the last decade the strategy has come under close scrutiny and much criticism because it presumes the need to maintain and replace components at pre-estimated stages in their life-cycle thereby meaning that components may be replaced before their useful working life has been exceeded. There is also a danger that operatives may fail to check or repair malfunctioning parts which are not on their work schedules.

Many organisations adopting a planned maintenance strategy are beginning to suspect that their buildings are 'over-maintained' to the detriment of funds for other facilities services and core business activity.

Perhaps the best solution to keeping maintenance costs down is based on 'planned inspection' and reporting followed by essential repair and replacement. However, following the principles addressed in Chapter 2.2 (Value Management) the benefits to the organisation of a maintenance regime which guarantees that there will be no failures may well justify a strategy which may appear on the surface to be over-elaborate and unnecessarily expensive.

---

[1] *BS 3811 (1993) Glossary of Terms used in Terotechnology*

Some operations can only be carried out outside of normal working hours. If routine maintenance must be carried out when premises are in use great care needs to be taken to keep intrusion and disruption to a minimum; otherwise savings in maintenance costs will translate into productivity losses of a far greater magnitude.

Whereas maintenance can only be carried out by seeking access to an adjoining property, time should be allowed for obtaining the agreement of the occupier. In the absence of an agreement, the facilities manager may need to resort to the court for an access order under the Access to Neighbouring Land Act 1990 (see Chapter 3.1.5).

Alterations disguised as maintenance

Fig. 5.2.B shows an analysis of the cost of so-called 'maintenance' produced in the course of a premises audit. On inspection it was found that only about one-half of the items included under the cost centre were truly maintenance (the services and fabric); the balance was made up of upgrading, alterations, and 'churn' (see Chapter 4.2). In spite of rigid interpretation by the taxation authorities of what constitutes revenue as opposed to capital expenditure, it is not unusual to find a lot of capital works included in the maintenance cost centre.

Fig. 5.2.B
Incorrect analysis - upgrading and 'churn' disguised as maintenance

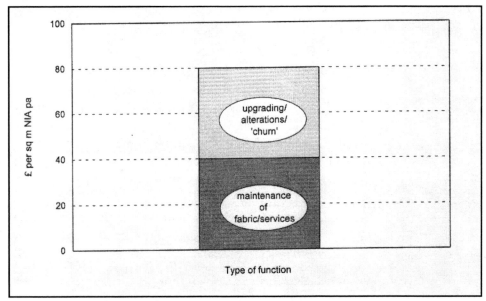

That may be good for tax relief in some taxation regimes but it does not help revenue budgets or assist management to identify and understand the problems which are presented by an inadequate building and/or poor space management (see Chapter 4.1).

Prioritisation

The need to prioritise maintenance is heightened by the pressure of funds available. It is doubtful whether any economic or political regime has ever over-funded maintenance of property and the 21st Century is certainly no exception - world-wide.

Unarguably first priority must always be given to health and safety (see Chapter 8.2) - inside or outside of the statutory requirements; in fact avoidance of adverse effects on vital core business is a far greater requirement in purely commercial terms and will follow closely on the tail of the statutory needs in pursuit of funding.

Any funds left over after dealing with the demands of these two main drivers will be fought over by:

- any statutory building preservation requirement

- any element needing significant attention in terms of its contribution to asset life and value.

Performance Indicators (PI's) should be geared to the priorities which should, in turn, be incorporated in the premises policy.

Subjectivity in prioritisation is to be avoided at all costs. If the managing director's carpet has a coffee stain under the desk it ought to take its place in the queue behind the threadbare safety hazard on the floor of the main reception.

Performance indicators

The maintenance provider will be expected to be targeted and monitored in a formal manner, particularly in respect of:

- response to emergency call-out
- down-time of essential plant and equipment
- physical inconvenience to occupiers
- quality of repair
- quality and appearance of operatives
- costs of operations.

One PI sometimes adopted sets a not-to-be-exceeded percentage of planned to unplanned maintenance. Such measures must however:

- be clear as to whether it is cost or number of events which is being targeted
- ensure that the proportion of planned v unplanned maintenance has been previously subjected to risk and cost/benefit analysis and set accordingly
- ensure that the items of unplanned maintenance have been prioritised in accordance with the maintenance policy.

Maintenance management programs

There are an increasing number of software packages available for assisting with the management of maintenance - particularly the planned preventative type. Some of these are linked into CAD for a visual effect and also to exchange information between the CAD drawn data and that in the database. These systems and their economics are described in greater detail in Chapter 2.6.4.

5.2.3 MAINTENANCE OF THE FABRIC

Typical expenditure

The Facilities Economics protocol for measuring and classifying the 'Maintenance of the Fabric' cost centre is given at Fig. 5.2.C.

Fig. 5.2.C Facilities Economics classification protocol - fabric maintenance

Sub-categories (contract bundle items)	Principal Examples / cost elements	Items commonly included in costs	Items excluded from costs	
			Item	Refer to category:
Fabric	Structure Roofing Partitions Doors Windows Surface finishes	Task management, handy-men, supervisors, blue-collar staff, maintenance equipment, tools, materials, tenants' areas service charge element, signage, essential spares, plantroom cleaning	New installations	Not applicable
			Alterations	Alterations / Improvements
			Improvements	Alterations / Improvements
			General management time	General facilities management
Decorations	Painting Wall-papering		Churn	Alterations / Improvements
			Office Equipment	Relevant business support services
Fixtures and fittings	Fixtures Fittings		Grounds maintenance	Grounds maintenace
			Furniture	Furniture

The typical range of annual expenditure on maintenance and repair of the fabric in the more common building uses is illustrated at Fig. 5.2.D.

Fig. 5.2.D
Typical spread of fabric maintenance costs pa for a range of common building uses

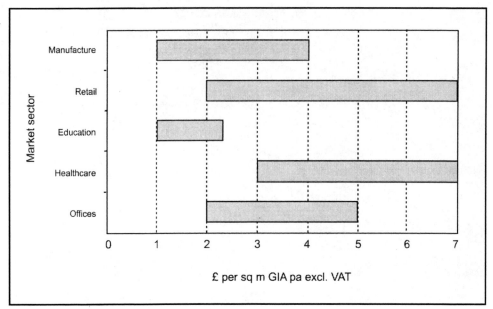

Among the more significant cost drivers, in no particular generic category or order of significance, are:

* the cost of labour and consumables

* the age of the building and its current state of repair

* the quality of the materials and workmanship as built

* its shortcomings with reference to Health and Safety at Work regulations

* the maintenance regime

* the service level requirements

* the inclusion of non-maintenance items within the cost centre (not a feature of the costs in Fig. 5.2.D)

* the intensity with which the premises are utilised (eg increased densities of personnel per sq m of the usable floor area will reduce lives eg of carpets and doors)

* any statutory listing in respect of building preservation

* affordability.

To interpolate the point in the range for high level maintenance costs for a specific building type refer to Chapter 1.3.2, in particular, Fig. 1.3.B.

5.2.4 MAINTENANCE OF THE BUILDING SERVICES

Typical expenditure

The Facilities Economics protocol for measuring and classifying the cost centres for Maintenance of the Building Services is given at Fig. 5.2.E (over the page).

Fig. 5.2.E
Facilities Economics classification protocol - building services maintenance

Sub-categories (contract bundle items)	Principal Examples / cost elements	Items commonly included in costs	Items excluded from costs	
			Item	**Refer to category:**
Heat and ventilation	Boilers Radiators Chillers Ductwork Filters Fire extinguishers Humidifiers	Task management, handy-men, supervisors, blue-collar staff, specialist services cleaning, tenants' areas service charge element, water treatment, PPM, emergency, ad hoc etc, smoke tests, statutory testing, emergency inspection and testing, PAT tests, legionnaire testing, hardwire testing, testing and inspection of earth bonding	Catering equipment	Catering
			New installations	Not applicable
			Alterations	Alterations / improvements
			Improvements	Alterations / improvements
Plumbing	Sprinklers Sanitary fittings Water supplies Drainage		Grounds lighting	Grounds maintenance
			General management time	General facilities management
Electrical	Switchgear Wiring Internal lighting Small power Floor out-lets Fire-alarms Generators Building management systems Energy management systems UPS		Security systems	Security
			Cleaning equipment	Cleaning
			Computer installations	ICT
			Data cabling	ICT
			Churn	Alterations / improvements
Lifts	Lifts Escalators			

The typical range of costs of maintaining the building services per annum in the more common building uses is illustrated in Fig. 5.2.F.

Fig. 5.2.F
Typical spread of building services maintenance costs pa for a range of common building uses

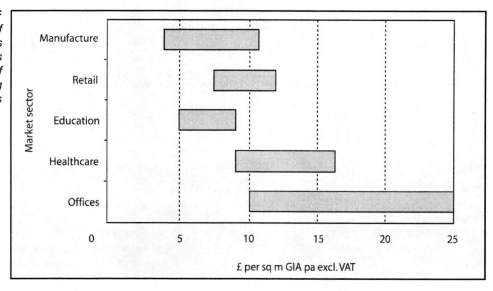

Among the more significant cost drivers are:

- whether or not the building has a mechanical ventilation/cooling/air-conditioning system

- the age of the mechanical and electrical installation, its unexpired life and current state of repair

- the quality of workmanship and materials in the installations as built

- the Health and Safety implications

- the maintenance regime

- the service level requirements

- the inclusion of non-maintenance items within the cost centre (not a feature of the costs in Fig. 5.2.F)

- the intensity of usage, eg increased density, will increase operating intensity and wear and under-usage may cause a system to fail through failure of the building to achieve the conditions it was designed to alleviate; over-specified power-loadings causing VAV boxes to fail to respond to minimum temperature changes are believed to be one of the primary causes of the 'sick building syndrome'

- the existence of a planned maintenance programme not accompanied by a planned inspection programme

- affordability

- payments for any landlord's approvals, for an access order and compensation under an access order.

The comparative annual maintenance costs for some of the more common cooling and heating systems are given at Fig. 5.2.G together with their typical energy consumption.

Fig. 5.2.G
Total energy and maintenance costs pa (HVAC only) - office building 4,250 sq m NIA

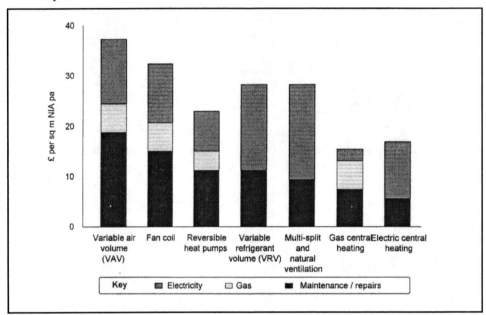

5.2.5 MAINTENANCE OF THE GROUNDS

Style and quality

Styles and quality standards for landscaping vary greatly according to region and policy. Companies increasingly tend to expect the highest standards and are prepared to pay for the service. They also favour plantings that are more natural in style reflecting the countryside around the facility. In some regions styles vary from the minimal to being very garden-like. Equally standards are very high or virtually non-existent, which is reflected in cost.

Drivers of policy may include one or more of the following:

conservation - increasingly companies may have policies on nature conservation in relation to their grounds. This will impact on grounds maintenance, for example in restriction on pesticide use and operations designed specifically to encourage wildlife.

environmental - the landscaping may be linked to the organisation's environmental policy on, say, rainwater recycling (requiring piping systems) or drought expectation (requiring special plants)

In line with current trends many grounds maintenance companies are working to or have been certified with ISO 14001 status indicating that their policies and practices are environmentally sound

child-care - provision of a nursery (see Chapter 8.3.4) for employee's children may require outdoor playspace with special play equipment, surfaces, landscaping and security

budget - the allocated budget may determine maintenance policies

historic conservation - the grounds may have features of a historic garden or archeological remains which require special attention. Membership of the Historic Houses Association or may give insights into the management of such facilities. Objects in a garden may be listed under the Town and Country Planning Act 1990 or scheduled as an ancient monument. In both instances, the law requires special procedures, care and attention for works otherwise a conviction may result

security - the level of perimeter security, with patrols, CCTV or other equipment may determine landscaping features and maintenance

staff recreation - for science parks and similar property, staff can be encouraged to use certain types of grounds during work hours for recreational pursuits, such as lunchtime picnicking

public opening - the national or local charity schemes to open gardens and grounds to the public are increasingly popular with business organisations.

Issues of location

Most city centre offices have only minimal requirement for exterior landscaping provision and maintenance. However, it is becoming more common to see roof and wall plantings as well as those found around entrances or in small courtyards. Much commercial and light industrial activity has now gone out of the city centre into places such as 'science parks'. In these cases exterior landscaping can be quite extensive and very prestigious. It can also involve water and rock features, accent and decorative lighting and sculpture, as well as plantings. In all cases standards for provision and maintenance are high compared to cost.

Costs and quality

Annual costs are usually in the service charge from the landlord managing a complex of buildings or are the direct concern of the facilities manager if the building is owned by the occupier. Compared to other factors in facilities management, ground maintenance is a low cost item. It is rare to have maintenance carried out 'in house' and the employment of a specialist grounds maintenance company is the norm. It is important to introduce criteria for quality, as the appearance of a scheme will depend not just on frequency of operations, but on the standards of performance. Quality of maintenance is directly related to training and motivation. Horticultural education is well established and the landscape profession is an accepted career.

Standards and codes of practice

The British Standards Institute (BSI) has published some 17 standards relating to landscaping. The following are the most relevant: BS 7370-4:1993 Grounds maintenance - Recommendations for maintenance of soft landscape (other than amenity turf); BS 4428:1989 Code of practice for general landscape operations (excluding hard surfaces); and BS 7370-2:1194 Grounds maintenance. Recommendations for the maintenance of hard areas (excluding sports surfaces). In addition, there are a number of BSI standards for plants, such as BS 3936-1:1992 Nursery stock: Specification for trees and shrubs.

The British Association of Landscape Industries (BALI) has codes of practice, which their members are required to follow.

Contents of the Cost Centre

The term maintenance as used in this context is rather different from its use in connection with the fabric and building services in that it also includes exterior landscaping which inevitably involves regular life-cycle replacement of components - ie plants and shrubs!

Of course not every building has any grounds at all whilst others may have several hectares.

The nature of the work is also often quite different from the works to and within buildings and is likely to be carried out by a wide range of contractors. (See Chapter 5.7 for Interior Landscaping and Decor.)

Fig. 5.2.H. gives the Facilities Economics protocol for this section. It contains items of cleaning as well as maintenance of surfaces, electrical equipment and other works which are sometimes analysed within the respective building-related cost centres. However, to include them in these other cost centres presents enormous disparities where there are extensive grounds as sometimes with hospitals, educational buildings and some offices.

Fig. 5.2.H *Facilities Economics classification protocol - grounds maintenance*	**Sub-categories (contract bundle items)**	**Principal Examples / cost elements**	**Items commonly included in costs**	**Items excluded from costs**	
				Item	**Refer to category:**
	Maintenance	Services Hard landscaping (fences, paving) Soft landscaping (planted areas, lawns)	Gardening, Horticulture, Tree surgery, Fences, Service charges, Snow clearance, Car park areas, Road maintenance, Task management, Handymen, Supervisors	Interior landscaping	Interior landscaping and décor
	Cleaning	Power washing Road sweeping Litter collection		Contract / directive management	General facilities management
	Utilities	Lighting and power Transformer sub-stations Incoming service mains Drainage / sewerage systems		Grounds security guards and surveillance systems	Security

Typical expenditure on grounds maintenance

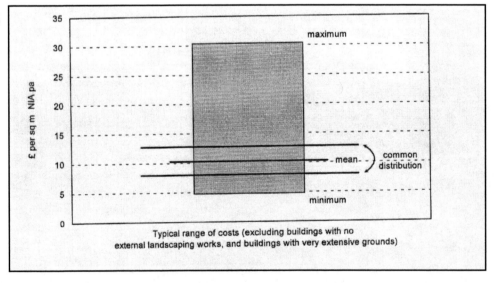

Fig. 5.2.J
Typical range of annual expenditure on grounds maintenance

Fig. 5.2.J gives a very 'high level' guide to the range of costs brought back to per sq m NIA pa which varies rather more extremely than most other cost centres depending upon the weight of the cost drivers. Among the more influential of these are:

- extent of grounds relative to building area (by far the most critical when using this parameter)

- extent of hard and irregular surfaces

- access and use by staff/general public

- extent of vandalism

- availability of litter bins (Note, a problem where terrorist activity is a threat)
- security
- extent of water features - health hazards abound
- required 'image'
- specification and service levels for maintenance
- quality of materials and workmanship as built
- affordability.

For larger estates expenditure normally lies between £1,200 and £3,000 per hectare pa.

In leasehold buildings this cost centre will nearly always appear as part of the landlord's service charge.

Ground maintenance is a rather mixed and non-conforming category and budgets/benchmark comparisons are best addressed by reference to the costs of specific works in the individual sections rather than the category as a whole.

Benefits of exterior landscaping

Although grounds maintenance is a comparatively low cost item even where it is extensive, as in the office parks or 'country house' offices, the importance of greenery around an office building cannot be over-stressed.

The impact of landscaping on an organisation's public relations, to both customers and employees, is now well established. A well designed building set in a pleasant well managed landscape, whether urban or less built up, sends nothing but positive messages. Also, the careful placement of landscaping can reduce the effects of cold wind in winter.

Good landscaping can make a positive contribution to the natural and man made environment. The planting of trees and other soft landscape elements can go some way in offsetting the greenhouse gas emissions produced by a building. Even where there is a preference for a more formally designed and even gardenesque approach, a well designed and maintained scheme is now expected to have a positive impact on the wider landscape.

Hard or soft landscaping?

The initial cost of hard landscaping is a lot greater than soft landscaping but the maintenance costs of the latter are often much smaller than people imagine. A simple example illustrating this point is at Fig. 5.2.K (over the page) which shows that, although paving a public area will save the costs - and hassle - of maintenance, its overall life-cycle costs do not provide any economic justification for the investment. Quite rightly landscape architects may argue that, if there is considerable wear and tear, maintenance of the soft area to peak condition may not be possible. Hard landscape is then desirable on aesthetic grounds. There can be a reluctance to introduce soft landscaping due to an inadequate appreciation of the overall economic picture. Nevertheless, it is important to recognise that, in spite of its maintenance requirements, soft landscaping is probably the most cost-effective design tool in terms of generating aesthetic acceptance and pleasure.

The Horticultural Trades Association (HTA) is a body that is a good point for general inquiries about plants and soft landscaping.

Fig. 5.2.K
Comparative annual equivalent costs of hard and soft landscaping

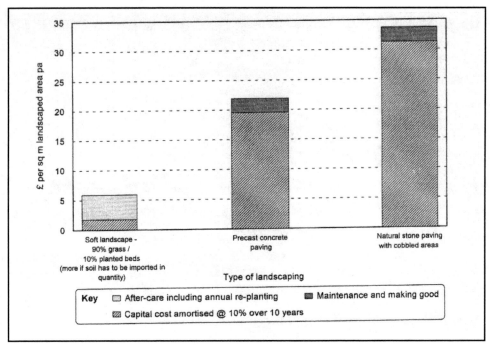

5.2.6 LIFE CYCLES

Building life

Whole-life building economics is considered and illustrated in detail in Chapter 10.6 - 'Whole-life economics'. One vital issue particularly affecting the maintenance cost centre is the design policy in respect of the planned life of components.

Indeed, there is much controversy over the total life span to which building design should be aimed. Commercial buildings are generally expected to have a useful life of 60 years. The concept of 'long life, loose-fit, low energy' was promulgated in the 1960's and reinforced by Dr. Frank Duffy's analysis of 'Shell, scenery and services'[2] in the 1970's.

Although the economics of low-cost short-life purpose-built buildings are powerful in business terms they do not marry with the view of the investment institutions that a building life should coincide with the terms of the favoured long lease.

However, radical change in the functional requirements of buildings has tested much of our commercial building stock in recent times. Perhaps surprisingly some of the older properties from the first half of the 20th century have proved more robust in the face of change than their modernist and post-modernist successors. This has probably less to do with architectural style than the meanness of post-war property developers in seeking to minimise storey-heights to save money and increase site coverage within planning/building regulation height restrictions.

Ironically, the 'meanness' of these latter-day buildings, which earned them the unwanted tag of 'prematurely obsolescent' in the 1980's as they failed to accommodate the information technology explosion, is now being forgiven as the technology itself becomes more sophisticated and less demanding of its accommodation at the start of the new Millennium. (The impact of depreciation on property values is explained with worked examples in Chapter 3.8.)

---

[2] *DEGW (1980) 'Planning Office Space' Architectural Press, London, UK.*

Component life

The life spans of building and services components are poorly documented. However much evidence exists in the collective experience of practitioners and examples of life-cycles of some of the more significant building and services components drawn from the authors' database are given in Chapter 10.6.4, particularly Fig. 10.6.K.

A research project under the LINK/CMR/SERC scheme in the UK developed the concept of the 'Performance-and-cost-managed building'[3]. This concept illustrated at Fig. 5.2.L relates to the process whereby the cost and performance of a building are managed throughout every phase from inception, through design, construction and occupation to refurbishment and, finally, demolition. The technical instrument for delivery of the concept (yet to be implemented) entails a building data-spine supported by, and linked to, a data-base of building component lives and costs of maintenance and replacement.

Fig. 5.2.L
The 'performance-and-cost-managed building' - the building data spine

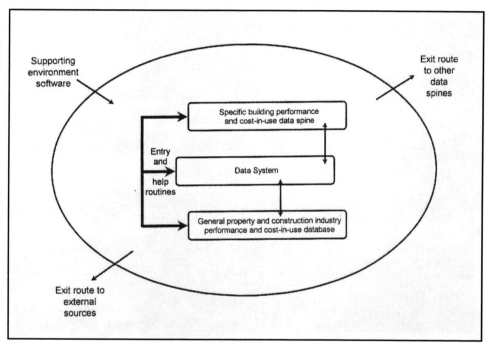

[3] *The Centre for Facilities Management / Arup R and D / BRE (1994)*

5.3 CLEANING

Introduction

Cleaning is one of those services which falls into both 'hard' and 'soft' categories.

The 'hard' facet relates to the importance of cleaning as a maintenance operation, protecting materials directly, or indirectly, from premature loss of performance or failure.

The 'soft' aspects relate to the image, health and safety, ergonomics and (sometimes) legal risk centres.

Because of the conspicuous nature of the operation - and any of its failings - cleaning tends to be a fairly emotive topic with users. Careful attention to both costs and performance is therefore needed and, in the case of the latter, the problem of how to measure cleanliness needs to be met head-on if value for money has to be established.

5.3.1 CLEANING AND BUILDING PERFORMANCE

Contents of the cost centre

The scope of the cleaning service varies quite considerably from one building to another; the premises auditor who does not analyse the cost centre into sub-categories such as suggested below will quickly become lost in financial mis-analysis.

The split between 'housekeeping' and cleaning is frequently confused - so the Facilities Economics protocol at Fig. 5.3.A shows 'special supplies' as a separate cost element.

Fig. 5.3.A
Facilities Economics classification protocol - cleaning

Sub-categories (contract bundle items)	Principal Examples / cost elements	Items commonly included in costs	Items excluded from costs	
			Item	Refer to category:
Windows and cladding	Windows External walls	Task management, Handymen, Supervisors, Deep clean toilets, Carpet shampoos, Stain removal, Cleaning materials, Tenants areas service charge element, Graffiti removal, Atria glazing, Roofs and integral gutters, Litter picking (interiors only) Cleaning equipment maintenance	Deep clean kitchens	Catering
Internal areas	Floors Internal walls Ceilings Sanitary fittings Toilet area surfaces		Catering area cleaning	Catering
Special supplies	Janitorial supplies (washroom and toilet)		Contract management time	General facilities management
Furniture and equipment	Furniture, fittings and business equipment		Cleans due to churn	Alterations and improvements
Special cleans	Exposed surfaces Catering special cleans Computer special cleans Lighting special cleans Ductwork special cleans Lift shaft special cleans (excluding tops and pits normally in maintenance contract)		Plantroom cleans	Building services maintenance
Pest control	Pest control		Grounds cleaning	Grounds maintenance
Waste management	General office waste disposal Waste recycling service Hazardous / environmentally sensitive waste disposal			

It should be noted also that works involved in cleaning to the external grounds and out-buildings such as litter collection, sweeping and hosing down paving is excluded from this cost centre: costs and commentary for these operations can be found under Maintenance of the Grounds at Chapter 5.2.5.

The reasons for cleaning

To the lay person cleaning is simply cleaning, but the facilities manager has to have in mind that there are five reasons for cleaning buildings:

- hygiene
- safety, eg of floors etc due to greasy or oily patches
- appearance
- function, eg of equipment likely to be affected by dirt and grime
- depreciation.

Protection against the latter is either through direct or indirect maintenance; an example of direct maintenance is cleaning of external cladding to avoid physical deterioration. The protocol at Fig. 5.3.A comes down on balance in favour of leaving such dual-function operations in 'cleaning', but it is important to remember the dual/multiple purposes of the cleaning operations when making the business case for the required budget.

Quality and performance

The quality of cleaning is a reflection of the aspirations of the organisation and its employees. The number of cleaners employed may influence the speed of the cleaning operation but the brown stains in the bottom of the coffee mugs will speak volumes for the inability of management to achieve an appropriate level of performance.

Management must set objectives for the facilities manager in terms of cleanliness as well as the other operating cost centres. How best to achieve those objectives within a sensible budget must be the facilities manager's decision. The facilities manager must also have a strong say in what is a 'sensible budget' and what the objectives ought to be.

The scope of the service will normally be universally constant in terms of what has to be cleaned: the only variable is the division of responsibility in a leasehold situation between the landlord and tenant - that is, the extent to which the service charge covers cleaning of common parts such as reception areas, staircases and toilets.

So, with the scope constant, the frequency of cleaning, the materials used and the supervision are the major determinants of the quality of performance.

The frequency of such cleaning operations as polishing desk tops, washing down partitions, vacuuming carpets and cleaning sanitary fittings has a marked effect on the cost of the service; it also has a marked effect upon the observed efficiency of the facilities operation, eg a facilities cleaning strategy may entail having the toilets cleaned four times a day. Apart from the obvious desirability of extra hygiene the policy may well be supported by core management on grounds of good Public Relations (PR). Perhaps in no other cost centre - even taking energy into account - is the diligence and efficiency of facilities management more open to comment (favourable or otherwise) than in cleaning. This PR feature is an integral part of the performance requirement: the premises policy must identify this feature and point out to management the risk management implications of the policy.

It is worth noting that the co-operation and goodwill of staff is extremely important to successful and economic facilities management. In that context spending a little bit extra on the cleaning budget in an attempt to improve relationships between management and employees may well generate benefits of a far greater magnitude in terms of core business productivity.

5.3.2 MANAGEMENT OF CLEANING

Supervision

The effect of good or bad supervision is felt in terms of cost and quality. It is, of course, a human factor and, despite the arguments often advanced to the contrary, is not directly related to the debate over contract v in-house cleaning. The responsibility stops with the facilities manager who will be concerned to see that standards achieved are in line with policy and costs. If performance is below standard for the price paid (and assuming market rates are being paid), it will come down to a question of whether or not the in-house or external supervising staff are being diligent in enforcing provisions of the specification.

As with all services the method and diligence of quality control must be stated, observed and itself monitored. Being a labour-intensive service generally involving fairly modest levels of pay and with a relatively high rate of operative turnover it can be a difficult task to manage especially with regards to quality control. Monitoring location of operatives on site can now be carried out electronically to good effect; logging on and off using modern biometric technology can also lead to greater control of labour input.

In terms of the output performance, apart from visible inspection the use of air quality gauges to set and monitor levels of invisible dust is gaining more and more acceptance in an area which has tended to be dominated and discredited in the past by use of subjective assessment.

Contract cleaning

The main cost difference between contract cleaning and direct labour is that the contract cleaners carry their own supervision, charge for their overheads and profit and carry a contract risk. Strictly speaking, direct labour costs, being minus profit and risk, should be lower than contract cleaning. However, this will depend on the ability of facilities management to exercise good cost control and quality supervision - which must include regular cost checks against the external contract benchmarks. Regular tendering of the cleaning is, of course, necessary, but too rigid a policy on selection by price alone can be counter-productive. By all means keep the existing contractors on their toes but do not jump out of the frying pan into the fire for the sake of a few pence per sq m pa.

The use of contract cleaning is an easy option for facilities management. It can ease an administrative burden but this ought to show in reduced administration costs, not simply in a quieter life and having the luxury of someone else to blame.

Cleaning and component life-cycle

As mentioned earlier a cleaning operation will influence the rate of depreciation of the treated surfaces such as carpets, furniture and cladding. Although it is likely that decay is reduced and the life of materials lengthened by frequent cleaning and treatment, there are some materials - carpets, being a good example - which can actually be damaged by excessive cleaning. Even where life-cycle replacement periods are extended by better cleaning performance these savings must be set against the extra revenue cost, to see if the extra specification is really justified on grounds of pure economics. The chances are that it will not be. However, once the argument spills over to functional as opposed to physical performance the true economic case will take a different turn.

5.3.3 THE COST OF CLEANING

Typical ranges of costs of cleaning in the major sectors, calculated by reference to the Facilities Economics protocol on Fig. 5.3.A are given in Fig. 5.3.B.

Fig. 5.3.B
Typical range of cleaning expenditure by sector per unit of floor area

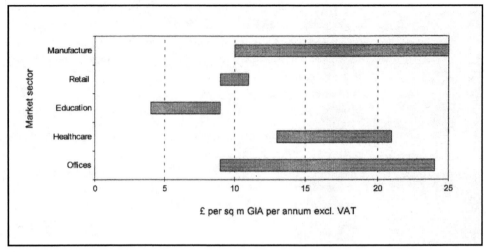

The cost drivers

The principal cost drivers in general terms are:

- the cost of labour, equipment and consumables

- the 'cleanability' of surfaces

- the nature and frequency of cleans - see Fig. 5.3.C for typical analysis

Fig. 5.3.C
General cleaning specification - task frequency comparison

Group category	Cleaning Items	Description of task	Cost band descriptions		
			A	B	C and D
			High standard	Average standard	Low standard
Externally	Windows	Wash and polish	Weekly	Monthly	Quarterly
Generally	Windows	Wash and polish	Weekly	Monthly	Quarterly
	Glazed partitions	Wash and polish	Daily	Monthly	Quarterly
Lifts	Doors	Clean and burnish	Daily	Monthly	Quarterly
Toilets	Partitions and walls	Thorough wash and clean	Daily	Daily	Weekly
	Floors	Machine clean	Weekly	Monthly	Quarterly
	WC's and urinals	Wash, clean and disinfect	Daily	Daily	Weekly
Office spaces	Floors	Vacuum clean	Daily	Daily	Weekly
	Bins etc	Empty and fit liners	Daily	Daily	Alt. days
	Doors	Dust/polish	Weekly	Quarterly	Half yearly
	Furniture (desks)	Dust/polish	Daily	Monthly	Quarterly
	Other furniture	Dust clean	Daily	Quarterly	Half yearly
	Reception desk	Clean/polish	Daily	Weekly	Monthly
Tea points	Walls	Wash and polish	Daily	Weekly	Monthly
	Floors	Machine clean	Weekly	Monthly	Quarterly
Staircase/ landing	Handrails	Wipe clean and polish	Daily	Monthly	Quarterly
	Glazing	Clean/polish	Daily	Weekly	Monthly

- the extent of wet areas

- adequate storage and access for optimum equipment - a cleaners' cupboard on every floor and wide doors to lifts and toilets can make a world of difference to the cost

- the intensity of utilisation of the premises
- environmental conditions internally and externally
- wet or dry carpet cleaning
- clear desk policy
- tidiness of local storage arrangements
- time available for cleaning function
- the existence of an atrium
- openable windows
- quality of air-filtering (if any)
- dust-free zones
- health and safety provisions
- affordability.

Typical distribution of costs

A typical analysis of the distribution of the costs of cleaning is suggested at Fig. 5.3.D.

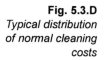

Fig. 5.3.D
Typical distribution of normal cleaning costs

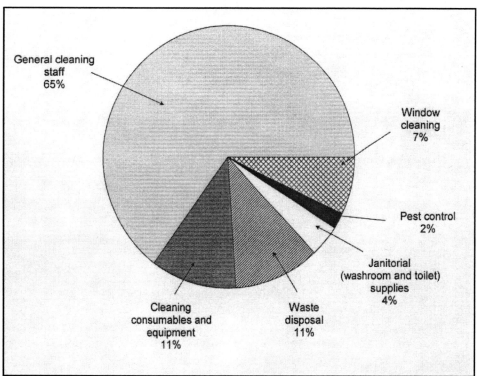

The 'general cleaning' sub-element is clearly the largest component and is almost exclusively about getting rid of dust, dirt and standard office waste. 80-90% of the dirt entering a building arrives on people's feet. If the facilities manager can devise an effective means of ridding those boots and shoes of their dirt before they enter the heart of the building (preferably in at least two strides) then the cleaning operation will be both quicker and more efficient and probably cheaper. These benefits, together with an improved life span for some of the surface materials, are the essential ingredients of the value for money which the facilities manager is seeking in every cost centre in terms of 'hard' returns on investment. Of course the biggest return, as always, will be in the 'soft' benefits such as improved productivity and image which are the main performance drivers of the cleaning policy.

5.3.4 SOME PRACTICAL ISSUES

Internal areas

Dry cleaning of carpets is known to be more effective than wet cleaning, avoiding discolouration and colour bleeding, shrinkage, stretching or splitting. Nevertheless, regular wet cleaning is essential to the control of microbes and reduction of static electricity.

Carpet tiles, with their stiff backings, are difficult for vacuum cleaners to suck air through; a light adhesive pat in each corner will facilitate the use of a more powerful vacuum.

Avoidance of too many changes of flooring surface can also speed the cleaning process. 'Track off' areas (where people drag dirt on to carpets from smooth surfaces and 'funnel areas' (where people congregate or traverse in intensive numbers) should be carefully controlled and minimised. Easily pitted surfaces should be avoided at all costs.

Cleaning of acoustic ceilings is probably best carried out by specialists to avoid discolouration and damage to the acoustic properties - painting the tiles is not a good preventative measure on both those grounds.

Lighting losses of up to 50% can result from inadequate lamp cleaning. Venetian blinds are a real dirt trap and the use of ultra-sonics in the cleaning process will ensure a thorough result.

The specification should also cover the ICT services, keyboards and telephones (in the latter case a regular hygiene service is highly desirable), especially where personnel are allowed to eat food at the workstation!

External surfaces

Apart from the obvious point about the proportion of glazed areas, adequate mechanism to permit cleaning from cradles or boats is clearly paramount. Abseiling from ropes is becoming increasingly popular and can be facilitated at a low capital cost. Reversible windows are appropriate in some environments and obviously save time and cost in the window cleaning process.

Windows cleaned with the wrong, abrasive, cleaner will become 'shot' over time making the process difficult and the result unrewarding in visual terms.

Again the proportion of walls to windows will impact - but not as much as the specification of surfaces requiring frequent treatment for maintenance purposes eg power-jet washing down the cladding system every three months - a product guarantee condition likely to be discovered by a facilities manager only upon handover of the new building.

Graffiti may be a problem in certain areas. Leaving it just encourages more artistry but it can be hard to remove. A preventative treatment using a polyurethane finish has been found to ease this serious cleaning problem.

5.3.5 TOILETS AND WASHROOMS

Consumables and appliances

The 'housekeeping' facet of cleaning, involving the provision and disposal of 'special supplies', such as soap, towels and toilet tissue, is of course fraught with problems, not least being the impact of health and safety legislation on the levels of hygiene to be achieved in toilets and washrooms.

Worthwhile economies can be found on a small scale. Products such as large roll theft-proof toilet-paper dispensers and sensor-triggered automatic flushing systems will save a few euros a week; however much more importantly they will ensure that the facilities are always properly provided and in a hygienic state.

Warm-air dryers are vandal-resistant and cheap to maintain but not suited to general office toilet areas - roller towels (linen fed) are best for the administrative areas with paper towels in the factory floor and food preparation area toilets. However, proper disposal of waste toiletry paper and sanitary towels is not only highly desirable but required by law.

5.3.6 HEALTH AND SAFETY ETC

Environmental and health and safety concerns are an important driver of cleaning services. Specialist cleaning services may be required in some instances and these may include emergency cleaning in connection with:

- radioactive contamination from core operations, from accidents or spillages
- asbestos, ie planned removal or accidental discovery or contamination
- oil or other fluid spillages or contamination
- contamination from bacteria, eg Legionaires disease, or other health or clinical hazards
- accidental fire damage or explosion
- flooding or escapes from blocked drains or sewers.

as well as 'special areas' such as

- computer rooms
- kitchens
- lift shafts
- ventilation ducts.

Where damage or loss arises and this is covered by insurance, any cleaning should be managed within procedures dictated by the way in which the insurance claim should be handled.

5.4 ENERGY

Introduction

Chapter 5.1, Fig. 5.1.B shows that the cost of energy as a building facility is unlikely to amount to more than 0.25 - 0.40% of an organisation's total expenditure. Yet consumption of energy assumes a level of priority in terms of national policies far in excess of its minor significance in micro-economic terms.

The reason is quite simple: burning of fossil fuels to create energy is strongly believed to be a major factor in global warming and environmental pollution. Global warming is a real and very serious issue, which affects the earth and every living inhabitant; this is the main reason why this chapter on energy goes into rather more depth than is offered for other facilities cost centres which are in many cases equally or more expensive.

This chapter considers how energy is produced, purchased, consumed, budgeted, monitored and conserved. It also illustrates the latest management techniques available to assist the facilities manager in saving the planet - well, contributing, anyway - in the course of keeping the facilities working properly and costs to an acceptable level.

Furthermore, it touches upon topics which impinge upon matters of relevance to the facilities manager, including energy targets, emission trading, renewable energy suppliers' credits, and the need for an energy survey when a building changes hands.

5.4.1 THE IMPORTANCE OF ENERGY

Economic importance

The economic importance of energy at a macro-level cannot be denied. Energy represents almost 10% of global economic activity. Energy companies still rank high in listings of the largest companies in the USA, Europe and Asia - and much of the wealth of the world's richest people from the mid-nineteenth to the late twentieth century was ultimately based either on energy itself - coal mining, oil - or the harnessing of energy - steel, railways and the like.

In the second half of the twentieth century, this dependence of economic development on energy has begun to create problems of its own. The main energy resources used at present are finite and non-renewable and there is the real prospect of the world's energy resources being used up at some stage. Indeed, though the entire globe has been mapped for oil resources since the 1970's, no new finds of oil compare with those already known before 1970. The peak of world oil production is expected to occur at some time between the years 2004 and 2012, after which it will be in inexorable decline. Natural gas has displaced oil in many buildings in Europe, but even gas is a finite resource.

In micro-economic terms one has to wonder what all the fuss is about. In the facilities context, even in a fully air-conditioned building energy costs are rarely more than about 20% - 30% of premises operating costs as shown in Fig. 5.4.A (over the page).

Certainly the occupier must try to avoid spending more than is necessary on any cost centre. In all facilities services the economic issue is not so much cost-efficiency as cost-effectiveness; however, in the case of energy consumption, there is an even bigger issue to be addressed.

Fig. 5.4.A
Energy cost in the context of total premises operating costs

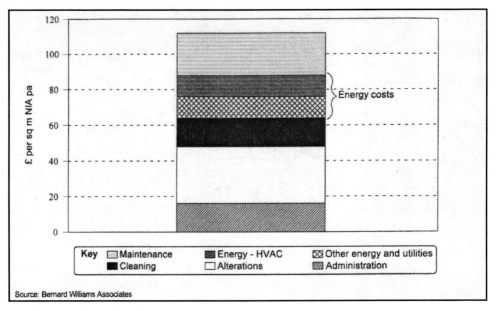

Source: Bernard Williams Associates

Environmental importance

The possibility that carbon dioxide produced by the burning of fossil fuels will lead to global warming - ie the reversal of warm ocean currents leading to occasional extremes of weather and modification of climate in northern Europe and raising of sea levels globally - has changed in only five years from a conjecture by scientists to a scenario accepted by policy makers. Because energy resources are not distributed over the globe in the same pattern as consumption, there is potential for disputes over energy to threaten world political stability in the long term.

In 1997 the meeting on Convention on Climate Change held in Kyoto, Japan committed the developed nations to reducing carbon dioxide (CO_2) emissions to 5% below 1990 levels by 2008-12. Some countries, notably the UK, have committed themselves to even greater reductions.

Fig. 5.4.B
Estimated CO_2 emissions from energy consumption by type of fuel

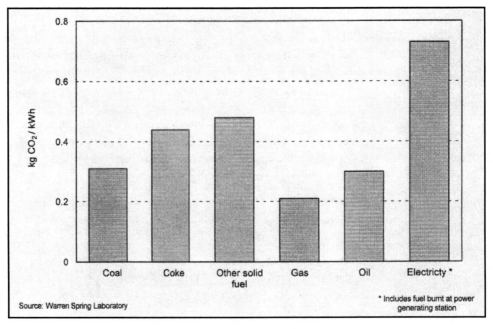

Source: Warren Spring Laboratory

* Includes fuel burnt at power generating station

5.4.2 ENVIRONMENTAL POLLUTION

Sources of pollution

The principal source of pollution is CO_2 which is emitted in the process of burning solid fuel, liquid and natural gas. Estimated CO_2 emissions from energy consumption by type of fuel are shown at Fig. 5.4.B. (previous page) Note that in the case of electricity the fuel burnt at the power station is included; however the use of nuclear fuel at the power stations is reducing this figure at a fast rate.

CO_2 emissions by sector in the EU are shown in Fig. 5.4.C.

Fig. 5.4.C
Estimated CO_2 emissions by sector

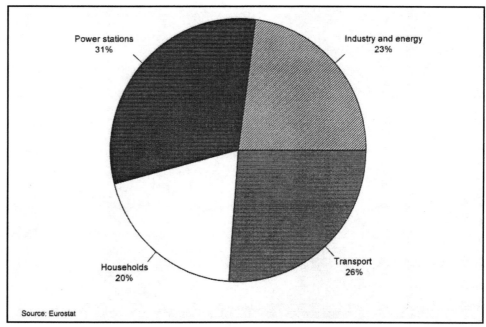

Clearly the emissions from power stations are all in respect of creation of electrical energy for consumption by households and industry/commerce; the figures include local emissions due to burning gas, oil, coal etc to produce energy on site or at home.

CO_2 emissions from transport account for about a quarter of the EU total which raises an interesting issue about the relative importance of energy consumed in buildings compared with energy consumed getting to and from them. An interesting

Fig. 5.4.D
Total energy consumption in two buildings

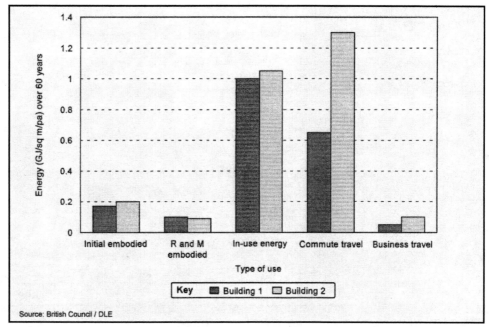

study carried out by the British Council and Davis Langdon Everest compared the predicted total energy consumption in the construction, use and travel to and from two major offices over a 60 year period - see Fig. 5.4.D. (previous page)

The researchers analysed not just the in-use energy but also that consumed in the construction process (initial embodied - see 5.4.9 below), in running and maintaining the buildings (R and M embodied) and in commuting and business travel. Interestingly the energy consumed in the provincial location was overall higher, due almost entirely to the need for travel by motor transport to and from the out-of-town site.

Fig. 5.4.E
Estimated CO_2 emissions from the two buildings

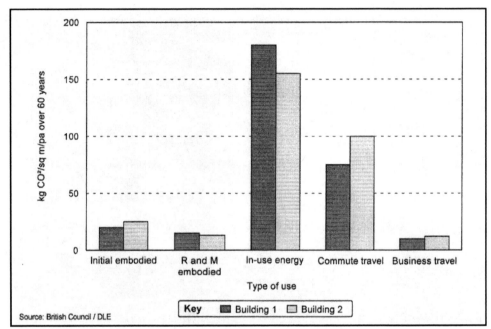

However, when these statistics are converted to CO_2 emissions (Fig. 5.4.E) the picture changes, ie 'building-in-use' energy becomes the critical source of emissions, dwarfing all but commute travel. The reason is that, whereas the building energy is predominantly derived from fossil-fuel-burning power station supplies of electricity, the travel emissions come from burning petrol and diesel fuel which are rather less toxic.

Fig. 5.4.F
Estimated CO_2 emissions from the HVAC systems and other energy uses in a building of 5,000 sq m GIA

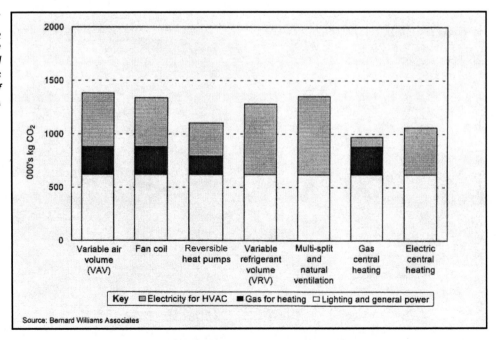

One of the biggest consumers of electricity in building is cooling (see 5.4.5 below) and, to a lesser extent, heating. Fig. 5.4.F. (previous page) is the analysis of CO_2 emissions pa from common air-conditioning and central heating systems in a 5,000 sq m building alongside that from lighting and general power.

Interestingly, although the more electrically-dependent heating and cooling systems consume more energy the electricity for the cooling component alone does not per se contribute greatly to the overall expenditure on energy or the additional CO_2 emitted through its production.

Natural cooling as an option is considered further at 5.4.5 below.

As well as CO_2 other gases such as nitrogen oxides, sulphur dioxide and other volatile organic compounds are also by-products of most aspects of energy consumption; however they are only a small fraction of the CO_2 emitted from the same sources.

Reducing carbon dioxide emissions

There are several ways to reduce carbon dioxide emissions:

- use energy sources that are not carbon based
- reduce energy consumption in buildings
- improve the efficiency of energy conversion.
- climate change levy
- emissions trading.

Non-carbon alternatives

In the case of the first option the main **non-carbon** alternative energy sources are nuclear, wind, wave, tidal, solar and hydro. Apart from solar, the choice of these tends not to rest with the energy user. Exploitation of nuclear, tidal and wave energy is entirely through electricity generation and the decision to use them rests entirely with the electricity generator.

Wind energy is attractive for facilities in remote locations but requires backup connection to the public supply to cover for when the wind does not blow. For this reason wind energy is also mainly adopted by generators for stand-by or back-up supplies rather than primary energy use.

Solar energy is a potentially important energy source where the decision to use it rests mainly with the designer and the operator of buildings. The potential for solar energy tends to be overstated by enthusiasts. Solar energy can be collected as heat or as electricity (photovoltaic conversion). The central problem is that the amount of solar energy available depends on season: the seasonal availability of solar energy does not match the season for consumption of heat energy in buildings and photovoltaic conversion is expensive. In any case, the amount of electricity wasted in buildings at the beginning of the twenty first century dwarfs the energy practically available through solar energy. The only practical use of solar energy in buildings is by the design of buildings to provide passive capture of solar gain, which is only applicable to new build but, even here, a much bigger opportunity tends to be the design of buildings to passively dissipate the heat generated in buildings to limit the need for air-conditioning.

Reducing energy consumption in buildings

Concerning the second option, ie the reduction of energy consumption, buildings still represent a large part of the potential for reducing global CO_2 emissions through positive action to reduce energy use. Although there have been significant developments in lowering the energy consumption of new buildings - through the technology of boilers, controls and lighting and by regulation applied to structures and controls - much of the energy saving potential in existing buildings remains untapped. This is partly because the techniques by which energy-saving opportunities in existing building are identified and appraised, and the investment in them financially justified, are comparatively new - mostly having appeared in the 1990's.

The identification of ways to reduce energy consumption and cost in buildings, including these newer developments in technique, as seen from an economic perspective, is the main emphasis of this chapter. The engineering detail is amply covered by the voluminous literature available in most countries.

The Building Regulations were reviewed for energy efficiency measures so that Part L now contains regulatory provisions to develop energy efficiency in buildings. Also, when buildings change hands there is the expectation that an energy audit will be undertaken with the view to improving energy efficiency thereafter.

Efficient conversion

The third option to reduce carbon dioxide emissions is to **convert fuels more efficiently** to heat and electricity. All fuels can be used to provide both heat and power, the proportions of each being determined by the technology used and the laws of physics, but most energy users buy these separately as fuel for heat and as electricity from the public supply. It is, however, possible to design systems that provide both power and heat at useful temperatures that are more efficient than a combination of separate supply of electricity from power stations and fuel burned in heating-only boilers. This so-called Combined Heat and Power (CHP) is used increasingly and forms a large part of the national strategy to reduce carbon dioxide emissions. In some cases this is through CHP generation in large power stations with sales of heat to the local community, in others it is by installation of combined heat and power within facilities such as universities, hospitals and industrial estates.

Emissions trading

The government's energy policy provides for emissions (or carbon) trading - both formally and informally. The formal arrangements are set down in Schedule 1 to the Pollution Prevention and Control Act 1999.

Briefly, emission totals or targets are calculated for an area. Companies who pollute, or want to, are then allowed or required to purchase part of the total. As soon as the total supply of emissions is thus exhausted, any new intending polluters will have to buy from the original purchasers. If demand to pollute increases, prices rise and holders of emissions will be encouraged to become more energy efficient - and so be able to sell off their surplus emissions.

A national approach, the Emissions Trading Scheme (ETS) commenced trading on 1 April 2002. About 150 companies joined in the auction on 25 February 2002 bidding for about £250 million of credit

Climate change levy

As part of a comprehensive energy policy, the government introduced a tax on energy usage, the 'climate change levy', from 1 April 2001. Energy suppliers, ie electricity companies and so on, will pay the levy. It will differ according to the type or types of energy supplied to businesses. The government's aim is to reduce greenhouse emissions, eg carbon dioxide, methane, ozone, nitrous oxide, CFCs but the effect will be to increase energy costs by as much as 10%.

Certain industries are exempt from the tax and others enjoy relief, eg some high energy using industries (80%) and horticulture (50%), but the rebate for an industry depends on achieving agreed targets.

No doubt facilities managers and others will need to address the impact of the climate change levy in terms of, for instance:

- energy saving schemes, eg the electricity from combined heat and power projects (CHP) is exempt

- applying for exemption or relief (although is should have been done by now)

- capital projects to change to cheaper supplies where possible.

Customs & Excise administer the levy and have issued explanatory guidance.

Fig 5.4.G shows the CCL rates of tax for the tax year 2001 to 2002

Electricity supplied from renewable sources, eg wind generation, is exempt from the levy

Fig 5.4.G
Rates of climate change levy

Type of Energy	Rate of Tax (pence per/kWh)
Coal	0.15
Electricity	0.43
Gas (natural)	0.15
Gas (Liquid Petroleum)	0.07

5.4.3 LEGISLATION, REGULATION AND STANDARDS RELATING TO ENERGY USE IN BUILDINGS

Energy has only become a significant issue at the policy level for EU countries in the third quarter of the twentieth century and over this time policy has been guided by a succession of changing imperatives - first the high rate of change of prices, then the integration of new supplies of natural gas as an alternative to oil, next the issues raised by the privatisation of national and regional monopolies in terms of supply and introduction of competition, and - last but not least - the response to climate change.

The development of the EU and hence national legislation and regulatory framework for energy has tended to reflect:

- the economic importance of energy

- the need to regulate markets with the introduction of competition in energy supply

- the extent to which emissions to the environment from energy use (sulphur, nitrogen oxides and particulates) can be accommodated within wider environmental legislation

- the health and safety aspects of energy (the flammability of fuels and the role of boilers and steam systems as pressure vessels)

- the fact that all developed countries have building regulations and standards that pre-date the first oil crisis and that have provided an existing but inadequate framework for the introduction of energy efficiency regulation into new buildings.

The result is that there is very little specific legislation or regulation affecting the use of energy in existing facilities but energy tends to be covered by a wide range of broader legislation and regulation on buildings, health and safety, environmental protection and competition regulation that is particular to each state.

European policy is broadly guided by the green paper For a European Union Energy Policy adopted by the EU Commission in 1995. This paper regards environmental protection, security of supply and industrial competitiveness as the core elements of EU energy policy but energy efficiency is mainly promoted by encouragement and exhortation and the injection of substantial resources aimed at supporting research and development, local initiatives, the promotion of combined heat and power and the promotion of renewable energy. This is likely to continue to be the strategy while confidence of reaching the Kyoto Commitment targets is high and the reductions agreed at Kyoto are regarded as enough.

The main alternative options under consideration are energy taxes to encourage lower energy use and a switch to fuels with lower environmental impact. In year 2000 this was under consideration as an amendment to Directive 92/82/EEC and would impose minimum tax rates on all energy products.

5.4.4 ENERGY PURCHASING

The end of energy monopolies

Until the 1990's, most forms of energy (except oil) were supplied by public or private, local or regional specialist monopolies. In other words, energy users had only one supplier for each form of energy and, furthermore, each supplier supplied only one form of energy and this was provided on a uniform price basis. Only for oil (and to some extent for small supplies of coal) was there any freedom to negotiate the price of energy.

The introduction of competition and the dismantling of key areas of monopoly in energy supply is the most significant change to have occurred in energy markets since the first oil crisis of 1973. Beginning in the UK with the privatisation of the electricity industry in 1988, then the introduction of competition in an already privatised gas industry from 1993; competition in energy supply is spreading across the world.

Competition and franchise

With the introduction of competition comes the concept of "franchise". Any part of energy supply that remains a monopoly is said to be franchised to the supplier. This may mean the whole of the supply of a utility or just some aspect of it. For example, in 1988 only electricity supplies to sites with a maximum demand over 1MW were opened to competition, the rest remained franchised to the regional distribution companies. Sites over 100 kW were disfranchised four years later and full competition was not achieved until 1998. It is important for facilities managers to be aware of the position of their energy supplies with regard to franchise at any time.

The other significant change is that the privatisation of state-owned and municipally-owned utility companies has allowed utility companies to combine so that their interests extend across several utilities - electricity, gas, water, telecommunications.

In the case of gas, electricity and heat from municipal CHP installations, where there is a fixed physical transmission and distribution network - pipes or wires - it is simply not an economic proposition to have more than one such system supplying a community. It is usual, therefore, for the transmission and distribution system to remain in franchise and to operate a single system of charging which is published and for competition to be limited to generation and supply of the energy itself - the m^3 of gas or kWh of electricity. This is important because this latter is the only part of the price of energy that is negotiable; prices for transmission and distribution are not negotiable and apply uniformly to everyone.

Factors in energy pricing

Energy prices vary widely, determined by the original source, nature and scale of the transmission and distribution network, local tax structures, extent of local subsidy (which applies particularly to nuclear power) and the extent of competition. Although all electricity is the same when it reaches the consumer, the mix of fuels used to generate it may be numerous.

The price paid is determined by four key parameters:

- quantity
- delivery
- quality
- security of supply.

The impact of these differs for each type of fuel according to the nature of the fuel, its distribution system and the way the industry is organised.

- **Quantity** - broadly speaking, the cost of selling and distributing a large amount of energy is cheaper than a small quantity so, in principle, a large consumer of energy should be able to get energy at a lower price than a smaller one, although this very much depends on how effectively the price is negotiated.

- **Delivery** - coal and oil are delivered by road or rail. A user who is able to take full loads and who is flexible about delivery dates and times - able to take night deliveries for example - can get a better price than one that requires delivery on specific days between 09:00 and 17:00 hours. Gas, electricity and heat as water or steam are delivered by pipeline and cable and are used as needed but use of plant to generate electricity and heat needs to be scheduled and through this the time of demand can affect the price. It is common, for example for electricity taken at night to be charged differently from electricity taken during the day. Electricity contracts and tariffs also often contain features that relate to a maximum demand - the highest rate of consumption in a given period - day, week, month.

- **Quality** is more an issue for oil and coal than for gas or electricity. There are three main characteristics of fuels that relate to quality. These are:

  - the calorific value (the amount of energy the fuel releases when it is burned)

  - the chemical content (how much sulphur, ash and other materials it might contain)

  - its burning characteristics (which for oil are mainly related to viscosity).

  There are specific grades of oil - gas oil, light, medium and heavy - which are offered at different prices. Which is used depends on the equipment installed to burn it. Even within these specifications there is still some variability and lower prices can be achieved by consumers who are able to accept a lower specification; nevertheless it falls on the user to ensure the supplier does not pass off lower quality for a premium price.

- **Security** of supply refers to whether the fuel is available when required and applies to all fuels. Oil is stored on the site in tanks; by managing the delivery of oil so that tanks are low when oil is cheaper in early summer (which is a usual rather than universal rule) rather than the common strategy adopted of "use one, buy one", can yield significant savings on cost but requires sophistication and the use of so-called stock models in which the rate of use is related to season and stocks deliberately run down in anticipation of seasonally low prices.

  For gas there are two types of contract - firm and interruptible. Firm gas is always available but has a higher price. An interruptible contract for gas allows the supplier to cut off (or ask the user not to take) gas when the supply network is under strain. The supplier offers a discount for this but the user then has to make other arrangements (usually to keep a stock of oil and to have and maintain the equipment to burn it) during interruptions. In those facilities where high security of supply is essential - hospitals, banks, supermarkets - there would normally be a back-up supply - oil to back up gas, a generator to back up electricity.

Comparing prices

The price paid for energy in a franchised market is either one price that applies to everybody or one from a limited range of choices offered to everybody. The price paid in competitive markets is negotiated between the supplier and user and, although in principle any basis for pricing could be chosen, in practice contracts are based on price schedules that depend on the type of meter installed. The essence of buying in these markets then is in the choice of price structure and negotiating the price elements within it.

Electricity tariffs and contracts fall into four categories, all of which contain fixed and variable charges:

- unit based - in which the only variable element is a price for kWh units, which may or may not differentiate between kWh's taken at night, during weekends and during the day

- maximum demand - in which the variable elements are kWh units, which may or may not differentiate between kWh's taken at night and during the day, and the highest demand in any half hour in the month

- seasonal time of day - where the price per kWh varies by time of day and season

- spot-related - where the price is linked to prices in a spot-market where traders agree on prices on the day of trading.

Unit-based, maximum demand and seasonal time of day are types of price schedule that were developed before digital metering was available (pre-1988). These are price structures which the supply side of the electricity market understands well and can be used with older analogue and new digital metering. Spot pricing and a range of other options between spot and seasonal time of day have only been possible since the introduction of digital metering. With the availability of digital meters, there are moves to apply the sophistication in tariffs and contracts to gas that had previously been limited to electricity.

Tariff and contract evaluation is an important skill for the facilities manager because reductions in energy prices can be achieved with no capital cost or disruption and any reductions achieved apply to the entire consumption bought under that tariff or contract - which can cover many buildings. By contrast, measures applied at the point of use only affect part of the energy use of one building.

There are two ways to make the choice between any two tariffs or schedules:

- costing out - in which the total costs are computed for the demand pattern in question and the one with the lowest price selected

- the criterion method - in which criteria are established from the structure of the tariffs that would determine which tariff would be optimal.

In practice, **costing out** is by far the most commonly used because is simple and seems to make such obvious sense that few people even wonder if there is an alternative. In truth, there are many circumstances in which costing out does not work well. Energy users not familiar with the alternative criterion method tend to gloss over the limitations of costing out, just on the assumption that there is no easier way.

Fig. 5.4.H shows how an organisation can determine the optimum demand choice from two tariffs from a given demand pattern.

Fig. 5.4.H
Calculating the optimum tariff

Annual day units	936,834 kWh
Annual night units	511,702 kWh
Availability	400 kVA

Maximum demand kVA:	Jan	Feb	Mar	Apr	May	Jun	Jul	Aug	Sep	Oct	Nov	Dec
	360	312	280	271	276	283	284	283	249	301	324	363

		Tariff 1	Tariff 3
Fixed charge £ per month		19.3	19.3
Availability £ per kVA per month		1.92	1.92
Maximum demand £ per kVA:	Nov and Feb	3.84	3.84
	Dec and Jan	11.85	11.85
Cents per kWh:	At any time	9.12	
	Day		9.17
	Night		4.14

Both tariffs		£
Fixed charge		12 x 30.88 = 370.56
Availability		400 x 12 x 1.20 = 9,216.00
Maximum demand	Nov and Feb	(324 + 312) x 2.40 = 2,442.24
	Dec and Jan	(363 + 360) x 7.41 = 8,567.55
Sub total		20,596.35

		Tariff 1	Tariff 2
		20,596.35	20,596.35
Day units	936,834 x 0.0912 =	85,907.67	
Night units	511,702 x 0.0414 =	21,184.46	
All units	1,448,536 x 0.0917 =		132,106.48
Total		127,688.49	152,702.83

So the tariff 3 is the lower cost for this site over a year, by £25,014.34

Costing out is simple to do but has three major drawbacks:

- to do it at all there has to be sufficiently complete information on the consumption pattern. If the tariff has different unit rates for consumption at different times of day, the unit consumption in each time zone must be known, as here. If the supply is not already on the most complex tariff, the split of kWh units between day and night is not available from the utility bills for that site and requires a separate measurement. This is not a problem for a single large supply but it presents an enormous problem for large number of small sites - it just is not an economic proposition for the money it saves

- although it indicates which is the lowest cost and by how much, it gives little idea as to how sensitive this result is to variations in the demand pattern unless this is tested by a repeat calculation, again a problem for large numbers of sites.

- costing out is time consuming because it requires all the requisite information on the demand and the tariff to be entered into the calculation. Although computer software is available, it still requires all the consumption data from all the bills to be keyed in.

The **criterion** approach is more sophisticated and is the one used by electricity suppliers to design tariffs and contracts. It determines from the structure of each tariff or schedule the circumstances under which one of any pair is the lowest cost and converts this to a simple criterion.

A common case is to decide, as in the example just used, the circumstances under which it is advantageous to pay a higher rate for day units in order to get cheaper night units.

The criterion for this decision is the fraction of all units used at night F_N. If the price on the single rate tariff for units used at any time is P_a, the price on the two price tariff for units used during the day is P_d and at night is P_n, then the two price tariff gives the lower overall price if:

$$F_N > (P_a - P_d)/(P_n - P_d)$$

In this example

$$F = \frac{9.12 - 9.17}{4.14 - 9.17} = \frac{-0.05}{-5.03} = 0.01004 \text{ or } 1 \text{ \%}$$

and the two-part tariff is the lowest tariff for all sites or supplies where the fraction of units used at night exceeds 1%.

There are three ways in which this serves the facilities manager:

- it enables a huge pile of bills to be scanned quickly for the right tariff because it can be applied by inspection - here the criterion is close to 1%, if the numbers of kWh units in the separate time periods are shown on the bill; checking that one is or is not more than 1% of the other can be done by eye;

- if the sites are similar in function, the data from sites in one region can be used to test the tariffs for sites in another region, especially in estates that extend across the boundaries of former regional franchise areas and when not all sites have the necessary metering to measure the consumption in different time periods, this is a procedure that is risky in costing out;

- in contract negotiations each element of a contract can be negotiated because the impact it will have is easily gauged.

This same formula applies to all pairs of tariffs of this kind. If the formula is entered into a computer spreadsheet the criterion for any pair of tariffs is calculated by simply entering the price information. Where tariffs or schedules differ in fixed costs or contain blocks of units at different prices the criterion is a minimum kWh consumption before the tariff with the lower kWh price becomes the cheaper. To compare maximum demand and units based tariffs and schedules the critical criterion is found to be the load factor (ratio of total kWh to the maximum demand) and there are criteria that can be deduced in the same way for power factor charges based on reactive units. (It takes quite modest mathematical skill to work out these criteria using simple inequality algebra - at a level that is taught in school at or around age 16.)

In most cases costing out is only better than the criterion approach for large buildings where there are schedules with four or more unit prices.

Negotiating energy prices

When negotiating prices in competitive markets there are two important factors in achieving the lowest price:

- market intelligence - knowing what range of prices is achievable

- negotiating skills.

There are two kinds of intelligence - general and price specific. A worthwhile amount of general intelligence can be gathered from public sources. The Financial Times, is a valuable source of information on movements in world prices, especially oil, company information on suppliers, general trends and industry comment. Also, there is dedicated European magazine called Utility Week, that is intended for the supply side of the industry but provides useful comment for large consumers. There are also reports by the regulatory bodies and the operators of the electricity and gas exchange. Some Internet sites give energy price information at the generation level.

There are several consumer interest groups - such as the Major Energy Users' Council, the Utility Buyers Forum and the Energy Intensive Users Group in the UK - which provide newsletters and share information between energy users that subscribe to these groups. There are also companies that specialise in price intelligence, usually provided on a subscription basis. This may extend to comparing prices from different suppliers on a brokerage basis - consumers report the prices they encountered in the previous month or fortnight, which is then returned in summary format, such as price ogives (a curve showing the proportion of the total sales offered at below each price in a range) and quantiles (the price at given points in a list of buyers arranged in descending order).

The essence of negotiation of contract terms is not simply the ability to combine the consumption pattern and the offer from the supplier in a way that enables rival offers to be costed reliably and compared quickly: a considerable factor is the relationship between the customer and supplier and elements of gamesmanship. It is not always obvious that much of the success of a negotiation depends on the suppliers' perception of what kind of customer they are dealing with. Before making an offer suppliers try to make an assessment of how far the organisation is capable of comparing offers and negotiating around them - and then act accordingly. The aim in energy purchasing should be to get the best initial offer possible and negotiate around that.

Successful negotiation starts with making sure the supplier is aware that the customer knows exactly what their energy requirements are and that they can evaluate quickly and reliably any offer the supplier comes up with. This is easier for a single supply but is just as important for a large estate. As a basic rule, no customers should ever go to their current supplier to request details of their consumption from the supplier's records - it is a certain sign that they are unprepared. If there is lack of cooperation between those who hold this information and those who need it, facilities managers should be prepared to make the availability of this information an issue within their own organisation.

Shared savings

Discussion of market intelligence would not be complete without mention of the activities of shared savings consultants; not least because, in terms of turnover, these dwarf subscription intelligence services. In a shared savings arrangement the consultant bases their fee on the money saved through their advice. The common formula quoted is 50% of the savings for five years but this should always be regarded as the ultimate aspiration of the consultant and is always negotiable. 10% over two years is more realistic but the key issue always is the contract terms and what precisely they mean.

Shared savings advice is usually very specific, relating to individual oil or gas contracts and particular tariffs for particular sites. The only way a consultant can police such an arrangement is by requiring the client to copy all bills to the consultant even though the savings will come from advice on only a tiny proportion of them. For large numbers of small sites the work involved for the user in servicing the consultant can be more time-consuming than the work of checking accounts themselves - looking at the bills instead of copying them. The effort required to compare tariffs does not depend much on the size of site and the cost of advice on a shared savings arrangement can be quite out of proportion to the effort or expertise in making the checks.

Deciding what the consultant has actually saved can also be enormously problematical. It is important both to assess accurately the savings actually achieved, (which should never be taken on trust), and to keep detailed notes on file to ensure that it is clear on whose initiative any particular actions were taken; this is to ensure the consultants do not claim savings that are not based on their advice, a common source of dispute between shared savings advisors and their customers.

5.4.5 ENERGY CONSUMPTION IN BUILDINGS

Consumption and costs

Most of the energy use that comes within the specific remit of a facilities manager is for buildings. The main energy uses are then fuel for heating, hot water and catering, electricity for lighting, cooling, office and other machinery such as elevators. The proportions of energy used in each of these applications varies widely from building to building, Fig. 5.4.J.

Fig. 5.4.J
Typical energy consumption in office buildings in kWh per sq m "treated floor area"

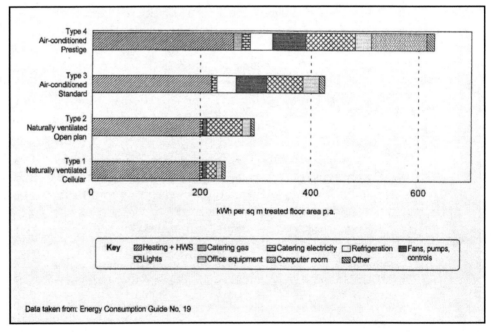

kWh per sq m treated floor area p.a.

Key: Heating + HWS Catering gas Catering electricity Refrigeration Fans, pumps, controls
Lights Office equipment Computer room Other

Data taken from: Energy Consumption Guide No. 19

Electricity prices on a kWh basis are two or three times that of gas or oil so, even though fuel for space heating is often the largest single use of energy, electricity usually accounts for the major proportion of energy costs, Fig. 5.4.K. (over the page)

Energy consumption also depends on the standard of management of the facility. Surveys of the energy use of large numbers of buildings indicates that, comparing like with like, the energy consumption of offices can vary widely. In offices good management can achieve energy consumption 25% lower than a typical office, Fig. 5.4.L (over the page).

When comparing energy costs between buildings it is important to take account of sources which are not directly charged - as for example in some district heating schemes where the cost of such energy is charged locally.

Fig. 5.4.K
Typical energy costs in office buildings per sq m of 'treated floor area'

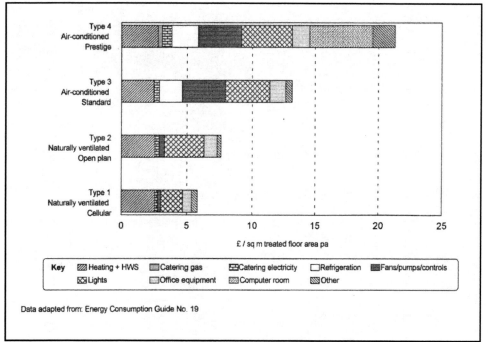

Data adapted from: Energy Consumption Guide No. 19

Fig. 5.4.L
Differences in energy costs of typical and good practice offices.

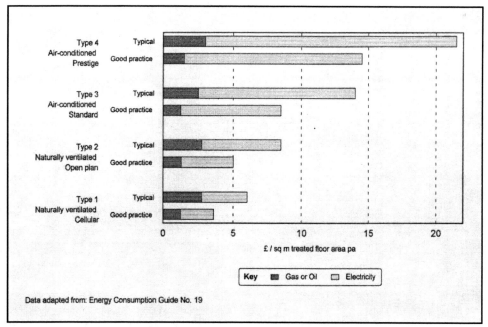

Data adapted from: Energy Consumption Guide No. 19

Space heating energy

The basic space heating needs of a building have been determined when the architect puts down their pencil. This has determined the size, shape and orientation of the buildings, the materials of construction and the number of penetrations that allow free ventilation.

The detail of the energy consumption is determined by the buildings services designer and installer. This has three parts:

- heating and/or cooling plant to maintain the difference in temperature between inside and out

- a margin to allow for making up this temperature difference after heating and cooling has been turned off overnight or over a weekend

- allowance for heat gains through heat emissions by people, lighting and machinery and solar gain.

This design process is guided by building regulations and design codes followed in each country. The installer then installs the plant according the designer's specification.

The result should be installation of an optimum heating and ventilation/cooling system in all buildings. In practice:

- the building regulations and design codes in all countries have evolved over time and the energy performance of a building can depend on age

- the design codes are not always easy to follow

- some buildings services designers work to rules of thumb of their own that are not always reliable

- there is a tendency for buildings services designers who lack confidence in their application of the design codes to build in contingencies that lead to oversized plant

- capital cost considerations often lead to installation of plant smaller or different from the optimum design

- the design of plant makes assumptions about heat loads that depend in turn on the activities in the building

- buildings last a lot longer than the design assumptions made when they were fitted out

- advances in technology have produced improvements in the efficiency of new plant such as boilers and air-conditioning systems

- improvements in control systems for both new build and for retro-fit to existing buildings that make it appropriate to replace plant in some cases even if the design assumption still hold and the plant still functions - this applies particularly to lighting and controls.

The result is that although most buildings operate more or less efficiently in energy terms, there is often some scope for improvement in many, and a small proportion of buildings have gross inefficiencies. The key problem for a facilities manager is to identify in which buildings these inefficiencies are, what corrective actions are required and how to justify capital investment in taking such steps.

Energy for cooling systems

Cooling systems are increasingly installed in buildings as part of an increasing level of expectation of levels of comfort from building occupiers and the prestige building owners and lessees associate with it. Cooling is also necessary for some buildings to reduce the impact of internal heat gains due to office machinery, especially information technology equipment, and the occupants themselves.

Fig. 5.4.M (over the page) shows the typical sources of heat gain per sq m of NIA in a large office building.

A major contributor to levels of discomfort in office buildings in recent times has been the invasion of a plethora of electric and electronic equipment which has revolutionised not only methods of working but the performance required of the building and its services.

In particular, the heat emitted by pc's, photocopiers, printers and the like have added considerably to the required cooling load, and reduced the mechanical heating load proportionately.

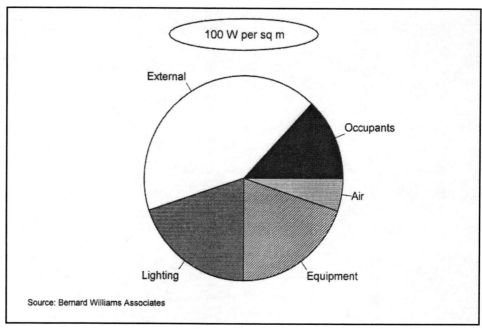

Fig. 5.4.M
*Typical heat gain
from various
sources in a large
office building*

A building wherein ICT take-up is around 1:1 will probably be generating additional heat of around 15 to 20 watts per sq m of net internal floor area.

Ironically, just as the world has come to terms with the problems - with engineers inventing enormously expensive and sometimes quite inappropriate systems of dealing with the cooling requirement - some of the main manufacturers have redressed the problem by introducing 'low energy' pc's and other equipment absorbing only 10% to 20% of the small power required by the older models with proportional reduction in heat gain. As many of the existing cooling systems are already designed to cope with two/three times the actual heat gain from equipment the move towards downsizing of such plant will be further encouraged. Of course, the heating capacity will have to be watched but extra energy costs in heating will be offset several times over if the process of handling the cooling load can be reduced to suit the actual needs.

Everyone knows that human beings generate significant heat via their bodies as a waste product from the energy used up in the processes of simply being and doing. The main problem with handling body heat is that it is less static and predictable in terms of location and concentration than equipment and solar radiation; six people gathering in a small meeting room will quickly generate a cooling problem which may or may not have a ready solution.

Identification of 'hot spots' involving people and equipment and designing for them in terms of both planning and services allocation is a key aspect of interior design and, indeed, building architecture as a whole.

Heat gain from outside the building can be delivered by radiation (from the sun or a process), conduction (via the fabric from a warmer environment) or by the air supply (forced or infiltrating).

Of these factors solar radiation is probably the most significant especially when arriving direct through windows; its warming effect on the fabric can also be important, although much of the heat retained in the fabric may well be returned to the ambient exterior at night time in the cooler northern climates. Careful attention to design and specification both to prevent the sun's rays penetrating the glass or fabric and/or reflect or absorb them can make a big impact on the gain and are or particular importance where a building is on the threshold of requiring mechanical cooling, eg shading of windows with blinds (preferably external) or overhangs/projections are effective and special glazing and window design can reject/absorb up to 70 to 80% of the solar gain.

The 'all-air' systems such as Variable Air Volume (VAV) are quite profligate when it comes to sucking in warm air from outside which then has to be cooled before being pumped round the building - and repeating the process several times an hour; and in their own way the simple open windows provide an uncontrollable source of warm air to an un-cooled building when it least wants it.

Of course, there are also systems which collect and use solar energy to good effect, thereby eliminating (or minimising) the need for mechanical heating in a highly cost-effective and environmentally friendly manner and also reducing the cooling loads.

Space cooling has all the generic problems of heating - the difficulty of the design process, the compromise of designs by installers and the passage of time - but to a greater degree. It is more common, as a proportion of installations, to find faults and inefficiencies in cooling systems than in heating systems. Particularly problematic in this respect is small package cooling systems because they have poor turndown control and it is very common to find cooling systems working continuously with the temperature controlled by using the heating system to offset the overcooling.

The other significant issue associated with cooling systems, although it is not specifically an energy issue, is Legionella. Legionella pneumophila is a bacterium that thrives in water maintained at between 20°C and 45°C, the typical conditions in the cooling towers of air-conditioning systems. In most countries there are specific regulations that require notification of the main kinds of evaporative condensers and cooling towers likely to be prone to infection by Legionella; for further discussion on this issue see Chapter 8.2.

Natural cooling

There is a growing stock of buildings designed to minimise or eliminate entirely the need for mechanical cooling. The capital costs of these buildings are not significantly lower than those with air-conditioning but the consumption of energy for cooling is reduced. The amount of energy saved is often overstated in appraisals and therefore viability in economic and environmental terms of such schemes has yet to be plausibly established.

Lighting energy

The largest use of electricity in non-industrial buildings tends to be lighting. There are many different ways to generate light, of which the three main ones are a glowing filament, excitation of a fluorescent material and electric discharge. In general, filament lamps are less efficient than fluorescent lighting which is less efficient than discharge lighting. Unfortunately, the colour quality of the light tends to be lower in the same order, so the most efficient lamps have the poorest colour rendering.

The output of a lamp is measured in lumens. The amount of light falling on a surface is measured in lumens/sq m (lux) the output of a lamp is measured in lumens and the efficiency of a lamp is called its efficacy and is measured in lumens per Watt. This provides a direct basis for stating the amount of light required for a given task and the size and number of lamps per unit area to provide the power required. It is not necessary to know precisely what a lumen is to appraise an existing facility because it will already have a lighting system with a known output.

The lamp is only one part of a lighting system. The fitting - usually now called the **luminaire** - is important because it determines how the light is distributed. The cabling and switching affect the ability to control the use of lighting. It is possible to improve the quality of lighting by modifying the luminaire but this tends to be at the same energy input unless it allows fewer lamps. Figs. 5.4.N and P (over the page) show alternative lighting layouts to achieve similar lighting levels and how capital and energy consumption costs are affected by the layout.

Fig. 5.4.N
Typical lighting layouts, performance and capital costs - 1500mm square ceiling grids

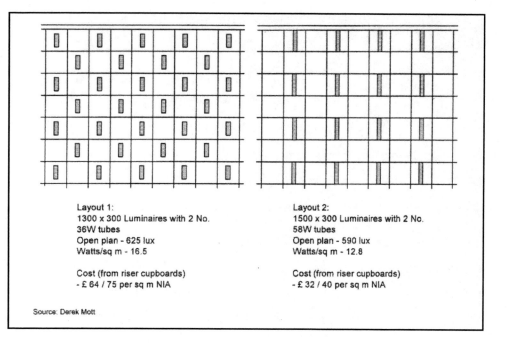

Layout 1:
1300 x 300 Luminaires with 2 No.
36W tubes
Open plan - 625 lux
Watts/sq m - 16.5

Cost (from riser cupboards)
- £ 64 / 75 per sq m NIA

Layout 2:
1500 x 300 Luminaires with 2 No.
58W tubes
Open plan - 590 lux
Watts/sq m - 12.8

Cost (from riser cupboards)
- £ 32 / 40 per sq m NIA

Source: Derek Mott

Fig. 5.4.P
Typical lighting layouts, performance and capital costs - 1800mm square ceiling grids

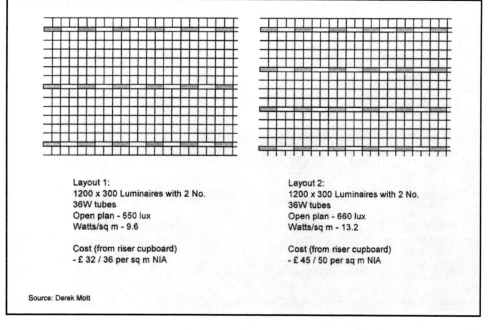

Layout 1:
1200 x 300 Luminaires with 2 No.
36W tubes
Open plan - 550 lux
Watts/sq m - 9.6

Cost (from riser cupboard)
- £ 32 / 36 per sq m NIA

Layout 2:
1200 x 300 Luminaires with 2 No.
36W tubes
Open plan - 660 lux
Watts/sq m - 13.2

Cost (from riser cupboard)
- £ 45 / 50 per sq m NIA

Source: Derek Mott

Changing the lamp type often requires a change in luminaire unless the lamp is specially designed; the most important development in design is the compact fluorescent lamp that fits a standard GLS (tungsten filament) lampholder. In the case of fluorescent lamps, the luminaire has an important function in that it contains the ballast, which is an important part of energy use (up to 20%) in older lighting systems. Replacement of any lighting system that is more than 20 years old is more than likely to prove to be financially beneficial.

A general feature of all lighting systems is that turning off lights that are not needed is a significant opportunity. Switching systems and control systems that facilitate this are often economically justifiable.

The widespread belief that it costs less to leave a fluorescent lamp on over short intervals rather than turn it off is a myth that originated from a calculation in the 1970's in which the engineer forgot to include the factor of 1,000 in working out the running costs of a lamp rated in Watts using electricity priced per kiloWatt hour.

Relying on people to switch off lighting when they leave a room only works for a short time and this is best tackled using physical controls, ie automatic switching systems.

The rest of electricity use in facilities tends to be associated with office machines, catering and ancillaries such as fans, lifts, etc. It is often difficult to establish any part of this that is not essential but it is possible to measure the total demand for electricity and characterise electricity demand patterns using an electricity demand profile.

Combined heat and power (CHP)

When a facility obtains its electricity and heat requirements separately, by taking the electricity from the public supply and the heat from fuel burned in a boiler, there are four places where energy is lost en route:

* combustion losses converting the fuel to heat at the power station

* converting heat to electricity at the power station

* losses of electricity due to electrical resistance in the transmission and distribution system

* the combustion losses in converting the fuel to heat at the facility.

When electricity and heat are produced simultaneously at the facility, the only loss is any heat produced at a temperature too low to use. As a rough indication of the scale of savings, the combined losses in generating electricity for the public supply are about 60%, making an efficiency of 40%. The efficiency of conversion of fuel to heat in a boiler at the facility are about 30%, the efficiency of conversion of fuel to both electricity and usable heat in a CHP system is about 60%, which can be higher if use can be made of low grade heat. The energy required to produce 1 kWh of electricity and 1kWh of heat is therefore

fuel input to power station for 1 kWh	$= 1/0.4 =$	2.50
fuel input to boiler for 1 kWh	$= 1/0.7 =$	1.43
total to provide heat and electricity separately		3.93
fuel input to CHP system $= 2/0.6 =$		3.33

The saving is 100 x (1- 3.33)/3.93 = 15% but in practice the savings vary with the ratio of heat to power. 1:1 is the typical optimum ratio for a gas engine system. If the amount of electricity required is higher than this the additional electricity is made up from the public supply. If less electricity than this ratio is required, the additional heat can provided by a boiler or other supplementary heating or the surplus electricity can be exported to the public supply.

CHP becomes an economic proposition when the savings in fuel input are enough to overcome the capital and operation costs. A factor is the economy of scale in purchasing the fuel for large power stations and the fuel used in operating them. Much of the electricity generating capacity in the public supply was planned and constructed before natural gas was available for electricity generation. This has significantly offset the economies of scale of the public supply in many countries. Other factors are the increased reliability of small scale gas turbines and the emergence of control technology that enables engine-driven generation systems to be monitored and controlled at a distance.

These have combined to change dramatically the economics of small scale CHP. For example, in the UK the payback of CHP based on natural gas in the size range 50 kW to 10MW, based on data provided in the trade and technical literature on actual projects, fell from 4 to 6 years in 1984 to 2 to 4 years in 1995.

After 1990 service companies began to be set up to provide operation and maintenance of small scale combined heat and power plant and with the liberalisation of gas markets could also become suppliers of gas. The economics of CHP became so favourable to service and maintenance contractors it became worthwhile for these to offer third party financing of the capital. Since then, although the number of installations has increased significantly, less information is now available in the public domain on the economics of CHP - financiers and operators of these systems became reluctant to reveal just how profitable CHP has become.

5.4.6 IMPROVING THE ENERGY EFFICIENCY OF BUILDINGS

Energy and comfort

In broad terms, an energy-efficient building is comfortable to work in and an uncomfortable building has poor energy efficiency. There are six determinants of comfort - air temperature, air velocity, humidity, radiant heat, metabolic rate of the individual and clothing. Of these, air temperature, air velocity and radiant heat are factors determined by the engineering of the building and its heating and cooling systems; and faults in these waste energy and affect comfort. For example a building heating system that provides too little heat to one part of a buildings and too much to another will lead to discomfort in both and expose the latter to risk of waste heat by opening windows. Too little insulation in a roof on which the sun falls in summer leads to radiant heat being emitted from the ceiling underneath it and often encourages installation of air conditioning which is unnecessary (and often ineffective because air conditioning does not remove the cause of the discomfort - the radiant heat).

Occupancy densities affect the cooling load in buildings; however, increasing them to get the most use out of the space has direct cost savings in other premises cost centres which far outweigh any extra cooling energy needed. Nevertheless, where the increases in cooling load are not able to be accommodated by the existing cooling system, the consequences of the subsequent discomfiture will, again, far outweigh the 'hard' value of any premises cost savings including energy costs per capita.

Diagnosis

Before specific action to improve the energy efficiency of a building can be undertaken, it is first necessary to locate what faults affect which buildings and the general nature of the action required to remedy it. There are four approaches of first resort for identification of inefficiency and its causes:

- **benchmarking** - compares the energy use between buildings at a distance and seeks out buildings with unusually high energy use

- **the energy signature** - compares energy use with degree days, or examines the electricity demand profile, at a distance to identify specific fault fingerprints

- **audits/surveys** - takes a person with specific expertise to a site to make a physical examination of the building and its equipment

- **checklisting** - uses a list of faults that are known to be common in buildings and uses personnel already at the site to carry out a physical inspection using the checklist as a guide.

These are not mutually exclusive; a facilities manager might use all four at some stage, but which is most effective as a first resort depends on the circumstances of the organisation and is not always, or indeed very often, chosen appropriately.

The main factors in determining the most effective approach of first resort are:

- **dispersion** - how many buildings there are to manage and how far apart are they geographically and

- **location** - location of the facilities manager in relation to the place(s) where the energy is used.

If the energy is all concentrated in one place, such as a college campus, large hospital site or industrial site, the energy costs are often great enough to justify employment of a full time resident engineer who either has, or can acquire through training, the expertise to recognise faults and to carry out a site survey, possibly supported by a checklist. In principle they must be able to see faults more easily through physical evidence on the ground than in information analysed at a distance, although in practice that is not always found to be the case. If the energy is dispersed over many widely separated buildings, the facilities manager is likely to be located in only one and methods that can be applied at a distance are appropriate.

Benchmarking

Benchmarking in the context of energy is based on the notion that buildings with similar characteristics used for similar purposes should have similar energy consumption. (See Chapter 12.2). Benchmarking compares energy use between buildings with the intention of revealing those with unusually high consumption. The idea is simple and readily understood but it is more demanding than many people realise.

The energy consumption of a building depends on three main factors:

- size

- the weather, which depends to some extent on where it is and the time period the energy use relates to

- what it is used for.

The effect of size is more complex than, for example, a crude expectation that doubling the floor area or doubling the number of rooms in a hotel doubles the energy consumption. If the energy use of a number of buildings is plotted against the indicator of size (such as floor area or volume), the graph is often (usually) straight but extrapolating the line of best fit to zero size cuts the energy axis. When this happens it is not possible to take account of the effect of size by simply dividing energy use by size because the resultant indicator - kWh/sq m, for example - will itself depend on size. This is seen in Fig. 5.4.Q (over the page) which shows a group of hotels. The inset shows the electricity costs divided by the number of rooms in descending order as a column diagram. There is a factor of 3.5 between the highest and lowest but none stands out particularly. The same data plotted as electricity cost vs number of rooms, however, shows up one large hotel with electricity costs 2.6 times the best fit prediction for its size.

There are similar problems with location of the facility and with time. The weather-related consumption of a building varies directly with degree days and degree days can vary, eg by as much as 15% for data gathering centres only 30 miles apart, and by 20% from one year to another. There have been various ways suggested to accommodate this of which the most popular is normalisation, which is to adjust the consumption to a standard number of degree days. Normalisation is not necessary for comparison between buildings in a close geographical region but is used to make standardised comparisons between buildings when there is a possibility that they are widely separated geographically.

Fig. 5.4.Q
Cost v size for electricity in the group of hotels

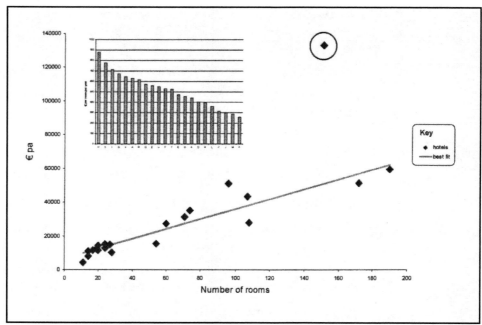

The UK Energy Efficiency Best Practice Programme publishes benchmark energy consumption data for a wide range of public and commercial building categories - such as prisons, schools, offices, shops, banks, sports centres, hospitals and hotels. There are also property management consultancies and energy management service providers who also gather this information and have large databases of buildings and can estimate the performance for typical and good practice for any category and pattern of use of buildings.

The disadvantage of normalisation is that it is time-consuming for the amount of useful information it generates - which may be limited to the fact that a particular building uses more or less energy than another building or than a standardised measure of performance - but it does not say what might be wrong with the buildings or what specific opportunities exist for improving performance.

Energy signatures

More informative is the energy degree day signature, which works from the same basic information as the normalised performance indicator, although it depends on a greater appreciation of the physics of the heat loss of a building.

The degree day energy signature is a graph of energy use v degree days with either a line of best fit or the points joined in time sequence. (Which of these is used depends on what is found and the choice only involves a couple of clicks of a computer mouse if the data are handled in a computer spreadsheet.)

The normal expectation of the energy use of intermittently heated building with constant boiler efficiency and ventilation rate independent of season is the relation.

Energy use = m x degree days + c

Where m = the slope of the line and c = the intercept.

This is a straight line when monthly energy is plotted as a graph against monthly degree days.

It is possible to show from physics that this straight line relation applies if the average boiler combustion efficiency is the same from month to month (which is usual - the key parameter is the combustion efficiency, not the overall efficiency), any internal heat generated is the same from month to month and the average ventilation rate is the same from month to month.

Departures from the conditions required for the straight line produce other features in the graph that are indicative of faults. Some examples are provided in Fig. 5.4.R. A graph of this kind contains four features:

- **the shape** - whether it is a straight line, whether there are bends, kinks, breaks or loops which are useful and very quick diagnostic tool for the presence of faults that can be applied at a distance

- **an intercept** - is where extrapolating the line back to zero degree days makes it cut the energy axis; the energy at this point is energy required even though there is no demand for energy due to the weather and if the intercept is on the degree day axis it indicates either a temperature inside the building lower than the degree day base temperature or a high internal heat gain

- **a slope** - which measures the additional energy required for each additional degree day and can be used to compute the heat balance of the buildings

- **the scatter** which is the amount by which energy varies for the same weather in a building and is indicative of the degree of control of energy use.

The significant point about the energy signature is that it only depends on information (utility bills and degree days) that is available at a distance from a site. As such, it can be applied more quickly and at lower cost than making a visit to a site to carry out a survey - one person can analyse several signatures in the time it might take a consultant to travel to just one site. Analysis of the energy signature therefore displaces the energy survey as a preferred approach of first resort. Also, since the energy information often comes from utility invoices, it follows that any feature that has a noticeable impact on the signature also has a noticeable impact on the energy costs recorded on an invoice.

Fig. 5.4.R (a)
Examples of energy-degree day signatures and their interpretation.

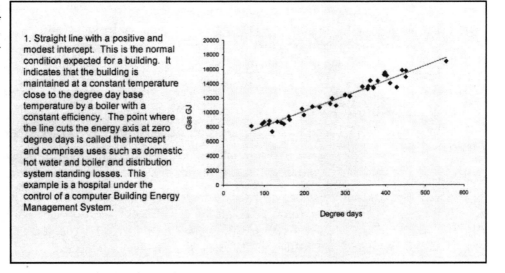

1. Straight line with a positive and modest intercept. This is the normal condition expected for a building. It indicates that the building is maintained at a constant temperature close to the degree day base temperature by a boiler with a constant efficiency. The point where the line cuts the energy axis at zero degree days is called the intercept and comprises uses such as domestic hot water and boiler and distribution system standing losses. This example is a hospital under the control of a computer Building Energy Management System.

Fig. 5.4.R (b)
Examples of energy-degree day signatures and their interpretation.

2. Straight line at higher degree days separated from a horizontal line at low degree days. The line at high degree days represents space heating, the line at lower degree days represents fixed loads outside the heating season. If extending the upper line back to zero degree days makes it cut the energy axis above the horizontal line this indicates a standing heat load present when space heating is in use which is greater than the summer load - a distribution system for heating, for example.

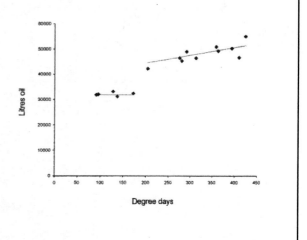

Fig. 5.4.R (c)
Examples of energy-degree day signatures and their interpretation.

3. Two straight lines with a break, the lower line with a higher slope than the upper line. The lower line indicates a rate of heat input higher than just a difference between inside and outside temperature. This occurs where heating is being used to offset overcooling by an air-conditioning system, as in this office. It is very common and very wasteful.

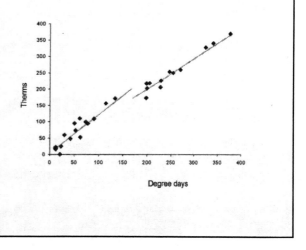

Fig. 5.4.R (d)
Examples of energy-degree day signatures and their interpretation.

4. A curve. There are four forms of curve encountered in practice. The extreme form is where it levels off to horizontal at high degree days. Higher degree days mean lower outside temperatures but the horizontal part means no increase in heating fuel. This may be because the system is designed only to take the chill off or may be because of an under-designed system, as in this example of sheltered housing where it is utterly inappropriate.

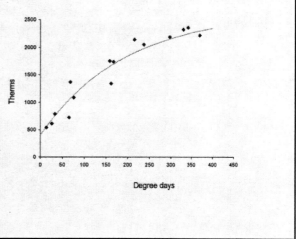

Fig. 5.4.R (e)
Examples of energy-degree day signatures and their interpretation.

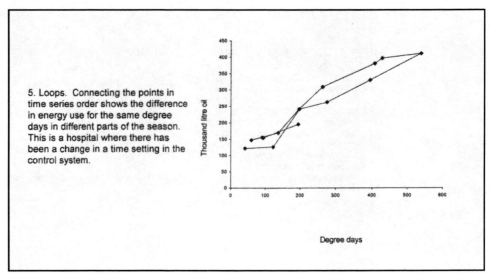

5. Loops. Connecting the points in time series order shows the difference in energy use for the same degree days in different parts of the season. This is a hospital where there has been a change in a time setting in the control system.

Energy-degree day signatures can be produced for electricity where this is related to the weather - for space heating or cooling.

It is also possible to obtained further quantitative information from the energy signature. The slope of a straight line can be used to estimate the ventilation rate. From physics it is possible to show that the slope of a line of energy v degree days is:

Slope = 0.024 KC ($\Sigma U_i A_i$ + 0.336 NV) / η

where $\Sigma U_i A_i$ is well known to building services engineers as the U-value of each element of the fabric of the buildings multiplied by its area and this added up for all the elements of the fabric - wall, roof, windows, N is the number of air changes, V is the volume, 0.336 is the volume specific heat of air, KC is a factor called the Knight Cornell factor that is related to the hours of intermittent heating and η is the boiler combustion efficiency.

If the graph is a straight line, the slope can be measured from the graph. The boiler efficiency of a well managed boiler system should be being measured regularly and is known or can be estimated, the areas of elements of the fabric can be taken from site drawings and the U-values looked up in standard tables. The factor KC can be looked up from tables. The only unknown then is the ventilation rate, N, and there is then enough information to evaluate it.

For example, take a building where the slope of the line of a graph of energy against degree days is 50.2 kWh/degree day. Suppose the structure is medium weight 30m x 10m plan and 6m high, 20% windows, located in London where the annual degree days are 2115, U-values are 0.4 for the wall fabric, 5 for the windows, 0.2 for the roof and heated 5 days a week, 12 hours a day, boiler efficiency 70%. KC factor looked up from tables is 0.64.

Area of wall   = A_{wall} = (30 x 6 x 2 + 10 x 6 x 2) x 80/100   = 288
Area of window = A_{window} = (30 x 6 x 2 + 10 x 6 x 2) x 20/100   = 72
Area of roof c   = A_{roof} = 30 x 30   = 900

So $\Sigma U_i A_i$ = 288 x 0.4 + 72 x 5 + 900 x 0.2 = 655.2   W/sq m/°

     V   = 30 x 10 x 6   = 1,800

50.2 = 0.024 x 0.64 (655.2 + 0.336 x N x 1,800) / 0.7

So:

$$N = \frac{0.7 \, (\, 50.2/(0.024 \times 0.64) - 655.2 \,)}{0.336 \times 1,800} = 2.7 \text{ air changes per hour}$$

which can then be compared with acceptable air exchange rates (such as those published by the Chartered Institute of Buildings Services Engineers); for example 2.7 air changes per hour is high for anything but a factory building.

The energy signature is a valuable input to an energy survey:

- where in the range of degree days a feature appears in an energy degree day signature it is indicative of the time of year that the physical feature associated with it is present in the building. It thus allows a survey to be timed optimally

- the energy degree day signature indicates the kind of opportunity to look for when the surveyor is there - whether a fault in equipment or a fault in control. Indeed, there are some kinds of faults that can be detected in this way that may not be seen by a surveyor unless they are specifically alerted to their presence - such as a broken shaft in a control valve or a fault in the programming of a heating control. The electricity half hour profile is also a very potent argument to justify the cost of an energy survey consultant to carry out a survey at night. Senior managers are often reluctant to sanction this because the consultant costs more to employ at night, but the profile deduced provides the justification

- the energy degree day signature offers a means to estimate the potential savings from measures in order to make the financial case for investment.

The direct form of electricity signature is the half hour electricity profile as shown at Fig. 5.4.S. Recording the half hour electricity profile first became a practical proposition in the 1970's. Profile recorders are widely available but are expensive and need to be taken to the site to measure the profile. With the introduction of competition in electricity supply, however, larger buildings are being fitted with half hourly metering for billing. Over time, given the rapid rate of advancement of digital technology, the same capability is likely to extend to smaller buildings.

Fig. 5.4.S
The electricity half hour demand profile signature of a large facility

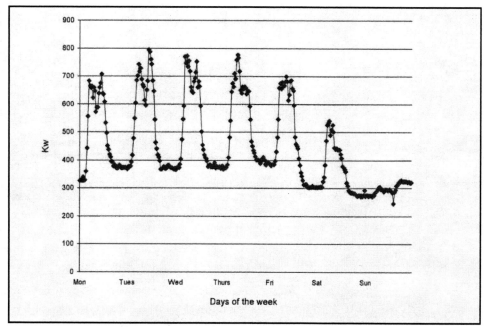

The example shown here, taken from a large industrial facility, illustrates the amount of inference that can be obtained from such a profile. The highest demand is on Tuesday afternoon. The profile on each day rises from 03:00 from an overnight baseload reaching the normal daytime level at 07:00. The baseload is almost half the level of the peak demand during the day and is 80% (calculated from the original data) of the total demand on weekdays.

It is therefore important to determine what the baseload comprises. The baseload demand is 60kW higher overnight on Mondays to Thursday than at the weekend, it would be worthwhile also to establish the reasons for this. The daily demand has two humps separated by a dip at mid-day. The hump on Thursday is less distinct for some reason. The electricity demand falls on each day is a different shape of profile to the way demand rises. On Saturday the baseload is lower, the peak is less high above the baseline and the afternoon peak is lower. Features like these can be linked to the activities in the building and the energy use for each activity established.

Energy surveys

Energy surveys are the longest established approach to locating energy saving opportunities with the first published account of this approach appearing more than 200 years ago.

Energy surveys are the mainstream activity of most energy consultants and they have been actively promoted by governments and other agencies since the first oil crisis in 1973. To meet the targets agreed under the Kyoto Commitment, several countries are considering the revival of public subsidies to support the cost of engaging consultants to carry out energy surveys. For all that, there is very little concrete information on what exactly consultants do in surveys, how they locate the energy saving opportunities they recommend, the basis on which they estimate the cost effectiveness of the actions they recommend or even of how cost effective the survey itself is.

The key issue with regard to surveys is who carries them out - whether an organisation uses its own staff (suitably trained) or a consultancy. This is important because there is a difference in objective between consultants working for a fee, energy user organisations managing their own energy costs and facilities management companies managing facilities on behalf of the energy user organisation.

Contrary to common belief, energy consultants, from whom most of the known repertoire of surveys derives, do not sell expertise, they sell their time. Where there is not active promotion of the energy survey by national Governments and/or other agencies, the survey is a difficult concept to sell and the consultants must expect to contact many potential customers before they find someone prepared to buy their service. They then have to recover the cost of marketing and this creates an incentive for the consultants to spend as much time as possible at large sites and to visit as many small sites as possible. Such evidence as there is indicates that:

- on large sites a competent surveyor knows within the first day or two what will form the bulk of the energy savings in their recommendations

- for small sites, the bulk of the energy savings comes from a relatively small proportion of buildings and better targeting of surveys, for example using the energy signature, is capable of providing almost as much in cost savings as surveys carried out indiscriminately and is therefore more cost effective; again, however, to recover the high cost of marketing consultants find themselves obliged to maximise the numbers of sites they visit.

There is also an issue of where survey consultants acquire the repertoire of skill to carry out the survey and, above all, on what basis they make their estimates of savings and paybacks. There is growing evidence that this is more ad hoc than has previously been assumed. A study published in the US in 1990 (LBL28568) analysed the results of some hundreds of surveys and found fewer than one in six of consultants' estimates came within 20% of the actual savings measured in post-installation audits. No comparable study has been undertaken in here but anecdotal evidence and various official published case studies and monitored demonstration projects indicate it is no better than this.

There are two strategies available to a facilities manager in a larger organisation:

- train internal staff in survey techniques to carry out surveys of buildings, supported by checklists

- engage consultants on terms that provide an incentive to the consultant to maximise the effectiveness of their paid time - perhaps engage them on a basis that links further work to the quantity of savings in, and the reliability of, the estimates they make from work already done.

There are initiatives being taken to improve the repertoire of technique in energy surveys and provide access to techniques beyond the consulting community. These will come to fruition by year 2005. In the meantime, whether surveys are carried out with the support of public subsidies or not, it is appropriate to link the work of consultants to the pattern and terms of such a publicly funded survey - at least those who have responsibility for managing publicly funded activities ought to have considered how best to manage the consultant and the energy users do not have to discover this for themselves.

Checklisting

The feature that characterises the energy survey as an approach is the physical presence of someone at the site with the ability to recognise the presence of a fault. In a survey it is usually found that the bulk of the energy savings are associated with a small number of recommendations - perhaps five would represent 80+% of the total. Across all the surveys that are carried out in all buildings and industrial sites, 80% of the savings are associated with fewer than 130 or so potential sources of wastage.

Checklisting is an approach that allows less experienced people than consultants to locate energy savings opportunities by checking the condition of plant and installations against a list, based either on a previous survey or against various compilations of checklists made by agencies that promote energy efficiency. None of these published checklists are ideal but for many facilities managers it is not difficult to draw on a number of these to produce a checklist that covers most of the areas of interest to them.

Energy audits

Over most of the time since the first oil crisis, the terms "energy audit" and "energy survey" have been used interchangeably to describe the physical examination of a buildings and site. Consultants prefer the hauteur of the term "audit" because it raises their clients' perception of their expertise which makes selling the activity easier and allows a higher fee rate, but there is little in what they do under the term audit that makes it significantly different from what most people would understand by the term "survey".

It is possible to trace origin of the term "audit" in this context to a first use in 1952 to describe the process of computing the heat balance of a factory site. It is also possible to trace much of energy survey practice to the same origins. Use of the term "audit" then was intended to draw parallels with the use of the term audit in financial accounting but the particular parallel drawn was mistaken and the term "audit" in that context is a misnomer.

There is, however, considerable benefit to be gained from exploring a separation of the identities of the balance, audit and survey.

- The **energy survey** is defined as a physical examination of the physical circumstances of a site and identification of energy saving opportunities that are visible or accessible to the simplest of measurements, such as:

  - leaks

- equipment in poor condition

- inadequate equipment

- abuses of equipment such as lighting in unoccupied areas, coats over thermostats, insulation removed and not replaced.

The survey depends entirely on a physical presence of someone at the site, which can be external expertise or someone resident at the site primed in what to look for.

- An **energy balance** goes further and attempts to account for energy in quantitative terms, achieving a quantitative separation of the energy for different purposes and the heat loss from energy conversion (boilers), fabric losses and ventilation. In the way the heat balance was first developed (in the 1940's) it too depended on a physical presence at the site but with recent developments the need for the physical presence of expertise at the site is reduced and in some cases the energy balance can be evaluated at a distance. For example, if one measures the slope of a straight line in an energy-degree day signature where the structural details of the buildings and boiler efficiency are known, the heat balance allows a computation of the heat balance and from this the ventilation rate.

- Reserve the term **energy audit** for something closer to its financial analogue, which looks beyond the faults and abuses identified in a survey to the organisational environment which has allowed them to occur and not be prevented or remedied. The audit would:

  - look at the management system, responsibility structures and accountability and the reasons why the organisation permits waste when it would be economic to prevent or repair

  - examine the effectiveness of the use of existing information, such as utility invoices, oil stock records and half hour meter data and how effectively monitoring, targeting and budgeting works

  - having identified inadequate or inefficient systems (whether mechanical or management) it examines the decision-making processes that caused them to be specified and approved.

The repertoire of the audit in these terms is as yet poorly developed. The only significant audit tool developed to date is the Energy Management Matrix, which emerged between 1983 and 1991.

The Energy Management Matrix recognises that organisations do not suddenly become imbued with energy efficiency but that the structures and activities that lead an energy efficient organisation develop gradually. It also recognises that there are several facets to energy management - policy, organisational structures, purchasing, information systems, investment, etc - and energy management is likely to be most effective if these support one another. An obvious example is that to use the energy signature requires information from utility bills to be available; once the signature has been characterised this provides supporting information for energy purchasing, with energy savings releasing financial assets required for further investment in energy efficiency.

Recognising the relationship between activities in each of these areas of energy management and ensuring they work with, and not against, one another is an important part of making these activities effective.

The Energy Management Matrix sets out the activities as columns and the different levels of development of those activities as rows. It then shuffles the levels in each column until the activities at the same level in different columns are mutually supportive. Once this is achieved the matrix is ready for use. Fig. 5.4.T shows a typical matrix.

Fig. 5.4.T
The energy management matrix

Level	Policy	Organisation	Information systems	Purchasing	Investment
Excellent	Policy reviewed regularly and updated by senior management.	Medium term strategy exists, organisation and resources available to deliver it. Reporting lines established through whole organisation.	Information system measures effectiveness of programme. System capable of identifying long term limits of efficiency.	Purchasing performance monitored and audited. Energy purchasing strategies look two years ahead.	Positive action to seek out investment opportunities. Discretionary investment in cost reduction has equal status with business development projects.
Very good	Policy agreed with senior management who set goals, ensure leadership. Resources are provided to ensure results.	Energy efficiency and utilisation evolved into a plan that extends beyond next two meetings. Current activities robust against changes of staff.	Monitoring monthly for all buildings for fuel, half-hourly data for electricity. Sub-metered electricity where appropriate. System has enough resolution to detect faults.	Purchasing includes negotiation of prices supported by market intelligence and budgeted requirements based on monitored usage.	Small projects funded from capital return budget. Larger projects have equal status with other cost reduction activities.
Good	Senior management declares a commitment to energy efficiency and exhorts middle management to give time to it.	Formal mechanism for co-ordinating energy-related activities, such as a committee. Designated person taking lead, such as an energy manager.	Collection of energy and production data co-ordinated. System capable of recording savings from measures as they are applied.	Minimum of annual contact with suppliers. Purchasing strategies take account of quality, security of supply and delivery.	Medium-cost and low-cost discretionary measures funded case by case, energy efficiency competes for opportunity funds.
Fair	Lead comes from middle management. Implied policy is results first, resources after.	Occasional contact between accounting, engineering and purchasing on energy matters. No specific responsibilities assigned.	Energy recorded in energy units. Information mainly handled as energy/production ratios. Collection of data on energy and production not co-ordinated.	Payment of invoices after checking by department responsible for cost. No negotiation of price or this is delegated to shared savings consultancy.	Investment in low cost measures within discretionary limits of engineering department.
Poor	Energy saving activities tacitly allowed but no actual or implied policy.	Energy efficiency assumed to be subsumed within normal maintenance, purchasing and accounting activities.	Energy recorded as costs only. Information on energy circulated for information but not action.	Payment against invoices. No negotiation of price. No checking of tariffs.	Investment capital for non-discretionary and business development projects only.

To use the matrix the energy management activities in the organisation concerned are compared with the activities described at each level in each column of the matrix, starting from the bottom of the column. When the activity described in the matrix represents the limit of activity in that column, a mark is made (the mark need not be in the middle). When a mark has been made in each column, these are connected by lines.

If the two outermost columns are considered special, there are seven possible forms of pattern this produces on the line on the matrix shapes shown in Fig. 5.4.U (over the page). Which of these best describes the state of energy management in an organisation then indicates balance in the energy management programme and the enables conclusions to be drawn on the most appropriate next action to take.

These seven shapes represent a complete, exclusive and non-redundant classification of the possible patterns found, although shapes five and six are only significant if the elements placed on the wings are deemed to have a significance not shared by the other elements. This is why **policy** and **investment** appear at the left and right end columns in most matrices.

Fig. 5.4.U
A simple classification of matrix shapes

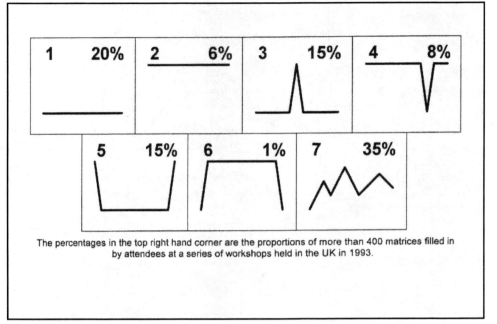

The percentages in the top right hand corner are the proportions of more than 400 matrices filled in by attendees at a series of workshops held in the UK in 1993.

- Shape 1 is a uniformly low development across all elements, indicative of an organisation that has still to make significant progress

- Shape 2 is a uniformly high development across all elements and is associated with a mature balanced energy management programme

- Shape 3 is highly developed in one element only. This is often an activity that aligns with the style and professional strengths of the facilities manager, such as motivation/organisation or information systems

- Shape 4 is highly developed in all but one aspect. This may be any element and could include programmes where one of the side elements lags behind, such as investment, although motivation/organisation or information systems often lag in this way

- Shape 5 is highly developed in policy terms and investment but lags in all other respects

- Shape 6 is highly developed in terms of activities but lacks financial support and authority to convert activity into effect

- Shape 7 has no particular strength or weaknesses and is probably not working effectively.

In principle, all organisations start at the bottom with shape 1 and should develop eventually to shape 2, although unless positively managed they may go through the others en route. The two end columns are special because they put two important resources at the disposal of energy management - the policy column measures authority, the investment column measures commitment in terms that means something to a business - money. The middle sections essentially measure activity. If the middle sections are lagging behind the wings, there is authority and money but inappropriately little activity. If the middle columns are running ahead of the wings there is activity but insufficient access to money and authority.

Having decided how far the organisation has progressed so far, it is then possible to decide what to do next. All that is required is to select one column in which it is appropriate to move forward one or part of one square. The action may be a grand gesture like proposing the adoption of a formal policy or setting up a committee, or it may be something more subtle like calculating a capital return budget or using existing data as the basis of monitoring buildings in a computer spreadsheet.

Different people in an organisation see things in different ways because of a different perspective. A useful feature of the matrix is that it provides an external window on the organisation and a vehicle to discuss the problems of the organisation in a detached manner. It is found in practice that there are significant differences between the scores given on the matrix by different people in the same organisation. A constructive use of the matrix is then to take the two different views, discuss why they are different and use this as a basis of discussion to decide how to make the organisation more effective. The logical extension of this is for the matrix to be applied as an audit tool by someone totally external to the organisation.

No one matrix is appropriate to all possible types of organisation and in practice organisations tend either to work out their own matrix as a kind of forward plan, possibly adapting a published matrix to their own needs.

As an approach to measuring organisational effectiveness the use of the matrix is still in its infancy. However as a tool it is already popular and clearly seen as beneficial by organisations that have used it. The design of some published versions of the matrix has departed enough from the principles on which it works, however, to advise caution. Always study carefully any published matrix before using it so as to ensure it is suitable.

5.4.7 MONITORING AND BUDGETING

Once the energy signature has been established, this can form the basis of continuous monitoring to pick up changes in energy use pattern, energy budgeting and faults as they occur.

Energy monitoring

The energy degree day signature can be formulated algebraically; for example, a straight line formulates as:

Energy use = m x degree days + c

where m and c are quantities that can be obtained from the line of best fit on the energy v degree day signature (see Energy signatures above). This can then be used to calculate a predicted energy consumption in each month for the degree days for that month. The difference between the actual energy used and the prediction can then be graphed as a **control chart**, Fig. 5.4.V.

Fig. 5.4.V
The control chart

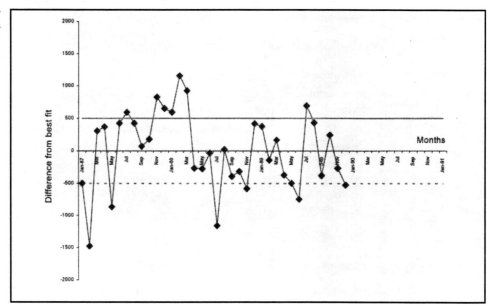

For signatures that are not straight lines, including signatures with bends, kinks and breaks there are other simple formulations for lines of best fit - see Fig. 5.4.R (b) to (e) above.

The same can be applied to electricity where the prediction is based on the repeating annual (for monthly meter readings), or weekly or daily (for half hourly metering) patterns.

Budgeting

The energy signature also provides a robust system for energy budgeting. The signature allows the energy consumption to be forecast on the basis of degree days interpreted from the historic record. A budget for energy consumption can be computed on this basis and consumption monitored against it, Fig. 5.4.W.

Fig. 5.4.W
The energy budget

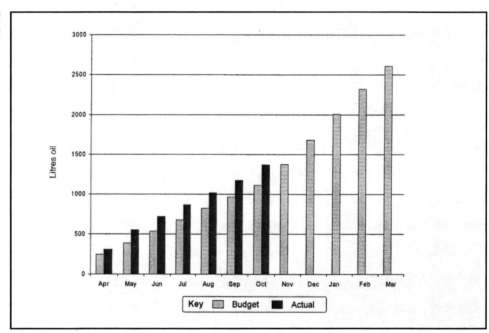

The forecast of degree days can be varied to suit different styles of budgeting. For example, organisations in the public sector tend to operate with prescriptive budgets in which the objective is not to exceed the amount budgeted for, but commercial organisations tend to operate flexible budgets in which deviations from the budget are allowed but must be managed.

In a prescriptive budget it is important to allow for the possibility of the coldest weather occurring but in milder years this will result in a surplus in the budget. It is important then to manage this surplus to avoid its re-absorption into the organisation's general funds or transferred to an overspent budget in some other part of the organisation by default. This can be achieved by basing the budget on the degree days in the ninth decile winter (the ninth coldest winter in the last ten) monitoring the budget surplus at each month and reallocating the surplus in a managed way - for example, by investment in low cost energy saving items such as thermostatic radiator valves, low energy lamps, insulation for pipe flanges and time-switches.

5.4.8 INVESTING IN ENERGY EFFICIENCY

The general issue of investment

Investment in energy saving has never been on the scale that straight economic criteria would justify. An apparent unwillingness of energy users, particularly in industry, to invest in energy efficiency has been both a puzzle and a challenge to policymakers because standard demand/supply economics tells us that if energy costs rise organisations must see it in their own interest to invest to reduce energy consumption. However, all studies have shown that high energy prices are not a stimulus to investment in energy efficiency.

Studies have shown that there are three reasons for the lack of investment in energy efficiency:

- capital budgeting practices in industry give the general class of investment to which energy efficiency belongs a low priority

- capital investment decisions in industry tend not to be very sophisticated

- the proportion of energy costs to total turnover in most organisations is not sufficiently large to merit detailed attention.

As it happens, energy is about the only cost centre where increased capital investment can show a meaningful return on that investment. Payback in many cases of investment in energy-saving strategies can be as short as two to three years, and even up to five or six years should meet the criteria for rates of return in most organisations.

The problem is usually of in-house facilities management resources and finding the time to focus on energy costs which may well be a less pressing issue than managing all the facilities cost-effectively (as opposed to cost-efficiently - see Chapter 2.3.2).

From a business viewpoint bogus 'affordability' arguments (see also Chapter 2.2.2 and below) are aimed at directing investment funds towards new, revenue-increasing (exciting) products and services, even though they are usually more risk- and capital-intensive.

This describes very well the situation in manufacturing industry. In buildings the situation is slightly worse if anything because maintaining older buildings is seen as yet more peripheral to organisations whose activities are based in them. In this respect, the tendency to describe buildings as facilities, to identify a specific aspect of a business as facilities management or even to contract it out under this heading, at least recognises the running and maintenance of buildings as a discrete aspect of the running of a business and gives it higher status.

However the issue of **sustainability** puts an onus on everyone to do their utmost to conserve energy regardless of any business model that says otherwise.

Investment appraisal

Many managers wrongly perceive the financial decision making process as driven by a shortage of money - as a means to decide whether or not a particular project is affordable. It is not intended to be like this at all. A healthy organisation is one which can see many opportunities for the development of its business and needs to make choices. Only when, taking all such possible areas of worthwhile investment over all its activities, the opportunities add up to more than the capital it has available overall, is it necessary to make this choice. This is best interpreted not as a shortage of capital but as a surfeit of opportunity within which the organisation must make choices.

The working definition of investment appraisal is then that investment appraisal is the means by which an organisation makes choices between investment opportunities in which measures of return on investment are the yardstick of value. This then contains four separate ideas:

- investment appraisal is designed to make choices between opportunities, not projects in isolation

- it assumes there are more opportunities than capital to fund them, not to proceed with some, seemingly viable, opportunities is normal

- this definition takes no account of where in the organisation these opportunities arise, so the choice may be between an energy efficiency project and something in a totally different part of the business of which the energy manager or facilities manager may not be aware

- it takes no account of timing; to choose not to invest in an opportunity is not rejection it is merely prioritisation at that instant.

Once this has been established investment appraisal is found to have three objectives to determine which investments make the best use of the organisation's money:

- to ensure optimum benefits from each of the investments from which this selection is made

- to minimise risk to the enterprise

- to provide a basis for subsequent analysis of performance of each investment made.

All the procedures of investment appraisal, eg the calculation of payback, the discounting of cash flows, arise from these. Where investment appraisal is conducted less than ideally in practice, this is because not all of these are given the weight they should have had. This will probably be of far greater significance than whether or not discounting has been applied to the cash flow.

The important point about investment appraisal is that the only inputs are the capital cost, savings in each year, number of years over which the project is evaluated and the discount rate (more usually now called the return on capital) as described in Chapter 3.5.3 above).

Clearly, if the energy savings are estimated wrongly the entire calculation is wrong, since the intention is to calculate the relative attractiveness of projects; unless errors in the estimates of savings from the project are wrong to the same degree such errors will change the ranking of projects.

On the other hand, if projects are assumed to have the same life (which is common because the choice of lifetime is a cultural issue) ranking by payback gives rise to the same relative order and if the cashflow statement has equal savings in each year, discounting the cash flow does not change the ranking and is thus unnecessary.

Prior estimates of energy savings from cost reduction measures

The weakness in investment appraisal for energy saving measures in buildings, tends to be the general lack of advice on how to estimate the savings. Most of the examples in textbooks (and even in research reports) tend simply to assume some fairly round percentage number level of savings like 5% or 10%. Only for a very small number of measures is there a well-established procedure, eg pipe insulation, change of type of lighting, boiler replacement (but not yet in year 2000 for condensing boilers). The poor success rate in estimating energy savings by survey consultants has already been mentioned.

One significant recent development in this area has been the use of the degree day-energy signature, which provides a ready means to estimate the savings for heating and cooling. This is best illustrated using an example.

Fig. 5.4.X shows the data for a hospital. Using a spreadsheet it is possible to establish a line of best fit through the data:

Fig. 5.4.X
Graphical appraisal of the savings from removal of an imbalance in a heating system using the graph of energy v summary degree days

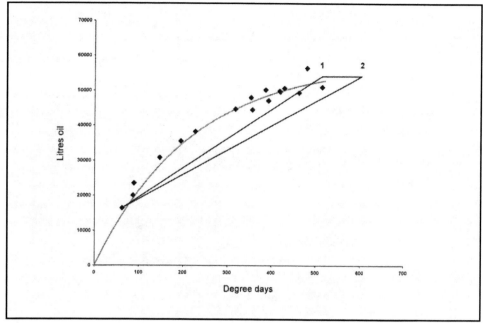

oil (litres in month) = (58000)(1 - e $^{-150/0.061\ \text{degree days}}$)

Using this to calculate the energy in each month using the 20 year average degree days for that month gives a consumption of 377,410 litres.

Consider the case if the strong curvature is found to be due to underheating in a corner of the hospital due to some factor such as inadequate capacity in part of the distribution system (this is very common). When this happens building occupants get around it in all but the coldest weather by allowing the rest of the building to be overheated. This is variable but can be measured using a thermometer. Suppose in the coldest weather it is found to be 3°C. Removing the bottleneck allows more heat to reach the underheated corner, and it reduces the temperature in the rest of the hospital (even in the coldest weather).

This can be modelled on the energy vs degree day graph:

- removing the bottleneck allows the underheated corner to be raised to the same temperature as the rest of the building, even though in the severest weather this is still too high. If we knew how much of the building is underheated - and by how much - we could be more precise, but for the time being make the point after removing the bottleneck slightly above the position of the present line shown as point (1) in Fig. 5.4.X

- better control produces a straight instead of curved line. The point at the lowest degree days does not change so join this to point (1) by a straight line, which is a chord cutting the curve

- this has so far only raised the whole building to a uniform temperature, it is still too high by 3°C. The effect of being able to reduce the temperature in the severest weather can be interpreted as either lowering the energy consumption by some amount or increasing the number of degree days that would require the same temperature

- At the degree days in the region of point (1) both the minimum and maximum temperatures are far below the degree day base temperature so lowering the internal temperature 3°C over a month of 30 days would give the building the same energy use as 30 x 3 = 90 additional degree days at the previous temperature. Move point (1) 90 degree days to the right (2).

The resultant pattern after these various changes would follow the formula:

energy = 12,060 + 69.44 x degree days.

For the 20-year average degree days of 2,407 this is:

energy = 12,060 x 12 + 69.44 x 2407 = 311,862 litres

and the saving is 377,410 - 311,862 = 65,548 litres a year.

Multiply by the cost of fuel to arrive at the estimate of savings.

There are similar procedures for the electricity half hour signature (see Fig. 5.4.S above).

Building energy management systems (BEMS)

Energy conservation cannot be discussed these days without reference to the adoption or otherwise of Building Energy Management Systems BEMS.

These gather information about environmental conditions in a building and use the data to adjust the performance of the services to optimise both comfort and energy efficiency. They can respond to predicted external environmental conditions - and override the inevitable mis-forecasts - as well as controlling peak loading to contain maximum demand.

Improvements in building management and maintenance often accompany the energy savings, but maintenance of the BEMS itself can be a problem, especially if the specification of the controls is inadequate, operator training is sub-standard or performance is tested inaccurately, too seldom or never at all.

However, the biggest draw-back to getting the full benefits of a BEMS is undoubtedly the problems occurring at the Man-Machine Interface (MMI). Manning the controls can be a soulless task, and the monitoring facilities are often too complex for the operator and are not implemented.

Some of the latest BEMS, particularly those arriving packaged in as part of the VRV (variable refrigerant volume) systems, can now run on automatic control response and diagnose their own operational efficiency; at a surprisingly low cost they cut out the bulk of the MMI problem.

An example of a pay-back analysis of a BEMS for an office building of 5,000 sq m GIA if given at Fig. 5.4.Y.

Fig. 5.4.Y
Payback analysis of a BEMS system

Typical example in a prestige air conditioned office building of 10,000 sq m NIA		£	£
Capital cost of B(E)MS	Full B(E)MS installed in a prestige air-conditioned building having 'typical' energy consumption	-	160,000
Annual costs	Monitoring – 25% full-time: Training – 5 days pa: Maintenance: LESS existing manual control – 50% full-time:	8,000 4,000 4,000 (16,000)	
	Net additional costs pa*	Nil	
Energy savings – on lighting and HVAC only	15% x 10,000 sq m @ £12/sq m	(18,000)	
Net annual savings £12			
* Excluding finance charges			11% ROI*

Clearly the percentage saving of energy costs used in this feasibility example should be tested more thoroughly, using appraisal techniques such as the degree day-energy signature described above, before final commitment to the investment.

The example is set at about the scale of operation when BEMS can show some kind of sensible pay-back. Some of the 20% energy saving suggested for lighting and HVAC might well be achieved by more conventional energy-saving measures. In fact a recent BEMS user survey gave a range of 15-30% savings - but whether on the whole energy bill or that which the BEMS controlled was not very clear.

The installation of a BEMS may well be justified by pay-back on energy-savings alone if the user starts from somewhere near the upper quartile of the range of energy costs given in the examples in 5.4.5 above. In the end, it is most likely that the effects on the workforce of good or bad environmental conditions, or a good or bad perception of management's attitude towards it, which are likely to be the really significant factors in the equation (or more probably left out of it!).

On the other hand, the costs of running and maintaining a BEMS properly may not always be adequately addressed when the appraisal is made.

Lighting control systems

A summary of many common techniques for reducing lighting energy consumption is given at Fig. 5.4.Z.

Fig. 5.4.Z
Some common sources of reduction in lighting energy consumption

Lamps and control gear	26 mm fluorescent tubes in lieu of 38 mm (-8%) Ditto, in luminaires and switch start control Compact fluorescent and integral control gear – replace tungsten Ditto, and separate control gear (NB plug-in adaptors) Display – tungsten halogen lamps (-40%) Metal halide lamps High pressure sodium lamps Low loss control gear (-10%) High frequency electronic control gear (-20%) Lamp cleaning and replacement
Luminaires	Apply reflectors
Design	Uniformity / localised

Fig. 5.4.AA is an illustration of how a reasonable pay-back might be achieved on a lighting control installation Where lighting energy costs are £21,250 pa (eg 4250 sq m NIA at £5 per sq m pa).

Fig. 5.4.AA
Payback analysis of a lighting control system

Lighting control system		£ pa
Initial cost: (£10,000)		
Saving on electricity pa	10% x £ 21,250	(2,125)
Saving on re-lamping pa	10% x £ 4,250	(425)
Total saving		**(2,550)**
£ 10,000 ÷ £ 2,550 = 3.92 ie approx 4 years payback on investment		

Budgeting for capital investment

One of the reasons why organisations attach low priority to the general class of investment to which energy efficiency belongs is what is known as the invoice problem. The main inputs to the financial records in organisations are those generated by the Accounts Department - invoices received from other organisations for purchases, including fuel and power, invoices raised against customers, other internally generated records such as salaries. Because cost reduction activities do not generate separately identifiable invoices other than for the purchase of the equipment, the Accounts Department has no record of the costs that would have been incurred in the absence of the investment. This is a problem which prevails across the whole of facilities management, not just energy.

The solution is very simple, ie to maintain a capital return budget. If an energy project reduces the expenditures of a business but the income remains the same - that is, the business does not take advantage of the saving to reduce its prices - funds that previously would have gone out as payments for energy are retained within the business. The retained funds are called a virtual fund because the vast majority of businesses are not managed with anything like the sophistication that would enable them to locate these funds in the financial system, although the principle of money out = money in means that they must exist. It is then open to the energy or facilities manager to argue that as the person responsible for generating the virtual fund (and usually the only one in a position to quantify the size of it), they should be involved in the management of the fund. This argument is put into effect by the energy managers setting up a capital return budget.

The capital return budget is a simple statement of the capital expenditures and the revenue savings achieved in each year, and the difference between them. This is shown in Fig. 5.4.BB (over the page) for a textile finishing works. In the example good housekeeping (needing no capital investment) resulted in modest revenue savings in all four years. However, in 1997/98 capital investment in additional energy-reduction measures produced substantial further revenue savings over the next three years. A further adjustment involving condensation return in 1998/99, carried out during maintenance without additional charge, also produced worthwhile savings.

Since the items tackled first tend to be those with the shortest payback, the capital return budget rapidly runs into surplus. If some measures which involve no cost are taken into account, the budget can always be in surplus. It is often the case that the greatest savings come from projects with longer paybacks. Once the short payback projects have been taken up the capital return budget demonstrates that funds are still being generated and longer payback becomes affordable.

5.4.9 EMBODIED ENERGY

Embodied energy is that which is consumed in the production process including mining of raw materials, manufacture and transport of materials/components, on-site assembly and in operation and maintenance.

Electrically powered heating and ventilating appliances have no intrinsic need for the energy storage facilities, gas emission flues, water pipes or ducts demanded by the 'liquid' alternatives. They therefore save not only in mechanical components but also in space to accommodate them, and consequently consume less embodied energy than other systems in their manufacture and installation.

For example, a VAV air conditioning system uses a gas-fired boiler for heating and needs massive ventilation trunking, fans and pumps and extra storey-height in the building to deliver up to ten air-changes an hour. It will consume considerably more energy in manufacture than a chilled ceiling system with supplementary electric heating. In terms of emissions the embodied energy in the more complex system must always be considered alongside its primary consumption.

As was shown in Fig. 5.4.D above, the whole-life implications of embodied energy consumption are not critical. However they need to be set alongside the other key environmental issue - sustainability - when evaluating the environmental implications of all major construction projects.

*Fig. 5.4.BB
The capital return budget for a programme of measures in a textile finishing company (a case study).*

Item	1996/97 £	1997/98 £	1998/99 £	1999/2000 £
Capital costs				
Good practice housekeeping				
Gas	0	0	0	0
Electricity	0	0	0	0
Heat recovery		(60,960.00)		
Inverter vacuum pump		(8,000.00)		
Boiler economiser		(38,400.00)		
Process insulation		(21,600.00)		
Inverter – dyeing machines		(144,000.00)		
Condensation return			0	
Revenue savings				
Good practice housekeeping				
Gas	74,787.20	74,787.20	74,787.20	74,787.20
Electricity	19,764.80	19,764.80	19,764.80	19,764.80
Heat recovery		70,560.00	70,560.00	70,560.00
Inverter vacuum pump		1,548.80	1,548.80	1,548.80
Boiler economiser		9,478.40	9,478.40	9,478.40
Process insulation		18,588.80	18,588.80	18,588.80
Inverter – dyeing machines		26,697.60	26,697.60	26,697.60
Condensation return			19,012.80	19,012.80
Totals				
Capital	0	(272,960.00)	0	0
Revenue	94,552.00	221,425.60	240,438.40	240,438.40
Net cash flow	94,552.00	(51,534.40)	240,438.40	240,438.40
Cumulative net	94,552.00	43,017.60	283,456.00	523,894.40

5.4.10 THE FUTURE FOR ENERGY MANAGEMENT

The first realisation of the need for energy efficiency came with the first oil crisis of 1973/74. Energy efficiency was then promoted by central government out of concern for security of supply. The main concern changed in the 1990's with the realisation that energy use was causing modification of the global climate. Alongside this, however, has been the gradual introduction of competition in energy supply.

When electricity reaches the consumer it is a mix of nuclear, gas and coal generated kWh, where it comes from or who generated it no-one can tell. The same applies to gas which can come from elsewhere. It is an important precept of economics that when there is nothing to distinguish the product, the price eventually becomes uniform and will gravitate toward the lowest price. This process is already well advanced in those countries where electricity and gas markets have had competition for some time and suppliers have begun to appreciate the need for some other way to distinguish their product on some other basis than price alone. They are therefore looking at ways to increase the value added to their product.

It is one thing not to be able to distinguish the product when it is a kWh but the real desire of an energy consumer is not a kWh but the effect kWh's produce - a given level of ambient temperature in living spaces, for example. Energy suppliers are becoming alert to the potential in providing a broader service than simply kWh for a price and to the provision of energy management services based on the information they hold in their customer for billing purposes - including monitoring energy consumption, benchmarking, the identification of energy saving opportunities using techniques like the energy signature.

Given the likely advances in information technology, in metering technology and in energy management technique over the next decades it is likely that much of the activity of energy management may pass from the energy manager or facilities manager to the energy supplier - except where there are individuals interested enough in the subject to take it on for themselves.

5.5 WATER AND SEWERAGE SERVICES

Introduction

The provision of drinking water and the collection and disposal of waste water was originally carried out on a local basis, usually under the control of the municipalities. As understanding developed of the importance to public health of good hygiene and water quality, national standards have come into force backed up by statute and enforced by central government. However over the past 30 years the harmonisation of quality standards has increased as a result of EU Directives. At the same time the standards themselves have in general become more stringent, requiring massive capital investment in water treatment, the supply network and in waste water treatment. Water and sewerage undertakings have been privatised. The companies have sought economies of scale to reduce costs and private sector finance.

This chapter examines water and sewerage separately with reference to sources, nature, policies and economics.

5.5.1 THE SOURCES AND NATURE OF WATER SUPPLY

Sources of water supply

Depending on geographical and geological characteristics, drinking water supplies arise either from surface waters, such as rivers, streams and lakes, or from groundwater via wells and boreholes. In England and Wales, for example, more than two-thirds of the total supplied comes from surface waters, although ground waters are common in the south and east.

Drinking water quality from public water supplies

Before 1980, the quality of drinking water was regulated by national legislation generally following advice from the World Health Organisation. Since then legislation is derived from the EU Drinking Water Directive[1] and all public supplies should comply with its provisions, ensuring they are safe to drink. Consequently on health and safety grounds alternative sources such as bottled water or drinking fountains should not be required in the workplace but some employees may find certain supplies of tap water unpalatable, especially in cases where relatively large quantities of disinfection chemicals or their by-products remain in the water.

Although compliance with the terms of the Drinking Water Directive ensures that harmful constituents will not be present, within these constraints quality may still vary. In particular, water may be hard or soft depending on the geology of the area from which the supply is derived. Hard water, containing high levels of calcium or magnesium salts, is more likely to be produced from areas of sedimentary rocks, especially limestone and chalk. These may provide some health benefit in protecting against heart disease but is also responsible for the build up of scale in water pipes and central heating systems which may increase maintenance costs.

Water supply from direct abstraction

An alternative to the use of public water supplies is the direct abstraction of water from surface or groundwater sources. In order to reach drinking water quality complex treatment may be needed but for some industrial uses it may be treated either not at all or to a less rigorous standard.

---

[1] *Council Directive relating to the quality of water intended for human consumption (80/778/EEC), Official Journal of the European Communities No L 229/11, 30 August 1980.*

5.5.2 WATER SUPPLY POLICIES

Policies

The current 1980 Drinking Water Directive prescribes limits for over 60 physical, chemical and microbiological determinants. Amongst the most important are those which require the absence of three types of bacteria (total coliforms, faecal coliforms and faecal streptococci) which act as indicators for pathogenic bacteria and viruses. Since the indicators are present in very large numbers in sewage and they are relatively resistant to the disinfection processes used in water treatment, their absence is a reliable indicator of the absence of harmful organisms of all types. Compliance with all standards is enforced by the Drinking Water Inspectorate (DWI), part of the Department for Food and Rural Affairs. A new Drinking Water Directive[2] has been adopted and most of its provisions will come into force by the end of 2003. Some limits have been tightened and other new ones introduced; some suppliers are having to invest in additional water treatment; some sources may be abandoned where such investment would not be economic. Expenditure is also required to improve many water distribution systems since water quality can deteriorate both microbiologically and chemically when passing through sub-standard supply pipes and storage tanks.

Water supply hierarchies

Since 1989 the water industry in England and Wales has been the responsibility of privatised water companies. Of these 10 provide both water and sewerage services; these are the successors to the Regional Water Authorities set up in 1974. The remainder are the relatively long-established water supply companies. however recently there have been attempts to provide a measure of competition for these companies and new entrants have the right to supply water in bulk. At present this right has been exercised to only a limited extent, but it may present a potential opportunity to negotiate lower water supply charges.

Since April 2002 water supply and sewerage services for the whole of Scotland have been supplied by Scottish Water, an authority answerable to the Scottish Executive who are responsible for setting charges. In Northern Ireland responsibility is with central government and charges are included in general taxation.

Facilities controls

Reducing the quantity of water used can lead to significant savings in charges for both water supply and waste water disposal. A useful means to achieve this is for the facilities manager to carry out an audit of all water use, questioning whether each use is necessary and, if so, whether the function could be carried out with less. Options that may be explored include the installation of water-efficient taps, showers and urinal flushing devices.

A further possibility is the use - after treatment - of 'grey' water from washbasins, showers, baths and washing machines for applications such as toilet flushing. Health and safety issues should be borne in mind, but as the price of water and sewerage services increase such re-use will become increasingly attractive economically. With this in mind criteria to protect public health have been under discussion in the UK[3].

(Conservation measures are discussed in 5.5.3 below.)

---

[2] *Council Directive on the quality of water intended for human consumption (98/83/EC), Official Journal of the European Communities No L330/32, 5 December 1998.*

[3] *Dixon, A. M. et al (1999) Guidelines for Greywater Re-Use: Health Issues J.CIWEM, 13, 322-326.*

5.5.3 ECONOMICS OF WATER SUPPLY

Basis of charging

Charges for water supply are calculated for any property having the benefit of the service, directly or indirectly.

Water can be charged on either a **metered** or **unmetered** rate. However the utilities are moving away from the unmetered charging and their policy is to ensure that all new and converted properties have meters installed, in which case the customer has no option but to pay on the metered charge.

Where there is no meter installed the customer may elect to continue to pay on an unmetered basis; but if the premises consume a low volume of water, users may find it beneficial to have a meter installed at their own expense and opt for the metered supply. Unmetered supplies are charged either as a fixed annual tariff, or as a combination of fixed charge and a charge per pound of rateable value.

Metered supplies

The metered supplies comprise two components:

- a standing charge

- a volume charge

In the case of commercial buildings the **standing charge** is calculated by reference to the size of the meter or the nominal flow rate. A current standing charge tariff from one of the water service companies is included at Fig 5.5.A. For the same company, the 2001/2002 volumetric potable water charge was £0.8825 per cubic metre consumed.

Fig. 5.5.A
Typical water supply standing charge tariff

Meter size (mm)	Flow rate (m³/hr)	Annual charge (£)
Up to 20	Up to 2.5	20
25	3.5	54
30		92
40		170
50		255
65		341
80		452
100		538
150 and above		693

Conservation measures

Metered water supply (and sewerage services) costs can readily be reduced by adopting measures to save water. In principle there are two ways of doing this. The first is the installation of water use devices which are designed to dispense only the quantity of water that is actually necessary. Examples of these include the attachment of sensors to toilet flushing devices and water taps to limit the amount of water wasted.

The second means of saving water is to take measures to limit leakage, whether through driping taps or leaking pipes. A regular survey of water consumption patterns can show if there is an upward trend of consumption which may point to a need for relevant action to reverse it.

Abstraction charges

Abstraction charges for industrial water supply are levied. The charges levied usually reflect only the costs of administering the licence so, if water of suitable quality is available, direct abstraction is usually more economic for non-drinking purposes than the public water supply.

5.5.4 THE SOURCES AND NATURE OF SEWERAGE SERVICES

Sewerage services - domestic

Most domestic properties, especially in urban areas, are connected to a public sewer which takes away waste water for disposal. The development of the sewerage systems originally gave rise to serious water pollution since the effluent was discharged to rivers and streams at a single point rather than diffusely as it had been before. This led to the development of sewage treatment, at first by settlement only but later including secondary biological treatment.

Sewerage services - industrial

Elsewhere in Europe a policy of separating industrial from domestic effluent has been pursued for many years. Harmful and toxic constituents such as heavy metals are removed by pre-treatment before the treated effluent is discharged either to sewer or to surface waters. However, until recently the UK has encouraged the discharge of industrial effluents into the public sewer. It was argued that a large municipal waste water treatment plant was capable of removing polluting constituents because of the dilution available with domestic sewage and the flow and load balancing capacity in the sewers and treatment processes. It is now known that the disadvantages associated with this policy include the inhibition by harmful constituents of the microbial capacity within the waste water treatment processes and the concentration of some toxic elements in the sewage sludge by-product. Consequently, it is increasingly likely that industrial effluents containing non-biodegradable and harmful constituents will require on-site treatment to remove them.

5.5.5 SEWERAGE SERVICES POLICIES

The Urban Waste Water Treatment Directive[4] (UWWTD) requires that properties in all towns of more than 15,000 people should, by 31 December 2000, have been served by public sewers and that the waste water should be given full secondary sewage treatment before discharge to river, estuary or the sea. Sufficient treatment must be given to meet a standard of 25mg/l Biochemical Oxygen Demand (BOD) and 125mg/l Chemical Oxygen Demand (COD). The requirements will be extended to towns of 2000 population (10,000 in coastal areas) by the end of 2005. Other environmental legislation[5] imposes additional requirements for dischargers of domestic and industrial effluents.

Compliance with the UWWTD has had major cost implications, both in terms of capital for the initial investment and the continuing running costs of the new treatment plants. The UK, as a maritime country, has incurred particularly high costs because of its previous use of long sea outfalls as an alternative to sewage treatments. Since a large number of smaller works will be required to meet the 2005 deadline,

---

[4] *Council Directive concerning urban waste water treatment (91/271/EEC), Official Journal of the European Communities No L 135/40, 30 May 1991.*

[5] *See especially Council Directive concerning the quality of bathing water (76/160/EEC), Official Journal of the European Communities No L 31/1, 5 February 1976.*

waste water treatment costs are therefore likely to increase steadily for at least the next five years and, assuming these costs are passed on to the water users, charges can be expected to rise until at least 2005.

Further EU legislation intended to improve surface water quality seems likely to continue this trend of investment in waste water treatment, particularly the Water Framework Directive and a forthcoming revision to the Bathing Water Directive. However the likely impact of these on prices and therefore costs is not yet known.

Sewerage hierarchies

In England and Wales sewerage services are supplied by the 10 large water companies derived from the Water Authorities; in Scotland they are provided by Scottish Water and in Northern Ireland by central government.

Facilities controls

Discharges of industrial effluent, whether to sewer or direct to the environment, are made under the terms of a consent issued by the environmental regulator. In England and Wales this is the Environment Agency (EA), in Scotland the Scottish Environmental Protection Agency (SEPA) and in Northern Ireland the Department of the Environment (Northern Ireland). The consent normally contains conditions specifying location of the discharge and the volume and composition of the effluent for BOD and/or COD.

Breaching such conditions may lead to the imposition of fines, especially in the case of direct discharge to the environment. Should significant pollution occur any proceedings may be heard in the Crown Court, where unlimited fines can be handed down. Cases causing major pollution have resulted in fines of over £100,000 and courts have the power to impose a penalty for each day that a polluting discharge subsequently continues.

5.5.6 ECONOMICS OF SEWERAGE SERVICES

There are three broad categories of sewerage service available to industrial facilities. The first, termed here commercial discharges, covers the discharge to public sewer of effluent which is comparable in strength to that of a domestic household and which does not contain constituents that are toxic or that render the sewage difficult to treat. Charges applied for such discharges from commercial and business premises are usually broadly in line with domestic volume-based charges. The volume used in the calculation is based on the volume of water supplied since most of this will be discharged from the premises.

However for those which do contain such high strength or toxic components, a special trade effluent charge may be levied. Here the charge is calculated in terms of the load volume and strength in COD which it imposes on the sewerage system and treatment processes.

The third service covers the direct discharge of effluent to the environment, if necessary following on-site pre-treatment to render it fit to flow direct to the environment, usually to a surface water body such as a river or to the sea. The main cost, particularly for highly polluting effluents will be incurred by the treatment processes but there will also be a charge from the environmental regulator to cover the cost of monitoring.

Such a discharge can only be made subject to a consent, and failure to comply with the terms of such a consent or the occurrence of pollution can lead to fines which may be heavy (see 5.5.5).

5.5.7 SEWERS AND WATER PIPES

The facilities manager may be required to deal with the laying of a sewer or water pipe by the relevant utility. Generally there is an entitlement to compensation to the owner of the property. Normally, the facilities manager will appoint a professional valuer to deal with the compensation and day-to-day estate management matters but will need to discuss various matters as they arise.

The following may be given as examples of concerns and issues:

- **line of the pipe or sewer:** a short route is desirable but may not always be the best, such as where the pipe would prevent future development

- **inspection chambers and above-ground accessories:** the fewer the better and make them as unobstructive and unobtrusive as possible

- **working space and access:** such works tend to have a 'width' of working space for installation and for future maintenance and repair; access to the work areas should be agreed and safeguarded

- **protection of existing features:** existing pipes, cables, trees, planted areas and so on should be protected; if necessary there should be diversions for pipes and cables

- **disruption to services:** interruption to telecommunications, electricity and other services should be minimised

- **finds:** any coins, archaeological artefacts and so on which are found should remain the property of the owner, subject of course to statute.

The means of compensation will be negotiated as recommended by the valuer. In the event of a dispute, there is the right of appeal to the Lands Tribunal. Compensation will reflect issues such as:

- the permanent effect of the 'width' of the pipe-line or sewer together with any accessories

- any adverse effect on development rights

- transient damage such as disturbance to surfaces and plantings and damaged or lost trees.

In a situation where the claimant's property is enhanced in value, the compensating body may reduce the amount paid, sometimes to zero. Reasonable professional fees are normally paid for work in settling the claim.

5.6 WASTE MANAGEMENT

Introduction

Waste is an environmental, economic, social and political problem, and it is a problem created by all of us. All wastes have the potential to cause environmental damage if not managed appropriately. The winning and use of raw materials constitutes an abuse of the natural environment by depleting non-sustainable resources and increasing the volume of wastes for disposal. In addition, improper disposal of waste can lead to pollution of land, water and atmosphere.

Economically, waste impacts both the producer and the consumer. The costs of waste management can make up a high proportion of the economics for certain products. These costs are then passed along the economic line to the customer. Social and political problems are borne by everyone. The NIMBY syndrome means that no one wishes to have a waste disposal site or incinerator located close to his or her home. Politically, it is difficult to develop suitable strategies for dealing with waste as the most technically feasible and economically viable alternatives may prove difficult through public objection.

The problem of waste disposal has led to a high level of regulation of the waste chain. Waste is produced from all business activities and the current focus on waste reduction places a responsibility on every business to reduce waste, and particularly to reduce the amounts of waste being sent to landfill. There are duties on producers, carriers and disposers of waste to prevent pollution. Compliance with legislation and regulatory requirements can only be achieved through good waste management practices.

Legislation takes a hierarchical approach promoting the minimisation of waste and placing controls on the storage, handling, treatment and disposal of waste to prevent pollution.

The reality is that, considered carefully, responsible waste management can create significant savings for a company in terms of lower raw material costs, reduced storage space requirements and lower disposal costs. These savings in turn allow the company greater market opportunity, reducing their impact upon the wider environments at the same time.

It may be noted that some pertinent matters, eg landfill tax and compensation for fumes, smoke and dust are dealt with in Chapter 11.4.3 and 7.5 respectively.

5.6.1 WASTE AND THE FACILITIES MANAGER

Waste arising within the responsibility of the facilities manager can be varied but are largely considered to be materials derived mainly from office wastes. These include:

- paper and paper-based products
- computer/printer/copier consumables, eg toner cartridges
- discarded furniture and equipment
- canteen wastes
- cans, bottles and other receptacles
- cleaning, decorating and other facility maintenance materials.

Fig. 5.6.A shows what good waste management practice would include, but is not limited to that shown.

Fig. 5.6.A
*Good waste
management
practice*

Issues	Good Practice
General Waste Issues	▪ Reduce, reuse or recycle where possible ▪ Provide dedicated waste storage areas ▪ Do not mix Special and Non-Special waste ▪ Do not mix incompatible Special Wastes ▪ Label all skips and containers with their contents ▪ Ensure that all skips and containers are in good condition and not leaking ▪ Ensure that all skips and containers are placed on hard standing ▪ Do not allow skips to overflow and change them regularly ▪ Undertake regular inspections of waste storage areas and areas prone to fly-tipping ▪ Do not dispose of (burn, bury or treat) waste on site ▪ Obtain copies of licensed waste carrier and waste disposal company certificates before allowing the waste to leave site ▪ Undertake periodic Duty of Care spot checks on transport and disposal companies dealing with the waste
Dealing with Controlled Waste	▪ Use covered skips where possible ▪ Ensure that each waste consignment off site is accompanied by a controlled waste transfer note ▪ Sign all appropriate documentation and provide a clear description of the waste ▪ Keep all copies of controlled waste transfer notes on file for at least two years
Dealing with Special Waste	▪ Use covered skips and ensure that liquid wastes are stored in containers provided with secondary containment ▪ Pre-notify the EA/SEPA of any consignments with a Special Waste Consignment Note ▪ Sign all appropriate documentation and provide a clear description of the waste ▪ Keep all copies of controlled waste transfer notes on file for at least three years

5.6.2. WASTE - POLICY AND STRUCTURE

Waste can be loosely defined as 'any substance which constitutes a scrap material or an effluent or other unwanted surplus substance arising from the application of any process; and any substance or article which requires to be disposed of as being broken, worn out, contaminated or otherwise spoilt'. This definition is taken from the Environmental Protection Act 1990 as amended by the Environment Act 1995, Schedule 22.

However, this definition does not provide for the re-use or recycling of another person's waste. (See 5.6.3 and Fig. 5.6.C, on page B-214)

Solid waste disposal continues to receive considerable attention from regulatory organisations. Recent developments in waste legislation can be divided into the following areas:

• development of a waste hierarchy to encourage waste minimisation, re-use and recycling, with disposal being a final option

• introduction of legislation to encourage the reduction of waste generation at source

• implementation of strict legislation controlling waste management activities.

A strong emphasis is placed on management at all stages of the waste cycle, from raw materials to end of use. Under section 34 of the Environmental Protection Act 1990, a duty of care places responsibilities on all persons involved in the production, handling and treatment of waste and is a central theme in the waste legislation.

Organisation	Responsibilities
Policy/Legislation	
▪ DEFRA ▪ National Assembly for Wales ▪ Northern Ireland Assembly ▪ Scottish Executive	▪ Set targets for waste recycling and recovery ▪ Establish the decision making framework ▪ Establish policy instruments to foster change ▪ Ensure roles and responsibilities are clear for all parties
Waste Management Regulation	
▪ Environment Agency (England and Wales) ▪ SEPA ▪ Environment and Heritage Service for Northern Ireland	▪ Ensure that waste management activities do not cause harm to human health or the environment ▪ Implement the waste licensing regime ▪ Advise on waste management issues ▪ Undertake data collection and information gathering ▪ Take a risk-based approach to waste management ▪ Implement firm but fair enforcement action where necessary ▪ Use legislative powers and advice to bring about waste reduction ▪ Publish reports for each region (EA)
Landfill Tax Regulation	
▪ Customs and Excise	▪ Ensure that Landfill Tax regulations are enforced ▪ Advise on Landfill Tax issues
Planning	
▪ Waste Planning Authorities (County/Unitary Council Level)	▪ Identification of suitable sites for treatment and disposal ▪ Implementation of planning policy guidance ▪ Determination of future requirements for facilities ▪ Establish BPEO ▪ Promote informed debate regarding waste management ▪ Work with the regulators to ensure that planning and licensing are complementary
Collection	
▪ Waste Collection Authorities (County/Unitary Council Level)	▪ Safe and efficient collection of household waste and commercial waste ▪ Duty to prepare and publicise Recycling Plans ▪ Review of plans and take account of Departmental Guidance ▪ Liaise with Waste Disposal Authorities ▪ Subject to Best Value
Disposal	
▪ Waste Disposal Authorities (County/Unitary Council Level)	▪ Safe management of household and some commercial waste ▪ Use contractors to remain at arms length from other council responsibilities ▪ Raise awareness of waste management and encourage recycling and recovery ▪ Development of appropriate facilities ▪ Develop effective working relationships to deliver integrated waste management ▪ Endeavour to meet UK targets for recycling and recovery ▪ Subject to Best Value

In the past, waste was an issue that could be addressed relatively cheaply and easily. In contrast, today it creates a whole series of problems that can impact on a company's profitability, if not handled correctly. Such problems include the segregation and sampling of waste, its labelling, packaging and storage. Moving the waste from its site of production highlights additional issues: is the waste hazardous? Is the haulier a licensed carrier? Legislation also demands that waste producers generate considerable amounts of paperwork to prove that they are fulfilling their duty of care and that they are meeting all current requirements. It is therefore of paramount importance that companies understand and review their waste management strategies and procedures to ensure legislative compliance and to determine whether there is the potential for identifying and implementing cost savings.

Plans and policies to deal with waste in the UK are to be implemented in line with the development of the national Waste Strategies developed for each of the four countries. The Waste Strategy 2000 for England and Wales, published in 2000, is currently subject to review as the National Assembly for Wales went to consultation on its own Draft Waste Strategy entitled "Managing Waste Sustainably" at the end of 2001. National waste strategies for Northern Ireland and Scotland were published in 2000 and 1999 respectively.

These documents set down the preferred hierarchical regime for each of the countries to develop sustainable waste management strategies that can be implemented within technical, environmental and financial constraints. They call for the implementation of statutory targets on local authorities to ensure that there is an appropriate diversion of waste away from final disposal to a more sustainable option through reuse, recycling or recovery.

The government and agency structure in the UK is shown in Fig. 5.6.B (previous page)

5.6.3 DEFINITION OF WASTE

The definition given in 5.6.2 does not provide for the re-use or recycling of another persons waste. Court proceedings in both UK and Europe have failed to come up with a satisfactory definition of what constitutes waste in these circumstances, although the current legal requirements relate to whether there is a need for recovery or treatment of material prior to its reuse. If so, it will constitute a waste material. There have been a number of attempts at achieving a practical definition of waste, but to date it has not been possible to reach final agreement. Fig. 5.6.C provides a general indication as to whether a material will be defined as a waste.

Fig. 5.6.C
Waste or not?

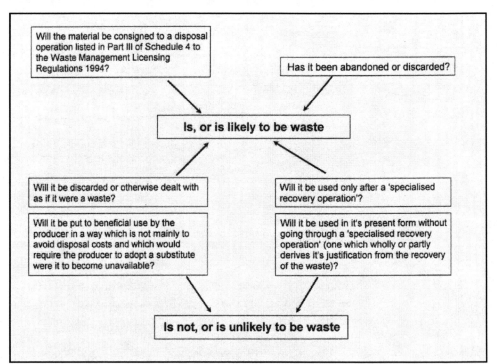

5.6.4 LEGAL FRAMEWORK

Much of the UK's policy is derived from that of the EU. The latter waste policy is based on the Directive on Waste of 15 July 1975 (75/442/EEC) as amended by Directive 91/156/EEC. The amended Directive provides the basic legal framework governing waste in the EU passing through all subsequent legislation in the UK. EU waste policy aims at prevention first, recovery second, and disposal (incineration or landfill) as a last resort.

The Directive defines the scope of "waste" and "hazardous waste", establishing permitting and registration requirements for those who handle, transport, dispose or recycle waste; it requires competent national authorities to draw up waste management plans with the object of achieving "self-sufficiency" in waste management, and allows those authorities to control waste movements which are not in accordance with those plans.

'Waste' is defined as a substance that the holder "discards, intends to discard, or is required to discard". The term discard is undefined, thereby leaving the interpretation largely uncontrolled. 'Hazardous waste' is defined as waste featuring on a list to be drawn up by the EC through a technical committee procedure (see Fig. 5.6.G (see B-218)).

Directive 91/156/EEC requires the national competent authorities to draw up waste management plans that are aimed at enabling the EU and member states to become self-sufficient in waste management. The authorities may then control shipments not in accordance with those plans.

As described above, each member state is obliged, under EU law, to define and develop ways of implementing the Waste Directive. As a result member states have developed environmental or specific waste management legislation to fulfil their obligations. The key legislation enabling the Directives on Waste is the Environmental Protection Act 1990, as amended.

The EC has singled out some waste items for priority treatment. These include, packaging, waste electronic and electrical equipment and end of life vehicles. These items will be incorporated into national policy and regulations.

Fig. 5.6.D shows the Directives which have been adopted and are to be implemented into UK legislation.

Fig. 5.6.D
Directives adopted and to be implemented

Landfill Directive (99/31/EC) (OJ L 182/1)	• Regulates the disposal of waste to land • Bans co-disposal of waste in landfill • All waste must be pre-treated prior to disposal • Phased reduction in the biodegradable content of waste allowed to landfill
Waste Incineration Directive (00/76/EC)	• Fill the gap between existing directives covering the incineration of hazardous and municipal wastes • Aims to reduce environmental impact from incineration of waste • Applies to new plants from Autumn 2002 • Applies to existing plants from 2005 • Plants must be authorised
End of Life Vehicles (ELV) Directive (00/53/EC)	• Prevention of waste from ELVs • Promotion of collection, reuse and recycling • Reduction in the use of hazardous substances in vehicle manufacture • Develop a system of deregistration upon presentation of a certificate of destruction • Free take back for last owner • Producers to meet all or significant part of the costs of applying this measure
Solvents Directive (99/13/EC)	• Encourages the reduction of solvent waste and reuse of solvents • Listed solvent based activities must be authorised when operated above certain annual consumption thresholds • Requires use of Best Available Techniques to reduce emissions • Compliance demonstrated by solvent management plan

The following Directives have been proposed:

• Directive on Hazardous Municipal Waste Collection

• Revision of the Packaging Directive

- Directive on Battery Recycling

- Directive on Recycling and Recovery of Electronic Waste

- Revision of Batteries Directive

- Directive on Composting

- New controls on Dangerous Substances in Water.

5.6.5. KEY STATUTES

Current UK waste legislation has been primarily based upon the Directives brought forward through the EU, and has a direct bearing on the way that business discharges its obligations. Fig. 5.6.E provides an outline of the requirements set down in UK law.

Fig. 5.6.E
Key legislation on the environment

Environmental Protection Act 1990	▪ Most waste management activities fall under Part II of the Act ▪ Implemented Waste Management Licensing Regulations 1994
Environment Act 1995	▪ Amended APA 1990 ▪ Established the Environment Agency and SEPA
Landfill Tax Regulations 1996	▪ Landfill Tax was introduced in October 1996 ▪ The tax applies to waste disposed to landfill, and is chargeable by weight (per tonne) at two rates: inactive and active ▪ Municipal waste is chargeable at the higher rate of tax which is currently £12 per tonne, and is set to increase by £1 per tonne per annum until 2004 when it will be reviewed
Producer Responsibility Obligations (Packaging Waste) Regulations 1997	▪ The Government introduced the Producer Responsibility Obligations (Packaging Waste) Regulations 1997 with the objective of implementing the recovery and recycling targets in the EC Directive on Packaging ▪ There are statutory requirements on UK organisations that qualify as "obligated producers" to recover and recycle set amounts of packaging waste ▪ Packaging waste is the only element of the waste stream currently subject to regulation ▪ Packaging accounts for about 9% of industrial, commercial and municipal waste. This equates to approximately 10 million tonnes annually, of which 4.5 million tonnes of packaging is estimated to arise in the household waste stream
The Waste Minimisation Act 1998	▪ The Waste Minimisation Act 1998 empowers local authorities to investigate and promote methods of minimising locally generated waste ▪ It is not a statutory obligation for local authorities to take such action but the Act does give them the power to explore the potential methods for waste minimisation
Pollution Prevention and Control (England and Wales) Regulation 2000 Pollution Prevention and Control (Scotland) Regulations 2000	▪ The Integrated Pollution Prevention and Control (IPPC) regime is a statutory tool for reducing waste produced by industrial installations ▪ Those regulated under IPPC will be required to abide by the general principle that waste production should be avoided, and that where waste is produced it should be recovered, unless technically and economically impossible
Special Waste Regulations 1996	▪ Hazardous materials subject to additional controls ▪ Defined in EC Hazardous Waste Directive 91/698/EC

Other primary and secondary legislation has an impact on waste management in England and Wales. It is shown in Fig. 5.6.F.

Fig. 5.6.F
Other legislation on the environment

- Control of Pollution Act 1974
- Local Government Act 1985
- Control of Pollution (Amendment) Act 1989
- Town and Country Planning Act 1990
- Planning and Compensation Act 1991
- Finance Act 1996
- Merchant Shipping Maritime Security Act 1997
- Local Government Act 1999
- Finance Act 2001
- Town and Country Planning General Development Order 1988, SI 1813
- The Sludge (Use in Agriculture) Regulations 1989
- Controlled Waste (Registration of Carriers and Seizure of Vehicles) Regulations 1991, SI 1624
- Environmental Protection (Duty of Care) Regulations 1991, SI 2839
- Controlled Waste Regulations 1992, SI 588 (as amended)
- Environmental Protection (Waste Recycling Payments) Regulations 1992, SI 426
- Control of Substances Hazardous to Health Regulations 1994
- Town and Country Planning (General Permitted Development) Order 1995, SI 418
- Town and Country Planning (General Development Procedure) Order 1995, SI 419
- Chemicals (Hazard Information and Packaging for Supply) Regulations 1996
- Packaging (Essential Requirements) Regulations 1998, SI 1165
- Animals By-Products Order 1999
- Ozone Depleting Substances Regulations 2001
- Landfill (England and Wales) Regulations 2001

5.6.6. WASTE CLASSIFICATION

Most products or materials discarded by businesses are considered to be waste. All companies are responsible for the safe storage, handling and disposal of the waste that it produces. Waste is defined in the Environmental Protection Act 1990 and European Directive 91/156/EEC.

Directive waste

The Directive on Waste (91/156) created the category "Directive Waste" as any material, substance or product which the holder intends to or is required to discard. Excluded from the definition of Directive Waste and covered by separate legislation are the following: gaseous effluents; wastewaters; radioactive wastes; natural non-dangerous materials from agriculture; waste from mining and quarrying; and decommissioned explosives.

European Waste Catalogue

Under Directive 75/442/EEC (as amended) the EC was required to draw up a European Waste Catalogue (EWC) to list all wastes and specify which are hazardous.

In late 1993 the EC agreed the basic EWC (Decision 94/3/EC of 20 December 1993). The EWC is not intended to be an exhaustive list and will be periodically updated. The inclusion of a material in the list does not automatically mean that it is a waste. This is the case only when the above mentioned definition of Directive Waste is satisfied.

The EWC is an extremely important guideline, because it lists many substances and materials that are not typically thought of as wastes.

Hazardous waste

The Council of Ministers approved, with the Decision 94/904/EC of 22 December 1994, the core list of wastes that are considered as hazardous for the purposes of implementing the Directive 91/689/EEC on hazardous waste. As a result of the approval of the list, the Member States had to transpose the 1991 Directive by 27 June 1995.

Annex III to the same Directive lists the 15 properties of wastes that render them hazardous (see Fig. 5.6.G).

Fig. 5.6.G
Hazardous Waste List

Hazard Code	Properties
H1	'Explosive' – substances and preparations which may explode under the effect of flame or which are more sensitive to shocks or friction than dinitrobenzene
H2	'Oxidising' – substances and preparations which exhibit highly exothermic reactions when in contact with other substances, particularly flammable substances
H3-A	'Highly Flammable': • Liquid substances and preparations having a flash point below 21°C (including extremely flammable liquids) • Substances and preparations which may become hot and finally catch fire in contact with air at ambient temperature without any application of energy • Solid substances and preparations which may readily catch fire after brief contact with a source of ignition and which continue to burn or to be consumed after removal of the source of ignition • Gaseous substances and preparations which are flammable in air at normal pressure • Substances and preparations which, in contact with water or damp air, evolve highly flammable gases in dangerous quantities.
H3-B	'Flammable' – liquid substances and preparations having a flash point equal to or greater than $21°C$ and less than or equal to $55°C$
H4	'Irritant' – non-corrosive substances and preparations which, through immediate, prolonged or repeated contact with the skin or mucous membrane, can cause inflammation.
H5	'Harmful' – Substances and preparations which, if they are inhaled or ingested or if they penetrate the skin, may involve limited health risks.
H6	'Toxic' – substances and preparations (including very toxic substances and preparations) which, if they are inhaled or ingested, or if they penetrate the skin, may involve serious acute or chronic health risks or even death.
H7	'Carcinogenic' – substances and preparations which, if they are inhaled or ingested, or if they penetrate the skin, may induce cancer or increase its incidence.
H8	'Corrosive' – substances and preparations which may destroy living tissue on contact.
H9	'Infectious' – substances containing viable micro-organisms or their toxins which are known or reliably believed to cause disease in man or other living organisms.
H10	'Teratogenic' – substances and preparations which, if they are inhaled or ingested or if they penetrate the skin, may induce non-hereditary congenital malformations or increase their incidence.
H11	'Mutagenic' – substances and preparations which, if they are inhaled or ingested or if they penetrate the skin, may induce hereditary genetic defects or increase their incidence.
H12	Substances and preparations which release toxic or very toxic gases in contact with water, air or an acid
H13	Substances and preparations capable by any means, after disposal, of yielding another substances, eg leachate, which possesses any of the characteristics listed above
H14	'Ecotoxic' – substances and preparations which present or may present immediate or delayed risks for one or more sectors of the environment

As with the EWC, the Hazardous Waste List is not intended to be exhaustive and its regular amendment is foreseen in the Directive itself. In addition the UK as a member state can identify any other material as hazardous waste provided it displays any of the 15 hazardous properties mentioned above.

Clinical waste

Generally these are any wastes arising from medical, nursing, dental, veterinary, pharmaceutical or similar practices.

Municipal waste

Municipal waste comprises waste collected by or on behalf of local authorities and includes household waste, street cleaning waste and some commercial and trade waste.

5.6.7 PRACTICAL WASTE MANAGEMENT

Industrial waste facilities controls

Most companies do not allocate clear responsibilities for the identification and management of material waste. The true cost of waste - which includes material value, manufacturing costs, disposal costs - can be as high as 10% of business turnover.

Waste minimisation not only reduces a company's operating costs, but also helps to maintain competitiveness and reduce its environmental impact. Senior management commitment is essential to the success of any waste minimisation initiative.

Waste minimisation should fit in with other initiatives that a company is undertaking such as:

- Total Quality Management
- Business Process Re-Engineering
- Quality Management Systems (BS EN ISO 9001)
- Environmental Management Systems (BS EN ISO 14001, EMAS)
- Investors in People.

However, focus must be maintained, otherwise effort and resources can become too thinly spread.

The waste management hierarchy

The waste management hierarchy is based on the principles of sustainable waste management and is the basis for waste legislation and waste management:

- waste prevention and reduction (minimisation)
- waste re-use
- waste recovery and recycling
- waste treatment
- safe disposal of any non-recoverable waste.

It should be noted that waste prevention, minimisation and re-use are, in principle, superior to recovery and recycling as methods of managing waste.

Life cycle analysis

Life cycle analysis (LCA) in the context of waste is the assessment and review of environmental impacts at each stage of the waste cycle, to ensure that wastes are managed in a sustainable way and environmental impacts are minimised. There has been an attempt to enforce LCA through packaging and packaging waste. It is considered likely that it will be some time before the LCA approach is fully adopted through waste legislation as debate surrounds the definition of the best waste management system and a global waste hierarchy.

Waste prevention and reduction

The overall aims of waste reduction are to maximise business efficiency and reduce environmental impact. The benefits of reducing waste at source include:

- reduced requirement for purchased materials
- reduced operating costs.

The waste reduction can be achieved by a change in technology, or by the removal of a process, or by substitution of a product with a similar product which has a longer lifespan. The application of this principle in terms of building component life-cycles is discussed further in Chapter 10.6.4.

Facilities managers should be aware that waste reduction will create cost saving in terms of raw materials and potentially in reduction of storage requirements. However, the payback period where investment is required, such as in changing a process or purchasing new technology, may have to be carefully considered.

A case study of this concept in practice originates from an organisation involved in paper intensive financial services and pensions administration. The company is required by law to retain all financial information for a number of years. Traditionally, large areas are dedicated to the storage of clean paper and the completed documents. The preparation and distribution of the documents together with disposal of the old records produces significant quantities of waste. The company now holds most brochures, application forms and confirmation documents on compact disc (CD) and transmits the information by electronic mail, or by posting a CD. Records are held on read-only CD for the required number of years and, since one disc can store 15,000 sheets of A4 paper, the storage areas are a fraction of the size traditionally required. In addition the CD's are reusable. The initial cost outlay for the new technology was paid back within one year.

Waste re-use

Many wastes can be returned to the supplier for re-use. This includes packaging materials, printer and copier toner cartridges, returnable bottles and some electronic equipment.

One good example of re-use is that by using recycled cartridges, a company reduced expenditure on toner cartridges by an estimated £48,000 per year. The use of recycled cartridges also reduces the quantity of material needed to produce new cartridges.

Waste recovery and recycling

Waste recovery is the process of converting a waste material into something that is useable. This term encompasses recycling, eg recovery of aluminium from cans for a new product, composting of biodegradable wastes to produce soil conditioners, and energy recovery from the incineration of waste or from the collection of landfill gas.

Use of workplace recycling containers are available, from small 15 litre deskside bins to larger mobile containers. These are generally available in clear uniform colours with clear recycling graphics for different types of recyclable wastes.

However, collections of recoverable waste materials may or may not be cost effective for a company. The paper recovery market is only marginally commercial and the provision of separate collection bins in a facility may be hard to justify in economic terms.

As an example of waste recovery, a company which manufactures paper and paper products optimised their waste paper collection which resulted in the reduction of rejects (wastes) of about 80 tonnes per year (equal to 95%).

Waste treatment and disposal

Waste treatment can include physical and chemical change to a waste to assist with final disposal of the waste. Final disposal of waste is normally to a landfill or incinerator.

On-site waste treatment, such as compaction, can provide an economic benefit through the reduction of the collection frequency or by reducing the space requirement for waste storage. Consideration needs to be given to potential savings on container hire costs and waste collection against the cost of an on-site compactor. Cost savings in the order of 30% can be achieved in offices where compaction may reduce waste volume by as much as 90%.

5.6.8 RESPONSIBILITY FOR WASTE MANAGEMENT

Duty of care

The concept of Duty of Care applies to all persons who import, produce, carry, keep, treat or dispose of Directive Waste. Effectively this applies to all of us and any office or place of work must be deemed to be producers of waste. In the UK, Duty of Care is enacted under the Environmental Protection (Duty of Care) Regulations 1991 (SI 1991/2839)

All organisations involved in the production and disposal of wastes must take an appropriate level of responsibility in preventing pollution from waste. Failure to comply is a criminal offence and there is no statutory limit for fines imposed for breach of Duty of Care.

Passing a waste to another person does not pass all the responsibility and there may be certain long-term responsibilities on the waste producer. Generally, the waste producer will retain some responsibility for the waste until its final appropriate disposal. It aims to ensure that waste never leaves the hands of an authorised person, that it is always accompanied by a written description and that it is safely contained at all times. Each waste producer has a duty to take all reasonable measures:

- to ensure that waste is securely contained

- to ensure that waste is only transferred to someone authorised to carry or manage it

- to ensure that appropriate records are kept

- to ensure that others involved in the handling and disposal of the waste do so in accordance with the legal requirements and that they follow the Duty of Care.

Authorised persons include Waste Collection Authorities, holders of waste management licences and registered waste carriers.

The facilities manager will most likely be the person responsible for ensuring that all waste is:

- handled in the correct manner by appropriately trained staff who are aware of environmental and public health risks

- correctly described and documented, with quantities recorded and analysis carried out where required

- contained in a secure storage place where the waste does not present a risk to employees or to the environment.

The responsible person on the waste production side will need to remain vigilant as the waste producer will still hold liability for waste that has left the site where the waste operator does not dispose of the material in an appropriately licensed facility. In such a situation, where reasonable checks have not been made, the producer could be liable for a breach of the Duty of Care.

The government has published a Code of Practice providing guidance on compliance with the Duty of Care, although this does not meet every possible contingency. Fig. 5.6.H identifies some of the means of compliance.

Fig. 5.6.H
Compliance with the Duty of Care

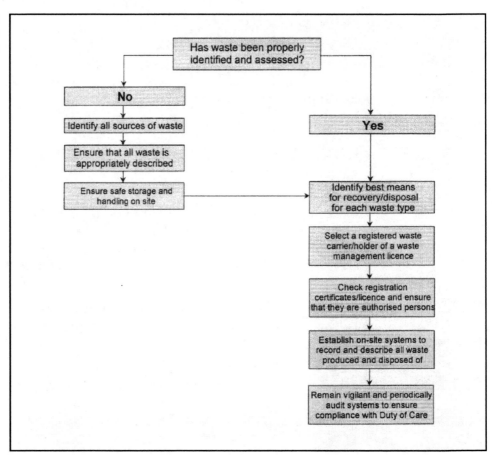

Suspected breach in the Duty of Care

If the facilities manager has cause to question operations the following steps may be needed:

- if there is an indication that waste is not being dealt with appropriately by the authorised person, check with them to ensure they have the correct records that left your site en route to their final destination

- if this does not provide satisfactory evidence, prevent further transfer of waste to the suspected party

- alert the local EA/SEPA office if a breach in the Duty is suspected.

Producers and Packaging

The facilities manager is likely to be the responsible person when it comes to the management of all types of waste on a site. The Producer Responsibility Obligations (Packaging Waste) Regulations 1997 (as amended) constitutes the UK's compliance with the EU directive on packaging and packaging waste. This places a legal obligation on those in the packaging chain to recover and recycle packaging materials. These regulations will only apply where a company:

- manufactures packaging raw materials
- converts materials into packaging
- packs and fills packaging
- sells packaging to the final customer
- owns the packaging and are not simply undertaking filling etc. for a third party
- has a group turnover of greater than £2m
- handles more than 50 tonnes of obligated packaging per annum.

Social responsibilities

There is a social responsibility on every individual and on every company to protect the environment for future generations. This embodies the concept of sustainable waste management. Training and raising the awareness of employees is one method of adopting social responsibility towards waste management.

Many companies are now carrying out environmental reporting, including sections on waste management costs and waste reduction initiatives, as part of their social responsibility.

The facilities manager can do much to encourage an economically viable approach to environmentally friendly waste disposal:

- recycling of waste paper can be encouraged by the installation of a second wastepaper basket - for recyclable materials only, particularly with high grade waste paper
- special collections or depositories for low-grade general waste such as newspapers and parcel wrappings
- purchase of paper products from low grade waste
- purchase of washable, not disposable, cups, saucers and plates
- cross-charging of waste disposal to departments where such a generic policy is in place
- pro-active stock control procedures checking consumption of paper against value-engineered and environmentally-friendly targets
- staff awareness programmes and campaigns.

5.7 INTERIOR LANDSCAPING AND DÉCOR

Introduction

Interior landscaping and décor is a small part of the total expenditure and activity of facilities provision. However, its benefits are well established and it is now recognised that carefully planned and costed plants and objets d'art can benefit customers, employers and (in the case of natural plants) the wider environment. It is also recognised that the key to success in landscaping depends more on the quality of installation and maintenance than the overall expenditure. In other words it is better to allocate a comparatively small amount of money and spend it on a well thought out sustainable scheme than try to be too ambitious. Works involving external grounds can be found in Chapter 5.2.5.

5.7.1 INTERIOR LANDSCAPING AND DÉCOR IN CONTEXT

The provision of services for interior landscaping is well developed in the UK. There is a reliance on the same tried and tested plants and materials. Installation costs of major projects, such as office building atria, may seem to be considerable; for example a single specimen palm will cost at least £3000. However such costs are usually quite insignificant in the context of the total costs of fitting-out.

5.7.2 THE COST OF INTERIOR LANDSCAPING AND DÉCOR

The protocol for interior landscaping and décor is given at Fig. 5.7.A.

Fig. 5.7.A
Facilities Economics Protocol - interior landscaping and décor

Sub-categories (contract bundle items)	Principal Examples / cost elements	Items commonly included in costs	Items excluded from costs	
			Item	Refer to category:
Horticultural	Trees Cut flowers Planters	Contract charges, Cleaning costs, Fireproofing, Special insurance premiums, contract hire charges, cleaning, restorations	External landscaping	Grounds maintenance
Objects d'art	Paintings Sculptures Bric-a-brac		Administration	General facilities management

Fig. 5.7.B indicates the sort of yearly expenditure range found from audits of interior landscape users. Apart from the rather exceptional "top of the range" settings, the costs are generally minimal for commercial office users.

The link between costs of landscaping and added value can be disproportionate, but the balance is definitely heavily in favour of the beneficial effects of small but wise expenditure.

These benefits evidence themselves predominantly in terms of improvements in:

- ambience
- health and safety
- public relations.

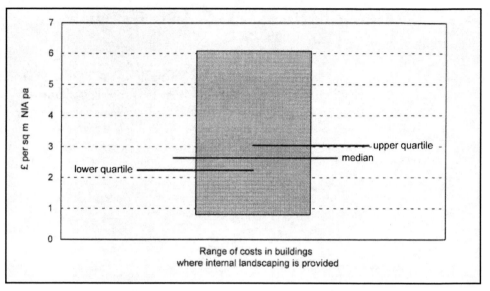

Fig. 5.7.B
Typical range of annual expenditure on interior landscaping

5.7.3 INTERIOR LANDSCAPING - PROCUREMENT

Options

Interior landscape can be provided as an in-house facility or by an outside contractor. The former can range from a casual tolerance of houseplants brought in from home or the formal provision of a range of plants and planters by the employer. The use of contractors should always be structured to meet the needs of the client. Reasonable ranges of both live and artificial plants are available and increasingly interior landscape has become part of a package that includes lighting, water, sculpture and other art.

Domestic provision

Provision and control of plants by individual members of staff is really only appropriate in the smaller organisations where staff are allowed to control what their environment looks like and take responsibility for buying, locating and maintaining their own plants. Sometimes in larger offices someone with an interest will take special responsibility for advising either staff or management on the types of plants to buy and how to maintain them.

However, rarely will a 'domestic' policy be satisfactory in a well-planned working environment and the inevitably haphazard solutions will most likely produce an unsatisfactory visual ambience to the visitor and many of the in-house personnel. Nevertheless, the feeling of being in control of the environment which seems to be so important in the case of comfort cooling and heating is also a factor to be taken into account before telling the amateur gardeners that the nurserystaff are taking over.

Outsourced services

This may merely involve the provision and maintenance of artificial plants or, as is more and more common, a full-blown exercise in horticultural planning, planting and maintenance.

It is best not to mix domestic and externally managed schemes as doing so results in visual anarchy. However, a properly designed and managed interior planting scheme can provide a highly cost-effective solution to functions such as screening and visitor-direction/guidance, in addition to providing a distinct ambience to the building.

Installations on any sort of scale should always be part of the interior design contract - or at least under the designer's direction - and large naturally-grown installations such as found in atria are best left to qualified landscape architects.

Outsourced office plantings are generally provided on a rental basis, with the plants remaining the property of the interior landscape company. Contracts often run for only one or two years and have to be renewed regularly. Installation of large scale interior schemes, such as atria, are normally on a design and build basis to install, with a separate maintenance contract.

5.7.4 SPECIFICATION OF PLANTS

Artificial plants

Artificial plants are cheaper than the natural variety but the pots, of course, cost the same - about half the price of smaller plants is in the container. Maintenance is much lower, the only requirements being a regular dusting and freshening (possibly even replenishing artificial fragrance) and occasional repair or replacement due to damage. However, it must be recognised that artificial plants represent a fire risk and so they must be treated with a flame retardant at least twice a year - see Fig. 5.7.C. Fire retardants should conform to BS 5852 Part 1 cigarette and match test and other retardant standards

Fig. 5.7.C
Comparative annual equivalent costs of artificial and natural plants

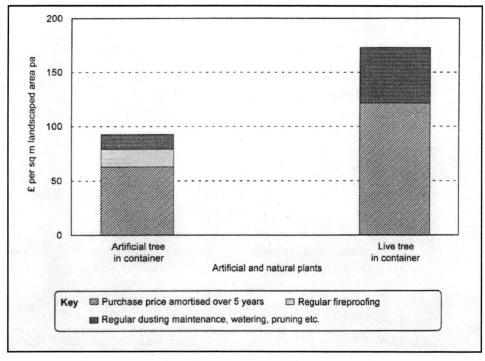

The better quality artificial plants made from polyester silk or preserved plants are really quite difficult to tell from the real thing on casual inspection but add nothing to the physical as opposed to the visual environment. Nevertheless they are a vast improvement on nothing at all, and can be used to good effect in darker or cooler parts of the building where the natural varieties might struggle to survive. Asthma and hay fever sufferers as well as well-intending but financially restricted management may also show a preference for artificial plants on totally practical grounds. The lack of any need for watering means that designers have a much wider range of containers from which to choose.

Natural planting

Natural plants are almost universally preferred to the artificial variety but owners do need expert advice on provision and maintenance; where natural plants are provided domestically, they have a tendency to grow out of control - or not at all - especially where the species has not been matched to the required climatic conditions.

Depending on whether the contract is full-rent-and-maintain or maintenance-only the contractor will replace plants as required within the annual charge or seek approval and funding for any reinstatement.

In atria, where tall varieties such as palms and weeping figs can reach eight metres, there is a problem of damage by natural pests. Some companies' environmental policies prohibit chemical spraying in which case (and why not?) biological control systems, whereby non-harmful insect varieties are introduced to see off the nasties, can be successfully implemented and are totally 'green'.

Fig. 5.7.C (see the previous page) considers the alternative life-cycle costs of an artificial and a natural plant which is typical of the generic economic argument. The cost of fireproofing artificial plants has been shown separately to emphasise the need for this operation.

Health and comfort benefits

Apart from the psychological benefit of working in a pleasant, green environment research in the USA[1] and England[2] has shown that certain pollutants commonly found in the office atmosphere can be countered and abated by various species of live plants.

Additionally, static electricity can be controlled and reduced by the presence of moisture in the live plants. As well as the filtering and oxygenating properties of the plants themselves many horticulturists and environmental scientists also hold that the soil from plants in well-maintained containers has a beneficial effect upon air quality within the office.

Care should be taken that floors, particularly timber floors, are protected from the watering of plants in porous containers.

5.7.5 OBJETS D'ART

Some organisations provide works of art for the enjoyment of staff and visitors and to enhance the decorative ambience of the facility. There is no evidence of any tangible benefits deriving from this practice in respect of the investment value of the works although many internal and external environments are undoubtedly made more interesting by well-chosen and aptly located pictures and sculptures.

Some organisations have a policy of changing their artworks on a regular basis; they can do this by renting from specialist firms or by promoting the work of local artists. One option is to allow employees to choose some or all of the paintings/sculptures; this is seen to be good for internal public relations. Nevertheless, some overriding control by the management is desirable, if not essential, to avoid displays of inappropriate or offensive (to some) paintings, photographs and so on.

The sums involved are rarely of any consequence so no cost ranges are given here. In the event of any objets d'art having a high investment value the impact will be felt in the security and insurance cost centres So, care should be taken to ensure that such objects d'art are properly covered by insurance, and that their provenance is sound at the time of acquisition

---

[1] *Wolverton, B.C. (1996) "Eco-friendly houseplants: 50 indoor plants that purify the air", Orion Publishing, USA*

[2] *Stiles J. (1995) "Human responses to interior planting" Unpublished, Oxford Brooks University, Oxford*

Some firms build up collections of objets d'art. The expert purchaser may be an employee, perhaps the facilities manager. However, more likely the organisation will have an art consultant to advise on both the acquisitions and the management of the collection.

Generally prices range from just over £100 to say £25,000; however some organisations may hold items of much greater value. In the UK, the annual art market for the business sector is worth around £400 million. Places for the purchase or hire of objets d'art include art schools and colleges, galleries, show rooms, exhibitions and, increasingly, the internet.

Management services for an art collection may include:

- pricing or bidding negotiations and strategies

- cleaning, repair or restoration

- cataloging, including labelling

- mounting and framing or re-framing

- security, including digitalisation, alarm systems

- lighting and other environmental controls

- insurance

- exhibiting and display controls within the organisation.

5.7.6 LEGISLATION AND STANDARDS

Legislation

Legislation on, for instance, employment practices and Health and Safety in the Workplace must be complied with to protect the occupants and users of facilities as well as gardeners and others working on the interior landscape.

Working at height in large atria or on large specimen plants will require the services of specialist climbers, equipment and insurance by the contractor. The facilities managers have a duty to ensure that working conditions are safe prior to work starting.

Standards

The British Standards Institute (BSI) has often produced standards that are applicable to interior landscaping. (However, countries in Europe, both inside and outside the EU are working with The European Committee for Standardisation (CEN) and International Organisation for Standardisation (ISO) to produce standards that are applicable across borders. To date there are few of these that apply to interior landscaping.)

A particular project may require a risk assessment, eg the installation of large containers involving lifting gear. In such circumstances good working practices will comply with any relevant standards.

A recent initiative by leading interior landscape companies and suppliers of plants has led to the establishment of the European Federation of Interior Landscape Groups (eFIG). This organisation will establish and monitor standards in the same way that BALI does for exterior grounds maintenance.

5.8   ENVIRONMENTAL MANAGEMENT STRATEGY

Introduction

Often the facilities manager will be responsible for, or at least contribute to, the development of the organisation's environmental management strategy and, in particular, its environmental land management plan. Concern for the environment may be reflected in many operational practices, which are dealt with in Chapter 5.6 - Waste Management. This chapter is concerned to introduce the following:

- government concerns, policy and laws on the environment

- as a landowner or tenant, duties toward neighbours and others

- contamination and pollution

- establishment and maintenance of an environmental land management strategy

- investigation, remediation and valuation of contaminated land

- sustainable new development

- environmental working operations

- waste management

- environmental liability insurance

- awareness of the importance of environmental taxation

- environmental accounting and reporting

- environmental records.

5.8.1 ENVIRONMENTAL POLICIES

Within the context of international, worldwide concern for Earth, the government is concerned with a dozen or so major environmental matters and has, or is involved in developing, policies and laws in respect of them.

These concerns embrace most aspects of natural and human existence. They include matters which arise from modern energy consumption and industrial processes, such as: changes in climate, loss of ozone in the stratosphere and rain acidification. They cover matters which arise from these activities and from sea fishing and agricultural production, such as: fish-stock depletion, soil degradation and desertification, biodiversity, tropospheric pollution, waste, chemicals, pollution of inland waterways and contamination of coastal and marine habitats. Also covered are the urban areas and the impact of natural and technology-based disasters.

It may be noted that major EU policy on the environment is covered by over 100 Directives and around 20 Regulations. Policies embrace:

- the environmental impact of large-scale developments

- environmental protection

- environmental taxation (Chapter 11.4)

- waste management (Chapter 5.6)

- eco-management and audit

- sustainable communities, development and buildings.

There are about 60 environmental pressure indicators published by European Commission Directorate General XI (ECDGXI (Environment)), eg transportation and local waste are two of the principal human activities in the EU causing negative pressures on the environment.

As far as the UK is concerned, the government has been or is involved in the developing the evolving legislation and its implementation.

5.8.2 STAKEHOLDERS

It may be borne in mind that the 'stakeholders' in the organisation's environmental management strategy include management and staff, customers and suppliers, neighbours, and the local population, together with any shareholders, funders, insurers and landlords. Indeed, in recent years, the last four stakeholders have become increasingly active in expressing their concerns and expectations. Thus, an ethical investment industry (although broader in concept than environment) has built up in recent years to the extent there is an expectation that companies and other bodies are pro-active towards the environment and are seen to be increasingly transparent in this respect. For instance, environmental reports (see 5.8.12) are increasingly demanded of organisations. Detailed analyses are undertaken by ethical investment analysts and the environment is seen to be within their purview.

Similarly, funders of property development or purchasers of land are concerned that contamination concerns are dealt with prior to advancing or seeking money for projects (this is covered in Chapter 10.4.1). Also, as will be seen in detail in Chapter 3.7, insurance cover is increasingly difficult to obtain without detailed investigation and action. Finally, landlords interested in protecting their property assets (and reputations) will look at tenants with the view to ensuring good environmental management practices.

Generally 'stakeholders' may look for certification of an organisation under ISO 14001, the recognised standard for an environmental management system (EMS) (see 5.8.8 below).

5.8.3 ENVIRONMENTAL LIABILITY

Liability for hurt or damage to neighbours and others arises under the law.

Originally, in England, the remedy for a person hurt as a result of environmental laxity would have been an action under the Common Law. Increasingly, however, statutes have resulted in remedies being available.

In addition, various authorities have powers to take action against polluters, both to remedy problems but also to punish.

Finally, where public bodies possessing powers to create infrastructure cause environmental damage to those nearly remedies may be available, eg in the UK statutory powers are given to pay compensation under the Land Compensation Act 1973 for depreciation of some kind of property due to such matters as smoke, fumes, discharges of solids and artificial lighting.

Apart from liability for actual hurt or damage as described above, liability may arise for the cost of the remediation of contaminated land (see 5.8.5 below). Thus, the polluter of land may be liable but if the polluter cannot be found, another may be liable under a contract, guarantee or warranty. The contract may be in respect of the sale or lease of land or of insurance. Similarly, a previous owner of land may guarantee its state as free of contamination; or perhaps a professional consultant or contractor involved in investigations or remediation has given a warranty or guarantee as to its state.

It follows that when the facilities manager is considering environmental investigation or remediation of property, which is owned, or being acquired, the question of who is liable for any risks should be established at an early stage in the process. Generally, however, the organisation as owner will be liable.

5.8.4 CONTAMINATION AND POLLUTION

Contaminated land is defined in section 78A(2) of the Environmental Protection Act 1990 as

" any land which appears to the local authority in whose area it is situated to be in such condition, by reason of substances in, on or under the land, that:

(a) significant harm is being caused or there is a significant possibility of such harm being caused, or

(b) pollution of controlled waters is being or is likely to be caused".

Contamination of land arises from so-called contaminative uses of that land or other land when one of the following happens:

- a one-off accident, involving the release of pollutants
- pollution due to inadequate or inappropriate working practices involving the use of contaminants
- an 'Act of God' or a force majeure causing pollution
- an act of sabotage or terrorism.

Generally, the one-off accident or force majeure might be expected to occur from time to time. Provided the prospect of such a peril is identified, it may be possible to protect a facility against destruction or at least mitigate the damage, eg not build on a flood plain or at least protect the facility against flood with barriers or levies.

Pollutants are transmitted in the environment by four principal means, namely:

- by air as a gas, as floating particles microbes or viruses
- by carrier, ie human, animal, bird or insect
- by water or another fluid on the surface, underground or as a spray in the air
- by radiation.

Prevention of contamination is, therefore, effected by good operational equipment and practices, including barriers and containers, cleaning and disinfecting at appropriate times, trained and aware management and staff. Also in the event of a happening causing pollution, a rapid response and clean-up operation.

In planning for the event of terrorists using explosives, virus or bacteria to cause a major incident, the facilities manager and other relevant staff should ensure that the organisation's policies and plans fit in with those of the police, fire and medical, and other emergency services, eg under NAIR, ie national arrangements for incidents involving radioactivity.

5.8.5 SUSPECTED CONTAMINATION OF LAND

Any land which has been used in the past may have had contaminative usage, ie one or more uses on it which might, but perhaps not, have led to contamination of it or adjoining land. The buyer or existing owner of such land needs to know whether or not it is contaminated and if it is how might it be treated so as to remove or mitigate any problem. Assessing the condition of contaminated land, doing works and monitoring is "remediation".

The facilities manager may therefore wish to consider whether any land which may be contaminated should be formally identified, whether it poses a high risk, and whether it should be treated. If it is decided to go ahead, they will need to establish who is responsible for dealing with the problem.

Remediation

Then, an investigation and survey should be commissioned by that person. In due course it will lead to a report on the state of the property and the steps which might be taken to treat the land. Where the land is to be re-developed the kind of treatment will most probably depend upon the kind and degree of contamination and the proposed type of development. For instance, the treatment needed for the site of an open car park might well be less than that required for a housing development.

The study will involve desk research and site investigation. The desk research will most probably include some of the following:

- a study of old maps and plans

- a reading of local industrial histories associated with the site

- talks with anyone known to have worked or been interested in the site

- reports and records of any companies who previously owned the site

- medical records or reports (where available).

The on-site investigation including boreholes might include evidence, such as:

- dead or dying vegetation, discoloured surface soils

- the giving off of smoke, vapours or chemical smells

- pools of coloured or 'dead' water, ie without vegetation or animal life

- the discharge of fluids from underground or 'methane' bubbles in water

- sample cores from trial boreholes (later) proved to contain chemicals or other contaminants

- foundations, tanks, buildings and other containers with perhaps suspect solid or fluid contents or structural members

- radiation given off by nuclear material.

Methods

The methods of remediation which might be needed will depend upon such matters as the topography, the level of pollution and the proposed development and use. Remediation might include one or more of:

- removal of all or part of the contaminated strata

- covering or sealing the contaminated ground

- washing or leaching soil

- chemical or microbe (biological) treatment to remove or mitigate the pollution

- vaporising or vacuuming

- planting vegetation which will remove or reduce the contamination.

Subsequent to treatment, it will be necessary to monitor the land for radiation or gaseous or fluid discharges.

As indicated the remediation should be appropriate to the future development and use. In essence, the purpose of the remediation is to break the "pathway" between the "contaminant" and "receptor" - the person, thing and so on which may be harmed, either in a current use or after development.

Historically landfill has been a source of contamination which should have been dealt with prior to any development on the site.

It may be noted that capital allowances at 150 percent of the cost of remediation may be available.

Remediation notices

Procedures exist under the 1990 Act, for a "remediation notices" to be served on one or more appropriate persons concerned with land which is contaminated or is considered to be contaminated by the enforcing authority.

The notices will specify works of remediation which must be undertaken by the appropriate persons. Failure may constitute a criminal offence. However, there is a right of appeal against a remediation notice, under section 78L of the 1990 Act. If the enforcing authority undertakes remediation itself under section 78N of the 1990 Act, it may be able to recover its costs under section 78P - subject to any waiver or reduced cost recovery policy.

Migration of contamination

Mention was made above of the "pathway" from the containment of the receptor. As existing or future stakeholders in a safe local environment, neighbours and purchasers of land should recognise that contamination may migrate from one piece of land to another. In essence, the cost of remediation should be borne by the polluters (unless they can pass the cost to insurers or others). In the event of contamination to a neighbour's property, the polluter is responsible for remediation or face action for damages and remediation notice action by the enforcing authority.

Land Condition Reports (LCR)

There have been moves to establish 'logbooks' for land, namely the Land Condition Reports. The Institute of Environmental Managers and Assessors (IEMA) has promoted the logbooks and has undertaken training and accreditation of individuals who may prepare LCR's.

Valuation

The valuation of land which is or is thought to be contaminated poses the valuer with major problems. Although a valuation by the residual method or discounted cash flow approach may be a starting point, direct comparison is probably a non-starter. However, the actual method needs to be applied after consideration of a number of practical issues and some intangible concerns - the latter probably posing major difficulties in identification and evaluation. They are often grouped as the "stigma" with which contaminated land is perceived.

The practical issues have two aspects, namely:

- the normal valuation constituents that the land would have if unaffected by contamination, ie rents, yields, construction costs, allowances and so on
- those constituents based on the land's contamination.

The former issues are dealt with in Chapter 10.3.1. Here, the latter are explored, albeit briefly. They include such matters as:

- **contaminants:** their nature, location extent and severity; and the cost of investigation
- **receptors:** bearing in mind the development options, who or what may be harmed by the contaminants
- **pathways:** if not dealt with, by what pathways might the contaminants reach the receptors and harm them
- **remediation methods:** for the various development options (and hence receptors), what remediation methods (in terms of cost, time and after-remediation monitoring costs) are needed to protect the receptors.

The brief list indicates, in effect, extra development costs to be "inserted" into the equation of the residual or discounted cash flow appraisal. However, the **intangible concerns** now need to be highlighted as items which call for a degree of judgement very much different from that needed in the valuation of land which is not impaired by contamination. The intangibles include:

- **remediation suitable for the use:** given the options, the valuer needs to assess whether the remediation will be suitable

- **certification, warranties and guarantees:** after remediation what protection does the developer have against receptors being harmed, ie professionals' and contractors' warranties and so on

- **polluters pay:** to what extent, if any, can the cost of remediation be shifted to others, eg the original polluters, previous owners or neighbours (migrating pollution) or their insurers, contractors or professionals

- **funding after remediation:** to what extent will funds be forthcoming for the development option chosen and will buyers or tenants obtain funds in due course.

To some extent, these concerns reflect the uncertainty in the standards for remediation, the possibility of future, post development, remediation, and a continuing perception of risk, perhaps undue, in the minds of those with knowledge of the real or alleged land's history.

5.8.6 SUSTAINABLE NEW DEVELOPMENT

Sustainable issues, eg Local Agenda 21 policies arising from the Rio Summit of 1992, underly much of what has become "sustainable development" in construction.

Sustainable development in the context of facilities relates to the principle that the use of any materials, designs and processes in construction should not impair nature's protective mechanism against environmental deterioration.

The set of principles for sustainable works which are established in an environmental management strategy might be used to brief consultants and contractors during the procurement of new buildings and structures. (See Chapter 7.5.8 on Intelligent Buildings.) The interpretation of the principles into contractual obligations may include the following:

- energy sources for heat, light and power are to be provided from renewable sources, eg solar or wind energy

- water is to be obtained from a sustainable source, eg surface water collected from the land and buildings and previously used water from operations, both cleaned appropriately and recycled

- construction materials to be procured from renewable or sustainable sources, eg timber from managed plantations

- the structure to be oriented to catch daylight, so reducing the use of artificial lighting

- provision of storage facilities, fire-fighting and health and safety equipment appropriate to protect those using the property

- appropriately built-in heat and noise insulation protection

- colour schemes suited to a stress-reducing environment

- "green transport" policies for cycling and cycleways, for car parking and links to public transport systems to reduce or eliminate staff travel by car

- provision of space for waste collection and recycling movements
- provision of hot desking (or teleworking) stations for itinerant staff.

As noted in Chapter 5.4.2, the building regulations require the adoption of energy saving materials, equipment and construction in new building works.

5.8.7 GREEN TRANSPORT PLANNING

The government's focus on green transport policies, eg in PPG13, require developers and occupiers to develop and use large new buildings with a green transport plan (GTP) in place. The facilities manager is likely to be involved in preparing any policies and implementing them. The aim is to increase the use of public transport and reduce dependence on the motor car. An integrated approach for a particular company may include some of the following:

- provision of cycle parking or storage
- changing facilities for those staff who become cyclists, joggers and walkers
- implementation of workplace parking levy policies (see Chapter 11.4.4)
- developing and running car pooling schemes for staff
- offering staff interest-free loans for season tickets or cycles
- providing staff with local travel information
- running a company bus shuttle to the local transport nodes
- introducing flexi-time or working times so that staff can avoid rush hour travel.

5.8.8 ENVIRONMENTAL WORKING OPERATIONS

A company's environmental management policies and practices may be independently assessed and accredited under ISO 14001, the recognised standard for EMS's. Thereafter the EMS must be reviewed. A company may achieve the standard on a site-by-site basis or for the organisation as a whole. Where the organisation already has a good approach to an EMS the process of quality assurance under the standard is likely to be much less expensive.

The environmental needs for the range of operations in all kinds of development, manufacturing, transport, research, power generation and so on are too extensive to be covered in this section. Generally, however, the following might be expected to be included:

- complying with environmental impact assessment (for major developments)
- health and safety clothing and equipment for managers, staff and visitors
- protective guards and other devices to ensure the safety of personnel working machines, processing plant, vehicles and so on
- appropriate storage facilities, spillage barriers and the like for hazardous chemicals, other materials and equipment
- adequate signs, signposting, route marking, vehicle/pedestrian separation devices and the like to ensure safe passage to all who are on site
- staff and visitor induction, training and development in safety and environmental awareness whilst on site
- accommodation, equipment and signs for first aid, accident and emergency services

- trained and developed staff to deal with accidents, fire and other emergencies

- security, staff, devices and equipment to deal with attempted perimeter and facility incursions

- arrangements for recycling of energy, water, waste materials and other substances

- use of pollution-free and noise-free vehicles for the transport of goods and personnel, eg sales staff

- use of ICT, hot-desking or teleworking to reduce space requirements and travel to work patterns (by allowing staff to work at home or away from the office)

- develop noise control policies and practices for machinery, vehicles and processes.

As indicated in the introduction to this chapter, many topics of operational concern for the facilities manager are dealt with elsewhere. See health and safety at work in Chapter 8.2; energy and waste management in Chapters 5.4 and 5.6 respectively; environmental taxation in Chapter 11.4 and insurance in Chapter 3.7.

5.8.9 ENVIRONMENTAL LIABILITY INSURANCE

The importance of insurance to meet claims for or against the facilities manager's employer cannot be stressed. However, whereas general policies covered such claims in the past such cover has generally been unavailable as many insurance companies have withdrawn from this market. Nevertheless there is cover available from specialist companies, albeit under pertinent conditions.

Briefly, limited insurance cover might be forthcoming if a company can show that its house is in order regarding the environmental concerns dealt with above. Thus, the organisation needs to demonstrate that it has achieved such matters as:

- having a transparent environmental management strategy in place

- working procedures and practices are in accord with good environmental standards

- having health, safety, welfare, security and emergency practices to meet appropriate environmental concerns

- any previous contaminative uses have been investigated and appropriate remedial action has been taken

- there are no outstanding environmental claims or actions against the organisation

- any documentation on previous claims, works and so on have been made available to the insurer.

Even so the insurer may well investigate and review the organisation on these matters before making a decision. If the insurer decides to offer cover it is likely to be offered on the basis of a one-off accident cover. In the event of an incident it is likely that the investigating process will be repeated or that the cover will be withdrawn.

As mentioned above, old policies may provide environmental cover, as a first resort it may be worthwhile checking the insurance register as to whether there are any. They may still provide cover!

5.8.10 ENVIRONMENTAL LAND MANAGEMENT STRATEGY

The facilities manager will need to manage within the bounds of the organisation's environmental management strategy and, will perhaps, be responsible for it or for the land and property elements of it.

In effect the strategy will draw together those aspects of sustainable new development, environmental working operations, treatment or remediation of contaminated land and, finally insurance and financial matters which form the principles and, hence, practices to which the organisation meets environmental concerns.

5.8.11 ENVIRONMENTAL TAXATION

The government has increasingly developed taxation policies designed to address pollution and the environment generally. The facilities manager may need to consider the impact that each kind of tax has on different aspects of the way in which the organisation operates.

Examples of environmental taxes are given as follows:

- carbon - energy taxes, eg fuel with a reduced rate of tax on unleaded petrol

- landfill tax, with differential rates of taxes according to the nature of the waste to be dumped

- city centre entry and vehicle parking taxes

- climate change levy

- aggregates levy

- car registration taxes, being varied according to engine capacity.

Chapter 11.4 discusses environmental taxes in much more detail.

It may be noted that environmental "taxation" has a 'carrot and stick' approach designed to penalise polluters and others, and to reward those who take advantage of exemptions and relief, eg by remediation of contaminated land (the cost of which enjoys capital allowances).

5.8.12 ENVIRONMENTAL ACCOUNTING AND REPORTING

For some years many companies have been preparing voluntary accounts and reports on the environmental aspects of their operations. The environmental accounts are usually incorporated into the company's annual report which may describe environmental policies and operations. However, many companies prepare a separate environmental report.

Features of good environmental practice or eco-management, and hence audit and reports, include:

- the setting of environmental objectives in managing operations and acknowledging compliance and failure to comply

- complying (or more) with all legislation, contracts and agreements covering environmental matters

- ensuring staff, contractors, suppliers and others are aware of and comply with environmental matters in company policy

- monitoring and improving environmental activities at all levels including operational sites

- consulting with outside agencies, neighbours and the community's representatives on policies and operations

- ensuring complete information and data which is verifiable, perhaps by independent assessment

- relating operations to financial outcomes and hence the annual financial accounts

- benchmarking to best previous performance, or preferably with any industry or sector schemes

- acknowledging any environmental liabilities and undertaking remedial action.

5.8.13 ENVIRONMENTAL RECORDS

Environmental records should be established and regular monitoring with resultant updating of records be undertaken. The kind of records which may need to be compiled include:

- environmental management plans and practices for control of contaminative uses

- emergency plans, practices and protocols which are at the ready in the event of an accident

- emergency services linkages which have been established and maintained for such as accident

- insurances which are in place with appropriate and adequate cover, together with proof or payment of premiums

- guarantees, warranties and undertakings which were received from third parties, eg vendors of properties

- held guarantees, warranties and undertakings which were given to purchasers, tenants, neighbours or others

- any land condition reports (LCRs).

Section 6

Fitting-out and Alterations

6.1   THE NATURE OF FITTING-OUT AND ALTERATIONS

Introduction

The days when 'fitting-out' meant a touch of paint, a new carpet and building a few more stud partitions are in the distant past for all but the smallest, or most backward or impoverished organisations.

Modern ways of working, following fast on the heels of the ICT revolution - on-going, of course - have focussed attention, as never before, on the importance of the working environment (in terms of flexibility, ergonomics and image) to the success of business operations.

Facilities managers are likely to find that there will be constant demand for change as a result of both 'churn' (see Chapter 4.2) and attempts to increase density of space usage. Ideally, changing the way space looks and functions is to be avoided wherever possible unless positive economic benefits in core business terms are obviously available. This chapter therefore examines the sort of work coming within the category of 'fitting-out and alterations' setting the scene for the economic issues discussed later in this chapter.

6.1.1 DEFINITIONS

Shell, scenery and services

It was Dr. Francis Duffy[1] who first highlighted the comparison between an office building and the theatre stage. He likened the theatre building enclosure to the office building shell, the scenery sets and props to the office interior and furniture, and the services to..... well, the services.

Fitting-out

Fitting-out is the process of creating and/or modifying the 'scenery' and modifying the services in the context of Duffy's analogy.

'Shell-and-core'

Perhaps spurred on by this analogy - and also by the costs of pulling down and replacing unwanted items of scenery and services provided by the developer - some developers in the UK took a leaf out of the American, Japanese and some EU entrepreneurs' books and opted to produce speculative buildings to 'shell-and-core' finish.

This meant that the office interiors to be leased had no finishes to floors, wall or ceilings and the heating, ventilation and air-conditioning (HVAC) and electrical services were capped off at each floor ready for the incoming tenant to do their own thing. This would avoid the waste accompanying the ripping out of the inappropriate finishes and services usually put in at the letting agent's insistence. Most letting agents believe passionately that marketing of a speculative development is severely prejudiced without carpets, false ceilings, wall coverings, fluorescent light fittings and variable air volume (VAV) boxes in place from the outset. In practice, the number of fully fitted speculative offices that could accommodate the incoming tenant's layout without serious, expensive and time-consuming modification is so small as to be statistically insignificant.

However, the shell-and-core developers' posture is not entirely philanthropic; by saving the three to six months needed for their own fit-out stage developers, if lucky

---

[1] DEGW (1980) 'Planning Office Space' Architectural Press, London, UK.

enough to have a tenant at shell-and-core stage, will save the interest charges on the whole development cost for that period which would otherwise have been incurred in the conventional rent-free fitting-out period at commencement of the lease.

Fig. 6.1.A shows the potential benefits to both developer and pre-let tenant of an office building in a shell-and-core deal.

Fig. 6.1.A
Shell-and-core development deal - comparative economics

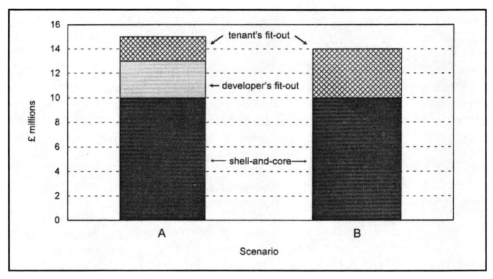

In scenario 'A' the developer provides a finished interior including service outlets which tenants have to modify before putting in their own divisions and 'special areas'.

In scenario 'B' the tenants save money because they do not need to modify the developer's finish and the developer only pays interest on the £6m shell-and-core development costs instead of on £8m during the rent-free period.

The shell-and-core process saves waste of time and money and some developers do offer a shell-and-core deal, but if no tenant is secured at completion of that stage, most of them will progress to developer's fit-out without delay. This rather strange decision is motivated by the belief - fostered by many letting agents - that prospective tenants will be unable to commit to a building without seeing what it will actually look like!

It is hard to conceive that facilities managers of large organisations in the New Millennium would prove to be so incompetent.

These various arrangements and their respective economics are further discussed below.

Alterations and adaptations

These terms can mean the same thing, though they are frequently used together to describe the process whereby the shell, scenery and services designed to be a permanent fixture of the absolute owner's premises are modified to perform their function differently - or to perform a different function.

Examples of alterations are extension, conversion or fundamental improvements to fabric and services. Frequently alterations form part of fitting-out projects but it is very important to separate the costs both for the purposes of accurate estimating from benchmarked comparables and for asset tracking and recovery of capital allowances against tax (where applicable) see Chapter 11.2.5. Alterations to items of 'scenery' such as demountable partitions, carpets and suspended ceilings can influence the recovery of capital allowances whereas holes in walls usually do not.

These terms should be restricted to changes to the basic configuration, appearance or function of a building and its primary service installations.

Inevitably changes to existing users' scenery will tend to get lumped in with this definition so, for the purposes of cost classification protocol, we have adopted the term 'primary alterations' to describe the category which has 'primary fabric alterations' and 'primary services alterations' as sub-categories.

Replacement

For purposes of cost benchmarking replacement of major replacement of components which have reached the end of their useful life-cycle (see Chapter 10.6.A) should not be analysed in 'alterations' but under 'life-cycle replacements'.

Refurbishment

Refurbishment describes the process whereby an existing building is substantially upgraded in quality either through restoration or improvements, or both. The process usually involves works to the fabric and services and is accompanied by increased investment value - unlike fitting-out which becomes a depreciating asset on the balance sheet from day one.

Refurbishment by an owner-occupier may entail both alteration and fitting-out works, in which case it is important to be able to separate these two distinct facets for benchmarking and possibly taxation purposes.

6.1.2 CATEGORIES OF FITTING-OUT

Developer's fit-out

This is often referred to by developers and their agents as Category 'A', 'B', 'C' etc fit-out (depending upon quality and extent of the finished article) and has already been discussed in principle above in the context of alterations to shell-and-core. Basically it comprises carpet/carpet tiles, plastered and decorated walls, a tiled suspended ceiling and heating/air-conditioning outlets and light fittings positioned in presumption of an open-plan layout. Prime locations will normally boast a fully accessible raised floor complete with floor boxes.

Any cellular space, be it for private workplace, meetings or conferences, will have to be provided at the expense of substantial modifications to finishes and services; preservation of privacy and operation of HVAC services at the point of compartmentation usually presents a problem on all perimeters - floors, walls and ceilings.

Open plan

As discussed in Chapter 4.1.2 this term implies an absence of individual rooms. Nevertheless, 'definable space' is acknowledged in most open plan solutions with screens and/or storage cabinets demarcating ownership. In some space 'management' regimes users are allowed to build up their own 'defence' but the inherent unstructured nature of such regimes leaves them prey to attack from the rigours of premises economics.

100% open plan offices are a rarity, although the open plan concept is sufficiently accepted as to be conventional for large parts of many organisations' premises. In economic terms much of the space saved at the open plan workplace is often re-allocated to meeting areas, which often need to be cellular. Provided the provision of meeting areas is adequate such an arrangement may produce premises cost savings without prejudicing the efficiency and effectiveness of meeting arrangements.

The success of an open-planned working environment is mainly dependent on the furniture system adopted. In many cases the cost of a successful furniture system may outweigh the savings in partitioning costs; however, the cost-inefficiency inherent in cellular space plans normally means that, on a cost per capita basis, the more open plan layout is more cost-efficient taking all the premises costs into consideration.

It should be noted, however, that there is no implication here that use of space in this **cost-efficient** way is necessarily more **cost-effective** in terms of value to the core business. As has been pointed out more than once in this text 'nothing is cheap if it is not what you want!'

Cellular layout

Generally, 100% cellular layouts are now an anachronism in most organisations, restricted to small firms working out of small premises. Modern cellular solutions are based on the concept of demountable partitions; these systems are much more expensive than builders' partitions which are actually just as demountable (in a low-tech and clumsy way) as their highly-engineered cousins, and rarely get moved anyway.

Part open/part cellular

This is the most common space-use strategy, usually based on open plan for clerical workers - or possibly money or share dealers working in very close proximity for cultural (surely not productivity!) reasons. Where tenants go into a previously fitted-out space the cost of providing this part-and-part accommodation is usually quite expensive. Not least of the problems is adapting the HVAC systems to the new layout.

Older buildings with perimeter induction air-conditioning cannot cope with cooling loads beyond the originally planned room-depth so partial de-cellularisation will become costly in respect of air-conditioning the open areas. On the other hand, VAV boxes positioned evenly for open plan will require major reconfiguration or supplementation to ensure equivalent comfort in the newly created cellular spaces; lighting and switching points may also turn out to be inconveniently placed relative to the required room and partition layout.

Non-territorial

The concept of shared workstations allied to enhanced common support areas was touched on briefly in Chapter 4.1.6. Clearly the balance of the facility as between general and special areas changes with shared workstations. The dramatic increase in density of space use more than compensates for the cost of this change. This cost may include higher quality fittings than previously as an inducement to staff to accept the new working environment.

6.1.3 SPECIAL AREAS

This term is used to define any part of the fitting-out which is not to general areas and includes such uses as:

- reception
- post room
- dining
- kitchen
- conference room
- computer room
- library
- central storage.

Further information on the cost of fitting-out special areas is given in Chapter 6.2.2.

6.2 FITTING-OUT COSTS

Introduction

The cost of fitting-out, when amortised over its normal life, can absorb up to 25% of the premises operating budget although it is unlikely to amount to more than about 1% of an organisation's total revenue expenditure. This chapter examines different ways of expressing this cost and the key factors that determine the bottom line figure.

6.2.1 FITTING-OUT COSTS IN CONTEXT

Fitting-out costs over time

Although fitting-out qualifies as capital rather than revenue expenditure, and the value of the work becomes a business asset on the balance sheet, the regularity of the expenditure and/or the rapid rate of depreciation means that many organisations annualise the costs for benchmarking purposes.

Typically, large commercial organisations refit their whole space on average every five years, although not necessarily all at one time. Those with excessive 'churn' (see Chapter 4.2) without a planning strategy to handle it will find the fitting-out cycle rather shorter than five years; those who do not need to refit (other than for cosmetic purposes) or cannot afford to do so may sometimes have to prolong the life of a fit-out on economic grounds. One way of 'annualising' the capital costs is to calculate a loan-purchase rate for the given period. In Fig.6.2.A a typical range of fitting-out costs is shown at a mortgage rate of 10% over five years and as a straight-line depreciation over the same period for balance sheet purposes.

Fig. 6.2.A
Alternative methods of expressing fitting-out costs in annual equivalent terms

Fitting-out costs (including fees) [1]	Pre-tax cost of 5-year 10% mortgage	Straight line depreciation over 5-years
£ per sq m NIA	£ pa	£ pa
480	126	96
640	170	128
800	211	160
[1] Excludes VAT, and other taxes		

Given the vagaries of interest rates it is best to use the straight line approach for benchmarking purposes with the life of the fit-outs being recorded as a key performance indicator as well as a major resource driver.

Fig.6.2.B (over the page) takes the highest and middle of the annual equivalent figures in Fig. 6.2.A and expresses them in the context of city centre and provincial premises costs respectively.

Clearly the fitting-out expenditure becomes a more significant component as rental levels become lower, particularly in the prestige buildings where standards of scenery tends to follow international, rather than regional, design and specification levels.

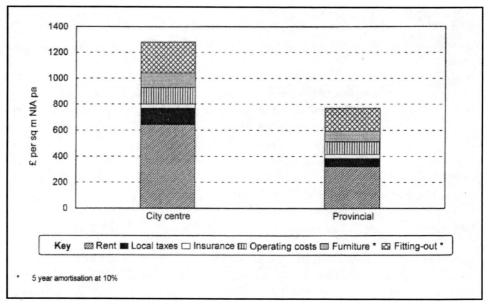

Fig. 6.2.B
Fitting-out costs in the context of premises costs pa

The cost drivers

As well as the local cost influences incorporated in the above index there are many other factors which influence the cost of a fitting-out project, including:

- quality

- scope

- performance requirements

- cost control, ie procurement budgetary control and value engineering

- nature and configuration of the base building

- extent of stripping out and demolition

- 'buildability'

- market conditions

- accessibility

- speed

- extent of cellularisation

- extent of 'special areas'.

6.2.2 GENERAL OFFICE AREAS

Fit-out from shell-and-core

Picking up from the general principles of premises economics introduced in Chapter 6.1. Fig. 6.2.C (over the page) shows the typical costs resulting from a fit-out of an office building involving modifications to the so-called 'developer's finish' for two layouts involving significantly different degrees of compartmentation. Compare this with a fit-out from 'shell-and-core' (Fig. 6.2.D, over the page) where the higher costs of the fit-out as carried out by (or on behalf of) the tenant would be abated by the developer's allowance for the finishes as a contribution to the deal. It should be noted that most developers insist on making a cash contribution rather than discounting the rent; this is because of the effect of the rental level on the investment value as well as the impact on market rents generally.

Fig. 6.2.C
Fitting-out general office areas from developer's finish - average costs for 10,000 sq m (NIA) building

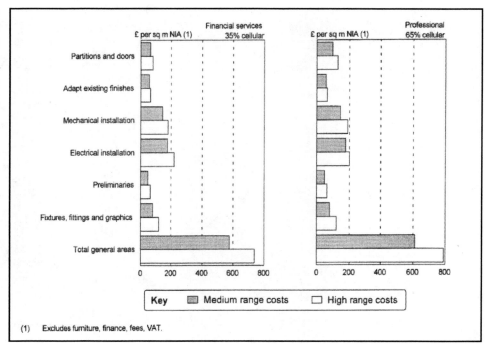

Fig. 6.2.D
Fitting-out general office areas from 'shell-and-core' - average costs for 10,000 sq m (NIA) building

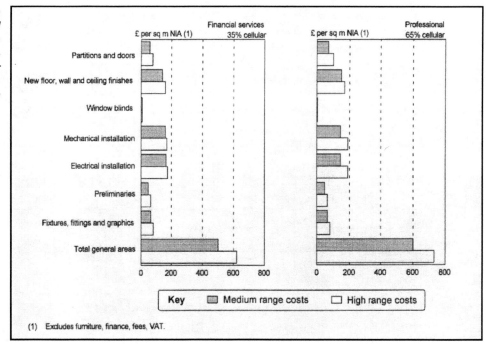

Where the developer does make a cash contribution to the tenant's fit-out the tenant should make sure the developer pays against work-in-progress, thus saving, in this example, maybe £60,000 in interest charges on the finishing works compared with a lump sum payment received on completion.

Open plan v cellular layout

In the examples above the overall costs of fitting-out the less cellular option is marginally cheaper. However the true economies are in the amount of space used in the largely open plan option where savings of up to 30% in space per capita will be the critical factor. A worked example of this thesis is given at Fig. 6.2.E (over the page) which also considers the total premises cost implications of the 35% and 65% cellular options - taking the fit-out from developer's finish.

Fig. 6.2.E
Average premises costs per capita pa for varying degrees of open-plan layout

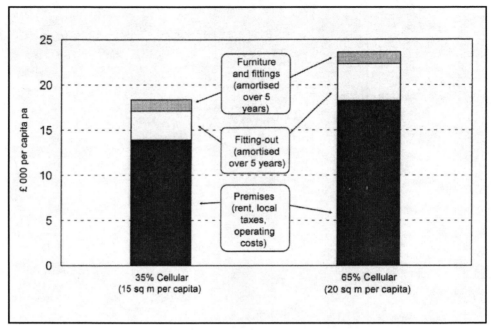

Capital allowances may be allowable on demountable partitions to offset against tax. In such a tax regime an organisation bent on a cellular solution might well consider the 'builder's option'; a notional comparison of the two alternatives, after tax and with and without capital allowances, is given at Fig. 6.2.F.

Fig. 6.2.F
Capital cost comparison of fixed and de-mountable partitions where business tax relief is available

Specification	Quantity	Unit rate £ / sq m	Total before tax relief (1) £	NPV (2) of relief through capital allowances (3) (4) £	Total net of discounted tax relief £
Metal panel de-mountable partitions	1,000	150	150,000	(38,000)	112,000
Fixed stud partitions faced with plasterboard and decorated	1,000	65	65,000	Nil	65,000

(1) Excluding: Fees, VAT, finance, periodic relocation costs, cleaning.

(2) See Chapters 2.2 and 10.4 for explanation of discounted cash flow. A 10% discount was used.

(3) May not be recoverable unless regularly moved – see Chapter 11.2.5.

(4) Assumes adequate taxable profits available and corporation tax at 30%.

It should be noted how the large cost differential, even if tax relief is available, clearly goes nowhere near justification of the demountable solution in terms of savings in use, unless only a short life is envisaged for the fitting-out layout.

Fitting-out special areas

Fig. 6.2.G
Fitting-out to special areas - typical average costs

Function	Fitted-out area
	£ / sq m [1]
Kitchen	2,060
Dining	440 – 705
Board room	1,765 – 2,650
Conference	440 – 705
Computer room	1,470
Reception	1,765
Vending	1,470
Post room	440 – 880
[1] Excludes VAT, fees, loose furniture. Area in sq m as fitted-out.	

Fig. 6.2.G considers the cost of fitting-out 'special' areas including support areas such as reception and restaurants, in an existing building. In the 'non-territorial' office planning strategies particular attention is usually paid to the common areas. For instance some of the meeting areas may take the form of pleasantly furnished coffee lounges and the reception area needs to be highly efficient as well as containing comfortable emergency 'waiting' accommodation for the occasional over-subscription of workplaces.

Common support may be as much as 10% to 20% of the total space to be fitted-out. So, where the fitting-out costs of the support space are significantly higher than the general areas, such as in the 'non-territorial' types of space regime, the impact on the overall cost of fitting-out per unit of floor area may be significant although on a per capita basis it will be subsumed within the overall premises cost-efficiency.

Since common support areas tend not be changed around as often as the general areas, they may have a longer life-cycle.

6.3   PROCURING THE PROJECT

Introduction

In the great majority of cases the sort of capital projects which come under the day-to-day direction of the facilities manager come into the category of fitting-out and/or alterations. For this reason the procurement of projects is dealt with in this chapter rather than in Section 10 (The Development Option) which is predominantly concerned with new works and total refurbishment.

However, the principles and procedures described here are totally relevant to any project of significance and readers are directed here from Section 10 (The Development Option) in respect of all aspects of project procurement.

6.3.1 THE PROJECT PROCUREMENT PROCESS

Objectives, responsibilities and project management

The facilities manager's task is to deliver up fitted-out space to accommodate the business requirements within a value-managed framework.

A major part of the procurement process will therefore be to ensure that the principles of value management described in Chapter 2.2 are enshrined therein. In particular, the use of the 'Value Tree' analysis at pre-briefing stage will be critical in ensuring that value for money gets a head-start in the process.

The objectives will encompass the intentions regarding quality, cost and time and the degree of risk exposure which is acceptable for each aspect of the project.

The principles of project management and the tools available for the job are considered in detail in Chapter 2.8. The decision as to whether or not the facilities manager handles or out-sources the project management should depend on the scale of the project and the experience of the in-house team.

Whoever acts personally as the project manager is not an issue with regard to the facilities managers' ultimate responsibility for their projects. If they undertake project management themselves there is an assumption of responsibility and a presumption of competence; if they out-source the function they will be responsible for the selection of the project manager, agreeing the brief and monitoring performance.

EU procurement rules

Public sector projects ie, works by public authorities and utilities, are governed by strict EU rules in terms of opportunities to bid for works above a certain size. These rules require projects to be advertised in the OJEC (Supplement to the Official Journal of the European Communities) and only contractors and consultants applying under these rules can be considered for selection.

Contracts covered by the rules include:

- works contracts
- works concession contracts
- standardised works contracts
- supply contracts
- standardised service contracts.

To comply with the rules it is first necessary to establish the type of contract to be awarded before adopting the appropriate procedure.

For works, services and supply contracts there are three types of procedure:

- open

- restricted

- regulated.

In the case of PFI/PPP projects a 'competitive negotiated procedure' is acceptable, although there is some controversy currently about the validity of the interpretation of this procedure, especially in the UK.

The other key area in EU procurement terms is the issue of 'framework agreements'. Framework agreements establish the business terms for purchasing one or more goods/services without prescribing the exact quantities. They are particularly relevant to bulk or repeated purchase of standard goods or services and can save a lot of time and resources in the purchasing process.

Framework transactions within the EU regulations can, exceptionally, be with one supplier, but normally it will only be permitted - and be economically sensible - if more than one supplier is included.

The regulations are far too complex to discuss in detail here. An excellent reference source is the EU procurement web-site - www.simap.eu.int

Procurement and cost control

Effective procurement is one of the three facets of cost control described in Chapter 2.3.2. Its place in the trinity is shown in Fig. 6.3.A. It should be noted that the term 'project' as used here relates to the whole process from inception to completion; a fitting-out project embraces a number of stand-alone procurement procedures.

Fig. 6.3.A
Competitive procurement as one facet of cost control

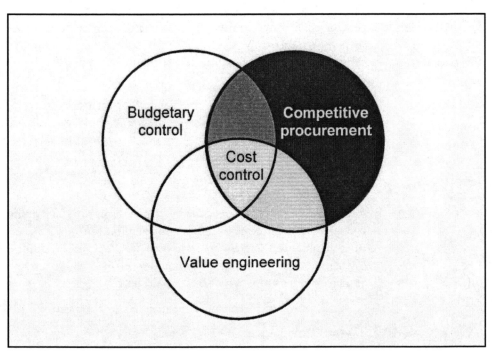

The stages of project procurement

The stages of project procurement are:

- feasibility study

- briefing

- procuring the design

- procuring the works

- procuring the furniture (where appropriate).

Fitting-out projects involve both design and construction; often the two processes are the responsibility of one person or company, but the main design work is most commonly the responsibility of an interior designer or architect independent of the principal constructor.

At an early point in the consideration of the process it is necessary to review the stage at which the designer should be introduced and the manner of their appointment. Since the designer should be expected to contribute to the feasibility and briefing process there is often a conflict where the intention is to adopt a 'single-point-of-responsibility' (design-and-build) route of procurement (see further discussion on the pros and cons of this route in 6.3.4).

The need for this early involvement at concept stage means that a design-and-construct contractor cannot be selected competitively for this work on the basis of a finite scheme. There are two ways around this: the first is to involve an independent designer at the briefing stage who may or may not be novated to (their contract assigned to) the contractor at a later stage; the second is to select the design-and-construct contractor by means of a preliminary 'two-stage' tendering process which will determine the relative design ability and competitiveness of the companies offering their services and incorporate a mechanism for ensuring that the level of quality and competitiveness established in the first-stage bid flows through into the pricing of the work and its final design and specification.

6.3.2 THE FEASIBILITY STUDY

The objective

The feasibility study is the process whereby changes in the organisation's space requirements are reviewed in the context of the available space (existing or new) and potential solutions. In its most fundamental form it will be the subject of a detailed value management study involving a 'Value Tree' as described in Chapter 2.2 - Value Management (see Fig. 2.2.D); it will also embrace all the accommodation options including those involving total or partial relocation (see Chapters 9.1.3 and 10.2.2). However, here the procurement process is discussed from the project brief stage, ie the point at which the fitting-out strategy has been finalised and agreed and the location and extent of the works identified.

The feasibility study must consider a sufficient number of generic solutions in terms of planning and quality together with their approximate costs, time-scales, risks and constraints to ensure that management is given the opportunity to make a well-considered decision with respect to formulating the design brief.

The study team

Ideally, the team assembled for the feasibility study will include:

- the facilities manager

- a space planner

- a designer

- a cost consultant

- structural, mechanical and electrical and other engineers (as required).

Subject to the caveat above regarding design-and-build appointments, the team for the study should ideally be the same team that will undertake the project. This will avoid the dangers of key points in the concept falling down the 'hole-in-the-middle' and also the loss of time and productivity resulting from a re-learning curve facing a new team.

It is usual to reimburse consultants on a time-charge or lump sum fee. In hard times, some consultants may work this stage for nothing in anticipation of being instructed to undertake any project which emerges. However, since it is at this stage that all the major influencing issues are explored and determined it is far better to pay consultants something - not necessarily a full fee, but enough to encourage them to approach the study seriously in the knowledge that some or all of the cost of their time is being recovered.

On large feasibility studies consultants should always be paid a full fee for their services. Popular idioms such as 'paying peanuts and getting monkeys' owe their existence not to disillusioned consultants but to the bitter experience of clients whose projects have failed because the feasibility stage was wrongly addressed and inadequately resourced.

The appraisal process

It may be that the generic layout is pre-determined by the organisation's premises policy, in which case it should only be necessary to carry out a quick check on any constraints which may prejudice a satisfactory design solution. For example, if a partly cellular layout is to be the basis of the scheme the mechanical and electrical engineer should check that there are no major problems including the nature and location of cooling system components or floor access boxes. Any performance problems such as acoustic transfer above ceilings or below floors should also be investigated. A quick check-over by the cost consultant either confirming previously predicted cost levels or identifying potential sources of extra expense will then enable the decision to be taken.

If constraints surrounding a particular design solution do pose a risk to cost then it is very important that the value engineering process (see Chapter 2.3.3 and below at 6.3.7) should be fully incorporated in the evaluation of more cost-effective solutions. The facilities manager should take a lateral view of the original brief and its potential design (even locational) solutions so as not to impede the application of value-management principles. The importance of commencing the value engineering process at this stage is stressed in Fig. 6.3.B which shows all the stages of financial control.

Fig. 6.3.B
Stages of cost control in building projects

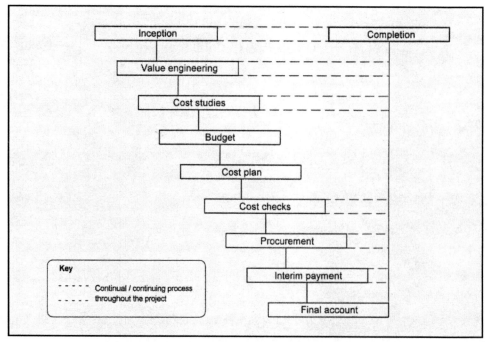

The cost estimate may be on a cost per sq m of the fitted-out area or, if there are a number of alternative layouts, estimates may require more detailed measurement and synthesis of contractor's prices (see below). It may not be necessary for the designer to plan floors in detail for each generic solution being considered, provided that the intentions are sufficiently clear for the facilities manager, engineers and cost consultant to conceptualise and report on the likely impact in the context of their own specialist disciplines.

The importance of having team members who can think conceptually cannot be over-stated; too often time and resources are frittered away as a result of detailed layouts being prepared only to be discarded on account of constraints which might easily have been foreseen (maybe even being ingeniously overcome) by professionals of the right calibre and experience. A truly conceptually-competent team should be able to carry out much of the feasibility study without any drawings whatsoever.

It is however important to note that in the absence of decennial insurance, discussed below in 6.3.5, team members often feel at risk when volunteering good ideas in a field in which they possess a sound working knowledge but do not hold insurance cover against professional negligence.

Many designers prefer to 'go away on their boat for a weekend' to produce the early schematics. However, this practice denies the opportunity for any creative contribution in terms of building economics, services or structure from the other specialists before the designer has become emotionally and irretrievably wedded to the solution he or she believes is 'right'! Getting the constraints and potential economics on the table at the outset for all to see is the only way to ensure that the feasibility study achieves its main objectives, ie to produce viable solutions capable of optimisation in terms of both performance and cost.

6.3.3 BRIEFING

The contents of the brief

As previously implied there are two types of brief - the project brief and the design brief.

Project brief: it comes from the core management, ideally as part of a pre-briefing 'Value Tree' analysis (see Chapter 2.2.5) carried out in consultation with their facilities manager in the capacity of 'intelligent client'. It identifies the problem to be addressed and may have been the result of a conceptual feasibility study. It will dictate the policy in terms of who, where and how; it may also pre determine how much by way of space and cost, and the generic planning style to be tested; in other situations these detailed considerations may be left to development of the design brief.

Design brief: it will confirm the requirements of the management brief and will also be concerned with such issues as quality of finishes, space norms or guidelines, workplace configuration, locations and extent of ancillary facilities such as storage and meeting spaces, and any special provisions of common support (see Chapter 4.1.2 for definitions of space use). The design brief will contain any policy on such items as signs and graphics, colour schemes, furniture systems and ICT. together with any critical guidelines emerging from the feasibility study which informs it. Usually there will be a target cost although sometimes the brief and the project programme will allow for a fully costed completed design solution without pre-determining cost levels; this is however a rather out-moded approach which usually evidences a faulty or non-existent feasibility study and is unlikely to generate a value engineered solution.

The importance of the brief

Having a properly documented brief is essential to a successful project. Too often the designer is left to make decisions about the client's requirements - a sure sign of sloppy or non-existent project management and also a guarantee that the designer's chosen solutions will be unchallenged; this often induces and encourages the 'weekend-on-the-boat' design syndrome discussed above, which is fatal to the value engineering process.

Of course, the design team will have to interpret - probably improve - the brief but they should not have to write it by default.

Performance specification

It would be most unusual to find a design brief which specified the client's functional performance requirements with such precision that all the design team had to do was to choose layouts, materials and systems which, efficiently integrated, would easily achieve the required efficiency.

Nevertheless, it should be possible for the facilities manager to define their major requirements in terms of physical performance characteristics, eg type, quality and quantity of space, acoustics, temperature, stability and durability, so as to challenge the design team to find cost-effective value engineered solutions. Whilst this may be asking a lot from the occasional user of the construction/shop-fitting industry the industry's regular customers really ought to hone down their performance requirements to non-product-specific specifications to encourage creative and cost-effective solutions.

Life-cycle implications

The brief must have regard to the expected life of the particular fit-out and ensure that materials chosen properly reflect this requirement. Most commonly designers over-specify materials and furniture, having insufficient regard to the realities of modern building usage.

A way to avoid this wastage, and also to encourage designers and facilities managers to consider the consequential effects of design and specification decisions, is to incorporate in the brief a set of cost benchmarks for all the operating cost centres. This forces the design team to demonstrate the impact of their proposals in respect of each building cost centre on these running cost targets. Fig. 6.3.C (over the page) shows a low-cost fitting-out example of this technique and is similar in principle to the new building example of a life-cycle cost plan given in Chapter 10.6.5. The point of the exercise is not so much to reduce running costs per se (although that is obviously a worthy goal) but more to ensure that the impact of the choice of materials and services on facilities management is properly thought through at the early stages of design thereby helping to avoid impractical solutions.

By testing alternative components and design in each cost centre optimum solutions will emerge ensuring high cost-efficiency in a whole-life - as well as simply capital cost - viewpoint. Cost-effectiveness, however, will depend upon the impact of each solution on functional performance requirements.

6.3.4 PROCURING THE DESIGN TEAM

Selecting the vehicle - the options

The facilities manager must decide from the outset the process by which to procure the fit-out design. In all but the most minor alterations an experienced, qualified designer should be engaged for the project; the only decisions will then be with regard to the vehicle by which the design is delivered.

Unless suitable designers are on the establishment the design will have to be outsourced.

The homes in which designers might then be found are:

Consultancies:

- architects
- interior designers
- space planners
- multi-disciplinary professional practices.

Contractors:

- design and build companies
- furniture suppliers.

Fig. 6.3.C
Life-cycle cost
analysis - low cost
fitting-out
components
(before tax)

Cost centre	Capital cost £ / sq m NIA	Annual costs per sq m NIA				
		Amortised capital cost over 5 years @ 10% £	Cleaning £	Maintenance £	Energy £	Total £
Partitions and doors	44.80	16.31	0.56	2.24	0	19.11
Wall finishes	16.80	6.12	2.24	1.12	0	9.48
Floor finishes	22.40	8.16	4.48	1.12	0	13.76
Ceiling finishes	22.40	8.16	1.12	1.12	0	10.40
Window blinds	11.20	4.07	0.28	0.11	0	4.46
Adapt HVAC	56.00	20.38	0	11.20	7.84	39.42
Lighting	33.60	12.23	1.12	5.60	4.48	23.43
Adapt power supplies	22.40	8.16	0	2.24	2.24	12.64
Fixtures, fittings and graphics	28.00	10.19	0	1.12	0	11.31
Builder's work and preliminaries	22.40	8.16	0	0	0	8.16
Total	280.00	101.94	9.80	25.87	14.56	152.17

Contractor design - pros and cons

Building contractors undertaking design services may have their own in-house specialists - usual where design-and-construct is a major feature of their business - or may engage consultants on a project-by-project basis; sometimes the client's scheme designer may be novated (the benefit of their contract passed across) to the contractor when the design-and-construct contract is struck.

The pros or cons of the design-and-build approach are discussed below. It is sufficient here to say that a client is entitled to, and has no reason not to, obtain the services of good designers of their choice without paying a premium. 'In-house' architects, however talented individually, may suffer from lack of design ambition and innovation due to their anonymity; they may also miss the cross-fertilisation of ideas which should inform their independent counterparts who are likely to be working across a broader spectrum of clients and building types.

While it would be wrong to be too categorical in this respect, the facilities manager should take extra care to explore the experience, credentials and track record of any design team put forward by a contractor. That is not to say that consultants should not be vetted just as thoroughly, only that control over the contractor's designer will be one step removed and therefore defence of quality will be more dependent on the integrity of both the designer and the employing contractor.

The independent or in-house designer will owe allegiance to the client and will also probably be the quasi-arbitrator for the works contract. Although in a perfect world this should not be a consideration the client will probably take some comfort from the fact that such a designer has the building employer's interests primarily to heart when matters of quality, cost and time are at risk.

There are, nevertheless, powerful arguments in favour of design-and-construct, eg it is an important feature of the Japanese construction industry which is perceived to be rather more efficient. The principal driver of the cause lies in the perception in some quarters that designers need to be controlled, particularly with regards to the consequences of their supposed economic naivete, and that the contractor is best placed to apply the necessary discipline.

Certainly a much closer collaboration between designer and builder, whatever the vehicle, is highly desirable.

Better project management encouraging the full introduction of value engineering activity from the earliest stages should bring its rewards without the client necessarily sacrificing control of the design process; the application of decennial insurance - discussed below - can bring independent companies together with all the positive benefits promoted by the pure design/build lobby.

Selecting the team

Choice of designer has already been considered from the point of view of their contractual status. The only other considerations are the background and qualifications most appropriate to the project. As with all the consultants this must be a key feature of the selection process to be fully considered alongside the fee bid.

Architect: few individual architects can offer a portfolio of projects embracing building design, interior design and space planning although some of the larger firms may have a reasonable range of experience across the board.

At this time, and since forever, architects have conventionally been pre-occupied with the exterior of buildings with varying degrees of detriment to the usefulness of the buildings to the occupiers. This is the result of the almost universal treatment of architecture as one of the liberal arts for educational purposes. This process tends to produce 'prima donna' architects whose reputation for distinctive design belies a relative lack of interest in clients' ergonomic requirements; this (fortunately obsolescent) band of individuals has to be avoided by facilities managers at all costs, not least because of the resistance to change or compromise which normally accompanies their utter belief in their self-glorifying design solutions.

Interior designers: by dint of qualification, or those few qualified architects who have moved into that field, are more likely to understand the client's fitting-out brief and the particular sector of the construction industry which will deliver it up in its built form. They may be less well versed in the management of the design process, building services, costs, and contract procedure than 'regular' architects which means that independent professional project management can have an important bearing on the outcome.

Interior designers also have a propensity to say what they want rather than specify or even draw it, and the shop-fitting industry which responds to them is geared up to accommodate this style of practice. Not surprisingly such an approach can play havoc with cost control; a good specialist cost consultant familiar with the fast-track financial control necessitated by the employment of such designers - and the nature of most fitting-out projects - will be a major bonus to the team.

Mechanical and electrical engineers: can usually adapt from new building to fitting-out work without adverse effects; their knowledge of life-cycle implications of mechanical and electrical design should be thoroughly explored by the project manager in advance of appointment. Wherever possible the estimated costs should be produced by an appropriately skilled cost consultant in consultation with the engineer: some services engineers have a reasonable knowledge of costs, especially if they have worked for contractors and their input can be valuable. Equally, a lot of cost consultants are weak on mechanical and electrical services costs and design principles; if one such cost consultant should slip into the team by default the engineer's ability or otherwise to help may prove critical to the financial outcome.

Cost consultant: the cost consultant should always be independently appointed, even if nominated by the designer, as is not infrequent. Teams of designers and cost consultants who have worked together regularly can often bring a smoothness to a project which is missing from ad hoc teams set up for specific one-off projects. If the project manager is satisfied that such an established team will benefit the project, it is well worth having the cost consultant appointed direct. The cost consultant should continue to wear a 'team hat' and report through the designer - this is essential to avoid misinterpretation of cost reports - but is still available to give independent cost advice on design proposals direct to the project manager if required.

Most important of all, the project team must really be a team. The project manager must take great care in their selection so as not only to get the calibre of professionals needed to do the job, but also the personalities which will determine whether or not the unit will function efficiently.

It is people, rather than systems or firms, which make or break any project.

Contract arrangements

Many professional consultants are quite happy to enter into a contract based on a simple exchange of letters. Professional institutions usually recommend standard conditions of engagement which may help to clarify the extent of services being offered and any rights and liabilities of the parties. The design-and-build contracts will nearly always be based on a formal document.

In the event, if things go wrong the most important thing is not who pays for them - which is what most formal contracts are about - but how to rectify the problems before they do irrevocable damage. This will probably be down to people and personalities as much as any written clauses, so carefully choosing players who know the rules and how to observe them will be more likely to influence the result beneficially than relying upon the rule book to control a nondescript mis-assortment of inadequately experienced professionals.

Reimbursement for consultancy services

Until recent years some of the professional bodies published fee scales which were mandatory for their members; serious breaches of the code could result in a formal warning or even expulsion. Where these fee scales still exist they are only a point of reference, sometimes as a basis from which discounts are bid or negotiated. If these scales are used as a discount base it is very important to clarify whether or not the discounted fee relates to all the services listed, and to the full service in respect of each component of the service offered.

Sometimes fees are bid on a percentage of the cost of the works, enabling the consultant to claw back the extra costs of administering post-contract changes to the scheme (presuming that these will be net extras to the building contract price); that is fine, but only if it is the client who has changed their mind, not the designer. A more usual method these days is the lump sum related to a specific project brief. This leaves the consultant free to claim extra costs for their client's scope changes and vice-versa. The lump sums may be built up from a resource schedule with related time-charges and, exceptionally, clients may accept open-ended time-charges where the scope of work is indeterminable at the outset. This is not usual with fitting-out projects unless accompanied by extensive refurbishment of old buildings.

Payments are either at pre-agreed stages or, more commonly in these hard economic times, on a regular monthly or bi-monthly basis, again on a pre-set schedule.

The design component of design-and-build is normally subsumed into the cost of works and paid monthly as part of valuations of the fitting-out works in progress. The VAT implications of such arrangements do, however, need to be carefully assessed - Chapter 11.5 refers.

6.3.5 PROCURING THE WORKS

Selecting the procurement route

As for getting the works built, the employer has only two generic contract choices:

- lump sum

- cost reimbursement.

However, within these categories there is a bewildering variety of bidding procedures and contract arrangements which are now discussed in detail.

It is important to distinguish between the processes of obtaining bids for the work and the execution of the contract under which they will be built.

Lump sum contracts

As the name implies a 'lump sum' contract is where there is a definite amount of consideration for executing a properly defined scope of works. The process normally acknowledges adjustments to the lump sum for a variety of changed circumstances such as revisions to the specification. The value of such changes is usually calculated by the client's agent by reference to a schedule of prices incorporated in the contract; however, in some countries the builder 'quotes' against the variation either for acceptance prior to execution or for negotiation at a later date.

Traditionally for major building works in some countries lump sum contracts based on either the industry's standard forms or some locally acceptable format were bid in open competition. Any builder could get hold of a copy of the bid documents - possibly drawings and schedules of quantities or simply specification and drawings - and put in a bid which, if accepted, would be the contract price. This system implied two conditions, ie independent design and adequate definition of the work to be built (see Fig. 6.3.D, over the page).

The quantity surveyor role is frequently formalised under the contract wherein the 'bill of quantities' may be a contract document.

It is becoming increasingly common for the independent cost consultancy facet of the quantity surveyor's role to be commissioned by clients as an 'insurance' policy against profligate design and/or over-commercially oriented contractors.

Fig. 6.3.D
Traditional lump sum contract with independent design

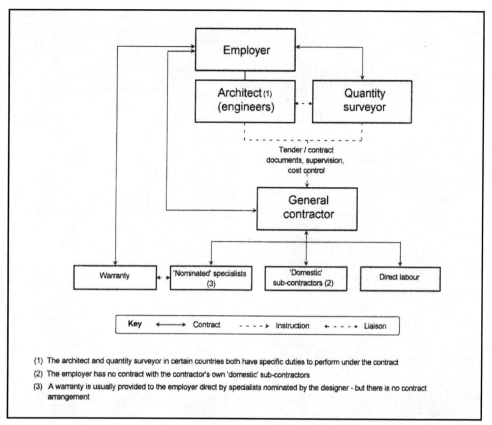

(1) The architect and quantity surveyor in certain countries both have specific duties to perform under the contract

(2) The employer has no contract with the contractor's own 'domestic' sub-contractors

(3) A warranty is usually provided to the employer direct by specialists nominated by the designer - but there is no contract arrangement

On construction management projects the cost control is often carried out by the construction manager; in the case of the larger CM projects employers sometimes appoint an independent quantity surveyor to overview this function.

Where bills of quantities are available the prices for measured work may become contract rates for adjusting the contract sum for any changes in design or specification. In some contracts, if the quantities are found to be wrong post-contract the contract sum may be revised following corrected measurement.

Of course, the designers rarely complete the contract drawings on time so the quantity surveyors or estimators often make up the specification, measure it in the bills of quantities and hope the cost of the eventual detailing will be covered by the price for the hypothetical measured work. In practice, there is the danger that if the final detail is more expensive than the quantity surveyors envisaged the contractor will claim extra, whereas if it is cheaper the matter may be left to lie quietly.

A bill of quantities or specification may contain provisional sums for work not yet designed - the costs are calculated post-contract in accordance with the method prescribed; the contract lump sum is then adjusted for the difference, plus or minus. Works by specialists such as air-conditioning or proprietary fittings are often included in the contract as prime cost (pc) sums to be expended in due course against a specialist (nominated) sub-contractor's quotation - the successful sub-contractor being contracted to the main contractor following the architect's instruction to accept the bid.

Standard building contracts have never been particularly popular for fitting-out works which at one time were often carried out by shopfitting contractors on a simple lump sum basis. However, with the advent of a much greater degree of sophistication and technology in fitting-out works the standard forms have come to be used much more frequently, with general contractors taking over from the shopfitters.

A new type of lump sum contract based on a loosely specified 'scope of works' has entered the picture via international construction managers (see below). This has been adopted by some developers to replace the standard industry versions which they deemed to be unfairly biased against the employers. Although 'scope' contracts are not common in fitting-out works the concept of the 'scope' contract has been used in some larger construction management projects. The object is to invite the contractor (main or trade) to estimate the cost of carrying out all the works indicated and implied by the designer's output performance brief. In fact, it is to some extent the extension of the concept of performance specification which has been used for many years to obtain lump sum bids for specialist works requiring contractor's design and guarantee.

Bidding for lump sum works can be by:

- open bidding

- selected list bidding

- straight negotiation

- competitive negotiation / two stage bidding.

Open bidding: where anyone may pick up the bid document and submit a tender, is rarely used nowadays for reasons which must be self-evident.

Selected list bidding: is the most common procedure whereby a 'short-list' of bidders is assembled from a 'long list' of applicants following a pre-qualification process.

Straight negotiation: is sometimes tried where projects need to start and (maybe, but not necessarily) finish quickly but is really only beneficial in special circumstances, such as where the client wishes to extend the scope of works already under construction, or the works are of a highly specialist nature. An independent cost consultant should be able to negotiate a competitive price with a contractor but sometimes lack of a viable alternative limits what can be achieved in this respect.

Competition negotiation/two stage bidding: where time is of the essence it is possible in most cases to get the project under way quickly by holding the competition on a two-stage basis, eg by issuing, at an early stage in the design process, measured approximate schedules of quantities or draft specification clauses, or by simply inviting profit margins on hypothetical trade values and/or any other of a great variety of ingenious methods devised by cost consultants and project managers. The object is to make sure that the builder selected in advance of design development can be seen to be demonstrably the most competitive and can be held to that pricing level in the negotiation of contract prices for the work as finally designed.

Given that designers rarely specify adequately in time for proper bid documentation, and also the wasted resource of contractors pricing five or six projects in full for every one that they win, there is, in fact, a very good argument for all lump sum projects being bid in this way. The process also gives the employer and their design team the potential benefit of the builder's experience in the design development phase, plus advice on material availability and other supply chain issues. Furthermore the cost consultant can develop the cost plan in the context of the chosen contractor's pricing and commercial regime rather than, as is the custom, forecasting costs at typical market rates - sometimes with embarrassing inaccuracy.

The main problem with this clever two-stage bidding technology is that unless it is properly explained to both designer and client they may be led into a false sense of security with regard to the adequacy of the information available to the contractor when they start on site. This can lead to very serious problems once the contract gets under way.

Cost reimbursement contracts

Again, traditionally, works which could not be defined sufficiently to enable lump sum bids to be sought and/or which needed to start ahead of design were sometimes let on a 'cost-plus' basis - the 'plus' being either a percentage or a fixed lump sum fee and the cost being the authenticated 'prime cost' of all the labour, materials and plant used up in the process.

This type of contract in the hands of any contractor worth their salt was a licence both to print and to waste money and has long been discarded as a serious procurement route.

In many countries the traditional approach to all construction projects has been some form of professional construction management - see Fig. 6.3.E - in which the builder acts as the client's agent procuring and managing the work on behalf of the client. It should be noted that although the construction managers prefer to take full responsibility for cost management and procurement many clients employ an independent cost consultant to audit these functions.

Fig. 6.3.E
Construction
management
procedures

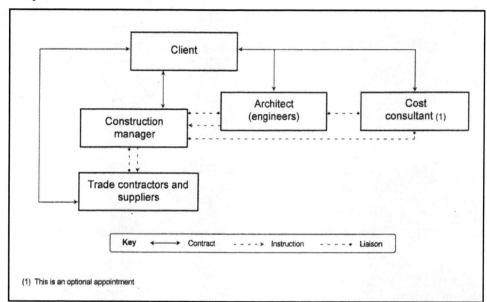

This sets on a totally professional footing the role of the organisation which will organise and procure the work of trade contractors. The construction manager has no contract with the trade suppliers or sub-contractors, all of whom are put into direct contract with the building employer. The construction manager normally draws a fee - again, a lump sum or percentage. Unlike the professional consultants, this fee normally includes an agreed value of overheads and profit, with the costs of all site managers and project-dedicated head office personnel reimbursed at prime cost.

The original concept of construction management had its roots in the role of the 'master builder' who tended to do everything associated with projects. However, the new wave of construction managers being developed in, or introduced to, projects is borne of a philosophy of doing the best for the client - something which they believe existing procurement processes fail to deliver.

Consequently among the many potential benefits a client can derive from construction management is the dedicated approach accompanying the pioneering of a cause which such companies really believe represents the optimum process; this leads to a greater contribution on the client's behalf at all stages from feasibility (where they would, and should, be involved) to completion.

The best of the new breed of construction managers now suffer from the problems of 'pale imitation' by traditional contractors 'jumping on the bandwagon' and giving the process a bad name. However there is a sufficient number of regular and large-scale building employers using construction management to guarantee its continued position as a credible alternative to lump sum contracting; it is, however, particularly suitable for any project where scale, complexity and time constraints merit the client bearing the risk of being contractually liable to reimburse all the prime costs incurred.

There are examples of construction management being spectacularly successful at lowering project cost levels, particularly through better organisation, improved buildability, avoiding 'middle-man' sub-contractors and encouraging prompt or otherwise beneficial payment terms to the trade contractors. In particular many clients have appreciated the opportunity to get 'hands on' the project through the construction manager being able to make strategic changes to scope and time with minimum exposure to risks of disruption and contractual claims. Major schemes in the 1990's such as the Broadgate development in London are testimony to the validity and success of the process.

Construction management is a particularly appropriate vehicle for procuring fast-track, fast-build fit-out projects. However, it is worth repeating and emphasising that cost management should be overseen and all costs audited by a competent independent cost consultant, even though the construction managers may try to persuade their clients they can carry out this critical function themselves. In the final event it is the adherence to programme and quality of the construction which predominantly motivates the construction manager and their natural aggression in achieving these goals needs both the support and the restraint of sophisticated, independent financial monitoring.

Partly as a compromise between the lump sum and construction management approaches the concept of professional 'management contracting' grew up from the late 1960's. Originally based on the prime cost reimbursement process denounced above, but laced with a philosophy that the client was there to be served rather than taken advantage of, the system was expanded into a process whereby the 'professional' contractor managed the work of sub-trades who were in sub-contract to them but on an 'open-book' basis; the client only paid the sub-contractor's agreed price with the management contractor taking a lump sum or percentage fee (see Fig. 6.3.F).

Fig. 6.3.F
Management contracting procedures

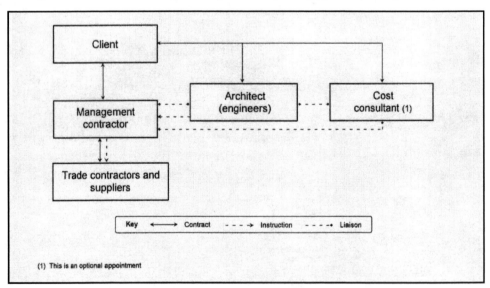

Management contractors usually encourage the appointment of an independent cost consultant, partly because it gives credibility to the 'open-book' approach to the trade contract prices and partly (a cynical viewpoint) so as not to discourage cost consultants from advising their clients against the fee management process.

Although the principle was much the same as the earlier prime cost reimbursement contracts the pioneers of management contracting tried hard, and with a certain degree of success, to instil into their managers that their main bias was towards helping the client deliver their project to time, to an agreed quality and within budget. Their main objective was not to look for opportunities to claim extras every time a problem threatened to disrupt the basis of the client's projections.

The system has lost some ground in recent times for several reasons, such as:

- lump sum bids offering apparently low mark-ups for overheads and profit whilst containing hidden profit margins have made the management fee seem expensive by comparison

- construction management has presented an even more professional, client-oriented image

- there has been a problem of recruiting and training managers who could readily aspire to a totally different philosophy

- the 'bandwagon' syndrome (also afflicting construction management) in which many contractors have sought to cash in on the vogue without properly understanding, or caring about, the underlying philosophy

- 'paid when paid' clauses in the contracts between management and trade contractors raising the level of trade contractors' prices.

Bidding procedures for both construction managers and fee management contractors usually seek separate fees for the pre-commencement period (anything from feasibility to start on site) and for managing the works on site.

'With-design' construction contracts

All the above variants of lump sum and cost reimbursement can be based on the 'with design' principle, ie the designer is part of the contractor's or manager's team as illustrated in Fig. 6.3.G. Whereas such arrangements make a lot of sense for simple projects such as industrial sheds requiring little special design input, they are harder to justify for 'quality' projects where many clients might expect to benefit from having the designer directly answerable to them at all stages.

In fact the current vogue for design-and-build springs from the inability of conventional design teams to get their act (and that of their clients) sufficiently together to avoid frequent and serious overruns of time and cost. Too often there are justifiable complaints from contractors that they are being impeded by poor design and inadequate project management in their genuine efforts to deliver good results.

The attraction of single-point responsibility, with the contractor or manager cracking the whip over the designers with respect to the provision of adequate and prompt information for building, is not difficult to appreciate. Nevertheless, contractors do

Fig. 6.3.G
Design-and-construction - lump sum and construction management alternative procedures

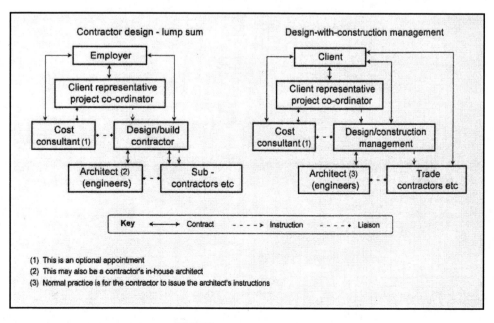

B-267

have a tendency to be philistine in their approach to business and there is an ever-present risk that the unwitting design/build client runs the risk of exposure to second-rate design and heavy punishment for daring to have a change of mind.

Decennial insurance

The liability system for construction projects has been described by John Goodall as 'the keystone of the construction process'[1]. In his view, the golden rule for any contractor or client about to get involved with a project is to begin by checking the system of liability. The continental system of decennial insurance has been introduced into this country.

The legal systems in France and Belgium are based on the Napoleonic Code which protects building owners against the consequences of latent defects for a period of ten years after completion of construction work. In both countries the risks arising from latent defects are covered under policies of insurance but there are important differences in the way these systems of insurance operate.

More significantly, the insurance system removes the risks for contractors participating in the function of design, so that contractors can offset risks when putting forward 'innovative' solutions in order to reduce costs and enhance the competitiveness of their proposals. More than any other EU nation, the French have exploited this advantage to the greatest effect. When French contractors price a project, they invariably look to find ways for submitting 'variantes' to reduce the amount of their tender. That is - they innovate! A persistent debate among French contractors is always over the intellectual property rights linked to 'variantes' which, they insist, must never be allowed to be exploited by another competing firm.

The insurance system in France is based on the 'Loi Spinetta' which dates from 1978. This measure was introduced to protect owners and the general public against latent defects and failures in buildings. The law does not however apply to public infrastructure projects including civil engineering works and alike. The 'Loi Spinetta' is itself based on the Napoleonic Code which provides for a ten year period of liability for which all parties involved in the 'acte de construire' are jointly and severally liable. A system of control has existed in France for 60 or 70 years by which it is compulsory in law that all parties must be insured and an inspection agency must be employed by the owner.

The principal advantage of the system is that in the event of an insurance claim, the insurance company pays out first and then asks questions about the source of the problem afterwards.

The perceived shortcomings of the system, however, are many, eg in the event of an insurance claim for liability, all parties are liable in the eyes of the law. Furthermore, apportioning liability between the parties to see which party's insurance company finally pays is a lucrative business for lawyers and makes for expensive insurance cover (see also below).

In the early years of the system, competition between insurers was so intense that they suffered tremendous losses and for a time were bailed out by the state; eventually premiums were increased to a more reasonable level.

With duplication of insurance amongst the parties, the total cost of premiums can now reach as much as 7% of project costs (very expensive).

Control agencies compete for work. Controls are often inadequate and both the quality of the actual controls as well as the quality of the works often fall short of what is required. This sometimes leads to an environment of 'poor quality' and 'poor control' and 'high risks' and 'high premiums'.

---

[1] John Goodall is Director of Technical and Environmental Affairs with FIEC, the European Construction Industry Federation, based in Brussels (here expressing his own personal viewpoint)

The Belgian construction process has five distinct features:

- no legally binding construction codes
- a 'qualified architect' must be employed for all works, however small
- a 'qualified contractor' must also be employed
- there is no legal requirement for technical inspection bodies (eg building inspectors)
- all contractors are required by law to pay 1% of turnover to the Belgian Building Research Institute (BBRI).

In common with Spain, Portugal, Italy and Greece, Belgium has a legally regulated system for the 'Qualification of Construction Enterprises'. This system regulates tendering for public projects.

In 1934, following a series of accidents and bankruptcies, the government threatened to intervene to protect the interests of owners and the general public. The industry however prevailed on the government to allow it to find its own solution.

In December of the same year, Professors Gustave Magnel of Ghent University and Eugène François of ULB founded SECO. This non-profit making organisation stems from the three essential professions in the field of construction, namely: architects, consulting engineers and contractors.

In contrast to France, the involvement of a 'control body' or 'inspection agency' appointed by the client is not compulsory in law although in large or complex projects the insurance company will usually insist on SECO being appointed. In fact only about 10% of construction projects are actually 'controlled' in this way in Belgium. All parties are liable in law and the court is unable to apportion blame between the parties.

The most important point however, is that when projects are 'controlled' all parties are insured under a single policy of insurance at a much lower cost (usually less than 1% of the value of the works) than in France.

The control body is paid either by the contractor or the owner, usually the latter and is normally involved in the project from inception to completion.

Although there are differences in the way that liability insurance is dealt with in France and Belgium there can be little doubt that the 'banging together of heads' which the system encourages - even demands - has a major impact on the ability of designers and builders to be innovative.

Most significantly, it serves to integrate the design and construction processes, since in the event of structural or technical failures both contractor and architect/engineer are covered under the same policy of insurance. In other words they are both protected under a 'common umbrella'. Moreover, this method of working eliminates many of the causes of litigation in the construction process and makes for a less confrontational approach.

This encouragement to think laterally is highly conducive to the value engineering process described above; it is this value engineering process which is most likely to produce cost-effective buildings and fit-outs and which goes a long way to explaining why the Belgian construction industry in particular is perceived to be one of the most efficient in the EU.

The best route

The merits and demerits of all the above procurement regimes arise continually in arguments as to the best way to go about getting works done. Nevertheless, as has been mentioned more than once in this text, it is the people who minimise risk and optimise solutions - not the systems or regimes under which they operate - although some systems and regimes are more conducive to efficiency of procurement than others.

6.3.6 BUDGETARY CONTROL

Introduction

The principles of budgetary control are described in Chapter 2.3.5 where it is defined as: 'the process whereby appropriate budgets are calculated and agreed, and expenditure against them monitored before and after commitment, to ensure that once budgets are set they are neither under-spent nor exceeded other than to meet variations in the performance criteria or market conditions upon which they were based'.

The principles

Briefly, budgetary control seeks to give the facilities manager or project manager an on-going picture of the progress, in financial terms, of a project or process. It differs from financial accounting in that the latter gives a financial picture at the end of a given period, usually a year. (Financial accounting is dealt with in Chapter 2.3.8.)

The facilities manager or project manager will use budgetary control to give one or more of the following:

- an overall budget for a project or process

- an estimate of the need for funds

- periodic reports on progress at predetermined intervals, eg weekly, monthly or quarterly

- the projected or actual profit or loss at any time during the life of the project, including the period in which it will break even.

Information of this kind, which arises during the project or process, may be used to take any corrective action which may be needed.

Budgetary control should be used pro-actively during the project, whereas financial accounting is a reporting device which may be used for analyses and corrective action, usually at corporate level.

Whereas the emphasis in this chapter is on the management of costs, it may be noted that 'break-even analysis' addresses the interplay of value and costs to arrive at estimates of profit or loss and when a project or process passes from 'loss' to 'profit'.

The applications

Budgetary control is another of the three facets of cost control (see Fig. 6.3.H, over the page) so necessary to the financial success of any project. As with the other two facets - effective procurement and value engineering - budgetary control is applicable on two levels, ie overall project costs and construction costs.

The principles and processes are no different at either level. However, in fitting-out projects of any size the budgetary control of the works will usually be exercised by a specialist (consultant or in-house) whose work will be concerned with much detail; he or she normally reports on cost of the works to the project manager who will feed that information into the overall project budgetary control system which may include design, legal and agent's fees, equipment, furniture and other non-building supplies.

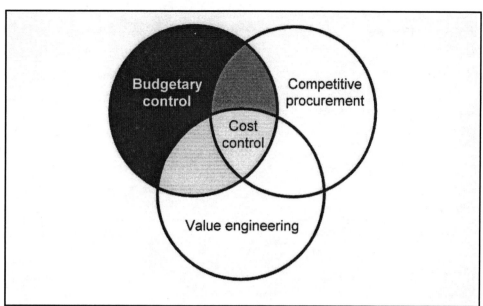

The estimating process

The stages of cost control are shown in Fig. 6.3.B above. The estimating process up to the time of appointment of contractors is usually carried out by the specialist cost consultant. In the feasibility stages 'ball-park' estimates will be provided - possibly per unit of the area to be fitted-out - based on experience of similar projects. Historic cost data has to be constantly updated for inflation, market conditions, quality and changes in statutory requirements. Once the scheme gets outline approval the cost consultant will usually present cost studies under standard cost centres, using either extrapolation of data, approximately measured quantities, budget quotations or, most probably, a combination of all three. Before considering these methods in more detail it is important to note the paramount contribution of the initial budget to the value-engineering process described in principle in Chapters 2.3.5 and 2.3.6 and, in more detail, below at 6.3.7.

Estimates may be made by 'extrapolation' from the cost consultant's database when the limited information available only merits forecasting the total cost of such components as partitions on a cost per sq m of floor area basis; this need not necessarily be unreliable for the purposes of early estimates and, sometimes, whole preliminary estimates are produced by simple modification and projection from the elemental costs of a previous similar project.

Nevertheless, as scheme design gets underway the cost consultant will soon be in a position to assess the quantities and specification of the major cost items. In this case the technique used is known as 'approximate estimating' in which the consultant attempts to forecast the unit prices the future contractor (or sub-contractor) will be applying to quantities of work deduced by measurement from the designer's contract drawings. The approximate estimating technique involves rough measurements of the item in question, eg the length or area of partitions to which is applied a unit pricing rate drawn from a database of similar work on similar projects.

Unit prices for the specification items making up a contractor's bid - the level of which will have to be forecast by the cost consultant ahead of the bidding process - are usually established by estimating the time needed to carry out an operation, the cost of the operatives' time, the cost of materials (allowing for waste including breakage or theft) and delivery, plus an allowance for overheads and profit. A simple example of this for carpet laying is shown at Fig. 6.3.J (over the page). It should be noted that many of these prices per unit of parameter are familiar to builders' estimators and are based on constants of labour, material, waste and machine output which the more sophisticated of them will vary to suit forecast conditions.

Work item	Sub-total	Total
Materials	£	£
Carpet and underlay 1,000 sq m at £ 32:	32,000	
Waste at 5%:	1,600	
Trims, etc say:	800	
Sub-total:		34,400
Labour	£	
0.25 hours / sq m at £ 16 x 1,000 sq m:	4,000	
Travelling and expenses:	160	
Sub-total:		4,160
Overheads and profit	£	
10% x (£ 34,400 + 4,160) £ 38,560:	3,856	
Sub-total:		3,856
Total:		**£ 42,416**
Unit rate (£ 42,416 / 1,000 sq m)		£ 42.4 / sq m laid

The difference between this form of quantified estimate and 'high level' extrapolated approximate estimates described above which are geared simply to the cost per unit of floor area should be noted.

Sometimes builders' estimators will build up a price for a complete task and may then be required to break the price back to cost per parametric unit for a bill of quantities or schedule of rates (as for example, the unit rate computed in Fig 6.3.J). These prices will be the basis of any variation requiring re-measurement; usually they are taken as they stand, but contracts often have provision for the rate to be modified if the forecast conditions on which a rate was calculated are materially different in the work as varied.

So, whereas the preliminary estimate for partitions was, say, £80 per sq m of the lettable floor area, once the design has developed it can be replaced by a calculation - say 100 sq m of partitions (measured across doors and glazing) at £150 per sq m of the surface area (one side) of the partition components. The cost consultant doing an early estimate will normally 'round up' the rate to provide a contingency to cover more expensive or additional work coming to light in the detailed design development of that cost centre.

At the early stages of, and indeed throughout a project, the cost controller may have to include forecast costs of items not yet depicted on drawings or specifications. When doing so it is critically important that the location and extent of such items is flagged up when costs are reported. The importance of communicating to the design team and the client in this way the basis of any forecasts cannot be over-stated; the whole team must own the budget and its composition, albeit that the cost consultant takes special responsibility for the level of costs forecast and the accuracy of the measurement.

Examples of preliminary and scheme design budget reports are shown at Fig. 6.3.K (over the page) and 6.3.L (on page 274).

The information in the 'cost study' at Fig. 6.3.K is based on the cost consultant's best estimate of the cost of implementing the designer's intentions; some of this information may not yet appear formally on a drawing or specification so the cost consultant has clearly stated the basis of all assumptions. As yet these costs are not yet 'signed off' by the client and do not constitute a cost plan budget.

Fig. 6.3.K
Preliminary budget report 'ceramic tiling' cost centre - extract

Project: Example				Work package: Ceramic tiling		
Cost study No.2 Date: October 2000				Work package No.: 7100		

Location	Specification	Source	Quantity	Unit	Rate £	Total £
	Wall tiling					
Servery / Finishing kitchen	White ceramic tiles in epoxy grout	Meeting 2.5.00	300	sq m	96.00	28,800
Servery	Ceramic tiles (£ 64 / sq m supplied) in epoxy grout	Meeting 2.5.00	65	sq m	152.00	9,880
Generally	Cut and fit around switches etc	Allowance		Item		500
Generally	Expansion joint	Allowance			Item	500
Generally	Mastic pointing at all junctions	Allowance			Item	500
Generally	Stainless steel corner guards to tiling	Architect 7.7.00		Item		2,400
Work package total to summary						**£ 161,000**

Fig. 6.3.L (over the page), on the other hand, reports the position one month later on the same cost centre as now estimated at scheme design stage and 'signed off' as part of the cost plan budget allowance.

Sometimes it is prudent to obtain budget quotations for specialist work or if market conditions are uncertain. These should be treated with caution as they may be under- or over-estimated depending on the trader's strategy and their view of the estimating risk.

Once the works are let, either on a main contract or in sub-trades, then the cost consultant's forecasts of quantities and rates are replaced in the budgetary control system by the contract estimates - hopefully not too far different. It is not at all unusual for the cost consultant's overall forecast to be close to the contract total even though there are significant variations, on a cost centre by cost centre basis, between forecast and contract price. This need not imply luck or ineptitude on the cost consultant's part: different contractors have their own special areas where they can procure particularly efficiently but the competitive total bidding process sees that the discrepancies usually cancel themselves out.

Post-contract changes will be forecast by the cost controller using the contractor's rates and pricing structure as described above, often with the forecasts being made jointly with the contractor's surveyor and ideally negotiated and agreed as contract prices at that stage. It should be noted that in some lump sum contracts it is the architect (or quantity surveyor) who assesses the value of a variation; the contractor

Fig. 6.3.L
Scheme design budget report 'ceramic tiling' cost centre - extract

Project: Example					Work package: Ceramic tiling		
Project Cost plan	Date: November 2000				Work package No.: 7100		
Location	**Specification**	**Source**	**Quantity**	**Unit**	**Rate £**	**Total £**	
	Wall tiling						
Servery / finishing kitchen	White ceramic tiles in epoxy grout	Dwg 1.2.004C	500	sq m	80.00	40,000	
Servery	Ceramic tiles (£ 64 / sq m supplied) in epoxy grout	Dwg 1.2.004C	50	sq m	128.00	6,400	
Generally	Cut and fit around switches etc	Allowance	100	No.	8.00	800	
Generally	Expansion joint	Allowance	50	m	16.00	800	
Generally	Mastic pointing at all junctions	Allowance	100	m	8.00	800	
All areas	Stainless steel corner guards to tiling	Architect 7.7.00		Item		4,800	
Work package total to summary						**£ 136,000**	

must provide sufficient information to enable the assessment to be made accurately, but the contractor's only recourse on disagreement is to arbitration or some other means of formal dispute resolution. In practice surveyors for each side normally sort it out by negotiation.

Cost reporting

In building projects there are various generic stages and types of cost reporting:

- feasibility study
- cost studies (of alternative design solutions)
- project cost plan
- pre-contract financial statement (sometimes called the cost check)
- report on bids received
- financial statements during the contract
- final account.

A detailed examination of all these process is beyond the scope of this work. However, the principles to be observed, in common with all systems of financial control, are that at all stages of cost reporting:

- the basis of any cost projection must always be communicated to client and design teams
- the project manager must get the team to confirm the assumptions underlying all cost-change projections and establish whether they are requesting to have them incorporated in the project

- the status of any projections presented in a cost report in terms of client acceptance, contractual commitment, legal obligations, risk etc. must always be made explicit, with the status of projections in terms of reliability, authority and priority categorised by prior agreement between the client and/or their project manager

- departure from the agreed basis of any budget should only be permitted with the client's prior approval.

Cost monitoring

In order to maintain budgetary control the following provisions will have to be securely in place:

- the basis of the budget must be published, disseminated, understood and accepted by client and design teams

- the presentation of the data must be such that the information becoming available concerning potential change can readily be identified as such by reference to the most recent amplified cost report

- the cost controller must have a pro-active approach to identifying and reporting the possibility that any potential decision, activity or event may impact upon the planned cost

- the client and/or their project manager must have the opportunity and time to consider any change proposals; in the event that cost increases are unavoidable - eg unforeseen structural problems - cost damage limitation techniques such as revision of specification or omission of non-critical works should be given as much time as possible to be considered and implemented.

With these disciplines in place the cost controller has a better than 50/50 chance of ensuring that unforeseen extras or savings do not turn up in the budget cost report without common ownership by the whole design team or denying the opportunity to consider them properly before their 'window of opportunity' has been finally closed.

Influences outside of the obvious ambit of a specific project must also be monitored. For instance, reliable reports of significant changes in market conditions should be brought to the table for consideration by the design team in the pre-contract phase. Of course, such a report will only be of use if the budget contains a coherent statement as to the conditions projected at the time the budget was agreed. One way this might be done is to quote the relevant point on any reputable published price index which may be applicable to the pricing of the project estimate.

Many people fulfilling the role of cost consultant hold back from the soul-baring philosophy advocated here. They do so through lack of confidence in their conceptual and practical estimating ability, and through failure to understand the reasons why budgetary control breaks down.

The 'Journal' system of financial control

The proformas used in the examples at Figs. 6.3.K and 6.3.L above are from the computer program called the 'Journal' system of capital cost control[2]. The original 'journal' system was devised in 1967 and was the first cost control system to introduce a pro-active approach to the management and reporting of financial change of building projects. In its manual form it was highly labour-intensive which discouraged most cost consultants from adopting the methodology even though it would potentially give a considerable lift to the calibre of the service offered to their clients. The computerised system developed in the late 80's has largely overcome these objections.

---

[2] The JOURNAL System of Capital Cost Control, Bernard Williams Associates (1988).

Project: Example		Work package summary		
Project Cost Plan	Date: October 2000		Gross internal area = 8,788 sq m	
Work package No.	**Work package title**	**Work package cost £**	**Work package cost £ / sq m GIA**	**%**
2500	General builder's work	240,000	27.36	3.13
2900	Fire stopping	32,000	3.68	0.42
3000	Suspended ceilings	387,200	44.00	5.04
4000	Raised floor	160,000	18.24	2.08
5000	Partitions and office fronts	1,480,000	168.48	19.27
5490	LAN room partitions	16,000	1.76	0.20
5600	Specialist joinery			
7100	Ceramic tiling	136,000	15.52	1.77
7500	Carpets and vinyl flooring	432,000	49.12	5.63
7725	Stonework	8,000	0.96	0.05
7760	Blinds and drapes	8,000	0.96	0.05
8200	Data and voice cabling installations	256,000	29.12	3.33
9222	Preliminaries	544,000	61.92	7.08
9500	Management contractor's fee	128,000	14.56	1.67
10000	Design and construction contingencies	348,800	39.68	4.50
Total		**£ 7,680,000**	**£ 873.60 / sq m**	**100%**

Project: Example			Cost Report No.: 08	
Report: Work package 7100 – ceramic tiling			Date: March 2000	
Change Order No.	**Introduced in cost report No.**	**Subject**	**Financial effect**	
			Add £	**Omit £**
Procurement 04/70	04	Omit: Cost plan; Add: White and Black's tender Add: Allowance for additional work	90,064 8,000	(105,880) 0
Client requirements 03/31	03	Tiling to dining rooms	6,400	0
05/104	05	25 x 25mm tiles in lieu of 50 x 50mm tiles to fitness centre, and addition of ceramic tiles to shower area ceiling	24,283	0
Co-ordination between budgets 04/86	04	Re-allocation of fitness centre finishes, joinery in lieu of tiling	0	(32,000)
Design development 06/171	06	Air freight tiles from USA to suit programme	3,200	0
Total			**131,947**	**137,880**
Net omission carried to summary				**(£ 5,933)**

Project: Example				Cost Report No.: 08		
Report: Executive summary				Date: March 2000		
	A	B	C	D	E	F
Cost centre	Authorised cost plan £	Adjusted cost plan £	Anticipated final account £	Shift from adjusted cost plan* £ +/(-)	Previous anticipated final account £	Shift since previous report** £ +/(-)
Construction costs	7,331,000	7,140,000	6,617,000	(523,000)	6,923,000	(306,000)
Budget costs for compression of construction program	480,000	480,000	454,000	(25,000)	454,400	0
Contingencies	480,000	480,000	480,000	0	480,000	0
Total construction costs	8,291,000	8,100,000	7,551,000	(549,000)	7,857,000	(306,000)
Client direct contracts	3,001,000	3,001,000	3,001,000	0	3,001,000	0
Total project costs	11,292,000	11,101,000	10,552,000	(549,000)	10,858,000	(306,000)

*   Difference between columns B and C
** Difference between columns C and E

Figs. 6.3.M and 6.3.N (previous page) give typical examples of a cost plan and a pre-contract financial statement from the 'Journal' system and Fig. 6.3.P shows a post-contract cost report. On a 'fast track' project, where some of the work is unlet post-contract and still the subject of the cost controller's predictions of future contract prices, the cost report must be expanded so as to reflect the level of price certainty in each cost centre.

The cost plan example at Fig. 6.3.M is presented in 'work packages' which coincide with the trade contracts expected to be procured by a construction manager on this particular project. In the Journal system the estimates and specifications supporting the budget for each package would have been considered in detail by the design team and client prior to signing off acceptance; Fig. 6.3.L above showed how this information would have been presented to them.

As the project proceeds changes will inevitably occur. Fig. 6.3.N shows how revisions to one work package are taken on board as they arise and both the financial effects and the underlying causes described on an 'open-book' basis.

This format is for the design team and project manager to use as a working reference tool. However, an Executive Summary showing the current financial status and comparisons with the original and modified cost plan is also provided - see Fig. 6.3.P.

The key feature in the 'Journal' system is the Estimate Note (Fig. 6.3.Q, over the page) which triggers not only the cost controller's forecast of a projected change to the planned expenditure but also provides information on a number of other key issues and required actions such as:

- who instigated the notion

- how it was communicated

- what it is

- how much it will cost

- its potential effect on programme

- whether the client has an option

- if so, how long it will remain open
- whether the client has authorised it
- which contingency sum, if any, is to be adjusted.

If the architects want the client to accept the alteration on the basis of the estimated time and cost impacts they signs the Estimate Note accordingly and pass it to the client with a formal request for approval; only if the client confirms acceptance will the proposal go ahead. This principle, enshrined in the 'Journal' system, not only applies to post-contract change proposals, but also to pre-contract change proposals where the cost plan is treated as a 'quasi-contract' between the client and design team pending the procurement of a formal works contract.

The 'cost study' is sometimes erroneously called the cost plan but it should not attain that status until the client and design team have collectively 'signed off' the bottom line figure for the selected option together with its detailed design and specification basis.

Fig. 6.3.Q
The 'Estimate Note' feature of the 'Journal' System

Cost plan / Contract sum – proposed change

Estimate note

Project: *Example*

Work package: Ceramic tiling	**Reason for origination:** 1 client requirement
Number: 7100 / 9	
	Authorisation status: Potential change order - Identified
Source: Architect	
Information received: 10 Jul 00	**Issued to client:**
Issued to architect: 12 Jul 00	

Subject: Revised specification to walls of staff toilets

Notes: Telephone conversation 10 Jul 00

Work package programme implications	Extend	Reduce	Contract programme implications	Extend	Reduce
	5 days			Nil	
Financial effect £	Add	Omit	Method of assessment: 2 - Approximate estimate		
	2,400				

	Signature	Date
Requested by architect On behalf of design team:	_____	_____
Authorised by client:	_____	_____

Incorporated in cost report: 08	**Classification:** Optional
Contingency fund to be adjusted: Design	
Architect's instruction:	**Latest decision date:** 19 Jul 00

B W A

Risks to budgetary control

The risks to efficient budgetary control are:

- inadequate outline and/or detail design resulting in excessive change

- estimating error in terms of quantity, quality, market conditions and (most important but often mistakenly taken for granted) the thoroughness of the ensuing cost control process

- re-active cost reporting

- inexperience - individually and collectively

- poor communications

- not enough time to consider alternatives

- poor or non-existent authorisation procedures

- inadequate contingency fund

- poor procurement

- lack of value engineering.

The inter-relationship between the three facets of cost control in this context can be demonstrated by reference to a notional scenario wherein a budget has been set for a project by a cost consultant envisaging the appointment of a team skilled in procurement and value engineering; in the event an inferior or less experienced team is appointed (possibly the result of low fee-bidding) resulting in all the budget assumptions being invalidated with consequent failure of the budgetary control process.

It is a constant source of amazement to those who understand cost control of building and fitting-out works that many clients and their project managers fail to grasp the bottom-line consequences of appointing a design team and cost consultants unfamiliar with, or not motivated by, the principles of efficient budgetary control described above.

6.3.7 VALUE ENGINEERING

Definition

In Chapter 2.2.3 the contribution of value engineering to the process of facilities management was discussed in principle. The authors' definition is repeated here: 'the process whereby products and services are provided to the required performance for the least cost'; the corollary is that value engineering requires 'the elimination of redundant performance and attendant extra costs'.

The applications

Fig. 6.3.R is a further reminder of the interdependence of the three facets of cost control of which value engineering is by far and away the most significant.

Whereas budgetary control and competitive procurement control the cost-efficiency of the procurement of the works, the value engineering facet also determines cost-efficiency in terms of the choice and form of components. However - and far more importantly - value engineering optimises the cost-effectiveness of the performance of components and elements in the context of core business demands on the building in which they are incorporated.

In fitting-out terms, although value engineering can influence the initial (and possibly running) cost of a project the fit-out is a depreciating asset which does not contribute long-term investment value to a company's balance sheet; so, whereas the cost of a

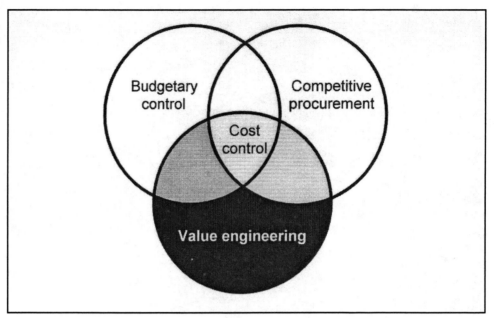

new building or refurbishment can often be side-lined in importance due to the gearing up of asset values the same can certainly not be said in respect of fitting-out.

In fitting-out there are, therefore, three main objectives and applications for value engineering:

- selecting the scheme which contributes most to (or puts at least risk) the health, well-being and productivity of the occupants and optimises the use of the premises

- choosing designs and specifications which meet these requirements for the least capital cost

- choosing capital cost solutions which do not invoke unreasonably high running and maintenance costs.

The processes

As previously explained and now illustrated again in Fig. 6.3.S the value engineering process should begin in the inception phase, being an integral part of the value management procedures for establishing the brief and testing design options.

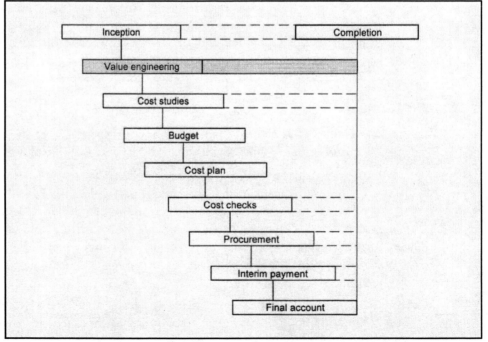

Probably 80% of the potential impact of the value engineering process will be made in this phase but the activity must be diligently pursued pre- and post-contract until all the important decisions have been taken.

The process will be greatly encouraged and improved if a 'challenging' but achievable budget limit is introduced at an early stage, bearing in mind always that it may need to be reconsidered once the cost studies are completed. Such a target cost may be derived from a reliable statistical base, initially by application of experienced conceptual estimating and then by cost studies of apparently appropriate design solutions.

A process which is gaining in popularity is that of the zero-based budget. An application of this technique illustrated at Fig. 1.2.C in Chapters 1.2.4 and 2.2.5 shows how both functional and physical performance may be submitted to the rigours of cost/benefit analysis without over-complicating the decision-making process.

Minimising costs

The scope for minimising costs is rather less in fitting-out than it is in the construction or refurbishment of a complete building. This is because one of the major determinants, ie the geometrical aspects of design economics, have limited application in the fitting-out design process.

Specifically, in any construction project, the initiatives which may be brought to bear in the process of eliminating redundant performance are in respect of:

Design economics:

- geometry

- specification

- spatial efficiency.

Construction economics:

- 'buildability'

- speed.

It is important to be aware of the influence that the size and shape of the building may have upon the quantities of different components of cost centres.

In particular, the effect of the building's configuration on the quantity of elements or components has to be taken into account in the context of the 'cost sensitivity' of that element or component. This refers to the relationship between the quantity of the element or component relative to the floor area or some other measure of the total scope of the project, eg where there is a very high floor-to-ceiling height and a mainly cellular layout is proposed the ratio of partitions to floor area will be particularly large. Fig. 6.3.T compares the ratio of partitions to floor area in such a situation, as also in a relatively open-plan layout.

Fig. 6.3.T *Cost sensitivity of partitions/doors element*	**Examples**		**Ratio of area of partitioning / doors to NIA**	**Element unit rate £ / sq m**	**Elemental cost £ / sq m NIA**
	Case A	Mainly cellular layout	2:1	100	200
		Floor-to-ceiling height 3.7 m		160	320
	Case B	Mainly open plan layout	1:2	100	50
		Floor-to-ceiling height 2.8 m		160	80

In the first case the choice of specification for the 'cost-sensitive' partitions will be important as they may represent between 15% and 20% of the total fit-out cost. Applying two alternative unit rates to the area of partitions the potential cost differential is highlighted.

Understanding these geometrical ratios is a very important key to understanding the effect of design on cost. The ratio of the element area to net internal area is called the 'Element Quantity Factor' (EQF) and the Element Unit Rate (EUR) is the total cost of the element divided by its overall area. As Fig. 6.3.U shows and explains, simply multiplying the EQF and the EUR will give the cost of the element per unit of floor area - a very handy way of quick appraisal of alternative proposals.

Fig. 6.3.U
Using the element quantity ratio factor for rapid appraisal of cost and cost-sensitivity

Full calculation				
A. Element quantity sq m	B. Element unit rate (EUR) £ / sq m	C. Element cost (A x B) £ .	D. Net internal area (NIA) sq m	E. Elemental cost (C /D) £ / sq m NIA
1,000	80	80,000	2,000	40

Simplified calculation				
F. Element quantity ratio factor (EQF) (A / D)	B. EUR £ / sq m			E. Elemental cost (F x B) £ / sq m NIA
1,000 / 2,000 = 0.5	80			40

Buildability

'Buildability' is defined as 'the extent to which the inherent characteristics of a building design and specification influence the efficiency and hence cost of the construction process'. The phenomenon of 'buildability', when it does manifest itself, usually falls to the benefit of the building contractor in terms of lower on-site costs. Provided the 'buildability' is appreciated (probably designed in) by the client's design team this bonus can be harnessed to the client's benefit through the procurement process, eg by designers explaining to bidders the inherent designed-in 'buildability' of their proposals. Mid-bid interviews with contractors present a good opportunity for the design team to introduce or reinforce what they are trying to achieve in terms of 'buildability' and also to get feed back both on the validity of their own strategy and ideas emanating from the prospective builders.

In value engineering terms design for fitting-out should address the following 'buildability' goals:

- reduce complexity

- minimise 'learning' time

- optimise on-site time

- optimise site-based assembly

- reduce return visits

- reduce sequential criticality

- improve workmanship

- minimise damage

- minimise waste

- reduce capital costs

- reduce maintenance costs.

Risks to value engineering

One of the easiest ways to lose the opportunity to value engineer a scheme is to permit the development of the design concept in an economic vacuum. Good designers are perfectly well able to express themselves creatively within economic constraints and should be made to do so. Procedures for managing this issue by target costing are discussed below.

Other risks to the success (or even application) of the process are:

• over-stated performance requirements

• excessive budget

• poor design management

• too little time - to consider alternatives

• intransigence - ie resistance to change by designers wedded to their own design concepts

• poor procurement

• poor budgetary control

• inaccurate estimating.

Good project management can overcome most of these risks. The first two simply allow the emergence and retention of redundant performance. The design management must allow proper time for considering change options while poor procurement and budgetary control can frustrate the most diligent value engineering effort.

The problem of inaccurate estimating can be particularly serious. Any architect who has been denied the use of a component on the basis that another is cheaper only to find the out-turn cost was greater, will resist the value engineering process at future stages - and with good reason.

If the risks can be overcome, the financial advantages of strategic value engineering can be quite startling for both capital and revenue expenditure.

Target costing

A major catalyst for value engineering is a budget which is set as close as possible to the minimum required to achieve the required performance (also see Chapter 2.3.3). However, it is often necessary to use typical input specification to imply or define performance requirements thereby discouraging efforts to seek even better alternative design solutions.

As an alternative to input specification, use of building or fitting-out quality 'scoring' systems, allied to challenging yet demonstrably achievable target costs drawn from a sound database, leaves all thinking in the 'lateral' mode - a pre-requisite for successful value engineering.

Fig. 6.3.V (over the page) illustrates how a fitting-out quality scoring system, such as available from the BQA system described in Chapter 9.1, can be used to set cost targets which will necessitate a value engineering approach from the design team.

The target costs are extrapolated from a vast database of fitting-out costs and BQA surveys. The costs represent the fitting-out work to be carried out by the user from shell-and-core; adjustments need to be made for the resource drivers given in Chapter 6.2.1 which should not cause a problem to an experienced cost consultant.

Users with large and regular fitting-out projects should consider developing their own target cost/quality models to ensure that the value engineering process is always applied using data which is directly relevant to their own circumstances.

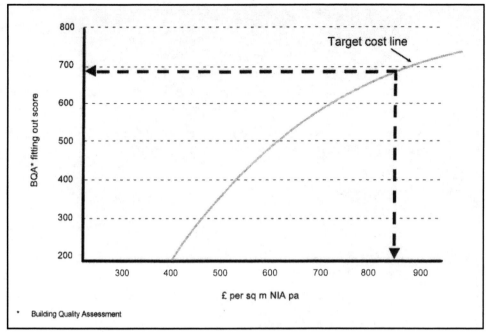

Fig. 6.3.V
Target costs against scored quality

* Building Quality Assessment

6.3.8 QUALITY CONTROL

Quality of design

The control of design quality is the project manager's responsibility. Getting the quality of the concept right is an elusive goal full of subjectivity and not necessarily influenced to any degree by the way the design process is carried out. That said, concept quality will be the better for having all the known constraints, such as cost or availability of materials, on the table at the initial briefing stage.

Design development through to working drawings may be improved by the application of standard quality control procedures such as EN ISO 9000 or Total Quality Management (TQM) as described in Chapter 2.4.3. However, the performance of most consultants is probably best assessed from their track record rather than their commitment to paper pushing. Project managers must make the quality control requirements known at the fee-bidding stage and then ensure that designers are chosen who patently understand what is required of them.

Project managers and designers must both make sure that there is adequate time in the design programme to do the job properly. Fast-tracking techniques as described elsewhere can make a programme look feasible on paper but the designers must defend their corner and the project managers should not pressure them unduly to accept the risk of an over-tight time-scale.

Quality of the works

Normally the architect or interior designer is responsible for supervising the quality of works on site. The project manager sometimes has this job, (for instance in certain central government projects) in which case an architect or interior designer will usually be engaged as sub-consultant in respect of quality control.

On some, possibly larger projects a Resident Engineer or Surveyor may be engaged to keep an eye on detail but economic constraints have seen a gradual disappearance of this noble discipline from the scene of the action.

Of course, the facilities manager should make it their business to visit the site regularly (and officially) and keep everyone on their toes by looking for, and reporting on, obvious deficiencies and praising good performance (both of course through the project manager, if there is one).

The use of 'sample' panels, areas etc. to set the standards is a worthwhile investment and will be rather more useful than woolly specification terms such as 'workmanship shall be of the highest quality'. Asking for it is one thing, but defining it is another.

6.3.9 THE PROGRAMME

Time and the fitting-out process

Almost without exception fitting-out projects are required to be carried out in the shortest possible time-frame. Most tenants have a 'rent-free' period at the commencement of a lease affording them sufficient time to fit-out to their requirements. Obviously this acts as a spur to the organisation to get up and running before the rent and the service charge become payable.

Once in occupation, re-fitting an area is even more time-critical, given that the organisation is:

- paying rent on the 'dead' space and/or

- possibly paying rent on temporary space or

- overcrowding the remaining stock.

Whilst allowing too much time for the process will not necessarily result in added value the converse is certainly not true - ie too little time will guarantee a bad job.

Any premises cost savings brought about by looking to save too much time in the fitting-out stage will probably be eroded in the short term by contract claims arising out of inefficient design and contract management. In the post-project era the loss of productivity resulting from a poor quality, ill-thought-out scheme will be many times more significant than any short-term premises cost savings.

The time drivers

Principles and applications for programme management are fully considered in Chapter 2.8.2.

Apart from the scope of works, factors which will determine the overall length of a project are:

Pre-construction:

- early involvement of the constructor - to advise on 'buildability', programme, availability of materials and labour and sequencing of drawings

- time allowance for thorough development of the brief

- time allowance for value engineering

- time allowance for the design development and working drawings

- experience of the team, collectively and individually

- previous working relationships between team members

- the bidding process - particularly time allotted to interviewing bidders and explaining the scheme to them.

Post contract:

- the knock-on effects of the pre-construction phase

- the time allowed for construction

- the calibre of the constructor's team

- the extent and timing of changes to the works

- time allowance for value engineering proposed changes

- degree of insistence on quality

- contractor's financial status - those in trouble may not get credit facilities for the resources they need for the job.

There are legitimate ways to shorten the overall process whilst keeping the risk low - or maybe lessening it. The easiest targets are:

- omitting the single stage tender period which conventionally has to await completion of the working drawings and specification

- overlapping the design and procurement processes

- shortening the construction period by better front-end planning.

These targets can only be achieved by involving the constructor at an early stage in the project, either by a two stage bidding procedure, management contracting, construction management or some form of design/construct arrangements (see over).

Fig. 6.3.W (over the page) shows the generic processes of single-stage lump sum, two-stage-bid lump sum and construction- or fee-management. It should be noted how the two stage bid claws back time by allowing negotiation of the price of the works as the scheme design, specification and possibly bills of quantities are being developed. In this process, as with the management route considered below, the contract time should also be reduced through the constructor's opportunity to plan the work more efficiently and also influence the specification, buildability and drawing production sequence.

The management route saves even more time through appointment of the manager on a fee without the need for a two-stage bid document. Their even earlier involvement and their client-orientated interest will be of particular benefit as trade contractors are brought in for discussions about their contribution to the works and the programme. The professional manager will also be trying hard to impress and their familiarity with the front-end process in which he or she is asked to participate may well be greater than that possessed by a traditional builder.

Provided that the fast-track programmes allow enough time for each activity and the cost control is sharp the management type of procurement process will not produce higher costs. In fact, the fast-building opportunities generated may save direct costs through simplicity of operations as well as cutting down project time.

In the event it will be the calibre of the team, its personnel and its management which will produce fast projects at reasonable cost to the required quality. Sophisitcated systems and procedures can help but in the wrong hands all the potential benefits will turn into unmitigated disasters.

Fast projects are more difficult and need more efficient people.

6.3.10 PERCEPTIONS OF RISK

Price certainty

The risk in a fitting-out project is in respect of cost, time and quality. It has been proposed above that it is not systems of themselves that reduce these risks, but people of the right calibre working within the appropriate regimes under competent management.

Fig. 6.3.W *Effect of procurement process on time*

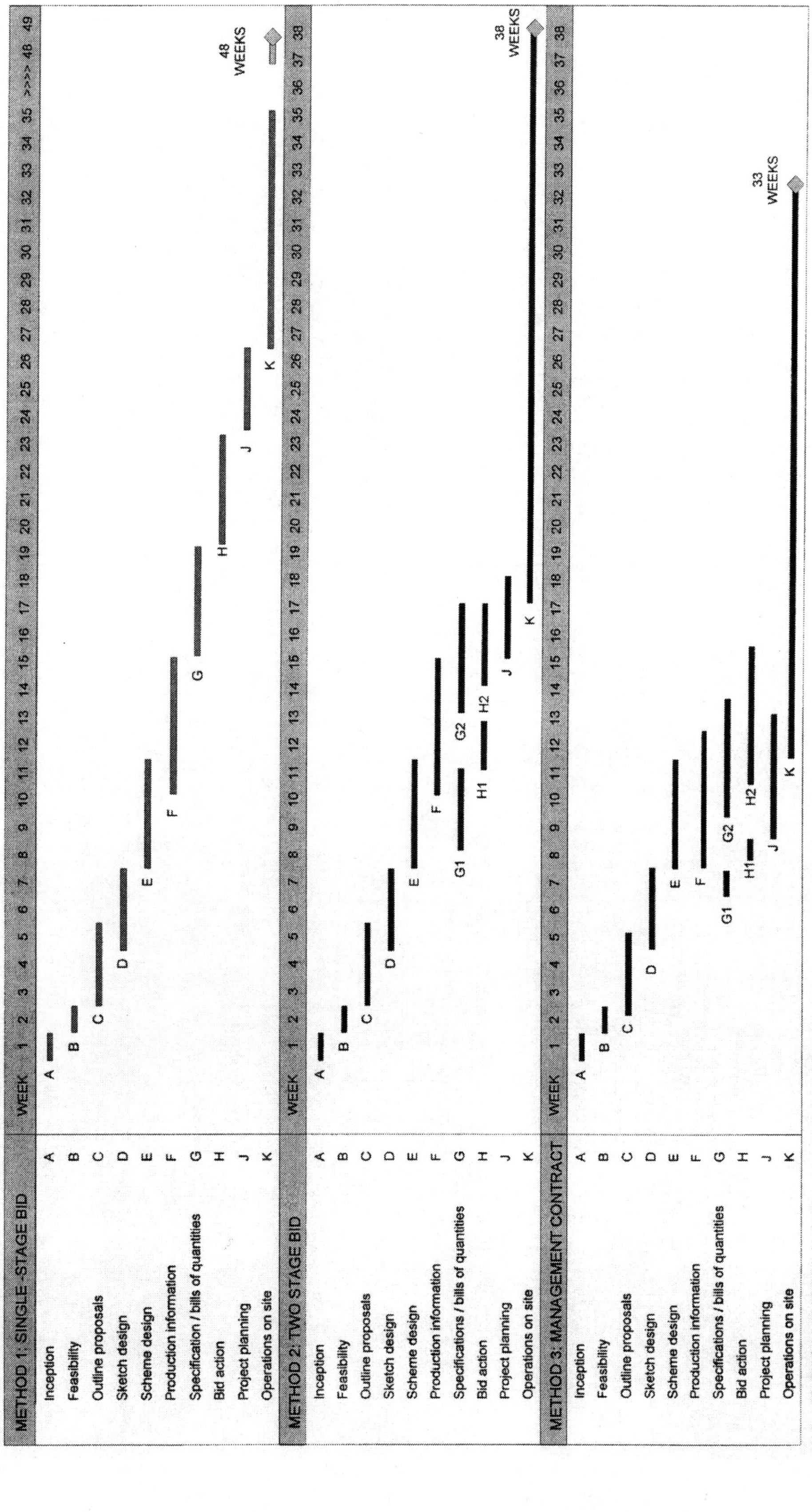

N.B: ASSUMES OPERATIONS ON SITE = 21 WEEKS IN ALL CASES

For example, many clients get concerned that they are at higher risk of cost over-run the further they move away from the single-source-responsibility procurement route. Fig. 6.3.X illustrates how the early certainty of price declines as the client gets more involved contractually in the selection and reimbursement of individual suppliers of services and goods for the project.

Fig. 6.3.X
Procurement process and the early achievement of price certainty

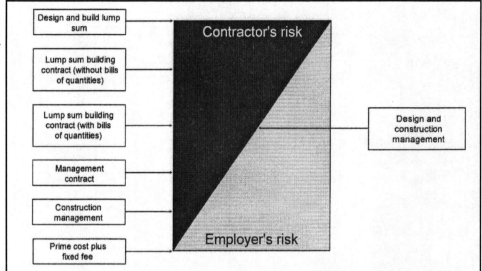

As seen earlier the ultimate in uncertainty of price is where the employer accepts liability for the cost of the work down to the number of packets of nails delivered to site. Nevertheless, good contractors make good profits from undertaking projects for a fixed price in the face of similar cost uncertainty themselves; it is therefore logical that, given the same calibre of management available to such a good contractor, the client would save the profit, risk and overheads margin he or she would otherwise have to pay to a builder within a lump sum contract price.

At the other end of the scale, making the designer answerable to the constructor rather than the employer affords the latter one point of redress if things go wrong but makes the designer one step removed from the client's authority and allegiance.

The 'design with construction management' process may not bring earlier price certainty; however, the close involvement of the construction manager with the

design process should reduce the risk of accidental over-expenditure against pre-agreed budgets, and is shown as equivalent risk to the lump sum contract.

As the procurement of work packages moves from contractor-led to client-led so price certainty reduces but project control (potentially) increases; so, when the price is firmed up - towards the completion phase - it may well be lower than it would have been on a lump sum contract. It is worth remembering that contractors charge for taking the price risk and, if the client is to take the price risk over, the need for high calibre professionals to provide 'insurance cover' - in the form of best practice management - is paramount; decennial insurance cover, properly implemented, affords the opportunity of using the most appropriate contract arrangements for a project with a hard financial indemnity as well.

Comparative costs

A hypothetical comparison between the price of a project as procured via either a good lump sum process or construction management is shown at Fig. 6.3.Y (over the page). This potential outcome was predicted by a project manager in support of a recommendation to a client to proceed along the construction management route on 'time' grounds; the 'lump sum' forecast was readily predictable from close and current comparables. In the event both client and project manager were rewarded by delivery of the project under a process of design-with-construction-management at 10% less than the predictions in Fig 6.3.Y and all to an incredibly tight programme; the contingency fund was handed back to the client intact.

Fig. 6.3.Y
Effect of procurement process on price

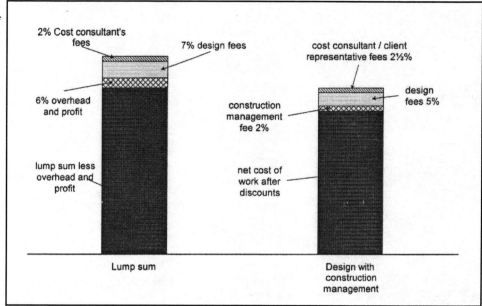

2% Cost consultant's fees

7% design fees

6% overhead and profit

lump sum less overhead and profit

cost consultant / client representative fees 2½%

construction management fee 2%

design fees 5%

net cost of work after discounts

Lump sum

Design with construction management

6.3.11 RISK AVOIDANCE

If a fitting-out project goes wrong in any respect, for whatever reason (and many are suggested above) proving whose fault it was is never going to be easy; no-one ever wins in building litigation so the best way to avoid losing is to go for excellence in every function needed to deliver the project. If that means paying a little more than peanuts to obtain such services then the extra should be the insurance needed against man-made disaster.

However, if the facilities manager does not thoroughly understand the process or does not take the trouble to consult someone who undeniably does, the decision as to which procurement route will deliver the appropriate quality at the right price, in time, with the least risk will be a lottery - and how many people win lotteries?

PART C

Support Services

Section 7

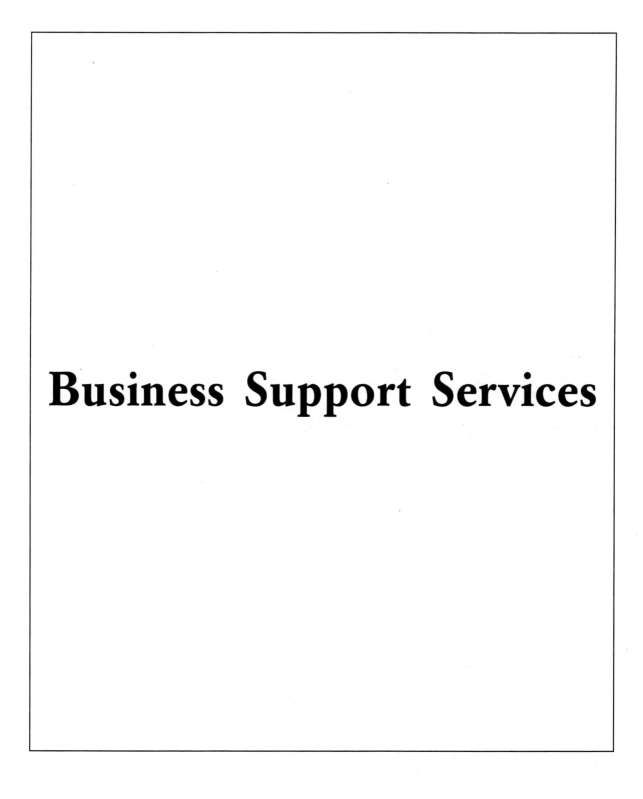

Business Support Services

7.1   SECURITY

Introduction

A dictionary definition of 'security' implies a state of freedom from danger, damage, fear, care, poverty - and the precautions taken to ensure against such disbenefits. In facilities management all these threats can apply - including poverty as a result of failure! But 'security' can also embrace other activities taking advantage of the by-products of the availability of personnel and technology engaged predominantly on prevention of one or other form of damage to the business.

So, security guards in the main reception area may double as receptionists and 'smart' cards for electronic access/egress may also contain the holder's medical history for use by the health and safety manager in case of accident.

Doubling up of business security with other key visitor and personnel services can be a key determinant in the economics of a security regime as also in the success, or otherwise, of its implementation. If visitors, staff and management all feel comfortable (or uncomfortable in appropriate circumstances) with, and supportive of, the security facilities provided, the chances of getting value for money will be enhanced by a large factor - not least because individual awareness of risks to security and the importance of reporting them are probably the single most important determinant of achieving secure facilities.

This chapter deals with risk centres, security management, methods and systems, guarding resources and regulation of the security industry.

7.1.1   THE RISK CENTRES

Categories of risk

Typically an organisation is exposed to risk in the following categories:

- premises
- personnel
- equipment
- data
- information systems
- public relations
- infrastructure and utilities installations.

In each category the threat is both external and internal to the organisation. The significance of that threat will also vary depending upon the nature of the business activity, the height of its profile, its location and other specific factors. The issue is further complicated by the fact that the physical design and performance of a building will itself both present and prevent threats in a way which does not facilitate cost/benefit analysis, eg a building over-provided with access points will require a greater degree of security but automatic access control may minimise the on-cost when compared to physical guarding by security personnel.

Premises

The principal risks to premises are:

Natural disasters:

- fire
- flood

- subsidence

- earthquake

- tornadoes / hurricanes.

Malicious damage:

- explosion

- vandalism

- fire.

Whereas it is normally possible to take out insurance cover against natural disaster it is becoming increasingly difficult to obtain cover against malicious damage, particularly the consequences of terrorist activity.

Chapter 7.9 - 'Disaster prevention and recovery' deals with the special measures needed to make buildings secure from terrorist damage and their associated costs.

Other risks to property such as failure of mechanical components and power supplies are maintenance problems which should not be the direct responsibility of the security manager - except insofar as they may be caused by vandals.

Infrastructure and utilities security

Security at many important infrastructure or utilities facilities is to be taken over by a special government security service. Its function will be to counter potential terrorist attacks.

Personnel

Apart from the risks to personnel arising out of the damage to premises described above, there are the following threats:

- theft of personal property

- assault

- kidnapping

- health and safety.

Risks to health and safety are considered in Chapter 8.2 and, again, are not the responsibility of the security manager other than protection from tampering with essential supplies such as water and air.

Theft of personal property may be covered by insurance but its impact on staff morale and trust goes way beyond the actual cost of replacement.

Kidnapping of prominent business executives is also sometimes a concern of the security manager. Protection of personnel against the risk is a specialist role involving trained consultants usually by former police or military staff.

Equipment

Theft and malicious damage in respect of items of equipment such as computers, fax machines and office furniture may be covered by building contents insurance - not that anyone should use this protection as other than a back-stop. In large organisations particularly, the loss of items of equipment is surprisingly common, frequently aggravated by the absence of proper inventory controls; very often theft of equipment is insidious and will go undetected over long periods if such control is lacking.

Data

Most organisations possess data which is either:

- essential to their own production process
- confidential to their business
- confidential to their personnel
- confidential to their clients.

Some may also possess government classified data.

Loss of or damage to this data will, one way or another hurt the business either through loss of output, removal of patronage, benefits to competitors or mere replacement costs. Insurance cover may be available against some of these risks but it is difficult to establish the potential consequential loss when placing the risk - and often even harder to justify it to the loss adjustor after the event.

Information systems

Anyone who has ever caused the network to 'crash' through faulty application of a program will know that this is an enormous risk which can only be controlled by a really high level of training for all who do, or might, load up a program.

Just as serious, and increasingly problematical, are the computer 'viruses' which find their way into a system via one program or another and infect it such that the whole system may malfunction with file structures on hard disks being destroyed, floppy disks contaminated and data lost irretrievably. These 'viruses' are maliciously introduced and are undetectable until triggered by a pre-determined event. The best way to protect against viruses is to produce regularly maintained anti-virus software and also to draft contracts of employment forbidding copying of unauthorised software on to office systems.

Backing up data is another well-understood but frequently overlooked risk management technique. Routines must be thoroughly drafted, understood and religiously observed. Once a day - at lunchtimes - is a good practice in most situations. Automatic recovery and 'mirroring' software are further sophisticated options to guarantee retrieval of 'lost' files - but do not provide protection against corruption from faulty power supplies.

Power supply variations - surges or reductions - can cause the power supply to fail with particularly serious consequences to data inputted but not backed up and also corruption to the data file header records. A line-conditioner is an economical first line of defence by maintaining the voltage level. However, to prevent loss of power at the computer as well as maintaining the voltage, an Uninterrupted Power Supply (UPS) is necessary. This entails a large store of batteries which are automatically available to pick up a failed power supply. The capital cost of a UPS might range from £800 to £1,250 per KVA depending on the extent of the computer installation and the size of the building giving a capital cost of around £13 to £20 per sq m of gross internal area.

In critical installations a dedicated 'clean' line can be supplied direct from the main distribution board to the processor. The capital cost of such a provision is not excessive - eg in a building of 5,000 sq m GIA, clean supplies to one sub-distribution board per floor - including sub-main cabling, earth boundary and final cable runs - will cost less than £5 per sq m GIA.

The risks to systems discussed above - plus unauthorised access to files by unauthorised system users - are the responsibility of the system manager, not the security manager.

The risks the latter will have to guard against are:

- access by unauthorised personnel
- theft of software and hardware
- malicious damage to software and hardware.

Public relations

External public relations, ie impact on the passer-by, visitor or casual observer - will be affected by:

- quality of reception
- exposure of any inadequacy or inefficiency, eg unsuccessful disaster prevention
- apparent, ie visible, efficiency
- courtesy
- delays or inconvenience.

Apart from the above external issues, internal public relations will be prejudiced by personal loss or injury, theft and regular vandalism, not to mention the effect on morale of a company's bad external image.

In this, as in so many operating cost centres, the consequences of a building's physical and functional performance on the performance of the occupiers can often be disproportionate to the amount of actual expenditure involved.

7.1.2 SECURITY MANAGEMENT

The cost centres

The Facilities Economics classification protocol for the Security category is included in Fig 7.1.A

Fig. 7.1.A
The Facilities Economics classification protocol - security

Sub-categories (contract bundle items)	Principal Examples / cost elements	Items commonly included in costs	Items excluded from costs	
			Item	Refer to category:
Reception	Reception Door guard / commissionaire		Fire alarms	Electrical maintenance
Guarding	External guarding Internal guarding	Staff costs, Day guards (external and internal), Night patrols (external and internal), Uniforms, Radios, Security cards, Camera operators, Tenants areas service charge element, Barriers, Swipe cards, CCTV, Pass issue, Task management	Alterations	Alterations and improvements
Surveillance	External surveillance Internal surveillance		Improvements	Alterations and improvements
Duties	Visitor escorting Lost property		Changes due to churn	Alterations and improvements
Security system maintenance	Car parking control Card readers CCTV equipment			

The security policy

The decision to provide security to one degree or another can only be taken by corporate management; the principles and objectives should, however, be stated positively in the organisation's premises policy statement.

The facilities manager's job is to make sure that the efficiency and cost of the security strategy is reasonable relative to the agreed policy, the potential loss and the degree of exposure to risk.

The grades of security may be defined as:

- Grade 1: deterrence of vandals and casual criminals (opportunists); reservation of minor confidentiality (for example, personnel files)

- Grade 2: protection of low values against the deliberate criminal; preservation of high confidentiality; protection of high values against vandals

- Grade 3: protection of moderate values against the deliberate criminal

- Grade 4: defence of high values against organised crime

- Grade 5: defence of terrorist targets (may be added to any of the above).

7.1.3 SECURITY METHODS AND SYSTEMS

Security control activities

Management of the security risk must address the following activities:

- external access/egress control
- internal access/egress control
- surveillance of activities
- reporting of events
- immediate and long-term remedy.

Most security systems use a combination of human, mechanical and electronic resources. They will seek to detect and/or deter intruders and to detect and prevent natural disasters.

Human resources take the form of:

- dedicated security personnel
- the general staff - through their alertness to dangerous situations and willingness to report promptly and clearly.

Mechanical resources include physical barriers such as doors, grilles, smoke detectors and sprinklers and electronic resources include means of opening and closing access points, detectors, video cameras and so on.

Each of these resources has a different measure of sophistication, cost, risk and effectiveness as is discussed below.

7.1.4 DEDICATED SECURITY PERSONNEL

In all but the smallest or lowest-risk premises it is essential that security staff be properly trained and carefully selected. In practice this condition is almost universally met by the use of security firms, which supply properly trained, uniformed staff on periodic contracts to an extent of provision agreed with the employer.

Security officers should be used to accepting responsibility, observant, resourceful and have good presence of mind. For special assignments they may need to be specially trained but in the normal course of events they will have been trained under the syllabus set up by their national or regional association. An example of such a syllabus is given at Fig. 7.1.B. They will also have received on-site practical training under supervision and at the security firm's expense.

Fig. 7.1.B
Typical training syllabus

Uniform	Maintenance and importance of the company's uniform and accoutrements
Standing orders	Standing orders regarding pay, sickness benefits, grievance procedures
	Standing orders regarding reporting for duty and performance of duties
	Reporting on/off duty, check calls
Security duties	Powers of uniformed security officer
	Security of keys, maintenance of key register
	Patrol activities
	Cash-in-transit procedures
	Key points - use of clocks and other key point systems
Static duties	Reception, access/exit control
	Security of keys, maintenance of key register
	Patrol activities
	Key points - use of clocks and other key point systems
Verbal communication	Methods of approach to staff at all levels, visitors and members of the public
	Use of telephone, radio, clarity of speech and 24 hour clock
Written communication	Use of daily occurrence/vehicle log book
	Other site books
	Incidence reports
Fire, first aid, bomb alerts-practical	Fire drills, use of basic appliances
	Basic knowledge plus 'when not to touch'
	Report and evacuation procedures
	Visiting sites - various types
	Site training - supervised training specific to site detail
Exercises	Radio exercise, voice procedure
	Report writing exercises
	Fire exercises

A key factor in choosing the security firm - apart from the quality and training of its employees - is the extent of management support available to the person on site or a mobile patrol. Security firms are normally set up on a regional basis. Each region will have a hierarchy of managers and inspectors. Operations are controlled through a 24-hour, heavily protected control room which usually doubles as a central alarm monitoring station. Managers and inspectors should make frequent visits to the site and these visits should be logged; any points noted by inspectors should be followed up immediately by the management.

It is quite easy to assess the quality of the security service from first impressions when calling at a site; it is particularly common for the service to fall away after the first few weeks of a contract.

7.1.5 GUARDING RESOURCES

Resource requirements

Depending on the degree of risk, cover may be:

- day time only - static guard
- 24-hours - static guard
- day time only - static guard plus mobile patrol
- 24-hours - static guard plus mobile patrol.

On an office building of up to, say, 10,000 sq m, the typical guarding hours pa for security cover for five days a week would be as in Fig. 7.1.C. Cover at the lower levels would only be acceptable in either a grade 1 or 2 risk or where there was a high level of security system back up.

Fig. 7.1.C
Typical cost for guarding a 10,000 sq m GIA administrative building

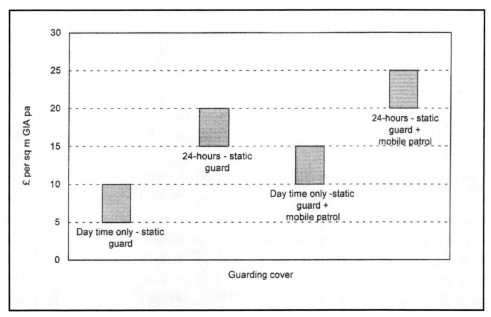

Across the board security guarding hours pa range from the low levels indicated above to as much as six hours per sq m GIA for high risk buildings such as data-centres. Use of security personnel for commissionaire duties or as receptionists can help to keep resource requirements down but this will not always suit the company's desired image.

Contracts are normally bid and are for a one-year period. The full range of supporting systems to be made available under the contract, eg central alarm monitors, key-holding, radio network, should be set down clearly. There should be adequate insurance for:

- public liability - £5m is common
- employer's liability - unlimited
- efficacy and contractual liability - £5m is common
- fidelity bond - £10,000 is common
- 'loss of key' insurance - £2,500 is common.

General staff awareness

However thorough or sophisticated the security personnel and systems may be, no organisation will have satisfactory security unless the general staff are fully aware of and willing to apply the necessary level of alertness, surveillance and speed and clarity of reporting required of them.

A simple real-life example of how important this attitude may be is where a multi-tenanted provincial office building opens directly on to the High Street with only a part-time security guard/receptionist and a proximity card reader/entry telecommunication system. At lunch-time, after the guard has gone home for the day, the office staff still come and go; some of them, in transit, will hold the door open for those outside (whom they may not know!) to let them come in out of the rain or merely out of 'politeness'. Not surprisingly breaches of security are regular and sometimes very serious. This is a very common situation in smaller buildings where the lessor's management leaves much to be desired.

The worst excesses of this type of breach can be avoided by including simple procedures not only for preventing illegal entry but also for challenging unauthorised personnel and/or alerting management to their presence. The same goes for training in respect of reporting fires, water ingress and other sources of natural or mechanical disaster.

Although it is the non-core visiting staff such as cleaners and guards who are the first to come under suspicion for petty theft or vandalism, it is surprising how often the culprit turns out to be a regular - sometimes popular - member of the core staff. While human resources can avoid the employment of undesirables the whole staff must always be aware of the need to leave their workplace and their personal belongings in a secure state; purses or wallets in pockets of coats over chair-backs are just asking to be stolen!

Intruder detection systems

Systems normally contain a combination of some of the following features:

- alarms
- detectors
- door viewers
- surveillance mirrors
- central control
- personnel devices
- closed circuit television (CCTV).

In addition to specialist systems, the design of buildings, and in particular external and internal lighting, can be important aids to detection. Fig. 7.1.D (over the page) reproduced from the manual, 'Whole Life Economics of Building Services'[1] shows a typical initial security control installation.

The system analysed is for the whole building and provides protection to all exits and entrances to the building with visual or audible alarm during periods of non-occupancy. There would be one security indicator panel at ground level connected directly to the internal/external security bells, infrared movement detectors, door protectors, night alarm switches and auto-dial unit - all at ground floor level.

Capital costs range from as little as £0.80 per sq m of GIA in very large buildings to around £3.50 per sq m of GIA on buildings of 2,000 sq m or less. These costs, as with all the other electronic systems described in this section, tend to be more or less constant as between different countries due to the fact that the systems are not normally locally manufactured and have to be purchased in the international market place.

---

[1] Hurst, Lay and Williams (2002) "Whole Life Economics of Building Services", BEB Ltd, Bromley, Kent

Fig. 7.1.D
Generic security control installation

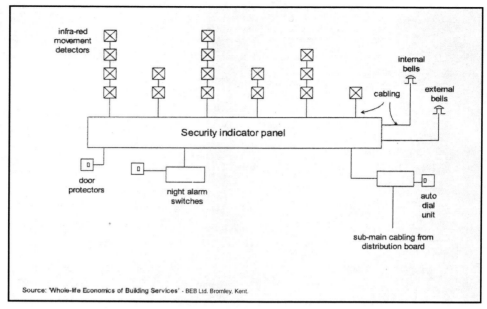

Source: 'Whole-life Economics of Building Services' - BEB Ltd. Bromley. Kent.

CCTV

Fig. 7.1.E, from the same source, looks at external CCTV. This system is usually used to supplement conventional systems particularly where there is a high 'footprint' area or a large level of external area requiring surveillance. The central control processor will include camera control positions and zoom facility, video recording and screen monitor. This is connected to remote, closed-circuit tv cameras by power and co-axial cable; in the example in Fig. 7.1.E, a building of 2,000 sq m might need four cameras whereas one of 30,000 sq m might need 10/12. Here again, the capital cost of providing CCTV security is many times cheaper per sq m GIA in the larger buildings dropping as low as £1.50 per sq m of GIA from the level of £10 to £13 per sq m GIA in the smaller premises.

Fig. 7.1.E
Generic closed circuit television (CCTV) installation

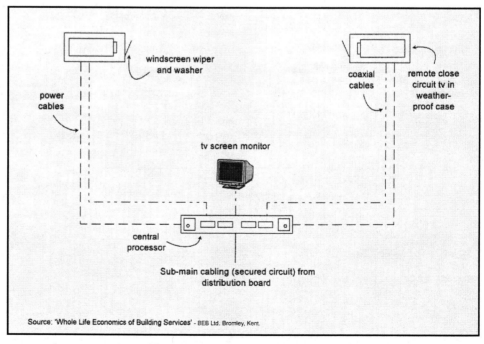

Source: 'Whole Life Economics of Building Services' - BEB Ltd. Bromley. Kent.

Care must be taken to ensure that the management of CCTV complies with the Data Protection Act 1998. Matters which should be addressed include:

- the on-site existence of CCTV is promoted on site with signs and notices

- procedures are in place for access by any person seeking 'on-camera' evidence of themselves

- access to monitors is restricted to authorised competent personnel, and the monitors are secure

- on film information is only kept for as long as necessary to meet management objectives

The Information Commissioner has developed code of practice on the management of CCTV. Facilities managers should have prepared a similar site specific code for their property; keeping it up-dated, as appropriate.

Sometimes systems are added which could enable the personnel complement to be reduced but, particularly where security staff are in-house, there is a tendency for management to turn a blind eye to the consequent over-manning. This is also often the case where the risk in a building changes as a result of departmental relocation.

Intruder deterrence systems

Barriers, barbed wire, plain or electrified fences and extensive external lighting are a highly effective first line of deterrence but some systems designed to hurt the would-be trespasser may be illegal in some countries. Close-up and internal security, door viewers, entrance telephones and entrance video systems are again very effective at putting off intruders.

Protection of designated areas from intrusion by members of staff as well as outsiders is usually controlled by some form of card-key system. Such systems have various levels of complexity and can be zoned to provide many levels of status or graded access.

Access control, with the aid of modern technology, is more and more concerned with controlling movement of people about a building rather than merely discouraging unauthorised entry. Systems will be either:

- self-contained ie electronically programmed to accept or deny access - cheap but relatively effective for low-grade risk

- on-line ie card-readers feeding information to a central computer

- networked ie provision of 'intelligent' readers on a network, the number and location being variable as user requirements are modified; this is the most sophisticated, but is cost-effective in larger buildings and estates, especially where 'churn' and change are prevalent features.

In each case the type of access card or token will be a critical decision. The type of 'key' will affect the cost of the reader as also ease of use, copying, issuing and up-grading and the speed and number-limitations of access.

The access control is normally either:

- proximity-based

- card-based

- remote.

The proximity-based cards or tokens can be kept on a key-ring and, as they are only held close to the reader, do not wear out or get damaged. They are more expensive than the plastic 'swipe' cards. The remote systems work like the 'proximity' keys but can be operated from a distance - just like the electronic door- locking devices on cars.

'Smart' cards can double as a medical records, 'phone cards or even as credit cards! They hold the data themselves, not the computer as in traditional card-access systems. Another newish development is of biometric devices which can 'read' personal characteristics such as images of face, fingerprints, iris or hand, and voice - expensive but 100% secure.

An analysis of the initial cost of a high-security proximity system in a building of 10,000 sq m GIA is given at Fig. 7.1.F. If the cost were to be annualised the ensuing figure would be midway between costs of the high and low level resources for day-time only human guarding given at Fig. 7.1.C.

Fig. 7.1.F
High security proximity based access control system - capital costs for a 10,000 sq m GIA office building

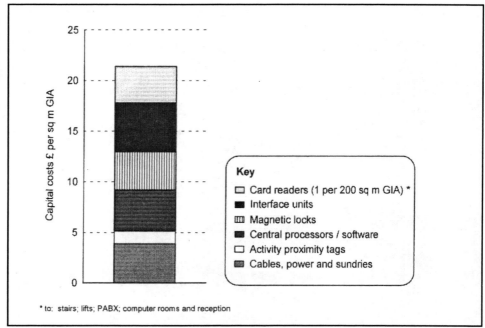

The example at Fig. 7.1.G is of a far simpler conventional system with two levels of access and costing between £1.50 and £5.00 per sq m GIA. The main control unit has a VDU screen and maintains a printed access record. It is linked by power cable/co-axial to fire alarm, card readers and door lock release. In this example, smaller buildings would have the whole of each floor independently zoned, whereas the larger ones would only be zoned to protect the main core.

Fig. 7.1.G
Conventional intruder deterrence system - generic layout

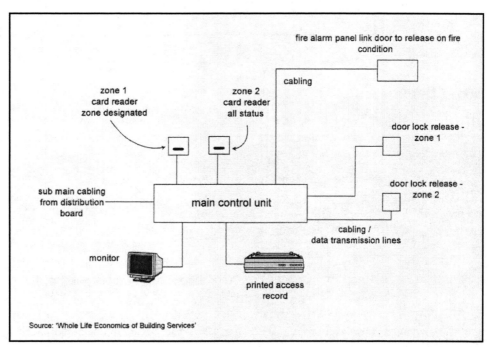

Building components such as security grilles, locks and enclosures together with 'strong' features like anti-bandit glass all make their contribution to deterrence and prevention. The technique of cost-benefit analysis should be applied to all these add-on design features rather than allowing them to be provided at whim. Also, the effect of the introduction of security features on the insurance premiums must always be investigated.

Fire protection

Fire and flood detection is normally solely a mechanical function comprising sensors and alarms. Control and/or extinction may be manual or automatic or both. The security staff should be trained to deal with the fire problem although often it will be the staff themselves who have to take initiatives. Larger premises usually have a dedicated fire officer - their costs should be allocated to security.

Fig. 7.1.H shows how the capital cost of the fire protection by different means varies between the four generic office types in the reference source.

Fig. 7.1.H
Capital costs of alternative fire protection installations - range of building sizes

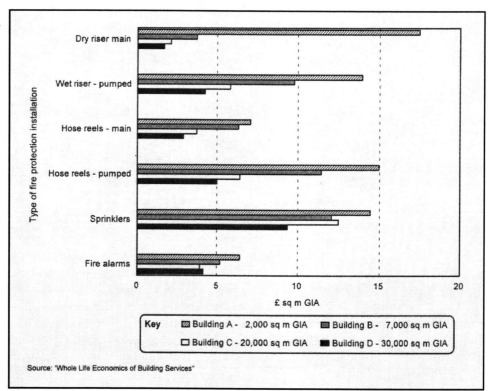

Guard Dogs

The facilities manager may need to be aware of the complex statutory provisions which govern the use of guard dogs on business premises. There are several areas of concern including:

- the management and control of guard dogs
- dogs attacking or worrying agricultural livestock off the premises
- dogs attacking persons off the premises
- dogs which are a nuisance to neighbours

Under the Guard Dogs Act 1975 whether a guard dog on the premises is inside or outside, generally it must be tethered or caged, ie it cannot roam by itself. If it is not tethered or caged, it must be on a leash under the control of a dog handler. The handler is strictly liable for the dog in these circumstances. Section 1 of the 1975 Act provides that where a guard dog is on business premises, warning notices to that effect must be displayed at entrances.

Escaped Dogs

Any dogs worrying or attacking livestock on another's agricultural land may result in the owner being criminally liable under the Dogs (Protection of Livestock) Act 1953. The owner of the animals may protect them, killing the dog if necessary; in some instances - there are conditions.

Where death or injury is caused to a person or an animal a civil action for damages may arise against the keeper (or owner) in some instances under the Animals Act 1971. (This may apply when a dog in under control.)

'Neighbourhood' law, eg against noise or fouling the footpath may be used by the local authority. Similarly, dangerous or stray dogs may be dealt with by the relevant authorities under the Dogs Acts of 1871 and 1906; even to the extent of destroying the dog.

Gauging the resource requirement

Security is a highly specialised field and one in which the cost of provision of personnel, components and systems varies considerably. Generally speaking, buildings suffer from too little rather than too much security. Nor can the 'right' level of security be easily gauged or interpreted from taking benchmarks from other organisations. In the sample given at Fig. 7.1.J the range is very considerable both within and between different uses and is obviously variable by many factors including, grade of risk, the mix of human and mechanical systems and procurement routes.

Fig. 7.1.J
Typical range of security expenditure by sector per unit of floor area

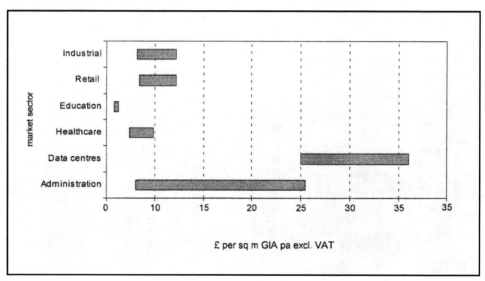

When appraising alternatives the capital and operating costs must be compared, eg as in Fig. 7.1.K (over the page) which compares a mainly human guarding resource with a 'mixed' human and electronic control system.

Reimbursement

Security guards are relatively low-paid. Apart from local labour rates the cost of employing security guards will be further influenced by:

- the risk
- the size, number, proximity, location and layout of the premises
- extent and nature of automatic security devices
- dress code

- formality of procedures
- qualifications and ability
- quality of management.

Fig. 7.1.K
*Comparative costs
of electronic and
human guarding for
access control*

High security access control system as Fig. 7.1.F		
Capital cost	£ 224,000	
Amortise over 10 years - say	£ 32,000 pa	
Maintenance	£ 2,400 pa	
Replacement tags	£ 1,600 pa	
Central monitoring - security personnel - say	£ 32,000 pa	
Patrol guards 3 @ £ 20.000 pa	£ 60,000 pa	
Total costs pa	**£ 128,000 / 10,000 sq m =**	**£ 12.80 per sq m NIA**
100% Human guarding		
Say 1 per 1,000 sq m : 10 guards @ £ 20,000 pa (inc O / H + P)	£ 200,000	
Total costs pa	**£ 200,000 / 10,000 sq m =**	**£ 20.00 per sq m NIA**

Cost-benefit analysis in respect of all three types of provision - personnel, components and systems - should be encouraged and when new buildings are on the drawing board the facilities manager must get the design team to set an operating budget for security in the context of their built-in capital cost provisions for security. Designers must always be encouraged to think about the security implications of their design; a great deal of capital and operating costs can be saved - and disasters prevented - by talking to security experts before finalising design proposals.

7.1.6 REGULATION OF THE INDUSTRY

The facilities manager will need to be assured of the calibre of the security staff supplied by security firms. Under the Private Security Industry Act 2001 the Security Industry Authority (SIA) has been created.

Its role will include the following:

- to establish and maintain a national register of licenced security companies
- to create and run an Approved Contractor Scheme on a voluntary basis
- to licence individuals who are employed in the security industry.

Other bodies concerned with the quality of the security industry include the Joint Security Industry Council and the British Security Industry Association. The latter is one of several accreditation bodies.

7.2   DOCUMENT STORAGE

Introduction

The economics of storage and retrieval are extremely complex especially when the productive output of the user is taken into account - as of course it must be to make any sort of economic sense of the decision-making process.

The chapter therefore examines the recording and distribution of information and the use of paper, microfilm and electronic storage and retrieval of information. The legal context for the management of information access, storage, destruction and so on is dealt with in Chapter 2.

It concludes with a brief look at off-site out-sourced storage.

7.2.1   RECORDING AND DISTRIBUTING INFORMATION

The problem

Although e-mail and e-commerce are taking great swathes out of the budget for paper-based products in the more advanced organisations in many parts of every country the 'paperless' office is no nearer than it was a decade ago. Most documents are still held in paper form - all that new technology seems to have done is increase the amount of data which can be generated by computer operators in a working day. Many letters are faxed prior to posting and the volume of redundant word-processed amended drafts lying around in files is bordering on the criminal.

Against this background employees' aspirations regarding the quality of the working environment and the cost of office space have put pressure on space planners to reduce the clutter of filing cabinets at and around the workstation, while many employees are in receipt of the greater volume of hard data referred to above.

Office space grows ever more expensive - a prime target for cost reduction - and the efficiency of the storage operation is at risk through the human factors ie mis-filing, and the prohibitive cost of manual filing per se.

The International Records Management Council has indicated that the average document is copied 19 times and costs £14 to keep stored. Worse, the cost of mis-filing a document is an average of £84 including time spent trying to find it and/or replacing it.

Local on-site storage can absorb up to 5% of gross usable area, with archive space on-and-off-site sometimes as high as 15% of an organisation's total space requirement - although the off-site space will be a lot cheaper per unit of area. Consequently more and more documentation is being transferred away from the office filing cabinet - either to remote storage or on to microfilm or electronic disk.

The classification protocol

The Facilities Economics protocol for 'Storage Facilities' is given at Fig. 7.2.A.

Fig. 7.2.A *The Facilities Economics classification protocol - storage facilities*	Sub-categories (contract bundle items)	Principal examples / cost elements	Items commonly included in costs	Items excluded from costs	
				Item	Refer to category:
	None	Physical documents Electronic media Film based media Document / file disposal	Dedicated staff and task management, Contract charges	In-house storage premises costs (see note below)	N/A

Note that although the cost of in-house storage space is not normally added into the budget for the cost centre it is essential to take it into account when comparing in-house with contract storage or with off-site self-managed storage as in Fig. 7.2.B (over the page).

7.2.2 STORAGE AND RETRIEVAL OF PAPER DOCUMENTS

The business requirement

Paper documents provide information to which reference may have to be made on many occasions. The decision as to whether the document should be on the desk, in the desk, adjacent to the desk, remote from the desk, or remote from the building should be dictated primarily by the needs of the user to access it, rather than the facilities actually available to contain it.

Documents obviously vary in importance. The routine business correspondence tends to have an active life of five to seven working days before being relegated to its place in the file where it may well live on or near the workstation for up to two years. Once the project is completed it may be shredded or, as in the case of legal documents, building projects and alike, stored remotely in one form or another either in perpetuity, eg a last will and testament, or for a term of years to comply with statutory requirements.

It is no longer necessary to generate or keep most documents in paper form - only certain legal records cannot sensibly be exposed to the risk of irretrievable electronic or photographic corruption. Nevertheless many people still correspond and record on paper and the facilities manager needs to find the optimum solutions for controlling access and storage.

On- and off-site document filing

Wherever practical in business and premises terms documents should be kept in the cheapest appropriate space available. Archiving in low-cost basement areas and/or off-site premises must be found for all but those files in regular use which have to be kept locally on site (unless available electronically or on microfile).

There are three main categories of local filing:

- drawer-based floor cabinets / lateral filing
- cupboard style wall units
- mobile track units.

Floor cabinets occupying 'dead' space under a work surface do not incur a premises cost penalty; where free-standing cabinets form a boundary within an open plan scheme this cost is mitigated but each unit still consumes several times the space of a free-standing screen.

Wall cabinets in theory do not take up floor space but care must be taken not to create dead space beneath them.

Mobile shelving systems running on floor tracks are relatively expensive to buy but save on circulation space associated with banks of group filing cabinets.

There are various ingeniously planned storage systems which can increase the volume of documents stored within the capacity of a storage unit and various types of filing systems can also impact on this form of space efficiency.

If the documents are needed locally on site for regular access then all these options need to be thoroughly evaluated in the context of space consumption and the commercial deals available on the products.

Where such access is not required then the on/off site storage equation needs to be worked through. Off-site storage facilities are known commercially in UK as 'self-storage'.

7.2.3 SELF-STORAGE

In recent years a fledgling service industry has been developing. Self-storage for business and personal purposes is well known in the USA but seems to be barely touching the potential market in the UK.

Such companies as Big Yellow Group; Lok N Store; Mentmore; and Safestore have been converting premises or building new. There has also been some acquisition and merger activity in the market.

The key 'product' is vacant storage space for self-use by the customer, usually for 24 hours a day. The size of the space starts at less than 10 square metres and is often variable. The premises are usually located off motorway or main road for ease of access.

A typical storage arrangement may provide for such items as:

- monthly rolling terms
- flexibility as to space requirements
- 24 hours access
- insurance
- loading facilities, including trolleys and fork lift and pallet trucks
- constant security with CCTV
- merchandise, including archive boxes, cartons, wardrobe boxes, dust sheets, tape, bubble wrap, and various locks.

The facilities manager should find the availability of self-storage facilities particularly useful in circumstances where on-site storage space is temporarily insufficient or not available. This may arise in such instances as:

- a build-up of inventory
- during rehabilitation or redevelopment works programmes or projects
- rapid growth of operations.

Fig. 7.2.B (over the page) shows how the physical (as opposed to image) document storage equation may be calculated. It may be noted that there is an allowance against the remote storage for the theoretical extra cost of re-fitting the floor space to achieve the more intensive use of the space freed by the removal of the floor cabinets; however, in practice this might well be achieved by simple re-arrangement of furniture and the provision of screens (not included in the calculation).

In the example a serious under-estimate of the numbers of retrievals would, in practice, erode the remote storage saving. On the other hand, if existing filing arrangements are inadequate then the cost per item retrieved by staff in-house could well be much higher than the estimate given.

If the extra space freed up by the elimination of the storage furniture avoided the upheaval of moving or taking on more space that might be a big bonus. Of course, a sensitivity test of various rental levels would also have a major impact. The example presumes a provincial town; central city costs could triple the on-site penalty with no counter-effect on the off-site alternatives. Equally, if you cannot use the extra space efficiently there is no advantage to be gained other than easier planning.

Fig. 7.2.B
Typical appraisal of on-site v self-managed off-site storage

On - site	£ / pa	Off - site	£ / pa
Leasing costs - say 100 x 4-drawer filling cabinets for group storage	1,600	Say 200 boxes leased at £ 8 pa (including sorting and boxing)	1,600
Retrieval by staff: 500 items at £ 5/each	2,500	Retrieval by staff: 500 items at £ 8/ each (excluding any charges)	4,000
Space occupancy costs (including circulation) 100 sq m at £ 350 sq m NIA	35,000	Re-planning and fitting out 100 sq m NIA at £ 350 sq m: £ 35,000 amortised over five years	8,000
Total costs	**39,100**		**13,600**

7.2.4 MICROFILMING

When paper records are in regular use, being continually referred to, amended, annotated and circulated it is really better to keep them on paper until they achieve 'passive' status. At this point off-site storage of the paper documents may be a viable option. The physical option has been examined above but another common solution is microfilming.

Microfilming, as the name implies, is a photographic process using either 16mm or 35mm rolls - roll microfilm - or 100mm flat microfilm which is called microfiche. The latter is most commonly used in normal day-to-day business.

Microfiche consumes only a tiny fraction of the space occupied by documents. Because the initial set-up costs are high the system comes into its own when large volumes are involved. Equally, the less retrieval required the better although 'active', as opposed to 'inactive' or 'passive systems', can be economical where retrieval at the speed of a paper system is necessary.

Here sophisticated indexing is the key, possibly linked to a database in the larger systems. However, since it is the cost of indexing which is the most critical factor in microfilming, the level of detail to which it extends must be considered most carefully. Microfilm rolls can store up to 2,500 pages without indexing whereas a fiche can hold as few as 60 pages - expensive but indexable to that level of detail.

For most microfilm users, however, it is the inactive or passive system which is in use. Simple indexing systems can separate those files which are most likely to be retrieved from those, such as important legal deeds, which may need to be accessed from time to time. The legal profession has taken quite extensively to microfilm (usually the microfilm rolls containing many more documents and being comparatively tamper-proof) and in many countries there are now official codes of practice dealing with its use in evidence.

Fig. 7.2.C (over the page) shows the cost implications of using microfilm when the volume of documentation used in the example at Fig. 7.2.B is substantially raised.

Fig. 7.2.C
*Comparative costs
of microfilming and
off-site storage*

Off-site storage	£ pa
Say 10,000 boxes leased at £ 5 pa including sorting and boxing	50,000
Retrieval by staff say 25,000 items at £ 0.30/ each (excluding any charges)	7,500
Total	**57,500**
Microfilm bureau	
Initial filming say 20M pages at £ 0.015 each = £ 300,000 (amortised over 5 years)	75,000
Film storage on-site: premises costs say 100 sq m NIA at £ 350 sq m	35,000
Staff training - say	8,000
Bureau management charge - say	80,000
Total	**198,000**

Where documents are required to be kept for a long time the amortisation period can be extended with a consequent large reduction in the annual equivalent cost of the initial filming; microfilm is expected to remain usable for up to 80 years.

Microfilming is shown managed off-site by a bureau in the example. On-site processing and storage means that the documents never leave the site which may be important where active papers are involved. Nevertheless in-house training costs - and, of course, the core v non-core activity argument (see Chapter 1.1.6) - must be taken into account at option appraisal.

In business efficiency terms microfilm provides a safe, well-organised, permanent, easily duplicated and distributed means of dealing with and avoiding losing/misfiling records. It is a well-established medium supported by sound bureaux and well-tried and tested technology.

Clearly it saves an enormous amount of space which would be financially more telling in a comparison with on-site document storage; in spite of the apparently much higher 'hard' costs in this comparison with off-site document storage it is still hard to fault in terms of both facilities and production economics once the volume border-line for viability has been crossed. Nevertheless its successful adoption will very much depend on whether the users will grow accept its rigours, slow rate of retrieval and the enforced changes of habit.

The change-over can, however, cause an enormous hassle; many organisations leave the backlog in physical storage and apply the microfilming process to new records only. Modern processes also permit direct filming from computers; a system known as Computer Output Microfilm (COM) replaces the line printer with a COM recorder.

7.2.5 ELECTRONIC FILING

These systems are variously termed:

- Document Image Processing (DIP)
- Electronic Data (or Document) Management Systems (EDMS)
- Optical Informational Systems (OIS)
- Electronic Information and Image Management (EIIM).

They all save a digitised copy of paper on a storage medium - usually an Optical Disk or a Large Hard Disk. The documents are readily retrievable at a pc or workstation and can, if required, be printed out.

One optical disk of around 640Mb can hold up to the equivalent of three fully-loaded four-drawer filing cabinets - about 20,000 A4 pages. Large Hard Disks are nowadays considered a more cost-effective solution than optical disks: a 40Gb IDE Hard Disk Drive (HDD) can be purchased for less than £180. However optical disks are now available that will store up to 5.2Gb giving space for up to 160,000 A4 pages. The pages can be scanned and stored up to a rate of up to 480 images per minute. However, this rate does depend heavily upon the condition of the documents, eg if there are a lot of staples, clips and other attachments which have to be removed prior to scanning/digitising the rate will drop and preparation costs increase accordingly.

There are three categories of system:

- stand-alone
- distributed
- integrated.

Stand-alone systems: these contain all the components needed to carry out image capture, processing, retrieval and display. They can handle thousands of documents but, of course, retrieval is limited to the one pc.

Distributed systems: they can have multiple personal computers networked with several servers. Resources of a system are distributed to provide the optimum file/facility performances and workstations for viewing and retrieval.

Integrated systems: they are large scale systems in which database and application software is run on a computer that will control the file server linked to workstations via Local Area Networks (LANS).

Any purchase of an integrated system must be considered a long-term investment and have the expansion and overall growth potential built in.

The types of disks are available for this application.

WORM (write once read many) - the files stored on here cannot be altered or erased; it was once the cheapest form of electronic filing but not any more and these days is only used for its robustness and security features, eg in archiving.

Re-writable - allow files that are stored to be updated when needed; it is ideal for files in current use and can also be used to transfer directly into store documents which have been viewed on email. However the hardware costs quite a bit more. Even with re-writable disks, the contents of the document itself cannot be re-written; the page is viewed only as a picture and that page may only be removed and replaced with another. Some companies tend to use the re-writable optical disk to store their live records, financial details etc. and at year end convert these files to the cheaper CD storage format. HDD holding very large amounts of data on-line.

With some systems it is possible to retrieve an archived filmed page and convert it into digital format if it is needed more frequently. This serves to provide a convenient bridge between fast access electronic media and low cost archival film media, in many cases providing an ideal solution to document management.

At present the initial cost of electronic filing limits its use to large, fast moving offices where information is needed very quickly. As more systems are developed and the supply goes up the costs will come down and the electronic systems will be available to the smaller business user.

These systems, once installed, can dramatically increase the productivity of the staff as well as saving considerable space. However, a great deal of these productivity gains rely on correct indexing and filing along with good systems management, especially where optical disks are used to store and manipulate live records such as invoicing. If the system is not thoroughly thought through in terms of indexing, cross-referencing etc., then the premises goal of achieving a cost reduction in terms of storage costs may well be totally outweighed by a dramatic loss of productivity.

Its speed of retrieval, computerised indexing, multi-user access and low operational costs make the system compare favourably with microfilm, which does begin to look a dated process in this age of ICT. Nevertheless the set-up costs both in terms of capital investment, digital scanning (one page at a time though still a lot faster than microfilming) and system conversion again make the system best suited economically to the larger volumes of documentation. The state of the organisation's ICT culture will obviously make a big difference to the ease of introduction and implementation of an electronic system.

Fig. 7.2.D shows the costs of a typical electronic filing system for comparison with the physical and microfilm examples at Figs. 7.2.B and 7.2.C.

Fig. 7.2.D
Typical calculation of large-scale electronic filing system costs

Cost Breakdown	£ pa
Initial data entry 20M pages at 2.5p each = £ 500,000 – amortised over 5 years	200,000
Staff training	8,000
'Re-writable' software	3,000
Maintenance - say	8,000
Total	**219,000 ***

*   Excludes any additional costs of ICT support installation.

N.B. Speed and frequency of retrieval may be a critical factor justifying the slightly higher annual expenditure.

Gauging the pros and cons

Of course, as with all the examples in this text, the actual levels of cost in these theoretical calculations will always depend upon the market conditions at any one time. The figures used to illustrate the issues must not be taken as categoric evidence of the economics of the various approaches.

In common with all facilities services, when benchmarking service expenditure, property and premises costs related to archiving, eg an off-site storage warehouse, are excluded from best practice comparisons; however they are clearly a relevant factor, along with retrieval time etc when comparing the options available. Archiving is of most importance in the administrative, educational and health sectors, however, facilities requirements vary considerably based upon:

- staff, patient or student numbers

- numbers of transactions

- availability of local and on-site storage

- ICT policy and electronic data storage/retrieval reliability

- legal records storage requirements of the business being served in terms of security, format and longevity.

Whilst high-level benchmarking can provide early indications as to relative cost comparisons, more detailed comparisons such as illustrated above taking account of the physical quantity of records storage and movement will be of greater value in identifying particular areas of concern, should they exist. At high-level, for example, annual archiving costs within an administrative organisation or building with an effective storage and ICT policy in place normally exceed £45 per capita. However, where the business requires regular retrieval of a significant quantity of important or sensitive records over a period of time, archiving costs may exceed £150 per capita.

Measuring capacity and performance

At the more detailed level hard storage quantities are usually measured in terms of boxes, cubic metres or shelf length depending upon the business sectors' requirements, while retrieval is measured in terms of both the quantity moved and the number of moves or transports. Here the service level, dictated by retrieval times, has a significant effect on cost, but of greater financial concern is the potential impact of the archiving solution upon the business in terms of service failures, lost records, delayed retrieval and the like.

7.3 STATIONERY

Introduction

Stationery as a cost centre is not universally accepted as belonging under the facilities umbrella. Nevertheless it is a business support facility with quite a sizeable budget; furthermore, the quality and availability of appropriate products can have an important impact on the end product - although this varies enormously from one type of business to another.

Certainly it merits more professional attention than available via the managing director's secretary or, worse, the office junior.

7.3.1 THE CONTENTS OF THE COST CENTRE

Definition

The term 'stationery' originally meant writing materials such as paper, pens, ink, blotting pads and rulers. Over time the true meaning has been distorted as a result of vendors - be they retailers, wholesalers or direct distributors - extending their activities across a whole range of consumer-related products.

So, for example, stationery retailers now also sell newspapers, tobacco and confectionery - and some provide a sub-post-office function. With regard to offices the suppliers of pens and paper a long time ago grasped the opportunity to sell in everything conceivable in terms of small workplace consumables, plus, in many cases, larger items of office equipment from waste-bins and filing cabinets to desks, photocopiers and pc's. Some will also plan the space and fit it out!

Consequently, the cost centre is one which, not having been subjected to the same sort of benchmarking rigours as its premises counterparts, is likely to be found analysed on the basis of the category of supplier rather than the nature of the items making up the bills.

The Facilities Economics classification protocol at Fig. 7.3.A is therefore suggested as a means of introducing a semblance of order into a cost centre which, though not particularly large, is still just as important financially as cleaning or building maintenance and often outstrips them for cost without economic justification.

Fig. 7.3.A *Facilities Economics classification protocol - stationery*	Sub-categories (contract bundle items)	Principal examples / cost elements	Items commonly included in costs	Items excluded from costs	
				Item	Refer to category:
	None	Standard paper products Bespoke paper products Non-paper consumables Storage materials Presentation materials	Envelopes, Writing materials, Other: cards / diaries / files, Flip-charts / foils / pens, Dedicated staff, Task management	Non-stationery items procured from stationery suppliers eg small items of office furniture and machines etc	As appropriate

In order to get to an overall figure in the first instance it may only be necessary to separate all the goods incorporated in this classification from all the rest of the goods coming through on the office supplier's bills.

Taken across the board, and excluding those non-stationery items, paper-based goods are by far the biggest component of the bill. Even where the hardware items (including computers and furniture) are left in the analysis, the costs of paper goods still outweigh the general consumable items by about 2 to 1. Fig. 7.3.B is one office supplier's estimate of the percentage value of goods supplied across the board. The low-ish percentage of items of furniture in the table reflects the fact that major purchases of office furniture are generally made direct with the manufacturer.

Fig. 7.3.B
Percentage value of goods supplied to all customers by a typical office supplies company

Goods supplied	Percentage
Paper consumables (cut sheet, labels, books)	22
Office furniture	14
Office Machines (computer, facsimile, copier)	11
Consumables (toners, inkjet cartridges)	9
Envelopes	9
Bespoke stationery (printing, special making)	8
Filing and storage	7
Catering supplies	6
Washroom supplies	4
Presentation and planning	2
Writing and graphic supplies	2
Office accessories	2
Packaging	1
Diaries	1
Personal accessories	1
Safes and fireproof cabinets	1
Total	**100**

Source: Office Plus Ltd.

7.3.2 THE USE OF STATIONERY

In most larger companies and in many others at the leading edge of their own area of business (large or small) the increased use of on-screen production, editing and e-mail transmission by ICT-aware and literate staff has dramatically reduced the use of plain and headed letter-quality paper for letters and reports and the envelopes they used to travel in.

In spite of this demand for paper products continues to rise, although at a slower rate. The biggest cause of the accelerating demand is the increase in production of printed and photocopied material as laser printers and high-speed photocopiers have become more and more an integral part of the office output process in many cases bringing in-house the reproduction of documents once put out to printing companies. Not only are users producing more copies - they are also matching the paper quality to the high quality of the graphic and printed output made possible by the modern equipment.

7.3.3 STATIONERY COSTS

Costs per capita

Fig. 7.3.C gives a range of stationery costs from a wide sample of commercial organisations of all shapes and sizes.

Fig. 7.3.C
Typical range of stationery costs per capita across a wide sample of disparate organisations

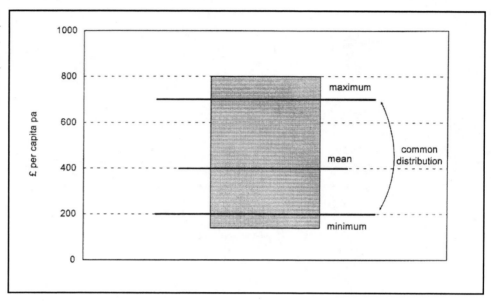

The resource drivers

The key resource drivers include:

- the nature of the business output
- the extent of e-mail activity
- quality of materials
- proportion of 'white-collar' workers
- extent of in-house document production
- effective stock management.

Economy measures

There are several ways to cut down on excessive expenditure under this cost centre. The first, and most cost-effective, is to dedicate one person to cost control of 'stationery' - the three facets of financial control as described in Chapter 2.3.2 (Fig. 2.3.A) and not just procurement or budget reconciliation. At the average cost of £400 per capita in the sample an organisation of 500 employees would be spending £200,000 pa on stationery. An employee dedicated for one day of their time per week to controlling the procurement and distribution, would need only to effect a 5% saving (or increase in value for money) to justify the role - and pro-active control of an otherwise unpredicted upwards spiral could be even more beneficial. In larger organisations the payback for the same investment would be even greater.

Critical measures to achieve effective cost control would be to:

- analyse the cost centre at budget stage into the categories suggested above or as practically convenient for benchmarking and budgetary control purposes

- prepare the budget analytically and by reference to benchmarks in a form such as suggested in Fig. 7.3.D - this will provide both justification for the estimate and a base from which to track change pro-actively.

Fig. 7.3.D
Preparation and presentation of the stationery budget

	Category	Components	Budget per capita £	Number of employees	Total £
1.	General office paper products	Headed notepaper Copier paper Fax paper Envelopes & labels Books and pads Business forms Packaging materials Sundries	180	850	153,000
2.	Personal desk consumables	Writing equipment Typing accessories Collating and adhesive accessories Sundries	60	850	51,000
3.	Storage stationery	Ring binders and files Filing systems Visible record systems Storage boxes Sundries	30	850	25,000
4.	Presentation materials	OHP foils and storage Slides and storage Presentation equipment Seminar / conference incidentals Sundries	15	850	13,000
5.	Administration	Clerical assistant 1/1.5 days / week			5,000
	Totals				**247,000**
	Total per capita				**290**

- set up a stock control system and monitor key categories on a regular basis; this will not only avoid running out of stock but also indicate areas where change in processes or type of project or numbers of personnel, or inherently wasteful practices are likely to break the budget

- dispense consumables from a central source - do not leave them to be picked up from an uncontrolled stock area (Editor's note: I recently found and counted 85 ball-point pens in my bedroom dressing-table drawer - there are about another 100 in a bag in a drawer of my desk, retrieved guiltily two year's ago from the same source!)

- check the prices of a key sample of goods on a regular basis against the supplier's competitors

- make sure that quantity discounts are always applied where applicable

- check each bill thoroughly and query any discrepancy, however trivial - it will keep the suppliers on the ball and your interest may draw a better service out of them

- take an interest in the processes consuming the stock, and look for ways to value - engineer the way stationery is used in every activity

- do not waste time trying to recycle waste paper in the office as scrap pads; it takes a lot of effort and people will not use them anyway. It is better to concentrate on recycling the waste paper externally; at least that way a token contribution will be made to the overall cost of paper from recycled sources

- try to purchase as many products as possible from low-grade recycled material - this will help to make its collection and re-processing commercially more viable

- always match the quality to the need - letter quality paper left in the photocopier paperfeed from the last report is apt to be host to many images not worthy of the quality it offers

- always remember that exceeding the stationery budget may be the result of increased or more profitable business compared with that forecast; the key to cost control is in identifying the changes in advance of un-budgeted excesses (budgetary control) and being all the time on top of the relationship between the business requirement and efficient use of the consumables supporting it

- remember the lesson based on 'Pareto's principle' - that 80% of the cost will be in 20% of the goods purchased - and pick out the key cost drivers for particular and constant analysis and monitoring.

If a dedicated cost controller cannot be resourced then there are firms who specialise in doing that job for no cost - just a share of the saving they will surely make from anyone's average spend on stationery.

7.4 PRINTING AND REPROGRAPHICS

Introduction

Possibly no other facility has changed as much as this one in terms of process and quality in the past decade. Dependence on 'hard copy' has lessened in many businesses due to the advent of email and the associated electronic filing capabilities.

Keeping abreast of developments in this field is critical to the ability of facilities managers to maintain control of the process - indeed, to win - and keep - responsibility for it.

7.4.1 HARD COPY REPRODUCTION

The processes

A meaningful and comprehensive analysis of the economics of printing and reprographics can only be achieved by the inclusion of all aspects of the organisation's printing and reprography process. The increased use of personal computers (pc's) in the workplace, with localised printers, has affected the usage of photocopying as the preferred process for producing duplicate copies of a document. The 'paperless office' has yet to materialise but the proper use of appropriate ICT systems by staff willing to adapt to current work procedures is beginning to generate a 'less-paper' working environment.

The technology behind these services continues to change significantly. Advancement in techniques for the electronic transfer of information, and the consequent effect upon the way business is conducted, will have an even greater impact upon the demand for reprographics and printing services in future. It is therefore necessary to be precise about the definitions surrounding these processes:

- plate printing is the process of reproducing an image through the application of ink

- electronic printing is the process of producing an original image directly from electronic data

- reprography is the process of copying documents by photography (photocopying) or digital scanning either by centralised, staff print-rooms or by local, self-service, 'satellite' photocopiers.

Current equipment offering a combined printer, scanner, copier, fax technology make the segregation of these definitions more challenging.

During the 1980's and 90's the production of printed matter increased in many market sectors due in part to the ease and falling costs of production of printed matter. However more recently the increased reliability of and improvements in standard office software and hardware, combined with more widespread understanding of the way staff should use these systems effectively, are gradually bearing fruit in a reduction in demand for printing and photocopying services. The ease, speed, efficiency and falling costs of printing to good quality direct from the pc has resulted in reduced dependence on photocopiers with increased electronic printing of multiple documents, where this is still considered necessary. Furthermore, during this period the improved software and printing techniques has led to increased expectations of the quality of printed matter, colour, paper quality, print clarity and the like.

The term 'printing' to the office worker is now as synonymous with the ink-jet on the end of their pc 'print' button as with production of the daily newspaper. Both processes stem from the same technology but bulk printing and graphics printing are not yet differentiated correctly in the minds of those who analyse office services costs.

Inkjet printers are cheap to buy but much more costly to run than either desktop laser printers or photocopiers and multi-functional devices (MFDs) which combine the functionality of scanners, printers, photocopiers and fax machines. In turn, desktop laser printers cost typically twice as much to run as a photocopier or MFD. Many offices are cluttered by a plethora of devices - desktop printers, copiers and fax machines. This can be avoided by the introduction of MFD technology: this achieves a two-fold improvement by saving space and reducing costs.

Central reprographic department (CRD) equipment now offers digital xerographic printing in both monochrome and full colour with attendant savings on plate-making and set-up time; the ensuing cost makes short-run 'print on demand' viable and also obviates the need to store the larger quantities necessary for a viable litho print run so avoiding the waste that can occur when stored bulk print becomes obsolete. CRD equipment can be found in the central printroom of a larger organisation or in a specialist digital print company or copyshop.

So, as the economics of the process are changing so is its location - not just the point of reproduction but also the origination.

The contents of the cost centre

Fig. 7.4.A gives the suggested protocol for this cost centre. Printing and reprographics is probably the most difficult of all the facilities services to analyse so many organisations will need to modify their accounting and equipment monitoring procedures if they are to begin to make real sense of what can be quite high levels of expenditure.

Fig. 7.4.A *Facilities Economics classification protocol - printing and reprographics cost centre*

Sub-categories (contract bundle items)	Principal Examples / cost elements	Items commonly included in costs	Items excluded from costs	
			Item	Refer to category:
Not applicable	Convenience copiers Central black and white photocopiers Central colour photocopiers Origination / DTP controller Off-site printing	Paper, task management, equipment leases and maintenance, dedicated staff, contract charges	Utilities General facilities management	Utilities General facilities management

Origination

A wide range of graphic and desk-top publishing software packages gives the organisation the opportunity to produce in-house those important prestige documents and visual aids which used to go out to the graphic design house for manual artwork. Those same houses these days use much the same software as the in-house originator; the difference is in the design skills of the professional which may not be available in-house unless dedicated graphic designers can be afforded and kept busy on a full-time basis.

For a special publication such as company report and accounts or a product operating manual, the cost of origination will be anything from 15% to 50% of the total cost; at the lower end of this range are found the low-circulation slim reports where printing costs of a small publication tend to be high due to 'make-ready' time, and vice versa.

Reprographics

Modern photocopiers are judged on six issues:

- quality
- productivity
- capabilities, ie range of functions
- reliability
- size
- price.

High quality is more or less taken for granted, with the increasingly sophisticated built-in electronic controls able to monitor performance and, in many cases, adjust the operating settings to correct any fall-off in the pre-set quality, eg variation in drum toner deposition, temperature, humidity and exposure may be picked up by a sensor and automatically re-adjusted to suit, and advanced all-digital machines can be connected by modem to the maintenance monitoring team for 'remote diagnosis'.

This improved performance does mean more capital cost but on the other hand can significantly reduce 'down time' as well as guaranteeing quality and speed of operation.

Two-sided copying obviously saves 50% on paper, which can reduce by up to one-third the total cost of producing a photocopied report. This process has been speeded up by better document-feeding and paper-handling: paper paths are now shorter and can handle a large range of different paper sizes including re-cycled stock. 50-100 gsm copier paper can usually be accommodated in cassettes, stackers and trays while manual by-pass feeders will cope with acetate film for transparencies as well as paper up to 200 gsm.

Operator time is a big feature of photocopying, especially where long repetitive runs are involved. Internal memory in the latest copiers enables complex sequels of instructions to be memorised, freeing the operator for other tasks. This is particularly important in smaller 'top heavy' businesses where senior and expensive specialists sometimes tend to do their own copying to cope with rush jobs.

On some machines commonly used sequences can be programmed by inserting a credit-card sized memory card or remotely using a desk-top editor which may be a battery-operated portable. The all-digital copiers are now making inroads into the mid-range market. Their increased productivity through digitally once-only-scanned images stored in memory, two-sided copies being produced without a duplex tray, electronic storage of pages in the correct order, plus creative features such as wide zoom range, merging of images, addition of text and comprehensive editing make them attractive to organisations highly dependent upon high resolution, high speed domestic copying.

All-digital copiers, or multi-functional devices (MFDs), can be networked together, depending on the configuration selected; they offer scanning, copying, printing and faxing from one device which can take the place of the conventional photocopier, desktop laser printer and/or workgroup printer.

Fig. 7.4.B
Typical capital costs for various grades of black/white photocopier

Reference	Generic features				Capital cost £
	Paper supply sheet	Copies per month	Basic speed A4	Duplex speed	
1	1,000	8,000	15 / min	1 / min	4,000
2	2,000	20,000	30 / min	10 / min	12,000
3 All-digital	4,000	50,000	50 / min	20 / min	24,000
4 All-digital	5,000	75,000	60 / min	45 / min	30,000
5 All-digital	6,000	100,000	80 / min	50 / min	35,000

Fig. 7.4.B shows a generic range of black/white photocopiers together with typical capital costs while Fig. 7.4.C works out on a theoretical base the cost per copy (excluding paper) in a typical copy run.

Fig. 7.4.C
Typical machine and operating cost per copy of each generic type of photocopier

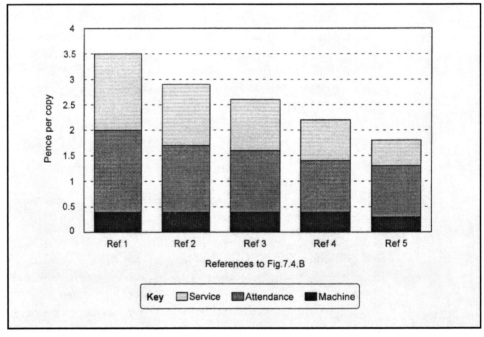

It is interesting to see how the machine cost per copy remains relatively constant as the runs get bigger, whereas the staff time in attendance reduces to a less insignificant figure. This is partly due to the programmable routines of the larger more sophisticated machines but also to the fact that the set up and retrieval time per copy are much less as the runs get longer - just like the economics of the old 'make-ready' time in traditional printing. Of course, where two sided copying is concerned the larger fast machines can halve the paper and machine cost per sheet with little penalty in terms of attendance time; (depending on volume of paper discounts) this means that the paper costs will come down by as much as 0.25p per printed side of the document saving almost 0.4p per side overall.

Note, however, that where local or satelite copying (see below) is a major feature of the regime, machine costs per copy will be substantially higher as will the costs of attendance - however, the latter will be 'indirect' so not shown as 'hard' costs.

Just as all-digital multi-functional device (MFDs) are taking the place of monochrome (black & white) photocopiers a new generation of colour/monochrome copier-printers is capable of taking the place of desktop colour inkjet printers, colour laser printers and conventional photocopiers. Speeds of 20cpm in full colour are now normal and the overall cost of copying and printing in full colour is steadily falling.

Local copiers

In most organisations of any size local or satelite copiers are used to supplement central reprographics.

The ratio of staff per copier will range from 50:1 to 300+:1; at the latter end of the range cost per capita increases will be significant - up to £100 per capita pa over a less locally-dependent regime.

There is also a tendency for organisations to 'collect' a disparate range of makes, models and contracts (including maintenance agreements and copy number discounts, bonuses and penalties) usually accompanied by lack of a reliable inventory of equipment and its annual costs; needless to say economic inefficiency will abound in such a regime.

The advent of digital technology presents the opportunity to rationalise this assortment of equipment with networked copier-printers that offer lower-cost printing and the ability to scan documents in, as well as the usual copying facility. This opportunity to rationalise may be missed if ICT departments ignore the convergence of copying and printing technologies and the scope for much lower running costs than traditional desktop and workgroup laser printers.

Machine printing

This process which was traditionally based on printing presses using hand-set lead characters was overtaken in the late 1960's by the off-set lithographic process. This has remained in place as the principal system with the machines developing in sophistication, particularly electronically, and now able to print direct from disks.

More economical than reprographics over long runs there is yet little difference discernible to the lay person between off-set litho and state-of-the-art 'industrial' photocopiers in terms of quality.

Few companies (other than major publishing houses) contemplating bringing their printing in-house (going against the trend nowadays) would consider other than high-quality reprographics for their commercial printing needs given issues of cost, quality and simplicity of operation and quality control.

Computer printing

The object of the computer printer originally was to produce the 'artwork' from which pages could be reproduced by photocopier or lithographically. However, the advent of laser (led) printing (see below) has led to a substantial increase in the use of computed print-out for volume reproduction purposes.

The generic printing types are:

- dot matrix
- ink jet
- laser
- light emitting diodes (led).

Dot matrix printer: is the cheapest in terms of capital cost although letter quality can only be achieved on the top 24 pin machines. Most organisations having dot matrix printers will use them only for internal reporting.

Output speeds are quite good, paper handling is flexible and some of the better quality machines can handle graphics and connect up to ink-jet colour printing. They tend to be a bit noisy and are rapidly losing out in the market to the laser printers.

Ink jet (bubble jet) machines: are the middle of the range with quality higher than dot matrix and approaching that of laser but usually with the advantage of being able to print in full colour. Print speed is now much improved and they are useful for printing business graphics in colour. Inkjet printers are cheap to acquire and are small, lightweight and reasonably quiet in operation. However, they are only suitable for very low throughput as consumable costs (ink cartridges) are higher than other forms of output. They are the slowest process and the ink is liable to smudge for a minute or two after printing. Small, lightweight, quiet machines, they have good colour options at a reasonable cost and are particularly efficient for putting graphic images on to paper.

Laser printers: have taken the market by storm with prices getting lower and more competitive all the time. They can produce professional looking documents at high speed, have excellent paper-handling capabilities and can produce high quality colours.

The caveat with such printers is that consumable costs (laser tone cartridges) are high and the cost per printed page is typically double that of a photocopier. Although acquisition costs are low this high running cost is rarely taken into account. Desktop printers tend to proliferate, sometimes reaching 'one per desk' in extreme cases with consequent adverse effect on printed output costs.

LED (light emitting diode): an alternative to laser printers is presented by similar-looking devices using LED (light emitting diode) technology. The acquisition cost is competitive but running costs are significantly lower and more comparable with photocopying.

7.4.2 PROCUREMENT

Important matters to consider when choosing a copier or printer are:

- monthly volume
- the expected growth of the company
- requirements for colour copies
- the main reproduction requirements
- how much space is available for the copying equipment
- quality
- extent of collating and stapling/binding
- speed of output
- extent of use of mainly A4 copies
- frequency of need for enlarged/reduced/two-sided copying
- networking issues.

Photocopiers and printers are all available with a full range of procurement options. They can be purchased outright or leased with a variety of plans and tax benefits similar to that described in detail for motor vehicles in Chapter 7.8.3 (Fig 7.8.C) below. However, lives of the printing and reprographic machines are normally only about three years, so depreciation and rental are comparatively high.

The majority of copiers are leased and only those used for low volumes are usually bought outright. The types of lease/rentals available are:

- **copy plan** - a rental is paid for the machine and then a charge is paid for the number of copies made

- **service plan** - a rental is paid for the machine and a monthly or quarterly charge is paid to cover any services necessary for the machine

- **straight rental** - a fee is paid for the rental of the machine only, any call-out charges being invoiced at cost.

There has been concern in recent years about copyplan and leasing contracts which has led to a number of major suppliers to issue codes of practice. The problems occur because most manufacturers deal at arms length with the end users of the machines. When getting into a copier contract it is important to know the monthly volume of copies.

A recent survey in the UK revealed that 63% of companies were paying too much for their copying services. Things to consider before entering into a contract are:

- monthly volume of copies

- length of contract desired

- type of contract wanted, eg copyplan, service plan

- future company needs

- the full contract implications, eg some contracts can only be changed by paying 45% of the remaining rental instalments, so getting the contract right at the start is essential

- many companies get taken in by 'X000 copies free' - this overhead has usually already been added to the capital cost of the machine.

The convergence of copying and printing, previously seen as two separate disciplines, the one handled by office services and the other by IT, is now such that a common approach should be taken to the procurement of copiers and printers. Multi-functional devices (MFDs), as mentioned previously, offer a real opportunity to reduce output costs and to save space and energy costs.

7.4.3 THE IN-HOUSE PRINT DEPARTMENT

It is a fact, that along with the 'first impression' of a company portrayed by the telephonist/receptionist, the quality of the printed material emanating from a company either by way of marketing/publicity material, mail-shots, annual reports, presentations, general correspondence, and even architect's drawings speaks volumes in today's highly competitive market place.

With the technology now available, the days of the dark and dingy printroom, billowing clouds of ammonia from the dye-line machines somewhere in the basement, are over.

The printroom now is very much an integral part of the business, working in close co-operation with every department in an organisation that calls upon its services.

Generally speaking, photocopiers are still to be found on every floor for use by all employees as required, but the large industrial photocopiers capable of producing direct copy (mono or colour), enlarging/reducing, trimming, collating, folding, stapling/binding documents at high speed, need to be sited where the resultant noise will not invade the general ambience of the organisation. The printroom is manned by specialist personnel with machines capable of producing high quality material.

The innovation of CAD, in recent years, has largely made obsolete the need for dyeline printing in those organisations with the necessary technology to enable the information to be sent direct to a plotter sited in the printroom from a pc anywhere in the building.

Given the requisite volume of business and relevant expertise there is no reason why the in-house print-room should not be just as efficient as the outsourced version. All other things being equal the in- or out-house decision will all be down to the quality of management, the funds available to fund the right equipment along with the inevitable and relentless upgrading of technology and the vigour with which the core versus non-core issues are raised and contested.

7.4.4 THE ANNUAL COSTS

Costs for a wide variety of organisations per capita pa are given at Fig. 7.4.D; although the larger companies have more expensive equipment the economies of higher volumes tend to even things out. They also usually achieve a consistently higher quality, which is a bonus due to the fact that the productive high speed copiers generate the better quality automatically.

Fig. 7.4.D
Sample range of printing and reprographic costs per capita pa

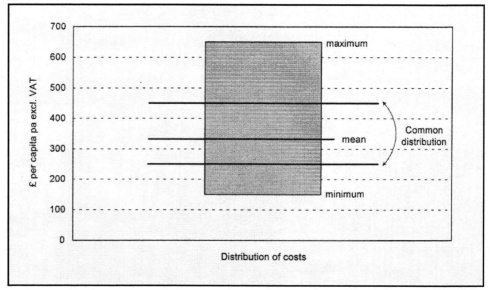

Usage within this range in most modern organisations is between around 5,000 - 15,000 printed sheets per capita pa. Depending on the efficiency of the set-up the more expensive local photocopiers may account for between 10% and 50% of the volume.

Per capita in this context always means per office-based worker.

Overall, as with 'stationery' in Chapter 7.3, there is no discernible pattern of difference in the wide-ranging sample of large and small organisations - however there are some critical differences in the way the cost centre is analysed. The principal issues are whether or not paper and attendance are included; this analysis excludes paper and includes attendance.

Where printing is outsourced the cost of the paper should be asked for separately to enable the costs to be analysed comparably with an in-house cost excluding paper. Most printers quote for large jobs on a separated basis anyway, so it should present them with no problems.

The cost drivers

Among the key factors affecting the overall costs within the range at Fig. 7.4.D are:

- centralised v localised facilities

- nature of business

- volume and quality of documents for distribution; (it should be noted that where an organisation's main output is in printed document form such as books, printed reports, brochures, leaflets and alike, this should be viewed as part of the core business activity and not benchmarked against the routine office expenditure levels in Fig. 7.4.D, previous page)

- efficiency of equipment

- contract arrangements

- extent of computer printing

- extent of colour copying

- extent of non-standard size paper usage.

7.5 INFORMATION AND COMMUNICATION TECHNOLOGY (ICT)

Introduction

Information and Communication Technology (ICT) is at the core of the business process. The office building has become a place to house and network computers so that staff can use ICT in the company of others with a degree of supervision. As the cost of wide-band communication falls the need for staff to work in an office for technology or cost reasons will disappear. Indeed 10% of the US working population is already working from home and in Europe the figure is approaching 5%.

However the social and supervisory aspects of office work will remain significant factors and working together in office buildings will not disappear. What will change is the move to location-independent working for more senior grades of staff. Professional information or knowledge workers are already benefiting from the flexibility of working part of the time in the office and part of the time at home. This trend will continue, with certain professionals only attending the office for specific meetings or social events.

The larger consultancies have many thousands of staff working in this way with dramatic impact on the cost of providing office space. Accenture in London has approximately one desk for every four consultants. The cost per sq m in fit-out cost was at the upper end of the spectrum for a city centre but the cost per head is only one quarter of that. This saving has been achieved by implementing voice and data networks that promote location-independent working and investing in web-based reservation systems that enable employees to book a desk by the hour or day according to need.

However, ICT is not predominantly a means of cutting back on premises costs; its primary goal is the improvement of the quality and speed of communications between and within organisations. An associated rationalisation of working methods and the facilities supporting them is inevitable, but in many cases the facilities cost savings feature too large in the business case.

7.5.1 ICT AND THE BUSINESS

The economics of ICT

Overall the cost of ICT for any given unit of function continues to fall rapidly, perhaps halving in real terms every five years. However, the extent to which modern business uses ICT is growing at a similar rate so that overall spend is more constant. There are very significant differences in the spend on ICT by industry sector. Fig. 7.5.A (over the page) shows the variation in IT spend per annum for different sectors. Companies in the financial services sector spend up to ten times as much as per head as some other sectors. There are also significant changes in where the money is spent. Mainframe computers costing millions of pounds have been replaced by large file servers costing tens of thousands. In contrast the money spent on mobile phone calls and Internet access has grown very rapidly and in many organisations now exceeds the fixed telecommunications costs.

One of the highest costs is in staffing the ICT function, whether this is done in house or by outsourced service providers. ICT professionals are scarce and good quality staff are well paid. Fig. 7.5.B (over the page) shows the growth in ICT salaries over the past 10 years.

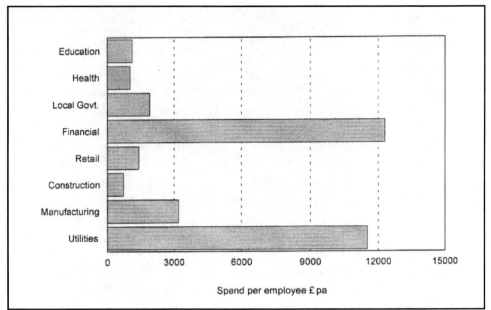

Fig. 7.5.A
ICT spend per employee pa

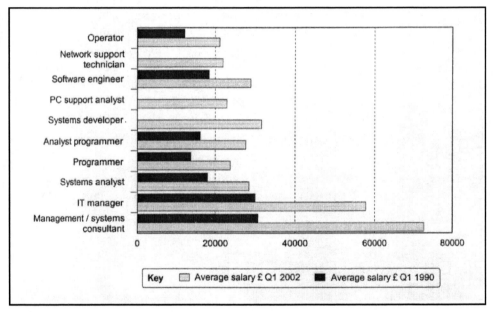

Fig. 7.5.B
ICT salaries over the past 10 years

ICT and the facilities manager

Certain specific aspects of the ICT are so closely inter-related with the premises that there is a very strong argument for integrating them under one manager - in particular the management of ICT distribution within the building from the wiring closet to the desk and in the future the reservation system necessary for location-independent working. The almost universal adoption of standard CAT-5 cable for voice and data services makes it no more difficult to manage than electrical power distribution. CAT-5 standard, which provides a four-pair, copper cable, and a standard RJ-45 outlet was originally developed by AT&T in the US and formalised in the EIA/TIA 568 standard. Compatible and compliant CAT-5 cabling systems are available from dozens of well-established suppliers such as BICC, Siemens and Alcatel.

The most logical split of responsibility is for the ICT department to deliver voice and data network capacity over the backbone to the wiring closet and the facilities department to be responsible for delivery from there to the desk. This includes taking responsibility for the horizontal voice and data cabling distribution, moves and changes of the physical elements, including floor boxes and cable patching to deliver the service to the correct desk.

Managing the investment in the core of ICT systems is becoming more and more complex and more of a specialisation. The overriding need is for close co-operation between ICT and facilities departments to deliver a safe, flexible and productive working environment. Fig. 7.5.C indicates a typical relationship between the costs of ICT and the other facilities in the context of annual turnover.

Fig. 7.5.C
Turnover, profit and facilities costs

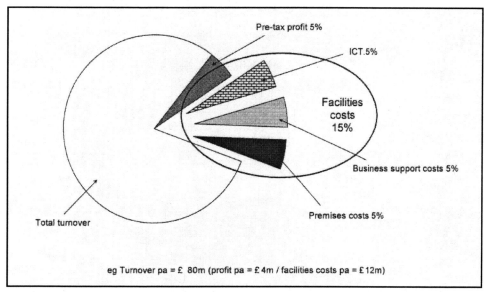

7.5.2 OFFICE NETWORKS

Over the last decade or so there has been a dramatic shift from proprietary computer and word-processing systems from suppliers such as IBM, BULL and WANG to a more or less standards-based architecture. That architecture comprises:

- personal computers with network connections
- shared networked printers
- structured voice and data cabling
- Radio LANs and DECT phones
- network hubs and switches
- backbone cabling
- central ICT equipment rooms.

Fig. 7.5.D shows a typical office computer network configuration.

Fig. 7.5.D
Office computer network

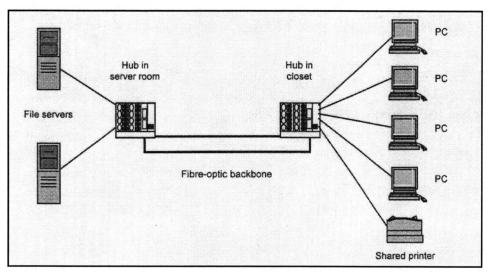

Personal Computers

The personal computer with a network connection is the visible element of the ICT infrastructure. The main suppliers such as Compaq, Dell, and HP offer similar products in a very competitive market. Microsoft has almost 100% of the operating systems market leaving hardware manufacturers little room for differentiation. Successive generations of operating system software including Windows 95, Windows 98, Windows NT workstation and now Windows XP and the associated office applications have brought limited business benefit over and above their previous versions but have demanded higher performance hardware for each generation. Typical office pc's are now specified with 800Mhz Pentium III processors, 20GB of hard disk space and 128 or 256Mb of memory and well as a CDROM or DVDROM drive.

A 17 inch (425mm) display screen is considered adequate for normal office work with 19 inch (475mm) or 21 inch (525mm) only required for graphics, typesetting and CAD work. However, organisations that have introduced document scanning have found that 19 inch (475mm) or 21 inch (525mm) screens with very high resolution are needed for staff to view scanned document images. This is particularly important for hand completed forms such as insurance claim forms.

Many companies are now looking seriously at replacing conventional CRT displays with plasma TFT displays that were originally developed for laptops. The technical benefits include:

- reduce glare and reflections

- lower power consumption and heat output

- elimination of high electrostatic fields and the associated dust problems

- elimination of magnetic fields.

Good quality 15inch (375mm) displays with a performance equivalent to a 17inch (425mm) CRT are now less than £600. Easynet, the Internet café operator, has equipped 2000 seats in London with TFT displays enabling the use of smaller desks and significantly more workstations per sq m.

Shared network printers

Shared networked printers allow several staff to share a single, high speed printer that can have multiple trays for plain, headed and continuation paper. The shared printer can be located away from an individual desk which reduces the impact of the noise, ozone, paper and toner dust that is inherent in the laser printing process. Newer printers have significantly lower standby power consumption and heat output, typically less than 10 Watts when idle compared with 500-600 when printing.

As indicated in 7.5.5, the new digital multi-functional copy/print devices (MFD's) offer the functionality of network printers, photocopiers and, optionally fax machines. A workgroup's output needs can be provided by one piece of equipment rather than two or three and they will also have the ability to scan documents and send to a central repository or their own PC.

Structured voice and data cabling

CAT-5 horizontal cabling has already been mentioned as the international standard. The latest European standard ISO/IEC 11801 (Channel D) has led to an enhanced version of CAT-5 called CAT-5E which is certified for 100MHz up to 90m and is able to support 100Mbps Ethernet over that distance. Typical installations provide between two and four outlets per desk that can be used for any mix of pc or printer network connection, digital telephone and analogue telephone, fax or modem connection. It should be noted that the structured cabling is only integrated for the last horizontal element to the desk and even then a given socket is being used for voice or data but never both at the same time. Many buildings adopt a convention where socket No1 of the four is used for the pc, socket No2 for the printer (if any), socket No3 for an analogue phone, fax or modem and socket No4 for a digital phone. **With the growing emphasis on location-independent working, visitors expect all meeting rooms to be equipped with analogue line sockets for them to use a laptop with a modem.** The same applies to hotel rooms where such facilities are still the exception rather than the rule.

Radio LANs and DECT phones

Alternatives to cable are becoming viable and attractive in certain situations. British Airways uses radio LANs in the café areas of its new HQ near Heathrow to allow visiting staff to log-on to email without making a physical connection. Similar applications in touchdown space where staff are also using a cell-phone or Digital Enhanced Cordless Telephone (DECT) cordless phone are also viable. Link speeds of 11Mbps are now commercially available but radio LANs are unlikely to replace all data cabling in conventional office buildings especially where cable-ways have to be provided for electrical power distribution to desktop equipment.

Network hubs and switches

Ethernet hubs or switches in wiring closets typically offer 24 or 48 Ethernet ports with auto-sensing of 10 or 100 Mbps equipment. An Ethernet hub effectively shares the 10 or 100Mbps network segment between the users. In practice a 24 port hub with a 100Mbps backbone connection is more than adequate for standard office applications because the users will not all be attempting to copy a file or print a document at the same time. Ethernet switches are different in that each port has its own dedicated bandwidth with no contention for the network segment. Switches are primarily used in server rooms to connect multiple servers to the backbone and for exceptional office applications such as CAD.

Backbone cabling

Fibre optic backbones for data are typically based on 12 or 24 core multi-mode optical fibre. Multi-mode optical fibre has a 62.5 micron diameter core and is acceptable for use in buildings up to one Gbps. For larger sites including campus situations the more expensive mono-mode fibre with its more difficult to work 8 micron cores is necessary. Conventional multi-core copper cable is still used for voice network backbones. Typically multiples of 50 pair cable are used to deliver blocks of 24 active telephone sockets to the wiring closets where they are patched through to the desk.

Central ICT equipment rooms

The backbone cables from each wiring closet are brought to central ICT equipment or a server room where all central equipment is housed in a secure environment. The growing importance of ICT demands that these rooms are operational 24 hours a day 365 days a year. Business managers expect to be able to send an email from their laptop at home any hour of the day or night and the equipment to provide that service is in the server room. Facilities managers are usually responsible for providing and maintaining the central ICT or server room. Typically these rooms require:

- standby diesel power generation
- redundant (spare) un-interruptable power supply
- duplicate electrical power distribution
- redundant (spare) 24-hour cooling
- fire rated walls and doors

- fire detection and fire prevention
- remote monitoring and alarms
- access control and CCTV surveillance.

7.5.3 EXTERNAL NETWORKS

External network connectivity is of growing importance to business and often partly falls under the responsibility of the facilities manager. The last 10 years or so have been dominated by the de-regulation of telecommunications such that Britain now has over 200 licensed telecommunications operators licensed under the Telecommunications Act 1984.

Access to multiple carriers has now become an issue for building acquisition. Property agents have been known to roam the streets looking at inspection chamber covers to find out which networks pass the building they are trying to let. For the acquirer the expectation is that a building will have duplicated, diverse duct routes to the principal carrier and enough duct entries for alternative carriers to ensure services are offered at competitive rates. This is easily achieved in the centres of capital cities or purpose built high-tech business parks but, at present, almost impossible in provincial or isolated locations.

New developments in broadband digital radio access will remove some of these limitations and provide economical and competitive connectivity and divers routing outside city centres.

The Internet

All commercial organisations require an Internet connection for communication with other organisations via electronic mail (email). In most commercial organisations and larger public bodies email has all but replaced facsimile (fax) and post for day to day business communication. An Internet connection is obtained from an Internet Service Provider (ISP). With the advent of free Internet service for the private residential sector those remaining in the business to business (B2B) market are able to offer a higher quality but paid-for service.

Smaller organisations can use an ISDN2 dial-up connection to their ISP. Typically this will cost £350 pa for line rental and perhaps £200 to £400 in call charges per month. ISDN connection charges and line rentals are significantly lower in Germany and France where they are almost the same price as analogue lines. The ISP normally provides a router as part of the package and will charge in the region of £225 per month for the service. The ISP will register an Internet domain name such as 'mycompany.com' or 'mycompany.co.uk' and allocate a block of 32 or 64 IP addresses for an internal network.

Medium size organisations (100 staff) will need to have a leased line connection with a capacity of typically 256Kbps while larger organisations will need up to two or more 2Mbps links with load balancing. Leased lines have high connection charges and annual rentals but there are no call charges. Typically a 256Kbps leased line will be £250 to connect and £1,200 pa to rent. A 2Mbps leased line will cost about £18,000 pa to rent.

The security and resilience of the email server and Internet connections are of key importance to business credibility. Firewalls and virus scanning software have become essential to keep out unwanted hackers and viruses from business networks. An ISP with a highly resilient server installation and duplicated and diversely routed connections are considered the minimum for all but the smallest organisations.

Wide Area Networks (WANs)

These systems enable inter-office communications by public network over longer distances nationally and internationally. In the past WANs have been constructed using networks of leased lines which can be costly to acquire and difficult to manage. Telecommunication carriers now offer a range of managed services as an alternative; these include frame relay, cell relay and Switched Multi-rate Data Services (SMDS).

The benefit of these managed services is that the carrier is responsible for all of the complex operational and management issues and for ensuring network resilience. Each business site requires only one (or two if duplicated) connection to the carrier's service. Bandwidth can be increased on demand with a simple phone call and only minimal capital investment is required.

Smaller organisations can use the Internet to replace their wide area network by using the Point-To-Point-Tunnelling (PTPT) protocol to send data securely between offices.

Value added networks

Value added network services such as Electronic Data Interchange (EDI) which were used for the exchange of business documents, like invoices and orders, are being replaced by use of the Internet. Large customers such as the motor manufacturers are establishing vertical Internet portals and forcing the component supplier to trade with them electronically. Their Internet sites encourage suppliers to bid electronically for each order with the business being placed with the lowest cost supplier of car seats, tyres or any other component.

It is anticipated that this practice will also become commonplace in facilities management and construction in the years to come.

7.5.4 TELEPHONE SYSTEMS

Facilities managers are more likely to be responsible for telephone services than any other aspect of ICT. This is partly because of the need to employ telephone operators who often double as receptionists and partly for historical reasons in that companies had telephones long before IT became important.

Despite the rise in the business use of email, telephone communication is still important to business operations.

The Private Automatic Branch eXchange (PABX) industry has consolidated with a relatively small number of suppliers offering very similar products. Modern systems usually have Direct Dial In (DDI) which allows an outside caller to dial extensions direct without going via the operator. This is often combined with voice mail so that the call will be answered if the extension user is taking another call or away from their desk. Typically only one in seven business to business calls reaches the intended recipient first time.

Operators are crucial to efficient telephone service and need careful training and a detailed knowledge of the company. An electronic directory that can be searched on line to find the correct person or department and business information such as who is responsible for a particular product or service can assist their task.

Extension instruments are proprietary to the particular PABX, which enables the supplier to charge £225 per phone compared to a fully featured analogue phone, which costs £40 to £60. Useful features are a display to indicate who is calling and the number being dialled and an indicator to show that a voice mail message has been stored.

Private networks

Larger organisations used to establish private voice networks of leased lines between offices. These were made up of 30-channel digital links on the backbone between larger offices and groups of two to ten analogue lines for smaller branch offices. Very substantial savings in call charges could justify the cost of the leased lines for these networks. Other benefits included the possibility of centralised operators working where a small team of operators at one location could answer the incoming calls for a national organisation. Lower dialled call charges have made these private leased line networks un-economic and many have now been replaced by Virtual Private Networks (VPNs). Telecommunications carriers provide VPNs using the public network but they appear to the user as a private network. So, for example, you can dial any extension at any site with a four or five digit number. Carriers offer substantial discounts over normal call charges to VPN customers and most of the cost is on a per call basis rather than the annual rental associated with a leased line network.

Voice Over IP (VOIP)

Some organisations are planning to route their voice traffic over their data networks so that there is only one network to manage. Most data networks now use the Internet Protocol (IP) and voice traffic can be encoded to produce Voice Over IP (VOIP). For the present there are some limitations in that there can be unacceptable delays on IP networks producing echo and other problems on speech circuits. For organisations that are already using a VPN for voice and a managed service such as SMDS for data there is little benefit and considerable complexity and capital cost associated with introducing VOIP.

Mobile 'phones

Mobile 'phones have become an accepted business tool and most companies provide them for managers and senior professional staff. The cost of the mobile phones is often subsidised by the cost of the call charges. There is considerable competition with several licensed carriers. The Group System Mobile (GSM) technology has been universally adopted resulting in compatibility between countries and networks. Although the service available is excellent the costs are very high. Business users are unable to make much use of the off-peak evening and weekend rates and typically pay £0.10 to £0.20 per minute for calls. This rises to £1.00 per minute for calls to phones in another country and an effective rate of several pounds per minute if the caller leaves a voice message, which is retrieved internationally. The mobile phone operators are making very large profits from business users and in part using this income to offer low off-peak charges to other consumers.

Wireless Application Protocol (WAP)

New developments in mobile phone technology will make them even more useful as business tools. The existing generation of phones are classed as second generation. Based on GSM technology they can send and receive data at up to 14.4 kbps. This is just enough to use them to access the Internet. The small screen and low data rate available on mobile phones has led to a dedicated protocol called Wireless Application Protocol (WAP). WAP is designed to allow the essentials of a web page to be condensed down to be presented on a mobile phone screen. It could indicate the balance of a current account, look up a train time, enable the purchase of a soft drink from a vending machine or list the runners and odds in a local horse race.

Web site designers now have to design two versions of a site, one for conventional PC users and one for WAP phone users. The screen on most mobile phones is so small that they will probably give way to Personal Digital Assistants (PDAs) with built-in mobile phones. PDAs such as the Palm Pilot and the Handspring provide a large enough screen to for short emails, diary, to-do list and an address book.

New generations of mobile phone technology including the intermediate General Packet Radio Service (GPRS) and the third generation Universal Mobile Telephone Service (UMTS) will provide higher data rates and 'always-on' Internet connections. Over the next five years these technologies have the potential to become a phone, PDA, satellite navigation system, ID card, credit card, cash, airline ticket and passport all rolled in to one hand-held package.

Controlling telecommunications costs

Controlling and managing telecommunications costs is an important issue for businesses. Several steps can be taken to reduce costs:

- call-barring
- least-cost routing
- call logging
- cross-charging
- break-out
- education and training.

The barring option simply stops the staff from making calls either at expensive times (time-barring), or to non-business numbers (number-barring), eg the range of consumer telephone services, or to subscribers outside of a certain call-charge band.

Least - cost routing is a system programmed to identify called numbers and takes the most cost-effective route available from the carriers at the time.

Call-logging is an in-house 'Big Brother' analysis of the destination, duration or originating extension of each call. In general, if staff know call-logging is in use the annual phone bill will fall by some 15%; larger productivity gains should, of course, accompany such savings. Most call-logging systems can produce a summary of call costs per department per month or quarter, which allows cross-charging.

Cross-charging regimes - both externally as expenses and internally via the internal market - are both extremely effective mechanisms for saving money on calls. Customers being charged abnormally high expenses will soon complain and get their way, and the internal cross-chargees will quickly get their minds around how to avoid running up a bill to a level which can easily equate to more than the annual building and services maintenance per capita.

Break-out is a facility whereby organisations with private leased lines between offices can use their private network to reach a distant node and then 'break out' onto the public network. In this way they only pay a 'local' rate for a long distance call. VPNs may offer similar local rates for national calls.

In the end, educating the staff (and directors) to use the telephone economically is an essential part of the facilities manager's role. Nevertheless, in spite of the high cost of the overhead it is a small proportion of the cost of employing the workforce; as such the savings regime must never be allowed to impede the efficiency of key staff going about their essential core business.

Fig. 7.5.E (over the page) shows a comparison of the total cost of calls from a mobile phone by an occasional, regular and constant user in conjunction with conventional static telephone calls.

Telephone system maintenance

The maintenance of the lines is included in the line rental charge for either analogue or digital connections. Maintenance of all PABX systems is mandatory from an approved contractor where there is more than one exchange line. The PABX manufacturer or the BSI certifies PABX maintenance contractors. It is normal to exclude the extension instruments since it is usually cheaper to replace them rather than repair. Similarly the extension wiring will normally be maintained by its installer as part of a larger building wiring scheme carrying both voice and data services. It is relatively easy for facilities managers to test a telephone port in the wiring closet with a spare phone to determine if a fault is in the central equipment, the wiring or the instrument.

Fig. 7.5.E
Typical mobile phone bills for an executive compared with PSTN

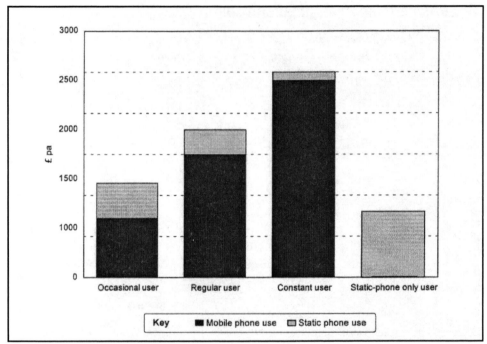

Depending on the call-out response time required the 'maintenance' will cost between 5% and 10% of the installed cost after the first year. This is very profitable business for suppliers since new digital electronic systems are very reliable and require no preventative maintenance at all.

Total costs of telephone services

A wide range of telephone service costs is incorporated in the sample range at Fig. 7.5.F which includes PSTN, cellular radio and cordless communications media but not facsimile transmission charges which are separately billed and deserve distinct analysis and cost control.

Fig. 7.5.F
Sample range of telephone costs per capita pa

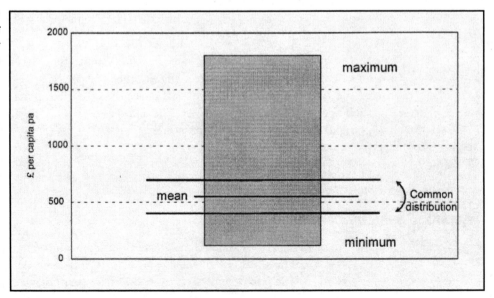

7.5.5 ADVANCED TELECOMMUNICATIONS

Use of Facsimile (Fax)

The use of fax has declined rapidly with the introduction of email. Its use remains strong in a number of specific business sectors, notably the legal and construction industries, which have been slow to adopt email. This is partly for legal reasons where a signed fax is accepted as a legal document and an email is not. Fax is also still widely used for international trade particularly with countries where Internet service provision is limited or unavailable.

Large organisations use fax-servers to integrate fax with email. Incoming faxes are distributed electronically to the recipient's email in-box where they can be read or printed on an ordinary laser printer on the local network.

The faster Group IV digital fax has failed to achieve significant market penetration and most organisations use analogue Group III Fax. Plain paper fax machines that use either inkjet or laser printing eliminate the need for special fax paper. The older thermal papers were expensive and tended to fade to illegibility if exposed to light for more than a few weeks.

Although memory features are useful in terms of flexibility of operation and use of cheap call-charge rates it is the speed of transmission which is the overall most critical economic factor.

Whereas the bottom end of the market will take about 20 seconds to transmit an A4 sheet, the top range Group IV faxes can go as fast as 1.5 seconds per page when linking to another ISDN subscriber. The effect of the low call-time and operator time of the fast machines in overall economic terms is quite startling.

Typical costs are from 3 to 20 pence per faxed page including the paper, call charge and the cost of the machine.

The figures excludes attendance time which is obviously considerably less for the faster machines; if included it would have a far more dramatic effect on the differential than the figures indicate. Of course, the cost of time taken to prepare a fax or transmission is a constant and, again, an infinitely greater number then the combined total of operational and attendance costs.

An alternative to dedicated fax machines is offered by MFD's which can offer Group IV fax capability in addition to copying and network printing.

Some useful additional features available depending upon the price paid are:

- error correction
- broadcast fax - for PR announcements to a regular list
- itemised billing of calls
- direct-to-accounts cost notification
- network integration - for direct-from-pc faxing
- mobile (including car-based) machines
- remote diagnosis and re-setting.

Finally, a sample from a large number of varied fax users at Fig. 7.5.G (over the page) gives the cost per capita excluding paper. This is a legitimate analysis convention given that the paper is not necessarily dedicated to fax in the growing number of plain paper models.

Nevertheless, it is important to analyse the paper **separately under stationery**, if possible by collecting and analysing the individual fax reports over the year for both annual budgeting and monthly cost monitoring. Of course, anyone who feels happier about including the paper in the cost centre may do so; as long as one knows the cost of a sub-component it does not, to a point, matter too much where it is finally deposited.

Fig. 7.5.G
Sample range of fax costs (excluding paper) per capita for a variety of users

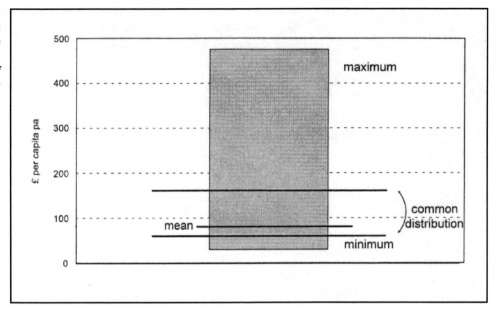

Video and audio conferencing

Meetings can consume up to 15% of an organisation's resources. Of that figure frequently more than half is spent in transit to and from the meeting incurring time costs and travelling expenses and often debilitating the travelling attendees to the extent that they under-perform at the event.

Meetings are expensive events, which may not always be necessary, or even desirable. The dichotomy primarily revolves around who should attend the meeting rather than whether it should actually take place. One point of view says that anyone who might have a contribution to make or need to hear the facts first hand should be there. The opposing view says to keep it small and make sure it is fully and accurately minuted.

If the former view prevails then the cost of those travelling will obviously be in direct proportion to the numbers.

Various forms of tele-conferencing are available to ease this problem but are considerably under-utilised, quite surprisingly so since they are invariably highly cost-effective.

Audio-conferencing

Public carriers offer very effective, high-quality audio-conferencing that can link participants in different countries. These work best if each participant uses an individual handset and dials into the conference bridge. The service is managed and must be booked. Participants must provide the operator with PIN before they are allowed to join in the call. It is possible to use a speakerphone for a group of participants in one room but the equipment must be of the highest quality to work effectively.

The simple ploy of gathering in a room to share a telephone conversation using an intercom telephone is little used. Many people would rather keep the conversation personal and relay a precis to whomever they deem appropriate rather than plan the call ahead and invite those who should really be participating in the discussion to sit around the phone for ten minutes or so - listening and contributing.

Conference adaptors costing less than £800 have been available for years, albeit that some of the pioneering models - designed primarily for hands-free use of the 'phone - made the speakers sound as if they were calling from the bathroom! However, the modern hands-free phones, especially those linked to the ISDN, provide excellent sound quality for this simple form of audio-conferencing.

So audio-conferencing has two main advantages:

- it enables colleagues to share a conventional telephone conversation

- it can help avoid travel to a formal meeting.

On the downside, the 'white of the eyes' cannot be seen, which may, or may not, be relevant and opportunities for social contact may be passed over to the general detriment of the marketing function.

To put the matter into economic perspective, two senior personnel travelling across a city for an hour-long meeting will possibly cost the organisation up to 4 man-hours (excluding the meeting time) plus two lots of travelling expenses - say £150 to £800 in total depending on the time-costs and distance. Against this, one hour on a 'phone, even at peak time, would cost less than £20.

Video-conferencing

Video-conferencing can also be effective in reducing the time and cost of business travel. Larger multinationals provide video-conference equipment at their principal offices. Typically these are in purpose-designed rooms where careful attention has been paid to the lighting and acoustics. It is quite difficult to achieve the optimum lighting and acoustic conditions for a video-conference.

A built-in system with rear projection, acoustic treatment and lighting controls costs from £70,000 to £100,000. Advanced equipment can combine two or more IDSN circuits to achieve better video quality. One 64Kbps circuit is only just useable whereas 384Kbps provides good quality pictures. The quality of the sound is very important for an effective meeting. The eye is more tolerant of imperfections and the video signal is less critical once the meeting has started. Telecommunications carriers provide videoconference-bridging services that enable you to connect audio and video with four other sites at the same time. A video-conference bridge is expensive at about £35,000 and it is usually more economic to use a carrier's service than to own and maintain the equipment.

An alternative to a purpose-built facility is to rent a video-conference room by the hour. These are available from telecommunications carriers and from serviced office providers. Even renting a room and the equipment in this way can result in significant savings. If the example includes inter-city travel taking a whole day plus two shuttle tickets then a cost of up to £3,000 for the meeting is quite likely. The cost of a bureau video-conference for a three hour meeting would be little more than £500 to £700 including time and expenses incurred travelling to and from a city centre bureau. The further the distances the more economical it becomes, particularly when international trips are involved. It also makes it possible for more people to attend the conference - which may or may not be beneficial.

Call centres

In many business sectors there has been a dramatic growth in the use of call centres for taking telephone orders or providing financial and other services. It is accepted that the cost of dealing with customers by telephone is significantly lower than by written correspondence. Typical costs are £1.00 to £2.00 by telephone compared to £15.00 to £20.00 by letter. The main users are those who provide services to large numbers of customers and include:

- airlines
- package holiday retailers
- electricity, gas and water utilities
- motor vehicle insurers
- banks and other financial services.

Call centres are specialised office buildings, often located outside capital cities where there is access to a large and mostly female labour pool. The occupation density is often close to the legal maximum. Agent desks are small with only room for a display screen, keyboard and telephone. The agents often wear a headset to keep both hands free for typing. All business information is provided on the screen to eliminate the need for paper on the desktop.

The core of the system is a PABX with automatic call distribution software that queues incoming calls and allocates them to the first free position. Large wall displays show the number of calls waiting and the average time to answer. Supervisors can listen in to any call for training purposes and the systems collect statistics about individual and team performance. Calling Line Identification (CLI) can be used to drive a connected computer system so that a customer's details can be presented on the screen at the same time as the call is presented to the agent. This facility is called 'screen-popping'.

The location of a call centre is usually determined by the availability of low cost office space and the local labour force. The use of freephone or local tariff numbers means that the caller is not charged or only charged local call costs for the call.

There is speculation that the Internet will reduce the demand for call centres since customers will be able to order goods and services on-line without talking to an operator. However, the increase in electronic transactions generally and the need to talk to a person when there is a problem with an Internet transaction may actually increase demand.

Businesses expect the cost of Internet transactions to be one tenth the cost of call centre transactions.

The cost of building a call centre is high requiring a substantial capital investment in the fit-out and ICT cost. Some organisations have chosen to outsource the whole function including staffing, hardware and software.

Typical costs for an outsource service are in the range £30 to £50 per seat per hour. This compares favourably with a basic staff cost of £15 per hour day-rate to £25 per hour night-rate taking into account employment taxes, vacation pay and an allowance for sick pay.

7.5.6 ICT COSTS

The cost of fitting out for ICT in a 4,000 sq m building for 300 staff is illustrated in Fig. 7.5.H (over the page).

A typical breakdown per capita of the annual costs of providing and operating such a system is given at Fig 7.5.J (over the page).

Because of the wide range of alternative configurations, it is neither feasible nor wise to provide typical costs against specific types of installation.

Fig. 7.5.H
ICT fit out costs for an office of 300 staff and 4,000 sq m NIA

Component	Qty	Unit	Unit cost £	Total £
Voice and data cabling	4,000	sq m	35	140,000
Telephone system	300	extns	600	180,000
Local area network				
Office ports	480	ports	250	120,000
Server ports	100	ports	600	60,000
Equipment room				
Floor	100	sq m	75	7,500
UPS	80	KVA	600	48,000
Cooling	60	KW	600	36,000
Fire protection	100	sq m	100	10,000
Electrical	100	sq m	225	22,500
Controls				22,500
Equipment cabinets	40	each	1,200	48,000
Desktop IT				
Personal computers	300	each	1,500	450,000
Software licenses	300	each	700	210,000
Network printers	30	each	2,200	66,000
Central IT				
File servers	20	each	10,000	200,000
Server software licenses	20	each	1,500	30,000
Routers and WAN				60,000
Total				1,710,500

Fig. 7.5.J
Typical range of ICT operating cost per capita pa

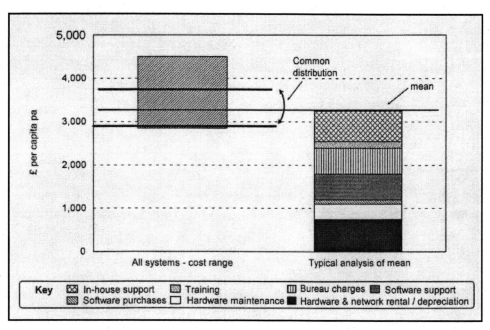

Hardware maintenance and support

These costs are fairly consistent with the complexity, and hence capital costs of the hardware. Depending on the exigencies of the call-out requirements the annual costs will normally be between 5% and 15% of the original purchase price.

Software maintenance and support

The better programs have a 'help-desk' facility to guide the user through operating difficulties. The main cost driver is the continual need to update; in many cases the purchase price will include for a certain number of updates, and/or offer them at large discounts.

Software licences

The licence is for a given number of users of the software and is a component of the price paid. Use of a program in excess of the licensed number is a breach of contract and copyright and is more easy to detect than many transgressors realise.

System management

The management of the system embraces:

- cable management

- condition and loading monitoring

- backing-up strategy

- application training

- pro-active advice on availability, performance and price of new hardware and software.

In a large installation a number of personnel will be dedicated to this function, possibly working to a director or senior manager with special responsibilities in the field. As a rough guide an organisation of 1,000 employees with a 1:1 terminal:user regime might need one dedicated systems manager with four assistants - say 0.25% of turnover. The ratio would be lower in a larger organisation and vice versa.

However, much depends on the complexities of a system, its age and the flexibility of the cabling system. Structured cabling (see 7.5.2 above) requiring only one type of cable to support all commonly available voice and data systems is a major bonus to the systems managers, especially given the usual proliferation and availability of useful equipment and systems and high 'churn' rates.

Some of the latest systems are designed with a special 'hub-based' connector enabling repositioning of workstations to be carried out in a fraction of the time required to relocate a conventional floor box.

7.5.7 SECURITY AND CONTINUITY

Business continuity plans and disaster recovery

Chapter 7.9 deals in detail with disaster prevention and recovery. With regard specifically to ICT, facilities managers have a leading role to play in developing and maintaining business continuity plans. Such plans need to be business-led not technology-led. Business managers must determine what is acceptable in terms of continuity. In some cases there will be legal minimum standards to be achieved. For example, the Financial Services Authority (FSA) will not grant a banking licence to a company that is planning to trade in foreign exchange, equities, bonds or other financial instruments until it can demonstrate an effective continuity plan.[1] For an investment bank this usually means a standby dealing room in another building no less than 400m away. The room must be available at all times and equipped to take over the trading 'book' within one hour of a major disaster. The cost of providing such facilities is so high that many companies pay a third party provider for the right to use a shared facility. Disaster recovery companies ensure that they do not sign up too many subscribers from a particular area of a city. This avoids a single incident resulting in competing claims for the same standby dealing room.

Where there are no legal requirements, shareholders expect the Board of Directors to take reasonable steps to secure the continuity of the business. In the past many companies affected by a major fire went out of business within a year or so of the disaster despite adequate insurance. The main reason for this is the loss of customer confidence or the simple loss of customers to competitors.

Business continuity plans must start with the main business process and determine how quickly each must be restored. For example:

- web site presence   30 min
- call centre   30 min
- telephone and email   4 hrs
- sales order processing   1 day
- production   3 days
- invoicing   5 days
- payroll   5 days
- accounts payable   10 days
- product development   20 days
- marketing   20 days.

One of the most difficult problems is providing office accommodation following a fire or terrorist incident. Organisations with two similar-sized offices deal with a major disaster at one location more easily than single-site businesses. One company with 500 staff in one office and 300 in another has a continuity plan that involves all staff working from home from both sites and the available desks then being used selectively for customer-facing functions like sales. The telephone and data networks are designed so that incoming calls can be routed to the surviving building and staff can log on at any pc at any location.

Asset management

Businesses need to maintain a database of their assets for statutory accounting purposes. Assets include furniture, computer and other office equipment and in a manufacturing environment will include production equipment. It is not usual to include air-conditioning and other fixtures in asset registers for accounting purposes because they cannot easily be removed from the building and would have only negligible value if removed; however, they may be recorded in a maintenance register.

Modern asset management software allows each asset to be labelled with a bar-coded label and for its physical location to be tracked. The software will record the purchase date and cost and calculate the annual or monthly depreciation for accounting purposes. For maintenance purposes the full maintenance history of components may be accessed via the bar-coded label.

---

[1] Financial Services Authority (2001) FSA Handbook - systems and controls, FSA, London, para 3.2.19.

Theft prevention

Careful controls are required to ensure that valuable equipment like laptop computers are not stolen by staff or others. These controls need to operate from the time a piece of new equipment is delivered until the day it is sold or disposed of. Particularly valuable items can be radio-tagged and detected by induction loops at exit points using similar technology to that used to prevent theft from shops. The radio tags need to be secured (possibly inside the equipment) so that they cannot be removed. The security tagging system should be linked to the swipe card access system so that staff authorised to take equipment out of the building do not need to be searched.

Data encryption

A number of high profile cases have demonstrated the risks of data falling into the wrong hands when laptops have been stolen or left in taxis. One senior military officer had his laptop stolen from a vehicle while he was looking at new cars in a showroom. The loss of the laptop itself was not serious; however the c-drive contained the NATO battle plan for the liberation of Kuwait in the Gulf war!

There is a legal requirement under the Data Protection Act 1984 to keep any personal information secure. If employees are allowed to carry laptops that contains personal information such as the names of clients or customers then this should be encrypted so that it cannot be extracted from a stolen laptop.

Domain names

An organisation's world wide web domain name ending in **.uk** should always be registered as soon as possible with an established domain name registrar. If not it may be subject to a genuine registration by another organisation with a similar name or by a cybersquatter with, perhaps, less than genuine reasons!

7.5.8 INTELLIGENT BUILDINGS

The concept of the intelligent building

The concept of the intelligent - or smart - building is now widely accepted and used in many countries around the world. In China, office buildings with integrated building management systems (IBMS) and structured cabling are marketed as intelligent buildings, and frequent intelligent building exhibitions attract vast crowds. In Poland, intelligent buildings are sufficiently established to support two magazines, one on commercial buildings and the other on the intelligent home. In mainland Europe and the UK, the European Intelligent Building Group (EIBG) continues to attract extensive interest in its programme of learning, research and market development. In North America, the membership and impact of the Continental Automated Buildings Association (CABA) continue to grow rapidly.

This acceptance has occurred despite the fact that there is still much discussion and debate on the precise meaning of the term intelligent building. However, extensive acceptance and use of the term illustrates that it has utility, and discussion is now more focussed upon the questions of why intelligent buildings are needed and how they can be designed, constructed and managed.

At the highest conceptual level, intelligent buildings are buildings designed for the information age. In an intelligent building, the aim is to optimise the use of information to deliver improved performance over the life cycle of the building. This is directly equivalent to the concept of a green building, in which the aim is to optimise the use of resources throughout the life-cycle of the building. From this it is apparent that intelligent buildings and green buildings are complementary in their objectives, a relationship which is indeed being used with considerable success by the Integer (Intelligent and Green) programme for housing innovation.

Intelligent buildings therefore represent a direction rather than a destination, the aim being to achieve buildings which are more successful than other buildings at using information to deliver building performance.

Intelligent building performance

In order to develop the idea of intelligent buildings further, we need to consider more fully the question of building performance. In this context, we must recognise that during its life-cycle a building has many different stakeholders and their own unique perspectives on building performance.

The stakeholders most often acknowledged are the building's users and managers. These are indeed key stakeholders, and the intelligent building must certainly provide information to support their performance objectives. At the same time, the requirements of the building's owner, financier, and builder must also be satisfied if the building is ever to be financed and constructed. Furthermore, the wider impact of the building upon the local and global communities - in social, commercial and environmental terms - has increasingly to be taken into account. Buildings which pollute their environment can no longer be recognised as intelligent buildings.

Understanding and managing the complex relationships between the performance objectives of the building's many stakeholders, in order to identify 'win-win' opportunities, is an essential part of any successful intelligent building strategy.

Facilities management and intelligent buildings

The emergence of facilities management as a recognised professional discipline is a critical element in the development of intelligent buildings. The relationship between facilities management and intelligent buildings is symbiotic. Facilities managers need intelligent buildings to provide the quality of information they need to manage building performance professionally. Intelligent buildings need facilities managers to specify, commission and manage the sophisticated information systems of the building.

Facilities managers are responsible for delivering building performance over time. Whether this responsibility is formally developed in contractual terms, as in a PFI/PPP contract, or whether it is implicit in the functional role, information is crucial to delivering improved facilities management performance. To achieve the levels of responsiveness, accuracy and timeliness that are needed in the information age, the real-time systems which are an integral part of intelligent buildings are essential.

Efficiency, effectiveness and opportunity

When considering the management of building performance, three categories of benefits are of relevance: efficiency, effectiveness and opportunity.

Efficiency benefits are directly related to the operational performance of the building. The objective of efficiency management is to achieve the maximum delivery for the minimum cost. Efficiency is normally measured in terms of cost per unit of delivery, and is independent of - and indeed may be in conflict with - the delivery of higher levels of organisational contribution. Efficiency is normally a necessary foundation for professional building management, but in itself is insufficient to justify the investment in intelligent buildings.

Effectiveness benefits are achieved by managing the building to achieve improved organisational performance. These benefits may be related to building characteristics such as flexibility, adaptability and responsiveness. Effectiveness benefits are measured in terms of contribution to organisational performance, and as such are valued far more heavily than efficiency benefits.

Opportunity benefits represent the highest level of performance contribution. They relate to ways in which the building, or buildings, may be used to deliver new and different forms of organisational benefits. Opportunity benefits are difficult to identify and deliver, but they represent a shift in the building paradigm from a cost-centred to a profit-centred focus, and as such represent the ultimate opportunity for facilities managers and intelligent buildings.

Characteristics of the intelligent building

How can we recognise an intelligent building? From the above analysis, it is clear that an intelligent building may be identified generically in terms of its performance contribution to the building's stakeholders. Physically, an intelligent building may be characterised in terms of its systems provided to optimise the use of information to deliver improved building performance. Such systems may be designed to deliver efficiency, effectiveness or opportunity benefits. The actual characteristics of the systems will change with time, as building and information technologies develop. At the present time, intelligent building systems may include integrated building management systems (IBMS), environmental management systems, security systems, energy management systems and change management systems.

The intelligent building process

Intelligent buildings and intelligent building performance, are increasingly inter-related to an intelligent building process ie the process of building with intelligence. Information systems to improve the design and construction of buildings are now commonplace, but the key characteristic of an intelligent building process is that information flows through from design to construction to building management. Physical entities in the building are identified in terms of their informational characteristics and these characteristics are made available at subsequent stages. Major international programmes are underway to standardise such informational entities in buildings, and to provide systems to support their transfer across process boundaries.

Implementation of intelligent buildings

The rate of implementation of intelligent buildings is related to changing expectations on building performance.

In the UK, buildings are being valued less and less in property or real estate terms and more and more in terms of their contribution - or otherwise - to organisational performance. In the information age, the value of buildings is increasingly related to their performance as nodes on information networks. Intelligent buildings are the ultimate manifestation of this perspective, and many successful intelligent buildings are now being implemented in the UK.

In some developing countries where major building and renewal programmes are underway, such as China and Eastern Europe, intelligent building concepts are being readily adopted. In these countries there are few legacy systems in buildings to constrain the adoption of the latest digital management and control technologies, and intelligent buildings are rapidly becoming the norm.

Integration of building management and office services

ICT is increasingly applied to building management and control systems to reduce energy consumption, and measure the performance of the facilities management function. The technology used for building management is derived from the mass-market office productivity systems and networks so that it uses pc's, Windows 95/98 2000 and Ethernet networks. However there is little or no merit in attempting to integrate building management systems with office systems. The main reasons are as follows:

- office systems and software are typically replaced every three years whereas building systems are expected to last seven to ten years

- office systems deliver services to desks whereas building systems monitor and control plant in plant rooms, doors and sensors in ceilings

- the occupier's business and IT managers are responsible for office systems whereas the landlord, managing agent or outsourced service provider are responsible for building management systems.

Another consideration is the way in which buildings are designed and procured. Typically the mechanical and electrical services and controls are purchased as packages. Each package such as fire detection, access control, and building management system is the responsibility of a separate manufacturer and installation contractor. Each system will have its own pc. To keep contractual and maintenance responsibilities clear the best integration that can usually be achieved is to give the Facilities Manager a chair with wheels so that they can move quickly from one pc screen to another! Most suppliers will usually accept that their software will run on any standard pc so that it is possible to impose the company standard pc on all systems that need a pc. There is also no real reason why several software packages cannot share the same pc especially if they are used intermittently for tasks like asset management or security card encoding and labelling. Functions like building management that run continuously, 24 hours per day, should have a dedicated pc and an uninterruptable power supply.

7.6 DOCUMENT DISTRIBUTION

Introduction

This service is concerned with the distribution of hard documents - including letters, reports and drawings - between and within organisations.

The terms 'mailroom (or postroom) services' and 'mail and messenger services' are traditionally more familiar than 'document distribution'. However changes that have taken place in many organisations in recent years have increased the importance and scope of the operation and the process by which it is carried out; the pigeon-holes are still there but facilities services such as the fast overnight international delivery carriers have brought a new dimension to the old, more sedate, routine.

7.6.1 CLASSIFICATION PROTOCOL

The protocol adopted by the authors for cost analysis of this cost centre is included at Fig. 7.6.A.

Fig. 7.6.A *Facilities Economics classification protocol - document distribution*	Sub-categories (contract bundle items)	Principal Examples / cost elements	Items commonly included in costs	Items excluded from costs	
				Item	Refer to category:
	General mail handling	Process and delivery of incoming mail Collection and preparation of mail for external distribution Processing and delivery of internal mail / messages Post room equipment charges and maintenance	Task management, supervisors, blue-collar staff, equipment hire, carrier charges	Fitting out post room Facilities services to post room	Alterations improvements Other categories as appropriate
	Charges	Postage stamps / franking Local couriers National couriers International couriers			

In an office environment such goods and products are largely paper-based - carrying information; in other environments the documents may be the product of the core business itself. It may be noted however, that in the context of this cost centre the distribution of goods and component parts is not included. Increasingly information is being created and conveyed not on paper but by electronic media including email. As such the distribution of this information will utilise email avoiding not only its hard copy capture (see Chapter 7.4) but also its physical transfer. However, at present there still remains the need for document distribution activities, but their scale is likely to continue to reduce significantly during the coming decade.

7.6.2 MAIL PROCESSING

The continuing need for physical processing

The process whereby letters and other packages are distributed internally and externally has not changed as radically as might have been expected given advances in information technology which threatened a paperless office by the late 1990's.

In spite of email and the direct computer linkages between customer and supplier considered in the previous chapter, people continue to produce data which is too bulky to fax or too late to be of use unless sent by express mail or carried physically by courier.

In many ways the office has twin communications engine-rooms - the switchboard and the post-room - each of which has a critical part to play in the way the organisation makes and maintains contact with its customers. But, whereas the switchboard has grown in sophistication at the expense of all but one or two operators, the army of people physically carrying letters and packages in and out of buildings has decreased but slightly - even in recession.

The post room

Post-room staff have a dual role:

- opening, collating, referencing and distributing incoming mail

- collating, packaging (if required) stamping, recording and posting/dispatching outgoing mail.

Depending on the size of organisation, post-room staff will either be dedicated - as in most medium/large business - or part of the secretarial function in the smaller organisation.

Typical costs of operating a post-room are given at Fig. 7.6.B.

Fig. 7.6.B
Typical costs of operating a post room

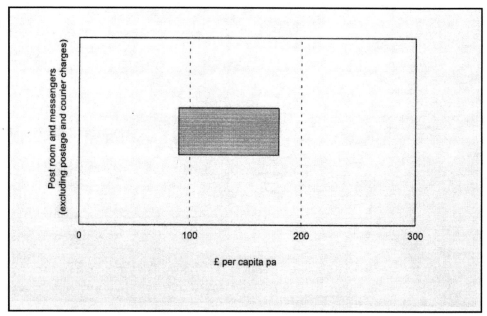

The principal resource drivers are:

- extent of mechanisation

- volume and type of mail

- the proportion of staff who are office workers

- variety of distribution centres

- the use of multi-skilling to optimise 'down-time'

- performance requirements for frequency of deliveries.

Typically one post-room employee should be able to service the mail of between 250 and 400 employees, the lower end being where there is a substantial element of mechanised handling internally, or electronic mail - both internally and externally.

In some cultures, the use of formal letters is discouraged so email has a substantial impact on the costs of all components of document distribution.

The design of the post-room is very important with mail sorting well arranged to facilitate handling by dwarfs and giants alike. Sturdy yet lightweight mail- and goods-handling trolleys should be in plentiful supply (with room for standby parking), plus electric letter openers, intelligent weighing machines which alert the user to under-or over-stamping (but franking in preference to stamping, please) and direct envelope printers for regular volume mailings.

Bomb detector screens in 'letter' and 'parcel' sizes cost only a few hundred pounds and are really an essential accessory for the more 'public' organisations.

Most of all a neat, tidy, decor backed up with a rigorous on-going 'keep clean and tidy' campaign can go a long way to making sure that an often under-rated task is not perceived to be under-valued by the management.

Internal document distribution

Porters involved with movement of goods, furniture and equipment (and people in the healthcare sector) are not included in this cost centre except insofar as part of their time is spent as multi-skilled assistants in the document distribution process.

The small-to-medium sized facility will probably rely upon the office junior to fetch and carry, almost certainly doubling up with secretarial or security duties. However, once mail is passing to and from more than say 150 staff then dedicated self-motivated personnel will become viable, especially if set performance targets.

Sorting of incoming mail is a straightforward task in a well-ordered mailroom, so the efficiencies will be made in the distribution. Here much will depend upon the horizontal and vertical transportation systems in the premises.

Larger buildings designed with facilities management in mind may well have special delivery services built in, eg a transit-box system working on the principles of a continuously moving paternoster-type elevator can be designed so that the mail can be distributed vertically direct from the mail-room. One such system involves proprietary tough plastic containers pre-coded for the various destinations by the mail-room staff; electronic devices scan the codes and mechanically deposit the boxes as required at each floor. Speed of operation, with box weights of up to 20kgs can make big inroads into delivery times and costs of messenger services, as well as allowing a steady flow of outbound mail to trickle down to the post room on a regular basis during the day.

As Fig. 7.6.C shows, pay-back on the capital installation cost of such a service in an organisation of, say, 750 personnel could be as little as two to three years with increased efficiency as an added bonus.

Fig. 7.6.C
Payback on a dedicated document conveyor system serving 750 staff on four floors - 12,000 sq m NIA

		£
Capital costs	Installation including builder's work, fees, finance and accessories:	48,000
	Loss of built floor area 12 sq m GIA at £ 800 sq m say	9,600*
	Total	**57,600**
Annual reduction in messenger staff	1 at £ 24,000 pa gross:	(24,000)
Payback period	£ 57,600 – (capital investment) £ 24,000 – (annual savings)	2.4 years payback
*	If the conveyor is inserted into an existing building, then this does not apply; instead the loss of rented floor space must be deducted from the annual saving. eg. at £ 320 sq m NIA this might amount to some £ 4,000 pa - and the installation costs would be about 20% higher	

External document distribution

Typical external document distribution costs per capita based on a broad-based sample are given at Fig. 7.6.D (over the page). These show that the conventional mailing services are

Fig. 7.6.D
Typical external distribution costs per capita pa

Component	Typical range of cost £ pa	Mean £ pa
Postage: home and international stamps	130 - 400	290
Overnight carriers	15 - 50	25
Courier/despatch riders	80 - 320	200
Totals	**225 - 770**	**515**

being challenged as never before by the 'overnight' carriers (who offer good delivery performance at excellent prices for the larger customers) and the 'biker' services which can deliver locally at high speed - as long as the forwarding address is written in large capital letters and located within 50 metres of a trunk road!

The cost of these express deliveries can amount to as much as 50% of the external distribution costs. At the more expensive end of the range costs of express delivery are about the same per capita as energy costs per annum in an air-conditioned building. All this suggests that the organisation can ill afford to leave delivery of its outgoing product to the last minute.

Affordability

In the event, the value of the document must surely always make the costs of conveyance to the customer fade into insignificance. If it does not, then either the mode of conveyance must be inappropriate to the product or the product is not appropriate to the mode of delivery.

In other words, low priority documents must be transported in bulk or via the letter box, whereas really vital products can go by whatever means can ensure their timely (and secure?) delivery.

Facilities must always support, not hinder, the product; however the right balance must be struck, for bad product managers often fail to understand how unnecessary overheads can impact on profitability. Fig. 7.6.E illustrates this point, showing the balance between document distribution, office services, turnover and profitability.

Fig. 7.6.E
Document distribution costs in the context of turnover, profits and office services costs

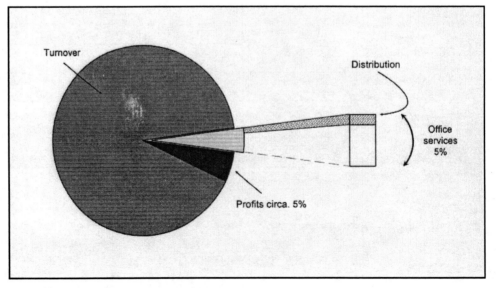

The exception is to be found in the offices of some major insurance, financial and professional organisations where the mail is opened and scanned in by post-room staff so that documents are then routed to recipients via the network. This apparent vision of the future is a reality in those offices: the technology is well-established and immediate availability of scanned images to any employee who may need to access a document offers significant advantages over traditional methods

7.7 OFFICE FURNITURE

Introduction

Most organisations have a need for furniture of one sort or another to facilitate their activities. Hospitals need beds and operating tables, cinemas and theatres have special seating, educational laboratories have work-benches and so on.

The special and varied nature of these fittings makes them too complex and detailed for cost analysis in this text. However, all organisations have office furniture to some extent, so this chapter concentrates on office furniture to illustrate the economic principles of furniture procurement and management in the general context.

7.7.1 THE COMPONENTS

Basic requirements

Office furniture may be provided for the purposes of:

- routine working
- storage
- meeting
- waiting
- dining
- display
- space division.

It comprises:

- work surfaces
- seats
- screens (division and/or display)
- storage units
- signs and graphics.

Performance

The physical and functional characteristics of furniture are very much driven by an amalgam of basic needs, image, life-span and initial cost. The impact of each of these factors is discussed within the category sections below.

Typical points to be considered are (in no particular order of significance):

- material
- form of construction
- strength
- weight
- appearance
- simplicity
- complexity
- appearance
- wear resistance

- size

- comfort

- adjustability

- statutory compliance

- cable management (for workstations)

- dedicated/multi-purpose

- availability (replacement etc.)

- space consumption

- durability

- cleanability

- sound integrity

- net cost (after discounts)

- after sales service.

7.7.2 THE FUNCTIONAL OPTIONS

The functions examined

The best way to consider furniture options and their economics is to consider each function in turn ie:

- the workplace

- the reception/waiting areas

- conference/meeting areas

- dining rooms.

However, in categorising thus it must be remembered that an increasingly important feature of office furniture is the need to standardise as much as possible between functions to improve the bulk order prices and to reduce the problems of storing and/or purchasing replacement units. So, for instance, there may well be a case for the chairs around the meeting table in the directors' offices to be the same as those in the main conference areas.

The workplace

The workplace may comprise simply a workstation or it may also accommodate storage and, in some cases, a meeting area. Whether it is in a cellular or open plan location will not necessarily determine the performance or quality, although if cellular accommodation equates to higher status then this can permit higher quality furniture without too obvious exposure of that policy.

The workstation itself will always have a working surface and a seat, in its simplest form a table and chairs; engineers and other designers will have a drawing board, normally accompanied by an adjustable chair (but they are no longer the only users who expect this one-time privilege). Most workplaces will have local storage either under the work surface (as part of a desk or a separate pedestal unit) and some may have additional storage nearby - on the floor or on the wall/screen or both.

The workstation itself may be designed specifically to accommodate information technology: desks may be designed to contain and manage cables, and worktops for the screens may be adjustable for tilt and height. Legislation on Health and Safety at Work (see Chapter 8.2) requires the adjustability for tilt in all workstations brought into use on or after 1/1/93 and in any case after 31/12/96; similarly, seats at Visual Disply Unit (VDU) screens must be capable of height adjustment under the new regime.

Fully adjustable tables and chairs are available, some beautifully engineered, for those organisations who recognise that staff over 2m tall cannot get their legs under a table by lowering the seat height without leaning backwards at 150°. Many modern workstations are modular ie they can be varied in their layout to suit a planning arrangement - particularly useful in open plan designs.

Depending on the job function (please **not** the job grade) personnel will require some measure of meeting support adjacent to the workstation. In modest cases this may mean a couple of chairs for visitors (internal or external), at higher levels a table and chairs and maybe easy chairs/settee for those responsible for clinching the big deals.

7.7.3 THE COSTS OF OFFICE FURNITURE

General workplace areas

The market will determine the actual price paid for office furniture - sometimes in a good deal one can purchase high quality fully adjustable workstations at less cost than the pretty but uncomfortable designer-favoured alternatives. Nevertheless, it is useful to compare the typical costs of workstations for various grades (the term used loosely here to define job function) across the broad spectrum of quality ranges - see Fig. 7.7.A. The higher end of the range may represent style, engineering excellence and uniqueness so value for money must be established by cost/benefit analysis; the performance characteristics given above may form a useful base for such an appraisal.

Fig. 7.7.A
Furniture and fittings requirements and budget capital costs per workplace

Grade	Furniture requirements	Cellular office Quality rating 1 £	2 £	3 £	Furniture requirements	Open plan office Quality rating 1 £	2 £	3 £
Secretary	Chair, desk, return, storage cabinets (2), pedestal	2,400	3,600	5,400	Chair, workshop, return, screens (3), cabinets (2), pedestal	3,000	3,900	5,700
Professional/ executives	Chair, desk, return, storage cabinets (2), visitors chairs (2)	2,000	3,200	4,800	Chair, workshop, return screens (4), screen storage, storage cabinet (1), visitors' chairs (2)	2,600	3,600	6,000
Manager/ director	Chair, desk, storage cabinet (1), meeting table, visitors' chairs (4), settee	3,600	4,800	7,200	Chair, worktop, screens (5), screen storage, storage cabinets (2), meeting table, visitors' chairs	4,100	5,400	10,500

Special areas

Fig. 7.7.B again looks at budget costs for three current levels of quality for 'special areas'. The comments above concerning value for money equally apply.

Fig. 7.7.B
Furniture and fittings requirements and budget capital costs for 'special areas'

Feature	Quality 1	£	Quality 2	£	Quality 3	£
Computers	Audio / visual workstation	3600	Audio / visual workstation	4560	Audio / visual workstation	6000
Kitchen/dining	Table, chairs (6), average of 3 sittings - cost per place	70	Table, chairs (6), average of 2 sittings - cost per place	175	Table, chairs (6), average of 1 sittings - cost per place	450
Meeting room	Table, chairs (8), 1 room per 80 staff - cost per employee	30	Table, chairs (8), 1 room per 60 staff - cost per employee	65	Table, chairs (8), 1 room per 40 staff - cost per employee	120
Plants & graphics*	1 plant per 20 employees, graphics £ 30 per employee - cost per employee	70	1 plant per 10 employees, graphics £ 50 per employee - cost per employee	160	1 plant per 5 employees, graphics £ 100 per employee - cost per employee	240
Accessories	Filing, general storage, etc. - cost per employee	160	Filing, general storage, etc. - cost per employee	220	Filing, general storage, etc. - cost per employee	300

* See also Interior landscaping – Chapter 5.7

In areas such as board room and main reception many organisations seek to indulge and impress by commissioning bespoke furniture such as the boardroom table and the reception desk. The latter investment is more likely to produce an appreciable return on investment by dint of its marketing implications (out of the marketing budget) than the former.

However, in truth, the amortised cost of the boardroom furniture (however apparently extravagant) as a proportion of the directors' remuneration is so small that it is either irrelevant or may indeed generate a return on investment by encouraging recruitment of better directors and/or helping them to be more efficient.

Fig. 7.7.C looks at the cost of three qualities of reception area and boardroom furniture in an organisation occupying a head office building of 5,000 sq m.

Fig. 7.7.C
Furniture and fittings - budget capital costs for reception and boardroom areas

Feature	Quality 1 £	Quality 2 £	Quality 3 £
Reception area	8,000	16,000	30,000
Boardroom	16,000	40,000	80,000

N.B. Examples relate to a head office building - 5,000 sq m NIA

7.7.4 PROCUREMENT

Design

Chapter 4.1 - 'Space - The Premises Cost Driver' - and Chapter 4.2 'Churn' discuss the relationship between furniture, layout and the efficiency and flexibility of space use. Here we must consider the fact that, in open plan space, the furniture does form part of the dividing function conventionally carried out by partitions in cellular space.

For this reason, the cost of furniture should always be included in any comparative study between cellular and open-planned space and the comparison must also address the cost per capita because of the differences in space-use efficiency between the layouts.

A typical range of fitting-out costs per capita for cellular and open plan office areas including alternative qualities of furniture is given at Fig. 7.7.D.

Fig. 7.7.D
Total furniture and fitting-out costs per capita (cellular and open plan arrangements)

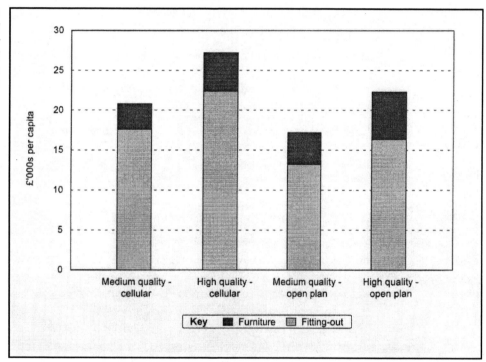

It is essential to have independent advice when procuring furniture in large quantities, or in small quantities as part of an incremental programme. There are many excellent interior designers whose experience of the pros and cons of the myriad generic types of furniture components and systems and their effect upon the working environment can be invaluable. However their recommendations should be supported by an independent cost consultant.

Unfortunately, 'hidden' discounts are sometimes made available to interior designers by unscrupulous distributors desperate for sales, so any undue bias by a designer in respect of one particular system may have to be viewed with some degree of scepticism; facilities managers ought to be given a full appraisal of performance v cost to enable them to be the final judge of value for money.

For the same reason - only more so - leaving the design and specification to individual suppliers is really asking for trouble unless a reasonably sophisticated 'single-point-of-responsibility' bid process (see Chapter 6.3.1) has been instigated and properly managed.

Specification and purchasing

Inviting large-scale bids from furniture suppliers should always be done on a thoroughly prepared performance specification. Unless bids are also requiring space planning (not a very good policy - far better to pay to have the planning done by independent designers) the precise quantities of each unit should be stated. As with all bidding processes it is always better to eliminate as many variables as possible; the consequence of contractors mis-calculating their estimates **never** works to the client's advantage.

The performance of each generic unit should be described in such a way that bidders can identify one or more of their products to suit the client's needs; exact compliance is not essential and suppliers will often offer more than one product type, drawing attention to any major departures from the given performance level, eg modular workstations may be offered in a choice of finish; however, if cable-carrying is part of the brief, then alternatives which cannot carry cables will obviously not be considered. Most reputable suppliers know the rules of the performance specification process and will bid sensibly.

It is important to identify the job functions of the intended users, the delivery requirements, and any statutory compliances, eg Health and Safety at Work (see Chapter 8.2). The bidders should be asked to show all discounts from list price and to confirm that all available discounts are being made to the client alone - this to guard against concealed discounts to third parties.

Care should be taken to ensure that product ranges offered are not likely to be phased out in the near future - or if so that the price reflects this obsolescence. Before placing the order, samples of each product should be inspected and labelled as a check against quality of the bulk deliveries. Where possible, products should be tested on site over a reasonable period, particularly workstations where the comfort of the user and his/her approval need to be established in advance of a major investment.

There is currently a trend back towards simpler, push-together styles away from the fully extensible systems. The Health and Safety (Display Screen Equipment) Regulations 1992 on provisions for VDU operation can be accommodated without excessive mechanical adjustment eg height adjustment by the use of wall brackets and slotted angles. Although the 'better engineered' solution will definitely be valuable to some organisations, if the users themselves do not want it there is absolutely no point in parting with the extra cash. However, employers have a duty to protect employees under the health and safety legislation.

However, the issue of 'adjustability' should be thoroughly examined with the 'staff side' before any major new acquisition programme; the users' comfort and convenience should be paramount in any furniture choice, for the effect on their productivity, one way or another, will far outweigh the cost of the furniture itself.

Finally, the decision as to whether to lease or purchase outright will be down to the finance director who will take into account the funds available plus the taxation considerations. Leasing costs in most countries go straight against profits whereas bought items of furniture may be subject to claims for capital allowances against corporate taxation (see Chapter 11.2.5).

7.8 VEHICLE FLEET MANAGEMENT

Introduction

Traditionally, the use of a motor vehicle provided and maintained by the firm was an accepted and almost indispensable perquisite, being added into salary for computation of earnings for mortgage transactions - but not for tax purposes. In 1971 this changed when the government introduced benefit in kind - BiK - tax on private motoring mileage; since then the government has levied increasing levels of personal taxation from the beneficiaries of a company car policy. The point has now been reached where there is scarcely any financial advantage at all to the beneficiary while the employer still has all the hassle of financing and managing or contracting a car fleet.

The company car can be an important part of the business, even if its management is not considered to be a key competence of the organisation. Frequently, with a services business, the company car is the only tangible asset of the organisation actually seen by the client or prospect; as a result the choice and quality of presentation of the business car can be important in projecting the right image.

The employer gains a number of benefits from providing employees with a car: the image of the business is protected by an appropriate car being used on business, the company car will be properly maintained and insured, and it will be replaced when necessary.

In terms of national economics there is no doubt that the motor industry gets more business via company cars than it would otherwise; and although roads should be safer with better maintained, more reliable vehicles on them, the human factor, whereby drivers treat their employer's property with rather less respect than their own, probably outweighs the benefits of fleet care.

Those organisations whose businesses depend on physical distribution of goods will probably have a dedicated transport manager rather than relying upon facilities management; control of driver hours, safety of loading/unloading, the sheer size of the vehicles and complexity of their mechanisms demand highly qualified and motivated management. Where a fleet contains just a few heavy goods vehicles, fully maintained contract hire or even complete out-sourcing of such transport is probably the best solution.

Because HGV fleets are an intrinsic part of industrial and retail activity as opposed to administration facilities they are not considered further in this chapter.

The market for the company car is mature and there may be some decline in the proportion of cars provided by the business. It may be noted that a growing proportion of fleets in the UK are international, belonging to subsidiaries of companies based elsewhere in Europe. Thus, management is somewhat more complex than simply seeking to manage a fleet in one country because of the different cultural approaches to company cars, the relative differences in car prices, residual values, operating costs, tax treatments, and attitudes to company cars.

Nevertheless, it is likely that over time there will be a convergence in the attitudes and expectations regarding company car provision and management.

In particular, this chapter examines fleet strategy, vehicle procurement, new and old vehicle prices, operating costs, telematics and provision.

7.8.1 DEVELOPING A FLEET STRATEGY

The model in Fig. 7.8.A highlights the principal stages through which most fleets need to pass so that common policies, practices and administration applies throughout the fleet, ie on all sites.

Fig. 7.8.A
Fleet strategy development

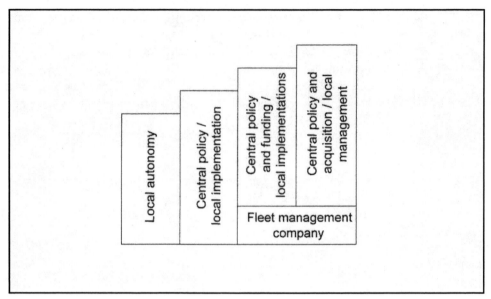

With the majority of business there is a high degree of local autonomy within the fleet. The relationship model shown in Fig. 7.8.A suggests that moving from that stage on the left of the chart there are a number of steps which might be needed to bring the fleet to the company status. Unless there are very special circumstances, it is generally most effective and less disrupting to introduce steadily tighter control rather than seek to move straight to a universal wide situation and replace vehicles, policies and systems in one go.

7.8.2 ISSUES INFLUENCING FLEET STRATEGY

Qualitative issues

Before one examines the pricing vagaries of the fleet operation, it is interesting to look at the other factors beyond the control of the fleet operator, but awareness of which can assist the operator to take corrective action and so minimise their impact. Consider the following issues:

- Provision practices regarding company cars; examine the practices of competition, to check which are the most cost effective

- Has the company had a consistent acquisition strategy historically? When was that last reviewed? What were the results? Policies justify annual review

- Does the organisation currently provide employees with cars - or pay a mileage allowance? Investigate the alternative cost/benefits to the company and to the employees

- What current models/makes are provided? How do those compare with competition and are they cost effective as new/used cars?

- Examine the implications of tax rules concerning the individual and the organisation regarding the most cost effective way of providing mobility.

Management issues

Before the individual cost elements are examined, there is a series of basic questions that the operator might consider. These include the nature of the individual fleet and the way in which the businesses are run with respect to the quality of fleet management:

- In-house or out-sourced - how should the fleet be provided?

- What is the size of the fleet within the market? Is it large enough to justify its own management - or should management be contracted out?

- What are the current car hierarchies? How do these compare with direct competition? They should be in broad parallel with competition

- What is the local fleet? If there are cars manufactured locally in line with requirements it is generally better to use these, provided quality and service are acceptable

- Is fleet financial control acceptable and in line with the rest of the business? If not, then the organisation might consider contracting out to a leasing or fleet management company

- How is the fleet acquired? (Methods and their relative benefits are discussed later.) More than one method, even if overall fleet management is used to control the fleet, may be necessary to achieve the best costs.

Research by the organisation can resolve most of these issues; discussions with the organisation's auditors/accountants should enable them all to be resolved.

It is important to note that any changes introduced will normally take 3 to 4 years to work their way right through the system.

7.8.3 PROVISION AND COST OF CENTRAL FLEET MANAGEMENT

The recent study - January 2002 - 'Business Car Expectations' suggests that the organisation typically employs a full-time fleet manager when it has about 250 units in operation, although that figure can vary enormously. Fleet manager salaries vary upwards from about £25,000 pa, depending on the total number of vehicles.

One critical issue to be examined is the means by which the fleet might be provided and to what level the fleet is to be taken. Earlier in this chapter the alternative methods of car provision were examined in some detail. The key question which still needs to be examined is how the fleet can be provided most cost-efficiently and cost-effectively in smaller markets.

The basic choices open to the business might be summarised as:

- **manage the fleet in house:** regardless of whatever method of funding is used, and either with a named individual or the driver made responsible for looking after the vehicle or vehicles. In theory the costs should be at their most effective because no third party is taking a profit element. However, the questions must be asked as to whether the business has the depth of management, or even administrative skills to be able to manage the fleet cost efficiently. It may require additional staff; capital may be involved; the number of units in operation may not justify the best possible terms from vehicle providers.

- **contract hire the fleet:** use a local contract hire provider or, even better, the local partner or associated company used elsewhere to provide the vehicles on contract hire. Such an arrangement would allow the business to call on the assistance of the contract hire company to plan the fleet and to ensure it matches the competition. Similarly, within a competitive situation, costs should be competitive. However, there is still the problem of managing the issues such as fuel for the fleet and providing the overall management of the operation.

- **fleet management:** a development from operational leasing, is the provision of full fleet management programmes - total outsourcing - is a viable option in many cases. It allows the business to outsource the management of the fleet for a known fee. The advantages are clear - but as with all business propositions, the situation has to be kept under constant review to ensure both the quality of service is being provided and the total cost of the service is competitive. It is a means of giving greater responsibility to the vehicle provider with that company taking responsibility for the management of the vehicle, handling the administrative burden of the fleet. Residual value risk remains with the owner.

Each of the following has an overall bearing on costs, namely:

In-house v out-sourcing: the decision is no different from any other cost centre - partly an issue of core v non-core and particularly one of availability of relevant skills. Even the contract operators mainly use the distributors' service agents for maintenance, but using in-house qualified engineers to vet their performance.

'Fleet management only' contracts are widely available and may be a visible solution where the user has strong purchasing power and cash flow but has a policy of contracting-out non-core activities.

Management reporting: management reporting on operating costs, values, condition, mileages, rental levels, tax efficiency, safety, insurance, etc is needed on a regular basis tailored to the company's needs (including any cross-charging) and is time-consuming, even when computerised.

7.8.4 VEHICLE PROCUREMENT

Acquisition Continuum

Within the business car market there is a range of alternative ways of funding. The Acquisition Continuum shown in Fig. 7.8.B summarises these alternative methods of acquiring business cars, using generic names for the different services offered.

Fig. 7.8.B
The acquisition continuum

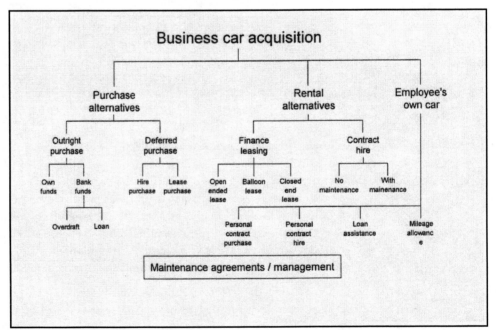

Procurement options

A purchase scheme, as defined by the Finance Act 1971, is one in which the company spends money under a contract which permits eventual ownership.

Purchase can take the form of:

- outright purchase
- hire purchase
- lease purchase
- contract purchase
- purchase of private cars by employees.

Leasing does not envisage eventual ownership. The contract may be for either:

- finance lease

    -open-ended lease

    -close-ended lease

or

- operating lease

    -contract hire

    -purchase and leaseback

Identifying the most appropriate vehicle funding strategy for your company is a complex and confusing task. The fleet operator is faced with the job of choosing cars that are most suited for the company's current tax and balance sheet position.

Outright purchase: using the organisation's own funds or borrowed money, a large initial expenditure is involved with this type of purchase which deprives potential profit-making core business of funds. The day-to-day management of the fleet can be a time-consuming task but does give complete control. Very careful consideration of purchasing costs and maintenance costs needs to be made to ensure that the best deals are obtained. It will be the responsibility of the company to get the best price for the vehicles when their useful life is over. Outright purchase really only makes sense for the organisation having the cash to spare and the time and resources to devote to fleet management. It is still - just - the most popular method of acquisition but it is gradually being replaced by more user-friendly alternatives.

Hire purchase: with this arrangement the business is effectively the owner but may not have title to the vehicles until the loan is paid off and the option to purchase is exercised. An initial deposit is paid and the balance of the capital sum and interest is paid back in monthly instalments over a specified period. The cost of the vehicle is spread over its useful life.

Lease purchase: this is not, strictly speaking, a lease but a hire-purchase scheme. Again, an initial low deposit is made and then monthly payments set at a level to cover just depreciation and interest. The option is then available of paying part of the capital amount at expiry and then paying or receiving a lump sum depending on the proceeds of sale, or having a normal full payout agreement. The cost of the vehicle is spread over its useful life; with hire and lease purchase the options do not attract VAT on the capital and finance elements and writing down allowance in respect of Corporation tax are available.

Contract purchase: this type of contract combines the service and operational benefits of contract hire with the tax advantages of outright purchase. The main advantage to the customer is that the capital and finance elements are completely exempt from VAT. Part of the vehicle cost is depreciation over the life of the agreement and the balance is paid as a lump sum at the end. Title passes to the customer when the lump sum is paid.

Purchase of private cars by employees: although the practice has been in decline, some companies still operate the option of reimbursing employees for the business travel that they undertake in their own car. This payment usually comes in the form of mileage allowance in pence per mile and may include a fixed monthly sum to assist with the running of the car. A few companies even provide low interest funding to assist employees with the initial purchase of the vehicle. With changes in Bik tax there is a steady growth in the number of employees taking "cash for car" and providing the vehicle themselves, claiming a mileage allowance for the use of the vehicle on business. If employees provide their own car, it makes it much more difficult for management to operate a consistent car fleet policy in that market. Equally, there can be problems in terms of mileage allowances insurance, and the control of the use of vehicles on business.

Finance lease: widely used in this type of lease the lessor company is the legal owner of the vehicles and can claim capital allowances while the vehicle user has possession and use of the car and can offset rental costs against profits; the lessor bears the risks of depreciation and the residual price achieved.

Finance lease agreements come in two forms - open-ended and close-ended:

With **open-ended leases**, equal monthly payments are made over a pre-determined period to recover the capital. Sale of the vehicle is usually undertaken by the leasing company who keep the profits in the first instance but then return them to the lessee company as a rebate on rentals. Subject to status VAT charges are recoverable.

Close-ended leases recognise the residual value of the vehicles in the funding calculations. This residual value is anticipated in the contract and the renting company will be charged with any shortfall and/or credited with any surplus when the vehicles are sold. Subject to status VAT charges are recoverable.

In both the above agreements the operation and administration of the fleet remains with the lessee company.

Operating lease or contract hire: in these types of leases the risks and rewards in operating the vehicles will remain with the lessor company. The vehicles will not show on the lessee company's balance sheet as assets although they have to be reported. The lessee company will retain the vehicles at the end of the lease and can then sell or re-lease them. Operating lease agreements also come in two forms - contract hire and purchase-and-leaseback.

With **contract hire**, vehicles are leased for a fixed monthly rental for a specific time and mileage and the operational and financial risk remains with the lessor. The majority of leases include a fixed price maintenance package or a vehicle maintenance programme operated by a fleet management company.

(Purchase and) Sale and leaseback contracts are useful when a company which has initially purchased a fleet wishes to inject some cash back into the organisation. Sale and leaseback enables the business to dispose of the depreciating assets and move to a position of leasing the fleet - and hopefully achieving best practice for the market. The company's fleet is wholly or partly sold to the leasing company and is then leased back on an agreed time and mileage parameter. This will then take on all the financial and operational aspects of conventional contract hire. It is a useful alternative source of re-financing core business activity if funds become short after the original non-core investment.

Fig. 7.8.C highlights the relative benefits of each of the methods of purchase as well as the leasing alternatives.

Fig. 7.8.C
Benefits of alternative methods of acquisition

Item considered	Outright Purchase / funds	Bank Overdraft / loan	Hire / lease purchase	Finance lease	Contract hire	Contract purchase
Minimum initial capital outlay		✓	✓	✓	✓	✓
Extra credit line			✓	✓	✓	✓
Interest rate Fixed			✓	✓	✓	✓
Fixed repayment assist, cash flow and budgeting			✓	✓	✓	✓
Vehicle security			✓	✓	✓	✓
Off balance sheet borrowing					✓	
Ownership of vehicle	✓	✓	✓			✓
Use of own writing down allowance	✓	✓	✓			✓
Rental allowable against taxable income				✓	✓	
No vehicle disposal problem					✓	✓
Administration reduced ·					✓	✓
Road fund licence included					✓	✓
Replacement vehicle in case of breakdown					✓	✓
Fixed maintenance cost					✓	✓
No depreciation risk					✓	
VAT on rental				✓	✓	✓
Input VAT recovery				✓	✓	

Considerations in procurement

In the purchase schemes the tax regime may permit Writing Down Allowances against a statutory computation of depreciation to be offset against corporation tax. When the vehicle is sold a balancing allowance or charge is computed by reference to the comparative values of the sales proceeds and the Tax Written Down Value. Eg a car purchased for £15,000 may be written down to £7,000 after four years: if it is sold for £4,000 the Balancing Charge of (£7,000 - £4,000) £3,000 is further allowable against profits, thereby allowing the whole depreciation, albeit part-deferred. Usually the interest component of purchase schemes is fully allowable as operating expenses except in certain categories of contract purchase where there is a sales option on completion.

On lease transactions both the depreciation and interest element of the rental may be allowable to the lessor subject to upper levels established in the tax regime.

In all cases of purchase and lease the service and maintenance charges built into the rental or contract (or directly incurred) are fully allowable as operating expenses.

Where employees are paid a mileage allowance by their employers in respect of business use they may be entitled to recover capital allowances themselves; alternatively they may obtain relief for the actual cost incurred in the business mileage - but only one or the other, not both.

Whereas VAT is payable on both capital and finance elements of a finance lease, a lease purchase, contract purchase or hire purchase transaction does not attract VAT on those elements.

Effect on trading accounts

In some organisations the value of motor vehicles may represent a potentially sizeable asset - provided they are purchased outright or on one or other of the purchase schemes discussed above.

In a leasing situation the test of whether the vehicle asset belongs to the lessor or lessee is 'who has substantially all the risks and rewards associated with the ownership of the asset, other than the legal title'? Thus, a finance lease and a hire purchase should be shown as the lessee's asset whereas an operating lease will not. Outstanding finance lease payments must be capitalised on the lessor's balance sheet.

Sometimes it will suit a company to minimise its book assets - possible to improve its return on capital employed (ROCE) or other performance ratio. This may influence the procurement route in favour of leasing - and vice versa where a patently strong capital base is sought.

A point to note is that where, in contract purchase, the customer has an option to sell vehicles back to the Fleet Service company for a guaranteed price they must always appear on the customer's balance sheet unless he or she can prove that they always have - and presumably always will - exercise the option. In the latter case an opportunity to go 'off-balance-sheet' may be available and attractive to the high-ROCE aspirants.

7.8.5 NEW AND USED CAR PRICES

Choosing the vehicle

As a general rule it makes sense to stay with one manufacturer for all the vehicles or at least for the generic categories such as used by sales reps, executives and directors. Not only will a better deal be struck on the purchase/lease but service charges will be lower than for a plethora of different machines.

Choice of colours may affect the price - fads have swung literally between black and white over the years.

Some foreign cars distributed in the UK do have difficulty replacing parts - especially on the older models - and component costs may be higher than one the mass-market models. However, since there are now no wholly-owned major UK motor manufacturers this bias is rapidly being eroded.

Low mileage nearly-new cars - usually ex-car hire vehicles sold at auction after just a few months - can be up to 30% cheaper than new and will run just as well.

The simpler the car is the less can go wrong with it and the cheaper the replacement parts. Nevertheless executives doing high mileage between high profile appointments ought to be afforded automatic gearboxes and power steering, even on smaller cars, but run-about-town reps may not benefit much from such added comfort, much as they might lobby otherwise.

There is patently a lot of choice, and not just in terms of makes and models but also of deals from particular companies and methods of purchase.

New car prices

Most people think they know about how to get the right deal on a new car, though the professional fleet operators have the financial muscle to do better than their potential customers. However, when dealing with an operator any 'hidden' discounts and short-term special offers should be squeezed out of the system to the customer's advantage - though this may only be possible through the exigencies of competition.

New car prices vary, even for the same model so it is important to research the market fully. Generally, although prices have fallen in recent years, manufacturers will seek to protect the status quo for as long as possible with the view to maximising revenues and profitability. The following are price drivers and issues which the operator should include in a review of the market:

- **base prices** - what is the manufacturer's pattern of base prices for a model or range of models? Except in the case of the least reliable foreign imports, cheaper, simpler cars have lower life-cycle costs in every cost centre and hold their value well so good discretion should be used in making the final choice.Except in the case of the least reliable foreign imports, cheaper, simpler cars have lower life-cycle costs in every cost centre and hold their value well so good discretion should be used in making the final choice.

- **taxation** - what taxes apply to particular models and the fuels that they use, and their usage (e.g. different congestion charges)?

- **discount** - what discount will be available for the quantum of vehicles to be ordered?

- **spares** - what is the availability of spares, discounts for bulk purchases?

- **warranties** - what is the cost of warranties and extended warranties; and policies on non-standard works and components used for business purposes?

- **accessories** - what is the range and cost of accessories?

- **servicing** - what are the service intervals and what restrictions are put on servicing, eg vis a vis the warranty?

- **training** - what training is provided by the manufacturer for the buyer's own fleet servicing personnel?

- **innovation** - what innovations are in the manufacturer's pipeline, eg telematics for fleet management fuel systems (eg fuel cells), new fuels (eg electricity)?

- **trade-in vehicles** - what is the policy on accepting and pricing of the previous vehicle?

- **cheap foreign cars** - beware of poor reliability and spares availability and poor second-hand value retention; which is not to say that most established imported models are likely to be any less satisfactory than the UK 'trusties'.

Used cars

Many of the points raised above for new cars are pertinent to the used car market. Prices vary considerably and the market is seasonal. Independent information is available in the like of Glass's Information Services (www.glass.co.uk).

Discounts of up to 35% may prove a good bargain, provided the users will tolerate the 'second-hand' stigma.

Summary

In summary, the whole field of new and used car pricing is a complex issue. It is further complicated where the facilities manager is responsible for an international fleet but that is dealt with elsewhere. In essence, the fleet operator might seek to minimise car prices by negotiating a fleet deal with a single manufacturer - provided there is sufficient annual volume to justify it. The overriding discount may well be claimed centrally and distributed.

7.8.6 VEHICLE OPERATING COSTS

This section highlights some of the key cost issues associated with the business car which should be considered by the facilities managers. The exact parameters will vary from one business to the next, so the notes give broad guidelines rather than seeking to micro-manage by fleet type.

The key cost drivers in a motor fleet operation are dealt with in turn as follows.

Finance charges: unless the borrowing for purchase is made directly by the customer the rate offered by the lender must be viewed with some scepticism. Most contract operators either have their own finance companies or have a close association with one. In either case it is common to put forward an attractive finance rate which is in fact to be subsidized out of some other profit centre. In terms of the total deal and tax efficiency, this may not alter the overall cost, provided that the purchasers do not ignore the opportunity for competition believing that the finance deal is too good to pass over.

Rate of depreciation: most fleet motor vehicles are written down over 4 years, usually representing 80,000 to 100,000 miles. The residual value is realised by the user company in the purchase arrangements and also in the 'open-ended' lease. The 'closed-end' lease may return a residual value to the lessees if there is a surplus over that originally anticipated by the agreement.

Wear and tear: where the residual value is to the benefit of the user the choice of vehicle and the standard of maintenance and driver-care are issues to take seriously into account. In the contract hire or some lease arrangements the supplier will insist on a 're-conditioning' charge for vehicles delivered up in a poor state of wear and tear on expiration of the agreement. In such cases the definition of 'poor' should be defined and benchmarked for the avoidance of dispute. Also, users should insist that rental payments do not have to continue through any re-conditioning' period.

Reliability: though not a cost centre in itself, the reliability of the fleet will drive not only the maintenance and replacement costs and residual values but also the productive output and morale of the users - probably a much more significant factor than any apparent saving by purchasing cheaply.

Servicing costs: servicing costs are driven to some degree by the warranty periods/mileages on individual models; there is a tendency for these periods to be extended so do check the warranty periods built into the vehicle and ensure this is reflected in the maintenance charges. Maintenance charges vary as could recommended service intervals, even for the same products. Read the brochures to check, as failing to follow rules could effect warranty; rarely are manufacturers willing to provide a single central set of data for a model. Check that best practice is being used and vehicles are being serviced in line with manufacturers' recommendations - at the best rates available within the franchise - or by alternative providers on a basis that will not damage the warranty.

Regular maintenance of the fleet is a fairly significant annual cost which can vary enormously between models and their manufacturers. As well as looking at the bottom-line whole life cost comparisons, the user should also look to secure absolute reliability in terms of quality and minimising time off the road.

Some service agents now operate a flowline service system where the car is only off the road for the hour or so it takes for routine maintenance or (by prior arrangement) major repairs. Facilities are available for the driver to have a snack, watch the tv or, even better catch up with some overdue paperwork. Waiting times are guaranteed subject to the need for repairs.

Replacement parts: availability and costs of components will vary greatly between makes and models. Major fleet owners can insist on minimum levels of dedicated spares in the service agent's stock or may carry them themselves, at the same time reaping the economies of bulk direct purchasing.

The lessee should be satisfied as to the suitability of the contractor's replacement parts strategy prior to entering the agreement; although most hire contracts offer a fixed maintenance/replacement price, the time off the road will probably be a far more critical risk to bottom line profits than the price of a spare part. The work is normally undertaken by cleaners with whom the contract hire company has a contract.

The use of non-standard components may damage the warranty and hence residual value. Check the small print and relative costs to determine the importance and risks of using alternatives. Contract hire agreements will have control over this issue - yet the looser carries the residual value risk.

Mileage: contract hire agreements often incorporate an 'excess mileage' condition, whereby the user has to pay a premium for every mile driven over the prescribed minimum. How accurately this level is assessed can make or break the economics of contract hire and needs to be the subject of thorough investigation - not only of historic mileage but of future requirements based on giving business trends. The facilities manager must be pro-active on this issue as in all management tasks!

Where possible the user should negotiate a universal mileage rather than taking each vehicle separately, thereby offsetting under-mileage against excesses.

Modern vehicles, even the smaller cheaper ones, conscientiously driven and maintained, can often go over 100,000 miles before ending their useful life; vehicles using diesel fuel can be expected to outlive their petrol-driven counterparts by as much as 10-20%.

Within the employees' terms of employment, do they have private use of the car - if so, are there norms and benchmarks for private use? This may vary by industry and by position in the hierarchy as well as by the competitive position of the employee, business and industry.

Type of fuel: as well as the above-mentioned longevity, diesel-fuelled cars may save up to 1.5p to 2.5p per mile depending on the model. There is a big question mark over the environmental impact of diesel fumes which may become the focus of legislation in due course. Meanwhile, the economics in running, maintenance and resale (at present diesel cars have a better residual value) have resulted in a steady increase in the numbers of diesel vehicles on the UK's roads - up from 18% of the marker in 1993 to 25% in 1994. It is therefore probably just as well that there has been a comparable increase in the proportion of petrol-driven vehicles using lead-free petrol over the same period.

The grade of fuel chosen also needs to be put under thorough scrutiny. Many drivers are under the false impression that high grades mean higher performance regardless of maker's recommendations. On the contrary, using Super grade where the maker recommends Premium will simply add to the mileage cost with no increased performance whatsoever.

New fuels and systems are currently a controversial and evolving issue. For the future it is important that the operator checks fuel preferences and the impact on total costs, new car price and residual values as well as potential tax allowances on capital cost for using innovative fuels and systems. These include electric and biomass fuels, and fuel cells and conversion systems.

Insurance: Insurance for business vehicles is often the poor relation of business insurance. Establish that local best practice is in line with corporate policy. Examine whether such insurance should be bought as part of the local unit's ongoing insurance need, or alternatively, whether the business is large enough to buy car insurance of the appropriate level, independently of the rest of the business. Regular review and the gathering of two to three separate quotes each year is recommended.

Where the vehicles are not purchased outright the users will almost always have to provide their own insurance cover, and the terms will have to be acceptable to the financier or hirer.

Always test the market at each renewal, and, where appropriate, give the fleet supplier or manager the opportunity to bid; they have a vested interest in the risk and its affect on their interests and will almost certainly have a far greater knowledge of the motor insurance market than does the facilities manager.

Where an employee provides the car, his or her insurance should cover business use on behalf of the employer.

Accident repair and management: The cost of accident repair and management can vary significantly depending upon the type of vehicle and the cost of labour as well as attitudes towards accident repair and insurance. Check how local contract hire companies would handle such a situation; how much they would expect to pay - and, of course check out how the local competition would handle accident repair. A further accident issue to check is the accident rate within the company. Check local figures; these vary annually and also can differ between regions.

All motorists know that once a vehicle has been repaired after collision damage it is never quite the same again 'I like the two-tone' says the smart second-hand car salesman when the discussion about trade-in value of your monotone pride and joy gets under way. Nevertheless, modern technology in skilled hands can achieve good repair results. Much more important than appearance is any structural damage caused by serious mishaps. The loss adjustors for the less scrupulous insurance companies will often resist a write-off claim; where this will obviously result in a loss of residual value the decision should be vehemently contested, if necessary with a threat of legal action to recover any loss.

Again, time-off-the-road will be a critical economic factor, and the fleet manager should ensure that his relationships with insurers and repairers are established in such a way as to minimise the time-lapses between:

- accident and estimate

- estimate and visit by loss-adjustor

- inspection report and repair works.

Some insurance policies and hire contracts will cover replacement vehicles for some or part of the time off the road. Otherwise 'down-sizing' of vehicles as well as simple daily hire as required are recommended ways to avoid the worst of the financial impact of the need for temporary replacement.

Better still, good up-to-date records of cars not in use through user's illness, holidays or business circumstances can throw up a pool of available cars at no cost at all.

Re-sale values: the implications for the user of re-sale values depending on the procurement route are discussed above.

Sometimes users are tempted to sell fully written-down cars to the employees at the written down price in the accounts. Where the true re-sale figure is substantially greater the Inspector of Taxes may take an interest in the transaction with a view to treating the employee's gain as income to be taxed.

Residual values are set in a highly competitive market. The range of guides available show fluctuations short term: there is some feeling that residuals are gradually declining although they can be influenced by new car sales 3 to 4 years earlier.

From April 2002, benefit in kind Bik taxes for the employees have been replaced by taxes that are related to the CO_2 emissions of the car and the list price of the vehicle.

These changes will be increased over the following three years. A number of web sites have excellent calculators available to assist drivers in determining their tax liability.

Tyre costs: as with other areas of expense, tyre costs vary between countries, as do local fitment practices. Some specialist organisations have built national networks so it may be highly beneficial for fleet managers to check with such organisations on relative tyre costs and usages in the areas in which they already work or plan to operate.

Taxation implications: the consequence of the various procurement routes with regards to corporation tax and VAT are discussed above.

From April 2002, benefit in kind BiK taxes for the employee have been replaced by taxes that are related to CO_2 emissions of the car and the list price of the vehicle.

These changes will be increased over the following three years. A number of websites have excellent calculators available to assist drivers in determining their tax liability.

7.8.7 VEHICLE TELEMATICS AND COMMUNICATIONS

Telematics is a growing technology providing a variety of fleet management and transportation services. In the UK, the sector has a small number of companies offering such services. It includes Itis, Minorplanet Systems, Toad, Trafficmaster and Yeoman. For businesses the telematic products and services assist in fulfilling the following activities:

- the management of the mobile sales force, including mapping, routing, detailing of trip deviations, times and location, route deviations and irregular usage

- the management of vehicles and trailers including the above and the status of loads, tyres and security, planning of journeys, reporting at location and on the road; audit of time-sheets and hence overtime claims; refrigeration temperatures

- integrated systems: much of the above can be linked into sales, order processing, payroll and overtime, and maintenance and repair scheduling

- travel by personnel may be influenced by in-vehicle devices for traffic congestion and mapping, door-to-door directions (with diversions), and facilities availability on route.

Generally, telematics has introduced a cost-saving perspective into route planning but, more importantly, augers well for more effective fleet management practice.

7.8.8 PERSONNEL PRESSURES

So far the business vehicle has been reviewed from the company viewpoint. The viewpoint of the employee is equally, if not more, important.

The company car is provided either to assist employees to undertake their role more effectively or as part of a total remuneration package. Little corporate benefit will therefore arise if the car fails to satisfy the needs of the business - or if it fails to satisfy and motivate the individual recipient. Equally, there is always a risk that the car will be maltreated if it does not meet the individual's aspirations.

It is therefore important that a number of headline personnel issues are examined when one considers the wider issues:

- is the market one in which a company car is normally provided? Check the 'entry level' for company car provision

- what are the personal tax implications of the company car? Tax may impact on engine size; total package provision; fuel type

- what model ranges are most suited to the tasks under consideration?

- what model ranges should be provided? There may be strategic requirements to provide locally manufactured products or to provide the locally dominant brand

- do new cars always have to be provided? In some areas there may be opportunities to provide nearly new or used cars; this may be influenced by the relative duty levels and the overall provision of new cars

- what is the cost of providing business cars? The relative cost of a new car might be prohibitive - or a smaller car than used elsewhere might be the acceptable strategy

- how important is the company car in local recruitment and retention? This may vary between companies but it is an issue that may move individual national companies out of line with others

- what are the company's policies on daily journey duration limitation, drivers tiredness, mobile telephone usage and training standards?

- what is the competitive situation? To attract and hold the best employees, the car offered will generally need to match the competition. This should be checked out.

With each of the questions raised here there is a list of subsidiary questions that the organisation may need to review as part of its fleet activities.

Throughout the exercise there is a serious risk of the so-called 'self reference criterion' creeping into the exercise. Quite simply 'what applies in the HQ market is not necessarily what will apply in each area market'. It is important to ensure that the fleet and the policy are totally suitable for the area market.

On the one hand such an approach could be expensive if cars are over-provided. On the other hand, if the level is too low, there is the risk that staff of the right quality will not be recruited - or retained.

C-91

7.8.9 CONCLUSIONS

At the beginning of the chapter some of the key issues relevant to pulling the fleet into a common pattern and structure across the country were examined. Given that the organisation seeks to achieve the best value for money from the total exercise then best value may well mean using different hierarchies and different models in the various markets depending upon the size of the local company and the numbers of vehicle in operation.

Quite simply, the right way to provide, operate and manage a fleet requires constant review of overall cost levels, local company requirements and the competitive situation.

7.9 DISASTER PREVENTION AND RECOVERY

Introduction

In its broadest context 'disaster' refers to any situation the totality of which could threaten the ability of an organisation to carry on its business in an effective manner.

A series of unfortunate events, possibly a combination of natural and man-made incidents, lies behind many disasters.

Man-made disasters may be accidental or intentional. Intentional disasters are motivated by war, politics or other causal dedication, malevolence or insanity - the latter arguably being at the root of all the atrocities committed under the guise of one or other of the above excuses for indiscriminate death and destruction.

Chapters 7.1 and 7.5.7 consider security in general and the problems facing the organisation deprived of its electronic communications facilities. This chapter therefore deals specifically with the nature of disaster, the risks of deprivation of the use of premises on a large scale, the costs of disruption and the costs of protection and recovery, even survival. Consideration is given to the recovery plan.

7.9.1 THE NATURE OF DISASTER

Natural disaster

Purely natural disasters, such as earthquakes, hurricanes and flooding, are not generally considered a threat to major properties although from time to time we experience unprecedented disastrous acts of nature. The full implications on flood levels of the global warming identified in recent years are still somewhat indeterminate with the underlying principles in dispute as between eminent environmental experts. Nevertheless it would be a brave person who would ignore the potential threats of the phenomenon.

Equally, earthquakes on a high point of the Richter scale are unknown so we do not have foundations designed specifically to counter seismic activity. But there is always a first time.

Violent storms are not in general a threat to the stability of modern city centre commercial building structures, but could cause a problem to some of the more lightweight structures sometimes found on the outskirts of provincial centres. However, climatic changes seem to be inducing increased risk of flooding, so facilities managers of vulnerable facilities, particularly those in flood plains, must review and plan accordingly.

A major cause of disaster - fire - is a natural phenomenon which can be brought about by accident or deliberately - either way it can have crippling consequences.

Man-made disaster

The principal cause of clearly identifiable man-made disaster in peace time is the terrorist attack. Terrorists attempt to advertise and enhance their cause by bringing public attention to their disastrous activity. It is often an insidious process, occasionally a one-off gesture. In every case severe personal or physical damage is sought or threatened. The whole activity is dependent upon each event - and its dire consequences - being broadcast to those parts of the world where it might be expected to be of concern, and, through fear, influence public opinion to turn against the stance of authority on a particular issue.

7.9.2 DISASTER RISK

Media responsibility

Given that publicity of the threat to human life and well-being is the sole cause of terrorist incidents, whether in the form of explosions or contaminated fish-paste, it does seem blindingly obvious that denying such publicity would eliminate the majority of incidents overnight.

The inherent risk to the perpetrator of a terrorist attack is such that it could not be justified in the absence of extensive media coverage of the incident. So, why international governments cannot collaborate in outlawing all media-reporting of claims made as to the responsibility for an incident is beyond the comprehension of most intelligent people giving the matter serious consideration.

It is only the claim to responsibility which needs to be quashed - the incident will publicise itself or, as in the case of food-contamination, require to be broadcast. However, a simple statement referring to 'a terrorist bomb' or 'intentionally contaminated fish-paste' without identifying the protagonist would surely satisfy the general public's curiosity; in fact, since the consequence would be to make such atrocities irrelevant to the various causes, there would soon be few, if any, such incidents to report.

The media will not regulate itself in this regard, believing implicitly (and erroneously) in the rights of people to be informed about every aspect of a newsworthy story regardless of the consequences. However, if governments can ban the broadcasting of information threatening their nations' safety then surely they should also classify media-orientated terrorism in a similar category - and ban all reference to claims of responsibility.

Only very tough and wide-ranging anti-broadcast measures will remedy this 21st Century phenomenon whereby TV, radio and press commentators almost fall over themselves to be first to convey the terrorists' propaganda messages and unwittingly (or carelessly) encourage the next incident.

Media relations

It is unlikely that the facilities manager will be responsible for public relations and media contacts in the event of a catastrophic event. Nevertheless, he or she should normally be a member of the group that feeds information to the nominated colleague for media contact.

Human response

Although flood barriers, anti-seismic structures, seismic readings and climatic analysis can mitigate against, or warn of, potential natural disaster, man cannot actually stop the elements from behaving in such a way as to cause widespread destruction.

It would seem that it is not possible to guarantee total security against disaster, whether natural or man-made, so what can facilities managers offer their companies by way of protection against the risks?

Protection against terrorist action

Explosion: The usual means of creating physical havoc are Improvised Explosive Devices (IED's) which are easily manufactured domestically, and carry little risk to the assailants either in the making, carrying or planting.

IED's are either incendiary or explosive. Incendiary devices are easily concealed and are usually planted in groups in and around combustible materials and furniture. They have a simple timer mechanism which is normally set to go off out of hours when the ensuing fire will do most damage before detection.

Staff must be trained to be observant and report unusual or unfamiliar objects although the installation of sprinklers may, in the end, be the best way of avoiding too much damage. Obviously sprinklers can themselves cause damage, so it is particularly important for all important papers and equipment to be stored or otherwise protected outside of normal working hours. The initial cost of sprinklers is considered in Chapter 7.1.5 (Fig. 7.1.H)

Explosive devices comprise the explosive, its detonator and a timer - all enclosed in some form of container. Placed close to its target a properly functioning device can, as we have all seen far too often, create havoc, death and destruction.

Explosive devices are unpredictable in the scale, direction and spread of the destruction and are particularly varied in the form of their containment and concealment, eg boots of cars, litter bins and parcels are but a few disguises commonly adopted by terrorists to conceal their weapons of destruction.

IED's can also be launched from a distance rendering external anti-terrorist security for a specific building almost impossible other than in the immediate location.

Physical anti-explosive construction is very expensive and is not yet a normal feature of design briefs for commercial buildings. However, it is possible to plan to mitigate the threat of explosion and its immediate physical consequences as also the disaster recovery package. For instance, at reception barrier doors may be needed to prevent a 'walk-in' terrorist gaining entry.

Nuclear devices: Although a pure nuclear weapon may be difficult for terrorists to put together, the threat should not be ignored. However, a relatively a more easy weapon would be an explosive device with a nuclear ingredient, ie a 'dirty' bomb.

Chemicals: the possibility of chemical weapons needs to be considered. They include mustard gas, hydrogen cyanide, phosgene and sarin.

Bio-terrorism: the terrorist's use of biological weapons, ie viral or bacterial, is a potential which should not be ignored. They include: anthrax, botulism, smallpox and Venezuelan equine encephalitis.

Preparations

Nationally, the government, local government and statutory agencies, as well as utilities companies and others, have levels of alertness to combat terrorism in general. Food and fuel supplies and medical, public health and emergency services are at planned contingency preparedness.

Locally the facilities manager's organisation needs to develop a similar approach - with a disaster recovery action plan. Fig 7.9.D sets out David Hyams' diagrammatic overview. It gives 14 steps to preparedness.

In the event of a major disaster of the types indicated above, deaths and injuries are virtually inevitable. However such matters as: careful planning; adaptations to buildings and facilities; protective clothing and apparatus; emergency plans for evacuation and rescue, medical treatment and vaccine availability; and, after-care and counselling should protect colleagues and mitigate some of the worst aspects of a catastrophic event.

7.9.3 PLANNED PREVENTION

The threats

Establishing the exposure of the organisation to risk of terrorist attack is the essential first step in planning prevention. Critical factors will be:

- the significance of the organisation and/or its business as a target
- proximity of other organisations to such target premises

- any history of terrorist activity in the locality

- ease and extent of public access to the main part of the building

- apparent security measures.

Having determined the nature and level of any identified risk the plan can then be drawn up. The plan will embrace protection and response, no different in principle from any other security management procedure as discussed in Chapter 7.1.2.

As with other security measures, anti-terrorist protection comprises deterrence and detection; however, some construction and planning measures can be taken to reduce the effect of explosion on fabric and personnel.

Physical protection

Existing buildings are not easily altered to provide protection. However, Anti-Shatter Film (ASF), secondary windows or laminated glass will all limit the internal hazard of flying shattered glass. Fig 7.9.A shows typical comparative initial costs for these measures. Of course, partitions give more protection than screens so locating cellular offices on the vulnerable perimeters may be popular with those in the open plan interiors - possibly less so with the occupants of the cellular space who might normally be pleased with the privilege.

Fig. 7.9.A
Typical cost ranges of alternative means of protection against flying glass

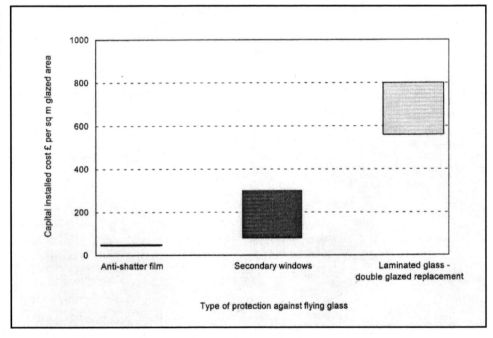

Many city centre buildings could benefit in investment value through a face-lift, so re-cladding or over-cladding with a blast-absorbent non-fragmenting material could perform a dual function; Fig. 7.9.B (over the page) gives some typical costs.

Fig. 7.9.C (over the page) shows how, by taking the opportunity to extend the floor area during re-cladding, the protective exercise will most probably pay for itself and leave a profit. The example is of an office building of 5,000 sq m GIA (4,250 sq m NIA) valued before re-cladding on the basis of rental payments of £480 per sq m NIA and 11 YP (9% initial yield). If it were only the added value of the extra floor space to be taken into account at the same rent and yield the costs would not be justified. However, because such an extension could not be carried out without altering the services and replacing the finishes the investor might expect that the improved image and perceived quality would generate either an improved yield or a better rent - or more likely both. The effects on the investment value of first a lowering of the yield to 8% (12.5 YP) and then a rental increase to £560 per sq m NIA show how the whole strategy can become cost-efficient. (See Chapter 3.5.3 for a fuller discussion on yields and YP's.)

Fig. 7.9.B
Capital cost ranges of alternative re-cladding/over-cladding options

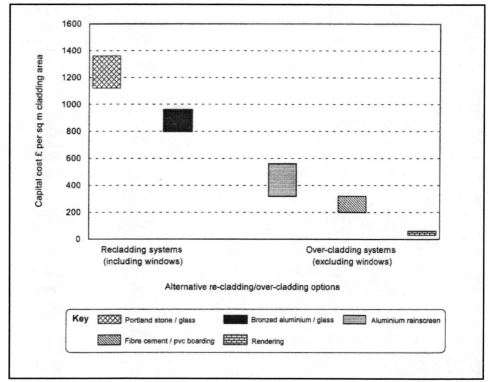

Fig. 7.9.C
Cost/value appraisal of re-cladding and refurbishing while increasing floor area by 14%

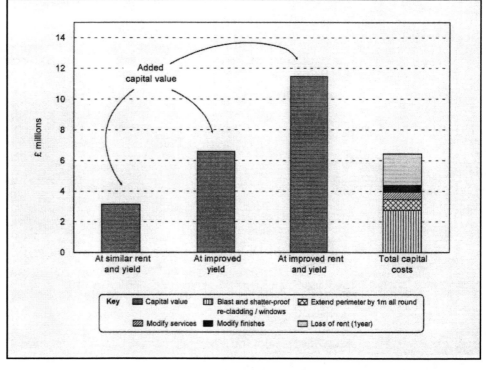

It is interesting to note that the loss of a year's rent costs nearly as much as the re-cladding works. However, such works are normally carried out at the end of a lease when a void might in any case have been anticipated and the loss of rent already written off; equally the investor may well have a sinking fund provision for the refurbishment. Either or both factors will make the profitability of the re-cladding/protection venture even greater in simple property investment terms.

Nevertheless, the location must be capable of sustaining a higher property investment valuation otherwise any such improvements will have to rely solely upon an occupier's business case - possibly a problem if the property asset is required to support the financing of the project.

The effects of blast can be contained in new building design by:

- use of homogeneous energy-absorbent materials such as reinforced concrete which do not easily deform or fracture and give warning signs of impending failure

- use of ASF materials as described above

- planning important areas away from the immediately vulnerable disaster zones

- simplifying perimeter shape to avoid blast-wave reflection.

Detection and deterrence can be helped by:

- light-coloured elevations to aid detection on dull days and at night-time

- floodlighting

- planning the car parking away from buildings (the latter also reducing the impact of any explosion).

(Other deterrent and detection methods relevant to basic security are discussed in Chapter 7.1.5.)

Alertness

Many organisations have coded states of alert which are useful for keeping the staff, visitors and potential assailants aware of the existence of a planned and manned security regime.

Natural disasters are frequently accompanied by broadcast warnings. The main security companies permanently monitor the radio and TV for such omens. Where the security manning is in-house there is a good reason to allow, even encourage, at least one security guard to stay tuned into the appropriate wavelength.

7.9.4 RESPONSE

Response to a threat

The team designated to deal with the threat, its duties and communications processes must be well established. Attack-response procedures should be written down and regularly rehearsed. Where appropriate, safe areas should be designated; blast-proof areas should be:

- internal

- away from primary circulation routes

- enclosed by solid, preferably reinforced concrete, structures

- equipped with communications media.

Liaison with the police and others in authority during a confirmed incident by nominated staff is essential and their advice must be sought on evacuation.

Recovery plan

The procedures recommended in the wake of a disaster affecting vital business are now well documented in all organisations where terrorism is even remotely a risk. It should not be forgotten, however, that natural disaster can present just the same

Fig. 7.9.D
'A guide to disaster recovery action planning'

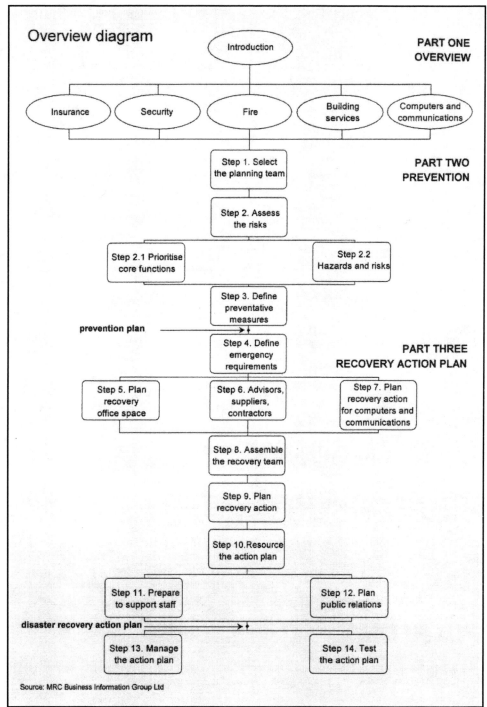

Overview diagram

Introduction

PART ONE
OVERVIEW

Insurance   Security   Fire   Building services   Computers and communications

Step 1. Select the planning team

PART TWO
PREVENTION

Step 2. Assess the risks

Step 2.1 Prioritise core functions

Step 2.2 Hazards and risks

Step 3. Define preventative measures

prevention plan

Step 4. Define emergency requirements

PART THREE
RECOVERY ACTION PLAN

Step 5. Plan recovery office space

Step 6. Advisors, suppliers, contractors

Step 7. Plan recovery action for computers and communications

Step 8. Assemble the recovery team

Step 9. Plan recovery action

Step 10. Resource the action plan

Step 11. Prepare to support staff

Step 12. Plan public relations

disaster recovery action plan

Step 13. Manage the action plan

Step 14. Test the action plan

Source: MRC Business Information Group Ltd

consequences as the man-made variety and needs just the same recovery procedures. The facilities manager may have a front line role in the recovery plan or just be a member of the core team. In either case he or she will certainly have to take up responsibility for reinstatement of all facilities and operating services and have a back-up pool of accommodation and suppliers to support the pre-identified key recovery job functions.

Some companies own their own fully serviced back-up premises for use in the face of discontinuity of business operation.

In some major centres 'disaster recovery centres' are available for short term rental with annual payment in advance for the possible use of the facility on a first call basis.

Security post-disaster will have to be particularly tight, especially with regard to malevolent supplementary damage by disaffected staff and also looting. A clear-desk policy is not only highly desirable with respect to cleanliness - it also provides major protection against one of the worst consequences of disaster - lost or damaged documents.

Photographic evidence of one form or another must be produced for negotiations with the insurance lost adjuster; for the same purpose all costs of the recovery and reinstatement must be carefully maintained by the facilities manager. A particular point to note is that the cost of immediate post-disaster construction work may not be allowed in full by the loss adjuster if the procurement route has not been planned and negotiated in advance to avoid 'blackmail' charging.

An excellent book by David Hyams[1] on the subject of 'Disaster Recovery Action Planning' contains the overview diagram reproduced at Fig. 7.9.D (previous page).

---

[1] David Hyams (1993) 'A Guide to Disaster Recovery Action Planning,' MRC Business Information Group Ltd, Oxford UK

Section 8

Staff Support Services

8.1   CATERING

Introduction

As with all facilities management cost centres, the decision as to whether, why, who, what, when, how and at what cost to provide catering must stem naturally from the organisation's facilities policy (see Chapter 1.1 - The Scope of Facilities).

8.1.1 THE CATERING POLICY

Policy considerations

The principal reasons for providing catering facilities at work are:

* employee satisfaction/convenience
* improved performance
* hospitality.

Employee satisfaction will become an issue for one or more of the following reasons:

* an isolated location offers limited or no alternative
* a special feature is needed to encourage recruitment and retention of staff
* as a gesture of social responsibility to ensure staff are properly fed, especially in shift situations where lunch may have to be the main meal of the day.

Improved performance may be influenced by:

* reducing time away from the workplace where critical to the function of particular tasks
* discouraging poor eating habits where fast food outlets and sandwich bars are the only alternative in a short lunch period
* discouraging lunch-time visits to inns or wine bars.

In-house hospitality catering is not just a highly cost-effective alternative to dining-out for it can also be a necessity if, in the normal course of business, confidential deals are frequently done over the dining table. Dining in-house can also be a great time-saver appreciated by today's time-pressured business visitor as much as by the host.

Hospitality dining is usually in a separate but adjacent facility, although the directors' areas are usually away from the staff dining and may have dedicated service. Alcohol is still served in most hospitality areas, but its provision in staff dining is now almost universally prohibited.

Policy decisions

Having decided, on one or more of the above grounds, to provide an on-site catering facility the organisation will have to make decisions in the following key areas, all of which will have important cost implications:

* catering numbers
* style of service
* range of menu
* price structure
* speed of service
* opening hours
* decor

- space

- food preparation technology

- location of catering facilities

- staff training and development.

8.1.2 THE CONTENTS OF THE COST CENTRE

The authors' recommended protocol for items included in this cost centre is given at Fig. 8.1.A.

Fig. 8.1.A
Facilities Economics classification protocol - catering costs

Sub-categories (contract bundle items)	Principal Examples / cost elements	Items commonly included in costs	Items excluded from costs	
			Item	Refer to category:
Staff dining	Staff dining: breakfast menu Staff dining: lunch menu Staff dining: sandwich bar Staff dining: snacks and beverages	Chef, Cooks, Supervisors, Waiters, Servers, Till staff, Table clearers, Preparation, Consumables, Equipment leases, Crockery, Disposals, Linen, Laundry, Deep cleaning / specialist cleaning, Caterers' fees, Task management	Fitting-out General cleaners	Alterations and improvements Cleaning
Vending	Vending: sandwiches Vending: confectionery and snack products Vending: Canned / bottled drinks Vending beverages		Utilities Subsidy	Utilities N/a
Hospitality	Hospitality: sandwich lunches Hospitality: beverage service Hospitality: cold buffet lunches Hospitality: hot buffet lunches		Till income	N/a
Private dining	Private dining rooms: breakfast menu (silver service) Private dining rooms: Lunch menu (silver service)			
Special functions	Special functions: seated dinners (silver service) Special functions: buffets (silver service) Special functions: cocktail parties			
Bar	Bar: coffee lounge Bar: alcoholic and soft drinks			
Maintenance and repair	Catering equipment maintenance			

The normal cost drivers associated with these components are considered later in this chapter.

8.1.3 CATERING NUMBERS

Proportion of staff dining

Where formal catering is provided on site the proportion of staff availing themselves of the opportunity varies widely from around 30% to 80%. Really remote sites may achieve 100%.

The minimum number to make formal catering viable in an organisation is usually considered to be 100 - also the number at which outsourcing of the facility becomes of interest to the contractor.

Generally speaking an organisation which has a policy of catering provision will want to optimise its use, partly for reasons of economies of scale but mainly to get as much good internal public relations as possible out of the provision.

Size of sitting

How many of the diners participate in one sitting obviously impacts on the space provision, but it is unlikely that space use considerations will drive the policy in this respect; time available for lunch will be the key determinant of the size and style of the facility.

8.1.4 STYLES OF SERVICE

The choices

Service levels and styles vary significantly between business sectors. Schools generally require a lunch-time only cost-effective service but offering limited choice. Hospitals may require a full-day service for patients with distribution towards, plated by catering or domestic staff to the bed-side, together with chargeable services for staff and visitors. The industrial production sector may provide more limited choice than in offices but covering all shifts over a 24-hour period. Service providers in all sectors are required to conform to all relevant statutes regarding the preparation and serving of food, and they will usually promote healthy eating alternatives, whilst being cost conscious for the paying customer business.

The catering options available are many and varied, due to the advances in technologies for preparation, storage, cooking, serving, clearing and disposal.

In ascending order of sophistication (and cost) the principal serving styles are:

- self-catering/vending
- self-service
- part self-service/part waited service
- waited service only
- 'remote' service.

In each case a decision will also have to be made as to whether the facility will be single - or multi-status with regard to importance or role within the business.

Self-catering/vending

The simplest form of self-catering is the snack/drinks vending machine. These are considered later in the chapter.

Few modern self-catering facilities now depend on gas/electric ovens with the associated pots and pans and domestic kitchen clutter. However, microwave technology has offered an acceptable quick and 'clean' alternative which can suit the smaller organisation.

It is important for the smaller organisation to know that the use of 'domestic' microwaves on business premises contravenes the food safety regulations . The reason for this stipulation is primarily that domestic units lose their capacity with continuous use thereby failing to meet the 70°C needed for proper cooking and putting the consumer at risk of food poisoning.

'Commercial' grade units up to 1,000 Watts are easily available in most localities at a cost of up to £1,000.

The commercial models have a greater capacity, better controls and sometimes alternative cooking processes. The degree of sophistication will depend upon whether the catering regime is truly self-catering or will have some assistants in attendance.

Avoidance of queuing is particularly important, especially as staff operating the ovens may become flustered under the scrutiny of their potentially (or actually) impatient colleagues.

Ready-made dishes can be sold or stored on the site and clearing away is usually left to the diner; disposable 'crockery' and cutlery are often provided free of charge.

Self-service

Self-service is now almost universally adopted for staff catering. Apart from the obvious saving in manpower and cost, the main advantage is speed of service - so important to staff wanting only a short break so as to take advantage of a flexi-time bonus, or just to leave time, eg social gathering, shopping. Options are becoming more and more innovative, catering for hot and cold food and sometimes 'fast' food.

The traditional self-service arrangement of one long counter with chef's assistants serving all menu items has largely been replaced by 'free-flow' service points, eg islands serving (or offering for self-serving) such menu variants as salads, hot dishes, sandwiches, fruit and drinks. Some restaurants have delicatessen-style refrigerated dispensers while others offer franchised speciality dishes.

The principal advantage of the 'island' type of layout is speed of service as also the prevention of queuing which is a counter-productive irritant. Of course, speed of service must be accompanied by speed of check-out.

A good performance speed benchmark for really sophisticated self-service is three minutes from entering the cafeteria to becoming seated at the dining table.

Methods of payment are also becoming more sophisticated mainly, again, with a view to increased speed and avoidance of queuing. Money is mostly out, being replaced by tokens or sometimes pre-encoded cards. Tokens may either be purchased to cover two or three course meals or provided free of charge if that is the catering policy. Cards can identify the user's tariff rating and either be 'loaded' by cash pre-payment into validation units or deducted from salaries by linking to the payroll program. Digital displays on the tills or vending machines indicate the current financial status of the card.

The payment point and beverage dispenser are usually the bottle-necks in the system. Payment can be speeded up by the various token/card arrangements and also by siting the cashier in such a manner as to permit calculation of the cost of down-queue meals pending settlement of the one immediately at the check-out.

Hot beverage service can be speeded up by attendant service, or by siting the facility outside of the main dining area, say in a coffee lounge; in this way only those wanting a hot drink with their meals will have to queue before check-out.

Waitress service

Such indulgence is only merited when neither speed nor cost is the main consideration. It is possibly appropriate to those organisations where a high proportion of employees frequently have cause to introduce visitors - in other words not a typical commercial company or public department.

Where waitress-service is deemed appropriate it is usually separate but adjacent to the main self-service restaurant using the same kitchen, but some Boardroom areas have dedicated catering.

Service may be 'plated', ie suitable for middle-management, with higher standards and great variety than in self-service, or 'silver-service' for senior management or anyone else who can afford it subject to status, where applicable.

Waiting staff are prone to accidents, particularly casual or seasonal staff. Awareness training and a safe working environment should help to avoid burns, cuts, falls and back strain.

Remote catering

Satellite offices or special locations within a campus may be served by smaller kitchens and dining areas, with meals delivered in heated trolleys or by hand or vehicle. Some organisations provide a trolley service of mainly cold snacks to the workplace; however, the provision of vending machines is now making this practice redundant.

Single or multi-status

The decision as to whether to go single or multi-status is relevant to all but 'silver-service' catering. Within the range to which multi-status is appropriate the golden rule is to set standards to the highest common denominator, which will have implications for the cost per meal, but offset by the increased usage and better internal public relations.

8.1.5 THE MENU

The factors influencing the range

Among the most important factors affecting catering policy with regard to what is available are:

- perceived importance of provision in respect of employee satisfaction
- length of lunch-break
- social and cultural groupings
- predominant age and sex of employees
- need to provide the main meal of the day
- dietary policy.

Apart from the long-distance commuter and singletons most employees prefer to have the main meal of the day at home, a trend which has led the demand away from heavy meals towards lighter lunches and snacks.

Where main meals are served, caterers try to avoid the sauces and trimmings of the private restaurant, to grill rather than fry and to encourage consumption of salads, pasta and other low calorie, low cholesterol products. Not only is peppered steak with french fries expensive, it also breaks a lot of healthy diet rules and, in any case, the glass of wine ideally to go with it is probably not available due to company policy - except maybe in the 'function' or 'silver-plate' dining rooms.

The range of food available will also depend on the location of preparation which, in turn, may depend on the size of the catering facility. Full site-preparation is usual in the largest kitchens, and does require a delivery point separate from any waste disposal operation; kitchens need to be laid out with separate areas for preparing and cooking each type of food to avoid cross-contamination.

Simpler provision is where the food is delivered chilled (for same-day service) or frozen (for consumption sometime in the future). Kitchens for such provision are smaller but the range of meals available need not be less than in the full-preparation regime. Similarly, required speed of service need not result in less choice of menu items.

8.1.6 THE PRICE

The pricing policy

Two factors influence the price of the meal to the consumer:

- the cost of providing the meal
- any subsidy.

The cost of providing the meal is discussed below. The policy with regards to subsidy is a matter for personnel rather than facilities management. A common policy is for the diner to pay the cost of food plus VAT with the company picking up the cost of management, preparation, equipment and service. Such an arrangement is normally considered as falling outside of the realm of taxable benefit, whereas 100% subsidy usually does not.

Other subsidy policies require the employee to pay a full price for 'special' dishes and beverages.

In the final event, the optimum level of investment per capita in terms of provision and subsidy will turn on the benefit thereby accruing to the organisation, whether measured by recruitment, retention, wealth or health of the employees.

Of course, if management gets any of it wrong then it would, in every economic aspect, be better not to have introduced the facility at all.

8.1.7 OPENING HOURS

Availability requirements

The range of time for formal catering availability is from two hours at lunch-time, through breakfast, coffee, lunch and afternoon tea-time to 100% full availability ie where full 24-hour shift-work is in operation.

The commonest provision is lunch-time only with vending areas catering for other requirements during the day.

A short unstaggered lunch-break necessitates a large facility with extremely sophisticated management; such an arrangement is not normal and is obviously expensive. More typically, an average of between two and three 'covers' per dining seat in a two hour lunch period applies to most self-service facilities.

8.1.8 DECOR

Design requirements

It is most important that the dining area should feel distinctly different from the main working areas. Lighting must be softer, colours warmer, servery counters and furniture crisp (and seats not so comfortable as to encourage a long stay!) and easily cleaned, and areas screened to provide a feeling of identity and possibly some privacy.

Changes of floor level are discouraged by the operators but can add considerable amenity; provided the main dining area is on the same level as the kitchen most operators will accept this feature, particularly in the self-service areas where diners clear their own tables.

Because of the space occupied by dining areas some organisations like the facilities to double as meeting areas outside of dining hours. Although this puts pressure on cleaning staff and is also very demanding in terms of compliance with the food safety regulations, it does make economic sense. The designer's brief will therefore require the decor to be appropriate for the alternative function. For this reason, and also to facilitate cleaning, the level of lighting must always be adjustable in dining areas.

The cost of fitting out

Fig. 8.1.B gives indicative costs for fitting out a range of dining area styles and configurations per unit of area and per capita. The actual space required is discussed below.

Fig. 8.1.B
Costs of fitting-out and equipping dining areas - various catering styles

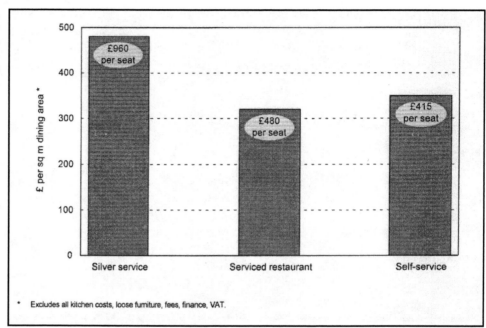

*   Excludes all kitchen costs, loose furniture, fees, finance, VAT.

8.1.9 FOOD PREPARATION

Types of processing

As discussed in the 'Menu' paragraphs above, preparation may be:

*   full on-site preparation

*   cook/chill/re-heat

*   cook/freeze/thaw/re-heat.

Space and equipment

Each process has a different space requirement and health and safety restrictions.

In particular, the delivery of fresh meat is only permissible during normal hours where there is a dedicated service access.

Modern kitchen equipment is multi-functional, space-saving, faster, energy efficient and mobile to facilitate both general cleaning of the rooms and specialist cleaning of the equipment itself.

The surfaces must be easy to clean and the hygiene generally scrupulous, eg lighting control should be by means of sensors to avoid spreading germs from one food to another via fingers and the light switches.

8.1.10 SPACE REQUIREMENTS

Space per meal

The space per 'cover' required in the dining area ranges from around 2 sq m in smaller establishments where there is waited service down to 1.2 sq m for a for a self-catering area. The coffee area is typically 0.7 to 0.8 sq m per cover.

Space in the kitchens will depend upon how much preparation takes place and whether it contains an active servery. Typically a full-preparation kitchen supporting a free-flow operation needs about 0.4 sq m per meal where large numbers are fed compared with 0.65 sq m for a 200-meal operation; cook/chill or cook/freeze operations can save substantially on space in some situations.

8.1.11 LOCATION OF CATERING FACILITIES

Geographical location

Ideally dining facilities should be provided in space not otherwise dedicated - or worse rented as - productive area. Some larger premises have catering dedicated in basement or lower-ground floor areas with rental values adjusted accordingly. As Fig. 8.1.C shows, if it is not possible to use space for catering which would otherwise be non-productive the space costs per meal, especially in high value locations, can be very considerable, even prohibitive.

Fig. 8.1.C
The impact of premises costs on catering costs where prime office space is dedicated to dining

Typical catering premises costs* £ per capita pa**			
Location	**200 Meals**	**500 Meals**	**750 Meals**
City of London	910	850	780
West End	850	780	650
Greater London	510	470	390
Provincial city	340	310	260
Out-of-town location	330	260	200
Typical catering premises costs* £ per meal per person dining**			
Location	**200 Meals**	**500 Meals**	**750 Meals**
City of London	7.20	7.00	6.50
West End	7.00	6.50	5.40
Greater London	4.20	3.90	3.30
Provincial city	2.80	2.60	2.20
Out-of-town location	2.70	2.20	1.60

*   Rent, local taxes and operating costs but excluding fitting-out and furniture.
**   Based on 50% of staff taking one meal per working day pa, ie double these costs per regular daily diner.

Location within premises

At an operational level, dedicated access to the kitchens/food storage areas is critical in avoiding the need for out-of-hours delivery of fresh foods, so provision of goods lifts may be necessary if the facility is above ground floor.

Where premises are formed in a local cluster it may be beneficial to use the least operationally strategic space for dining rather than that most convenient for the more senior staff. Much will depend on the time available for lunch, the desirability or otherwise of a short walk in the neighbourhood and how important the provision is in personnel terms.

As a general rule it is best for catering to be in the building containing most potential diners. However, if the 'flag-ship' is smaller but reasonably accessible then many satellite staff will make a short trek, just to be 'seen'. Again, if the cost of space in the flagship is high the decision must be made particularly carefully taking all costs and benefits into consideration.

8.1.12 THE COST OF CATERING PROVISION

Typical costs per capita

The recommended protocol for this cost centre has been provided at Fig. 8.1.A.

Similar to other facilities services, catering costs comprise labour (including supervision and management consumables (food, disposable items, utilities) and equipment (kitchen and dining areas), together with profit and overheads payable in the case of an external contract. Food costs maybe as much as 50% of a basic plated meal prepared on site, but this proportion tends to decrease as the more labour-intensive higher service level meals are provided.

Published high-level catering benchmarks, eg expenditure per unit of floor area or per building occupant are of little benefit due to the variety of service levels and the indefinite relationship between consumption and either floor area or staff numbers. One of the most obvious reasons for these cost differentials is take-up of a service. This will vary significantly according to service level quality, the presence or absence of alternative sources of sustenance and the organisation's subsidy policy, amongst other reasons. A fully subsidised good quality staff restaurant will attract a daily lunch take-up of 75% of the potential building occupancy, even where local alternatives exist, whilst a low quality, poorly-situated partly-subsidised catering establishment will have difficulty attracting 25%.

To give some idea of the danger of using the wrong parameter for estimating or benchmarking catering costs Fig. 8.1.D (over the page) shows cost per capita from a number of headquarters office buildings in different organisations but in a similar peer group.

As previously shown the ratio of diners is typically from 30% to 80% of the workforce. Several of the specimens in the example are locally clustered offices; in all cases the catering is provided in the head office building. For this reason the costs per unit of area and per person have been calculated on the basis of the whole building stock and workforce in the clusters - ie the Headquarters catchment area - as well as just for head office.

Of significantly greater benefit is cost by unit of consumption, ie cost per cover, per bedside meal or per vended drink.

Fig. 8.1.D
Average catering costs per capita depending upon usage

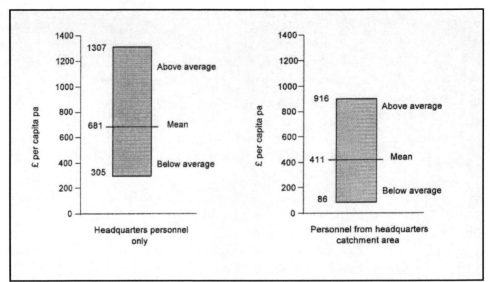

Typical meal cost analysis

Fig. 8.1.E shows typical costs per meal (excluding subsidy, premises costs and sales income) for self-service and serviced facilities. Typically a basic self-service plated hot meal can be provided in a staff canteen for as little as £2.50 however, this cost can quickly rise to over £6 per cover in higher quality 'restaurants' where greater choice, fewer covers and a higher quality of environment food and service is expected. Whilst these costs purport to be the full cost of meal provision, in a canteen situation they will in fact normally be exclusive of property costs (rent, local taxes, insurance) and premises operating costs (including maintenance, utilities and cleaning of the dining area); the omission of premises costs from the costs of catering clearly conceals a massive subsidy in many areas which may reflect business strategy - or just ignorance. Who knows?

Fig. 8.1.E
Typical costs per meal excluding premises costs

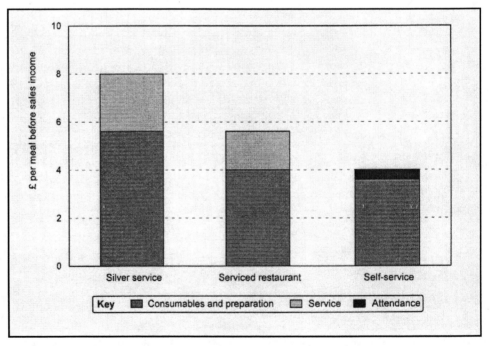

8.1.13 MANAGEMENT

In-house v out-source

The core/non-core argument takes on significance once the catering numbers rise above 100; below this the contractors do not find the work profitable or must charge excessively to achieve the desired return on investment.

In-house catering can be effective and efficient just as in provision of any other specialist service. Nevertheless the purchasing power, labour resources and fundamental commitment to hygiene of catering contractors are powerful (but not overwhelming) arguments in their favour.

The catering contract

Choosing and monitoring the contractors is critical; reputation alone will not necessarily guarantee quality, so the in-house liaison person must insist on the letter of the agreement, in particular with regard to:

- availability and calibre of trained staff

- diet balance

- management reports (monthly is preferable)

- cost accounting (up to date and accurate)

- management audit.

Sometimes contractors will design the facilities and organise construction, purchasing and funding; they will always insist on controlling cleaning and maintenance.

There are two principal mechanisms for paying the catering contractor:

- cost-plus

- single fee.

In both cases the catering contractor runs the whole operation, with all costs (net of all trade and cash discounts) being reimbursed to the contractor plus an agreed percentage or sliding scale fee.

In the case of the cost-plus arrangement the client has potentially more control over what is provided in terms of quality, cost, portions and alike, whereas in the single fee arrangement the level of provision is fixed subject only to inflation of raw materials and labour.

A variation on the theme relates final reimbursement to performance against performance indicators - much as in some types of maintenance agreement - including financial and management as well as quality targets.

Care must be taken to ensure that, where different styles of catering such as 'self-service' and 'silver-plate' are being sought under the same contract, the caterer has the experience and staff levels necessary to provide both services efficiently.

In all cases, as well as in-house provision, regular, independent questionnaire surveys must be conducted in the interests of staff, caterer and business management alike.

Multi-skilling

Because catering staff are usually only required on a part-time basis some caterers use 'multi-skilled' staff for some of the more basic operations. So cleaning operatives may double as table-cleaners or counter-servers to provide a full-time equivalent role; this may prove more cost-efficient and make it easier to retain staff; however, it may not always be possible to effect such flexibility unless the catering is 'bundled' together with the appropriate alternative service.

8.1.14 VENDING MACHINES

Services available

Vending machines can these days provide each and every refreshment requirement from a cold drink to a hot meal.

The range of consumables available through vending machines comprises:

- cold drinks
- hot beverages
- confectionery
- snacks
- water
- hot meals.

Cold drinks come refrigerated in cans and cartons bearing 'well known' brand-names. Hot beverages (in-cup or fresh brew) include tea, coffee (cappuccino, espresso, au lait), savoury drinks, fruit cup and alike. The confectionery merchandisers selling chocolate bars, crisps and nuts are operated on a commission basis to the employer, which should return a profit after rental payments and maintenance.

Employers who provide water for employees should ensure that it comes from a reliable source and meets health and safety purity standards, eg the criteria for cleanliness, freedom from chemical and bacteria - as under the Workplace (Health and Safety Welfare) Regulations 1992.

The chilled merchandisers operate on a similar basis offering packaged snacks (eg biscuits and cheese) and sandwiches and pies or whole meals for microwaving. The latest models can now incorporate a microwave oven, thereby offering a complete (if limited-menu) on-site catering service.

Quality and maintenance

Nearly all goods purveyed are quality name brands. The hot beverages can be freshly brewed and the ingredients mixed to taste; most users of good machines consider that the taste is about as good as that produced in the kitchen via the kettle. Upkeep such as keeping the machines stocked can be contracted-out if necessary. Troublesome coin-in-the-slot machines are fast being replaced by the far more efficient token or electronic-card operating equipment, both of which are better from the security viewpoint than coin-in-the-slot.

The 'in-cup' and sachet systems avoid release of ingredients amongst the working parts, so dramatically improving efficiency of performance, and reducing down-time maintenance costs; such systems also avoid the need for filling on site by contractors.

Vending-machine policy

The decision to use vending machines will normally be covered by the need to:

- provide a minimum on-site convenience
- augment a primary catering or snack facility in 'remote' locations
- provide a drinks and beverages facility about the site in lieu of, or to augment, a central facility
- to make a profit.

The latter is not a serious consideration since by far the over-riding purpose of the provision is for staff convenience, internal public relations and hygiene/safety. However some organisations do subsidise the vending prices by allowing the vending operator to take normal profits from non-essential goods like confectionery and toiletry/pharmaceutical consumables.

From a health and safety perspective, the substitution of mobile beverages facilities, eg kettles, with fixed vending machines should reduce the likelihood of accidents. However, care is needed in training cleaning staff to properly clean vending machines.

The economics of vending

All the services can provide a return to the employer by way of commission on sales, rebates, or free maintenance or even free rental. It all depends upon the numbers of machines, volume of sales and any subsidies available.

In some situations the need for an on-site catering facility can be avoided, without loss of face, by providing a combination of beverage dispenser and chilled merchandise.

Machines take up less space than kitchens, are easier to keep clean, keep the Health and Safety Officer happy (or less miserable) and may subsidise or eliminate the rental cost of this facility.

Monthly rentals currently range from £6 per month for in-cup beverage dispensers to £7,000 per month for hot/cold fresh brew machines and chilled meal merchandisers with built-in microwave.

When considering the time spent by employees making tea/coffee from the kettle, vending machines do provide a good return on investment. Surveys have shown that on average 45 minutes a day is spent (outside of formal breaks) per capita on making tea and coffee. Even at a low average time-charge of £24 per hour this means an average loss of output of over £20 per day per capita. Perhaps for this reason alone the Americans and Japanese now have one machine per 25 head of population; given that this phenomenal development is largely the result of electronics replacing the old coin-in-the-slot and dispensing mechanisms now available, no doubt the present modest average of one machine per 100 head of population will soon whittle down.

As it is, over 5bn cupped drinks are sold in the UK Vending machines each year, yielding around £2.5bn of sales. This average of 50p per cup can be as little as 10p in the lower quartile so, taking the £20 per day time-loss calculated above, the economic argument does seem to fall in favour of the machine (see Fig. 8.1.F).

Fig. 8.1.F *Theoretical calculation of self-catering v vending for break-time beverages*	Cost breakdown	Free beverages – self-catering	£ per capita per day	Free beverage vending machine	£ per capita per day
	Lost output per capita per day	5 x 10 min at £ 24 per hour	20.00	5 x 5 min at £ 24 per hour	10.00
	Ingredients and maintenance	5 beverages per capita day at £ 0.30 per beverage	1.50	5 beverages per capita day at £ 0.65 per beverage	3.25
	Total		21.50		13.25

The only thing not quite certain is how the time spent around the machine equates to the kitchen time, or whether people would otherwise be productive in the time saved - perhaps they need frequent breaks to function efficiently the rest of the time.

Nevertheless the arguments in respect of availability, cleanliness, health, safety, security, space and convenience, probably win the day for the automatons.

8.2 HEALTH AND SAFETY AT WORK

Introduction

Health and safety is an important part of every business operation. Legislation places a responsibility on every employer to identify, assess and control workplace risks that may potentially harm their employees. However, considerations of health and safety at work are not just restricted to the employees of one organisation working from its premises. Just as much at risk are:

- visitors to the premises on official business from other firms (including contractors and suppliers)

- visiting relatives and social acquaintances of employees

- members of the general public affected by activities, emissions and waste associated with the premises

- also, conceivably, intruders, trespassers and users of any public footpaths and the like.

The consequences of disaster resulting from failure to afford adequate protection will fall upon both the individuals affected and the organisation responsible for the event; responsibility may be passed onto a third party in certain circumstances.

The role of facilities managers is to assist their employers with the identification, risk appraisal and control of such hazards.

This chapter looks at the legislation, the main players in the field, the risks encountered, assessment of risk, management of risk, economic and legal aspects, and, finally, the 'sick building syndrome'.

8.2.1 HEALTH AND SAFETY LEGISLATION - AN OVERVIEW

Sources of legislation

The majority of health and safety legislation is derived from EU Directives brought into the statute book. The key directive being the 'The European Framework Directive on the Health and Safety of Workers' 89/391/EEC. The main objective of this directive is to introduce measures to encourage improvements in the safety and health of workers at work.

To achieve this objective the Directive establishes a number of obligations for employers and a variety of obligations for workers. An employer's obligation is to be aware of health and safety issues in the workplace and of employees' capabilities, to identify health and safety workplace risks and minimise their impact, to develop and implement an overall coherent prevention policy, to train and consult staff in health and safety issues and report to the appropriate authorities any occupational accidents/illnesses. Employees are obliged to follow company safety policies and work safely in the workplace.

A set of six EC Directives - known as the 'EC Six-pack' - became part of UK statute law on 1 January 1993. They derive from Article 118A of the Treaty of Rome and have now been incorporated into the following regulations:

- Workplace (Health, Safety and Welfare) Regulations 1992

- Manual Handling Operations Regulations 1992

- Management of Health and Safety at Work Regulations 1992

- Personal Protective Equipment at Work (PPE) Regulations 1992

- Provision and Use of Work Equipment Regulations 1992
- Health and Safety (Display Screen Equipment) Regulations 1992.

Most of these merely augment the provisions of the Health and Safety at Work Act 1974 - but there are new concepts, especially concerning how health and safety should be managed and dealing with hazards at the computer workstation. A particular requirement now is for management to assess the health and safety risks in their premises, devise antidotes and put them into effect, measure their effectiveness and appoint competent persons to be engaged on these activities.

Further directives have brought about new requirements in respect of consumer products, fire precautions, asbestos, pregnant women and new mothers, young workers and construction sites.

In addition to the formal Health and Safety at Work regulations, enactments which are also relevant to the subject include:

- Control of Substances Hazardous to Health Regulations 1988
- Electricity at Work Act 1989
- Food Safety Act 1990
- Environmental Pollution Act 1990.

- Fire legislation (which is due to be consolidated).

8.2.2 RISKS TO HEALTH AND SAFETY

There are a number of groups of persons who are potentially at risk of health and safety hazards in the facilities environment. These include employees, contractors, visitors and members of the public.

Under the legislation employers have a general duty of care to ensure the health and safety of all employees while at work. This general duty of care is extended to others who work at or visit the premises. In the case of visitors, the Occupier's Liability Acts 1957 and 1984 cover those who enter with permission and those who do not, eg trespassers (see Chapter 3.3.1).

The Disability Discrimination Act 1995 concerns both workers and visitors, requiring adaptations to premises to comply with the Act in meeting their needs.

What are the risks?

The following are the types of risk to which employees, contractors, visitors and members of the public are potentially exposed:

- **biological risks** - micro-organisms such as bacteria, fungi and viruses can be common around moist and or poorly ventilated areas such as sanitary conveniences and in water-cooled ventilation systems.

- **chemical risks** - cleaning solutions, paints, pesticides, adhesives and thinners can all contain substances hazardous to health. Exposure to these contaminants can cause short-term health problems such respiratory and/or skin irritation or longer-term health complaints such as asthma and cancer.

- **physical risks** - physical risks can include trip hazards, excessive noise from machinery and equipment, too much or too little lighting, electrical and fire hazards, inadequate heating or cooling.

- **musculoskeletal risks** - these include sprains/strains of backs, upper and lower limbs due to the lifting of heavy objects or repetitive work.

- **psycho-social risks** - these can include, stress, anxiety or 'burn out' as a result of poor organisational design, long working hours and/or workplace aggression.

There are a number of health and safety risks of particular concern to facility managers. These include:

- **humidifier fever** - an illness affecting those who become sensitised to certain biological materials growing in the recirculating water or air - characterisics of illness include a high temperature, chest discomfort, sometimes a dry cough and general malaise, symptoms very like those of mild influenza. It can be avoided by proper attention to the design and maintenance of air conditioning systems to avoid the accumulation of stagnant water in any part, which can grow a mixture of organisms.

- **Legionnaires Disease** - a type of pneumonia caused by bacteria commonly associated with water systems in large buildings. The characteristic symptoms begin with a high fever; chills, headaches and muscle pain ending in a dry cough that is frequently accompanied by breathing difficulties. Water contaminated by Legionellae only presents a risk when it is dispersed into the air in the form of an aerosol (very fine water droplets/spray). Systems presenting the greatest risk are air conditioning plants and industrial cooling systems involving cooling towers and evaporative condensers; in these pieces of equipment typical temperatures are around 30°C, there is a presence of sludge, scale, rust and/or algae and water droplets are readily generated. Legionellae can be easily controlled by the regular application of biocide to the cooling water.

- **sick building syndrome** - a condition associated with symptoms of frequent headaches, dry throat or sore eyes that increase in severity with time spent in a building. The cause is unknown; however it is now almost universally accepted that the phenomenon is most likely due to a combination of physical or environmental factors such as ventilation, lighting, cleaning, maintenance and workstation layout and job factors such as variety and interest of particular jobs and ability of persons to control certain aspects of their working environment (see 8.2.6 below).

- **construction safety** - in the course of the erection, refurbishment and/or demolition of buildings and plant is by far the most hazardous work undertaken in the industrialised world in term of fatalities. This type of work is of particular relevance to facilities managers as they are often responsible for managing construction work on the premises. It is a special focus for government. The health and safety risks associated with construction work are well known and include falls from heights, head injuries, manual handling, slips, trips or falls, contact with machinery, being struck by moving vehicles, trapped by collapse or overturning, electrocution and exposure to hazardous chemicals. Interestingly the highest risk occupations in the construction industry include labourers, roofers and management/professionals. The Construction (Design and Management) Regulations 1994 set out to influence the design and construction processes for building works, particularly with the health and safety of construction workers in mind. A key role is the 'planning supervisor', required in all projects (other than those which are relatively small). The role functions include:

  - ensure all health and safety requirements are met in the designs

  - prepare a health and safety plan and ensure it is in the tender documents

  - prepare a health and safety dossier or file for materials impact and design impact on those who will clean and maintain the premises.

- **building design** - the Building Regulations and other legislation seek to ensure that health and safety are taken into account in the plans for new buildings or for conversions and other alterations to existing buildings. For large projects the planning supervision is principally concerned with inclusion, planning and implementation. However the designer also has a particular responsibility for ensuring health and safety law is not infringed by the manner in which it is necessary to construct the building.

Full responsibility for compliance is currently placed with the building owner, who for certain construction projects engages the 'planning supervisor' to advise on health and safety implications of design and construction proposals. Although the safety record in this field has been amongst the best in Europe there are currently calls from the UK industry's clients to fall more into line with less stringent (less costly) regimes in the rest of the EU!

Common health and safety risks

The European Foundation for the Improvement of Living and Working Conditions found in 1996 that the most common work-related health problems in Europe are:

- back pain   (30% of workers)

- stress   (28% of workers)

- muscular pains in arm and legs   (17% of workers).

They also found that exposure to physical hazards (noise, vibration, dangerous or polluting products or substances) and poor workplace design remains very common (28% of workers are exposed to intense noise, 45% to unsatisfactory working positions). Interestingly only 32% of employees had had job-related health and safety training provided by their company in the previous 12 months. (Risks from bio-terrorism were considered in Chapter 7.9.)

8.2.3 ASSESSMENT OF RISK

Identifying risks

In Chapter 2.5 risk was defined as 'the possibility of incurring misfortune or loss'. So, in a health and safety context, it is necessary first to identify the hazards which expose personnel to the danger of illness or injury. In fact the legislation places obligations on employers to undertake and be in possession of an assessment of the risk to safety and health of employees at work. The risk assessment should be undertaken by a person who has the necessary skills, training and experience to adequately identify and assess workplace risks. In addition, the risk assessment should be regularly reviewed to ensure it is current and valid. This function is normally the responsibility of the facilities managers or their agents.

A vital component of risk assessment is the identification of hazards, hazardous situations and hazardous events. A hazard can be described as something that has the potential to cause harm. Typical hazards in the facilities environment include the handling of hazardous substances, walking upon floor surfaces, climbing up or down ladders, and the use of electrical equipment.

There are many procedures for hazard identification, ranging from sophisticated techniques used in the process industries, for example hazard and operability studies (HAZOP), to straightforward observational techniques.

In the facilities environment, straightforward observational techniques would normally be considered a sufficient method for risk assessment. This involves seeking out relevant sources of information about risks including legislation and supporting approved codes of practice and guidance from the national legislating bodies, product information, relevant national and international standards, industry or trade association guidance, accident and ill-health data; it also involves touring the workplace to systematically identify the hazards associated with equipment and activities in each work area. A preliminary checklist such as the one in Fig. 8.2.A., outlining the main hazards in a facilities environment may be also be useful.

Hazard	Issues to consider
Work Equipment and Machinery	• Electrical safety • Access for maintenance • Guarding • Lock out systems and emergency stops • Preventative maintenance • Training • Suitable signage
Fire	• Means of escape • Fire alarm and fire fighting • Housekeeping • Storage • Smoking • Training of fire wardens • Evacuation drills
Hazardous Substances	• Inventory of substances used • Collection of material safety data sheets • Safe procedures for use • Local exhaust ventilation • Personal protective equipment • Training
Noise	• Assessment of noise levels • Isolation of noisy processes • Hearing protection devices • Training • Signage
Manual Handling	• Heavy loads • Frequency of lifting • Lifting equipment available • Training
Slips, trips, falls	• Maintenance • Housekeeping • Dealing with spillages • Training
Confined Spaces	• Identification of confined spaces • Safe systems of work • Signage • Training
Contractor Safety	• Approval of contractors systems of work • Work permits • Training
Working at Heights	• Safe system of work • Work permits • Training • Ladder and scaffolding safety
Falls of Objects	• Adequate racking • Storage of items at heights • Handling of pallets • Personal Protective Equipment
General Workplace	• Toilets • Washrooms • Lighting and temperature • Traffic • Welfare • Waste disposal
Driver tiredness	• Journey durations • Use of mobile phones • Training

Assessing risks

Once a hazard has been identified, the risk that is poses to an individual or group of individuals should be assessed to determine if the risk is acceptable or is in need of control. To assess risks, you need a similar knowledge of activities and working practices as required to conduct hazard identification.

The extent of the risk can be quantified by examination of existing controls, then estimating the likelihood of the event taking place and the nature and severity of the harm. The simple risk calculator produced by British Standards and outlined in Fig. 8.2.B is useful for estimating risk.

Fig. 8.2.B
British Standard 8800 - simple risk level estimator

Likelihood	Severity of harm		
	Slightly Harmful	**Harmful**	**Extremely Harmful**
Highly unlikely	Trivial Risk	Tolerable Risk	Moderate Risk
Unlikely	Tolerable Risk	Moderate Risk	Substantial Risk
Likely	Moderate Risk	Substantial Risk	Intolerable Risk

Source: British Standard 8800 (1996) A guide to occupational health and safety management systems

An example of a typical risk assessment using the BS8800 Simple Risk Level Estimator is included in Fig. 8.2.C.

Fig. 8.2.C
Example of a risk assessment

Hazard/Risk	Who might be harmed?	Existing controls	Likelihood	Severity	Estimate of Risk	Future Actions for Control
Portable electrical equipment / Electric shock	All Staff	Planned Preventative Maintenance Routine Visual checks by users Sufficient sockets provided Staff instructed to report faulty plugs and cables to manager	Highly Unlikely (due to current controls in place)	Extremely harmful (electric shock can be fatal)	Moderate	Install trip devices to isolate equipment in case of electrical fault. Staff instructed not to bring own portable electrical equipment onto premises
Hazardous substances / Handling and use of solvents	Maintenance staff	Only use solvents infrequently and in well ventilated areas Staff employ no touch techniques Staff are provided with appropriate gloves Staff are trained in safe use of hazardous substances	Unlikely (due to infrequency of use and controls in place)	Harmful (Risk of inhalation - short term effects)	Moderate	Examine substitution of solvent degreasers with aqueous degreasers
Slips, trips, falls / Floors, staircases, entrances	All staff Visitors	Reasonable housekeeping standards maintained Repairs and maintenance carried out when necessary Stairs and entrances well lit, hand rails provided	Likely (stairs slippery in wet weather, no internal lifts)	Severity of harm - Harmful (Risk of strain/fracture)	Substantial	Improve housekeeping standards Examine placement of non-slip treads on stairs

To use the estimator first establish what controls are in place, then estimate the likelihood of the event, that is, either highly unlikely, unlikely or likely. Pinpoint this outcome in the first column of Fig. 8.2.C. Once the likelihood is established, estimate the severity of the harm of the potential risk, ie, either slightly harmful, harmful or extremely harmful. Once the severity of harm is established scan across from the likelihood outcome to the column that represents your estimated severity of harm. The cell that correlates to the combination of likelihood and severity of outcome is the estimate of risk.

Prioritising risks

The risk assessment should enable the employer to prioritise the remedial measures to be undertaken to control the risks. In many cases it will be clear to the facilities manager that some risks require attention before others. Where there is uncertainty, a "risk rating" may be attributed to each identified hazard by using a simple formula, such as that given in Fig. 8.2.D, which has been adapted from the British Standards 8800.

Fig. 8.2.D
Prioritising risks adapted from British Standard 8800

Estimated	Risk rating	Action and timescale risk level
Trivial	1	No action is required and no documentary records need to be kept.
Tolerable	2	No additional controls are required. Consideration may be given to a more cost-effective solution or improvement that imposes no additional cost burden. Monitoring is required to ensure that controls are maintained.
Moderate	3	Efforts should be made to reduce the risk, but the costs of prevention should be carefully measured and limited. Risk reduction measures should be implemented within a defined time period.
Substantial	4	Work should not be started until the risk has been reduced. Considerable resources may have to be allocated to reduce the risk. Where the risk involves work in progress, urgent action should be taken.
Intolerable	5	Work should not be started or continued until the risk has been reduced. If it is not possible to reduce risk even with unlimited resources, work has to remain prohibited.

Using this risk rating strategy for the risks identified and assessed in Fig.8.2.D a priority action plan may be developed as below in Fig.8.2.E.

Fig. 8.2.E
Action plan for identified facilities risks

Hazard / risk	Estimate of risk	Risk ranking	Action / timescale
Portable electrical equipment/Electric shock	Moderate	3	Install trip devices - within 6 months Staff not to bring own portable equipment onto site -within 6 months
Hazardous substances/Handling and use of solvents	Moderate	3	Substitute solvents with less hazardous substance - within 6 months
Slips, trips, falls/floors, staircases, entrances	Substantial	4	Replace treads with non-slip - within 1 month Improve housekeeping standards - within 1 month

8.2.4 MANAGEMENT OF RISKS

Planning for improvements

Planning for health and safety involves designing, developing and installing suitable health and safety management arrangements, risk control systems and workplace precautions such as planned preventative maintenance, lock out systems and safe working procedures. To ensure cost-effectiveness of these systems they should be proportionate to the hazards and risks identified and the needs of the organisation.

The facilities manager needs to consider the following in terms of effective planning for health and safety:

- design of structures/buildings/plant/equipment

- control of structural and design changes

- selection of buildings/workplaces/plant/equipment

- supply of plant and substances

- purchase of buildings/workplaces/equipment/substances

- construction and installation of plant

- transport of plant and substances

- maintenance of buildings/workplaces/plant

- changes to process/plant/equipment/substances

- commissioning

- selection of equipment on hire

- security

- emergency arrangements, eg first aid, fire fighting, evacuation planning and practice

- decommissioning/demolition

- staff induction, training and development

- disposal of plant and substances.

Implementing controls

Once risks have been identified and assessed, decisions can be made about the types of controls to be put in place to minimise the risks. Decisions about the types of controls to be used can be guided by reference to the preferred hierarchy of control which are:

- eliminate the risks by substitution or avoidance of the risk, eg substitution of hazardous substances with less hazardous ones

- combat the risk at source by engineering such as guarding, installation of local exhaust ventilation, or isolation of noisy equipment

- minimise the risk by designing suitable systems of working and/or using personal protective clothing and equipment. Note the use of personal protective equipment should be used as a last resort only.

The method of control used will be based upon the degree of health and safety risk identified and the costs associated with implementing the desired control.

Audit and review of risks

Controls put in place to manage risks can deteriorate over time or become obsolete as a result of change. Periodic reviews or audits are necessary to ensure that the risk assessment process is on track and that controls put in place continue to be effective.

To make a judgement about the adequacy of health and safety, it is important to compare what is found against a relevant benchmark. The most reliable benchmarks are the national legal standards and/or industry standards.

The nature and complexity of the audit will vary according to its objectives and scope. There are three important information sources on which to base the audit, ie examining documents, interviewing individuals and visual observation of the workplace. To assist in limiting bias associated with the audit, it is often useful to appoint an external individual or company to conduct the audit.

8.2.5 ECONOMIC CONSIDERATIONS

Implications for non-compliance

The human and financial costs associated with work-related injuries and diseases are an ongoing concern for all industries across the world.

In 1999, the European Agency for Health and Safety at Work have estimated that the costs of work-related injuries and diseases in the EU vary from 2.6% to 3.8% of the GNP. This would indicate a total cost of between £110 billion and £160 billion for the EU as a whole ie between £600 and £900 per capita of the workforce per annum. These costs include direct costs paid out such as compensation and medical treatment and indirect costs such as loss of quality of life, loss of output and costs associated with recruitment and administration.

Of course, sickness and injury can be caused by events outside the place of work - at home, in transit, at leisure - and many contagious illnesses contracted at work cannot be prevented by the Health and Safety regime, however stringent. Nevertheless, absenteeism is a major source of lost productivity, accounting for an average of eight to ten working days pa; most of this is put down to avoidable ailments and injuries directly resulting from an unhealthy or unsafe working environment. On the simple basis of eight hours work to eight hours play a 50/50 split of sources of hazards seems probable.

How much of this lost time is due to genuine illness and how much to malingering cannot be accurately assessed. However, it has been shown that where management has taken up an inquisitive and caring approach to employees' absenteeism, days lost have often fallen significantly.

Pre-return interviews have sometimes identified situations where the employee is in fact not ready for work (or possibly ready for part-time only) and provide a useful record for reviewing staff performance and health statistics.

One survey[1] shows that those who keep computer records of sickness suffer 30% less absenteeism from sickness than those who do not keep any at all.

It may, of course, be the fact that management seems to care which encourages better attendance though whether the response is motivated by appreciation or fear almost certainly varies from one employee to another.

---

[1] *CBI Benchmarking Survey, Focus on absence: absence and labour turnover survey 1995, Confederation of British Industry, London, UK.*

The costs of compliance

The costs associated with implementing effective occupational health and safety programmes have been estimated to be far less than the cost of human financial losses associated with work related accidents and injuries; however the actual costs associated with effective programmes are much harder to establish due to the broad range and number of variables associated with implementing them.

The current stage of health and safety at work can be summed up as having two phases - the project and the monitoring. Most major organisations have by now completed the project phase, ie they have appraised the risks, and devised and implemented the precautions.

The resource to achieve this in a large organisation may be one or two man-years.

The on-going monitoring within the ICF need not be a major draw on resources - possible £0.60 to £1.20 per sq m GIA pa depending on the size. Some companies have been sharing the services of experienced health and safety executives.

The cost of health and safety management and training within contracting companies (or in-house service provision teams) is probably between 1% and 10% of the cost. At the lower end companies are already well up to speed with the regulations and health and safety has been absorbed into the process; at the other end there is a culture shock and there will be a significant closure of the cost gap between facilities services in developed and developing states as the legislation becomes more rigidly applied.

The other cost factor relates to the quality of specification required to meet the new standards. Again costs involved in new ergonomic furniture, improved maintenance and cleaning and environmental control will be net extras in the weaker companies and in some of the less well-provided facilities in better-off companies .

Nevertheless, the effects of poor health and safety at work risk management on the external image of an organisation as well as on its internal self-respect and morale are so potentially serious as to dwarf these more personally distressing direct consequences of failure and any costs of containment.

Legal considerations

Another impact of non-compliance with health and safety legislation is the potential for legal action. This implication primarily occurs where there has been a non-compliance with legislation that has resulted in a fatality or serious bodily injury/disease, eg with regard to the duty of care.

Whereas the individual may suffer death, disability or illness, the perpetrator may also suffer in several ways, for instance:

ccriminal prosecution under statutory provisions against:

- the organisation
- its directors
- its employees

- civil action under the laws of contract or tort against:
  - the organisation
  - its directors
  - its employees

- expense and loss of employee productivity through
  - sickness
  - re-recruitment

- loss of morale

- absenteeism.

This can affect a company financially through prosecution and/or civil actions costs, downtime and poor public image. In addition, individuals of companies may be liable to charges of corporate manslaughter resulting in imprisonment. This is of course in extreme circumstances of negligence, usually those resulting in a fatality of employees or others.

Various duties concerning health and safety are imposed by legislation. It is too big a field to cover here in detail but the principal concerns or risks include:

- **asbestos:** regulations now require building owners to survey their premises for asbestos, to prepare an action plan for its treatment, and to create awareness, particularly for workers carrying out repairs, maintenance and other works - so providing for their protection and safe work arrangements

- **electricity**: maintain electrical works to prevent danger - the Electricity at Work Regulations 1989

- **first aid:** have on hand first aid equipment and trained staff, and, inform staff of their whereabouts - Health and Safety (First Aid) Regulations 1981

- **hazardous substances**: transportation, storage, use and signage of hazardous substances should be such as to prevent harm to employees - Control of Substances Hazardous to Health Regulations 1994 (COSHH)

- **fire fighting equipment etc:** certain buildings require a fire certificate, fire fighting equipment and means of escape; fire risk may lead to restrictions or closure until the risk is removed - there are several statutes and order including Fire Precautions (Workplace) Regulations 1997, and the Fire Precautions (Factories, Offices, Shops and Railway Premises) orders 1976 and 1989

- **employer's liability**: compulsory cover against certain risks, eg injury to employees, is required and certificates must be displayed at the place of work - Employer's Liability (Compulsory Insurance) Act 1969.

The regulatory environment is not going to diminish - many initiatives are emerging including requirements on passive smoking, road safety policy, stress management, and the payment of NHS costs of treatment and transportation for those with work related injuries.

The human factor

Many workplace accidents/injuries lead to partial or complete incapacity to work and generate income. These can be cited as the 'human costs' associated with accidents/injuries and include the pain and suffering associated with the injury or illness, the worry and grief caused to family and friends and the loss of amenity resulting from incapacity.

The 1996 statistics from the World Health Organisation show that the new cases of work-related injuries and deaths per 100,000 in the manufacturing, agriculture and utilities sectors were 263.32 and 0.38 respectively.

Insurers are concerned to mitigate loss by seeing that injured employees and those with work-related illnesses are rehabilitated as speedily as possible. Ideally, they see prevention as a principal thrust. To this end many will offer to review and advise on work operations and processes with the view to reducing or eliminating accidents or illnesses. Also, insurance cover may be available to employers, including private medical services, personal accident, death at work, critical illness and product liability.

Other bodies provide information and advice including:

- occupational health - NHS Plus in some local hospitals
- accidents - Royal Society for the Prevention of Accidents
- repetitive strain injury - RSI Association
- HIV/Aids - National AIDS Trust
- flu - Department of Health
- smoking - Action on Smoking and Health.

8.2.6 SICK BUILDING SYNDROME

Definition

This condition has received considerable media attention in recent times, as much because of the 'mystery' nature of the issue as for the consequences to employee and their employers. It relates to ill-health symptoms which manifest themselves during time spent at the workplace but which tend to reduce or disappear completely once out of the office environment.

Typically such symptoms comprise many or all of the following:

- runny nose, sneezing and blockage of the nasal passages
- sore, dry throat
- eczema and other skin irritations
- itching, reddening and watering of the eyes
- headaches
- dizziness
- a general and uncharacteristic lethargy at, or disaffection with work.

The causes

As these symptoms are transient they are unlikely to be caused by infection; rather the source of affliction will be some local irritant, allergen or toxic substance. No single factor has been identified as the primary cause of 'sick building syndrome' (SBS); although causes of other occupation-related diseases such as asthma, humidifier fever and legionella are now well documented.

SBS is of concern because it not only causes great personal distress but also results in loss of productivity, absenteeism and, sometimes, enforced retirement. It is quite likely that some employees may be hyper-sensitive to the causative conditions but that does not let the employer off the hook.

Air-conditioning systems may possibly be a source of the problems and also a protection. For example, all-air systems are thought to improve air quality and humidity but require a high level of maintenance. The induction type of system, where air introduced at the point of heat exchange is often not humidified, creates a deficiency which is a commonly held cause of SBS. However, 'sealed' air-conditioned buildings have been found to give more exposure to SBS than other simply (mechanically or naturally) ventilated buildings.

One building fitted with an induction-based air-conditioning system in the London area in the 1970's was a constant source of complaints about feeling sick from its government employees. On refurbishment in 1981 it was discovered that none of the duct joints had been properly taped; the system had never worked since 'commissioning'!

Other inadequacies in factors such as temperature, airflow and lighting may encourage employees to complain when they otherwise might not have bothered. In particular, the opportunity to control local environmental conditions and the apparently caring (or otherwise) attitude of management towards maintenance and environmental conditions, have been found to have a significant effect on the incidences of lost productivity and absenteeism.

8.3 SPORTS, SOCIAL AND WELFARE FACILITIES

Introduction

The types of facilities considered in this Chapter are generally optional (as indeed is Catering, already considered in Chapter 8.1) and are not to be confused with the 'special areas' discussed in Chapter 6.1.3 and 6.2.2 - although they do come into that category with regards to costs. Unlike those 'special areas' such as reception and meeting areas, staff support facilities are provided either as a philanthropic gesture aimed at better public relations with the staff side (and incidentally to impress visitors), or genuine investments geared directly to perceptible improvements in productivity. Sometimes both benefits may arise, but, like so many other attempts to add value by enhancing the functional performance of the facilities, the measurement of any payback is usually highly dependent upon subjective assessment.

8.3.1 STAFF SUPPORT FACILITIES

Categories of staff support facilities

The range of facilities within this category encompasses:

- catering and vending
- restrooms and lounge-rooms
- residential accommodation
- workplace nurseries (crèches)
- physical fitness centres
- changing rooms/showers
- indoor sports facilities
- banking facilities
- travel agency
- retail outlets
- club room (with/without bar)
- playing fields, perhaps with stands and covered accommodation
- club house.

Catering and vending facilities have already been fully discussed in Chapter 8.1.

8.3.2 REST ROOMS AND LOUNGE AREAS

Rest rooms for staff are not mandatory under the Health and Safety at Work regulations. However, organisations of a size sufficient to warrant a first-aid room may find it beneficial to provide sufficient space for a bed for the employee feeling unwell.

Lounge areas are usually part of the catering facilities but may be provided specially as part of the 'non-territorial' 'new ways of working' space arrangements considered in Chapter 4.1.5. Sometimes the reception area may extend into a coffee lounge though this is a difficult format to control both with regards to tidiness and security.

8.3.3 RESIDENTIAL ACCOMMODATION

This may be in respect of a resident caretaker or, alternatively, offer overnight-stay facilities for senior executives who may need to make frequent overnight stops near the office locality (possibly to meet early-morning travel times) or due to long spells of late night/early morning headquarters-based activities.

Unless it turns out to be a business 'perk' without a foundation in productive benefit, a residential facility in city centres will usually pay back quite quickly. An example of such a valid proposition is given in Fig. 8.3.A which assumes that residential accommodation may be provided above commercial offices in a situation where the space thereby created would not otherwise attract planning permission for office use; the land value hypothesised therefore relates to residential rather than commercial values which, in important locations, would be substantially higher.

The issue of council tax on 'composite' property, ie mixed property, is dealt with in Chapter 11.4 Business Rates and Council Tax.

Fig. 8.3.A
Payback on residential accommodation through savings on hotel bills

Initial costs		£	£
Residential accommodation costs (including site-works)	1 – bed apartment 60 sq m GIA at £ 960 per sq m	57,600	
	Fees, finance and other development costs	19,200	
Total building costs (excluding land costs)			**76,800**
Notional residential land value		32,000	
Fees, finance etc. on notional land value		8,000	
Total land costs			**40,000**
Total development costs			**116,800**

Annual costs	£ pa	£ pa
Commercial mortgage at 10% for 10 years £ 116,800 x 0.163 =	19,000	
Running and maintenance costs	3,400	
Total annual costs		**22,400**

Payback analysis	
Minimum number of overnight stops pa to cover the alternative cost of hotel bills (room-only charges)	at £ 320 per night : 70 No.
	at £ 160 per night : 140 No.
	at £ 80 per night: 280 No.

8.3.4 THE WORKPLACE NURSERY (CRÈCHE)

The social case

Women constitute about one-half of the total labour force in the UK. However, the number of mothers with children under five years old in employment is significantly less than this, which reflects the almost universal lack of crèche facilities at work.

Because the extent of daycare facilities in nurseries is negligible mothers who want to go to work are generally restricted to a part-time occupation.

The equal opportunities case for providing nursery care to make it easier for young mothers to get straight back to work - and possibly a career - as soon as they are ready and able is overwhelming. Nevertheless, the welfare of the children is equally if not more important, both for their own wellbeing and the benefit of a society which will suffer at large if children are not given an appropriate and fair start in life.

The Children Act 1989 lays down standards for the accommodation and provision of childcare facilities. It is now generally recognised that having the childcare at the workplace, as opposed to local childcare centres, is preferred by families on grounds of:

- avoidance of additional travel to and from work/childcare centre
- better monitored care quality
- better facilities
- easy access by mother to child.

The biggest demand is for places for babies under 12 months, a fact that has surprised more than one workplace nursery provider forcing them to re-fit the facilities to suit. On the other hand, much depends on the location. For example, a mother with a three month old baby may not be attracted by a nursery in the city centre workplace given the problems of peak-hour travel; for that matter they may not be too keen about having to escort a two and four-year old pair through the metropolis at any time. In both situations, however, the alternative may well be a difficult circuitous journey around town to work via the local child carer's premises. The organisation should test the strength of demand for the facility together with the performance requirement by interviews and questionnaires to avoid making the wrong decision based on the personal preference or opinion of the Director of Human Resources.

The business case

According to a survey conducted by the national voluntary organisation 'Working for Childcare', in May 1994 there were nearly 500 organisations in the UK providing childcare facilities for their employees.

Rather less than half the number of childcare facilities are provided at the actual workplace; the majority are 'partnership nurseries', ie places at day nurseries allocated to, or taken by, one or more employers for use by their staff.

Among other important statistics unearthed by the Working for Childcare's survey were that:

- less than one pre-school child in every 250 has access to an employer-sponsored nursery place
- the average fee for a full-time place in such a nursery is £76.00 per week
- the public sector subsidises more nurseries for its staff than the private sector
- the greatest concentration of identified nurseries is in the more affluent regions
- over half of all identified nurseries are provided for use by staff (and students) in hospitals, colleges and universities.

So what are the business arguments in favour of providing or sponsoring childcare facilities for employees?

Probably the strongest case revolves around the loss of productivity plus the recruitment costs in the process of losing and replacing a valuable employee who wants to return to work after having a child, but who cannot manage to find a suitable childcare facility to enable them to do so.

It costs employers quite a lot of money to train an employee in particular clerical skills; at the high-end of the business structure women in senior positions often carry their share of the business' goodwill which is lost on premature and avoidable retirement.

The combination of training time, learning curve, decline of productivity on an employee's permanent retirement, plus recruitment costs, training time and learning curve for the replacement, obviously add up to a large financial loss in each case - not to mention the inevitable increase in absenteeism where mothers experience temporary difficulties in securing adequate childcare facilities.

Various independent studies have concluded that the costs of replacing a member of staff can be in excess of £100,000 in the case of key personnel.

One employer introducing nursery facilities recorded a near doubling of staff returning to work after taking maternity leave; an example of the economics of a case built up from these statistics is given later in the chapter, drawing from the costs and income data discussed in the following text.

Apart from the cost-efficient direct returns the facility will also be highly beneficial in respect of the morale, concentration and enthusiasm of the beneficiary and will also promote a good public image externally, so it should present a bonus to personnel recruitment on more than one count.

The facilities required

Under the 1989 Act and guidance notes the premises should ideally afford access to the open air, which may present problems in the more expensive inner city complexes - though access to an atrium may effect a suitable compromise.

The accommodation should afford both structured and play activities as well as providing for the disabled. It should have a 'friendly' ambience (not particularly easy to achieve in a commercial building) giving children and their parents a sense of security and confidence.

Fig. 8.3.B
Minimum desirable workplace requirements for a nursery

Age of child	Minimum overall open floor space (excluding hallways, toilets and kitchen)
	sq m
Under 2 years	3.7
2 – 3 years	2.8
3 – 5 years	2.3

The minimum desirable space requirements under the Act of 1989 are given at Fig. 8.3.B. About 25% to 30% should be added to provide space and storage for equipment, furniture etc. Where possible a room should be made available where older children can get down to concentrative activities in peace and quiet.

Facilities must be 'user-friendly' and, in addition to the nursery area itself will need to provide space for administration, a staff-room and a kitchen or other catering area. The recommended use of industrial microwave ovens for reasons given in Chapter 8.1 'Catering' is equally applicable in the childcare catering facility.

The 1989 Act specifically requires separate toilet facilities for adults and children - one wc and wash-hand basin per ten children - plus a 'mother's room' for changing nappies. Provision of the facility in a commercial building will require the acquisition of all the usual licences including planning consent, fire and building regulations approval and registration with the local authority's social services department. All furniture and equipment should meet legislation on safety standards and pictures, books, and graphics should portray multi-cultural activities by both sexes in many and varied roles.

Where gardens or grounds and equipment are provided for children outside, special concerns may arise (see Chapter 5.2.5 on Grounds Maintenance).

Managing the facility

The quality of the service will depend upon:

- the ratio of staff to children
- the qualifications, personal integrity and application of the staff
- staff remuneration
- the facilities available.

Fig. 8.3.C gives the minimum staffing levels laid down under the Childrens Act 1989. It should be noted however that additional staff will be required:

- at the local authority's discretion (1:1 may be required for children under one year old)
- for nurseries open longer than 10 hours per day
- for overall supervision - where there are more than 20 children
- for catering, administration and cleaning.

Fig. 8.3.C
*Minimum staff -
children ratios
according to the UK
Children's Act 1989*

Age of child	Ratio of staff : children
Under 2 years	1 : 3
2 – 3 years	1 : 5
3 – 5 years	1 : 8

Ideally, at least half of the staff should have a suitable qualification - either for nursery or sick nursing. Any employment of trainees on employment training schemes should always be properly structured and supervised, additional to core staffing levels and with adequate allowances being made for staff-time in training and monitoring on top of basic duties.

Under Childrens Act 1989 local authorities are obliged to inspect every nursery at least once a year to check on standards of facilities and care.

The cost of providing and operating workplace nursery

Unless the facility is to be new-built the capital costs will relate to:

- conversion
- fitting-out
- equipment.

Typical costs for these components are given at Fig. 8.3.D (over the page).

Fig. 8.3.D
Typical capital cost of providing, fitting-out and equipping a workplace nursery

Space requirements		sq m
Free area : say 20 children at an average of 3 sq m per child		60
Add : storage, furniture and equipment space, catering, circulation, administration etc. 100%		60
Total dedicated area		**120**
Capital costs		**£**
Building costs	Conversion of existing space 120 sq. m NIA at £ 320 sq m	38,400
	Fitting-out of existing space 120 sq. m NIA at £ 480 sq m	57,600
	Fees at 10% x £ 96,000	9,600
Total conversion and fitting-out cost		105,600
Equipment and furniture	Say 20 at £ 1,600 per child	32,000
Total capital costs		**137,600***
Annual equivalent at 10% pa over 10 years x 0.163		**22,430**

*   Excludes VAT and any loan finance costs

The annual costs

Fig. 8.3.E estimates the cost per child per annum taking the amortised capital cost of the 20-child example used above and including a notional rent, operating and staffing costs. The rent assumes that space is taken from a fairly expensive commercial area and that any circulation areas are part of the common areas of the main building area and not rentable.

Fig. 8.3.E
Typical annual costs of a 20-child workplace nursery

Premises costs	Amortised capital costs as Fig. 8.3.D	£ 22,430
	Notional rent, local taxes and operating costs – 120 sq m NIA at £ 500 per sq m pa	£ 60,000
Operating and management costs	Support services / consumables at £ 960* per child x 20	£ 19,200
	Staffing at £ 7,200* per child x 20	£ 144,000
Total annual costs before tax and fees		**£ 245,630**
Total cost (at 100% occupancy) per child	per annum	£ 12,280
	per week	£ 236

*   Source: Sue Finch

The significant item of expenditure in operating a crèche is clearly the staff and consumables. Staff pay levels for carers has been pitifully close to any minimum wage due to the lack of appreciation of the benefits they bring to their charges and vocational nature of the work; however with increasing training requirements and legal obligations, this situation has begun to improve.

Fees, funding sources and taxation factors

Employers usually subsidise the costs, often on a sliding scale according to income. So, for example, a cost per child place of say £170 (in a lower-rental area than the example and after the employer has claimed tax relief on any plant/machinery content of the works and all the revenue expenditure) may be charged to the working parent at say £70 per week.

There is normally no tax payable by the employee receiving the subsidy. It is important to note that the provision of childcare allowances and vouchers are usually still regarded as taxable benefits whereas the subsidised amount of the fee is usually not!

Further tax concessions are often available to employers in the industrial sector. The supply of childcare is exempt from VAT provided it is usually registered under the appropriate legislation.

The business payback

The £100 or so per child per week which is left to the employers to subsidise has to deliver a payback: this can only be in terms of saving the cost incurred in staff retiring prematurely due to lack of convenient childcare facilities.

For the 20-child facility in the above example, a taxable organisation would probably be spending a net £200,000 or so (£10,000 per child) each year. Given that the cost of one premature retirement might cost up to £100,000 it is clear that, if only two of the 15 to 20 mothers of the children in the group goes back to work because of the provision, the facility should quickly pay for itself, ie a £200,000 pa total investment can be recovered with just two premature retirements avoided - not to mention the internal public relations bonuses.

8.3.5 THE PHYSICAL FITNESS CENTRE

The medical case

'Healthy body, healthy mind' goes the adage but does it have any foundation in fact? Physical fitness represents the achievement of an optimal state of both physiological and psychological performance with low health risk factors, thus increasing our overall well-being. Exercise stimulates the production of endocrines in our bodies with a net result of improved neuro-muscular motor skills, eg improved concentration, speed of response and clarity of mind.

In addition, adequate cardiovascular exercise is also known to relieve stress and also lower and regulate our blood pressure levels. As a major contributor to the prevention and combat of Coronary Heart Disease (CHD), cardiovascular exercise reduces the risk of artherosclorosis (furring of the arteries) due to its effect on our liptoprotein profile, by the production of High Density Liptoprotein (HDL) cholesterol and the reduction of Low Density Liptoprotein (LDL) cholesterol.

In plain language, adequate exercise is generally acknowledged to be a major contributor to health-related fitness in terms of our overall well-being and all round performance.

Adequate exercise - yes, but there are question marks over many aspects of physical exercise of a violent or repetitive nature such as the heart-muscle extension resulting from exacting activities like squash and long-distance cycling or running - the latter especially damaging to back and limbs when carried out continually on punishing hard surfaces.

A general description of physical fitness is defined by Dr Kevin Sykes of Liverpool University as "the ability to carry out daily tasks with vigour and alertness without undue fatigue and with ample energy to enjoy leisure-time pursuits and to meet unforeseen emergencies".

It would therefore be reasonable to assume that physically fit individuals would perform better than average in their day-to-day tasks.

Fitness and productivity

Whereas there is some logic in the assumption that regular participation in fast-reaction sports such as squash, badminton and (to some extent) tennis make executives sharper about their work (unless they have played one and a half hours at lunch-time and pushed themselves to near exhaustion) the case for non-competitive fitness routines is a little less clear-cut.

Body-building per se develops muscles and reduces fat (in the short-term) without sharpening the reactions - although education of the flow of oxygen and adrenaline to the brain may well be a beneficial by-product of fighting against the spring-loaded paraphernalia now finding its way into corporate expenditure on facilities.

According to Fitness for Industry (FFI), who own and run some 30 corporate fitness clubs regular use of the facilities available in the gymnasium can make the difference between an executive who stays the course of the day sharp, and one whose performance falls off over the last hour or so. They point to a NASA exercise control programme in the USA which showed that regular exercising produced a 12.5% increase in productivity.

Another company reported a cut of about 50% in absenteeism over the course of a six-year corporate fitness programme. Whether this was due to fitness or because people were keen to come to work to indulge in the fitness routines may need further research to clarify - not that the findings would in any case be too relevant, it may just be the fact that management seems to care (a common theme running through many of the cost centres in this text) or it may be some physically beneficial consequence which generates the increased productivity; either way, it does not really matter as long as it works - not just in the short term but over time.

Capital and running costs

A typical corporate gymnasium will be about 300 sq m including an area for aerobics plus changing/shower/toilet facilities in the proportions shown at Fig. 8.3.F (below).

The cost of converting and fitting out the space together with the equipment is predicted at Fig. 8.3.G (over the page) and the extension of this calculation of the annual equivalent cost (before tax) to the total annual cost of the fitness centre per member is given at Fig. 8.3.H (over the page).

Fig. 8.3.F
Fitness centre - distribution of area by function

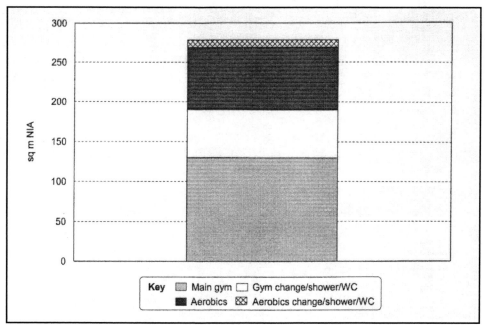

Capital costs	£
Conversion costs 300 sq m NIA at £ 320 sq m	96,000
Fitting-out costs 300 sq m NIA at £ 450 sq m	144,000
Fees and finance at 10%	24,000
Total conversion and fitting -out costs	**264,000**
Equipment in gym area: 140 sq m NIA at £ 1,120 sq m	156,800
Total capital costs	**420,800**
Annual equivalent at 10% pa over 10 years x 0.163	**68,590 pa**

Fig. 8.3.G
Fitness centre - capital costs of conversion, fitting-out and equipment

Annual costs	£ pa
Amortised capital costs as Fig. 8.3.G – say	70,000
Notional rent, local taxes and operating costs – 300 sq m NIA @ £ 480 sq m pa	144,000
Equipment maintenance / replacement	16,000
Supervision	48,000
Total annual costs before tax and fees	**278,000**
Assuming 200 club members	**1,390 per member pa**

Fig. 8.3.H
Typical annual costs of a corporate fitness centre

The business case

Clearly the cost per capita is such that, even if after tax relief by way of capital allowances and revenue expenditure the cost is reduced to say £650 per capita pa, subsidised membership may not be easy to justify as an investment.

On the other hand, if but one quarter of the 200 members of the club in the above example benefit to the extent of increasing their productivity by the suggested 12.5% (see 'fitness and productivity' above) then the annual improvement in productivity for an average staff cost of £32,000 pa per employee using the facility might well amount to, say, £32,000 x 50 x 0.125 = £200,000.

The annual cost of £278,000 in the example may well be substantially less due to lower rental levels, tax relief and membership fees and might well be enhanced by reductions in absenteeism and recruitment costs as well as a small improvement in productivity of the remaining 150 club members. So the facility might well be seen as justifying its investment in commercial terms with a public relations bonus in addition.

8.3.6 SIMPLE EXERCISE AND HEALTH TESTING FACILITIES

The sceptics will suggest that employees using the in-house gym or squash court would have done the same thing somewhere else if the facility was not available on site. Where such facilities need to be subsidised an alternative low-cost solution may achieve similar results. This simply involves the provision of equipment for helping employees to assess, target, attain and thereafter monitor their fitness level.

Space requirements, capital and running costs are low and gentle peer group competition encourages take-up and continuation of the courses. Though not as much fun for the committed sportsperson the overall cost-effectiveness of this type of keep-healthy facility is likely to become increasingly attractive in the cost-conscious facilities environments of the new millennium.

8.3.7 SPORTS FACILITIES

Few organisations these days can afford the luxury of providing and maintaining sports facilities either at the place of work or remotely based.

Most major centres have local public or private facilities for swimming, fitness, squash, badminton and (sometimes) indoor tennis, so the need for special provision does not often arise.

Nevertheless, many of the bigger organisations which have had the capital investment in a sports facility written-off over time still consider the public relations benefits to outweigh the not inconsiderable costs of running and maintaining grounds and clubhouse for the use of only a small proportion of their workforce who either:

- live near the centre, or

- prefer not to join a private club or use public facilities.

Because of the wide range of facilities available and given that provision of new facilities on a grand scale is a feature of another economic era, details of capital and running costs are not provided in this section.

For stands with covered accommodation for over 500 persons, the facilities manager should check the need for any safety certificate issued by the local authority under the Fire Safety and Safety of Places of Sport Act 1987.

Provision for safety, eg construction of barriers, at stadia may be eligible for capital allowances income taxation relief.

PART D

Relocation and
Development

Section 9

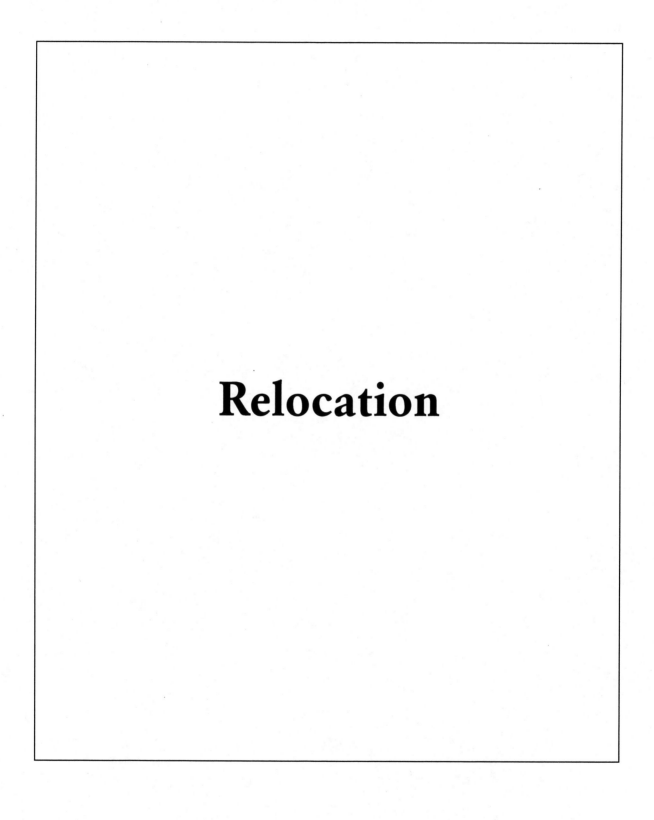

Relocation

9.1 PREMISES AND BUSINESS PERFORMANCE

Introduction

The location and performance of business premises affects the success of the business directly and indirectly. The direct, or 'hard', implications impact upon the 'property' costs, ie rent, taxes and operating costs, whereas the indirect or 'soft' implications are much greater and relate to key issues such as corporate image, production costs and output.

Clearly the close inter-relationship between premises and core business success needs to be fully appreciated by both the facilities manager and core business management but too often this appreciation is missing on one or both sides.

This chapter expands on the issues introduced in Chapter 1.1 - The scope of facilities, which looked at the relationship between premises and business needs and considers the premises options available to accommodate them. It also assesses the economic implications of the generic options in terms of both initial setting-up and relocation.

There is also a most important cross-reference to the value management process described in Chapter 2.2

9.1.1 THE PREMISES POLICY IN PRACTICE

Premises costs in perspective

Fig. 9.1.A replicates Fig. 1.1.C in Chapter 1.1.5 which considered the essential linkage between the business requirements to be accommodated and the premises performing that function.

Fig. 9.1.A
Premises and the corporate plan - premises policy

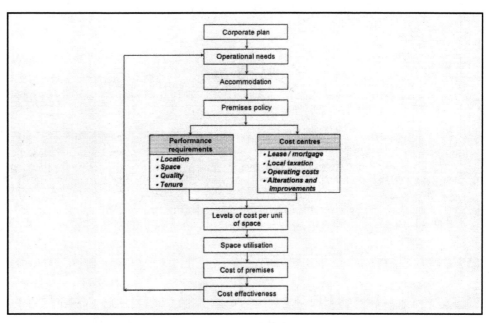

That the quality and location are critical factors in the business plan from the point of view of production, sales, marketing or personnel is undeniable. However, it is not unknown for top management, under embarrassing scrutiny in their attempts to improve bottom-line efficiency, to propose cheaper premises costs as the main reason for a relocation which is in practice designed to reduce *staff* costs; such savings will amount to at least ten times the saving on premises costs. The relationship between premises costs, support services and total turnover at Fig. 9.1.B illustrates this point graphically (over the page).

Fig. 9.1.B
Turnover, profit and facilities costs

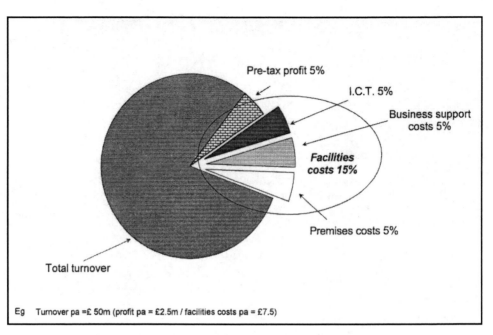

It is obviously hard to see how a decision to cut the 'property' components of premises costs as a proportion of turnover could justify the attendant upheaval unless such costs were substantially above this high-level benchmark; of course there are many hidden agendas.

However, politics aside and looking at the matter of accommodation purely from a premises perspective, what issues should a facilities manager consider when setting up from scratch or when the ability of the existing premises stock to accommodate the business requirement comes into question?

9.1.2 FITNESS OF PREMISES FOR PURPOSE

Problems and issues

The answers in respect of setting up for the first time can easily be gathered from consideration of the problems normally encountered by organisations established in their premises; facilities managers must learn from their own and others' experience and address all of these problems from the outset.

The circumstances which will require the organisation to review the suitability of its accommodation will be triggered by any or all of the following underlying issues:

- shortage of space

- too much space

- inefficiency of space

- inefficiency of facilities

- inadequate internal environment

- image

- location - staff availability, access to customers, environmental problems

- corporate centralisation

- corporate de-centralisation

- flexibility

- premises costs
- staff costs
- redundancy policy
- mergers and acquisitions
- real estate factors
- accountancy policy.

Solutions and options

The solutions available to overcome these issues as and when they become problems affecting business performance come down to just two generic options:

- stay and make alterations as necessary (make do and mend)
- move away to new location(s) (total relocation and partial relocation).

A combination of these options and some further sub-options are considered below.

It is, however, most important to recognise the importance of approaching such decision-making in the context of value management as described in detail in Chapter 2.2

9.1.3 THE PREMISES OPTIONS

Make do and mend

This option may be dictated by economics - principally affordability (cash flow in real terms) and probably means making some compromise. The scope and quality of the alterations together with any tenure factors will determine the extent to which this option is economically viable; sometimes, in the case of over-supply of space, part of the existing premises may be prepared for leasing or sub-leasing. The effect of making radical and expensive alterations to the leasehold property - for example, upgrading for ICT - must be carefully weighed up in the context of the terms of the lease. It is not at all unusual for tenants to have their rents revised to a level reflecting the improvements they have paid for themselves, unless the lease or statutes provide otherwise (see detailed discussion at Chapter 3.2.2).

It is far better to do a deal with the landlord and sign a new agreement whereby some or all of the costs are rentalised on the basis of a low institutional investment yield. This will normally be a better deal in cash flow terms than the organisation funding the works as a lump sum out of its own cash-flow or on a commercial mortgage at a higher interest rate for a finite period (see Fig 9.1.C over the page); there may, of course, be normal upward reviews on the extra rent in the rentalised option. The risks inherent in refurbishment are discussed in Section 6 - 'Fitting out and Alterations'.

The taxation implications for a tenant funded option are similar in principle to those involved in payment out of revenue expenditure (but possibly not for capital allowances - see Chapter 11.2.5) where tax relief is available except that with any mortgage the relief is generally only on the interest component for the duration of the loan whereas the rental affords tax relief in full throughout the tenancy.

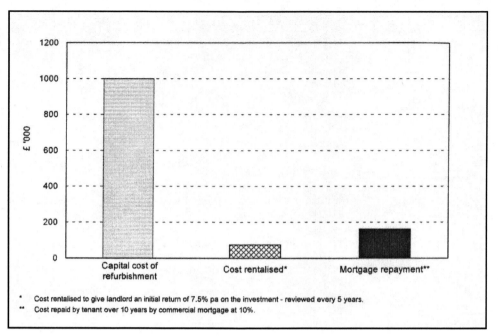

Fig. 9.1.C
Alternative funding options for refurbishment of a leased building

* Cost rentalised to give landlord an initial return of 7.5% pa on the investment - reviewed every 5 years.
** Cost repaid by tenant over 10 years by commercial mortgage at 10%.

Total relocation

There is a rich variety of sub-options.

The tenure may be:

Freehold:

- newly built speculative development (outright purchase from developer)
- existing building
- purpose-built development.

Leasehold:

- newly built speculative development
- existing building
- proposed speculative development
- purpose-built development on sale and leaseback terms.

The nature of freehold and leasehold interests are discussed in Chapter 3.1 and will be dictated by such issues as availability, accountability, financial status, flexibility, image, location or, probably, a combination of all or some of these factors.

There can be advantages in getting into a development early enough (either as a tenant or owner) so as to have the building tailored to suit one's requirements - often without a cost penalty.

Fig. 9.1.D (over the page) draws from Fig. 6.1.A - The nature of fitting-out and alterations - in Chapter 6.1 to show the potential cost penalty to be paid in speculative development where it is necessary to adapt a finished building to meet individual requirements. Up to 40% of the cost of a re-fit can be spent on taking out and/or altering what is put there by a developer or a former tenant - one reason why the 'shell and core' type of development has gained favour.

It may be noted that although the costs from 'shell-and-core' at Fig. 9.1.D are higher than from the 'developer's finish' the cost of the latter should be allowed to the tenants by developer if the building is leased on a shell-and-core basis. Tenants not only avoid the non-beneficial costs of changing the developer's finish but also get a substantial contribution from the developer to the cost of the fitting-out . In addition tenants are also able to co-ordinate both sections of the work to their best advantage.

Fig. 9.1.D
The fitting-out cost penalty for works to a building with 'developer's finish'

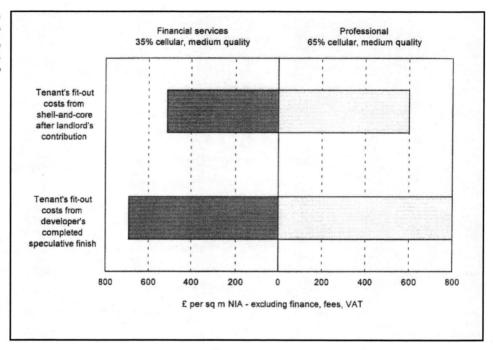

The temptation to optimise the real estate benefits - particularly for balance sheet purposes - is often very strong. However, the purpose of the premises is to accommodate the corporate needs; unless itself a property development or investment company an organisation would do best to think of premises as plant to aid the business function. The real estate implications should not be ignored but equally should not dictate the decision.

The location will have a big impact on:

* premises costs
* cost of staff
* turnover of staff
* availability of staff
* image
* access by and to customers
* travel times to, from and during work.

Ways to assess the benefits or dis-benefits of these issues (some of which are 'hard' and others 'soft') alongside actual premises costs are considered below. It is quite common for major decisions about location to be based on the personal convenience of the key decision makers and/or their spouses. The best way to discourage such appallingly bad practice is to make a watertight financial case for the best strategy.

The performance of the new premises against which the hard costs are assessed should be looked at under headings such as:

* efficiency of design, layout and specification
* comfort
* convenience
* image - external PR, internal PR
* flexibility

- resilience

- capacity.

Although it is not usual for the benefits of these factors to be valued in monetary terms there are techniques for bringing them into the financial equation to help consider the issue of value for money. An example of how to bring these issues to the table for discussion alongside the costs of provision was given at Fig. 1.2.C in Chapter 1.2. - The performance of facilities. Alternatively they can be considered in a more analytical fashion such as illustrated in Fig. 9.1.E.

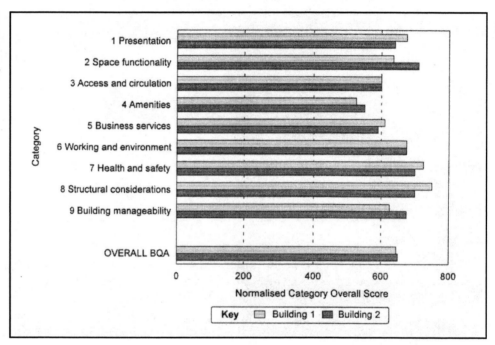

Fig. 9.1.E
Performance comparison of two buildings using the BQA method

This example is taken from the Building Quality Assessment (BQA)[1] program which provides an index of quality based on modelling the consensus view as to the theoretical relative usefulness of 137 individual aspects of building design/specification. The assessor tests each of the 137 factors in the building under evaluation 'scoring' them on a scale of 1 to 10 against pre-determined examples of quality within the range. The result gives a 'weighted' (normalised category) score for each of the nine categories to which the factors are allocated; these category scores are then weighted and combined into one overall BQA index.

It is possible to set cost targets using a model relating BQA scores to historic cost data - see Fig. 9.1.F (over the page).

By reading off the target cost for the relevant BQA score £ x per sq m NIA in this example, it is possible not only to budget accurately for buildings of a particular quality but also to set 'challenging yet demonstrably achievable' cost targets to encourage value engineering by the design team.

---

[1] *Available from QAI (Europe) Ltd - c/o BWA Tel: (+44) (0)20 8460 1111*

Fig. 9.1.F
BQA target costing

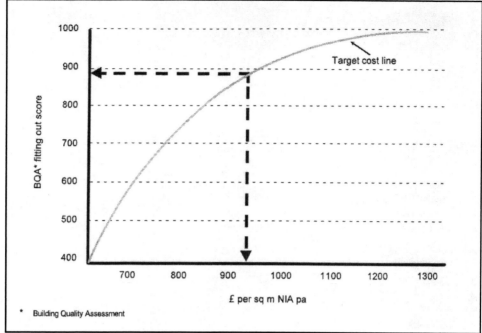

Partial relocation

When new accommodation is provided to meet space demands the original building is sometimes retained as a 'flagship'. In this case if business circumstances allow it is often best for the satellite premises to be a good distance away where both premises and staff may come a lot cheaper.

Where there are a number of premises in a cluster the tendency is, over time, for either new all-embracing corporate premises to emerge or, alternatively, for a 'flagship - plus scattered support premises' policy to be adopted.

9.1.4 TECHNIQUES OF EVALUATION

Degrees of sophistication

There are many ways of looking at the costs and benefits of a premises strategy and for comparing one with another. These range from the simplistic 'annual premises costs' calculation to highly sophisticated techniques of cost/benefit analysis.

Annual cost method

Here the cost centres are calculated for a given point in time (normally current) and a simple comparison made of merely the 'hard' premises costs. This is normally only a 'first strike' process to aid discussion and to eliminate obvious non-starters. Fig 9.1.G (over the page) illustrates this technique where Building X is the current tenancy to which the annual cost of essential improvements is added to the passing rent for comparison with alternative rented options at Buildings Y and Z - also upgraded to a similar standard.

Life-cycle cost analysis

This is a more sophisticated technique of premises cost appraisal, the principles of which are described in Chapter 10.6.3. The appraiser must attempt to forecast such cost variables as:

- size of rent reviews/indexation

- changes in taxes and duties

- payments, if any, on leases surrendered
- re-active v pro-active maintenance
- service charges and operating costs
- alterations caused by 'churn' (see Chapter 4.2)
- inflation.

Fig. 9.1.G
Alternative
premises strategies
- preliminary
appraisal by
comparison of
annual costs per
unit of area

Item	Building X 7th floor (1,700 sq m NIA incl. Mezzanine storage)		Building Y 10-14th floors (1,600 sq m NIA)		Building Z 3rd and 4th floors (1,650 sq m NIA)	
	£,000	£/sq m NIA	£,000	£/sq m NIA	£,000	£/sq m NIA
Rent (analysed over first five year review period)	360	210	440	270	616	370
Local taxes (current)	45 District A	25	135 District B	85	133 District B	80
Operating costs (including service charge)	105 (non a/c)	60	144	90	150	90
Fitting-out costs (includes building works, professional fees and bridging finance)	195	120	100	60	100	60
Additional cost for comfort cooling	70	40	Inc.	Inc.	Inc.	Inc.
Furniture * (includes fees)	70	40	70	40	70	40
Total annual costs	845	495	889	545	1069	640

* Amortised over a seven year period at 13%
N.B. The above figures exclude any allowance for: VAT; work to landlord's WC's and sublet areas; data cabling and telecommunications; decanting.

The resultant cash flow projections will normally be discounted at a rate (or rates) indicated by the user. Organisations may wish to introduce certain additional quantifiable 'hard' costs such as:

- moving
- replacement
- redundancy payments.

They may also wish to consider certain indirect costs of a move - loss of productivity caused by the move, say, both during the move itself and through loss and recruitment of staff. In more sophisticated appraisals they may wish to look at changes in the level of organisational productivity as a consequence of the move - for example, shorter journey times for employees moving around the premises, for key executives travelling locally and abroad, and genuine improvements in productivity at work.

Fig. 9.1.H (over the page) shows how such a cost/benefit analysis may be prepared. In this case the productivity change assumptions are calculated by simple percentage addition to (or deduction from) total costs of the staff affected. As discussed further at 9.2.1 below such an appraisal is most useful when sensitivity testing of the assumptions is employed. This particular example is adjusted for inflation and it should be noted that inflation in the rent is calculated at the estimated (mid-year) rent review figure for the five succeeding years, whereas other costs are inflated annually. Discounted cash flows and the pros and cons of including inflation are considered in detail in Chapter 10.6.3.

The key factor which this example does not take into account is any direct savings in staff costs due to any differential local economic factors. This factor is often at the root of relocation decisions and, where present, will certainly drive the business case.

Fig. 9.1.H *Cost/benefit analysis of a premises strategy taking account of potential impact on productivity - inflated and discounted*

Cost centre		Year 1 £,000	Year 2 £,000	Year 3 £,000	Year 4 £,000	Year 5 £,000
Premises	Rent	(2,979)	(3,211)	(3,211)	(3,555)	(3,555)
	Local taxes	(2,372)	(2,491)	(2,615)	(1,247)	(1,322)
	Operating costs	(1,392)	(1,462)	(1,535)	(1,247)	(1,322)
	Routine alterations	(290)	(305)	(320)	(210)	(223)
	Total	**(7,033)**	**(7,469)**	**(7,681)**	**(6,259)**	**(6,422)**
Fitting-out	Fitting-out	0	0	(5,226)		0
	Furniture	0	0	0	(3,102)	0
	Total	**0**	**0**	**(5,226)**	**(3,102)**	**0**
Real estate	Premiums	0	0	0	2,000	0
	Disposals & acquisitions	0	0	0	(180)	0
	Total	**0**	**0**	**0**	**1,820**	**0**
Productivity	Organisational	0	0	0	2,477	2,614
	Physical communications -internal	0	0	0	2,319	2,447
	Physical communications - external	(335)	(353)	(373)	(552)	(582)
	Total	**(335)**	**(353)**	**(373)**	**4,244**	**4,479**
Relocation	Removals including general temporary loss of productivity	0	0	0	(3,218)	0
	Replacement of staff	0	0	0	(3,130)	0
	Total	**0**	**0**	**0**	**(6,348)**	**0**
Total		**(7,638)**	**(7,822)**	**(13,280)**	**(9,645)**	**(1,943)**
Net present value factor		0.87	0.76	(0.66)	0.57	0.49
Net present value pa		**(6,407)**	**(5,915)**	**(8,732)**	**(5,515)**	**(966)**
* Rounded to 2 decimal places						

Fig. 9.1.H *(Continued)*

Cost centre		Year 6 £,000	Year 7 £,000	Year 8 £,000	Year 9 £,000	Year 10 £,000	Total £,000
Premises	Rent	(3,555)	(3,555)	(4,278)	(5,000)	(5,000)	(37,899)
	Local taxes	(1,401)	(1,499)	(1,604)	(1,717)	(1,837)	(18,105)
	Operating costs	(1,401)	(1,499)	(1,604)	(1,717)	(1,837)	(15,016)
	Routine alterations	(236)	(253)	(271)	(290)	(310)	(2,708)
	Total	**(6,593)**	**(6,806)**	**(7,757)**	**(8,724)**	**(8,984)**	**(73,728)**
Fitting-out	Fitting-out	0	0	0	0	0	(5,226)
	Furniture	0	0	0	0	0	(3,102)
	Total	**0**	**0**	**0**	**0**	**0**	**(8,328)**
Real estate	Premiums	0	0	0	0	0	2000
	Disposals & acquisitions	0	0	0	0	0	(180)
	Total	**0**	**0**	**0**	**0**	**0**	**1820**
Productivity	Organisational	2,758	2,909	3,069	3,238	3,416	20,481
	Physical communications -internal	2,581	2,723	2,873	3,031	3,198	19,172
	Physical communications - external	(615)	(648)	(683)	(721)	(760)	(5,622)
	Total	**4,784**	**4,984**	**5,259**	**5,548**	**5,854**	**34,091**
Relocation	Removals including general temporary loss of productivity	0	0	0	0	0	(3,218)
	Replacement of staff	0	0	0	0	0	(3,130)
	Total	**0**	**0**	**0**	**0**	**0**	**(6,348)**
Total		**(1,869)**	**(1,822)**	**(2,498)**	**(3,176)**	**(3,130)**	**(52,553)**
Net present value factor		0.43	0.38	0.33	0.28	0.25	
Net present value pa		**(808)**	**(685)**	**(817)**	**(903)**	**(774)**	**(31,520)**
* Rounded to 2 decimal places							

For the purpose of these examples all payments are deemed to be made at the beginning of each year

9.2 RELOCATION

Introduction

As discussed above the decision to relocate can result from a wide range of pressures. Common examples include company growth and change, shortage of space, financial pressures, organisational inefficiency, the need for company rationalisation and operational problems.

However, it must be subjected to thorough testing within the organisation's value management regime (see Chapter 2.2).

The motivation may be seen as corporate led (that is, by business factors) or premises led (that is, by accommodation issues). The distinction is important because it is likely to dictate the stage at which the facilities manager becomes involved in the decision-making and, therefore, their ability to influence the parameters of the relocation project. This chapter examines the practices and economics involved.

9.2.1 TOTAL RELOCATION

The use of consultants

The complexity of relocation is such that many companies hand over responsibility for day-to-day planning and implementation of relocation to specialist consultants. This frees the facilities management team to meet existing responsibilities; it can be more objective and it will provide a buffer for resolving internal disagreement. Other companies, particularly those with large and experienced facilities management teams, will choose to handle the project internally. This approach avoids the learning curve needed by consultants, and it centralises project management.

A compromise between these two extremes is often favoured, whereby an internal team is given responsibility for the management and implementation of the relocation plan, while appointing consultants at key stages to provide expert help where necessary. This approach fits into the two-tier strategic and tactical plan model outlined below.

Thus, once locational criteria, key operational and budgetary considerations have all been decided internally, outside help may be sought as and when necessary to evaluate a short-list of locations, undertake cost/benefit appraisals, cost development options and assess space planning options.

The identification of available sites or buildings is but one example of the necessity for specialist advice at particular stages of preparing detailed plans. A company cannot hope to cover all lines of enquiry. In appointing specialists, time will be saved and more comprehensive appraisals will be made. The recommendations of the specialist can then be absorbed into the overall relocation strategy.

Planning - strategic and tactical

For a relocation, whatever the cause, a 'to move or not to move' appraisal is appropriate as it will help to clarify the issues, set the objectives and involve the facilities manager with the board in developing a strategic plan of action. It will fulfil the requirements of the value management process described in Chapter 2.2. and, in the process, ensure that premises and business management will become more inter-dependent.

The early development of a strategic plan highlighting the key decisions necessary for the relocation project and endorsed by the board will help to address the pre-conceptions and priorities of those concerned with managing the move. Moreover, detailed tactical plans to deal with specific stages, such as site finding, cost/benefit analysis or building appraisal can be addressed within the framework of an agreed masterplan. This approach affords the facilities manager much needed flexibility through the relocation project.

Relocation will involve exhaustive planning and co-ordination. Once the master plan has been approved by the Board, a series of tactical plans can be drawn up to address specific issues.

These will work within the framework of the master plan, forming separate packages of work. A relocation management team, with individuals responsible for sets of tactical plans, will simplify the complexities of planning.

Detailed programmes and costings of the studies needed, together with the collection of all relevant internal information and data at this stage, will pay off at later stages of the project.

Each tactical plan will form an element of an overall critical path network (see Chapter 2.8.2), which provides a schedule of actions and decisions. This schedule will run through until after occupation of the new premises allowing for post-relocation assessment. Such a schedule tightens overall control of the project.

The detailed studies necessary for the relocation will revolve around three main areas, in addressing which the priorities of the business plan again overlap with premises management. These areas are:

* organisational

* personnel

* premises.

Details of these studies are as follows.

Organisational: the first main area involves organisational issues. Can the organisation operate effectively in the new location and what factors will enhance this effectiveness? Flows of information between parts of the organisation, inter-departmental communication, the uptake of ICT and functional space requirements may all be relevant considerations here. The ability of the organisation to meet its customers' needs has to be central to the relocation process.

The most efficient and well designed building will ultimately become a non-productive cost factor if its location, function or use fails to meet operational needs.

Personnel: the second key area of concern is personnel. Is the relocation inspired by a need to shed staff? How many staff are likely to be lost, and how many is the company prepared to lose? On the positive side, the tactical plan can recommend ways of informing staff of key decisions and setting up 'internal PR'. Most companies move only short distances, and the shorter the distance, the fewer staff are lost. However, in a move from, say, a low cost to a high cost area, the difficulties encountered by staff may need to be addressed by the company itself. In some instances, particularly with qualified or skilled staff, incentives may be necessary.

Premises: the third and final area for detailed studies is the premises themselves - the type of building required (how big, what level of specification, what image, and so on), the servicing requirements, the space available. A review of the existing space will make an invaluable contribution to refining requirements.

The extent to which these and other significant factors are taken in to the economic evaluation depends on the appraiser's belief in the merits of cost/benefit analysis. Below the pros and cons of this sophisticated approach will be considered in more detail.

Economic appraisal

The need to consider a relocation option should never be considered in the light of premises costs alone. Indeed, as was in shown in Fig 9.1.B the cost of the premises in the context of the cost of the operations going on inside them is relatively insignificant. Therefore, the simple 'annual costs per sq m' appraisal of rents, local taxes and running (operating) costs can only be of use as a background for further and more sophisticated evaluation. The same applies to the life cycle cost analysis technique which, though more sophisticated through the use of discounted cash flow, still preoccupies itself with premises costs rather than the real issue - the operational efficiency of the user.

Fig. 9.1.H gave an example of how certain consequential 'non-premises' effects of relocation could be introduced into the life cycle cost plan to provide a cost/benefit analysis. The effect on productivity within the organisation was projected by applying a percentage reduction to staff costs, to take into account easier communications internally (movement around the premises) and easier communications externally (such as movement to and from the premises, as affected, say, by a closer proximity to the airport).

Although such analyses are subjective and open to valid criticism they do have the effect of focusing the mind on issues which, though cost significant, are not easily quantified. Premises costs can be calculated easily but is that a good reason for leaving other, probably more important and cost-sensitive values out of the argument? Most certainly not. Cost-sensitivity analyses - that is, taking a range of values for the assumptions on productivity increases and so on - will normally enable management to take these issues into account without the need to argue the case for and against a specific value judgement: 2.5% or 10% may not tip the balance of the appraisal but if it does, then everyone will have found something important to look at.

Fig. 9.2.A
The penalising effect of DCF appraisal on options involving early capital investment and delayed sales income

Rented option		Year 1 £,000's	Year 2 £,000's	Year 3 £,000's	Year 4 £,000's	Year 5 £,000's	Year 6 £,000's	Year 7 £,000's	Total £,000's
Annual expenditure	New premises	(1,750)	(2,500)	(2,500)	(2,500)	(2,500)	(2,500)	(2,500)	
	Existing premises	0	0	0	0	0	0	0	
Capital expenditure		(2,000)	0	0	0	0	0	0	
Capital income from sale		6,000	0	0	0	0	0	0	
Net annual cash flow		2,250	(2,500)	(2,500)	(2,500)	(2,500)	(2,500)	(2,500)	
NPV at 15%		2,250	(2,174)	(1,890)	(1,644)	(1,429)	(1,243)	(1,081)	(7,211)*

Freehold development option		Year 1 £,000's	Year 2 £,000's	Year 3 £,000's	Year 4 £,000's	Year 5 £,000's	Year 6 £,000's	Year 7 £,000's	Total £,000's
Annual expenditure	New premises	0	(500)	(1,000)	(1,000)	(1,000)	(1,000)	(1,000)	
	Existing premises	(800)	(400)	0	0	0	0	0	
Capital expenditure		(9,500)	(6,500)	0	0	0	0	0	
Capital income from sale		0	6,000	0	0	0	0	0	
Net annual cash flow		(10,300)	(1,400)	(1,000)	(1,000)	(1,000)	(1,000)	(1,000)	
NPV at 15%		(10,300)	(1,217)	(756)	(658)	(572)	(497)	(432)	(14,432)*

* This is a net negative figure: all figures in parenthesis denote negative cash flow

On the subject of tenure, the cash flow analyses can be quite distorted by the decision as to whether to rent or buy (and if to buy, whether to develop a site or purchase an existing building) and in either case whether to lease back, mortgage or finance out of cash flow.

The effect of different options is illustrated in Fig. 9.2.A (previous page) and 9.2.B. In a discounted cash flow (DCF) calculation, the reducing effect of discounting on up-front capital expenditure is much less significant than on future revenue costs, especially at the high-ish discount rate (15%) used in this example, so renting always comes out looking much better economically on paper. It may be noted that because the example is not based on inflation there is no increase in the rent over the period.

In Fig. 9.2.A the freehold interest development option, which is shown here as being financed out of cash flow, has a discounted net cost at Year 7 twice that of the rented option. This is for two reasons: first, the capital cost occurs at the beginning of the cash flow so is not discounted by a very large amount; second, the existing building cannot be sold until the new one is built, so the income is discounted over the two years elapsed time.

Under the freehold development option the annual expenditure on 'new premises' is reduced to merely the operating costs.

Fig. 9.2.B shows what happens to the same example if the effect on the company's assets is superimposed on the cash flow (net capital value) - note how the result in Fig. 9.2.A is completely reversed.

Fig. 9.2.B
The effect of introducing created asset value to a discounted option appraisal

Freehold development option (including capital value)		Year 1 £,000's	Year 2 £,000's	Year 3 £,000's	Year 4 £,000's	Year 5 £,000's	Year 6 £,000's	Year 7 £,000's	Total £,000's
Annual expenditure	New premises	0	(500)	(1,000)	(1,000)	(1,000)	(1,000)	(1,000)	
	Existing premises	(800)	(400)	0	0	0	0	0	
Capital expenditure		(9,500)	(6,500)	0	0	0	0	0	
Capital income from sale		0	6,000	0	0	0	0	0	
Net annual cash flow		(10,300)	(1,400)	(1,000)	(1,000)	(1,000)	(1,000)	(1,000)	
Net capital value of asset created		0	19,005	0	0	0	0	0	
Net total		(10,300)	17,605	(1,000)	(1,000)	(1,000)	(1,000)	(1,000)	
NPV at 15%		(10,300)	15,309	(756)	(658)	(572)	(497)	(432)	2,094

Of course, because the asset value is not cash income it has no logical place in a discounted cash flow example. Nevertheless the expenditure incurred in creating the asset is not money lost as Fig. 9.2.A implies and, of course, the asset can be used as security for borrowing money. However, to be correct management accountants would show the asset value only at the end of the life-cycle, possibly discounting it back over 40 to 60 years.

A further method of appraising rent v buy options is to treat the capital cost as funded out of external borrowing at a commercial rate, maybe allowing for a down-payment of 10% to 20% of the total. This is probably the best way to do it, and Fig. 9.2.C (over the page) shows how its adoption affords a much fairer comparison with the rented option in Fig. 9.2.A.

Fig. 9.2.C
Option appraisal as Fig. 9.2.A but expressing capital expenditure as a commercial mortgage at 10% over 15 years

Rented option		Year 1 £,000's	Year 2 £,000's	Year 3 £,000's	Year 4 £,000's	Year 5 £,000's	Year 6 £,000's	Year 7 £,000's	Total £,000's
Annual expenditure	New premises	(1,750)	(2,500)	(2,500)	(2,500)	(2,500)	(2,500)	(2,500)	
	Existing premises	0	0	0	0	0	0	0	
Capital expenditure		(2,000)	0	0	0	0	0	0	
Capital income		6,000	0	0	0	0	0	0	
Net annual cash flow		2,250	(2,500)	(2,500)	(2,500)	(2,500)	(2,500)	(2,500)	
NPV at 15%		2,250	(2,174)	(1,890)	(1,644)	(1,429)	(1,243)	(1,081)	(7,211)*

Freehold development option		Year 1 £,000's	Year 2 £,000's	Year 3 £,000's	Year 4 £,000's	Year 5 £,000's	Year 6 £,000's	Year 7 – 17 inc. £,000's	Total £,000's
Annual expenditure	New premises	0	(500)	(1,000)	(1,000)	(1,000)	(1,000)	(1,000)	
	Existing premises	(800)	(400)	0	0	0	0	0	
Capital expenditure		(9,500)	(6,500)	0	0	0	0	0	
Development loan 100%		0	16,000	0	0	0	0	0	
Loan repayments years 3 - 6		0	0	(2,100)	(2,100)	(2,100)	(2,100)	0	
Loan repayments years 7-17 inc. NPV at 15%		0	0	0	0	0	0	(10,500)	
Capital income from sale		0	6,000	0	0	0	0	0	
Net annual cash flow		(10,300)	14,600	(3,100)	(3,100)	(3,100)	(3,100)	(11,500)	
NPV at 15%		(10,300)	12,702	(2,343)	(2,040)	(1,773)	(1,541)	(4,968)	(10,263)*

* This is a net negative figure : all figures in parenthesis denote negative cash flow

It may be noted that the loan commences in year 3 once the building is completed; to save space the remainder of the loan repayments from years 7 to 17 (inclusive) are shown 'rolled-up' to the end of the period. Although the mortgage is at a 10% interest rate the Net Present Value of 15% is being used to discount all future payments and that discount rate has been applied to the accumulated cost of the loan repayments in years 7 to 17 inclusive.

Management accountants will argue forever about the merits and shortcomings of such presentations. However, in order to understand economic arguments a bending of traditional rules (provided the logic behind both rule and deviation is understood) can often be a big aid to management in decision-making.

Implementation

Once the studies have been completed, the results will have to be co-ordinated and re-cast as a strategy for implementation. Again, the importance of the critical path will be underlined, because it will provide the continuity for moving from planning to implementation.

If findings seriously question elements of the master plan, these will have to be resolved within the context of the business plan. The critical path, however, should allow for this period of reconciliation as the company pauses for breath.

Where construction of a new building is involved, the company will need to prepare for relocation during the building programme. Rationalisation of leases, organisational changes and moving-in strategies can all begin. Relocation to an existing building will telescope these stages so that they can proceed simultaneously.

The actual move can be an extremely disruptive exercise, but if the earlier stages have all been completed successfully, disruption can be minimised. Thorough consultation with user groups through formal channels can pre-empt many problems. Needless to say, involving a skilled and reputable removals contractor in the plans from an early stage is essential.

Post-occupancy

The relocation exercise does not end with occupation of the new building. Inevitable teething problems will need to be ironed out. The relocation team will be required to respond to the problems and worries of staff as well as ensure the smooth running of the organisation as a whole.

9.2.2 PARTIAL RELOCATION

Reasons for splitting locations

Fundamental issues forcing organisations to consider moving part of their operations away from the single place of business include the following:

Shortage of space coupled with:

- lack of extension capacity

- high cost of extension

- no particular need for centralisation

- desire to reduce overall level of premises costs

- ready availability of suitable location space

- desire to reduce staff costs.

Desire to maximise existing central space by:

- improving space standards, or

- generating income from valuable space freed up by partial relocation.

Desire to move part of the organisation to a better location in terms of:

- image

- staff recruitment

- salary levels

- customer access.

The solutions to all of these issues have implications for the cost of premises. **However, they should not stem predominantly from the desire to make or save money on the real estate side even though that goal, per se, is far from invalid.**

All the better though if that can be done without impairing business efficiency. The calculation needs to be thoroughly investigated during the 'business case' stage and a good attempt made to express all the 'knock-on' effects in money terms - not just those which are easily and traditionally quantifiable - such as rent, local taxes and operating costs.

Partial relocation - reduced premises costs

There is a wide difference in the cost of premises nationwide.

High premises costs in the major commercial centres often cause management to think seriously about relocating those staff who do not need to be in such prestigious accommodation. Of course, staff costs can also be saved in provincial locations, but the following examples address both sets of considerations.

Thus an organisation of 400 employees occupying 6,000 sq m of net internal (lettable) floor area in a major city centre electing to relocate 320 staff to a back office in the provinces might calculate its prospective premises costs as shown in Fig. 9.2.D which presumes that the required back-office space is immediately available to rent.

Fig. 9.2.D
Premises cost appraisal of partial relocation (rented) option by comparison with status quo

Option 1 – Status quo		Year 1 £,000's	Year 2 £,000's	Year 3 £,000's	Year 4 £,000's	Year 5 £,000's	Total £,000's
City Centre	Rent	(1,800)	(1,800)	(1,800)	(1,800)	(1,800)	(9,000)
	Local taxes	(750)	(788)	(827)	(868)	(912)	(4,145)
	Operating costs	(480)	(504)	(529)	(556)	(583)	(2,652)
	Fitting-out / 'churn'	(300)	(315)	(331)	(347)	(1,800)	(3,093)
	Rental income	0	0	0	0	0	0
Total £,000's		**(3,300)**	**(3,407)**	**(3,487)**	**(3,571)**	**(5,095)**	**(18,890)**
Present value factor at 15% pa		1.0000	0.8696	0.7561	0.6575	0.5718	
Present value		**(3,330)**	**(2,963)**	**(2,637)**	**(2,348)**	**(2,913)**	**(14,191)**

Option 2 – Partial relocation		Year 1 £,000's	Year 2 £,000's	Year 3 £,000's	Year 4 £,000's	Year 5 £,000's	Total £,000's
City Centre	Rent	(1,800)	(1,800)	(1,800)	(1,800)	(1,800)	(9,000)
	Local taxes	(188)	(197)	(207)	(218)	(228)	(1,038)
	Operating costs	(120)	(125)	(132)	(139)	(146)	(662)
	Fitting-out / 'churn'	(375)	(75)	(79)	(83)	(450)	(1,062)
	Rental income	1,350	1,350	1,350	1,350	1,350	6,750
Provincial location	Rent	(675)	(675)	(675)	(675)	(675)	(3,375)
	Local taxes	(225)	(236)	(248)	(260)	(273)	(1,242)
	Operating costs	(270)	(284)	(298)	(313)	(328)	(1,493)
	Fitting-out / 'churn'	(1,013)	0	0	0	0	(1,013)
Overall total £,000's		**(3,316)**	**(2,042)**	**(2,089)**	**(2,138)**	**(2,550)**	**(12,135)**
Present value factor at 15% pa		1.0000	0.8696	0.7561	0.6575	0.5718	
Present value		**(3,316)**	**(1,776)**	**(1,579)**	**(1,406)**	**(1,458)**	**(9,535)**

The amount of lettable space taken on board in the new location allows for similar space standards to those previously adopted for clerical grades in the city centre but there is an addition for improved space standards for supervising grades. Also provision is made within the initial fit-out for 5% p.a. growth in the back office over a five-year period (which explains the absence of fitting-out costs in years 2 to 5, although there probably would be a bit of 'churn'). There is a partial recovery of the extra costs through short-term leasing out (see 'Rental income' in the Figure). Head office space and quality standards are also improved.

All costs have been inflated at 5% p.a. but there are no rent reviews for the five years period in the example. Due to the high discount rate costs and income beyond the first five years have been excluded from this and the following related examples.

9.2.3 BENEFITING FROM A SUCCESSFUL LOCATION

An important point about the premises costs of relocation - and one which is often missed in appraisal - is the effect of successful judgement on the cost of premises in the area of relocation, and the further influence of the rent/buy decision on that appraisal.

For example, an organisation locating at low cost in a newly-established business park ten years ago might well now be paying a rent 100% higher due to the popularity of the area in subsequent years.

They may well continue to pick up regular upwards-only rent reviews, so they will be exposed to the ups and downs of the market which will probably be disproportionate to the much slower growth in the original central location. The hoped-for saving in annual premises costs is effectively reduced following this calculation so the organisation is penalised for its successful judgement of the quality of the new location.

On the other hand, if they had bought and developed a site or bought a freehold interest, the capital value of their asset would have benefited substantially from the same market in real terms even allowing for temporary rises in investment yields. However, if the business park in the example had turned out not to be a success, the organisation buying a building or doing its own development there might well have difficulty getting its money back when trying to move on.

Fig. 9.2.E (over the page) shows how the sums in Fig. 9.2.D would be varied using a development option. Because of the development period the move and subsequent benefits are not shown until year 3. It may be noted that a continuance of 'churn', albeit at a lower level, is included in 'fitting-out' in the city centre office but written out - maybe rather optimistically - in the newly planned provincial office building.

The option is shown financed out of the business cash flow which both penalises the heavy up front expenditure and discounts down the income from sub-letting in the city centre.

Fig. 9.2.B showed how the inference of such a calculation would be reversed if the effect on assets were to be shown in the DCF appraisal. However, expressing the capital costs by way of instalments of a commercial mortgage as in Fig. 9.2.F (over the page) makes the back office development option look fairly attractive in this case especially given that the company owns the provincial asset.

Fig. 9.2.E
Partial relocation appraisal as Fig. 9.2.D but with self-financed development for the provincial location

Development option		Year 1 £,000's	Year 2 £,000's	Year 3 £,000's	Year 4 £,000's	Year 5 £,000's	Total £,000's
City Centre	Rent	(1,800)	(1,800)	(1,800)	(1,800)	(1,800)	(9,000)
	Local taxes	(750)	(788)	(225)	(236)	(248)	(2,247)
	Operating costs	(480)	(504)	(132)	(139)	(146)	(1,401)
	Fitting-out / 'churn'	(375)	(75)	(79)	(90)	(95)	(714)
	Rental income	0	0	1,350	1,350	1,350	4,050
Provincial location	Land purchase	(1,000)	0	0	0	0	(1,000)
	Construction	(1,200)	(3,000)	0	0	0	(4,200)
	Fitting-out	0	(1,013)	0	0	0	(1,013)
	Local taxes	0	0	(248)	(260)	(273)	(781)
	Operating costs	0	0	(293)	(307)	(322)	(922)
Overall total £,000's		**(5,605)**	**(7,180)**	**(1,427)**	**(1,482)**	**(1,534)**	**(17,228)**
Present value factor at 15% pa		1.0000	0.8696	0.7561	0.6575	0.5718	
Present value		**(5,605)**	**(6,244)**	**(1,079)**	**(974)**	**(877)**	**(14,779)**

Fig. 9.2.F
Partial relocation appraisal as Fig. 9.2.E but incorporating the capital cost of development by way of annual loan repayments

Development relocation		Year 1 £,000's	Year 2 £,000's	Year 3 £,000's	Year 4 £,000's	Year 5 £,000's	Total £,000's
City centre	Rent	(1,800)	(1,800)	(1,800)	(1,800)	(1,800)	(9,000)
	Local taxes	(750)	(788)	(225)	(236)	(248)	(2,247)
	Operating costs	(480)	(504)	(132)	(139)	(146)	(1,401)
	Fitting-out / 'churn'	(375)	(75)	(79)	(90)	(95)	(714)
	Rental income	0	0	1,350	1,350	1,350	4,050
Provincial location	Development loan	5,200	0	0	0	0	5,200
	Loan repayment	(846)	(846)	(846)	(846)	(846)	(4,230)
	Land	(1,000)	0	0	0	0	(1,000)
	Construction	(1,200)	(3,000)	0	0	0	(4,200)
	Fitting-out / 'churn'	0	(1,013)	0	0	0	(1,013)
	Local taxes	0	0	(248)	(260)	(273)	(781)
	Operating costs	0	0	(293)	(307)	(322)	(922)
Overall total £,000's		**(1,251)**	**(8,026)**	**(2,273)**	**(2,328)**	**(2,380)**	**(16,258)**
Present value factor at 15% pa		1.0000	0.8696	0.7561	0.6575	0.5718	
NPV		**(1,251)**	**(6,979)**	**(1,179)**	**(1,531)**	**(1,361)**	**(12,841)**

9.2.4 TOTAL ECONOMICS OF RELOCATION

Cost/benefit analysis

As previously emphasized the premises cost argument should never be paramount: the costs and benefits should always be gathered into one equation to find the true picture.

In the case of partial relocation the advantages of such savings as premises costs and possibly staff costs have to be read against possible increase of overheads in supervision, travelling between offices, disruption and so on.

Of course, forecasts of productivity changes are always going to be challenged, so a sensitivity testing of these assumptions is absolutely essential. The easiest way to calculate and justify figures for such analysis is by taking minimum/maximum percentage savings (or increases) in the total salaries bill for all the staff whose productivity is likely to benefit (or otherwise) from the change.

Fig. 9.2.G shows how the provincial location example might look in the context of a cost/benefit analysis.

Fig. 9.2.G
Partial relocation appraisal as Fig. 9.2.F but as a cost/benefit analysis introducing personnel costs and improvements in productivity

Development relocation		Year 1 £,000's	Year 2 £,000's	Year 3 £,000's	Year 4 £,000's	Year 5 £,000's	Total £,000's
Premises costs - city centre	Rent	(1,800)	(1,800)	(1,800)	(1,800)	(1,800)	(9,000)
	Local taxes	(750)	(788)	(225)	(236)	(248)	(2,247)
	Operating costs	(480)	(504)	(132)	(139)	(146)	(1,401)
	Fitting-out / 'churn'	(375)	(75)	(79)	(90)	(95)	(714)
	Rental income	0	0	1,350	1,350	1,350	4,050
Premises costs - provincial location	Development loan	5,200	0	0	0	0	5,200
	Loan repayment	(846)	(846)	(846)	(846)	(846)	(4,230)
	Land purchase	(1,000)	0	0	0	0	(1,000)
	Construction	(1,200)	(3,000)	0	0	0	(4,200)
	Fitting-out / 'churn'	0	(1,013)	0	0	0	(1,013)
	Local taxes	0	0	(248)	(260)	(273)	(781)
	Operating costs	0	0	(293)	(307)	(322)	(922)
Business costs - both facilities	Direct moving cost	0	0	(50)	0	0	(50)
	Indirect moving cost	0	0	(500)	0	0	(500)
	Productivity benefit - city centre	0	0	32	64	67	163
	Productivity benefit - provincial location	0	0	64	128	134	326
	Dual location costs	0	0	(150)	(158)	(165)	(473)
	Salary saving	0	0	450	473	496	1,419
Overall total £,000's		(1,251)	(8,026)	(2,581)	(1,314)	(1,316)	(14,488)
Present value factor at 15% pa		1.0000	0.8696	0.7561	0.6575	0.5718	
NPV		(1,251)	(6,979)	(1,951)	(864)	(752)	(11,797)

Fig. 9.2.H summarises the results of the various strategies. In this case the rental relocation option looks more favourable than owner-occupation using pure discounted cash flow methodology which ignores the asset value created until the end of the building's life when its NPV is of minor significance.

Fig. 9.2.H
Partial relocation study - summary of alternative appraisal calculations

Premises costs only		NPV cost £,000's
Fig. 9.2.D	Option 1 – status quo (city centre) option	(14,191)
Fig. 9.2.D	Option 2 - partial relocation (rental option)	(9,535)
Fig. 9.2.E	Partial relocation (development option)	(14,779)
Fig. 9.2.F	Partial relocation (development option – loan repayment)	(12,841)
Premises plus business costs		
Fig. 9.2.G	Partial relocation (development option – including cost / benefit analysis)	(11,797)

The introduction of business efficiency/cost assumptions from Fig. 9.2.G indicates a further beneficial effect which would, of course, similarly influence the other appraisals if applied.

The 'front and back offices' premises policy does usually make economic sense, and in the example has helped to avoid the worst symptoms of the 'churn' disease. However, not a few organisations have found to their cost that the second centre has been more trouble than the expected saving was worth and either re-relocated or re-centralised at further expense.

Sometimes an argument is made that renting affords more flexibility than purchase or development of a facility. Whereas this is undoubtedly true when leases are short or with easy 'break' options it rarely holds good in the case of long, inflexible leases: if a building is good it can be disposed of regardless of the tenure - and vice-versa. (See Chapter 3.2 for an analysis of lease terms.)

If the business logic is sound, the premises advice well informed and the appraisal technique flexible and comprehensive then the right decision will be made - **but only if the business decision drives the premises policy and not vice-versa.**

9.3   REMOVAL

Introduction

Relocation or partial relocation will involve the transfer of all or some of the staff and, depending on the nature of the business, may involve removal of such items as:

- furniture and equipment
- plant and machinery
- vehicles
- raw materials
- stock and work in progress.

This chapter examines the removal process including issues arising from an international removal.

9.3.1 THE REMOVAL PROCESS

Project management

Whether it is just another piece of internal 'churn' or a major premises relocation the actual move needs to be meticulously planned and executed if the organisation is not to suffer from delays and disruptions leading to extensive loss of productivity.

In major moves a dedicated project manager will almost certainly be needed, possibly externally appointed but in close liaison with the facilities manager.

Issues relating to staff notifications, relocation allowances and alike, are down to the personnel department but the project manager must liaise closely with them to ensure that the date and time of the operation are agreed well in advance - changes of plan can be disastrous in terms of employer/employee relationships at these times.

Preparing to move

The following is a checklist of key issues to be addressed by the project manager in preparation for the move once the relocation decision has been taken:

- the budget
- staff requiring special treatment, eg people with disabilities or key executives
- lead times for installation of new or relocated facilities such as: security systems, telephones, ICT networks, power supplies
- permissions and licences, eg loading/unloading, parking, rubbish containers, liquor licence (for the caterers)
- identify equipment and/or substances requiring special handling (by external suppliers or contractors) such as photocopiers and toxic materials
- design production and delivery of new headed stationery
- advice to customers and suppliers of the move date and new address etc. and also any temporary arrangements pertaining to the period of the move
- internal telephone/fax/email directory
- security requirements for two or more properties
- notification of move to insurers and consideration of any special cover which may be required, including the removal contractor's insurances.

Choosing the contractor

It will be advisable to tender the work on a fairly specific document; however, because the best way to handle dealings with removal contractors is in fully co-operative mode it is well worth making the appointment as early as possible getting their input to the logic of the process from the outset of planning. These apparently opposing requirements can be solved by the sort of two-stage tendering process described for selection of a building contractor at Chapter 6.3.5, leaving the tying up of a comprehensive contract to be negotiated at the second stage by reference to key competitive factors established in the first-stage bidding process.

The programme for the removals

Depending on the nature of the business it may be possible to carry out the whole operation at one go. However, some organisations cannot afford a complete shut-down - even for 24/48 hours - so for them a staged programme, or weekend operation will be essential. Although weekend and out-of-hours working may be more expensive (this can be determined at the first-stage bid) the cost of the move per capita will normally be insignificant in the whole financial scheme of things when the effect on employee productivity is brought into the equation.

Every good programme has a float and a contingency. The float may be concealed but the contingency, both in terms of time and recovery plan, must be made known to all key managers.

Moving out and in

Key issues to be addressed relating to the actual move are:

- the insurance of both new and existing properties

- availability of all utility services and disconnecting as appropriate

- security and fire protection services in place and fully operational at both locations

- a condition survey completed and agreed by the landlord/assignee of the old premises and the new landlord if applicable

- washroom and catering facilities must be up and running for the workforce and any 'pioneering' staff

- only move goods and equipment which are needed in the new location - it is surprising how reluctant people are to 'out' rubbish and the move is a perfect time to insist on it

- make sure of the times at which legal possession and relinquishment actually take effect to avoid the embarrassment of being locked out of one or both properties while the contractor's vans wait in the road outside

- the contractor must take full responsibility for the protection of both buildings during the move - specify the performance rather than the method, and check the contractor's insurance cover for damage to goods and property, as well as loss in transit

- thoroughly check the inventory on leaving and arrival; companies with bar-coded equipment for asset tracking will find this easier, but remember that the code-readers are not usually intelligent. Someone with a live pc (possibly a lap-top computer) should be able to keep well on top of the inventory from beginning to end - also checking accuracy of drops to various floor levels and locations in the new buildings

- with the contractor check out the access points (again) before commencing to unload; in particular, dimensions of openings, lift and floor loading capacities must be reviewed in case last minute changes to the arrangements prove to be illegal or impossible or both

- the contractor will have a formal modus operandi for labelling crates, mechanical handling and transportation and marking up the drawings. Always check it, but make sure that the contractor takes full and sole responsibility for its accuracy and efficiency.

Post-move activity

The commissioning of any new or modified services needs to be reset once the building is ready for occupation, and a 'deep clean' is essential prior to any staff taking up their posts.

Finally, having had the foresight to prepare a new telephone/fax directory/email do make sure that it is in place and distributed from day one - it is amazing how often this simple but critical operation is overlooked risking the goodwill of the staff at a time when plaudits are potentially there for the taking.

The cost of moving

Fig. 9.3.A gives an approximate guide to the cost of removals per capita across town and further afield. It may be noted that if the move were to take place over a weekend the costs would be from 15 to 30% higher - but still only a tiny amount compared with losing two days output per member of staff!

Fig. 9.3.A
The approximate cost of weekday removals per capita

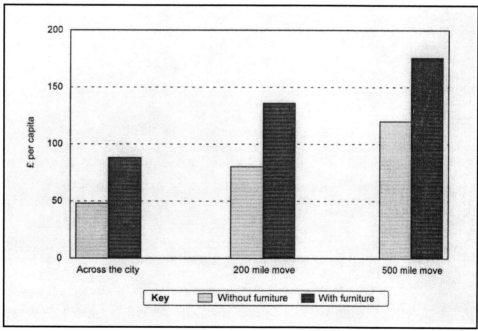

9.3.2 COMPULSORY PURCHASE

Where the move results from the compulsory acquisition of property belonging to the company, the project manager will need to liaise with the company's professional advisers and those of the acquiring authority on such matters as the move and the compensation which may be claimed. Broadly, the actual removal will follow the process described in 9.3.1 above. However, care will be needed to observe the principles underlying the assessment of compensation. Briefly, the company should be put, as far as financial compensation can determine, in the same position afterwards as it was before the acquisition. The following conditions need to be observed:

- the claimant company should mitigate the claim

- notice to treat determines the nature and extent of the interest to be acquired

- the claim for the property taken is based on open market value

- the claim may include a claim for disturbance.

A claim may be based on the higher of either open market value as it is together with disturbance, or open market value including development value reflecting actual or assumed planning permission.

It is outside the scope of this volume to go into detail on the law of compulsory purchase but an indication of some of the items of claim for disturbance in respect of the compulsory purchase of, say, a factory and ancillary offices are:

- reasonable costs of finding alternative premises

- adaptions, removal and settling in costs

- additional overheads for two premises whilst removal is in progress

- temporary and permanent loss of profits

- redundancy payments and keyworker removal costs and expenses

- legal costs and surveyors fees on the acquisition of new premises.

This is in addition, of course, to the value of the property being acquired together with the associated legal costs of disposal and surveyors' fees in dealing with the compulsory acquisition.

9.3.3 INTERNATIONAL REMOVAL

The UK facilities manager may be involved in international operations of removal. Removal across national borders requires of the facilities manager an understanding of the special problems and techniques involved.

The need to locate in another country requires a consideration of all the factors discussed above. The decision will follow an evaluation of the business-specific requirements for such resources as the following:

- land and buildings

- plant and machinery

- managers and other staff

- raw materials and other consumables

- power, telecommunications and other utility services

- road, rail, air passenger, and air freight and other logistics services.

The business development options may include one or more of the following:

- a merger or takeover involving a company in another country, resulting in a rationalisation at one or more relocations

- a new facility in another country for manufacturing or other purposes

- a rationalisation of one or more business functions, eg accounting, currently located in several countries, resulting in a Shared Service Centre (SSC)

- expansion of the business franchise or a 'brand' facility into other countries.

Facilities implications

Where a trans-border merger or take-over is taking place the facilities implications of particular concern may be:

- corporate dissonances arising from the marrying of different national business cultures

- problems arising from a lack of knowledge and skills in a second language, perhaps in terms of technical vocabulary and, in particular, lack of linguistic communicative competence for the tasks to be carried out

- staff relocation and movement following rapid recruitment or redundancies

- different house styles which need to be superseded by new logos, signboards, stationery, livery on vehicles and so on.

Shared service centres (SSC)

The creation of a SSC is likely to require:

- the recruitment of new staff from the locality of the SSC

- the transfer or redundancy of staff made surplus as a result of the new facility.

The brief for the location of a SSC is likely to include:

- a strong telecommunications infrastructure

- staff with multi-language skills and the willingness to adapt to the new location

- for existing staff, a change of perspective from being a cost-centre employee to being a profit-centre employee

- a flexible employment environment, particularly in terms of accepting foreign workers.

Franchise/branded development

Where a franchise or a branded development is to be expanded into other EU member states or elsewhere, it will be necessary to consider a number of matters, including:

- the development of common facilities management and information systems

- the induction, training and development of managers and staff (through the entrepreneur franchisee in the first instance for such facilities)

- the translation of all manuals, posters, sign boards, accounting and other instructions and so on into the appropriate second languages

- a culture check, so that all expected business behaviour and all promotional material is carried out or prepared in accord with the new country's norms of behaviour of a moral, religious or legal nature.

Languages

Where business operations take place between those without a common language English is often, perhaps usually, adopted as the third language unless interpreters are used.

For overseas locations and operations the facilities manager may need to recruit multi-lingual staff with a sufficiently good measure of fluency in a second or third language to get work done. There are internationally recognised levels, standards and qualifications or awards in languages. However, although the comprehensive basic skills are in speaking, listening, writing and reading, it is important that the linguistic communicative functioning member of staff has skills at least appropriate for the tasks to be performed. In other words it is not always necessary for them to be completely fluent in other European languages.

The approach that might be adopted for a particular individual at a given level comprises the following:

- undertake an audit of the role, job or task to ascertain the language skills and knowledge needed

- translate the skills and knowledge into objectives for vocabulary, linguistic, functions, grammar, situational needs and pronunciation

- identify business or technical vocabulary likely to be needed

- develop situational language needs, such as business socialising, travelling, bookings for hotels, meetings and the like, making company presentations and so on

- develop transactional linguistics, usually at a higher level, involving negotiating, conducting meetings, presenting research findings or in-depth technical material including responding to questions

- develop working documents in the required second language

- prepare a programme of linguistic training and developmental work to achieve the objectives

- monitor and evaluate the individual's progress; broadly, the individual's programme should be based on usage in the work situation for the foreseeable future.

Culture and ethics of business

It is not easy to cover the culture of business in a text-book. It is likely that dissonances in relations between individuals or groups arise from a number of sources. These may include:

- language

- body language

- age, gender, race and religion

- dress

- business practices, ethics and style, including litigation

- property ownership.

As far as language goes, misunderstanding due to misuse of words or to misinterpretation may cause problems. Sometimes the difficulty arises from attempts to transfer expressions literally. Often the nuance of meaning of words or phrases is lost on a listener in a second tongue. Similarly, whereas a particular joke may be appropriate and acceptable in one culture, it may be regarded as offensive in another.

Most cultures have taboos on the parts of the body which may be touched by strangers or how eye contact may be made. Whilst the handshake may be common to most business cultures, kissing in a business context may be alien to some.

The treatment of age, gender, race and religion varies in different societies despite legislation which may prohibit certain practices. Sexual and racial harassment and bullying still prevail, such that corporate cultures may need to address these issues head on.

Dress may be an issue in some business cultures. Customs and conventions on religious dress, casual or formal dress, health and safety dress and corporate uniforms are examples of problem areas that the facilities manager may need to address in a multi-national context.

A business's practice and style in one country may conflict with underlying national practices and style in another. At a simplistic but important level it covers working hours, lunch and break periods and the like. At another level it concerns fundamental issues of differences in business ethics. The list below is not exhaustive but indicates the range of matters where, potentially conflicts could arise. It covers several areas of ethical concern, such as relations with customers, relations with staff, the organisation and the law.

In relations with clients or customers the following practices might be considered:

- the need for clients' accounts

- the need for any cover, by insurance, for third parties, professional indemnity and product liability.

In relations with employees the following areas might be considered:

- transparent employment practices for recruitment, induction, training, development, promotion, personal resources, eg a car, and succession

- equal opportunities in relation to such matters as gender, life-cycle, race and religion

- appropriate safeguards concerning health, safety, welfare and comfort in the workplace.

For suppliers consideration of:

- the fairness of the terms of the business relationship, including its termination with notice

- a complaints procedure

- appropriate terms of payment of goods and services supplied.

Increasingly society is adapting an ethical approach to assessing a business, perhaps for the purposes of doing business or for the purposes of judging whether or not to invest in the business. The ethical investment concerns include the environment, treatment of animals and sourcing of sustainable supplies.

Generally, failure in some of these areas may lead to claims for compensation and, perhaps, litigation. Whilst in many countries the appetite for litigation does not seem so well developed (compared with say, the United States) there does seem to be a growing awareness of rights and processes in law.

In particular the law and practice of real estate varies widely between the member states. Given the importance of this facet of facilities to facilities managers these issues are discussed in depth in the text.

Section 10

The Development Option

10.1   THE DEVELOPMENT PROCESS

Introduction

This chapter covers the three main aspects of the development process for a new project. It opens with a consideration of the facilities manager's role in a new development project.

Whereas the project manager's role in a project is likely to be taken by a consultant, the project liaison role falls to the facilities manager in many instances. The chapter gives an analysis of the principal functions which are broken down into the main tasks undertaken by the professional and other participants. This is portrayed later on in the chapter in Fig 10.1.B which, however should be regarded as a schematic representation and does not relate exclusively to owner-occupation.

The last section of the chapter considers the principal stages of the development process, from acquiring the land to handover and commissioning. Again, the order in which the stages are dealt with is not to suggest the order for an actual project.

It may be noted that from time to time in this chapter titles have been given to those who carry out certain tasks. However in practice the configuration of tasks differs from one project to another as does the title of the task executor.

10.1.1 THE DECISION TO BUILD

The decision to build or not should have been reached only as a result of strict adherence to the principles of value management as described in Chapter 2.2.

Carrying out a new development may seem daunting to the facilities manager without previous involvement in such a project.

It is likely that the choice of location would stem from a corporate decision at a strategic level concerning the development of the company's business. Even if the facilities manager was not involved in the decision it may, nevertheless, be useful to understand the basis of the decision in terms of any important potential economic, technological, financial, legal or social factors.

For a specific location some of the factors given in Chapter 3.6.3 might form a fuller basis or checklist for the facilities manager's eventual understanding of the decision. Of course, many of these matters will be dealt with by the various consultants employed to advise on the development project.

10.1.2 SETTING UP THE PROJECT

The facilities manager's involvement

In Chapter 9.2 on 'Relocation' the issue of whether to rent or build was explored and the financial implications of both options considered in detail.

Once the management board has made up its mind for a new-build project the facilities manager can expect to be pushed into the front-line role in the commissioning and managing of the project. If not, then they ought to volunteer; not just because it is a fascinating process - which it is - but because the facilities manager's constructive involvement is essential to the success of the venture.

The project management decision

Whereas the facilities manager may be capable of managing fitting out projects - albeit possibly on a smaller scale - without external assistance, project management of the development process is strictly for the professionals (see Chapter 2.8). Few facilities managers will have the background in real estate, finance and construction to be able to deliver a project of any size to time, quality and cost without exposing the organisation to an unacceptable level of risk.

However, there are two facets of project management: the delivery process referred to above, ie the development project management, and the liaison process. The facilities manager must carry out the latter to ensure that the requirements of the premises policy are met in full and that the organisation is fully and properly involved in, and informed about, the whole process from start to finish.

Project sponsorship

Project sponsorship is an obvious extension of the 'sponsorship' facet of the Intelligent Client Function (ICF) (see Chapters 1.1.1 and 2.1.2).

The project sponsor is, ideally, an in-house appointment from amongst the ICF team although it is not unusual for consultants to be appointed to this role where a suitable candidate is not available internally.

The role is quite distinct from that of the development project manager in that it entails forging that critical link between the client and the development process.

The project sponsor will probably be involved from the early stages of developing the brief, commissioning the feasibility study, guiding and informing the decision-making process. Once the process begins in earnest, they should take up the role at the interface between the participants as depicted at Fig 10.1.A.

Fig. 10.1.A
The role of the project sponsor

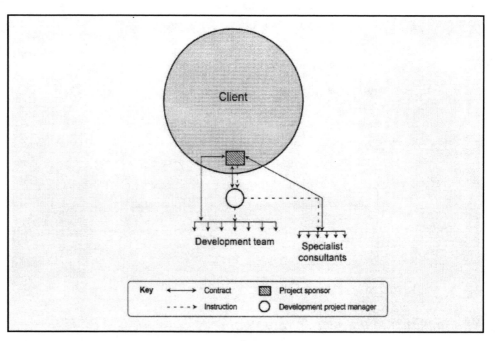

Note, however, that although the figure reflects a conventional contract arrangement in terms of client/development team, the development project manager and the team are sometimes part of the same organisation, eg in sales and leaseback provision of buildings.

Internally, the project sponsor will need to be the organisation's focal point with regards to:

- developing and refining the brief
- determining the method of building procurement
- reporting on progress

- ensuring appropriate records are maintained, eg for taxation purposes
- dealing with the decisions required of the client
- issuing instructions
- liasing on finance, incentives and taxation matters
- authorisations, eg payments and charges
- dealing with other consultants, eg agents, solicitors, valuers, funding agents (possibly in conjunction with the development project manager)
- liaison with personnel management concerning the move and staff requirements, approvals and the like
- management of the move - or liaising with a dedicated move manager.

It is important that the project sponsor and the development project manager work closely together; really a side-by-side structure should be established in practice, although the project sponsor is theoretically superior in the hierarchy. In spite of this, it must always be totally clear as to who carries what responsibility, and that clarity must prevail in-house as well as to the outside world.

It may be noted that although Fig. 10.1.A (previous page) shows the specialist consultant directly in contract with the client it is quite common for some or all of these appointments to be as sub-contracts to the development project manager.

10.1.3 PARTICIPANTS AND ACTIVITIES

The qualities required of the development project manager

The development project manager will have many tasks to control and many disparate people, companies and authorities to manage by whatever means available. They need experience, intelligence, common sense, vision, tact, tenacity, patience, charm and resources - to list but a few of the qualities essential to successful delivery of a project. Very importantly they should have a thorough understanding of the philosophies and strategic roles of the key consultants, contractors and authorities with whom work is carried out.

The development activities

The key processes coming under the development project manager's overall direction, more or less in consecutive order are:

- preparation of the briefs for consultants
- feasibility study
- site finding
- planning/building permission
- short-term (bridging) finance (possibly)
- land acquisition
- site management
- insurances and performance bonds (possibly)
- design
- health and safety plan
- construction
- cost control

Fig. 10.1.B *Typical functions and activities in the development process*

Appraisal and estates management	Cost management	Architecture	Structural engineering	Building services engineering	Project management
Pre-contract					
• Seek and appraise site. • Prepare case for building permission. • Assemble site by agreement or compulsorily. • Negotiate acquisition prices and take possessions. • Site management and clearance. • Prepare rent and value estimates. • Negotiate development finance. • Prepare lettings plan and tenant mix. • Prepare marketing program. • Obtain consents from local and national bodies. • Obtain consents of owners of adjoining land and superior landlords.	• Advise on cost in use and total cost. • Undertake cost/value analysis. • Prepare cost plan and targets. • Set up cost control systems. • Advise on building standards. • Prepare documents for competitive bids. • Report on bids. • Advise on detail of specification and contract documents.	• Survey the site. • Prepare initial sketch design and plans. • Prepare final sketch design. • Prepare design details. • Ensure health and safety requirements are incorporated in the scheme ie planning supervisor roles. • Establish building finishes. • Prepare working drawings, specifications and schedules. • Obtain approvals, building time etc. • Advise on bids.	• Site investigation, test soil samples. • Assess bearing pressures for foundations. • Prepare alternative framing schemes. • Compare costs. • Advise on foundation frame and materials. • Prepare working drawings, details and specifications for structure.	• Advise on design of services. • Prepare sketch and working drawings. • Or prepare schematic layout and performance specification.	• Initiate scheme. • Appoint professional consultants. • Draw up consultants brief. • Prepare feasibility and risk studies. • Establish development budget. • Advice on 'planning supervisor' requirements. • Advise on insurances for construction. • Appoint contractor. • Monitor national, local landlord and other consents. • Monitor insurance's. • Monitor public relations. • Chair team meetings etc. • Select main contractor. • Agree contract.
Post-contract					
• Undertake lettings program. • Give estate management advice on leasing property insurances, management, car parking etc. • Prepare valuations for national and local taxation and for finance. • Advise on disposals by sales and lettings. • Prepare management procedures for retaining property.	• Monitor cost program and report to all parties. • Value interim applications for payment on account. • Measure and value variations from original drawings. • Prepare final account.	• Project planning. • Site supervision. • Variations and instructions. • Certification for payment. • Defects Liability. • Agree final account. • Final certificate.	• Monitor structural work. • Prepare details for any agreed variations.	• Advise on variations to building services. • Monitor and advise on progress of work. • Advise on insurance's. • Advise on maintenance, breakdown and emergency plans.	• Monitor progress on site and on estate management. • Control variations. • Authorise changes. • Chair team meetings etc. • Draw up 'house' manual (for occupiers and users).

Source: Adapted from Parsons GB and Redding BG (1976) Planning, Development and the Community Land Scheme, Rating and Valuation Association (now IRRV) London pp 106 -7

Contractor	Legal services	Environment	Insurance	Finance and taxation	Facilities manager	Planning supervision
Pre-contract						
• Prepare bid • Prepare programme for the use on site of time, manpower and other resources.	• Land acquisition searches, contracts, and completion. • Termination of leases. • Terms and conditions for any wayleaves and easements. • Building procurement contracts. • Building leases and ground leases. • Other legal documents, contracts etc.	• Site appraisal. • Desk research. • Site survey. • Analysis. • Report. • Remediation. • Action plan. • Contract and supervision for remedial works. • Advice on environmental management strategy • Supervise archeological study, if any. • Consider and set up insurances, if appropriate.	• Fire and title insurance on acquisitions of property. • Advise on insurance in leases and other matters. • Financial insurance. • Advice on all insurances on site management operations and construction. • Environmental liability and archeological delays. • Review security arrangements	• Method of funding project. • Mortgages etc. • Currency matters – hedging. • Bank presentations. • Tax record systems. • Negotiations on incentives.	• Develop brief from premises policy. • Sponsorship / liaison with project manager. • Advise on impact of design / specification on functional and physical performance over time. • Agree life-cycle cost plan. • Devise security strategy • Devise environmental management strategy. • Revise the asset arrangement programme	• Project notification to HSE. • Check liaison between designers. • Ensure pre-tender health and safety plan is drawn up. • Advise client as requested. • Ensure designers fulfill requirements.
Post-contract						
• Demolition / clearance • Construct / build • Supervise variations. • Monitor site progress and site organisation • Monitor contractors drawings, program, labour and materials. • Fencing.	• Leases taken. • Leases to sub-tenants. • Other legal documents, contracts etc.	• Supervise remedial works. • Monitoring for pollution. • Environmental plan for future operations. • Liaise on insurance matters, if any.	• Insurance liability for operations. • Insurance on commissioning, fire, contents' and other cover of perils.	• Arrange payments and receipts. • Assessment, payment for national and local taxation. • Devise records for capital allowances.	• Consider and authorise (or not) major change proposals. • Prepare occupation budget. • Take delivery of site for occupation. • Prepare move management plan. • Arrange move management contract. • Liaise on 'house' manual (for occupiers and users).	• Make sure health and safety file is prepared. • Advise client as requested.

Source: Adapted from Parsons GB and Redding BG (1976) Planning, Development and the Community Land Scheme, Rating and Valuation Association (now IRRV) London pp 106 -7

- change

- asset management plan

- handover

- removals

- occupation and commissioning

- long-term finance (possibly).

Depending on the arrangements which best suit the project and the relevant experience and skills of both the project sponsor and development project manager, some of these activities may be carried out directly by the client or by the two managers together.

Participants in the process

In the course of these extensive and often overlapping activities the development project manager will have to deal with (again possibly in conjunction with the project sponsor) any or all of the professions who are essential to various stages of the process.

The professional team will be drawn from some or all of the following disciplines: lawyers, letting agents, insurance consultants, funding brokers, valuers, architects, structural engineers, mechanical engineers, civil engineers, highway engineers, quantity surveyors, cost consultants, planning supervisor, planning consultants, landscape architects, building control officers, planning officers, and so on. Fig 10.1.B (previous page) shows some of the main functions and activities undertaken in the process.

The activities listed are not always carried out by the person to whose function it is allocated in the figure. Nevertheless, all the relevant activities need to be identified by the project manager and delegated to the most appropriate (or willing!) member of the development team; however, some, e.g. marketing for tenants, may not be appropriate to a development for owner-occupation.

10.1.4 PRINCIPAL STAGES IN NEW DEVELOPMENT

Acquiring the land

Once the location has been decided the hunt for a site begins - unless the whole concept has been initiated by the availability of a piece of land which meets, or has kindled the idea of, a relocation strategy.

Generally, the facilities manager will be concerned to buy or lease property but other methods or means of acquisition include:

- exchange

- gift

- dedication to the public

- adverse possession

- expropriation or compulsory purchase (by a body so empowered).

Usually private treaty negotiation is used in transactions but the owner may deal with the property by one of the following:

- open (to all-comers) or closed (restricted numbers) bids

- auction.

The process of putting together a site from disparate but adjacent land components may be complicated and frustrating; it can also be rewarding for the speculator, but rarely for the serious owner-occupier. Ironically the 'cleverness' of speculators in this respect has produced some of the least appropriately designed premises imaginable.

The worst thing a prospective owner-occupier can do is try to compete for land with the professional developers in a seller's market. Apart from the obvious lack of commercial market intelligence - even if supported by the expertise of a real estate consultant - there are the 'hidden agendas' of the developers and investors which can turn the true value of an individual site on its head, eg where it has a 'marriage value' with adjoining sites making the whole site value infinitely greater than the sum of the individual parts.

It is most important to understand that development land has no intrinsic value; its value is a residual figure the calculation of which is explained in Chapters 10.3.1 and 10.3.2. Furthermore, although the residual figure has to be estimated prior to purchase the true residual will be whatever figure turns up in the post-project reconciliation statement. Fig 10.1.C is a graphic representation of the calculation showing the 'true' residual land value after allowing for a 'normal' development profit rather than the 'windfall' profit portrayed in that example which has arisen through a post-land purchase improvement in the YP multiplier (and hence gross development value).

Fig. 10.1.C
Development budget out-turn compared to forecast - effect on 'true' residual land value

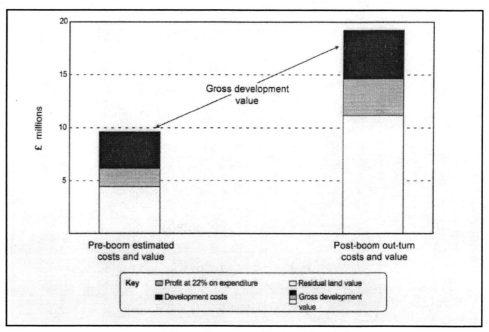

Profit made by the developer in effect comes primarily from the increased residual land value. This is another good illustration as to why no-one should ever buy land on the basis of some 'comparable' transaction on another site which may be based on a completely different set of cost/value parameters.

The nature of the interest in land, eg freehold interest, leasehold or building lease, will need to be considered. Where existing buildings are acquired and some are occupied by third parties on a continuing basis, the need arises to consider such matters as insurances and other obligations.

Site Management

Site management in a particular instance may require attention to such matters as:

• obtaining possession from any remaining occupiers

• cutting off and securing utility services and apparatus

• demolition of buildings and structures

- fencing and controls against waste dumping, trespassers, squatters and the like

- security services, as appropriate

- archaeological investigation - particularly important in heritage cities, eg York

- previous contaminative use investigations

- remedial works for any contamination

- insurances.

Planning permission process

Planning permission for 'development' is required under the Town and Country Planning Act 1990 prior to commencing the work. Development is defined in section 55 of the 1990 but it may be noted that certain works are not development and some development is 'granted' planning permission by the Town and Country Planning (General Permitted Development) Order 1995, as amended. Similarly, the Town and Country Planning (Use Classes Order) 1987 also 'grants' planning permission for certain changes of use within given classes.

Once full permission is obtained development may start. There are powers by order, rarely used, to modify or revoke permission (under the 1990 Act) before the work is completed or the change of use is operational. If such an order is confirmed compensation for loss or damage may be claimed.

Whether the chosen site is green- or brown-field the prospective owner-occupier may well be able to use the company's pulling-power as an employer - or attractor of employment opportunities - to obtain a valuable building consent which the local planning authority might be reluctant to award to a speculator. The prospect of jobs may sway the views of elected representatives and public officers who might otherwise throw up their hands in horror at the idea of the local environment being offended by a new high-tech building on the edge of their neighbourhood.

In the end, 'politics' will determine the fate of development sensitive on sites, and the best strategy is to try to recognise them and then avoid them unless the political bias is strongly and patently supportive.

The planning permission process may overlap with the acquisition of property. It follows that the property acquisition may best be achieved by a 'conditional' contract, eg a contract to purchase land subject to the grant of planning permission.

Prior to a planning application and decision, the permission process will necessarily involve negotiations with the local planning authority's officers and others on such matters as:

- access to and exit from the site

- uses to which the site will be put

- buildings and structures - including nature, form, height, massing, design and materials to be used in construction

- layout of buildings and structures including loading facilities, open storage, parking and landscaping

- community benefits to be provided by the applicant developer as part of the conditions for allowing the development.

It will, of course, be necessary to obtain approvals under the Building Regulations. Also, it may be necessary to obtain special approvals, eg a listed building consent for heritage property.

Mention has already been made of 'marriage value', and its influence on site values; it may also influence planning control officers where comprehensive, as opposed to piecemeal, development is preferred. Other matters which may affect a particular project at the development control stage may include:

- local government's development planning objectives - resulting in a willingness to support the proposal with incentives, the use of expropriation or compulsory purchase to obtain badly needed land

- public consultation, objection or protest - resulting in excessive delays when not well handled

- special arrangements for reallocation of land in the estate in which the chosen site is available - this may involve private or public exchanges of land with similar valuations (for a fair exchange value)

- where the site is part of an estate - regard to any overall development brief and also the avoidance of adverse effects on the use and value of the owner's retained property

- title insurance for any identified deficiency in an otherwise good title to the land.

Insurances prior to construction

As well as title insurance care should be taken to consider the need for all relevant insurances from the date of contracting to buy the land. Where the buildings on land are to be demolished or land otherwise cleared, the owner and/or potential developer should consider the need for insurance. Thus, land awaiting development may be subjected to trespass, (particularly by children) - and third party liabilities may arise. During demolition contractual insurances should be in place. However, delays may arise if archaeological remains or evidence of previous contaminative uses are discovered.

If either of these last two are suspected earlier in the acquisition process, it may be prudent to have archaeological or environmental studies undertaken and any necessary remedial works carried out thus making it possible to obtain insurance.

Apart from the demolition contractor's insurance, operators of advertisement hoardings, fencing contractors and so on should have appropriate insurances. (See Chapter 3.7 for a fuller treatment of general insurance matters.)

Finance

Unless the developing owner has substantial surplus holdings of cash external funding will be needed. The sources and conditions for obtaining funding are considered in Chapter 10.4. Here it is sufficient merely to understand that there are normally two phases in funding:

- bridging, or development, finance

- long-term finance.

Bridging finance is short-term borrowing - sometimes from the bank or out of cash deposits; as the term implies it helps the developer to carry the costs of the land purchase and the execution of the project up to handover. It is usually paid for at a commercial rate and is expected to be repaid on completion, by which time the owner should have secured the long-term finance, usually by a sale-and-leaseback arrangement or a medium-term commercial mortgage. Both these exit routes will require payment at a lower interest rate than the bridging loan reflecting the fact that the risk of carrying out the development to successful completion has disappeared from the equation.

How to estimate the likely cost of bridging finance is shown in Chapter 10.3.1 (Notes 3A to Fig. 10.3.A) while the various types of short-and-long-term financing for a property development are discussed in greater detail in Chapter 10.4.

An essential feature in obtaining the long-term finance to pay back the bridging loan is that the value of the completed development must be significantly greater than the original amount borrowed (see development cash flow below). Indeed, the initial funds cannot normally be raised unless the development appraisal indicates that the requisite surplus value is available in the completed development to cover the financier's risk.

Where there is some form of leaseback arrangement from an investment institution, eg an insurance company, it is quite common for the bridging finance to come from that same source.

However the bridging finance is raised the project manager will be responsible for producing a development cash flow showing the rate of expenditure, the amount required to be borrowed at any one time and the forecast interest charges. A simple example of what is often a highly complex calculation is given at Fig 10.1.D. In practice interest would be calculated monthly or even daily rather than quarterly as shown here for simplicity. The cash flow is not discounted in this example because it is produced for the purpose of calculating actual funding requirements.

The system presumed in the cash flow is one in which the developer employs a design team to procure and manage a separate construction contract for the works.

In other arrangements such as design/build the cash flows would not be dissimilar although the developer's payments would be going into different pockets at slightly different times.

Fig. 10.1.D
Development cash flow (simplified)

Expenditure	1st quarter	2nd quarter	3rd quarter	4th quarter	5th quarter	6th quarter	7th quarter	8th quarter	Totals
	£ 000	£ 000	£ 000	£ 000	£ 000	£ 000	£ 000	£ 000	£ 000
Land acquisition	(3,200)								(3,200)
Legal and agent's fee	(56)								(56)
Pre-contract design etc. fees	(80)	(240)							(320)
Construction works			(400)	(1,600)	(1,600)	(800)		(400)	(4,800)
Post-contract professional fees			(32)	(32)	(32)	(32)	(16)	(16)	(160)
Marketing / agent's fees								(80)	(80)
Sub-total per quarter	(3,336)	(240)	(430)	(1,632)	(1,632)	(830)	(16)	(500)	(8,616)
Cumulative balance	(3,336)	(3,659)	(4,182)	(5,918)	(7,697)	(8,726)	(8,964)	(9,690)	
Income from sale / investment value								12,800	12,800
Interest on balance at 2.5% per quarter	(83)	(91)	(104)	(147)	(197)	(222)	(229)		(1,074)
Totals	(3,419)	(3,750)	(4,286)	(6,065)	(7,894)	(8,948)	(9,194)	3,110*	3,110*

* This is the gross profit from the development before tax.

The value of the investment on completion shown in the example as £12,800,000 will either be the amount which might be expected to be realised on sale of the building(s) or their value to the beneficial owner.

In the case of commercial buildings like offices and shops developer/users may wish to retain the buildings as an investment probably seeking long-term borrowing; alternatively they may sell or lease the building to an investor and take a lease back to themselves. In either case the value in the open market needs to be established so as to prove the viability of the development in real estate terms.

However, many organisations (such as multi-nationals and institutional users, eg, schools, hospitals and prisons) developing their own sites may choose to ignore market values; they must then make a business case for a development which does not meet normal commercial property profitability criteria. In such cases external funding will not usually be available for the whole amount leaving the user to fund some or all of the development costs out of cash flow. The residual figure of £3,110,000 is the theoretical 'profit' on the development after all costs have been met. Although this profit is unlikely to be realised in cash from an immediate sale of the facility (although user/developers do sometimes manage to profit from sale or leaseback deals) it needs to be there as a risk buffer, as discussed above, if long-term finance is to be secured for the whole cost.

Procuring services

The facilities manager may need to order directly or to liaise with architects and other professionals (advising on a project) about the procurement of services from the statutory supplier, eg electricity, gas, water, for the project. Fig 10.1.E shows the principal services and the legislation governing them.

Fig. 10.1.E
Principal services and legislation

Service	Legislation
Electricity	Electricity Act 1989
Gas	Gas Acts 1986 and 1995
Pipelines	Pipelines Act 1962
Roads (adopted)	Highways Act 1980
Sewers	Water Industry Act 1991
Telecommunications	Telecommunication Act 1984
Trade effluent	Water Industry Act 1991 Part III
Water	Water Industry Act 1991

Electricity: electricity is supplied by the area's privatised supplier at the request of the consumer. If new works, such as cables, pylons or transformers are needed the consumer may be required to pay for them.

Gas: the local licenced gas supplier will normally respond to a request to supply gas to a property provided it is within 23 metres of a gas main (there are exceptions).

Pipelines: pipelines, eg for oil, are an unusual service in that the private 'user' provides the pipeline and uses it thereafter subject to the obtaining of a compulsory rights order under the 1962 Act. Under the order a private person may lay a pipeline on other persons' land, subject to paying compensation.

Roads or streets: generally, highway authorities maintain the principal roads and streets in their area. Where there is a proposed private street, the highway authority may be prepared to adopt it (for future maintenance) after it has been made-up by the developer. (Similarly, an existing private street may be adopted after it has been made up to an approved standard and paid for by the frontagers.) As a general rule developers undertake to construct and pay for new roads but the highway authority will normally require a bond under the 'advanced payments code' of Section 219 of the 1980 Act (to cover the developer's default). As an alternative, the parties may agree to a Section 38 agreement under the 1980 Act. Here the highways authority is covered against a defaulting developer by the frontagers or by a bond put up by the developer.

Sewers, trade effluent and water: the designated water supply company deals with water supplies and connection to sewers for waste and trade effluent. (However, in some places statutory water bodies may still exist in a largely privatised industry in England and Wales). For trade effluent, there are 'trade effluent notice' procedures but negotiated agreements may be a better approach to the body concerned.

Telecommunications: there is a highly competitive industry for telecommunications. Suppliers are governed in what they can supply by the statutory licence they hold. Private negotiation is the norm for such suppliers.

Dispute resolution: where disputes arise in relation to the above various resolution bodies are in place, eg: the Director General of Water Services; the Director General of Gas Supply; the Lands Tribunal (for pipelines); the Director General of Electricity Supply.

Wayleaves and easements: the facilities manager may find that a supplier needs to supply a neighbour and therefore affects one of his or her properties by laying a water or gas pipe, a sewer or a cable (on, over or under the land) with pylons or poles, if necessary. It may be noted that such events require detailed attention and frequently lead to compensation payments. (A brief account of matters to be considered for water mains or sewers is given in Chapter 5.5.8.)

The construction project

The various participants in, and stages of the procurement of a new-build project are all similar to those examined in detail under the fitting-out process in Section 6. However, the nature of a new build is such that there is a far greater scope for error and default than in the simpler interiors projects and the designers and constructors tend to specialise in one field or the other - in a normal market!

Where public buildings or infrastructure are being procured, the facilities manager should ensure that EU requirements for competitive procurement across national borders are observed - see Chapter 6.3.1.

The whole new-build process is infinitely more complex than fitting-out so any decision to increase the pace of the design or construction process, eg as suggested in Chapter 6.3.9 (Fig 6.3.W), needs to be considered most carefully and particularly in the light of the calibre of firms and individuals likely to be available to participate.

The facilities manager is particularly vulnerable at this decision-point and has to take the project manager very much on trust if a fast-track route is agreed, which may be needed to meet the organisation's accommodation requirements. For this reason, some large organisations who procure several buildings over time now find it useful to enter into 'partnering arrangements' with consultants and contractors for several jobs, rather than one.

Chapter 6.3.5 considers construction project insurance in greater detail and only the key issues are summarised here. The all-party 'decennial' insurance cover for construction projects not only provides the relevant risk cover but also appears to have a significant impact on overall efficiency of the process. Elsewhere the professionals need to carry professional indemnity insurance (PII) and the contractor's 'all risks' and 'latent defects' insurances needs to be most carefully scrutinised.

Insurance of the works against damage by fire is normally covered by the builder's all risks insurance but works in existing buildings are often insured separately by the building owner.

Also, consideration of the need for 'performance bonds' might be made. Liability to third parties should be prudently addressed.

The asset management programme

The best time to produce an asset management programme is when the cost plan has been 'signed off' at 'outline proposals' stage of the design and construction programme; in fact the asset management plan, eg as shown in Fig. 2.7.B in Chapter 2.7.3 should emanate directly from the life-cycle building cost plan which informs the decision-making process prior to the building cost plan being adopted by all sides.

The property being developed may well form an important component of the organisation's asset base and requires to be planned and designed with its physical performance under thorough - though not dominant - consideration; remember, it is people and their equipment which are the organisation's biggest assets and their functional interface with the property must always be at the forefront of the facilities manager's mind when dealing with the project manager over matters of building quality and performance.

The handover

The facilities manager will wish to ensure that any defects which arise after handover are dealt with at no cost to the organisation. Ways of dealing with defects include:

- a 'snagging' period for minor 'seen' defects
- insurance cover held by the contractor or professional consultant (or all parties as in 'decennial' insurance policies)
- defects insurance held by the organisation
- guarantees, warranties or bonds held over by the contractor or consultant
- action in law.

Minor defects are usually dealt with in a relatively short period - normally six or twelve months - during which time the builder has to make good any defects arising out of the works but not evident at the handover stage. Usually the architect or engineer, with the project manager's consent, will allow the builder to go around after handover making good the items on a practical completion 'snagging list' of a relatively minor or decorative nature.

For latent or hidden defects practice, once the 'final certificate' is issued, the contractor is liable only for a period of six years (twelve years where the contract is under seal), although there is a longstop of fifteen years under the Latent Defects Limitation Period.

Insurance against latent defects is a highly specialist area and one in which there are currently some interesting new approaches available which the facilities manager should insist upon being fully explored by both the company's and the contractor's insurance broker well before the project is commenced.

Commissioning and occupation

The move into the new premises is considered in Chapter 9.3. On commissioning a number of matters will need to be dealt with, including:

- assessments for local taxation
- execution of any agreements for long term finance, and conclusion of any short term finance agreement
- execution of any lettings to tenants or sub-tenants
- valuation for fire insurance and other insurances, probably as an update
- as required, any registration with the relevant authorities, eg business name and address, cadastre, national and local taxation offices

- liaison with the local bodies for fire, health and safety, police and so on

- the divestment of any shares or interest in the development

- setting up of services, such as security, cleaning, catering and nursery.

Insurance of premises in occupation

As far as insurance is concerned Chapter 3.7 deals with property and other insurance in some detail. Briefly, therefore, issues of insurances for common perils and special perils which might affect the buildings, contents, and occupiers or visitors need to be reviewed. The owner-occupier will either self-insure (to the extent that there is no statutory or contractual obligation to take external policy cover) or seek to pass the risk to an insurer. Where owners sub-lease all or part of the premises the risks may be passed to tenants with an obligation to insure.

Such cover is likely to include:

- fire, flood, tempest

- occupier's liability to third parties

- contents

- employer's insurance against accidents to employees

- insurance against failure of plant and machinery such as boilers and lifts.

10.2   OBJECTIVES UNDERLYING THE DEVELOPMENT PROCESS

Introduction

The facilities manager involved in a new-build development will come upon one or more kinds of developer-entrepreneur, each with somewhat different objectives. Therefore, this chapter begins by identifying the five kinds of developer and then goes on to briefly describe each with reference to such matters as finance, taxation and ownership.

Where the organisation is making a disposal of part of its estate to a developer the facilities manager may need to consider the need to protect the retained property.

10.2.1 PROPERTY DEVELOPERS' ACTIVITIES

Categories

The activities of property developers fall into five categories:

- developer/dealer
- developer/investor
- developer/owner occupier (business, residential or leisure)
- developer/public sector
- developer/voluntary sector.

The facilities manager may come across the developer/dealer in the course of approaches or negotiations to sell part of the organisation's estate to the dealer for the purposes of development or redevelopment. Occasionally organisations may purchase buildings or sites from dealers direct, ie before they have been sold on to real estate investors.

On the other hand the developer/investor may well become the organisation's landlord - even its partner in the provision of new-build facilities leased or sold to the developer and leased back to the organisation on completion of the project as described in Chapter 3.2.5..

A cynic once defined a property developer as 'someone who follows you through a revolving door and comes out in front!' Although this is grossly unfair to very many of the legitimate old-established developers who generate a goodly slice of the country's wealth, the facilities manager should be aware that the apparent rich pickings from development attract some inexperienced but shrewd 'fly-by-night' characters who may act unscrupulously in any dealings.

It is essential to use a reputable and experienced consultant in any property proposal but particularly in dealings with developers.

Developer/dealer

An individual or other 'person' who buys and sells land and buildings as a way of trade is known as a property dealer and is broadly similar in function (for taxation purposes at least) to a property developer who trades by buying land, building on the land and selling the completed properties. Both may act as landlords or even occupy the premises during the period of ownership; nevertheless the intention is trade rather than to invest. Builders of residential property for sale also fall into this group.

Generally, the dealer/developer does not have a long term perspective in the property to be sold, so 'pride of ownership' will not be an underlying motive for design and so on. Nevertheless, good design sells!

For taxation, it is usually clear when a person is trading and usually liable, under the Income and Corporation Taxes Act 1988, to income taxation on trading profits but in some instances recourse to law will require a review to determine the objectives of the taxpayer. It is outside the scope of this work to examine the subject in detail.

A developer/dealer does not usually pay tax on capital gains on the disposal of land which is stock-in-trade. However, disposal of any capital asset, eg the premises from which the business is run, may give rise to tax on capital gains under the Taxation of Capital Gains Act 1992.

As the prime purpose is trading or dealing, the duration of borrowing the funds required for this purpose is likely to be short term or medium term or both.

Commercial, industrial and other developers, eg for offices, shops, and industrial premises, who intend to sell are likely to use short term borrowing for the duration of construction, obtaining funds from merchant banks, joint stock banks and other 'short term' providers of funds. Whilst agreeing such finance, long term arrangements will be explored so that repayment may be at the end of the development period. This may be by way of outright sale of the freehold interest or headlease held by the developer.

Sometimes one of several forms of sale and leaseback (see Chapter 3.2.5) may be arranged, so enabling the developer to retain an interest for a longer period; but this implies an investment policy rather than dealing.

Developer/investor

An individual or other body may buy land, develop it, and hold the completed building as an investment for letting. There are numerous ways in which funds may be made available for this operation.

In the main direct property investment outside the institutional sector has been by property investment companies with shareholders' funds sometimes being relatively highly geared (with a high ratio of borrowings to initial investment value) by debentures and loans. Sometimes in the past the institutions would lend on a long term basis but this has not generally been the case in the last twenty years, with equity participation tending to supplant such loans.

In the past, the property investment companies have also adopted project funding arrangements by mortgages or by sale and leaseback arrangements of various kinds. In more recent times bank lending, debentures or rights issues have become prevalent, particularly as the institutions have tended to move into direct development through partnering with developers or using development project management consultants.

Generally, the traditional mortgage and sale and leaseback may be described as the most popular means of funding for long term retention of the property. People have different views on the relative advantages and disadvantages of these methods. The commercial mortgage, subject to interest rates, may seem more attractive in times of high inflation but the sale and leaseback enables the retention of realised capital profits whilst exposing the tenant to commercial market rents (possibly less than full market levels) in the future.

Motives underlying ownership vary considerably. Long term ownership is a perspective so pride of ownership in the sense of meeting tenants' requirements or needs will often be apparent, particularly where the developer/investor is involved with heritage or image pointers.

The net income of a property investment is taxed under the Income and Corporation Taxes Act 1988.

Also, the taxpayer will probably be able to offset against taxable income interest on loans provided if there is a 'qualifying purpose', eg the purchase of land, or improving or developing land or building on the land.

Disposal of an asset usually results in liability to some form of capital gains tax, subject to any exemptions or reliefs which may be available. The charge is more often than not the current corporation tax rate applied to the chargeable gain as far as companies are concerned, unless the company is a small one. It is likely that individuals pay capital gains tax at standard and top rate income tax, as appropriate, but an annual relief is available.

Developer/owner-occupier

The facilities manager is almost certain to be heavily involved where the organisation is developing land for its own occupation. The property thereby created will be a capital asset and will usually be procured with the view to long term ownership. One or more of the various forms of corporate or project funding are likely to be available (see Chapter 10.4). In some circumstances public funds may be available under various financial incentive schemes (see Chapters 10.4 and 10.5).

Development for owner-occupation often involves a prestige commercial building of a style which would not usually be available from an investor landlord. Similarly, industrial property may involve modern conventional buildings but often requires bespoke buildings or extensive structural elements, plant and machinery or both. Disregarding these special aspects of owner-occupational needs in terms of appraisal, the decision to invest in property, ie land and buildings, for owner occupation may be measured by reference to the internal rate of return. Whereas property returns may be expected to be generally very much lower than "business" returns, some organisations will, nevertheless, invest in property for their own occupation to establish full control and to avoid paying future market rentals. The reverse happens when a sale and leaseback is transacted by the owner-occupier.

As far as the taxation of profit is concerned, the profit due to rent saved by owner-occupation of buildings whether absolute in possession interest or long leasehold without rent reviews, is normally reflected in the assessment of the business as such.

Similarly, any premium paid under a short lease or certain other transactions may attract taxation. If the buildings or plant and machinery are eligible, capital allowances may be claimed under the relevant legislation (see Chapter11.2).

Developer/public sector

The facilities manager in the public sector will probably not be involved with buildings in the common categories, such as offices, shops and industrial premises. Their concern is more likely to be procurement of bespoke hospitals, schools, clinics, town halls and the like. Apart from the usual development and building controls, these institutional buildings are likely to be regulated by specific standards and requirements.

Sometimes, they will involve political and public participation processes which do not usually arise in the provision of more commonplace buildings by the private sector. Increasingly, the Private Finance Initiative (PFI)/Public Private Partnership (PPP) approach to procurement has been required of public bodies (see Chapters 3.5.13, 6.3 and 10.4.6).

Funding of public projects may involve allocations from public authority' revenues or by way of bond issues, specific or general. Where PFI/PPP is involved a mix of public and private funding might be expected.

Developments in this sector usually have to be in accordance with fairly stringent tests of affordability based on conventional and/or historic cost levels.

Many public bodies may have available to them powers of expropriation of land.

Developer/voluntary sector

As far as the voluntary sector is concerned, the buildings will often be unusual, linked to charitable purposes such as a hospice, clinic, orphanage or refuge. Funding may involve a protracted public fund raising process and/or application to charitable trusts, such that the facilities are provided in stages.

Cost levels are usually geared to available funds rather than any perception of value, and often suffer functionally through under-funding.

10.2.2 THE DEVELOPMENT OPTIONS

Premises options

In Chapter 9.1 the principles of relocation were examined and examples given of the various appraisal techniques. As far as whether or not to develop is concerned, where an organisation needs more or better accommodation the facilities manager might consider the options at any particular time as being:

- do nothing, ie rationalise the existing space - or hope the problem will go away!

- expand on the existing site with new development (see Chapter 3.8.2 on configuration obsolescence)

- acquire adjoining property for expansion

- acquire land or a property - new site - elsewhere for development or redevelopment.

Do nothing

There is actually no such thing as a 'do nothing' option: it exists only in the minds of finance directors who do not (or will not) have access to the funds needed to meet the organisation's accommodation needs.

The least the organisation can do is to re-arrange its furniture, weed out under-utilised or redundant facilities and/or increase the numbers of people reporting to or temporarily occupying each designed space.

However, sooner or later something has to give, and usually the delay in acting costs a lot more indirectly than any direct savings in premises costs.

Expand on the existing site with new development

The property has vacant space or options for space to be created by alterations, improvements, or redevelopment. Generally the facilities manager will be concerned to minimise disruption of the company's existing operations and to maintain the appropriate level of services.

This option involves building works to different levels of complexity, such as from the basic fitting-out in existing space to the redevelopment (in stages, no doubt), of the whole building. (The expansion may involve, in due course, vacating part or all of the old space, and either closing it down or letting it to one or more tenants.)

Acquire adjoining property for expansion

The purchase of an existing adjoining freehold interest or taking a lease in it will involve the kind of analysis described in Chapter 3.5. This is strictly not a development option though in most cases a bespoke fit out will be necessary and some alterations will be required.

Acquire land and/or a property and develop/redevelop as a new site

This option may result from a long term strategy to consolidate the company property holdings on one site. It requires a fuller analysis than the previous options but can be carried out by occupiers under their own project management or with the help of professional development project managers. These professionals must have skills mirroring those of their counterparts employed to do a similar job in property development companies. Provided the skill base is strong enough there is no reason why the internally managed project should be any less successful than one carried out by a property development company and in the process avoid the latter's substantial oncost for overheads, risk and profit.

10.2.3 DISPOSAL FOR REDEVELOPMENT OF PART OF A HOLDING

From time to time the facilities manager may be involved in disposing of part of a property for redevelopment.

The need for professional advice cannot be over-emphasised, eg for valuation, planning, building, legal and taxation matters. The facilities manager is likely to be involved in such matters as the following:

- ensure retention of sufficient lands/property for the organisation's future requirements

- with regard to the retained property, what needs to be safeguarded, eg rights of way, light, cables or pipes, views

- restrictions on the property to be sold or leased, eg the form of any development, use of materials, boundary fencing, overlooking windows

- the legal rights being disposed of, eg a freehold

- the method of disposal, eg private treaty negotiations, auction or tender

- the documentation required, eg agreement for lease and lease, building lease, development brief, auction or tender particulars

- scope to realise so-called "marriage value", eg by sale to an adjoining owner or to a developer who has a land assembly operation in the locality

- limitation of the use or uses to which the property may be put, eg by imposing restrictive covenants.

Where a public body is using expropriation or compulsory purchase, the compensation and "accommodation works", eg, new fences will need to be evaluated by professionals, maybe in conjunction with the facilities manager.

10.3 THE ECONOMICS OF DEVELOPMENT

Introduction

Many of the technical terms used in this chapter are explained in Part B - Real Estate - and in other chapters in Section 10. This chapter considers how costs and value are used in various forms of financial appraisal of development opportunities.

10.3.1 THE DEVELOPMENT BUDGET

The development equation

Like economic appraisal of any other product, the development equation says simply that:

Value less Costs = Profit.

Although this is a simple concept the difficulty in creating a successful project lies in the fact that not only are the end value and demand difficult to predict but also the level of costs tends to be volatile at every stage from inception to completion. So it is the prediction, rather than the mathematics, which makes development appraisal a minefield for all but the expert.

The development process gets under way with a prediction of the out-turn costs, values and profits emanating from a development of a specific building type (or complex) and of a predicted size - usually described by floor area. This appraisal is based on what is commonly termed the 'development budget'; its first practical application will be to calculate how much the developer can afford to pay for the land.

Components of the development budget

The developer will have to take account of four main groups of factors in preparing the project development budget and they can be briefly summarised as follows.

Types of property: for any type of property the value of which is not conventionally geared to its rental or trading income potential, eg residential property for sale with vacant possession to owner occupiers, these factors comprise:

- selling price.

- annual ground rent (where applicable)

- expected market yield (of ground rent, if any)

- selling costs.

For income or investment property, eg commercial, industrial or residential for leasing, these factors comprise:

- rentable floor area

- achievable annual rent from rentable floor area

- non-rental income

- annual management expenses (where not recoverable under a service charge)

- expected market yield (or market capitalisation rate)

- leasing costs and commissions.

Land costs: factors related to the cost of the land:

- basic cost of the land

- acquisition costs (agency and legal)

- finance charges on the land and acquisition costs.
- costs of obtaining possession from any occupiers
- any site management costs prior to commencement of construction
- any remedial works due to past contamination
- costs of any archaeological investigation.

Building costs: factors related to the developer's building cost:

- basic cost of building and site development
- professional fees, eg architect, cost consultant, structural, mechanical and electrical engineers and soil analysts
- finance charges on the building cost and professional fees.

Risk and profit: a margin to cover the developer's overheads, profit requirement and development risk.

The facilities manager is unlikely to be concerned with any form of residential development, so the chapter concentrates solely on the 'commercial' category of property development. However the principles are applicable to any category of user.

Applications of the development equation

The development equation which, as illustrated above, shows how to calculate the residual profit, is adapted in practice to calculate each of the four principal development budget components using actual or predicted values for the other three. Most commonly it is used by the developer to calculate the residual land value, ie the maximum amount they can afford to pay for the land given specific assumptions on end value, development costs and a required profit margin.

Land value: in this case referring to the four budget components above - the Building Costs (BC) and required Development Profit (P) are subtracted from the Capital Value of the completed Development (CV) to arrive at the Residual Land Value or Land Cost (LC). Thus:

$$CV - (BC + P) = LC$$

Profit: second, where the developer knows the land cost and has estimated the building cost and end value they are able to calculate their profit margin or return on investment. Thus:

$$CV - (LC + BC) = P$$

Building cost: third, where the developer has been offered a plot of land at a fixed price, has estimated the end value and decided on the minimum profit required for the development, then a target building cost, ie the maximum that can be spent on the building, can be calculated. Thus:

$$CV - (LC + P) = BC$$

Property value: the fourth use is for the purposes of valuations based on cost (see Chapters 3.5.6 and 3.7.5) where the appraiser wants to know the end 'value' produced by adding together all the costs plus a required profit margin. Thus:

$$CV = (LC + BC + P)$$

The 'value' in this case is, of course, highly unlikely to equate to the true market value of a conventional development, and would only be used where no such value could be assessed.

Explanation of the components and factors

The following are brief explanations of the above components (or their factors) as they would normally appear in a development budget.

The capitalised value of completed commercial development is the net annual income from the development (gross rental income plus 'other' income less outgoings), capitalised by use of an appropriate 'multiplier' (or 'years purchase' figure) to reflect the interest rate required to attract investors to purchase the property (ie expected market yield). Thus, if investors expect initial net earnings to show an 8% return on investment (100) then the investment (or capitalised) value of the property is the years purchase (100 ÷ 8 = 12.5) x net earnings; this calculation is considered in detail in Chapter 3.5.3.

This method is the one most widely used in the property industry for assessing investment values and corresponds to the simple 'rate of return' formula where initial or current net income is expressed as a percentage of the purchase price to calculate the investment yield. The capitalisation rate is then the reciprocal of the yield,

ie $\frac{100}{X}$ where X is the percentage rate of return.

(The result is frequently called the 'years purchase'.)

Leasing, selling costs and commissions include any real estate agent's commission and advertising or any costs of a direct sale. Costs here normally constitute up to 10% of the initial gross annual rent, ie between 0.5% and 1% of the capital value of the completed development.

At initial feasibility study the basic cost of building and site development will normally be calculated per square metre of the gross internal area. The unit price must include the cost of any demolition and site management/development work. On schemes of any size the works will normally be costed in some detail prior to committing to land purchase, but in a 'bull' market speculators may take a chance on the unitary rate method. Costs of the remediation of contaminated land or archaeological investigation may need to be considered.

Professional fees (building work) include the costs of services provided by the architect and cost consultant and in many cases, the services of a structural, mechanical and electrical engineer and soil analyst. Fees are conventionally expressed as a percentage of the building costs, and the appraiser should round the percentage figure upwards to allow for incidental expenses - such as printing etc. Fees should be calculated separately even where a design-and-build contract is envisaged.

Acquisition costs include any agent's fees for introducing the site and the legal costs of establishing title, preparing contracts, payment of stamp duty, effecting indemnity insurance and the like.

The allowance for developer's overheads, profit and risk provides a return to the developer for devoting their skill and time to the development, for the risk that they undertake, and to offset the overhead costs of their organisation.

Finance charge covers the interest chargeable on the loan or equity capital required to carry the costs of the land, building and professional fees, during the period of the development. A notional interest charge should always be included for the equity capital element since, by using their own capital, the developer forfeits the opportunity of gaining a return from an alternative investment - 'the opportunity cost' in management accountancy terms.

Chapter 11.5 examines Value Added Tax (VAT). For present purposes it is sufficient to note that VAT is generally chargeable on construction cost and all fees in connection with commercial development and refurbishment, subject to exceptions.

The tax may also be chargeable on the sale of absolute in possession interest or leasehold land if the vendor so elects; otherwise it is exempt. The same applies to the onward sale of the completed building. However, once the land has been charged VAT through 'election to waive exemption', all subsequent transactions must be charged at applicable rate.

The tax is ultimately recoverable providing the developer is registered for VAT, and is considered to be the builder for VAT purposes. The only costs incurred by the developer are the extra finance charges on the tax until recovery, and some overhead and administration costs. These may, however, be deductible for income taxation.

Therefore, when calculating the building cost when VAT is standard rated, or selecting a percentage to cover professional fees or acquisition costs, the cost of VAT should be included so that the finance charges will automatically be included as well. The recoverable amounts should then be deducted as appropriate. However, it is quite common for VAT to be excluded from preliminary development appraisal unless the developer is unable to recover it.

The development budget in use - example

Although the development budget is normally worked through a detailed cash flow appraisal programme most developers still tend to appraise schemes at an early feasibility stage using simple arithmetical calculations with rule-of-thumb calculations for interest charges. The following examples demonstrating the practical use of the development budget are therefore worked on these simple principles.

The first example shows how a developer would normally set about estimating profit margin (or the annual return on investment) on the construction of an investment property, on the basis of known land and building costs [Equation as above: CV - (LC + BC) = P].

Example A:

An office development with a gross internal floor area of 930 sq m is to be built. If the factors given below are expected, what profit can the developer expect to make, assuming a sale to an investor? The factors are:

- non-rentable floor area is expected to be 15% of gross internal area (ie net internal area is 85% of gross)

- annual rent will be £300/sq m of net internal (rentable) area

- the expected market yield (or market capitalisation rate) will be 8% (12.5YP)

- total building costs (including demolitions, site development etc.) will be £1,300/sq m of gross internal area

- professional fees will be 10% of the total building cost

- construction contract period will be 1 year

- finance charges on building costs and associated professional fees will be 11% pa compound

- purchase price of land is £927,550

- land acquisition costs will be 3.5% of the land cost

- development period will be 1.5 years (assuming immediate letting)

- finance charges on land and acquisition costs will be 11% pa compound

- initial leasing commissions will be 10% of first year's gross rental income

- value added tax is omitted for simplicity.

From the above data the developer would normally estimate their before-tax development profit as shown in Fig. 10.3.A.

Capital value of completed development						
Gross internal area sq m GIA	Less non-rentable area: 15% sq m GIA	Rentable floor area sq m NIA	Rent / pa per sq m NIA £	Total rent pa £	Capitalisation factor at 8% initial yield	Capital value £
A	B	A-B	C	(A-B)xC=D	E	DxE
1000	(150)	850	300	255,000	12.5YP	3,187,500

Development cost			£	
Land costs	Purchase price	(927,550)		
	Acquisition costs (3.5%)	(32,464)		
	Finance charges at 11% pa compound over 1.5 years (note A1) development period on £ 960,014 x 0.165	(158,402)		
Building and site development costs	1,000 sq m gross floor area at £ 1,300 per sq m GIA	(1,300,000)		
	Finance charges (monthly cash flow basics) 0.5 x 11% pa for 1 year construction contract period (note A2)	(71,500)		
Professional fees	10% of building cost	(130,000)		
	Finance charges (monthly cash flow basis) 0.75 x 11% pa for 1 year construction contract period (note A3)	(10,725)		
Other costs	Initial leasing commissions (10% of gross rent for first year)	(25,500)		
Total development cost		**(2,656,141)**		**(2,656,141)**
Residual profit (before tax)				**531,359***
* This represents a profit of 20% on capital expenditure (total development cost)				

Notes to Fig 10.3.A:

Note A1: Because the land is usually purchased before the building contracts are produced it is necessary to add a period on to the building contract period to cover this elapsed time.

If it is anticipated that there may be a 'void' between completion and rental income then a further period should be added to the development period and a similar allowance made in respect of the full amount of the building and site development costs for the whole amount of the elapsed time.

Note A2: Most building contracts provide for monthly payments to the contractor based on valuations of the work carried out in the particular month; for the purpose of calculating finance charges on the building cost, it is sufficiently accurate at the first feasibility study to assume that the monthly payments are equal throughout the building contract period for each phase of the development. Since the employer will only borrow money to make the monthly payments as they become due, it follows that finance charges will average out at the full interest rate over half of the building contract period. This rule-of-thumb therefore approximates the results of a cash flow forecast and probably is as accurate as a full cash flow analysis given that all figures are normally only predictions anyway.

Note A3: the greater proportion of architects' and engineers' fees are normally due to be paid on completion of the contract documents (ie drawings, specifications, etc). The remainder of the fees are then paid in instalments over the building contract period.

As with the building costs the employer will only borrow to make the payments as they become due; practice has shown that it is sufficiently accurate, at the first feasibility study, to assume that the finance charges on the professional fees, for each phase of the development, will average out at the full interest rate over three quarters of the building contract period.

Example B:

The second example at Fig. 10.3.B is of the same project but illustrates how the developer can calculate how much to offer for the land given that they must make a given capital profit of 20% on their development expenditure.

Fig. 10.3.B
Development appraisal - calculation of residual land value

Capital value of completed development						
Gross internal area sq m GIA	Less non-rentable area: 15% sq m GIA	Rentable floor area sq m NIA	Rent / pa per sq m NIA £	Total rent pa £	Capitalisa-tion factor at 8% initial yield	Capital value £
A	B	A-B	C	(A-B)xC=D	E	DxE
1000	(150)	850	300	255,000	12.5YP	3,187,500

Development cost		£	
Profit	20% of expenditure, ie 16.67% capital value (note B1)	(531,356)	
Building and site development costs	1,000 sq m gross floor area at £ 1,300 per sq m GIA	(1,300,000)	
	Finance charges (monthly cash flow basis) 0.5 x 11% pa for 1 year construction contract period	(71,500)	
Professional fees	10% of building cost	(130,000)	
	Finance charges (monthly cash flow basis) 0.75 x 11% pa for 1 year construction contract period	(10,725)	
Other costs	Initial leasing commissions (10% of gross rent for first year)	(25,500)	
Sub-total		(2,069,081)	(2,069,081)
Gross residual land value			1,118,419
Land finance and acquisition costs	Eliminate finance at 11% pa over 1.5 years development period ÷ 1.165 (note B2)		960,016
	Eliminate acquisition costs 3.5% of land costs ÷ 1.035 (note B3)		927,552
Net residual land value			927,552

The resultant residual land value is virtually the same as used in the first example; this is because a minimum profit figure of 20% of the capital expenditure is used here and the actual profit in the first example was deducted on the same basis.

The residual method of land valuation described here is preferred for development appraisal. The merits and demerits of other approaches such as the 'comparative method' are discussed below.

Notes to Fig 10.3.B:

Note B1: the allowance for developer's overheads, profit and risk is normally expressed as a percentage of the capital expenditure. However, when preparing a 'residual land valuation' the capital expenditure is not known to start with, since the cost of the land (to be found) is part of that capital expenditure. It is therefore necessary for the amount to be reserved for profit on capital expenditure to be expressed as a percentage of the expected capital value of the completed development.

To convert Profit as a percentage of Capital Expenditure (PE%) to Profit as a percentage of Capital Value of completed development (PV%) the formula is:

$$\frac{PE\%}{100 + PE\%} \quad x \quad \frac{100}{1} = PV\%$$

The principle behind the calculation of that percentage can best be demonstrated by considering a development budget to calculate developer's profit, expressed in the simplest possible terms in Fig. 10.3.C.

Fig. 10.3.C
Development appraisal - calculation of profit on capital value

Item	Development Costs £	Capital Value £
Capital value of complete development (CV)		120,000
Less :		
Total cost of land (LC)	(50,000)	
Total cost of building (BC)	(50,000)	
Total capital expenditure		(100,000)
Developer's risk an d profit incl. overheads		20,000
Profit as a % of Capital Expenditure (PE%)	= $\frac{20,000}{100,000}$ = 20%	
Profit as a % Capital Value (PV%)	= $\frac{20,000}{120,000}$ = 16.66%	

Fig. 10.3.D (over the page) illustrates this concept graphically.

Note B2: the gross land value which has been calculated at this stage of the valuation includes the net cost of the land, land acquisition costs and finance charges. The simplest way to eliminate the finance charges is to multiply by the appropriate 'Present Value Factor' for the particular interest rate over the development period. Discount or Valuation Tables can be used to obtain the 'PV Factor' (see Chapters 2.3.7 and 10.6.3). Since the Present Value is the reciprocal of the compound interest the example shows how to make the adjustment if discount tables are not to hand; in this case 1½ years @ 11% gives a compound interest multiplier of 1.165, so the present value factor is $\frac{1}{1.165}$ which makes a divisor of 1.165 to eliminate the finance content of the gross residual value.

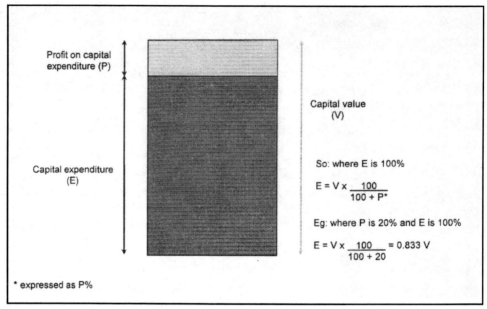

Profit on capital expenditure (P)

Capital expenditure (E)

Capital value (V)

So: where E is 100%

$$E = V \times \frac{100}{100 + P^*}$$

Eg: where P is 20% and E is 100%

$$E = V \times \frac{100}{100 + 20} = 0.833\ V$$

* expressed as P%

Regardless of the various patterns which developments take, the development period in this context is deemed to be between the date of completing the purchase of the land and the selling or letting of the completed development; therefore since the land acquisition and fees must be paid for at the start of the development period, it then follows that finance charges must be allowed for on the whole amount over the whole period - see also Note A1 to Fig 10.3.A above).

Note B3: the figure now arrived at, say Z, includes the net cost of the land and land acquisition costs. Land acquisition costs are expressed as a percentage of the net land cost (A%).

Therefore to eliminate land acquisition costs:

Deduct $Z \times \dfrac{A}{100 + A}$

Say Z = £100,000

A = 3.5%

Net cost of land but including acquisition costs at 3.5%	=	£100,000
Deduct land acquisition costs: £100,000 $\times \dfrac{3.5}{100 + 3.5}$	=	(£3,382)
Therefore Residual Land Value	=	£96,618

(As a double check on this calculation 3½% of £96,618 = £3,382).

In the calculation in the example at Fig. 10.3.B a short cut has been taken, eliminating the acquisition costs by dividing by the factor representing the inclusive figure ie 100 + 3.5 = 103.5 therefore:

$\dfrac{103.5}{100}$ is the dividing factor

The visual representation of this calculation at Fig. 10.3.E (over the page) illustrates this calculation, as also does the profit elimination described in Note B1 above.

Guide to selection of development budget factors

When calculating the 'Residual Land Value', 'Residual Profit' or 'Residual Building Cost' for a particular development it will often be the case that not all the values of the development budget factors are known. However, in such circumstances it should

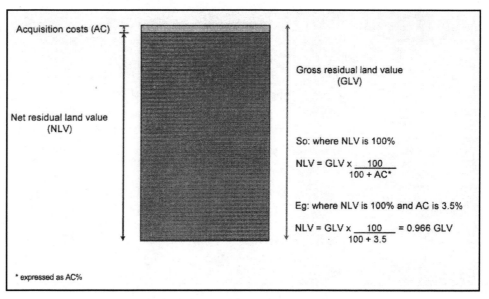

Fig. 10.3.E
Graphic illustration of mathematical relationship between acquisition costs and gross and net residual value

Acquisition costs (AC)

Net residual land value (NLV)

Gross residual land value (GLV)

So: where NLV is 100%

$$NLV = GLV \times \frac{100}{100 + AC^*}$$

Eg: where NLV is 100% and AC is 3.5%

$$NLV = GLV \times \frac{100}{100 + 3.5} = 0.966 \ GLV$$

* expressed as AC%

always be possible to make a reasonable assessment and non-experts may find this guide to the selection of the various factors helpful.

Non-rentable floor area percent of gross internal area: generally, it will be the architect's aim to create the maximum permissible rentable floor area. As shown in Chapter 4.1 this area is calculated by measuring between the inside faces of the external walls (this calculates the gross internal area) and then, in the case of offices for instance, omitting staircases, landlord's, ie public, circulation spaces, toilets and amenity areas, plant rooms and any other non-usable space.

Unfortunately the term gross floor area (or gross floor space) is often used in development control to calculate the ratio of built area to site area (plot ratio). When used in this context it is the total area of the building measured from the outside face of the external walls. The actual area of external walls will normally be between 2% - 6% of the 'gross' depending on the thickness of the wall construction and the shape of the building (ie the wall/floor ratio).

In blocks of offices and multi-storey apartments the proportion of non-rentable floor area to gross floor area can be expected to increase with the height of the building. The variation is such that in a typical four-storey block the non-rentable floor area might be approximately 15% of the gross floor area, whereas in an 18-storey block it could even be as much as 25 to 30%. Much depends also on the amount of plant and riser space required for any air-conditioning system.

In single storey shops, warehouses and factories it can generally be assumed that the whole gross floor area will be rentable, ie non-rentable floor area is 0% of gross internal area. The productive floor area of hotels and restaurants should be assessed by inspection.

Minimum profit required on capital expenditure: the amount of profit to be included in the development budget will be determined by such factors as risk, overheads and competition. Assuming that all items of capital expenditure (including 'opportunity costs') are taken into account, most developers (and their financiers) will require a minimum profit/surplus of between 15% and 33.33% of capital expenditure.

Expected initial yield will undoubtedly be the single most important factor to assess in any budget for a commercial or industrial development. To arrive at a realistic result this factor should be assessed by an experienced valuer but for purposes of initial high level feasibility studies reference can be made to guides published by some of the more reputable real estate consultancies an example of which is given in Chapter 3.5.

Rent reviews at intervals of less than five years will cause the expected initial yield to drop and conversely reviews at longer intervals will cause it to rise, perhaps by as much as 1.5%.

At the early feasibility stage investors and developers do not always make a separate allowance for the provision of a sinking fund as part of the outgoings but adjust the expected market yield to allow for it. Discount and valuation tables include a dual-rate table for calculating the necessary adjustment - see also Chapter 3.5. It must be stressed however that any 'rules-of-thumb' described above should only be used for preliminary appraisal and only when the services of an experienced valuer are not readily available.

Annual rents recently commanded by prime properties (generally new buildings in good locations) in various EU locations are given in Fig 10.3.F. For investment appraisal purposes, it may be deemed prudent to inflate the figures presented here in making an assessment of future rental growth.

Fig. 10.3.F
Office rents across the EU

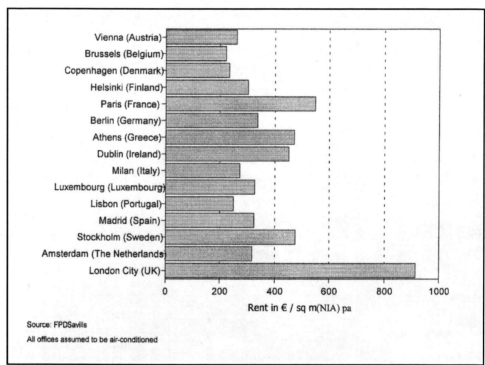

Construction contract period is a factor which will obviously vary considerably depending on the type of building, form of construction, size, site conditions and the like. Various methods of speeding up the construction/development period are available but often carry a higher risk; this should be reflected in the construction cost forecast, the required profit margin - or both.

Professional fees on building cost payable to the architect, cost consultant, structural engineer and mechanical and electrical engineers usually amount to between 3% and 12.5% of the building cost for commercial and industrial development. The actual level will depend on the size and complexity of the project and the state of the market at any one time. Developers can sometimes get a very good price from construction professionals - time alone will of course show whether the savings made will be offset by expensive problems down the line. Where applicable the technical audit process necessary in support of the 'decennial' insurance policy can add between 1% and 5% to the cost of the project.

Finance charges: rate of interest per annum compound; bridging finance charges for property development can normally be obtained at standard commercial rates of interest. If the developer intends to invest capital the calculations should be based on the 'opportunity cost' of an interest rate equivalent to the company's internal rate of return adjusted for the risk factor.

Building costs: quite clearly, a realistic estimate of the likely final building costs of any particular building, can only be prepared by an experienced cost consultant from drawings and specifications. However, this is not always possible and for the purposes of a preliminary feasibility study it is not necessary to be so precise.

With the advancement of cost data-bases and cost planning techniques it has become possible to state with a reasonable degree of certainty that, at any given time, a particular type of building could be built within a given cost limit.

Figs 10.3.G and H give a range of prices in Euros per sq m of gross internal area for construction of offices and industrial buildings in UK and other EU locations.

Fig. 10.3.G
Typical international office building costs per sq m GIA across the EU

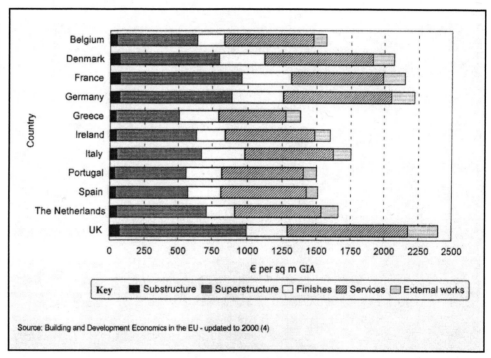

Fig. 10.3.H
Typical industrial building costs per sq m GIA across the EU

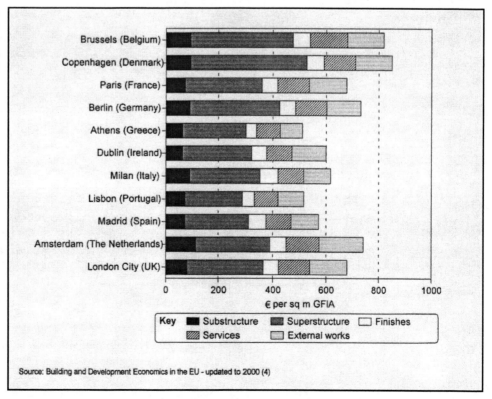

All the prices in these figures exclude external works, furniture, equipment and professional fees and assume a basic set of conditions:

- that the prices reflect the national average (due to market factors such as demand and supply of labour and materials, workload, taxation, and grants, a location factor should be applied to allow for abnormal regional variations).

- that no exceptionally difficult site conditions pertain

- that the building will have 'normal' foundations relative to local conditions

- that the contract prices will be obtained on the best terms available

- that adequate cost control will be exercised during the design and construction stages

- that a normal building period will be available

- that the prices are as tendered by contractor to developer - they may not be applicable to builder/developers, ie builders undertaking development also sometimes subsume their net building costs into the budget before development profit is calculated.

Land acquisition costs (agency and legal): professional fees for acquiring land are charged by the letting agent and solicitor in respect of the following services:

- agent's fee - for introducing the site and negotiating the sale

- solicitor's fee - for establishing title, preparing contracts, payment of stamp duty and effecting indemnity insurance and the like.

Fees and costs together usually amount to a total of between 3.5% and 5% of the land cost.

Development period: regardless of the various patterns which developments take, it is assumed in the examples above that the development period is between the date of purchasing the land and the date of selling or renting the completed development.

As discussed briefly in Note A1 to the worked example above the development period can be considered in three parts: (i) between the purchase of the land and the start of the building contract period, (ii) the building contract period; (iii) the 'void' between the end of the building contract period and the selling or renting of the completed development. It will obviously be in the interest of any developer to restrict the development period to a minimum to keep down the costs of finance and overheads.

Between the date of purchase of the land and the start of building it may be necessary to obtain planning permission (except, of course, where there is an option or conditional contract subject to planning permission and other statutory consents). Designs have to be developed, tenders obtained and building contract documents prepared. For most conventional developments this should take between three months and nine months.

Depending on the economic climate and quality of the development, it can sometimes take several months after completion of the building to sell or let the finished development. Therefore in the absence of details six months to one year might reasonably be added to the building contract period in estimating the development period to cover for this risk. The 'void' period would, of course, only be relevant to owner/occupier (or any other user concerned with the development) if part of the space was to be leased out for the short/medium term.

Selling costs on sale price include any agent's commission and advertising or any costs of a direct sale. Agency and promotional costs normally constitute up to 2.5% of the sale price.

10.3.2 LAND-USE ECONOMICS

Enhancing the land value

Even the most casual observers of the activities of property developers will be aware that there are three principal ways in which a developer, land-owner or land-speculator can make an increased profit out of development land:

- to obtain valuable building consent on land without consent and bought cheaply
- to get an improved building consent on land bought on the basis of an earlier approval
- 'marriage value', ie assembling two or more sites cheaply then merging them into one site for development purposes with a total value greater than the sum of the two parts taken in isolation
- acquiring key sites which unlock development value on other land, eg to provide access to back-land owned by others.

Depreciation of land value

Fig. 10.3.J
Negative residual land value resulting from changes in the value assumptions at Fig 10.3.B

Capital value of completed development						
Gross internal area sq m GIA	Less non-rentable area: 15% sq m GIA	Rentable floor area sq m NIA	Rent / pa per sq m NIA £	Total rent pa £	Capitalisa-tion factor at 10% initial yield	Capital value £
A	B	A-B	C	(A-B)xC=D	E	DxE
1,000	(200)	800	200	160,000	10YP	1,600,000

Development cost			£	
Profit	16.67% x £ 1,600,000		(266,720)	
Building and site development costs	1,000 sq m GIA at £ 1,300 per sq m gross internal area		(1,300,000)	
	Finance charges (monthly cash flow basics) 0.5 x 11% pa for 1 year construction contract period		(71,500)	
Professional fees	10% of building cost		(130,000)	
	Finance charges (monthly cash flow basis) 0.75 x 11% pa for 1 year construction contract period		(10,725)	
Other costs	Initial leasing commissions (10% of gross rent for first year)		(16,000)	
Sub-total			(1,764,945)	(1,764,945)
Gross residual land value				(194,945)
Land finance and acquisition costs	Eliminate finance at 11% pa over 1.5 years development period ÷ 1.165			N/A
	Eliminate acquisition costs 3.5% of land costs ÷ 1.035			N/A
Net residual land value				**Negative**

Generally speaking most landowners have become wise to these clever ruses and it is unusual for developers these days to 'beat the system' in the spectacular manner of some of their predecessors. However, it is not always win/win for developers; sometimes land can have a negative residual value as is shown in Fig 10.3.J (previous page). Here the dual causes of the problem lie in the inefficient ratio of rentable to gross floor area and a market yield of only 10% compared to 8% in Fig. 10.3.B combining to reduce the value of the completed development by a substantial amount.

Fig 10.3.K indicates how the impact of dramatically falling development values affected land values across the range of UK locations in the severe recession of the early 1990's. It may be noted how the 1993 reduction in rent and increase in initial market yield reduced the City of London capital value (and hence land value) from the 1989 level in this example. In spite of lower construction costs the residual land value in 1993 was less than one-third of its 1989 boom figure.

Fig. 10.3.K
Changes in the development equation in a city and a provincial centre over a period of severe recession

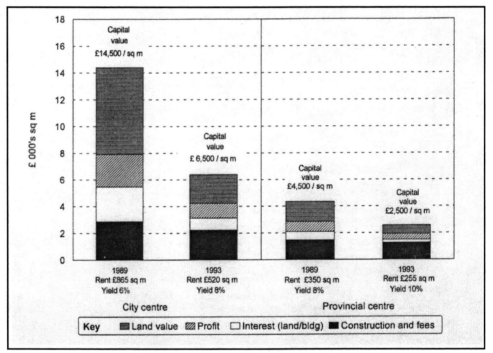

The land value has reached rock bottom in the provincial centre in the example, even with a lower building performance and cost and easier finance rates - if available at all for such a project. The problem is that the capital values are decimated by the high yield of 10% which gives only ten years' purchase of the lowish rent. Of course, when supply dries up through lack of a decent price structure pent-up demand will coax it back to the market merely because of the 'weight of money' available to drive the price up in a market short of suitable property.

Normally yields recover quite quickly post-recession, for two reasons. First, there are pent up funds anxiously looking for a home in the generally inflation-proof property investments. Second, the initial yield will most likely be geared to depressed rental levels, giving hope for large increases in values and returns when the market fully recovers.

One problem of low land and total property values is that security for borrowing for development finance is eroded; at times of recession the gross value of security held by financiers has been known to fall to as low as 70% of total development funding advances. Funding of property development is considered in more detail in Chapter 10.4.

10.3.3 THE BUILDING

The construction process

The various contract arrangements available for design and construction in the fitting-out process as described in Chapter 6.3 are equally applicable to new construction works and are not further elaborated upon here. Nevertheless it should be remembered that there is a big difference in the complexity of the new construction process compared with fitting-out; not only are the large contracts considerably larger, they also take longer and are subject to much greater risk in terms of quality and cost as well as time.

The new-build construction process is surprisingly complicated, especially when one considers that many of the works activities themselves are comparatively straightforward. The problem seems to lie with the peripatetic nature of the industry where every site is a new production plant involving new teams, new techniques, often new materials and equipment - and one which is normally disbanded on completion, never to be reconvened in the same form again.

The building design

Worse still, every brief is perceived as a design challenge; consequently the learning curve is always in evidence, particularly being made worse by the fact that designers (especially of the independent variety) seem to relish the opportunity to replace a good old familiar detail with a bad new one.

The 'design team' has traditionally comprised:

- architect
- structural engineer
- mechanical engineer
- electrical engineer
- cost consultant
- quantity surveyor
- planning supervisor (health and safety).

The architect is the traditional team leader, with the other consultants usually appointed direct by the client but under the architect's direction. Sometimes the design team is part of the contractor's organisation in the design-and-build type of arrangement.

Works and supplies

On large projects in most countries the work is carried out by general contractors who 'outsource' the tasks to sub-contractors who will often again sub-contract without people further up the line knowing about it - often in spite of contract conditions strictly forbidding that situation.

Builders' merchants supply the materials and plant for smaller contracts but the larger contractors usually deal direct with the suppliers, taking advantage of bulk order discounts; these do not always get declared in those cost-reimbursement contracts - including various forms of construction management - where the customer pays all the suppliers' bills direct.

Refurbishment

The 'cut-and-carve' process is fairly cyclical, alternating with new construction at times when money is scarce and/or new development is not financially viable in the context of current property investment valuations. The economics of refurbishment are generally not well understood. John Desmond[1] highlighted and analysed the critical factor in the economics of refurbishment, ie that unless the building is modern or in a good state of repair it may prove more expensive to refurbish than to demolish and re-build.

Apart from that key consideration the other feature of refurbishment which is often overlooked is the risk factor. It may seem reasonable on paper to show a door opening being formed in a plastered brick wall but not unusual for the whole wall to need re-plastering once the first coal-chisel has been applied to the ageing surface.

Any facilities manager contemplating, or being involved in, a refurbishment project should be insistent upon a contingency sum appropriate to the nature of the base building and the extent of alterations proposed.

In certain circumstances a contingency of up to 25% may be prudent - and may possibly tip the scales against that process as an option. A fundamental rule for any feasibility study involving refurbishment as an option is that a thorough structural and condition survey must be carried out professionally in advance of any financial commitment.

---

[1] *Partner of Bernard Williams Associates, cited in The Re-use of Redundant Buildings for Small Enterprises, ed. Peter Eley and John Worthington, Architectural Press*

10.4 FUNDING OF PROPOSALS

Introduction

At any time an organisation is likely to want funds for various purposes including:

- business start-up

- merger with or takeover of another company

- service or product development

- development of a franchise strategy for an existing business

- acquisition of property

- acquisition and installation of facilities

- development, redevelopment or refurbishment of owned land or property.

Although this chapter is oriented to the last of the above-mentioned purposes, in general the content applies to all of them.

Facilities managers may not be involved directly with obtaining funds for a project. However, whether it is a property acquisition, a new development or a refurbishment, they may be involved with some of the professionals dealing with the matter. Some facilities managers may have responsibility for:

- liaising with the fund providers

- accounts and records for the purposes of payments, drawings, taxation and on-going services

- authorising payments on behalf of the organisation.

It is important, therefore, to understand the nature of funding.

Although facilities managers are most likely to be concerned with funding their organisation's own development projects, this chapter explains funding from other perspectives; it is always useful to know the other side's objectives.

Initially, this chapter looks at how a proposal for funds might be approached together with the funders' requirements - a kind of overview. It then considers the sources of funding in different sectors. Finally, the chapter examines the types of funding under two broad headings, ie 'corporate funding' and 'project funding'. Although financial incentives, eg grants, are mentioned they are dealt with more fully in Chapter 10.5 - Financial incentives and mobile investment.

10.4.1 FUNDERS' REQUIREMENTS

Introduction

This section gives the facilities manager involved in funding an overview of the matters which funders are likely to want when considering or offering funds. Many impinge on the operational responsibilities of the facilities manager.

Making a proposal

The nature of the project in terms of, for instance, its location, size, duration and complexity will, no doubt, govern the nature of the initial information required of the fund-seeker by the provider of funds. In general for commercial projects, details of the likes of the following may be appropriate:

- the business plan

- the management team

- the resources, both material and financial, dedicated to the project
- any grants or incentives from public sources
- the partner organisations, if any, and their contributions or support.

More specifically, projects may have one or more 'characteristics' which require more specialised information some of the more significant of which are as follows.

- **Environmentally sensitive projects** eg 'brownfield' development, and commercial projects involving contaminative uses. Details of the following may be sought:
  - environmental management strategy and plans, particularly evidence of ISO 14001
  - consultants' environmental assessments
  - remediation works completed or proposed
  - environmental impact assessment (as required for local authority planning purposes).

- **Development and refurbishment projects**: generally, details of the following, including the above two categories if appropriate, may be required:
  - confirmation of planning permission and other statutory consents
  - plans and specifications of the proposed layout, buildings and structures
  - evidence of planning agreements for financial or other contributions to the community
  - cash flow, break-even, discounted cash flow or other forms of investment or financial analysis pertinent to the application.

- **Design-build-fund-operate projects and other very large projects**. Details may include:
  - confirmation of the stage reached, eg pre-qualification as prospective bidder
  - at pre-tender stage, details of any negotiation or tendering progress to date
  - at post-tender stage, details of any final negotiation, contract or legal issues.

However for this type of project the funder may be a partner to the proposal, albeit that other financial institutions may be required to provide guarantees.

- **Smaller projects**: perhaps before any loan is offered, the lender or mortgagee may seek some or all of the following:
  - a valuation of the property offered as security
  - accounts or a statement of income, earnings or joint earnings
  - copy of documentary evidence of company or partnership status
  - references from employers, trade suppliers, landlords or bankers
  - guarantees, warranties, performance bonds or collateral available from contractors, the applicant, professional advisors, or others
  - any deposit, grant or equity share put in by the applicant or others
  - tenancies and sublettings.

These items may apply generally to all projects depending on their nature.

Valuation of security

A funder will inevitably require a valuation of property offered as security for funds. Any valuation will normally be at the prospective borrower's expense, similarly for any structural survey that may be needed. In Chapter 3.5 a consideration of valuation methods is given. In essence, the mortgagee secures the loan with the mortgagor's property. In the event of default on the loan, the mortgagee may need to sell in order to recover the outstanding debt in connection with one or more of the following:

- the outstanding principal of the loan
- any arrears of interest
- any holding costs prior to disposal, eg insurance, repairs, management
- cost of making ready for sale, eg promotion
- agent's and solicitor's fees and expenses on disposal.

The safeguard for the mortgagee lies in the 'loan to value ratio'. If the valuer values the property at say £10m a loan/value ratio of 70% will result in a maximum loan of £7.0m. The deficit of £3m is the sum available to meet losses on default of the loan, provided the property can be sold at £10m. In times of recession property values are likely to have declined and the full recovery may not be achieved. The appropriate approach to valuation is, therefore important.

It may be noted that the above is a general account endeavouring to cover many situations; its primary purpose is to give the facilities manager a background knowledge of the issues involved. In practice the facilities manager will usually have recourse to colleagues or consultants who are able to offer expert advice in any particular situation.

10.4.2 TERMS AND CONDITIONS

The terms and conditions for a loan are likely to include the following:

- in development, complying with planning and other statutory requirements
- user restrictions
- period of the loan
- rate of interest, variable or fixed
- insurance of the property
- mortgage protection or endowment provisions for the life of the mortgagor
- putting the property into good condition
- maintaining the good condition of the property
- repayment of the loan by instalments, or at the end of the loan period.

10.4.3 TYPES OF FUNDING

Funding and the facilities manager

For many facilities managers funds for facilities operations and projects will come from the cash flow of the business operations or from the finance department's corporate financing operations, (of course, if an organisation operates an 'internal market', facilities will be charged to internal 'customers' but the sources of their funds are likely to be the same). In many of these instances, the facilities manager has a budget for facilities and may not be concerned with the types or sources of funds used by the organisation. In other instances, facilities managers may be actively involved in obtaining funds; they may need, therefore, to develop an understanding of many aspects of the subject, including:

- particularly, funders' requirements and terms and conditions (10.4.1 and 10.4.2)

- distinctions between equity and debt (see 10.4.3)

- the duration of funding arangements (see 10.4.3)

- sectoral arrangements for obtaining funds (see 10.4.4)

- types of corporate and project funding arrangements (see 10.4.5 and 10.4.6).

Equity and debt

The scope for property funding is growing and it is likely that innovative means to meet novel funding problems will continue to emerge. The subject is too wide to be dealt with adequately in this chapter, which gives a general overview of 'corporate' and 'project' funding.

It may be noted that an important distinction is that of 'debt' and 'equity' funds, the latter implying ownership in the enterprise. Thus, equity is the use of one's own funds to buy and develop for investment, dealing or owner-occupation, by owning shares or units in some business, property or intermediary. Debt funding involves borrowing, eg by mortgage or by issuing interest bearing bonds. The relationship between the proportions of equity and debt, ie 'gearing', which underpin the ownership of property may have important implications on obtaining the next tranche of monies. The gearing will also affect the returns to the equity portion in times of changing rental levels or interest rates or both (see Chapter 3.5, 'Introduction' for the effect of over- or under-valuation on gearing).

Taxation

It may be noted that the various ways and means of funding have different taxation implications. In any appraisal, taxation and any relief therefrom is likely to be a material factor affecting the outcome of the proposal being considered.

Corporate and project funding

The facilities manager seeking funds from the private sector for property acquisition, development or rehabilitation will find them grouped into the following:

- corporate funding

- project funding.

They will find that status of the 'person' seeking funds may influence the outcome of the search. ('Person' here is used for legal persona.) Thus, corporate bodies may seek both corporate or project related funds. On the other hand, individuals intent on maintaining control over development may seek project funding on their own account. However, the individual wanting to plan for taxation may wish to create a company for future property holding or dealing; and then seek corporate finance.

Similarly, the 'objective' of a landowner as an investor will tend to long-term funding (similarly for business ownership), whereas a dealer will tend to favour short-term finance. Of course, both may operate within a corporate structure.

Thus, corporate funding seeks to provide or raise funds through a corporate vehicle, such as a company, a charity or a trust. Devices or means of such financing are dealt with in 10.4.5 they include:

- creation of a private company

- the flotation of a company on a national or an international stock exchange

- the issue of debenture stock

- the issue of preference shares, which are, perhaps, convertible to equity capital

- the issue of paper script
- the issue of bonds of some particular type, eg a Eurobond or a deep discounted bond
- the securitisation of assets, eg a portfolio of loans
- the creation of a joint venture.

On the other hand, project funding (which is detailed in 10.4.6) seeks to raise funds by virtue of the project itself. In practice it is likely that the use of project funding would have an impact on the capital structure of the fund user. It may be noted that joint ventures or 'partnership' arrangements may be regarded as vehicles for funding development projects.

Examples of project funding include:

- leasing
- mortgage
- sale and leaseback
- forward funding
- funding by contractors
- franchise.

The essence of project finance by borrowing is the repayment of the loan from income, ie from the business to be conducted or from rental income. This will enable funds to be repaid over a period of medium duration.

Public bodies

Public body users of funds obtain their finances from a number of sources. Government may issue, for instance, government stock and raise funds from tax revenues which are redistributed to local authorities and other bodies by function-specific or programme-specific tranches of funds. Local authorities and other public bodies may also raise funds by the issue of bonds, fees, and fines or penalties.

Duration of funding arrangements

Generally the duration of funding is described as 'short-', 'medium-', or 'long-term'. Those who require short-term funds in the form of bridging finance, eg funding a development which will be sold (such as a speculative office development), may only need funds to cover the construction and disposal period. The sources include overdrafts from banks, trade credit from suppliers, stage payment arrangements with the purchaser's funders and advances from contractors employed to carry out the work.

Loans from banks and similar bodies which are made available for periods which range from, say, five to ten years are regarded as medium period. They may or may not be secured on property. The kind of borrowers will be those wanting to buy to improve property, eg proprietors or owners intent on running a small hotel, guest house, restaurant and the like. Also, dealers in property may seek such funds, sometimes on a 'flexible; or 'revolving' basis.

Long-term project funds are upwards of 10 years and may be as long as 60 years, eg for agricultural property, but 20 or 30 years is common.

Large projects may need funding for a long term, say 25 years, and mortgages suit this need. However, in these cases the relative risk the parties face tend to result in different forms of funding, ie other than the mortgage. Leases, sale and leaseback and other devices are used in this context.

10.4.4 EXTERNAL SOURCES OF FUNDS

The facilities manager may work in one of the three main sectors of the economy, ie private, public or voluntary. Each sector has its own 'culture' of funding but the facilities manager is likely to be interested mainly in the sources.

Private sector sources: a host of private sector funding sources may be identified. They include:

- international or national stock exchanges

- the clearing banks for overdraft and other short-term facilities and for mortgages

- the merchant banks for short-term funds and mezzanine finance

- the finance houses for equipment and plant leasing arrangements

- the insurance companies, pension funds and other financial institutions for sale and leaseback arrangements, mortgages, forward funding arrangements with ultimate purchase

- venture capitalists

- mortgage houses.

Public sector sources: in the public sector numerous local, regional national and international bodies are sources of grants or loans or both. Some such bodies may be seen as underpinning development with powers of land acquisition, planning powers, provisions of infrastructure and, perhaps as a catalyst, providing grants and loans in prescribed policy areas. In some instances, the lending of public funds is intended to 'seed' the start of apparently marginal or speculative public projects so as to generate a substantial injection of private sector funds, of the order of, say, one to four.

With their grants, loans and other means from various government initiatives, public bodies tend to be project-oriented funders. However, they may have powers in a given instance to enter into 'partnership' either as lessor, eg of a ground lease for a development site, or as a shareholder in a corporate body.

Funding criteria may be categorised as follows:

- area of location, eg regional or zonal support

- business function, such as 'research and development' or 'export'

- industry or business, eg agricultural or oil

- financial device, eg subsidised or guaranteed loan, grant, rent-free period or insurance subsidy.

In addition, the EC regulates grants and loans under various programmes (see Chapter 10.5 - 'Financial incentives and mobile investment'). Also, the European Investment Bank of the EU may make loans or guarantee loans for private or public projects involving development.

Voluntary sector sources: a very wide and varied range of organisations provide funds in the voluntary sector. Charities and trusts provide funds (as well as raise funds) for voluntary projects. Generally, charities come within four categories, namely:

- education

- religion

- maintenance and improvement of property to be preserved

- public benefit.

10.4.5 CORPORATE FINANCE FOR DEVELOPMENT

Flotation of company

A company may be created from a family or partnership business, as a subsidiary of an existing private or public company or as a joint venture by two or more 'persons', eg companies. The facilities manager may be involved in such a creation. Floating a company on a stock exchange is probably the most onerous. Also in the case of a major project it is fairly common for a new company to be established as the vehicle for development.

The flotation of a company requires several months of intense work for its directors, senior staff and consultants. In a sense, every issue of shares is a test of the board and management of a company and its advisors in the eyes of the public. The matters likely to require detailed consideration include:

- the business strategy and business plan
- the taxation position of existing shareholders
- the taxation position of future shareholders
- control of the new company
- the disposal of surplus assets
- the settling of debts and taxation liabilities
- board representation on the company
- the status of any occupational pension scheme.

The kind of issue selected is important. It may involve a quotation on an international or national stock exchange. Various approaches to the flotation may be considered including an 'offer for sale', an 'offer for sale by tender' a 'placing' or a 'share introduction'.

A number of criteria are used, such as:

- the cost of the issue in money terms and in terms of management involvement
- the loyalty of shareholders in terms of holding the shares
- practical support of the shareholders in providing further funds
- the degree of control given by the existing proprietors or shareholders
- the support of shareholders in times of difficulties.

The 'equity shares' resulting from a flotation carry the risk of ownership in the assets of the company (a separate entity in law). Entitlement to dividends is one benefit as is the prospect of any growth in value. Shares are often used as consideration for acquisition of property, other companies and so on. They may also be issued to staff in the form of 'share options' to aid recruitment, retention and productivity of employees.

Once it is created a company may raise funds in other ways, such as the following.

Rights Issues: for any existing company another way of raising funds is an approach to existing shareholders with a 'rights' issue in equity or stock, invariably at a discount to the current market price.

The advantage to the issuing company is that the company's 'gearing' of equity to debt is reduced, as no extra borrowing is incurred. Some dilution of earnings may follow and this may result in a drop in the value of existing shares. However, if the discounted price is low enough this will not result in a loss to the rights issue shares, although much depends on timing and market conditions. The success of the activities or ventures supported by the project will, in the end, be the major influence on the success of this funding policy.

Bonds: a bond is issued by a development company or other organisation as a way of raising funds as debt. The bond usually carries the right to earn interest on the capital invested but there are also other types of bonds.

International bonds: an international bond, eg a eurobond, is a means by which governments, international companies and others may raise funds on the international market, much of it centred in London and other major cities. A company issuing such a bond usually does so to raise funds for an overseas project or the acquisition of a foreign business. The cost of such funds depends on the prevailing strength of that currency in terms of supply and demand which is affected by such factors as the political, economic and social stability of the 'home' country.

A bond may be issued in one of several currencies including the deutschmark, the dollar, the yen, and sterling. The euro has become increasingly used in Europe.

Some bonds are convertible into the issuing company's equities, which has the effect of by-passing the traditional way of issuing shares on a stock exchange.

Prospectuses as such are not issued but the bonds are dealt with by licensed bond dealers, eg a merchant bank. Generally, dealers are regulated by the Financial Services Authority with powers, perhaps, to suspend, reprimand or expel them from business.

Deep discount and deep gain bonds: a device which some property development companies and others have used in recent years is the 'deep discount bond'.

The basic advantage of this type of bond is the partial or total deferral of interest payments. Where a capital sum is required but cash flow for the payment of interest is tight or not available, these bonds enable nil or low rates of interest, often until maturity of the bond. In effect all or some of the interest is paid as capital on redemption.

Preference shares: another form of risk investment is the preference share, a loan stock which ranks ahead of equities for dividends and taking a fixed dividend. They are, therefore, relatively less risky than ordinary shares but do not usually benefit from capital growth or further profits/dividends.

Debentures: a debenture is a type of long-term corporate borrowing which may take one of several forms, eg mortgage debentures secured against assets and convertible debentures secured against equity shares. Interest is normally paid on the capital of the loan (which may be secured as a fixed charge against a specific asset, or a floating charge across all, or a selection of the assets). Debentures 'gear' a company's financial structure and almost all are redeemable (unlike equity shares).

Securitisation: a company or financial institution with assets producing a positive cash flow may securitise them to raise funds. Thus, a development company with several design/build/fund/operate schemes ongoing (see below) may issue bonds backed by the profitable cash flows from the projects.

10.4.6 PROJECT FINANCE (FROM EXTERNAL SOURCES)

When the facilities manager considers project funding, availability is likely to be as follows.

Leasing: the most readily available means of funding the use of commercial property is a lease which enables the lessee to acquire an interest in and use a capital asset without any immediate outlay other than the rental instalments (unless a premium is paid to the landlord or a capital sum is paid for an assignment of the lease). The landlord's capital asset is used by the tenant; the rent being paid represents the return to the lessor, and quasi-interest to the lessee. The terms and conditions upon which the grant of a lease are made will partly determine the capital worth of the asset to the lessor. Generally, rent paid under the lease will be an allowable expense for corporation tax purposes. See Chapters 3.1 to 3.5 for a discussion of the characteristics of leases and sale and leasebacks.

Franchise: the facilities manager may be concerned with a franchise operation. In effect, a business which is franchised uses funds generated by other operators to expand its own core business. It is a growing sector of business enterprise. A successful entrepreneur with a suitable type of business (frequently, but not exclusively, retail) can become a 'franchiser'. In essence the franchisee buys a package which enables him or her to run an already proven business. The franchiser is able to build up a network of businesses each generating initial acquisition capital and a stream of 'royalties' and sales in the provision of supplies. An added advantage for the franchiser is the likely keenness of self-motivated entrepreneurs who carry the operational component of the business risk in the venture. The franchiser offers a marketing mix which may include many of the following: the name, house-style, specification for premises, detailed manuals on trading systems and operations, advice on the selection and fitting out of premises, supplies of stock and equipment, promotional services and advice, access to funding arrangements, and training of staff.

The impact of franchise operations has become apparent, especially in town centres and the trend is likely to grow in the next few years. In a sense, the franchisees indirectly fund the growth of the franchised business through the borrowing they are able to make in support of their operation of the franchise.

The cost of a franchise to the prospective franchisee could be from say £5,000 to over £800,000. Several of the clearing banks have created specialist departments to deal with applications for loans with which to fund the acquisition of a franchise and to proffer advice in this respect, eg by providing information packages.

National associations, eg the British Franchise Association, exist to promote good practice and regulate members, and may follow the European Code of Ethics for Franchising.

Mortgages: basically, the mortgagor (the one borrowing) offers the mortgagee a property as security for a longish term loan. The loan may be repaid during the term as an annuity (interest and capital) or at the end of the term (interest only being paid during that period). Terms and conditions are attached to the mortgage by the mortgagee, ie a bank, building society or other lender.

Funding by contractors: building contractors employed on development projects sometimes provide funds for a client developer as part of the contract for the scheme. The loans may, for instance, be on deferred payment terms and secured by mortgage arrangements. Such arrangements are, however, fraught with difficulty in situations where the contractor's building performance falls below standard with regard to cost, time or quality since onerous protective clauses are not acceptable to the contractor/funder. Repayment may include an issue of shares by the developer to the contractor.

Forward funding: a developer may obtain short-term finance to carry out development and at the same time obtain agreement to sell the project or fund it on a long-term basis. Generally, this reflects a 'forward funding' approach. The long-term finance may involve 'vertical' or 'horizontal' shares in the rental quality of the project: so-called mezzanine financing.

Design-build-fund-operate projects: a package approach offered by some contractors with others is to design, build, fund and operate a project for a period, eg 10, 20 or 30 years.

A special instance is the Private Finance Initiative (PFI)/Private Public Partnership

(PPP) originally conceived in the UK (see Chapters 3.5.13 and 6.3.1). It may be seen either as project funding or as a vehicle for a mix of corporate or project funding. It seeks to shift the funding of some public sector projects, such as roads and bridges, offices, hospitals, schools from central government to the private sector wherein a company or consortium of companies and others bid a 'unitary charge', ie a fixed annual repayment by the user, in return for undertaking to design, build, fund and operate a facility for a given period, eg for 20 or 30 years.

PFI/PPP has not been without problems. For instance, groups intending to bid find that the bid preparation costs can be substantial and with no guarantee of success. Also, the nature of many projects requires a knowledge base and skills not held by traditional contracting or property companies. One of the biggest problems relates to the prediction of future facilities services costs and life-cycle replacement costs. In funding a project a consortium may find traditional bankers reluctant to commit themselves; specialist and innovative financing arrangements need to be developed. Also, the contractual arrangements may require a substantial legal input covering several areas beyond traditional property and construction matters.

10.5 FINANCIAL INCENTIVES AND MOBILE INVESTMENT

Introduction

The attraction and retention of mobile investment has become an important feature of national and regional economic development policies. The location decisions for such investments are driven by a wide range of factors that embrace both broad issues such as the general business climate, the state of the labour market and taxation, as well as firm or sector-specific needs such as access to markets, site availability or existing clusters of related activity.

As barriers to trade between EU member states have come down, there has been increasing competition between governments to attract mobile investment. One of the few ways in which national, regional or local government can influence investment location decisions on a case-by-case basis is through the use of financial incentives.

Financial incentives have often been viewed as one of the most effective ways for governments to influence the individual location decisions of firms. However, incentives tend not to be key in the choice of country but rather in the selection of region once possible locations have been narrowed down to a shortlist. In many major investment decisions, a number of sites in different countries are chosen on the basis of cost and other location factors, but the final decision can depend on the incentive package available.

Notwithstanding the high levels of aid sometimes offered, the use of financial incentives is subject to a body of rules that flow from the competition policy provisions, basically Articles 87 to 89 of the Treaty of European Union. These are outlined briefly before discussing the incentives on offer in the UK.

10.5.1 EUROPEAN COMMISSION CONTROL OF FINANCIAL INCENTIVES

The control of "state aids"

Unlike the United States where states and cities offer tax breaks or other forms of aid apparently unfettered by any code of discipline, the use of so-called "state aids" is monitored by the EC. The essence of the approach to state aids is that they are banned, subject to a number of exceptions where it is considered that the use of aid can be beneficial.

The broad thrust of policy has been to allow the use state aids for general investment (land, buildings, plant and equipment) by small and medium-enterprises; however, for large firms, the EC has restricted general investment aids to areas designated for regional policy purposes - typically underdeveloped regions or areas affected by industrial restructuring. This approach has reinforced the role of regional aids as the main incentives used for the attraction of mobile firms in such areas.

Importantly, the areas which a member state proposes to designate for regional aid (the assisted areas map) must be approved by the EC in advance of implementation; it must also approve the proposed award maxima.

New regional aid guidelines

On 10 March 1998 the OJ contained the EC's new rules, 'Guidelines on National Regional Aid', set to come into effect from the start of 2000. The member states were to submit their proposed regional aid schemes and associated maps during the course of 1999 (in principle by end March 1999) with a view to their being reviewed, and if necessary revised, prior to implementation at the start of 2000. In practice, there were significant delays in many countries, including the United Kingdom. Nevertheless, in the course of 2000 a new UK assisted areas map was approved for the period 2000-6, along with new (lower) aid ceilings. In considering the various forms of assistance on offer, it is important to note that the assisted areas map and associated upper aid limited concern financial incentives from all sources - national, regional and local - whether alone or in combination.

In general, European Commission approval of aid schemes means that the administration concerned can operate the aid measure in a discretionary manner, subject to the parameters which the Commission has approved. However, the European Commission also has a role in certain individual cases. Aid to certain sectors, notably the motor vehicle and synthetic fibre industries must be notified to the Commission on a case-by-case basis. In addition, in all sectors, aid offers exceeding certain limits must be examined by the Commission individually. The limits for current projects are either:

- total project costs exceeding 50 million where the aid level proposed is more than 50% of the authorised ceiling for large firms in the region or more than 40,000 per job, or

- total aid is more than €50 million.

As already mentioned, the intervention of the EC has tended to make regional aid the principal source of financial incentives. Outside the designated assisted areas, the scope for large firms and projects to receive financial incentives is much more limited (in this context, large firms broadly means those with over 250 employees, a turnover in excess of £40 million or a balance sheet total of more than 27 million); under the EC rules on state aids, incentives are likely to be limited to certain types of "horizontal" investment such as research and development or environmental protection expenditure, or to be very limited in scale; the EC considers aid of up to 100,000 in a three-year period to be de minimis and essentially outside the scope of the state aids rules, but such sums are unlikely to be of significance to large firms. More flexible provisions apply to small and medium sized enterprises (SMEs) and the Commission permits governments to aid SMEs throughout their territories, albeit at higher rates of award in the designated assisted areas.

(It may be noted that a multi-sectoral framework was published in March 2002. It will operate from 1 January 2004, except for motor vehicles, synthetic fibres and steel industries.)

10.5.2 ASSISTED AREAS AND AWARD MAXIMA IN THE UK

The UK assisted areas approved by the European Commission cover the whole of Northern Ireland and almost 28% of the population of Great Britain. Within Great Britain, the assisted areas are mainly focussed on former industrial areas such as Merseyside, Tyneside, South Yorkshire, Clydeside and the Welsh Valleys. However some predominantly rural areas - Cornwall and the Scilly Isles and the Highlands and Islands of Scotland are also eligible.

In principle, the Commission relates the maximum rate of award it will authorise to the perceived severity of the regional problem. In the UK, the highest rates of award are available in Northern Ireland where the ceiling is 40% of investment. In the so-called Tier 1 areas - Cornwall and the Scilly Isles; West Wales and the Valleys, Merseyside and South Yorkshire, the maximum rate if 35%. In the Highlands and Islands, the ceiling is 30%, reflecting the low population density of the area. Elsewhere - the so-called Tier 2 areas - rates of award vary between 10 and 20% of investment. In some of the assisted areas higher rates of award may be available to small and medium-sized enterprises.

It is important to note that these ceilings apply to aid from all sources - they cannot be exceeded simply by combining assistance for the same project from different agencies. In practice, however, the ceilings should be treated with some caution. Although they are theoretically attainable, a key trend in recent years has been to try and achieve 'value for money' in incentive expenditure by spending the minimum thought necessary to attract a given investment. As a result, actual award values have typically been well below the advertised maxima.

10.5.3 SUPPORT FOR MOBILE INVESTMENT PROJECTS

For large and/or potentially mobile projects, it is commonplace for 'packages' of financial assistance to be assembled. These are typically co-ordinated by agencies (who may not themselves provide direct assistance) who aim to provide a 'one-stop-shop' for investors. In England, the lead bodies at regional level for co-ordinating inward investment are the Regional Development Agencies. In Scotland, Scottish Development International undertakes promotional activities and co-ordinates the financial package for investors. Similar functions are performed by the Welsh Development Agency and the Industrial Development Board for Northern Ireland.

Regional Selective Assistance

The main form of general investment aid for large firms in Great Britain is Regional Selective Assistance (RSA) (a parallel but separate measure is operated in Northern Ireland). Regional Selective Assistance is a discretionary project-related capital grant. In the last decade or so there has been a tendency for the administration of financial incentives to become more discretionary. Until the 1980s many countries, including the UK, operated incentives that were essentially automatic - firms which met the advertised criteria in terms of location, eligible investment and so on simply claimed the amount due. Growing public expenditure constraints, combined with concerns at the possible lack of influence of such automatic schemes over the investment decisions of firms led policymakers to become increasingly preoccupied with getting 'value for money' from incentive spending. In practice, this means that there is discretion over whether a firm should receive assistance and, if so, what the level of any assistance - the rate of award - should be. In general, the larger the project and the more attractive it is to potential host countries, the greater the competition for it between potential sites, and the more the incentive package is likely to involve extensive negotiations between the investor and the relevant government agencies.

An important factor in the administration of RSA which may favour mobile projects is the 'need' for assistance; so-called 'additionality' is a key eligibility criterion. This means that an award offer will only be made if the award will lead to a significant change in the scale, timescale or location of the project; the aim is to avoid subsidising investments that would have gone ahead anyway on the same basis. In this context, awareness of award offers from competing locations can be an important factor in determining award values. International competition for investment may lead policymakers to consider what level of aid is necessary to bring a given project to their location.

Other forms of support

Regional Selective Assistance may be complemented by property-related aid. This is operated at the sub-national level by, for example, English Partnerships and the Local Enterprise Companies in Scotland. Not all such support contains a subsidy element; however, where it ides, this counts towards the aid ceilings described earlier.

Support may also be available for training and re-training of employees to the needs of incoming investors. In addition, the New Deal provides a short-term subsidy in relation to new job creation for young people.

A distinct package of measures is operated in Enterprise Zones (EZ). These are designated for 10 years, but all the current zones expire before end 2006. There are seven EZ in the East Midlands region, six in South Yorkshire and East Durham, 11 on Tyneside and one in Lanarkshire. Assistance comprises a package of benefits including 100% first year tax write off for new commercial and industrial buildings. Local property tax exemptions and a simplified planning regime.

10.5.4 SOURCES OF FURTHER INFORMATION

As mentioned earlier, a number of organisations are engaged in assembling 'packages' of assistance to firms. The agencies concerned might not offer assistance directly themselves, but play a co-ordination and advisory role. In England, the regional development agencies (RDAs) are the lead organisations for co-ordinating inward investment, but the Government Offices in the English regions generally administer RSA (although the Department of Trade and Industry takes the lead in large cases). In the case of smaller firms especially, so-called Business Links provide advice as well as some forms of financial support. In Scotland, the lead role is played by Scottish Enterprise, its network of Local Enterprise Companies and, for inward investors, Scottish Development International. For Wales and Northern Ireland, the WDA and the IDB respectively both provide support and can direct investors to further sources of aid.

Further information is available from the following websites:

UK: Invest UK: www.invest.uk.com

England: Department of Trade and Industry: www.dti.gov.uk

Wales: Welsh Development Agency: www.wda.co.uk

Scotland: Scottish Enterprise: www.scottish-enterprise.com

Northern Ireland: Industrial Development Board: www.idbni.co.uk

10.5.5 CONCLUSIONS

This chapter has outlined the circumstances and conditions surrounding the use of financial incentives for mobile investment. In part as a consequence of EC intervention, regional aid policy has become the main incentive instrument for the attraction of foreign investment.

However, the current climate is somewhat uncertain given the EC's role in authorising the regional aid plans of the EU member states. Nevertheless, past trends with respect to incentive administration are likely to continue - policymakers will tend to offer the minimum possible in order to secure an attractive investment project, but compete actively where there is locational choice. On the other hand, the new rules mean that coverage of the assisted areas have become lower in most countries, limiting the scope for incentives for large projects. Similarly, maximum rates of award are set have fallen across the board; in practical terms, this may not impact greatly on award offers - typically, national policymakers have opted to offer much less than the EC would allow. Also, as the EU expands to the proposed 25 member states the availability of incentives will be spread - it seems that in the UK only Cornwall will be eligible for them.

In short, financial incentives seem set to remain an important, if not vital, consideration in any mobile investment decision; while few firms would locate solely on the basis of the aid available, and this would generally be unwise, financial incentives can enhance the attractiveness of locations that might not otherwise be considered by investors. Moreover, such locations may offer an additional bonus in that other costs (such as labour and land) may often be below the national average.

10.6 WHOLE-LIFE ECONOMICS

Introduction

The building life-cycle is from birth (first occupation) to death (demolition). Its gestation period, ie conception (design) thru pregnancy (construction) is, totally analogously responsible for most of the factors contributing to its performance throughout its life.

As in human life, neglect, accident, care, attention will impact on the performance of the product but its intrinsic physical qualities will be the overriding factor in the usefulness of its contribution to those depending on it.

During its life a building will undergo many changes. Apart from the washing and scrubbing to keep it clean, the repair and replacement of parts which go wrong, the redecoration to keep it looking smart, the building will also be subjected to considerable change throughout its life; the main cause will be obsolescence in terms of the basic design and specification no longer being totally appropriate to the basic needs of the user.

To carry the human analogy further than is probably advisable, a building emulates the re-training and redundancy phases of a working life and tends to be similarly indiscriminate in the timing, location and extent of those phases.

The concept of 'shell, scenery and services' was discussed in Chapter 6.1.1. The shell, comprising the structure and the envelope, will remain unchanged throughout the building's whole life (subject to extensions, change of use, re-cladding and the like).

The scenery, ie the components applied to the interior to make it fit for a specific purpose, might have a life of say, five to seven years before becoming redundant through change of one sort or another and subsequently being replaced.

The building services have a longer life-cycle - say 10 to 20 years - conditioned by the physical capacity of the components and natural obsolescence in a fast-changing business/technology environment.

Of course, these phases and time forecasts are only indicative: a lift motor, well maintained, might last 30 years in a building just growing old gracefully whereas the scenery in the same building might get altered within a couple of years due to 'churn' or simply change of user.

Nevertheless, the ephemeral nature of this regime tends to compound even medium-term prediction and is a nightmare in terms of depreciation and asset valuation - issues discussed in Chapters 3.8.

10.6.1 ATTITUDES TOWARDS WHOLE-LIFE ECONOMICS

An academic concept

When Dr Stone[1] introduced the principles of cost-in-use to the construction industry in the early 1960's; his efforts were greeted with well-merited academic recognition and complete apathy from the industry's practitioners.

The reasons for this apathy - then as now (or until quite recently) are quite simple:

- the data is not generally available to make the cost-in-use appraisals realistic

- even if it were, the sums involved are relatively minor in the whole financial scheme of things

---

[1] *Dr. P A. Stone (1968), 'Building Design Evaluation, Costs in Use', E and FN Spon, London, UK*

- the effects of discounting on future cash flows makes the impact of future expenditure much less significant in the investment appraisal
- relief from tax on revenue profits is usually available for all the costs of running and maintaining buildings.

So, with clients interested in the bigger financial fish, consultants unlikely to command an additional fee for applying their skills in this direction and the constructors not in the slightest bit interested, the principles and techniques of cost-in-use preached by Dr Stone were left more or less unapplied throughout the rest of the century; interest in his theories was confined mainly to the lecture room.

The influence of ownership

One very important factor to be taken into account when considering whole-life economics is that the user is not always the owner. Therefore, in buildings designed in the past speculatively on behalf of developers and/or investor there has been no immediate incentive to improve the life-cycle performance above the conventional norm because the investor cannot be certain of directly benefiting from it. Because building performance is inadequately reflected in rents and value - as discussed in Chapter 1.2.3 - pressures have remained on designers to pare capital costs at the expense of the ultimate physical performance.

Challenging the apathy

However, three things have occurred in the past decade to cause this apathy to be challenged.

First, the increasing complexity of the modern commercial building has caused the whole level of the life-cycle costs to rise significantly. This has led not only to greater pressure on budgets but also engendered much higher profile for the way the building performs in physical terms - especially if under-performance has adverse consequences in terms of the business operation.

In tandem with (and mainly because of) this sea-change is the advent of a new breed of facilities managers, with a greater influence on the way their buildings are put together, and under constant pressure from the finance director to contain expenditure on premises.

The final, and probably most significant, factor has been the advent of total premises outsourcing wherein users pay a unitary charge for fully serviced accommodation. This latter regime first came to the fore in the various forms of public sector/private sector partnering arrangements under the loose term Private Finance Initiative (PFI)/'Private Private Partnership' (PPP). Such schemes, which now are also available for purely private sector applications, place the risk of predicting replacement cycles and costs fairly and squarely on the shoulders of the building provider: so what are minor costs and risks in terms of the user's commercial interests become critical cost and risk centres to the entrepreneur providing the premises for a fixed annual price.

Possibly the days of completely speculative development are nearly through, to be permanently replaced by buildings with bespoke design for the owner of pre-let occupier. If so then the techniques considered here will become the rule rather than the exception. however, as we shall see. their application may be in a different economic context than that envisaged by Dr Stone and the educational pundits who have slavishly taught his valid but unfashionable logic over the past 30-odd years.

10.6.2 WHOLE-LIFE COSTS

Cost analysis

The whole-life cost of a building comprises:

- its initial construction cost

- the cost of operation, maintenance and repairs

- the replacement costs

- cost of fitting-out, alteration, adaptation and extension

- demolition costs.

As discussed above the fitting-out, alteration, adaptation and extension costs are not normally predictable in terms of time or cost so most life-cycle forecasts ignore them unless they are part of a phased programme. The fitting-out is cyclical and, if accommodated in the appraisal, both costs and life-cycles will be based on subjective estimates.

The initial construction cost will include all fees and finance charges. Land is not normally included since it is not deemed to be a wasting asset; the cost of demolition clears the way for re-use of the land, presumed to be still useful at the end of the physical construction's life-span.

The protocols for analysing and measuring the cost of maintenance in Chapter 5.2 should be re-visited before reading further into this chapter. In particular the separation of replacement of secondary components from replacement of primary components needs to be thoroughly understood in theory and applied in practice: both of these items are normally considered to be capital as opposed to revenue expenditure on routine maintenance which includes replacement of minor parts such as filters and stop-valves. The important thing to recognise is that primary components of elements - such as boilers in a heating system or cladding panels in an external walling system - may have their lives extended by replacement of the secondary components, ie by refurbishment. So the boiler may last 60 years provided the burners, flue pipes and circulating pumps are replaced when their time is up; probably the only secondary component of the boiler that will service the whole of the primary component life-cycle is the boiler casing itself.

How such principles of analysis affect the way life-cycle costs are defined and predicted is considered in detail later in the chapter.

The cost of managing the premises should be allocated to the operating and replacement costs. The operating cost centres themselves are as discussed in Chapter 5.1. It may be noted that business costs as incorporated in the cost/benefit appraisals in Chapter 9.1 are not usually included in life-cycle appraisal since they reflect specific aspects of the user's business rather than the inherent performance of the building. Some overlap is inevitable but excessive consideration of hypothetical productivity benefits can take over from practicality.

However, in most cases whole-life appraisal is a 'personal' issue and the appraisers may include whatever they deem to be appropriate - provided they observe consistency in any cross-comparisons.

Building performance, cost and value

Fig. 10.6.A (over the page) is a reminder from Chapter 1.2.3 (Fig. 1.2.D), which suggests that the costs of providing and operating premises reflect their physical performance; this, in turn, influences the functional performance which generates the real value to the user.

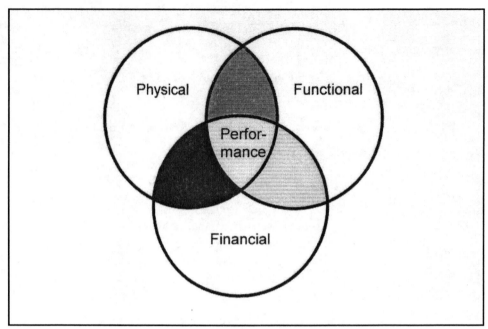

Fig. 10.6.A
*Three facets of
building
performance -
inter-relationships*

Conventional life-cycle cost analysis will therefore only be concerned with the physical - ie 'invoiceable' aspects of the premises over the life-cycle; however, as previously stated, there is no reason whatever why the life-cycle cost analyses should not be extended into cost/benefit analysis for the purposes of option appraisal on behalf of an occupier, thereby bringing both physical and functional aspects of building performance into the equation.

10.6.3 APPRAISAL TECHNIQUES

The principal methods

There are three principal methods of evaluating the life-cycle costs of buildings:

*   simple aggregation
*   Net Present Value (NPV)
*   Annual Equivalent (AE).

The net present value and annual equivalent methods both rely upon the concept of 'Discounted Cash Flow' (DCF) which is described in detail below.

Each of these three methods can be calculated with or without inflation and with or without tax relief.

Simple aggregation

The simple aggregation method simply adds the total capital costs to the total of all expenditure on operating, repairs, maintenance and replacement over the building's life. Most lay people - and many building professionals - expect proposals which spend more on the capital cost to result in reduced annual expenditure.

However, as the histogram in Fig. 10.6.B illustrates (ignoring inflation), this is by no means usually the case. This is due to the fact that although the better quality building 'B' is slightly cheaper to run and maintain pa (which is not always the case - especially if the higher quality specification involves greater complexity or high cost parts to replace during maintenance), the cost of replacing the more expensive components at the end of their life-cycles is rather higher - though deferred.

Fig. 10.6.B
Aggregated life-cycle cost analyses of alternative building specifications - not discounted

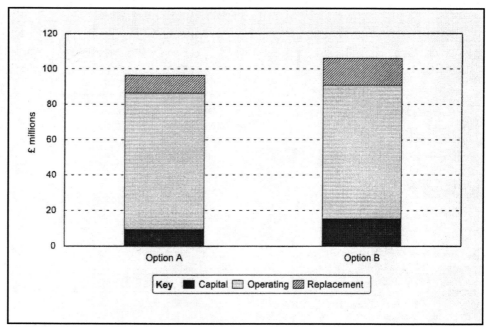

A more compelling argument for focusing attention on the operating and replacement costs is that (as Fig. 10.6.B shows) the aggregated annual operating costs of a building (excluding inflation) will be many times the initial costs - even before costs of fitting-out and alteration have been taken into account.

Fig. 10.6.C depicts the cyclical effect of operating and replacement costs.

Fig. 10.6.C
Graphical depiction of life-cycle cost analyses of alternative building specifications - not discounted

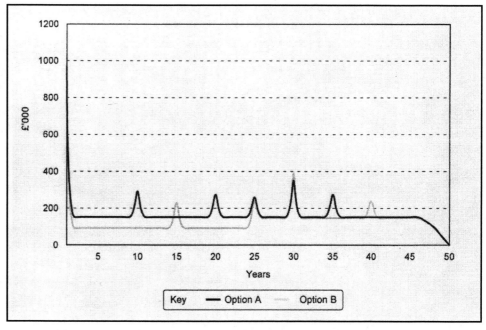

The lower capital cost of Option A produces slightly higher operating costs pa and the replacement cycles are shorter. However when the replacement of the major components of Option 'B' come around they tend to be more expensive - reflecting the higher quality of the original specification. And, of course, at the end of the buildings' lives Option A costs much less to replace - albeit that it needs to take place a few years earlier. (It may be noted that the final total replacement is not included in the replacement costs at Fig. 10.6.B.)

Furthermore, in practice, although the operation of 'B' would probably need less investment in reactive maintenance the costs of planned preventative maintenance would probably be higher, reflecting the relative complexity of services and the higher specification of the components of the fabric. Of course, this is all very theoretical and is merely illustrating a 'fact of life' that is generally misunderstood.

Although sometimes used to make a point, (in this case that it is important to get the life-cycle costs right because they are so much greater than the initial costs) the 'Simple Aggregation' method has no standing in management accountancy terms; this is because it ignores the highly significant effect of DCF on the real value of deferred expenditure. DCF, considered in more detail below, takes into account the interest potentially earned on capital invested elsewhere pending the deferred expenditure.

The Net Present Value (NPV)

In the case of the Net Present Value method, the aggregation of initial and annual expenditure is modified by deduction of the interest (at the chosen rate) theoretically earned on the money invested during the period from inception of the project to the actual date of payment for the component. The effects of this calculation, using a discount rate of 6%, on the previous aggregation examples are shown at Figs 10.6.D and 10.6.E.

Fig. 10.6.D
Aggregated life-cycle cost analyses of Options 'A' and 'B' - discounted at 6%

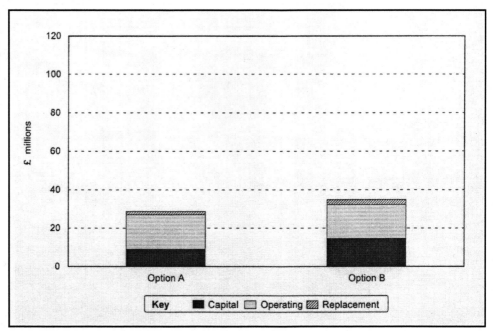

It may be noted that in Fig. 10.6.D the operating expenditure in both options has sharply reduced due to the effect of discounting a deferred expenditure. Similarly the costs of life-cycle replacement are much less significant. How this all works is more easily understood from the whole-life graphic representation at Fig. 10.6.E.

As each year goes by the cumulative effect of the discounting erodes the significance of both the operating and replacement costs reflecting the concept that money not yet needed to invest in the buildings is invested somewhere else in the interim at 6% pa compound interest. The longer the deferral the more interest rolls up; this means that when the expenditure is incurred it will be net of the rolled-up interest.

It may be noted how the order of the comparative costs of the two options remains unchanged; in spite of the overall reduction in the aggregated costs after discounting; this situation holds good in the example whatever the discount rate because the annual operating costs are similar in both options. The low discount rate of 6% still exaggerates the NPV of the operating and replacement costs as a proportion of the whole-life costs; however, at a high rate of say 15% they would show less than the capital cost (see Fig. 10.6.J below).

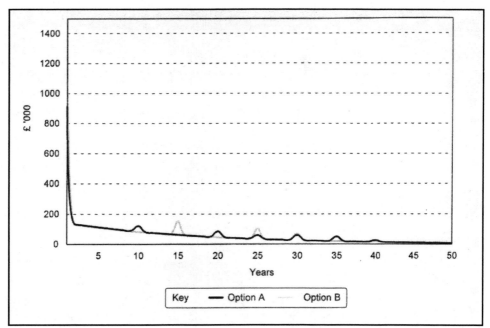

Fig. 10.6.E
Life-cycle cost analyses of Options A and B - discounted at 6%

The effect of discounting is therefore to penalise up-front expenditure in the context of the whole-life costs which makes it difficult to justify higher quality/lower maintenance investment decisions in the context of a management accountancy appraisal regime.

Taking relief from corporation tax in the year end following this expenditure and adding tax on the interest earned during the deferred expenditure period will obviously change the figures again, as would the inclusion of inflation; both these aspects are discussed more fully below.

The Annual Equivalent (AE)

The third method, the annual equivalent cost expresses the aggregated amounts in terms of the 'mortgage payable' on the initial cost added to the typical annual costs of operating, repair and replacement usually related to the unit of floor area. A mortgage payment is the same as a hire-purchase payment and includes both the annual interest on the purchase price and a sinking fund payment to replace the initial capital at the end of the term.

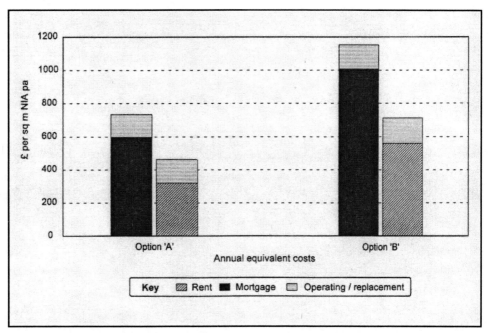

Fig. 10.6.F
Life-cycle cost analyses of Options 'A' and 'B' - annual equivalent cost per sq m NIA

Fig. 10.6.F (previous page) introduces another new variable with the same example, ie the 'rent or buy' option.

Taking Option 'A' first we see that the operating costs are the same (but more of this below) but the rental cost is quite a lot less than the mortgage. Because, as we stated above, the mortgage payment includes a sinking fund payment to repay the original capital the annual payments are normally higher in a 'purchase' scenario than one involving leasing. The shorter the period of the loan, the higher the mortgage repayments pa and the greater the differential from a rented option.

The example also shows that, whereas property costs may vary from one location to another, operating and replacement costs tend to be relatively comparable.

Rent reviews after one or more years (or perhaps annual indexation) are the norm (see Chapter 3.2.2, Fig. 3.2.B) so it is sometimes suggested that the annual equivalent technique does not give the full picture over time; however since indexation or rent reviews are predominantly there to accommodate normal inflation and since normal inflation should not be incorporated in investment appraisals these 'snapshot' results are valid for any given period between indexation and rent reviews although they do not reflect the benefits or ownership accruing to the mortgagee at the end of the loan period.

The capital cost of Option 'B' being substantially higher than 'A' there is a proportionate increase in both the mortgage and the rental alternatives. A point to watch out for is that if the example was the comparison of two existing buildings and, say, Option A rent was due to be reviewed earlier than that in Option 'B', there would not be a like-for-like comparison. For this reason the use of the annual equivalent cost is normally restricted to quick, early comparison, eg as in Fig 9.1.G in Chapter 9.1.

Discounted cash flow

The discounting effect of interest earnings on the worth of deferred expenditure as described above is, in practice, calculated from tables of factors produced for the purpose from first principles. For instance, the calculation of the interest earned on the expenditure deferred until year one on the example at Fig. 10.6.C can be calculated from the formula:

$$PV = (1+i)^{-n}$$

where:

- PV = Present Value

- i   = Rate of interest

- n   = number of years

so, at 6% interest over 50 years

$$PV = (1+0.06)^{-1} \text{ or } \frac{1}{(1.06)} = 0.9433$$

By the same formula the factor becomes 0.8899 at year 2, 0.8396 at year 3 and so forth - allied to the net amount of the cash flow for the period. It may be noted that this same formula can be used to calculate factors for any period, eg monthly or quarterly.

The annual equivalent of the initial cost is calculated rather like a mortgage instalment table, ie it is the annual interest rate per £ added to the sinking fund required to be set aside to replace £1 capital by the end of the period.

So, the annual equivalent factor applied to the initial cost is calculated from the formula:

(i+s) where

- i = the remunerative rate of interest
- s = the sinking fund for an n year life accumulating at 6%

In this case (0.06 + 0.0034) = 0.0634 (where n = 50 say).

The sinking fund, also used in the calculation of depreciation is calculated from the formula:

$$\frac{i}{(1-i)^n-1}$$

ie it is the amount required to be invested annually at a given rate of interest (before/after tax) to repay the initial sum borrowed by the end of the period. It is the reciprocal of the amount of £1 pa at the remunerative rate.

Given the tax relief may be available in the form of capital allowances and against most revenue expenditure the effects of such savings need to be calculated prior to discounting.

Inflation and DCF

The effects of inflation on DCF are at one and the same time a problem of forecasting and an argument against the whole process.

Inflation is not normally incorporated in life-cycle appraisal. The reason for this is that at the time the inflated amount comes to be spent it would be normal for the economy to have grown by a similar amount; in other words, although it costs you more you are earning more money which cancels out the increase. Obviously there are lots of situations recorded when inflation and growth have not run strictly in parallel but the problems of predicting inflation lead most appraisers into using this excuse for ignoring it.

The only time that inflation does get incorporated is where a particular commodity is expected to have a rate of inflation which is significantly different from the normal level. An example of such a differential rate might be that energy prices were expected to grow abnormally quickly as a result of world supply shortages. The inflation rate to be included for that component would therefore be the net differential between the expected rate of inflation on energy and the normal inflation rate.

Nevertheless it is worth considering the effects of allowing a rate of inflation (whether gross or net differential) into the life-cycle cash flow prediction.

Although DCF will whittle away at the future cost of deferred expenditure, inflation will be compounded and will counteract and outweigh the effects of discounting in most cases - ie money spent at the beginning of the life-cycle may well be seen to give an apparently satisfactory return on investment through future savings. Nevertheless the standard procedure has been to ignore inflation entirely - for the sound reason given above.

An example of Fig. 10.6.D taking inflation at 5% is shown at Fig. 10.6.G (over the page).

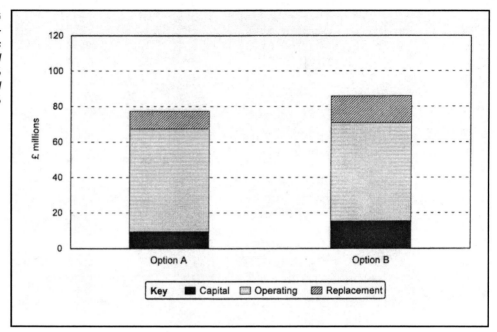

The calculation is simple - just add the inflation percentage, in this case 5%, to the discount factor for the period in question, giving the formula:

$$PV = [1 + (i + inf)]^{-n} \text{ where}$$

'inf' = the inflation per £ pa - ie 0.05 is the figure for inflation at 5% pa

A summary of the NPV of the two schemes for two rates of interest, tax and inflation are given at Fig. 10.6.H and J.

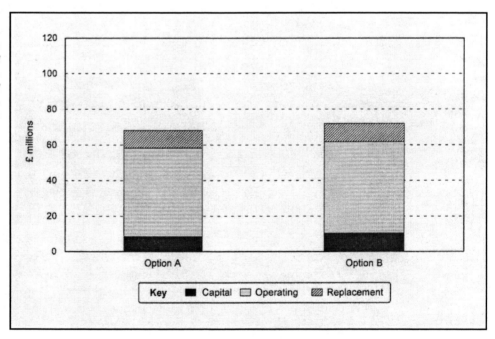

In Fig. 10.6.H the 5% inflation rate has virtually negated the effects of the 6% discount factor but the 30% (hypothetical) tax relief on the running costs is causing the significant fall below the original levels in Fig. 10.6.B.

In Fig. 10.6.J the 15% discount rate is still effectively at 10% after 5% inflation which obviously minimises the significance of the life-cycle operating expenditure in the context of the whole-life costs comparison.

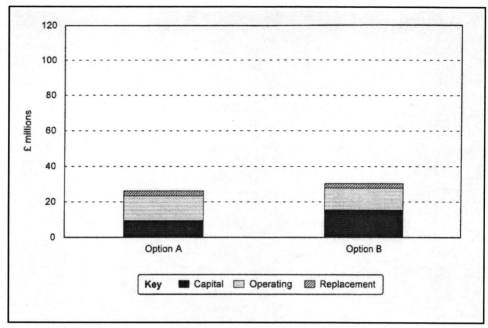

Fig. 10.6.J
Aggregated life-cycle cost analyses of Options 'A' and 'B' - inflated at 5% pa (compound) and discounted at 15%

One could be forgiven for being cynical about the consequences of letting two management accountants loose in support of (or opposition to) this or any such proposal. Nonetheless, it is submitted that the process, like any other predictive exercise, encourages full consideration of the issues.

In any case, a sensitivity analysis - of which the latter is but one example - can be extremely useful in knocking out irrelevant objections to the benefit of consideration of the real issues.

10.6.4 COMPONENT LIFE-CYCLES

Factors influencing component life

As if the machinations and manipulations of the choice of DCF factors were not enough, a further major obstacle to the acceptance of life-cycle cost analysis in conventional practice is the problem of getting hold of good data about the life of buildings, their component parts and the associated costs-in-use.

There is a widely held view - which is not without substance - that it is virtually impossible to predict with any degree of accuracy how long a component can be expected to last before it becomes unserviceable; even the definition of 'unserviceable' has no consensus, except nine as it happens in PFI/PPP projects where its impact on 'non' availability can give it a more determinate meaning.

The life of components is influenced by myriad factors, some of the more important of which are:

- quality of production
- intelligence of design
- relationships to other materials/components
- quality of workmanship on site
- exposure to the elements
- exposure to wear and tear
- maintenance regime
- quality of maintenance

- obsolescence

- change of use.

A technique for identifying and controlling the risks attendant upon these and other life-cycle drivers is introduced and explained below.

The 'shell' of the building will have different life-cycle characteristics from the 'scenery' and the services.

The 'shell' is the structure and enclosure; the 'scenery' is the internal finishes, fittings and fixtures and the 'services' are the mechanical, electrical and electronic facilities.

The structural components such as the frame, external walls and structural floors should last the building's life; however, structural settlement due to adverse ground conditions or unexpected problems such as 'concrete cancer' (caused by the presence of sea-salts in reinforced concrete) very occasionally occur resulting in the need for premature replacement.

The scenery will either become obsolescent and require (but not always get) replacement in five to seven years or be overtaken by changes brought about by organisational re-structuring ('churn') - see Chapter 4.2. The impact of this phenomenon is universal but the less important the user and location the more the 'make-do-and-mend' regime prevails so that component lives of carpets, ceilings and alike get stretched - sometimes to a point where working conditions are sub-standard and inappropriate to the organisational business needs. PFI/PPP contracts will define the point at which this represents; 'non-availability', but the need for a 'change project' as opposed to a piecemeal replacement of components seems to be the biggest 'grey' area in computing life expectancies.

The 'services' in a new building will last up to 20 years but, again, churn usually brings about a lot of modifications and replacement of the lesser components such as radiators, air extracts and the like. The impact of life-cycle replacement periods on the whole-life economics of building services in considered in detail in the book "Whole Life Economics of Building Services" (as referred in Chapter 7.1). So the life-cycles of the 'scenery' and 'services' are to some extent influenced by usage and changes in user requirement whereas the 'shell' life-cycles have only very occasional replacements due to alterations. however, the protective elements of the shell, eg roof coverings and external renders may well need to be replaced due to physical deterioration and wear and tear before life expiry of a building.

Life-cycle prediction

The advent of PFI/PPP-type outsourcing of whole building or estate provision has focussed the contractors' attention on life-cycle prediction as never before. Unfortunately there exists little valid or verifiable data on how long components have lasted - at least not in a form in which entrepreneurs could make reliable future predictions. The problem facing the PFI/PPP contractors is that the cost of running, maintaining and replacing buildings and their components is critical to the financial success of their venture and, as such, is a very high risk centre. This is a dichotomy because, from the user's perspective, such amounts are relatively trivial and non-sensitive in terms of financial risk (see Fig 10.6.CC below).

The irony of it all is that the risk to the user lies not in the relatively trivial cost of the maintenance and replacement of components but in the impact of any future facilities deficiency on business efficiency. By outsourcing the provision and maintenance of premises the users lose control of the critical 'functional performance' risk factor.

Nevertheless, as a result of this new and popular procurement route the contractors' need for good life-cycle data is suddenly of paramount importance; but where to find it?

Sources of data

There is now a proliferation of publications suggesting 'normal' life-cycles of components. This data can only be based on the opinions and experience of experts in the field because very little (if any) formal collection of such data is carried out anywhere. In any event the predictions can only relate to 'average' conditions - whatever that may mean - and cannot directly address the life-cycle drivers listed above which will easily shorten or extend the life-cycles by substantial amounts.

The anecdotal evidence contained in these published schedules is useful as a basis of sensitivity analysis on the traditional building components used in conventional design solutions. However the schedules cannot, of themselves, provide finite proof of life-expectancy; where new materials and techniques exist there is no experience at all to go on so we have to guess. All new technology is suspect and the construction industry is not clever enough or sufficiently adequately invested in research to second-guess potential failures with any degree of reliability.

In order to predict life-cycles of new buildings (and their systems and components) with reasonable accuracy there are three pre-conditions:

- good data must exist on the life-cycles of the relevant components

- control over the design and construction process must lie with the life-cycle fund manager, or

- sufficient due diligence must be carried out by the purchaser of a new building from the constructor - preferably exercised throughout all stages of the project.

Such conditions will minimise the risk of human predictive and implementation error (without eliminating it) but will not be able to address the consequences of change of use; insofar as the ICF is able to keep one step ahead of the business requirement their premises policy should hold the key to change of use prediction.

In the case of existing buildings the facilities manager will have to find out by inspection what to expect by way of residual life-cycles. The only optimisation they can make relates to the influence of their maintenance regime on the residual life, and that will be the subject of financial modelling and sensitivity analysis.

New and more recently completed buildings will contain some components and design features of which there is little or no precedental life-cycle data: these will have to be the subject of intelligent life-cycle appraisal. However, in the case of traditional (or neo-traditional) construction the condition, and hence residual life-cycles, of components should be able to be assessed and replacements costed with some degree of reliability.

Given a typical 20 year period of one user's occupation it is likely that many of the 'services' components and most of the 'scenery' components will face life-expiry during the period whereas relatively few buildings should need much in the way of replacements of the 'shell' components - perhaps failures such as the odd badly leaking flat roof or some 'shot' glazing here and there being the most likely cost centres.

Unfortunately there are too many examples of failure of new products which did not perform as promised, and this is a real problem when designers want to be innovative.

Fig. 10.6.K (over the page) (repeated from Chapter 2.4.3, Fig 2.4.C) gives some guidance in respect of average life-cycles of typical materials and components.

Computerised techniques will also generate more information on physical performance, eg maintenance management data-bases. If the data-bases are properly kept up to date they will provide good data for future analyses. Better still, the pro-active financial management control systems now coming to the scene can provide, not only ready access to actual life-cycles and costs but also an audit trail back to the original predictions via the maintenance and performance history.

Fig. 10.6.K *Typical economic life of some common components*

Elements from BCIS[1] standard form of cost analysis			Estimated life years	Preventive maintenance
2.C.2	Roof coverings	Slate	30+	Replace damaged or slipped slates as necessary.
		Asphalt	15-30	Recoat with solar paint every 3 years. Replenish chippings as necessary.
		3-layer felt / chippings	10-20	Inspect annually and repair localised damage.
		Clay tiles	30+	Replace damaged tiles if necessary.
		Concrete tiles	20+	Replace damaged tiles as required. Colour may fade.
		Copper	50+	None.
		Aluminium	35+	Annual inspection and maintenance. Regular cleaning with non-alkaline detergent. Renewal of side / end lap seals as necessary.
		UPVC	15-20	Replace damaged sections as required.
2.E	External walls	Stone	50+	Visual inspection every 5 years. If necessary cleaning, repointing and surface repairs.
		Brickwork	50+	If efflorescence occurs salt deposits to be brushed off.
		Concrete blocks	40+	None.
		Reinforced concrete	35+	None.
		Rendering	20-40	Can be washed by water jetting at mains pressure. Cracks and damaged render to be cut out and repaired.
		Timber framing	20-40	None.
		Timber cladding	25-30	Redecorate-stain every 3 years or paint every 5 years. Renew creosote every 3 years.
		Curtain walling	20-40	As manufacturers' instructions
2.F.1	Windows	Softwood	25-40	Stain at 3 years, paint at 5 years. Replace unpainted.
		Hardwood	40-60	Stain at 3 years, paint at 5 years. Replace glazed.
		Galvanised steel	15-35	Redecorate steel after 20 years and every 5 years thereafter. Replacing glazing gaskets, weatherstripping, etc. as required. Replace unpainted ironmongery plated at 10 years or stainless steel at 20 years.
		UPVC	10-25	Clean every 5 months with non-alkaline detergent to maintain appearance. Renew weatherstripping and gaskets every 10 years. Renew hardware every 10 years if plated or 15 years if stainless.
		Aluminium	20-35	If painted, repeat every 5 years. Renew weatherstripping and gaskets every 10 years. Renew hardware every 10 years.
2.F.2	External doors	Softwood	20-30	Redecorate: Stain every 3 years, paint every 5 years. Lubricate ironmongery when required. Replace weatherstripping as required.
		Hardwood	30-50	Redecorate: Stain every 3 years, paint every 5 years. Lubricate ironmongery when required. Replace compounds and seals as required.
		Galvanised steel	15-30	Occasional cleaning with non-abrasive cleaner. Repaint every year.
		UPVC	15-25	Clean every 6 months with non-alkaline detergent. Adjust and lubricate ironmongery as required by manufacturer. Clean track regularly. Replace draught strips and gaskets every 10 years.
		Aluminium	20-30	Clean every 6 months with non-alkaline detergent. Adjust and lubricate ironmongery as required by manufacturer. Clean track regularly. Replace rollers and locking mechanism every 10 years. Replace draught strips and gaskets every 10 years.

[1] Building Cost Information Service, RICS, UK.

Elements from BCIS[1] standard form of cost analysis			Estimated life years	Preventive maintenance
3.A	Wall finishes	Plaster	35+	None.
		Plasterboard	20-40	None.
3.B	Floor finishes	Vinyl	10-20	None.
		Woodblock	40-70	None.
		Terrazzo	40+	None.
		Quarry tiles	50+	None.
3.C.1	Finishes to ceiling	Mineral tiles	15-40	None.
		Carpets	5-10	Regular cleaning to manufacturers' instructions
5.D.2	Cold water service	Pumps	10-20	Clear pump regularly. Clean strainer regularly. Service pump as recommended by manufacturer.
		Pipework	10-35	None.
		Tanks	15-35	Maintenance of ball valve, checking of overflow pipe, retaining insulation / covers in place.
5.D.3	Hot water service	Pumps	5-20	Visually examine for leaks and if necessary renew gland packing and seals every quarter. Change overdue pumps every quarter.
		Pipework	20-35	None.
		Calorifiers	20-35	Every 2 years inspect scaling to calorifier shell and tubes. Cleaning and descaling when required. Monthly inspection of safety valves and gauges etc.
5.E	Heat source	Steel boilers	10-20	Annual service and maintenance contract.
		Calorifiers	20-35	Every 2 years inspect scaling to calorifier shell and tubes. Cleaning and descaling when required. Monthly inspection of safety valves and gauges etc.
		Tanks	15-35	Maintenance of ball valve, checking of overflow pipe, retaining insulation / covers in place.
		Pipework	20-35	None.
		Control equipment	15-20	Regular inspection / testing
5.F.1	Water / Steam	Steel radiators	15-20	Regular dosing with inhibitor.
		Pipework	10-35	None.
5.F.4	Local heating	Gas burners	15-20	Annual service and maintenance contract
5.F.7	Heating with ventilation (air treated centrally)	Heater batteries	15-20	Annual service and maintenance contract
5.F.8	Heating with cooling air (air treated locally)	Water chillers	15-20	Annual service and maintenance contract
5.F.9	Heating with cooling air (air treated locally)	Cooler batteries	15-20	Annual service and maintenance contract
		Cooling towers	10-25	Water treatment, regular cleaning
5.G	Ventilating system	Air handling systems	8-15	Annual service and maintenance contract
5.H.1	Electric source and mains	Switchgear	15-30	Regular inspection and testing
		Main cables	25-35	Regular inspection and testing
5.H.2	Electric power supplies	Electric motors	20-25	Annual service and maintenance contract
		Main cables	25-35	None.
5.J	Gas installation	Gas burners	15-20	Annual service and maintenance contract
		Pipework	20-35	None.

In summary, data is required under the following categories:

- the life of buildings
- the life of systems
- the life of components
- the cost of maintenance
- the cost of repair
- the cost of replacement
- the causes of deterioration and failure
- the consequential effects of deterioration and failure.

Until better data is available facilities managers have to use the best evidence they have; better an intelligent prediction than no thought at all - which seems yet to be the convention in many new-build and refurbishment projects where the risk of life-cycle replacement resides with the building user.

Intelligent life-cycle prediction

Fig. 10.6.L
Risk appraisal - life-cycle replacement prediction proforma (1)

Project: Example	Element: External walls	Life expectancy projection			
Scenario - 1	Component: Curtain walling	Maximum life-years		30	30
		Minimum life-years		(10)	-
Risk exposure centre	Risk exposure factor	Contribution to loss of life-years		Maximum loss	20*
		Worst case	Probability %	Probable loss	
1. Component	Quality Manufacturer Obsolescence Complexity of operation	(8.0)	80	(6.4)	
2. Specification / Design detailing	Adjacent materials Adjacent detailing	(3.0)	90	(2.7)	
3. Installation	Complexity Site management Familiarity Competence Protection Accessibility Site conditions	(5.0)	70	(3.5)	
4. Local factors – in use	User activities Environment Location of Building Redundancy	(4.0)	35	(1.4)	
5. Others	Specify	-	-	-	
Maximum loss - years		(20*)	-	-	
* The 'worst case' total must always be the same as the 'maximum loss' prediction	Probable loss - years		(14.0)		
	Total predicted loss - years				(14)
Note: Tinted areas to be written by hand	Total predicted life-cycle - years				16

Source: Bernard Williams Associates

State-of-the-art life-cycle prediction makes extensive use of statistical modelling to help to minimise and contain the risks inherent in predicting component lives. The principles of this approach are discussed below; however, first consider the more practical and 'intelligent' approach to risk management of life-cycle prediction.

Fig. 10.6.L shows a useful proforma which enables any or all members of the design and construction team to contribute to the predictive process.

The objective of the technique underlying this proforma is that an estimate of the 'normal' range of years between minimum and maximum life-cycle of a component or system is usually available from one source or another; the list at Fig. 10.6.K above is typical of the most commonly used components and some of the published schedules contain details of a much wider range of components.

The factors which cause component failure before its natural life-expiry date can be identified; the proforma lists the most important of these 'Risk Exposure Factors' under the heading 'Risk Exposure Centre'. The initial objective of this system is to get a consensus view from the project team as to the likely impact of each of these factors on the life of the component under scrutiny.

The first step is to list the normal life-range, eg in the case of a particular proprietary curtain walling system the range might be from 10 to 30 years. This range is inserted in the box headed 'life expectancy projection' on the proforma and the difference between the two - ie (30-10) = 20 years - is the maximum amount of life-expectancy which the 'risk exposure factors' can influence.

Having established this 'range of influence' the team must next set about discussion of the 'relative weighting' of each 'risk exposure factor' in a worst case scenario. At this stage they must ignore any decisions which have been, or are yet to be, taken concerning the procurement process and the actual status of the local factors in use.

In this example the team will be asked to apportion the 20 years 'range of influence' between the four risk exposure centres according to their view as to the relative seriousness of the factors with regard to the early failure of the windows in question.

The views of one member of the team are shown here, ie

- component   -   8
- specification/detailing   -   3
- installation   -   5
- local factors   -   4

    Total   -   20 years.

The total must always equal the life-expectancy range - in this case 20 years. The other team members may have different views, and the discussion around the selections will be a valid contribution to the design development process in its own right. The complete range of views may be averaged at this stage; alternatively, the individual opinions may be taken forward for statistical processing.

Whichever route is chosen the next step involves 'scenario planning'. The scenario we are concerned with here relates to the specific circumstances of the design, installation and use of the component. Taking each of the 'risk exposure centres' in turn the following scenario is proposed:

- component   -   new, untried product
- specification/detailing   -   inexperienced architectural practice
- installation-small local builder   -   little experience of non-traditional construction
- local factors   -   high levels of pollution in the area.

The team is then asked to assess the 'probability' of the 'worst case' failure occurring given the scenario being painted. In the case of the view presented in the Figure the probability forecast is a percentage likelihood: so the view is that in generic terms 8 of the potential 20 years (maximum) lost could be down to component failure and that given the untried nature of the product and its manufacturer there is an 80% chance of this worst case failure occurring.

Working through all the risk exposure centres for the relevant scenario the 'probable contribution to the loss of life-years' is established. The total loss is expected to be 12.9 years. So, instead of 30 years maximum life the windows are expected to last only (30-14) years, ie 16 years. If all the probabilities were shown as 100% all 20 years would be lost and the windows would only be predicted to last the minimum 10 years in the range.

Obviously this is quite a theoretical calculation. However, it focuses attention on the risks inherent in the process - not only the risk of life-cycle prediction but also the causes of failure upon which those predictions are - or should be - based.

The life-cycle fund manager, presented with this curtain walling system and this scenario, not only knows the basis of the team's prediction but also the issues that must be addressed in order to control the life-cycle risk.

As discussed above the team's average views can be taken as a consensus. Alternatively the views of all the team members can be taken through to the risk modelling stage to be treated as if they were real-life data.

Fig. 10.6.M shows an alternative forecast for a scenario in which:

- the component is well-established

- the architect/detailer is skilled and experienced in the use of the component

- the builder is well-established and has good quality control procedures

- there are no local environment problems.

Risk modelling

There are various statistical techniques for risk modelling which are used in prediction of life-cycles of components and systems. One which has been gaining in popularity in recent times is the Monte Carlo simulation and Latin Hypercube methodology. Clearly the detail of such systems is outside the scope of this text. However, readers should know that these programs can accommodate:

- individual cost variables

- individual time variables

- combined cost and time variables

- other variable assumptions.

The results will either be represented as a uniform or skewed triangular distribution: the 'uniform distribution' emphasises the average life-cycles and costs in the sample whereas the 'skewed distribution' represents the 'weight' of the sample's responses. The differences in the results are shown at Figs. 10.6.N and 10.6.P (over two pages).

Fig. 10.6.M
Risk appraisal - life-cycle replacement prediction proforma (2)

Project: Example Scenario - 2	Element: **External walls** Component: **Curtain walling**		Life expectancy projection			
			Maximum life-years		30	30
			Minimum life-years		(10)	-
Risk exposure centre	Risk exposure factor	Contribution to loss of life-years		Maximum loss	20*	
		Worst case	Probability %	Probable loss		
1. Component	Quality Manufacturer Obsolescence Complexity of operation	(8.0)	20	(1.6)		
2. Specification / Design detailing	Adjacent materials Adjacent detailing	(3.0)	30	(0.9)		
3. Installation	Complexity Site management Familiarity Competence Protection Accessibility Site conditions	(5.0)	20	(1.0)		
4. Local factors – in use	User activities Environment Location of Building Redundancy	(4.0)	10	(0.4)		
5. Others	Specify	-	-	-		
Maximum loss - years		(20*)	-	-		
* The 'worst case' total must always be the same as the 'maximum loss' prediction		Probable loss - years		(3.9)		
		Total predicted loss – years - say				(4)
Note: Tinted areas to be written by hand		Total predicted life-cycle – years				26

Source: Bernard Williams Associates

Fig. 10.6.N
Distribution for annual life cycle replacement cost for average specification office building using uniform triangular distributions

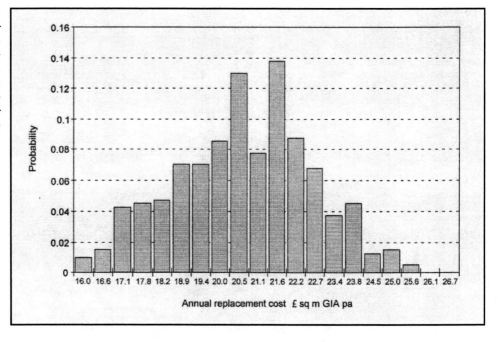

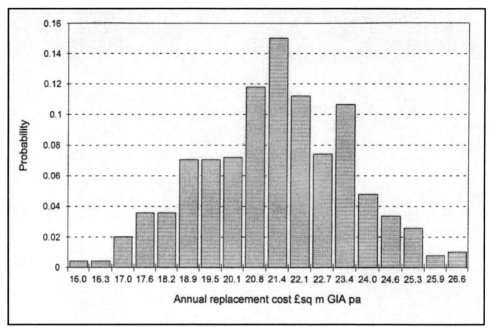

10.6.5 LIFE-CYCLE FUND MANAGEMENT - THE ROLE

A new role identified

It will be apparent from the previous section that there is more to component life expectancy than merely putting predictions into a statistical model and relying implicitly on the answer.

The risk of both life-expectancy and replacement costs have to be borne by the life-cycle fund managers. They will either form part of the ICF or be members of PPP-contracting consortia. In either case they have the job of making sure that:

- the financial equation gives value for money

- there is enough provision in the budget to meet future demands

- all risks are identified, addressed and maintained

- all available risk-buffers, eg guarantees, warranties and indemnities, are identified, secured and monitored over time.

To carry out this task effectively life-cycle fund managers need to have a properly identified role and authority. They need to be present from briefing stage onwards, as part of the project management team; however, unlike the project manager, their role continues beyond project completion.

The process of life-cycle cost planning and control is described below. It is the life-cycle fund manager who has to ensure that the design decision-making processes - such as the prediction risk analysis (Fig 10.6.L) and zero-based performance option appraisals (see Fig. 10.6.W below) - are incorporated in the design development programme.

When the decisions are taken on the strategies in terms of design, installation, maintenance and replacement the life-cycle fund manager has to monitor the progress of all the strategies through planning and implementation.

Upon completion of the project the life-cycle cost model, as finally delivered, becomes the financial expression of the asset management plan. The monitoring of this plan, and all decisions subsequently taken with regard to it, are the life-cycle fund manager's responsibility - right through to demolition.

10.6.6 CONTROLLING THE LIFE-CYCLE FUND

Application of cost control principles

The three facets of cost control - budgetary control, procurement and value engineering (see Chapter 2.2.1, Fig 2.2.A) are, of course, totally applicable to the process of life-cycle cost control.

However, the emphasis between the various components of the equation, ie initial operating and replacement costs, will shift depending on the financial interest of the building developer. Developer/dealers (see Chapter 10.2.1) are likely to be more concerned with minimising their capital cost at the expense of revenue cost which will be incurred by other parties; this is a historic tendency which is, thank goodness, starting to be changed due to the advent of a buyer's market, a more discerning and powerful user lobby and PFI/PPP-type contracts as discussed above.

The owner-occupier will probably be seeking a better balance between initial and running costs than is conventionally available in speculative buildings to rent where the tenant normally has full responsibility for all repairs, maintenance and replacement of building components. Concentrating therefore on the owner-occupier's equation, let us consider how cost control principles should be applied from inception to completion.

10.6.7 WHOLE-LIFE BUDGETARY CONTROL

Principles and application

The principles and application of budgetary control described in Chapters 2.2.4 and 6.3.6 apply to new-build and refurbishment schemes in just the same way as to fitting-out. In such projects, as with major fitting-out work, the budgetary control will nearly always be carried out by specialists - either independent consultants or members of a packaged one-stop-shop team.

Facilities managers should be closely involved with the development of the budget cost plan and they or their project managers must have power of veto over any proposal to depart from the cost plan agreement; specifically they have three critical functions to carry out.

First, to make sure that the cost plan is right for the performance required of the building, ie its physical, functional and financial performance. This will not be easy, given the conventional wisdom (or lack thereof!) in this area.

Second it is also (as has been discussed in Chapter 2.2.3) an integral part of the value engineering process to set the budget at an optimum level, ie challenging yet demonstrably achievable in terms of these performance requirements.

Although such analysis of the functional value of a scheme design is undeniably difficult, the third task of the facilities manager, ie correctly balancing the initial expenditure of a scheme against the revenue cost implications of its physical performance, is achievable - but only within a discipline which must be imposed on the design team from the outset.

The whole-life capital cost plan

Turning back to the life-cycle cost analysis at Option A in Fig. 10.6.B let us assume for present purposes that this is the forecast out-turn from a cost plan proposal put forward by the design team at sketch design stage. Fig. 10.6.Q analyses the total initial and replacement costs into the detail needed to enable a whole-life cost centre procedure to be operated; the figures can either come from a model or be the outcome of a fully costed scheme proposal. The facilities manager should require the design team to demonstrate in detail the basis of their forecasts for building and component life-cycles and costs of operating, maintenance, repair and replacement.

The figure illustrates how the model works in respect of the 'roof' cost element which is part of the primary element 'superstructure'. The figure incorporates all the factors needed to calculate the initial and replacement cost components of a high-level whole-life budget, as follows:

- primary element (column 1) is the principal generic grouping of building cost elements for capital cost budgeting

- element (column 2) is a typical protocol for elemental analysis of capital costs

- components/systems (column 3) are in effect sub-elements; in this example the sub-elements of the roof element are extracted from the model

- the outline specification of the principal features of the component/system are given in column 4

- columns 5,6 and 7 produce the total estimated capital cost of the sub-elements and elements (column 8) using the technique of elemental cost estimating described in Chapter 6.3.6

- the conversion of these estimated costs to £ per sq m of the gross internal area of the building (column 9) is for convenience of estimating off-line

- column 10 gives the estimated proportion of the component/system which is subject to replacement

- the replacement quantity (column 11) is derived from multiplying the original quantity in column 5 by the column 10 percentage

- the estimated addition at column 12 is to the original unit rate in column 7 and allows for the problems of taking out and replacing existing components in existing buildings; the product of the multiplication is in column ...

- column 13, the cyclical replacement unit rate is the product of columns 7 and 12

- the total cost of one cyclical replacement (column 14) is the product of columns 11 and 13

- the result of an off-line calculation of the number of replacements anticipated during the building life-cycle is given in column 15

- the total cost of replacement (column 16) is the product of columns 14 and 15.

Whole-life capital and operating cost plan

Fig. 10.6.R (over the page) takes the results (such as these computed in a model like Fig. 10.6.Q) and sets them alongside the operating cost centres. It may be noted that these are not just those which are premises related such as maintenance and cleaning; they also include some of the relevant support services cost centres, like archiving and mail and messenger service, the costs of which may possibly be influenced by the design and specification of the building.

This model is constructed as follows.

The initial replacement costs taken from the previous Fig. 10.6.Q are included in columns 1A and 1B. (It should be noted that the calculations for these two figures are shown separately for convenience of illustration - in practice they are all part of the same modelling process).

Section 2 matches the premises services costs to the building elements to which they relate. So, in 2A the costs of services maintenance are apportioned between 'plumbing', 'mechanical'. 'electrical' and 'lifts'. The predicted energy consumption from these elements is also apportioned between them.

Fig. 10.6.Q *Typical life-cycle cost model - initial and replacement costs of roof elements (part only shown)*

Primary element (1)	Cost-element (2)	Components / System (sub-element) (3)	Outline specification (4)	Total unit Quantity (5)	Unit (6)	Unit rate £ (7)	Total initial cost £ (8)	Initial cost sq m GIFA £ (9)	% subject to replacement (10)	Adjusted replacement quantity (11)	% increase to unit rate (12)	Cyclical rate £ (13)	Cyclic replacement cost £ (14)	Number of times replaced (15)	Total replacement costs £ (16)
Substructure	Substructure														
Superstructure	Frame														
	Upper floors														
	Roof		*Details omitted for clarity*												
		Pitched roof coverings	Concrete tiled dormers	680	sq m EUQ	120.00	81,600	4.80	50%	340	150%	180	61,200	1	61,200
		Flat roof coverings	Asphalt	2,380	sq m EUQ	96.00	228,480	13.44	50%	1,190	135%	130	154,224	1	154,224
		Roof structure	Reinforced concrete	3,400	sq m EUQ	200.00	680,000	40.00	100%	3,400	150%	300	1,020,000	-	
		Glazed rooflights	Double glazed, UPVC	340	sq m EUQ	640.00	217,600	12.80	100%	340	125%	800	272,000	2	544,000
		Roof drainage	Cast Iron	3,400	sq m EUQ	7.20	24,480	1.44	100%	3,400	125%	9	30,600	1	30,600

CONTINUED

	Total initial and replacement costs						27,064,317	1,592.02							20,868,901*

* This is the total replacement cost of all the elements

Fig. 10.6.R *Typical whole-life cost model - initial replacement and operating costs (part only shown)*

Element	1A. Initial costs £'000	1B. Replacement costs £'000	2A. Services maintenance	2B. Building maintenance	2C. Cleaning	2D. Pest control	2E. Utilities	2F. Reception security	2G. Grounds maintenance	2H. Total	3A. Mail and messenger	3B. Archiving and storage	3C. Furniture	3D. Catering	3E. Porterage	4. Capital allowances	4. VAT
Substructure	3,090																
Frame	3,040																
Upper floors	1,600											✓					
Roof	1,970	2,460		610						610							
Staircase	825																
External walls	3,155			1,200	815					2,015							
External doors	110	290		610	210					820							
Windows	3,620	4,180		610	815					1,425							
Internal walls	66			305						305			✓				
Internal partitions	50			610	815					1,425			✓			✓	
						CONTINUED											
Plumbing	1,060	1,300	11,200		2,400		350			13,950							
Mechanical	7,230	8,350	9,120				9,600			18,720			✓	✓	✓		
Electrical	5,090	12,015	5,600				3,710	1,680		10,990			✓	✓	✓		
Lifts	510	1,300	1,120		Inc		350			1,470	✓		✓	✓	✓		
External hard landscaping	1,820	2,610							130	130							
External soft landscaping	260								655	655							
Unallocated	0					1,250		15,040	655	16,945							
* Total	43,302	33,390	16,960	5,744	6,592	1,250	14,496	16,720	785	625,547							

* These are the totals for all of the elements

At the early cost modelling stage these costs would not be attributed to a detailed design or specification, more likely emanating from a 'target' whole-life-cost benchmarking program modelling best-performance economic solutions.

Cost-checking design development

However, as the design develops the proposed design and specification solutions must be tested against this model (including the part illustrated in Fig. 10.6.Q). Of course, the option appraisal test described below at Fig. 10.6.W (previously introduced in Chapters 1.2 and 2.2) should be used prior to the formal testing against this model; equally the life-cycle prediction appraisal tool discussed at Fig. 10.6.L above would be used to test the validity of the assumptions culminating in the totals in column 1B (taken from Fig. 10.6.Q).

Ideally the total whole-life out-turn cost should not exceed the theoretical target from the model, and this may or may not be subject to DCF calculations, depending upon the purpose of the study.

The columns in section 3 of Fig. 10.6.R are there as a reminder of the 'knock-on' effects of building design on the 'non-premises' facilities support services, eg the cost of internal partitions needs to be assessed in the light of the 'furniture' budget (column 3C) wherein may be found the cost of screens and dividers in open-planned space. Equally the 'mail and messenger' services (column 3A) may be based on automatic vertical distribution in which case the operating costs will be lower but the capital costs higher.

Section 4 is a reminder that the tax implications of both capital and income expenditure (see Chapter 11.2) may need to be reviewed if the true costs to a taxable organisation are to be reflected in the cost model.

Given the state-of-the-art in terms of culture, philosophy and lack of data this whole process will undoubtedly stretch everyone involved including the facilities manager. Nevertheless, it will make the design team think through the consequences of their proposals in a way which should avoid the worst excesses of the traditional process. In that connection a recent anecdote concerned the case of a facilities manager taking over a brand new bespoke building and discovering, for the first time, that the external cladding required to be power-jet cleaned every three months to stay within the conditions of the product guarantee.

Guarantees and the like

While on the subject of guarantees it is important to be aware of the great variation which exists between the length, quality and cost of guarantees, warranties, indemnities and post-installation maintenance available from suppliers and contractors. The implications of these insurance policies for life-cycle costs and performance must be thoroughly examined at bid evaluation stage; furthermore, the life-cycle implications in terms of cost, particularly in the earlier 'protected' stages, must be built into the life-cycle cost plan and kept under constant review during occupation.

The significance of operating and replacement costs

Except where the buildings and services form a PFI/PPP contractor's core business the relatively insignificant impact of running costs on the overall business finances, coupled with the effect of discounting on deferred expenditure, means that the most important reason for this exacting process of appraisal is the avoidance of unexpected problems such as that with the external cladding as described above. It is, however, as well to remember that the facilities manager who unwittingly inherits a building which is difficult or expensive to operate and maintain will face a running battle over the years with customers or the finance director - or probably both.

Although the operating and replacement costs are never likely to sway the option appraisal one way or another, to the facilities manager five years into the life of a building on the inevitable tight budget it can be a matter of life or death as to whether there are enough funds to run the building properly. In any case, if there is no good reason to build a problem for the future then it should not be allowed to happen.

Detailed cost appraisal of options

An example of calculations which might be offered in support of the cost plan proposed at Figs. 10.6.Q and R is given at Fig. 10.6.S. This examines the proposals for the lift installation and the estimated consequences in terms of maintenance, overhaul (ie replacement of secondary components) and energy consumption.

Fig. 10.6.S
Calculation for comparative life-cycle cost analyses of alternative lift installations in Options 'A' and 'B' - not discounted

Lift A Low specification - 8 - person	£ Life cycle costs – 50 year period						
Cost centre	Year 1	Year 2	Year 3	Year 4	Year 5	Year 6 etc	50 - years Total
Initial installation	100,800	0	0	0	0	0	100,800
Energy	4,320	4,320	4,320	4,320	4,320	4,320	108,000
Maintenance	19,200	19,200	19,200	19,200	19,200	19,200	480,000
Cleaning	9,600	9,600	9,600	9,600	9,600	9,600	240,000
Overhaul every 5yrs	-	-	-	-	7,096	-	180,000
Total	**133,920**	**33,120**	**33,120**	**33,120**	**40,216**	**33,120**	**1,108,800**

Assumptions	Floor to floor height of 3.5m
	Standard finishes to cars, doors and gates
	Electrically operated 8 or 10 person lifts
	Serving 6 levels at a speed of 1 m/s

Lift B High specification - 10 - person	£ Life cycle costs – 50 year period						
Cost centre	Year 1	Year 2	Year 3	Year 4	Year 5	Year 6 etc	50 - years Total
Initial Installation	115,200	0	0	0	0	0	115,200
Energy	4,000	4,000	4,000	4,000	4,000	4,000	100,000
Maintenance	20,800	20,800	20,800	20,800	20,800	20,800	520,000
Cleaning	12,640	12,640	12,640	12,640	12,640	12,640	316,000
Overhaul every 5yrs	-	-	-	-	3,813	-	94,000
Total	**152,640**	**37,440**	**37,440**	**37,440**	**41,253**	**37,440**	**1,145,200**

Assumptions	Add £ 6,400 for –	Stainless steel finishes to cars
	Add £ 6,400 for –	Enhanced efficiency motors and energy saving controls
	Add £ 1,600 for –	Serving 6 levels at a speed of 1.25 m/s

In the more sophisticated appraisal processes the consequences of 'non-availability' or 'unserviceability' of premises due to failures and/or works necessary to remedy or prevent them can be built into the decision-making process.

As designs are progressed all these assumptions should be formally tested by the whole team and the client's representative using the tools described above and changes of substance not permitted without the client's formal authority.

Budgetary control in occupation

The third function which the facilities manager must carry out in budgetary control is to set up from the outset a fully pro-active budgetary control system for the operating, maintenance, repair and replacement costs during occupancy. Such a system should be linked into an asset management program and, ideally, will contain the following features:

- automatic end-of-year accounts reconciliation
- pro-active budgetary control forecasts of potential commitment
- reports on contractor exposure and performance
- audit trail through all pre/post-budget activity
- risk appraisal of budget change proposals
- automatic VAT liability computation
- options to transfer excesses to contingency budget
- record of contract and contractor details
- built-in benchmarking parameters and performance indicators
- record of leases, rents and service charges
- option to specify the facilities managers own cost centres and risk categories
- graphic and tabular outputs.

The important thing to observe is that any control system is only as good as the people charged with operating it. A budgetary control system requires the basic assumptions underlying the budget estimates to be recorded in such a way that potential changes can be identified by simple reference back. This takes expertise, and the process of picking out events or proposals which will lead to cost over-runs (or under-spends) requires a discipline which does not come naturally to line managers. Even in the finance departments themselves it is rare to find genuinely pro-active financial management; most are content with reactive budget control by reference to committed expenditure. The corollary of such a reactive approach is that once the budget for one cost centre is spent reductions must be made in other works to recover the position, if that is indeed possible and/or practical.

Ironically, the state-of-art financial control systems now becoming available to cope with the dynamic processes of construction and facilities management may well be the forerunner to changes in the financial management of core business activity.

10.6.8 PROCUREMENT

The role of efficient procurement of both capital and revenue works is considered in Chapters 2.2 and 6.3. One specific issue perhaps worth considering in the whole-life economics context is the concept of 'one-stop-shop' building provision and management discussed earlier and including PFI/PPP-type procurement strategies.

Clearly, the risks to both parties are quite high and both need to provide adequate contingency against deficiency of performance in both building and premises management terms.

As an exercise in risk management 'one-stop-shopping' does have a high cost penalty and is more likely to be to the advantage of the contractor - who gets a lot more work out of it - than the user, who may lose control of the vital management information in an attempt to transfer the risk (and bother) of facilities management. Nevertheless, the principle does have a basis in logic and it should have the effect of encouraging the sort of holistic approach to project appraisal and design development recommended above as an integral part of design development.

10.6.9 VALUE ENGINEERING

The right balance

Here again observance of the principles described in Chapters 2.2 and 6.3 is of paramount importance to the life-cycle fund manager. The process of properly equating initial and deferred expenditure is an essential part of value engineering the building through its whole life.

Presuming that the life-cycle budget has been set at an appropriately 'challenging' level it will remain for the many components, systems and elements to be tested individually for economic efficiency.

Each capital cost centre should have its life-cycle costs forecast in a format such as suggested in Fig. 10.6.S above which compares the un-discounted whole-life costs of the alternative lift proposals. This is depicted graphically in Fig. 10.6.T and the results are compared with the discounted appraisal at Fig. 10.6.U.

Fig. 10.6.T
Aggregated life-cycle cost analyses of alternative lift installations in Options 'A' and 'B' - not discounted

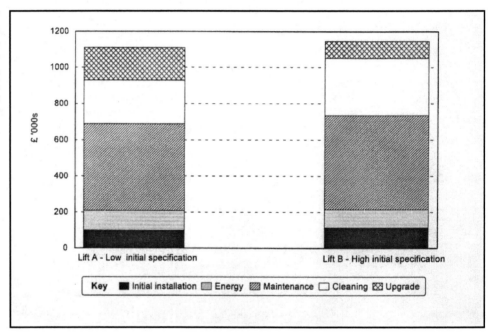

Fig. 10.6.U
Aggregated life-cycle cost analyses of alternative lift installations in Options 'A' and 'B' - discounted at 6%

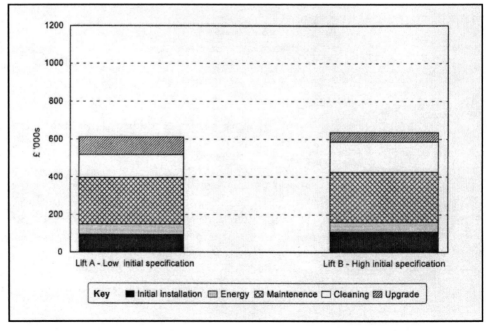

In both these examples the incidence of corporation tax relief on revenue expenditure and via capital allowances will impact on both examples proportionately so may be ignored; however, some sensitivity analysis testing of various tax rates and depreciation regimes could be valuable on larger items of expenditure.

It may be noted also that a comparison of two design options, eg builder's partitions, which do not normally afford tax relief, against 'demountable' partitions which may, (see example in Chapter 6.3.3, Fig 6.3.C) always need to be tested for tax as well as construction efficiency.

Pay-back analysis

A further example of value engineering computation based on the simple 'pay-back period' is shown in the example of energy conservation of lighting installations at Fig. 10.6.V.

Fig. 10.6.V
Lighting energy pay-back period on conservation measures

Lighting energy	Net internal area (NIA) – sq m		Cost per sq m NIA pa £		Total pa £
	4,500	x	8		**36,000**
Lighting control system					
Capital cost					**16,000**
Saving on electricity pa	10%	x	36,000		(3,600)
Saving on re-lamping pa	10%	x	6,800		(680)
Total saving					**(4,280)**

£ 16,000 ÷ 4,280 = 3.74 ie approximately 4 years payback on investment

The three-year pay-back shown on this lighting control proposal (before tax) is, of course, equivalent to a 33% return on initial investment (ROI). Although this looks very good many organisations will not commit management time and resources to such improvements if the pay-back is more than three years. Because the pay-back period is short DCF is not normally applied to such calculations.

Whole-life performance appraisal

A step in the right direction with regard to value engineering the 'whole' performance (ie functional and physical - see Chapter 1.2) is illustrated at Fig. 10.6.W (over the page).

This example was originally developed in the context of a value engineering exercise where the client wished to challenge the design team's principal 'cost drivers' in terms of both functional and physical performance. In the example, using a long list of items suggested by the whole team collectively, the provision of the higher quality lift installation was considered in a round-table discussion by the facilities manager and the design team in the context of the criteria listed. Quite rightly, the client knew they could not easily value the functional criteria but equally realised that the physical performance cost consequences would be much smaller - so did not request detailed financial appraisal of the latter.

Fig. 10.6.W
Performance evaluation - alternative lift installations in an office building

Subject:	Lift installation	Estimated Costs
Location:	Main core	
Zero-base specification:	Option A	£ 100,800
Proposal:	Option B	£ 115,200

Benefits analysis - subjective evaluation		
Effect of proposal on functional performance	Perceived quality	better
	Visual ambience	better
	Comfort	better
	Ergonomics	better
	Flexibility	better
	Safety	N/A
	Speed	better
	Waiting time	better
	Capacity	better
Effect of proposal on on operating costs	Cleaning	better
	Energy	worse
	Maintenance and repairs	better
	Security	N/A
	Insurance	N/A
	Replacement	better
	Management	worse
Effect of proposal on on environment	Energy consumption	N/A
	Embodied energy	N/A
	Sustainability	N/A

As a value engineering tool for all major design decisions this method has much to commend it. Not only does it make sure that all three facets of performance are properly considered by the facilities manager at design stage - it also meets the requirements for the team to give proper consideration to performance consequences of their proposals in principle, even in the absence of good data for in-depth appraisal.

Resourcing the value engineering process

The importance of spending the right amount of time (and costs if necessary) at the right time in order to optimise performance (or reduce the risks of failure - much the same thing) cannot be over-emphasised. Fig. 10.6.X illustrates how the opportunity to influence costs through eliminating wasted resources in the construction and use phases falls sharply away during the early design stages. A small amount of fees paid to experts to thoroughly examine the cost/benefits of design decisions in those early stages will have a big payback down the line.

Shakespeare wrote:

'There is a tide in the affairs of men which, taken at the flood, leads on to fortune; omitted, all the voyage of their lives is lost in shallows and in miseries'.[2]

He might well have been advocating whole-life cost planning!

---

[2] *Julius Caesar Act IV, Scene III*

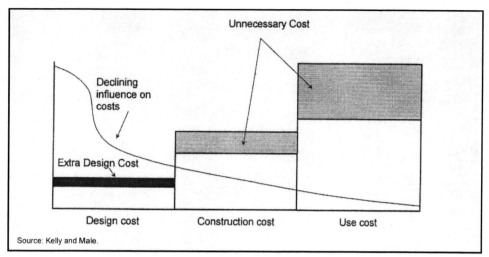

Fig. 10.6.X
Whole-life cost management - the briefing and design stage

10.6.10 LIFE-CYCLE COSTS IN A WIDER CONTEXT

Initial costs in context

Because the initial costs of building development, viewed as a one-off payment out of cashflow, would present a non-affordable investment option for most organisations they are invariably amortised over a medium or long-term - either by way of commercial mortgage for the owner-occupier, or in the rent for the tenant.

Taking two current examples of commercial offices in a city centre and provincial location, costs of development and amortisation over 15 years might be as shown on Fig. 10.6.Y.

Fig. 10.6.Y
Initial development costs and amortisation - front-and-back-office examples

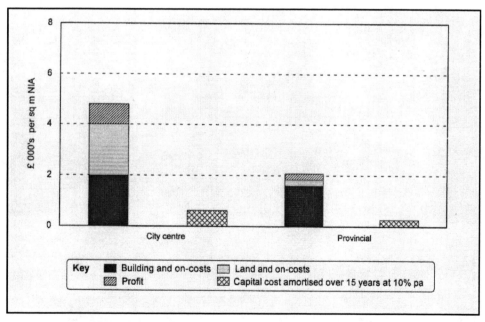

The City centre building having an annual amortisation cost of £600/sq m of net internal area (NIA) including land, finance, fees etc, costs £6m pa. In the context of an organisation of 400 employees the turnover generated in the building might be say £200m pa. Similarly, the Provincial building with an annual amortisation cost of £250/sq m NIA (ie £2.5m pa) might be set in the context of a 'back office' turnover/business cost of £100m pa.

Fig. 10.6.Z (over the page) shows both these sets of relationships as pie diagrams, graphically and perhaps dramatically highlighting the relatively small impact of the initial costs on the whole financial scheme of things - City centre building is about 3.5% and Provincial building 2.5% of turnover.

Fig. 10.6.Z
*Amortised
development costs
in context of annual
turnover*

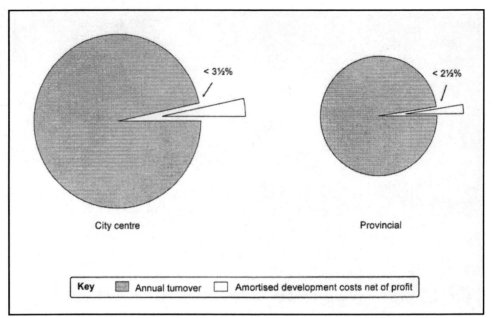

Rentalised by a developer the cost pa would actually be less. Fig 10.6.AA shows the previous example but with capital costs adjusted to include for developer's profit and initial rental being based on initial investment yields of 7% for City centre building and 9% for Provincial building - the latter representing the out-of-town nature of the investment (see Chapters 3.5.3 and 10.3.1 for detailed consideration of investment yields and the effects of location thereon).

Fig. 10.6.AA
*Developer's budget
rentalised - front-
and-back-office
examples*

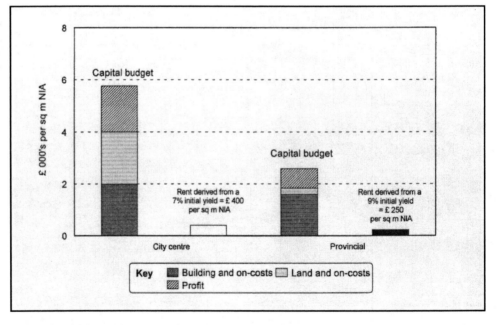

In fact after taking business taxes and operating costs into account the total cost of premises is rarely more than 5 to 6% of turnover unless the space is being under-utilised or there is a need for extremely high quality premises in a specific location.

It may be noted also that when the land and ancillary costs are removed from the equations at Figs 10.6.Y and 10.6.Z the 'building only' component drops to around 1.5% of turnover in all cases - see Fig. 10.6.BB - much less when rental values rise with high demand and rent reviews.

This low ratio of premises costs to total business expenditure is very significant when considering the cost/benefit of buildings in relation to functional performance (see Chapter 1.2.3).

Fig. 10.6.BB
Amortised building and associated costs (fees, interest etc) in context of annual turnover

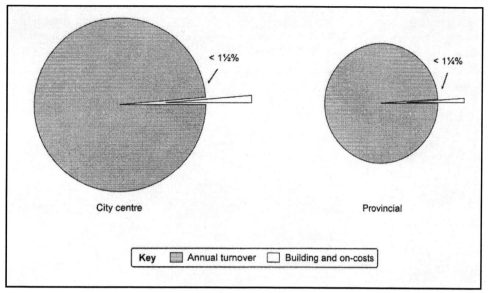

Operating and replacement costs in context

Taking the same examples the typical operating and replacement costs pa are shown in Fig. 10.6.CC and are seen to be no more than about 1% of turnover at maximum; it is interesting to recognise how items as important to facilities managers as maintenance and energy have so little significance in this overall context - though it is not wise to belittle the importance of getting them right in terms of performance, cost and affordability (in cash flow terms).

Fig. 10.6.CC
Premises operating and life-cycle replacement costs in the context of amortised development costs and annual turnover

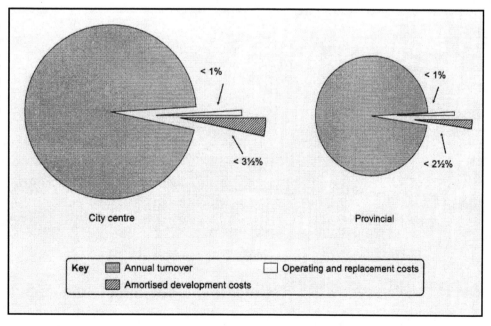

Whole-life v 'people' costs

Fig. 10.6.DD (over the page) looks at the 'city' head office situation showing that the typical level of pre-tax profits at 5% for an administrative operation roughly equates to the premises costs. Clearly any saving in the premises costs which might be effected without loss of performance of the staff in occupation should go straight to the bottom line profit.

However, it is only administrative buildings which are mainly used by employees; service-type accommodation including schools, hospitals, shops and cinemas are mainly used by non-staff personnel. In expressing ratios of premises costs to core business finance it is best to use 'revenue expenditure' as a parameter for administrative buildings (as above) and 'income generated' for the buildings providing serviced accommodation for the core business clients (eg hospitals, theatres and hotels).

Fig. 10.6.DD
Premises cost in the context of typical corporate turnover and profit

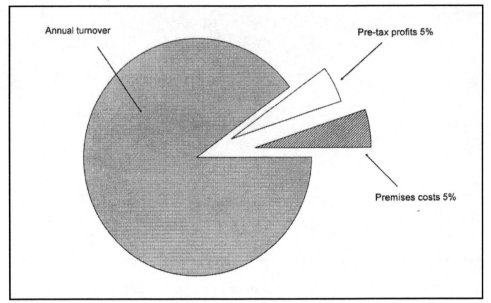

Either way, the influence of the buildings and how they operate will impact on the productive output (in terms of quality of resulting performance) of the core business; consequently the low ratio of premises costs to business costs/turnover will always make it axiomatic that business operational requirements must always drive the premises budget - not vice versa!

10.6.11 WHOLE-LIFE BUILDING QUALITY

Implications for user and provider

A constant theme running through this text relates to the futility of addressing costs in the absence of consideration of quality. With regards to this section on whole-life development economics it is important to understand the issue of whole-life quality - what it means, how to measure it and its implications for both user and provider.

Single-source provision of premises, such as PFI/PPP-type arrangements, mostly measure functional performance in terms of 'availability'; this term usually relates to the condition of the premises measured against a set of performance parameters which purport to describe the point at which the premises are no longer fit for their designed purpose. Such parameters may include air temperatures and quality, fabric disrepair and malfunctioning of key operating systems such as lifts and escalators and, of course, ICT.

In most cases the term 'availability' does not encompass hazards such as 'image', the significance of which is discussed in detail in Chapter 2.5 - Risk Management, or obsolescence.

Any building, taken over a reasonable life-cycle, will be likely to fall foul of both these hazards. Taking, for example, the external enclosure, however prestigious the construction may be at first handover there are many factors such as local pollution, vandalism and simple neglect which can leave it looking very sorry for itself after a time.

Equally, components such as lifts, in spite of diligent maintenance and cleaning, may simply be out of fashion after 10 to 15 years both in terms of image and operation.

Not always, but often - it would be quite wrong to be too dogmatic on the point.

However, the prudent life-cycle fund manager will attempt to identify the quality drivers relating to the building, its environs, its usage and the facilities management and service level regimes to be put in place.

Measuring whole-life quality

The Building Quality Assessment (BQA) system described in Chapter 9.1 2 is a good starting point for whole-life quality planning since it provides an identifiable measure of initial quality for the whole building and the nine generic quality categories.

Fig 10.6.EE shows the level of expenditure on maintenance and replacement for a building having a BQA score of 500. The average operating costs are £200,000 pa with major replacements of components at years 15 and 25; expenditure between years 25 and 30 (end of life) reduces as the need for planned maintenance and other operating expenditure diminishes.

Fig. 10.6.EE
Whole-life building quality

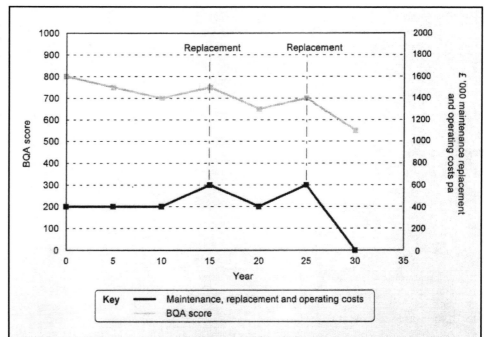

The BQA line on the graph starts at a designed performance of 800 BQA points but drops to a score of 700 over the first 10 years. This theoretical scenario presumes that a combination of deterioration and obsolescence would detract from the quality; however a major replacement in year five partially redresses the loss, taking the BQA score back to 750. By year 20 a further combination of deterioration and obsolescence has knocked the score down to 650 and the year 25 replacement gets it back up to 700. From then until the 30 years end-of-life the graph anticipates a more dramatic tailing off to around 550 BQA points.

It does not have to follow this pattern and much will depend upon the quality of both initial design/specification/construction and life-cycle quality management. The important thing about the exercise, however, is to force all the participants to properly consider the implications of their proposals and decision over time in terms of functional as well as physical and financial performance. After all, the value chain is controlled by functionality, and this must always be at the forefront of any consideration of whole-life facilities economics.

PART E

Taxation

Section 11

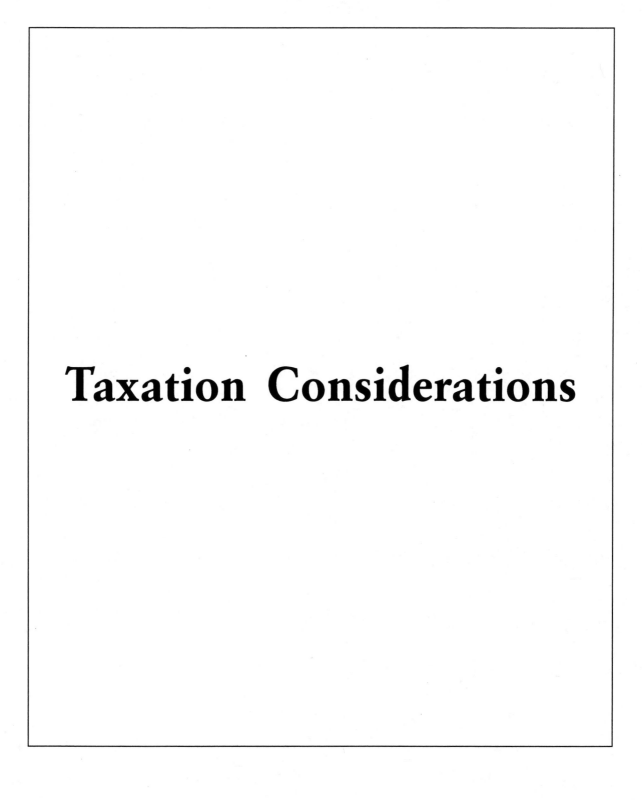

Taxation Considerations

11.1 TAX EFFICIENCY

Introduction

In this chapter the national and local taxation systems are outlined with regard to:

- the principles of taxation, including tax planning

- taxation and the facilities manager

- taxation policy and structure

- the importance of classifying expenditure for tax purposes

- the management of taxation.

The underlying theme is that the facilities manager's role is a pivotal service in ensuring tax efficiency within the organisation, particularly with regard to expenditure on premises, equipment and support services.

11.1.1 PRINCIPLES OF TAXATION INCLUDING TAX PLANNING

Principles

In considering the approach of the government to taxation, it may be useful to visit the principles of taxation:

- **tax base:** it seems that almost everything can be taxed. In recent years, items which have come within the tax base include landfill loads, "congestion" trips by motor vehicles, insurance premiums, carbon emissions and workplace parking spaces. Of course, the tax base is much wider and includes personal and corporate incomes, capital gains on disposals, wealth passing on death, and gifts.

- **fairness or equity:** the principle that like taxpayers should be treated in the same manner and that the application of taxes should be progressive and not regressive.

- **certainty:** the taxpayer should be certain of the nature of a tax, how it is applied and that evasion will be tackled by the authorities.

- **efficiency:** the principle that a tax is administratively efficient as to compliance, and that the cost of collection is small compared with the amount collected.

- **neutrality:** a tax does not distort the market in some unforeseen manner.

Tax planning

In general, tax planning and operations for tax avoidance (not evasion) are legal. Taxation professionals should be able to structure any acquisition, development works, on-going operations, and disposals so as to mitigate taxation effects, and maximise the benefit of any exemption, relief or concession which may be available. For tax planning the facilities manager would normally require the professional services of an accountant, lawyer and, perhaps, a real estate consultant.

As far as property and taxation is concerned the facilities manager may wish to develop a 'feel' for the following question 'areas':

- what is the underlying objective for the transaction, works or other proposal?

- what corporate vehicle or legal status would be the most appropriate?

- what kind of transaction (acquisition, disposal, works and so on) would best serve the purpose?

- what alternative locations are available?

- what taxes apply to the status, proposal, location, business, industry or option to be considered?

- what funding arrangements might suit?

- what exemptions, reliefs or concessions might be available?

- what is the best net-of-tax outcome for each alternative approach to the proposal?

- will the underlying objective be achieved?

Of course, this list only highlights the taxation issues.

In summary, taxation implications are almost certain to arise under the headings of:

- legal status as an entity

- transaction or works

- location

- funding

- industry or business.

11.1.2 TAXATION AND THE FACILITIES MANAGER

Even in the best organised companies, the dialogue between the accounts department and facilities management may become perfunctory and negative; as a result facilities managers all too often fall into the trap of controlling expenditure against the budget without planning, or at least considering, the most tax-efficient solution to a problem, whether it is procurement, maintenance, fitting-out or any other operational cost.

Equally, some accounts departments split costs and budgets for taxation accounting purposes without letting the facilities manager know the implications of the methodology. In every area of expenditure on premises there may be the possibility of an alternative solution or strategy which has different exposure to one tax or another. Very often the decision is not made by the facilities manages; choices such as whether to lease or buy, rent or mortgage will almost certainly be taken with the benefit of the advice of the company's tax specialist.

However, such is the range of choice of specific solutions to premises problems that it is quite easy for the facilities manager unwittingly to choose solutions to day-to-day problems which are not tax-efficient. Facilities managers do not need to be tax experts but they must have a sound working knowledge of the basic principles of taxation and allowances to avoid making decisions which lead to loss of valuable tax exemptions, reliefs or concessions and so optimise the tax efficiency of the operation.

With this in mind it may be useful, perhaps with professional advisors, to review events, transactions, works and so on with the following sequence in mind, namely:

- identify the organisation's status (company, partnership, etc), objectives (dealing, investment, etc) and proposed actions

- determine the nature of any proposed transaction or works (repair, maintenance, new works)

- identify any taxation consequences of the proposed transaction or works (VAT, income taxation, capital gains taxation, etc)

- determine the kinds of computations required

- obtain data and make assumptions needed to carry out valuations or computations

- identify any exemptions, reliefs, allowances with reference to "the person" (status), property (capital allowances) or place

- carry out computations

- prepare a report and present findings and advise the relevant parties in the organisation.

In this sequence, the facilities manager will have or could develop appropriate records or be able to provide estimates of costs, etc.

11.1.3 PROPERTY OWNERSHIP AND TAXATION

Ownership of interests in property is inseparable from property taxation and the importance of taxation on property cannot be over-stressed - and not only with regard to expenditure on fitting-out and operating the premises. Before implementing any proposal for a transaction or a development, an evaluation should be made of the prospective tax burden arising from investment in property; from construction of certain buildings and structures; and from certain ways of disposal of occupation or property.

Generally, and at the risk of over-simplification, a person may arrange affairs to take advantage of the tax exemptions and reliefs which are available. However, statutory provisions which seek to counter avoidance of tax do exist, eg section 776 of the Income and Corporation Taxes Act 1988; also, case law has moved against avoidance of tax.

It follows that property taxation is an area where professional advice should be obtained before transactions or works are commenced. In the context of property this usually requires joint consideration by the accountant, lawyer and surveyor as well as the facilities manager, perhaps liaising with others in the organisation.

11.1.4 TAXATION POLICY AND STRUCTURE

Government policy over about two centuries has laid down the broad structure of national taxation, with increasing detail since 1945. The annual Budget and consequential Finance Act provides incremental changes each year, sometimes with wide-ranging effects. From time to time the legislation is consolidated as follows:

- the Inheritance Tax Act 1984

- the Income and Corporation Taxes Act 1988

- the Capital Allowances Act 1990

- the Taxation of Chargeable Gains Act 1992

- the Value Added Tax Act 1994.

Each year the Finance Act may amend any of these Acts. Thus, there are four principal groups of taxes: income taxation, capital taxation, consumption taxation and environmental taxation:

- income taxation covers income tax and corporation tax, together with capital allowances (see Chapter 11.2)

- capital taxation covers capital gains tax, stamp duty and inheritance tax (see Chapter 11.3)

- environmental taxation covers a range of energy taxes and other green taxes (see Chapter 11.4).

- consumption taxation (for the purposes of this section) covers value added tax (see Chapter 11.5), business rates and council tax (see Chapter 11.6).

Income taxation

The Income and Corporation Taxes Act 1988, as amended, provides for incomes to be taxed on an annual basis. Assessments are categorised under schedules under the 1988 Act.

Generally, income taxation falls into two broad categories:

- income tax which is charged on the taxable incomes which individuals have each year

- corporation tax on the taxable income and gains of large companies.

The government's policy in recent years has been a general lowering of both income tax and corporation tax rates but this has been tempered by the need to redress the effects of excessive public borrowing.

Where the company has let out property, the rents from leases in the United Kingdom and premiums on short leases (50 years or less) and certain other items are assessed under Schedule A (certain premiums and deemed premiums on the grant of short leases may also suffer capital gains tax).

The assessment of rents to income taxation of unfurnished property is based on the gross rent receivable less permitted deductions. The chargeable amount of a premium is that premium reduced by 2% of the premium for each year of the lease except the first. Where a lease is let at a 'full rent' there are rules governing the right to carry forward losses during the currency of the lease or to offset in the same year a loss on one property against the profit from another (the so called pooling arrangements). Generally, the facilities manager may need to consult with the company's accountant or other professional advisor in developing a strategy to deal with tax efficiency.

Where the company is dealing in property, it is assessed under Schedule D Case I of the Income and Corporation Taxes Act 1988, ie on annual profit. Where the company is trading, expenditure on land and buildings or on the erection of buildings is treated as revenue expenditure and where wholly and exclusively incurred for the purposes of trade, it is brought into the computation of profit. Section 74 of the 1988 Act sets down the limitations on revenue expenditure.

The facilities manager should beware of complicated transactions in property, perhaps linked into financial transactions. Thus, section 776 of the Income and Corporation Taxes Act 1988 provides a pitfall for those seeking to avoid tax in certain kinds of land transactions. Cases pertinent to section 766 include: Yuill v Wilson (1980); Page v Lowther and Another (1983) and Sugarwhite v Budd (1988).

Dividends from shares in property companies are assessed under Schedule F. The low rate of income tax is deducted at source from dividends received by shareholders.

The above is by no means exhaustive and belies the technical minefield of taxation confronting the investor, dealer or business. It may be borne in mind that numerous exemptions, reliefs and concessions exist. For instance, capital allowances under the Capital Allowances Act 1990, as amended, may be available to the taxpayer whereby the cost of construction of a building or of plant and machinery may be set against rental income or business profits to arrive at taxable income.

Capital taxation

Capital gains tax is chargeable to any capital gains accruing on a disposal which, basically, relates to a period of ownership since 1965 except where accruing to those who are in the business of 'dealing', eg property developers, or who are eligible for some exemption or relief.

Inheritance tax applies to the estates passing on the death of an individual and certain lifetime gifts.

Stamp duty may affect the cost of acquiring certain kinds of property.

Consumption taxation

The Value Added Tax regime was introduced to construction and real estate in 1988 following sustained pressure from the European Union. It's effects are widespread and profound.

Aside from VAT, business rates and stamp duty also affect the cost of procuring and occupying premises.

Environmental taxation

A range of taxes have been developed with the view to protecting the environment, including landfill tax, energy tax, carbon tax, congestion tax and workplace parking levy.

11.1.5 CONFIGURATION OF ORGANISATION FOR TAXES

It may be useful for the facilities manager to understand the way in which taxation is organised. Thus, up to four levels of taxation may be expected:

- national government
- provincial or regional government
- county government
- municipality.

For instance, the Scottish Parliament was set up with limited powers to impose taxes within Scotland. Also, the new 'congestion' tax is available at the discretion of the appropriate local authority, although probably less than 30 are interested at the moment.

Generally the organisations in the national taxation system need to cover policies and practices which are included under:

- fitting taxation policy to other policies, eg energy or transport
- law-making
- the making of assessments
- the demand and collection of taxes
- interpretation of the law
- enforcement of payments and other matters.

11.1.6 EXPENDITURE ON PROPERTY

It is important to identify expenditure on property as either capital expenditure or revenue expenditure. It will then be allocated to the correct assessment for the purposes of taxation. For instance, investors tend to hold property for long periods and expenditure by the landlord on such matters as repairs, maintenance, insurance, management and services are generally set against gross income to find the profit or loss under Schedule A. A similar approach is adopted in determining the profit of trades, professions or vocations under Schedule D, eg for retailers, manufacturers, farmers and architects.

Generally, investor landlords (or businesses owning and occupying buildings) will find that the expenditure on acquiring them and on improving them will be treated as capital expenditure. Capital expenditure is not normally allowed against income as a revenue deduction, but may be allowable for capital gains tax at the time of disposal of the property.

The only depreciation of capital assets allowed to landlord investors or businesses for income taxation purposes is that given as 'capital allowances' by the Capital Allowances Act 1990 and various Finance Acts. Thus, for certain types of building and for qualifying plant and machinery, capital expenditure is deductible under the regime for capital allowances. Large sums may arise and it may be prudent for the facilities manager to initiate a review of all development projects where no claims have been made previously (see Chapter 11.2.5).

It should be borne in mind that, unlike the case with dealers in land, the cost of land and buildings occupied for commercial purposes is expenditure on capital assets and may feature in future capital gains tax computations on disposals, subject to roll-over relief or retirement relief (see Chapter 11.3.1).

11.1.7 MANAGEMENT OF TAXATION

Government

Towards the end of the calender year (November), the Chancellor indicates aspects of fiscal policy in his Pre-Budget and follows up with the Budget and Bill at the end of the fiscal year (March). The Bill receives Assent (becomes a statute) at the end of the Parliamentary year (July).

Executive

Statutes lay down government policy as law which is applied and managed by the Board of Inland Revenue and the Board of Customs and Excise.

Assessments to income taxation are made by Inspectors of Taxes, demands for payment and collection are made by Collectors of Taxes and the District Valuer (or Valuation Officer for rating) deals with much of the work of property valuation.

Of course, VAT and excise duties are dealt with by the Commissioners of Customs and Excise.

The taxation authorities publish numerous booklets and have web sites. The published information covers advice on procedures, computations and numerous other matters. Nevertheless, many are only advisory and the interpretation of the law is a matter for the courts and tribunals.

Court action and appeals

In some instances a complex series of transactions to avoid tax may be challenged by the Inland Revenue under section 776 of the Income and Corporation Taxes Act 1988. Alternatively, the avoidance scheme may result in legislation to block a potentially serious tax revenue loss should the scheme be taken up by many taxpayers.

Appeals of various kinds are heard by the General or Special Commissioners of Inland Revenue with appeals to the hierarchy of courts, ie the High Court, the Court of Appeal, and the House of Lords. The Lands Tribunal deals with valuation appeals in most instances, but there is a local valuation court system to handle rating matters prior to the Lands Tribunal.

Tax year

The Tax year runs from 6 April to 5 April in the following year. It is not likely to be the same as a company's accounting year.

11.2 CORPORATION TAX AND INCOME TAX

Introduction

The broad aim of this chapter is to outline for the facilities manager the importance of a general understanding of corporation tax and income tax. It covers the assessment of profits for tax purposes; the liability for tax; the treatment of revenue expenditure, ie the way it is allowed in calculating profit; the statutory allowances for capital expenditure, ie the "capital allowances"; and finally, aspects of tax planning.

The main impact of such matters on the facilities manager's role lies in:

- identifying and recording expenditure accurately for taxation purposes

- timing works and the procurement of goods, equipment and services so that expenditure is deducted to best advantage for tax purposes.

Broadly, the assessment regimes for corporation tax and income tax are the same. The principal differences are:

- the accounting year

- the rates of taxation

- the timing of payments

- the allowances applied to net incomes.

Corporation tax applies to companies, whereas income tax applies to individuals, sole traders and partners in business partnerships.

It is not possible within this chapter to provide a comprehensive treatment. The main concern of facilities managers is likely to be corporation tax - this is therefore emphasised.

11.2.1. SOURCES OF INCOME

"Income taxation" is applied to assessments of each source of taxable income. The "sources" include:

- **trade or business**: which gives rise to profits

- **property investments**: giving rise to rents and premiums under leases

- **employment**: giving salaries, wages, pensions and other "emoluments"

- **property avoidance schemes**: giving profits and gains

- **investment in shares and securities**: giving dividends, special dividends and interest.

Schedules of income taxation assessment

Traditionally, the statutes categorize the sources of income under "schedules" for the purposes of assessment. Figure 11.2.A outlines the sources, schedules and assessments. As shown it applies to corporation tax and income tax but it should be borne in mind that the detail is more complex.

Taxpayers

Taxpayers are different according to legal status and the source of income. The principal groups of taxpayers are:

- **individuals:** partners in a firm, sole traders are examples; they are charged to income tax

Fig. 11.2.A
Schedules for income taxation

SOURCE	SCHEDULE	ASSESSMENT
Rents (unfurnished)	A	Gross rents less allowable deductions, eg repairs, insurance management
Rents (furnished)	A	Gross rents less allowable deductions, eg repairs, insurance management, cleaning (property rents to Schedule A by election)
Premiums under short leases	A	Chargeable amount = Premium − $\dfrac{\text{Premium} \times (T-1)}{100}$ where P = Premium T = Term (21 years or less)
Profits from trade, professions and vocations	D Cases I and II	
Interest and annual payments etc.	Case III	
Avoidance schemes in property (Section 776 Taxes Act)	D Case VI	"…as is just and reasonable"
Miscellaneous (not elsewhere)	D Case VI	
Salaries, emoluments, pensions (individuals)	E	Gross salary etc. less allowable deductions
Overseas securities	D Case IV	
Overseas possessions	D Case IV	
Shares	F	Gross dividends and other distributions

- **partnerships**: the income is, in effect, calculated on the entity partnership but the income is then divided between the partners and income tax paid is on the individuals as such

- **companies**: are treated separately from their shareholders (owners) and taxed to corporation tax (see Fig. 11.2.B, over the page)

- **trusts**: are treated separately from their beneficiaries (and indeed trustees as individuals or corporate bodies).

11.2.2 RATES OF INCOME TAXATION

Generally, income taxation rates are progressive and under corporation tax a distinction is made between small or medium companies and large companies. Fig. 11.2.B (over the page) sets out the rates of tax for 2001-2002 and 2002-2003.

11.2.3. EXEMPTIONS AND RELIEFS

Non-taxpayers: certain organisation are exempt from income taxation. They include the following:

- local authorities
- charities

- small companies (see Fig. 11.2.B).

Fig. 11.2.B
Corporation tax
rates

Profit level	Rate %	
	Year to 31 March 2002	Year to 31 March 2003
New company up to £10,000	10	0
Intermediate rate from £10,001 to £50,000	22.5	23.25
Small company up to £300,000	20	19
Intermediate rate £300,001 to £1.5m	32.5	32.75
Full rate	30	30

Capital allowances: wide range of items of a capital nature, eg certain types of building, plant and machinery and other items, are given capital allowances, ie the expenditure may be set off against profit (see 11.2.5).

11.2.4. DEDUCTIONS IN RESPECT OF REVENUE EXPENDITURE

As a general rule, for a business such as retail, industrial, commercial and so on, all the premises costs incurred in the normal running of the business can be offset against income before calculating taxable profit. Allowable revenue expenditure is offset in full against profits for the accounting year in which it is incurred (whereas allowances for capital expenditure are normally spread over a number of years at varying rates depending on the current tax legislation). Revenue expenditure embraces routine premises costs such as rates, cleaning, energy, routine maintenance, repairs, and any rent and service charges if applicable.

Section 74 of the Income and Corporation Taxes Act 1988 provides that the expenditure must be wholly and exclusively incurred for the purposes of the business. However, when a building is first acquired the cost of repairs in, say, the first two years may be treated as capital expenditure rather than revenue expenditure, but there may be exceptions. Also, if works comprise repairs and improvements to premises, the Inland Revenue will probably allow an apportionment of the costs to revenue and capital accounts.

11.2.5. CAPITAL ALLOWANCES

Government policy

From time to time governments have introduced capital allowances as a means of recognising the consumption of assets by a business or more pertinently to encourage particular forms of investment, eg thermal insulation in industrial buildings and safety at sports stadia.

Nature and amounts of capital allowances

The capital allowances are as follows:

- **initial allowance**: where the whole or a relatively large proportion of the expenditure is set against taxable income - generally, initial allowances have been abolished, except in one or two special cases

- **writing down allowance**: where a relatively small percentage is given each year against taxable income - they are either 'straight line', ie a fixed percentage of the original cost (eg on industrial buildings at 4%), or 'reducing balance', ie a fixed percentage reduction of the last calculated written down value (eg plant and machinery at 25%).

- **balancing allowance**: which arises when, on a disposal, the written down value is greater than the consideration attribution to the asset (or vice versa for a balancing charge).

For buildings, the eligible expenditure includes site clearance, cost of construction and associated professional fees. Care has to be taken that the building qualifies under the relevant statutes, ie the Capital Allowances Act 1990 as amended by provisions in later Finance Acts. Also, a substantial body of case law has developed to interpret the Acts, particularly on the different types of qualification for buildings and on qualifying plant and machinery, eg the latter must be 'functional' rather than part of the 'setting'.

However, for the facilities manager, the most significant aspect of capital allowances is the substantial amount of fitting-out and refurbishment works which can count as 'plant and machinery' making them eligible for off-setting against revenue tax.

Occasionally the service charge may contain items for capital expenditure which attract capital allowances in due course. These may only be reclaimed by the landlord. The tenant may claim the whole of the service charge as revenue expenditure. The landlord receiving the service charge payment will have to add it to income and potentially some or all of it will be taxable as the landlords profit. It is important to note that the capital allowances may now be claimed against actual expenditure and not, as in the past, delayed until the project is completed and operational.

The plant and machinery element is not defined by statute but case law is important. However, it is commonly accepted that, in its ordinary sense, the term plant and machinery "includes whatever apparatus is used by a businessman for carrying on his business - not his stock in trade, which he buys or makes for sale, but all goods and chattels, fixed or movable, living or dead, which he keeps for permanent employment in his business" (Yarmouth v France (1887)). Section 117 of the Finance Act 1994 provides some restrictions on the scope of plant and machinery but should not affect previous case law.

Fig. 11.2.C (over the page) shows common items of expenditure which may be deemed to be plant and machinery for tax purposes. The main borderline area is the one concerning repairs - when does a repair become refurbishment? Repair expenditure is generally taken as that sum spent on maintaining the original performance of an asset. It is regular expenditure, usually budgeted annually, and is required throughout the life of a building.

Fig. 11.2.C

Typical items of capital expenditure on buildings normally qualifying for capital allowances

Items of plant	Comments
Blinds	-
Demountable partitions	Where regularly moved in the course of trade
Carpet	Where readily removable in the course of trade (eg carpet tiles)
Suspended ceilings	Where acting principally as a plenum as part of the air conditioning system
Loose furniture & furnishings	-
Fittings & equipment	Tea points, credenzas inc. 'fridges, dishwashers etc.
Office equipment	-
Sanitary appliances	Wash-hand basins, baths, urinals etc.
Hot water system	Includes pipework, tanks, builders ' work
Heating system	Includes pipework, builders' work
Control panels	Eg temperature controls – but not switchboards
Air-conditioning & ventilation systems	Includes ductwork, builders' work
Emergency generators & transformers / UPS	-
Task Lighting	Where attached to furniture
Ambient lighting	Moveable fittings connected to a circuit not dedicated solely to lighting
Emergency lighting	-
Wiring from outlet to loose equipment	No other general electrical wiring included
Sprinkler systems	Includes pipework, tanks, builders' work
Fire alarms / fire fighting equipment	Includes builders' work
Security systems	Includes builders' work
Lifts & escalators	Includes electrical work and builders' work but not lift shaft
Preliminaries	Proportion of preliminary costs (foreman, scaffolding, temporary work, insurances)
Professional fees	Proportion of total cost
Telephone & data	-
Cabling	-

Note: some items may be excluded as a result of section 117 of the Finance Act 1994.

The impact of expenditure on certain new buildings which can also qualify for capital allowances at varying rates is shown at Fig. 11.2.D (over the page). Capital allowances are available only to the person who incurs the expenditure. Capital expenditure is usually that which has a benefit that extends beyond a single accounting period.

Much capital expenditure frequently goes on upgrading premises to accommodate information technology. If management were fully aware of this, they might reconsider the whole of their premises policy. Whether expenditure is finally allocated to capital or revenue it is important that all associated overhead costs such as consultants' fees and contractors' 'preliminaries' are identified and added to the net cost of actual work items.

An example of an ongoing assessment of the amount of plant and machinery in a fitting-out contract is given at Fig. 11.2.E (over the page). Note that there is a distinction between what the team believes is certain to be acceptable by the Inspector of Taxes and those items where negotiation may need to take place; the Inspector may well take a much harder line on the "grey" areas as a result of the 1994 statute.

The communications component of the fitting-out is allowable in full and Fig. 11.2.F (on page E-19) shows this in the context of overall fitting-out project costs.

Capital allowances are an important source of funding for projects and can make a sizeable contribution as Fig. 11.2.G (on page E-19) illustrates.

Fig. 11.2.D
Capital allowances on new building work for the most common user categories

Building type		% of capital allowed against tax in each year	
		Year 1	Subsequently
1. Industrial	Introduced from 6/4/46 at 2% per year upto 5/11/62, thereafter 4% per year (NB various rates of initial allowances were available at different times)	Now 4	4% p.a. until year 25
2. Commercial, trade or professional		NIL	(Plant and machinery items only)
3. Industrial, commercial, trade, professional, or hotels in an enterprise zone		100	Or 25% straight line available, ie 4 years
4a. Scientific research	Expenditure before 1/1/85 (or before 1/4/87 under a contract pre 20/3/85)	100	On cost, including land and any dwellings
4b. Research and development (new definition for tax years from 1/4/02)		100	(subject to restrictions concerning plant and machinery)
5. Dwelling let on assured tenancies	After 9/3/82 and before 1/4/87, then to 1/4/92, but abolished in effect from 14/3/88	Varied according to period in which expenditure occurred	4% thereafter, ie to 0 (but transitional from 14/3/88 to 1/4/92)
6. Residential buildings (other than qualifying as scientific research)		NIL	
7. Qualifying hotels of a commercial nature (e.g. at least 10 bedrooms, open 4 months a year, 25% ancillary offices)	Expenditure and in use before 1/1/95 if contract entered into 1/11/92 − 31/10/93	24	4% p.a. until year 20
	Otherwise expended after 11/4/78	4	4% p.a. until year 25

Fig. 11.2.E
Preliminary appraisal of plant and machinery content of a fitting-out contract

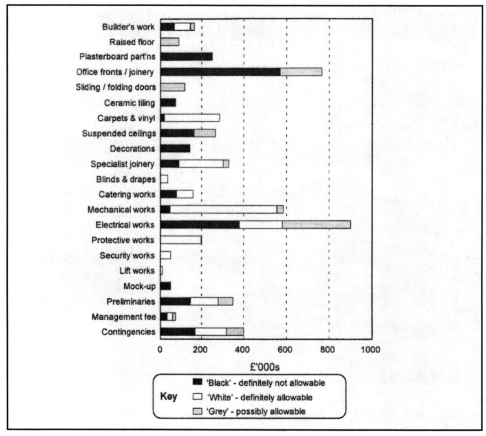

Fig. 11.2.F
*Preliminary analysis
of plant and
machinery content
of complete fitting-
out works*

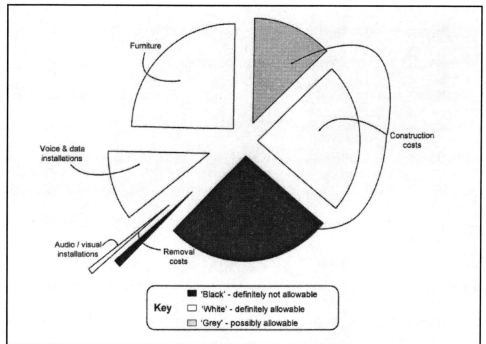

Fig. 11.2.G
*Potential
contribution of
capital allowances
to funding complete
fitting-out works*

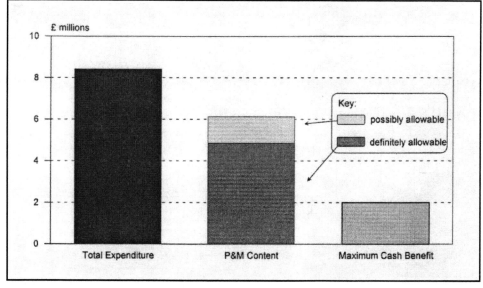

Corporation tax planning

The organisation has some scope to control the amount of tax it pays. Thus there are three approaches to the use of tax allowances which can be fruitful. The first relates to the choice of **specification**, the second to the method of **purchasing** and the third to the **timing** of the expenditure. In all cases the facilities manager, in consultation with the accountants, tax consultant, or both, will need to establish the potential liability to corporation tax in the current and immediate future tax years. They can then exercise their choice to optimise efficiency.

Specification: the decision to create new rooms in an office building gives rise to specification options with variable tax allowances. For example, fixed solid plastered partitions are inexpensive but do not attract capital allowances nor do they rank as revenue expenditure. On the other hand, demountable partitions can cost two to three times as much but may rank as plant and machinery for tax purposes, bringing the appropriate capital allowances. Also, demountable partitions may make 'churn' (see Chapter 4.2.) easier and hence increases in productivity may be obtained more readily than with fixed solid plastered partitions.

Purchasing: as far as purchasing is concerned the company may be able to enter either a contract-leasing or hire-purchase agreement for the demountable partitions; this gives the alternative of claiming the annual cost against revenue expenditure rather than claiming capital allowances against a one-off cash purchase. The facilities manager must try to discover the extent to which these issues are actually considered in depth in the facilities decision-making process. Where the methodology fails to meet the criteria, he should try to see whether it is apathy, ignorance or arrogance in the organisation which is at the root of the problem.

Timing: as for timing there is not much sense in acquiring tax allowances in excess of profits. In a bad year firms are usually keen to defer expenditure in any way so it makes sense to do so and get the tax allowances against next year's prospective return of profit.

Disposals

Finally, when disposing of an existing property both parties to the transaction may have an interest in the history of any capital allowances enjoyed by the transferor. The transferor may have a balancing item to deal with and the transferee enjoy 'outstanding allowances'.

It is important, therefore, for the owner to keep comprehensive on-going records, including:

- the kind of works carried out and their costs

- the times when the works were carried out

- the allowances claimed in respect of each lot of works

- the dates of starting to use the building (and those of any changes of use).

11.3 CAPITAL TAXES

Introduction

For this chapter capital taxation covers three taxes, namely:

- capital gains tax
- inheritance tax
- stamp duty.

The last mentioned is, perhaps, unusually classified. However, since it relates to property and share transactions, it is not inconvenient to deal with it in the context of the main capital taxes. Of these, inheritance tax will not be very common to facilities managers in a work context unless they are concerned with private companies or estates.

Generally, facilities managers may find it useful to have a general overview of the workings of these taxes since they affect most capital transactions. In particular they may need to know about such matters as:

- who pays the tax
- what assets are exempt or relieved in some way
- what records need to be kept for tax calculations
- the broad nature of the calculations
- the rates of tax and the amounts that are charged to tax.

11.3.1 CAPITAL GAINS TAX

Brief History

Capital gains tax was originally introduced by the Conservative government in 1963 as a short-terms gains tax. In 1965 the current long-term tax was implemented by the Labour government - it has been substantially modified and is now embodied in the Taxation of Capital Gains Act 1992, as amended.

Taxpayers and non-taxpayers

Individuals, companies and others are liable to the tax on the disposal of a chargeable asset. Those who do not pay tax include the following:

- charities
- pensions funds
- local authorities.

Disposals

A wide range of transactions or "disposals" of capital assets are caught to capital gains tax, including:

- a sale
- an assignment of a lease
- the grant of a lease at a premium
- a gift
- an exchange
- a transfer on death (but this is subject to exemption)
- proceeds of insurance.

It should be borne in mind that the assets are of a capital nature: stock in trade, eg land held by a dealer in land, would not be liable to capital gains tax.

Date of disposal

Generally, for land the date of contract is the date of disposal but there are exceptions, eg for a conditional contract, the date is that when the condition is satisfied. On death, the date of death is the effective date for the tax, eg, capital gains tax runs from that date for a beneficiary.

Exemptions and reliefs

The principal exemptions and reliefs from capital gains tax include:

- an individual's sole or main residence, provided conditions are met
- 'roll over', ie where the proceeds of disposal of a business asset are used to acquire assets for business, subject to qualification
- 'retirement relief', but this is to end after 2002-2003
- 'roll over' on compulsory purchase, ie sales under actual or prospective compulsory purchase of non-business land which is not the claimant's sole or main residence.
- **death of an individual**: no liability to capital gains tax arises
- **annual exempt slice**: of £7,400 for individuals for 2002-2003
- 'indexation': of 'costs' from March 1982 to March 1998 (now replaced by 'taper' relief)
- 'taper' relief: from 6 April 1998 chargeable gains are reduced by a prescribed percentage according to the period of ownership in whole years
- **certain shares and securities**: are exempt.

It is not likely that the facilities manager will be concerned with the full range of exemptions and reliefs most of which concern individuals. However, it may be useful to have an overview of those which may relate to disposals of business assets and certain shares. These include:

- **shares**: losses on shares in certain Business Expansion Schemes and Enterprise Investment Schemes. These are subject to conditions, and it may be possible to set them against income tax
- **irrecoverable loans etc**: loans to companies or unincorporated businesses and costs of meeting loan guarantees which are lost may, subject to conditions, be treated as losses for capital gains tax purposes.
- **retirement relief**: for 2002-2003 subject to conditions, relief of 100 percent up to £50,000 gain, then 50 percent relief up to £200,000 on disposals of certain businesses assets or shares in a business. It applies to persons of 50 or more years unless illness forces retirement. (However, for year 2003 to 2004 onwards the relief will not be available - taper relief is deemed its replacement.)
- **taper relief and indexation relief**: from 6 April 1998 gains on disposals will be given an inflation indexation relief (for assets acquired before that date) together with taper relief from that date. The taper relief depends on the period of ownership, subject to condition. The nature of taper relief for business assets is more generous than that for non-business assets (it may be noted that assets acquired after 6 April 1998 no longer enjoy indexation relief). Generally, the provisions for taper relief on business assets contain many circumstances and conditions, eg the period of ownership, the definition of business assets, quoted and unquoted company shares distinguished. It is outside of the scope of this

chapter to enter into detail as this is another aspect of taxation generally requiring specialist professional advice.

Computations

The basic form of computation for capital gains tax is given in Figure 11.3.A. However, numerous forms of computation exist depending on, for instance, the nature of the asset, eg a lease, the duration of ownership and the date of disposal, and type of disposal.

Fig. 11.3.A
Basic form of CGT computation

Consideration / Market value costs or allowances	£	£
Consideration / Market value at acquisition		A
Less: the sum of:		
• Incidental costs of disposal	a	
• Enhancement expenditures	b	
• Costs of defending title	c	
• Incidental costs of acquisition	d	
• Cost of acquisition (or market value at acquisition or market value at 31 March 1982)	e	(B)
Capital gain (or loss) (unadjusted)		A - B
Less: allowances for indexation (if any)	f	
Less: taper relief (if any)	g	(C)
Capital Gain		A - (B+C)

Indexation applies to expenditures incurred before 6 April 1998. It may, therefore be necessary to calculate different indexation amounts for enhancement expenditures at different times, likewise for defending title (but it must not apply to any expenditure incurred after that date). If an asset was acquired before 31 March 1982, "rebasing" may be taken, ie the market value at that date may be substituted for the earlier acquisition cost (or market value), so the resulting gain is less. However, where the asset was acquired before 6 March 1965, the market value at that date may, or must, be used unless "time-apportionment" about that date gives a better result. (Generally, however, the date rarely features in computations.)

Taxes interaction

Of course, a transaction may give rise to one or more other taxes, eg stamp duty, income taxation, or value added tax. Issues of taxes interaction are, however, outside the scope of this work, but see Chapter 11.5.2 for a brief treatment of VAT and capital gains tax.

11.3.2 INHERTITANCE TAX (IHT)

Brief History

Inheritance tax is a gifts tax and a tax on death (which it replaced) which has its origins in estate duty and capital transfer tax. It arises when an individual dies and, put simply, is charged on the estate which passes or is deemed to pass on the date of death. The provisions of the Inheritance Tax Act 1984, as amended, govern the tax.

Facilities manager and IHT

This part of the chapter gives a broad overview of IHT and indicates some areas of particular interest to the facilities manager, including:

- what passes and how it is taxed

- favoured assets

- tax planning

- treatment of business assets.

Facilities managers concerned with private family companies or large landed estates are likely to need a detailed knowledge of the workings of the tax.

Taxable estate

The values of the deceased's properties transferred on death, including any gifts made in the seven years before death are totalled. Subject to exemptions and reliefs, tax is applied to the net value of the estate, eg after debts and funeral expenses are deducted and certain gifts enjoy relief according to when they were made.

Where exemption is claimed in respect of business property it must be owned for at least two years and not be subject to contract for sale. Certain businesses do not qualify for exemption or relief, eg dealing in shares or property or holiday investments.

Sale proprietor's or partner's interests in qualifying businesses obtain 100 percent relief - assets owned by a partner but used by the business obtain 50 percent relief.

As far as shares in trading businesses are concerned, a different treatment is rated to unquoted and quoted shares. Thus:

- unquoted shares (including AIM shares) obtain 100 percent relief

- quoted shares obtain 50 percent relief (the transferor must have control).

Similarly, assets used by the business obtain a 50 percent relief for transfers intervivos or on death of the controlling shareholder.

The above has been a brief look at some of the more relevant aspects of the calculation. All of these exemptions and reliefs are subject to conditions, generally requiring professional advice as to their availability and application in a given instance.

Exemptions and reliefs

The IHT legislation provides for numerous other exemptions and reliefs, eg exempt gifts of a family nature, which are outside the scope of this chapter. However, the following are likely to have a bearing on the role of some facilities managers:

- **a trust of a business created for the benefit of employees**: a transfer of share to an employee trust are exempt, subject to conditions. Briefly, the trustees must control the company within one year and beneficiaries must be employees (but not participators in the company)

- **favoured assets**: woodlands, agricultural property and heritage buildings and the like and their contents. All favoured assets obtain exemption or relief provided conditions are satisfied. Briefly, the following apply

- **occupied farm land**: total exemption provided it has been occupied for at least two years

- **tenanted farm land**: a 50% or 100% percent relief, depending upon whether the tenancy was granted before, on or after 1 September 1995 respectively

- **woodlands**: may enjoy either business relief (see below) or 'woodland relief' (subject to the duration of ownership)

- **heritage property**: buildings of historic or architectural interest, 'scenic' land, and artefacts of quality obtain conditional relief. Briefly, such property must be maintained and preserved and reasonable access by the public must be permitted.

Tax planning

Again, because of the personal nature of IHT, facilities managers will not usually be involved in tax planning for the individual and the family. However, the proprietor's tax planning for the business side of a large private company, a sole trader's business, or country house gardens, park and estate may well impinge on several members of the family. Issues likely to arise may include:

- succession to the proprietor's position in managing the business

- transfers of property to others, eg for an unincorporated business, the creation of a company and the distribution of shares

- the payment of tax, eg either by gifting heritage property in lieu or by stage payments over 10 years

- the transfer of 'favoured' property subject to undertakings, eg not to sell, to keep open to the public, or not to fell trees

- skipping a generation by transferring a business or property to grandchildren

- the creation of trusts

- insurance, eg to protect gifts from the tax

- managing assets in accord with undertakings made to the Treasury, eg opening a heritage house, garden and park to the public.

11.3.3 STAMP DUTY

With many amendments introduced since, the Stamp Act 1891 and the Stamp Duties Management Act 1891 provide for stamp duty. However, it seems likely that the tax will be simplified and, no doubt, consolidated.

Even now the Finance Act 2002 provides for changes. With these covered below, stamp duty is imposed on a wide selection of 'instruments', usually documents, involved in transactions, eg those in property sales, leases and share purchases. (but this will change to 'transactions' as a result of the Pre-Budget Report 2002).

Shares

Stamp duty on shares is imposed at 0.5%. There are exceptions, including disposal by way of gift.

Land and Buildings

Commercial and residential property purchasers are required to pay stamp duty in accord with the sale shown in Fig 11.3.B.

Fig. 11.3.B
Stamp Duty on sales of land and buildings, and other property (not shares)

Consideration for Property (£)	Stamp Duty (%)	Comment
Up to 60,000	0	
60,001 to 250,000	1	The charge is rounded up to the next £5
250,001 to 500,000	3	
500,001 and over	4	

The facilities manager concerned with a purchase may like to note that it is only the consideration for land and buildings which suffers stamp duty. Money or money's worth for chattels and so on does not suffer the tax. It may be necessary in some instances, therefore, to agree an apportionment of the purchase price with the vendor, therefore identifying the worth of the chattels.

Leases

It may be noted that lease transactions have their own scale for rents, ranging from 1 percent to 24 percent, depending on the duration of the lease, eg 24 percent for a term over 100 years (see Figure 11.3.C).

Fig. 11.3.C
Stamp Duty and leases

Term	Rate of duty on rent %
Under 7 years or not definite	1
7 years but not over 35 years	2
Over 35 years but not over 100 years	12
Over 100 years	24

Exemptions, reliefs and tax mitigation

To some extent stamp duty is at present considered a 'voluntary tax' (see 'New proposals' below); notwithstanding the proposed revisions to the way it is operated the following exemptions may be noted:

- **goodwill**: stamp duty on sales of goodwill has been chargeable hitherto; however, the Budget 2002 provides for exemption from 23 April 2002

- **receivables**: the Budget 2002 provides that no stamp duty will be levied from late 2003

- **property in specified disadvantaged localities**: no stamp duty is imposed on sales and leases of land in areas specified by Treasury Order (see Finance Act 2001 which may, however, be blocked by the EU)

- **marginal price**: bringing the price of property just below the upper limit of a band on the scale in Figure 11.3.B will mitigate the charge (similarly, if the price for chattels reduces the overall price below the limit)

- **patents**: an exemption is afforded to patents

- **exchanges**: where property and cash is exchanged for a higher value property, the contract should show the lower value property as £80,000 plus "equality" cash - the stamp duty on the lower value property will then be on £50,000 not £100,000. However, purchases of new property from a builder for the old building value plus cash will only result in stamp duty on the new property, not the old

- **structuring land transactions**: hitherto it has been possible to mitigate the charge to duty by structuring large land transactions in particular ways. The Budget 2002 provides anti-avoidance measures to challenge such structuring

- **leases**: transactions in leases suffer duty according to their duration, the amount paid (or value), the rent or rental value. Briefly, the rate ranges from 1 percent to 24 percent of the average rent or the rental value. In negotiating the terms of a lease, advice should be sought as to the implications of its terms with regard to any mitigation of the tax.

The above has ranged over some existing provisions. A 'simplification' has been mooted and further changes are underway as a result of the Pre-Budget Report 2002 (see below - "New proposals).

Stamp Duty Reserve Tax (SDRT)

Certain shares and securities transactions are paperless and attract stamp duty reserve tax. Also, where an oral or written agreement for a shares or securities transaction is agreed, SDRT will be applied. However, where an instrument is executed and stamped, the SDRT will be refunded (provided the stamping is within six years).

Stamp duty is sometimes lower than SDRT so an advantage accrues to the user of a stamped instrument.

New proposals

The Pre-Budget Report 2002 shows an intention to preclude the 'voluntary' nature of stamp duty by imposing it on transactions in land which the purchaser must, firstly notify, and then pay the tax (unless an exemption applies).

Land transactions cover two types; namely:

- major interests, ie freeholds and leaseholds

- minor interests, ie conditions, covenants, easements, profits à prendre and rentcharges.

Transactions in major interests will have to be notified, but only those in minor interests which breach the lower threshold (see Fig 11.3.B).

Full details of the above proposals are not yet available.

11.4   ENVIRONMENTAL TAXATION

Introduction

Environmental taxation has become more common and innovative in recent years. The taxes and their exemptions and reliefs take many forms but may be broadly classified into:

- energy taxes

- health taxes

- pollution taxes

- transportation taxes

- disadvantaged areas relief.

Even so some taxes may be listed under more than one of these groupings.

In some instances differential rates of tax are imposed with the view to encouraging better environmental effects, eg lower tax rates on cars with lower engine capacity or on the use of unleaded petrol.

Historically, what might now be regarded as environmental or green taxation has been used to raise revenues. However, a modern approach in fiscal policy has been to make environmental taxation a major way to deal with societal problems, such as: congestion, pollution, waste disposal, energy-saving or global warming. In some ways a 'carrot and stick' approach is apparent.

This chapter examines the implications of such taxation for facilities managers, particularly with regard to mitigating or avoiding a tax or by taking an exemption or relief.

11.4.1 ENERGY TAXATION

For many years, the conservation of energy has been a feature of taxation, particularly since the oil crisis of 1973; measures take many forms including:

- fuel taxes

- relief for insulation of buildings

- control of heating in buildings.

Fuel taxation

Motor fuels: generally, fuels such as petrol and diesel bear heavy taxation although the tax on diesel is lower, so as to encourage commercial vehicle use.

Company car tax: from 6 April 2002 a carbon dioxide emission related tax based on the price of a car was introduced. The charge is 15% of the cost of the car for a CO_2 emission of 165 grammes/kilometre. It increases by steps of 1% for increases of emission up to 35% maximum. A 3% supplement is added for diesel cars, again to a maximum of 35%. The tax sharply increases the impact of this type of tax.

Buildings: taxes on fuels for heating buildings have been common, eg VAT was imposed at 8% from 4 April 1994 (but has since been reduced). (However, home insulation grants are commonly offered to reduce fuel consumption.)

Capital allowances: capital allowances at 100% of the cost of insulating buildings used for trade were introduced long ago, under the Finance Act 1974 (in response to the oil price increases of that era).

From April 2001 certain energy-saving equipment enjoys 100% first-year allowance.

11.4.2 HEALTH TAXATION

Excise duties: the principal health taxes may not interest the facilities manager - at least in a professional capacity! They include excise duties and taxes on tobacco products and alcoholic beverages.

Also to the extent that exhaust fumes and particles are injurious to health, the taxes on petrol and oil may be included under this heading. Thus for vehicle fleet management, differentials on petrol may suggest that alternative fuels may be more common in future. Similarly, higher energy costs arising from taxes may induce improved insulation specifications.

Life policies: premiums on certain term life policies, eg those designed to protect a company for loss of profits on the death of a key-person, are tax deductible (but the proceeds are taxed) (see ICTA 1988 section 540).

11.4.3 POLLUTION TAXATION

Climate change levy: the climate change levy has been looked at in Chapter 5.4. It is designed to reduce carbon emissions by taxing energy suppliers who then pass the tax to customers. However, the tax is said to be neutral for industry as a whole because employers' national insurance contributions will be reduced by the amount of levy raised. Opportunities to trade in emissions have been created as described in Chapter 5.4.2. No doubt, facilities managers will be involved in this field and some will need to develop operational policies to move towards the optimum tax position.

Landfill tax: pollution has resulted in governmental pressure for extensive recycling and other waste management policies for industry. (See Chapter 5.6 - Waste Management). An example of taxation in this field is the taxation of landfill deliveries, with higher charges for the relatively more contaminative waste. The tax is provided by sections 39 to 70 of, and schedule 5 to, the Finance Act 1996. It is charged on the site operator by the tonne of waste delivered to a licensed landfill site. The rate is currently £13 but rises by £1 pa until 2004. Site operators will try to pass the tax on to customers; it is designed to induce in the customers alternatives to landfill, such as recycling, composting, and other forms of disposal involving energy recovery (However, further increases are proposed in the Pre-Budget Report of November 2002).

Aggregates levy: from 1 April 2002 the aggregates levy is imposed at the rate of £1.30 per tonne on sand, gravel or crushed rock which is quarried in the UK or imported. It is intended to balance the environmental costs, eg noise and dust, of quarrying, processing and transportation of the aggregates.

Contaminated land relief: capital allowances relief of 150 percent of the cost of remediation of contaminated land is available under the Finance Act 2001. After 11 May 2001, the Act covers the cost of the removal of asbestos from buildings.

Fuel taxes: fuel taxes have to be considered under 11.4.1 and 11.4.2 above.

11.4.4 TRANSPORTATION TAXATION

The principal taxes are the workplace parking levy and the congestion tax.

Workplace parking levy (WPL): this is likely to make its appearance in a few towns and cities in the next few years. It is a local tax designed, in due course, by the local authority under the enabling provision in the Transport Act 2000.

Considerable concern has been expressed by businesses in places where the WPL has been moved. It may be noted that in Greater London the approach will be by "congestion tax", rather than WPL.

For the facilities manager involved in due course in WPL implementation at site level, company policy will need to determine how, if at all, staff who use parking spaces may be affected. Variations of policy as to who bears the cost of WPL may include:

- the company alone

- the company (as company fleet owner and provider of visitor's spaces) and staff who park on-site

- staff who park on-site (with the company bearing the tax on any visitors' spaces)

The intention of the taxing authorities is to reduce congestion, particularly during the journey to and from work, ie peak times. The dilemma for the company is cost of the tax and issues arising from any passing on of the charge to staff, including:

- should any staff be exempt, eg staff who have disabilities

- staff who use their own cars for company purposes and may be off-site for much of the time

- staff who do not regularly use on-site parking but use a space from time to time, for either personal or work-related reasons

- if staff are given "free" parking, the views of those staff who never use (or give-up) a parking space (does it come to be regarded as an extra, differential perk?).

Although it is likely to be a medium to long-term (or never) problem for the facilities manager, it may be useful to develop a prospective policy in the event of WPL being raised at one or more sites. It may be noted that the formulation of such a WPL policy by the local authority is not likely to be rapid.

- **Travel or green transport plan incentives:** incentives are in place to encourage alternatives to the use of the motor car for travel to work. The alternatives include:

- a works bus - free or part supported

- public bus subsidies

- parking for bicycles and motorcycles at work

- normally, such benefits are taxed and liability for national insurance contribution arises; however, for travel plan incentives such taxes or liabilities are exempt or given relief in some way.

- **Congestion tax:** the tax is intended to reduce traffic congestion. In London, a fixed charge of £5 a day for entry into the central area commenced in 2003. For the Greater London area it is intended by the mayor that there will be no workplace parking levy. Exemptions or reliefs exist, eg for electric cars

11.4.5 DISADVANTAGED AREAS

Local or community environments which are disadvantaged are supported under the tax regime in several ways, they include:

- **stamp duty:** abolition of stamp duty on business property transactions. Residential property enjoys an exemption for transactions up to £150,000 in very disadvantaged areas.

- **Community Investment Tax Credit:** a CITC of 25 percent of the investment will be given for private sector funds put into not-for-profit and profit-seeking bodies in certain disadvantaged areas (see Budget 2002). However, aspects of such regeneration support may fall foul of the competition policy of the EU as undue state aid.

11.5   VALUE ADDED TAX (VAT)

Introduction

Value added tax was first introduced into the United Kingdom on 1 April 1973 as a result of the country joining what is now the European Union. The regime from the 1 April 1989 was based upon the Value Added Tax Act 1983, as amended. It is now consolidated again and mainly contained in the Value Added Tax Act 1994 and the VAT Regulations 1995.

The latter legislation severely affects the way in which provision of goods and services, development, construction, leasing and investment involving landed property are approached.

There are two principal aspects of any legislation - the wording of the law and the interpretation by its administrators. In the case of the VAT legislation on construction, land and property, it is Her Majesty's Customs and Excise who have the task of letting the taxpayers know what they believe the law really says, eg by notices and leaflets. However, in a dispute the VAT Tribunals and the courts are the final arbiters.

The indications to liability etc given in this section rely upon the legislation, HMC&E's published Notices and leaflets and the authors' interpretation of the data as a whole. Nevertheless, the subject is wide ranging and many nuances in the detail have not been covered in this text.

Aspects of enforcement, fraud and appeals are dealt with in Chapter 11.1.

11.5.1 VAT AND THE FACILITIES MANAGER

For the facilities manager VAT impinges on many situations involving the supply of goods and services. This chapter examines the principles of VAT and seeks to give the reader insights to VAT on such situations as:

- the purchase or sale of bare land

- the purchase or sale of land with buildings

- the letting of land or land with buildings

- the works of construction involving new works or repair and maintenance

- the employment of professionals, contractors and others

- the type of building and the kind of buyer or tenant or grantor and so on

- the purchase of every day goods, services and works.

The subject is complex but warrants the pointers given to it below.

11.5.2 GENERAL PRINCIPLES OF VAT

Taxable persons

Under the legislation Customs and Excise charge VAT to a taxable person for the supply of goods and services in the course of business which is a taxable supply, ie a supply which is not exempt from the liability.

The VAT legislation seeks to tax the final consumer. Curiously, although the final consumer is taxed, or may be said to be taxed, on standard-rated (or other rates) or zero-rated supplies respectively, he or she is not the 'taxable' person.

A taxable person is one who in the course of business makes taxable supplies and is registered for VAT because he or she has a turnover of more than the statutory sum per year or per quarter (or expects to have these levels of turnover for such periods). Subject to conditions, the statutory sum is a gross taxable turnover of at least £55,000 (2002/03). Voluntary registration is allowed on a lower turnover.

Input tax and output tax

The tax on a taxable supply is known as an 'output tax', whereas tax paid on supplies received are known as 'input tax'.

The taxable person's liability may be expressed as:

L = To - Ti

where L is the liability, To is the output tax and Ti is the input tax.

If the result is positive, VAT must be paid: if the result is negative, the taxable person is eligible to a credit or remittance of VAT.

VAT is an invoice system of taxation with the 'tax from tax' feature of net liability or net credit.

VAT returns and payments

Briefly, registered persons are required to submit regular, (usually three-monthly) VAT returns (other periods are allowed on request). Payment for VAT, if any, is due within one month of the end of the VAT return period, together with the return.

Recovery of VAT

VAT paid to suppliers is recovered by being set-off against output tax in the VAT return. If in excess, there will be a repayment by the taxation office.

Kinds of rates and exemption

At present supplies are subject to VAT as follows:

- at standard rate
- at a lower rate (of 5 percent currently)
- at zero rate
- exempt.

Standard rate: the taxable person who supplies goods or services which are standard rated must charge tax (output tax) - currently at 17.5%. However, any tax on goods and services received which are taxed to VAT (input tax) may be offset against the liability to pay the output tax to the Customs and Excise. Works for new commercial buildings, certain self-supplies (ie, commercial DIY operations), certain demolition services, repair and maintenance, alterations etc and certain disposals of new buildings are standard-rated.

Zero rate: Section 16 and Schedule 8 to the 1994 Act provide that zero-rated goods and services are those where no tax is payable by the customer but the taxable person, ie the supplier, may recover any input tax paid in respect of goods and services provided. Zero-rated supplies are 'taxable supplies' despite the fact that no tax is chargeable to the customer.

As a matter of historic interest as far as land and buildings are concerned, zero-rated supplies were defined in Schedule 5 Group 8 of the 1983 Act. Briefly, and oversimplifying, construction works, demolition services and disposals of buildings by builders were at that time zero-rated, except for 'protected buildings'.

Under EC VAT Second and Sixth Directives, zero rating may only be used 'for clearly defined social reasons and for the benefit of the final consumer'. Hence the challenge in the European Court of Justice which was decided in June 1988.

Under the current regime only the following buildings and works are zero-rated:

- new dwellings

- almost all new communal residential buildings, so-called "relevant" residential buildings

- new buildings for non-business activities of charities, so-called "relevant" buildings

- certain approved works to protected buildings.

Listed buildings and monuments etc.

Certain buildings, eg "protected buildings", are afforded special VAT treatment. Essentially, they are certain kinds of both listed buildings and scheduled monuments. Generally, works of repair and maintenance are standard rated but other works, eg those requiring listed building consent, are "approved alterations" and enjoy zero-rating.

Exempt supplies

Exempt supplies are covered by schedule 9. Here no output tax is charged on supplies to the taxable person's customers. However, unlike zero-rated or standard-rated goods or services, input tax cannot be recovered by the taxable person.

Examples of bodies who make supplies which are mainly exempt include:

- banks

- financial agents, such as stockbrokers and mortgage brokers

- charities

- educational bodies, eg universities and private schools

- hospitals in the private sector

- insurance companies, agents and brokers

- pension funds

- building societies

- finance houses

- betting shops

- undertakers

- non-profit making sports clubs.

An exempt supply is said to provide a hidden tax charge which is passed on in the price to the consumer who cannot recover it. Under the old regime many disposals or grants in land were exempt. However, under the new regime some are now standard rated or the supplier has the option to tax, eg rents under leases.

Where supplies are partly exempt and partly zero-rated or standard-rated, the taxable person may be required to only offset part of the input taxes incurred. In recent years the regime for this 'partial exemption' has been tightened to prevent avoidance.

Lower rate

Schedule 7A covers the lower rate on specific items, eg certain building works, energy, security and grant-aided heating.

Treatment in account and in taxation

Input tax which is irrecoverable, eg on exempt supplies for partially exempt business, is attributed to the cost of the property acquired.

Thus, under Statements of Standard Accounting Practice, VAT on fixed assets is included in the capital cost of the item. In the long term this may be relevant to any Capital Gains Tax computation and may feature in calculations for capital allowances.

For VAT purposes, no substantive difference is made between capital and revenue. Thus, a taxable person pays input tax on taxable supplies of a capital nature as well as those of a revenue nature. Similarly, output tax is charged on standard-rated capital items and revenue items.

Taxes interaction

It may be useful to note that VAT may interact with other taxes in some circumstances. A brief indication is given here. Thus, where input tax is completely recovered against output tax, the following computations should be made without taking VAT into account:

- income tax or corporation tax

- capital allowances

- capital gains tax.

Where input tax is not recoverable by a trader, eg for an exempt business, it may be available for setting against income tax or corporation tax liability.

Input tax charged to a person on a capital item and not recovered by or credited to the taxable person, may be used in a subsequent computation for capital gains tax purposes. Of course, any VAT charged as output tax is not included in the consideration on disposal.

Persons who are not taxable persons for VAT may compute profits for income taxation and gains for capital gains tax by deduction of any VAT paid as an input tax. Capital allowances are treated in a similar way.

For a person who is partly exempt, VAT on inputs must be apportioned to taxable outputs and exempt outputs; only the input tax relevant to taxable outputs is allowable. Generally, unrelieved input tax is allowed against income or capital taxation as described above.

Recovery of overpaid VAT

Where a person has overpaid the amount of VAT actually due to HMC&E there is now a separate mechanism for obtaining a refund of that amount.

Incorrect certificates as to zero rating etc

If, subject to the satisfaction of HMC&E, a person gives a certificate in the prescribed form to a supplier that the supply or supplies are to a building qualifying for zero rating and that certificate is incorrect, then that person will be liable to a penalty.

'Capital goods' scheme

From 1 April 1990 a new scheme came into force applying to certain capital items which are used for non-taxable purposes. The scheme only applies to a very small percentage of companies which are not fully taxable. It will not apply to any capital items acquired or brought into use or costs incurred before 1 April 1990.

The capital items affected are:

- computers and items of computer equipment worth £50,000 or more

- 'land and buildings' (or part of buildings) worth £250,000 or more.

'Land and buildings' includes both freehold and long leases of buildings; extensions and alterations to buildings are included, as are buildings which owners construct for their own use.

The scheme generally operates by making adjustments to the original input tax reclaimed by the business where the taxable use of the relevant goods changes.

The adjustments are made where a change in use occurs for:

- computers etc. (as above) within 5 years

- 'land and buildings' etc (as above) within 10 years (subject to the adjustment being only 5 years for building interests of less than 10 years).

Various regulations and controlling principles have been included to govern changes of ownership of companies and the goods themselves, theft, damage etc, and special calculation rules in limited circumstances.

The facilities manager may need to keep or contribute to the maintenance of the records required by the HMC&E.

11.5.3 RELEVANT SUPPLIES

'Relevant Supplies' are those which fall within the VAT regime; in connection with premises these are:

- disposals of interests in land and buildings

- construction services and goods

- professional and specialist services.

Disposal of interests in land and buildings

Technically this only applies to the sale, or granting a lease, of land and buildings. However, for the sake of brevity, the term is used here in connection with 'disposal of interest' to embrace also grants of rights and licences.

Generally, the interests and rights are described in Chapter 3.2, however, for purposes of the VAT legislation there is a special definition of a 'long lease':

- leases for over 21 years including those providing for:

  - periodic rent reviews

  - right for either party to terminate within 21 years

  - assignment by a person of his lease of the site on which he has begun to construct, or first constructed, a building provided that the lease has over 21 years to run at the time of assignments.

However, assured tenancies and the like are excluded.

Perhaps not surprisingly a 'short lease' is any lease which is not a long one!

Land includes buildings, walls, trees, plants and other structures and natural objects attached to the land so long as they remain attached.

Fixtures supplied under the disposal of a freehold or leasehold interest in land are regarded as 'flowing' with the land. Their liability will follow that of the land, that is exempt, zero-rated or standard-rated.

Construction services and goods

Supply of services takes place when a person does something, other than supplying goods, for a consideration, so construction services need to be separately identified in respect of each of:

- **construction only of new building**: the sole purpose of this term is to distinguish straight-forward building construction from the 'design-and-build' process. Procurement processes involving payment of separate fees to management contractors, construction managers and the like are included in this definition.

As explained in Chapter 6.3 the management contractor employs contractors to do the construction works and the client pays the management contractor a fee and the cost of the contracts executed directly by the management contractor. This total is zero-rated or standard rated depending on the type of building construction work. A construction or project manager's fee is treated as payment for professional services as it is considered separate from the works consideration. Therefore the 'accountable sum' in these contracts for the purpose of this definition is the total of the works contracts excluding the construction or project management fee.

- **design-and-construction of new building**: generally, design work in design - and - construct projects follows the VAT situation for the building, ie where the contractor supplies the design services under the contract within a lump sum package. Where design etc services are, however, supplied outside the lump sum package they are standard - rated.

- **alteration - only works**: the sole purpose of this term is to distinguish straight-forward building construction alterations from the 'design-and-build' process for alteration works, discussed below:

- **design-and-construction in alteration works**

- **sub-contract services in new building**: this refers to sub-contractors working to a main contractor or another sub-contractor. For VAT purposes it is not currently necessary to distinguish sub-contractors from 'works' or 'trade' contractors working to management contractors or under the direction of construction managers

- **sub-contract alteration - only works**

- **sub-contract design and construction of new building**: a client may obtain the necessary design work for a building project from a sub-contractor as part of a design and build package deal with the sub-contractor. The principles with regard to the taxation of the design element are as for the main contractor in design-and-build

- **sub-contractor design and construction in alteration works**

- **supply of goods without services**: goods supplied to purchaser where the supplier does not provide services in connection therewith. Typically this would cover supplies of materials from builders' merchants to contractors and any supply where exclusive ownership passes from one person to another. It is interesting to note, in connection with real estate, that 'goods' includes a major interest in land, ie a freehold or long lease. Other disposals of interests in land, eg rights licences and short-leases are held to be supplies of services rather than supplies of goods.

Professional and specialist services

Professional and specialist services may be either independent or integral.

- **independent professional services**: comprise work of a design, legal, surveying, engineering, agency or project management nature which are typically provided for a fee to clients by independent consultants in relation to land and property development

- **integral services**: are provided within the total consideration for the supply to which they relate. If they are separately billed then they will normally be treated as independent professional services.

It must be noted that whereas this situation is expressly confirmed by HMC&E in their explanatory publications in respect of 'design-and-build' contracts there is no such statement in respect of other comparable situations, eg property dealers employing their own conveyancing staff.

- **specialist services**: are treated in the same way as professional services. They comprise such supplies as site investigations (prior to offering a building contract), concrete testing, site security, site cleaning, site catering and temporary lighting.

Supplies of certain specialist services in the course of zero-rated construction can be zero-rated if they come with HMC&E's definitions of 'demolition', 'site restoration', 'hire-plant with operator' or 'the erection and/or dismantling of scaffolding, formwork and falsework' (but not the hire).

11.5.4 STAGES OF DEVELOPMENT FOR VAT PURPOSES

Primary conditions

Liability for VAT and the rate to be charged on such supplies is primarily conditioned by the development stages of the site under consideration. In the manual 'Property Experts Guide to VAT'[1] the authors defined these stages as:

- non-development land
- land under development
- land with mature development.

Each of these stages as defined below, relates to 'trigger' points in the legislation which determines whether a supply will be exempt, zero-rated or standard-rated.

Definition of 'non-development land'

All land which, at the time of disposal of an interest etc is:

- not yet 'land under development' as defined below, ie does not contain any new building construction that has progressed beyond foundation stage; and
- not 'land with mature development' as defined below.

Definition of 'land under development'

Land with new building construction that has:

- progressed beyond foundation stage, and
- has been completed and unoccupied for 3 years or less.

The term new building includes all work of building construction other than works to buildings which are part of 'land with mature development' as defined below. By definition it specifically excludes:

- conversion
- reconstruction
- alteration
- enlargement
- extension or annexation which provides for internal access to the existing buildings
- extension or annexation for which the separate use, letting or disposal is prevented by the terms of:

  - any covenant

---

[1] *Bernard Williams Associates (1983) Property expert's guide to VAT, BEB Ltd., Bromley, Kent.*

- any statutory planning consent

- any similar permission.

For the purposes of this section it also includes civil engineering works such as roads, sewers, drains etc, carried out concurrently and in association with other new building construction.

11.5.5 THE STATUS OF THE SUPPLIER

Status in construction and development

It is important to distinguish between the developer and the contractor.

The significance of the difference lies in the fact that the disposal of an interest in 'land under development' by the developer as defined below must be distinguished from the provision of the construction services for VAT purposes.

In relation to a building or works, 'developer' as owner, means any person who:

- constructs it (person constructing)

- orders it to be constructed

- finances its construction,

with a view to granting an interest in, right over or licence to occupy it (or any part of it) or to occupying or using it (or any part of it) for his own purposes.

Where a body corporate is a member of a group and is a developer in relation to a building or work and it grants an interest, etc to another body corporate which is a member of the same group, then that body corporate is also a developer in relation to that building to work. The above applies to any body corporate which:

- was a member of the same group as the body making the grant at the time of the grant; or

- has been a member of the same group at the same time as the body making the grant has an interest etc in the building or work (or any part of it); or

- has been a member of the same group as any other body corporate which had an interest etc in the building or work (or any part of it).

11.5.6 OPTION TO TAX INCOME FROM PROPERTY

The principle

From 1 August 1989, subject to certain exceptions (mainly residential, relevant residential and charitable property), there has been an 'option to tax' (officially called an 'election to waive exemption' from) what would otherwise be exempt grant of interests in and rights over land, and licences to occupy land. (See VAT Act 1994 Schedule 10 paragraph 2.)

From 1 August 1989 a company (or a body corporate or relevant associate) can opt to tax the - otherwise exempt - sale, assignment, leasing or licensing of any other type of building or civil engineering work, or part of it, any agricultural land, including a building on agricultural land in which it has an interest which is identifiable as separated from any other agricultural land in which it has an interest, or any other land it specifies. Once having opted to tax any supply of these, however, every subsequent supply must always be taxed. The option is irrevocable (except in limited circumstances).

If premises are linked by a walkway or similar means, or groups of separate units within a parade, precinct or complex these are to be treated as a single building (but the nature of the "link" is important).

Where making an inclusive supply of qualifying accommodation (qualifying for zero-rating or exempt from the option to tax) together with other, commercial or industrial accommodation, the supplier must apportion the consideration, eg if he lets a shop with a flat over it at an inclusive rent he must apportion the rent between the standard-rated element for the commercial premises and the exempt element for the residential accommodation.

If, having opted to tax a building, it is subsequently completely demolished and another building is constructed on the site, the supplier is not bound by his option for the previous building.

On acquisition of a freehold interest in land or a building in which the purchaser in turn intends to grant an interest, he is not bound by the previous owner's option.

Similarly with acquisition of any other interest in land or a building or any part of a building in which the purchaser intends to grant a sub-lease or licence he is not bound by the option exercised by the freeholder or head lessee.

Eligibility for 'option to tax'

Eligibility to opt to tax in relation to a building/land so that the building or land is changed into a taxable supply (at standard rate) from an exempt one depends on the type of disposal and/or the category of use:

- 'qualifying' building
  - any transaction
- freehold sale
  - of land with mature development
  - of all undeveloped land
  - of agricultural land or buildings thereon where elector has an interest, right or licence
  - of agricultural land or buildings thereon
  - of any other land or building
- leasing
  - of all land
  - of buildings on agricultural land where elector has an interest, right or licence
  - of any other buildings on agricultural land
  - of any other building
- grant
  - of any leasehold at a premium
- assignment
  - of any leasehold at a premium.

Consequences

Once the option has been made it cannot be revoked.

As a direct consequence of the option, a taxable person will then be able to recover any input tax attributable to his taxable outputs in respect of the building or land from the date of election only. In the long term input tax incurred before the option will not be recoverable.

Timing

For VAT purposes there is no imposed time limit within which a supplier must exercise the option to tax. His responsibility for accounting for tax on an 'opted' supply runs from the time that he exercises the option.

Notification

Suppliers must give written notice of an option to tax to the local VAT office not later than 30 days after it is exercised. If they are not already registered for VAT, but will become registerable by exercising the option to tax, they must include written notice with the application for registration. They need not, however, give written notice where they opt to tax and the total consideration for all the supplies for the buildings or land for which they have opted is expected to be less than a presented amount in the next 12 months.

Where they give written notice, they can do this by:

- naming the individual buildings

- opting for all their buildings without naming them

- opting for all their buildings with specific named exceptions

- opting for their buildings, together with any that they may subsequently acquire.

They must be careful, however, when they make any option which does not specify actual buildings because they will be bound by any option which they exercise to account for tax on all future supplies of the land or buildings concerned. Remember that the option is irrevocable.

Records

The facilities manager should ensure that records of options are kept on a long term basis, including copies of notifications, and any acknowledgements.

Tax point for chargeable leases

There are special provisions which determine the point, ie the time when the supply is treated, for VAT purposes, as taking place.

Existing leases

If the company making the supply is a lessor or licensor, it has the legal right to add VAT to the rent agreed in the lease or licence unless the lease specifically says it cannot. If it has opted but cannot, under the terms of the lease, add VAT to the rent, it must still account for VAT which is deemed to be included in the rent.

Input tax

The supplier cannot claim his input tax on supplies (or importation's) attributable to his building or land if the supplies were made to him before the effective date of his option except where he has made not previous exempt supply in respect of his building or land.

Advice to landlords and tenants

Landlords are advised to tell their tenants in advance if they plan to exercise their option. This could avoid getting enquiries from them when the rent demands go out and help maintain good relations. The VAT will be a new expense for them: not all will be able to claim it (or all of it) as their input tax, and even those that can may incur a cash-flow disadvantage. Any who sub-let would appreciate notice so that they can consider charging tax on the rents they receive.

They should check that the lease entitles them to require payment of the VAT by the tenant.

Tenants not currently being charged VAT on their rent should check with their landlord.

How far tenants can recover as input tax any VAT on the rent they pay will be governed by the normal rules of input tax. If they cannot recover and the landlord has merely indicated an intention, it may be possible to pay a higher rent and avoid VAT, but this is not likely.

If tenants sub-let they will particularly wish to know whether their landlord intends to exercise the option so that they can decide whether to do the same and so recover, subject to the normal rules, the VAT they will pay to him. Their own tenants would appreciate knowing what the plans are.

11.5.7 SELF SUPPLY OF LAND

Companies falling within the above definition of developer using land already in their possession may be liable to a special VAT self-supply charge on certain of the building or civil engineering works which they construct or arrange to have constructed.

Liability of charge

What this means is that even if they did purchase the land specifically for the development, they may have to account for tax and to value according to a formula.

Fig. 11.5.A shows how to determine if there is a liability in this respect

Fig. 11.5.A
'Self-supply' of land - how to determine any liability to VAT charge

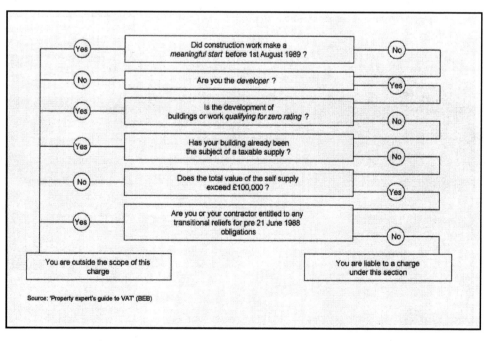

Source: 'Property expert's guide to VAT' (BEB)

If liable the charge will rise on the first occasion of:

- the exempt supply of part, or all, of the building, work or the land on which it is to be constructed; or

- use of the building, work or any part of it when not a fully taxable person (or if the representative member of a group of bodies corporate is not a fully taxable person) during the period commencing with the day when the building or work is first planned and ending 10 years after completion of construction.

The value of the self-supply is the total of:

- the value of grants relating to the land on which the building or work is constructed, made or to be made to the developer, other than grants to be made for consideration in the form of rent the value of which cannot be ascertained by the developer when the supply is treated as made; and

- the value of all the taxable supplies of goods and services, other than any that are zero rated, ie paid before 1 August 1989, made or to be made for or in connection with the construction of the building or work; which includes: professional and managerial services, demolition and site clearance services, security services, hire of equipment, haulage services, landscaping services, fitting out services etc.

11.5.8. SELF SUPPLY OF CONSTRUCTION SERVICES

If a company is using its own labour to perform construction services for its own occupation or use then there are various mechanisms which determine the level of tax to be paid, if any; the logic of these provisions is illustrated in Fig. 11.5.B.

Fig. 11.5.B
'Self-supply' of construction services - how to determine liability to a VAT charge

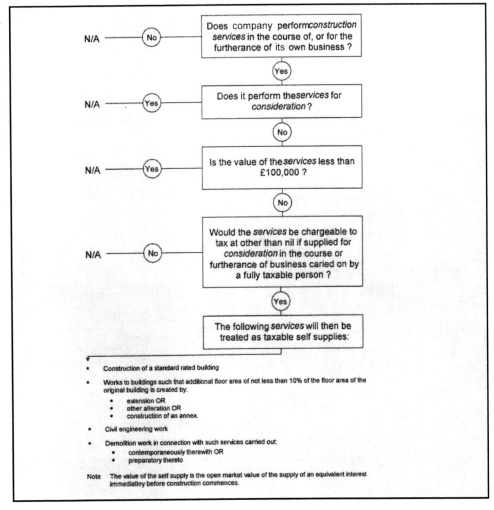

11.5.9. SERVICE CHARGES AND THE LIKE

The provision of services

It is common for leases between landlords and tenant to lay down that the landlord shall provide, and the tenants shall pay for, the services required for the upkeep of the building as a whole. The lease may provide for an inclusive rental, or it may require the tenants to contribute by means of a charge additional to the basic rent. These charges are sometimes called 'service charges', 'maintenance charges', 'further rent' or 'additional rent'.

Provided the services supplies in return for the charges are towards the general upkeep of the structure and common areas of the premises and grounds or for the services of a person such as a caretaker or warden they are regarded as part of the consideration for the grant to the tenants of their right to occupy the premises.

Therefore, where rent, including ground rent, is consideration for an exempt supply, then the service charge is further consideration for that exempt supply.

If the rent is consideration for a standard-rated supply, eg under the 'option to tax rent' then the service charge is further consideration for a standard-rated supply.

The main supply

The main supply is the main benefit passing under a disposal of interest etc to which the main consideration relates.

Where companies meet costs relating to premises which they share with others the precise terms of the sharing arrangement will dictate whether such payments are a main supply as opposed to a separate supply or disbursements.

The main supply is one which is rendered in respect of the shared facility rather than one where the partner in the facility gains the whole benefit of the separately identifiable supply, ie a separate supply.

For example, tenants recharging part of the rent invoiced to them will be making a main supply to the other occupier whereas cleaning of their rooms in the building is a separate supply.

Separate supply

Where companies sharing premises with other occupants make a supply which is separately identifiable as being in respect of facilities they use, they are making a separate supply. See also 'Main supply' above for further explanation of the distinction between the two categories.

11.5.10 OPERATING FACILITIES

Facilities provided by the landlord

Supplies which are further consideration are defined above.

The supplies by the landlord which may be described as operating facilities include the following:

- day-to-day maintenance
- general upkeep
- fixtures and fittings
- water and sewerage
- fuel and power

- cleaning

- telephones

- reception and switchboard

- administration

- management

- security

- office staff and services

- office equipment

- staff facilities

- car parking.

11.5.11 'NON-RELEVANT' CONSTRUCTION WORK

Definition

'Non-relevant' construction work is the definition used to describe construction goods or work that must always be standard-rated regardless of whether or not the building to which it is supplied otherwise qualifies to receive zero-rated supplies.

The following are examples of goods which are standard-rates because they do not fall within the general description of goods for which zero-rating is allowed - for instance, because they are not fixtures, or because the law specifically excludes them from zero-rating (ie, most fitted furniture and domestic gas and electrical appliances):

- fitted furniture, both domestic and non-domestic, (other than units and work surfaces installed in the kitchens of dwellings or other qualifying buildings) whether supplied ready assembled or as materials, or part-assembled and finished-off on site. Examples in commercial buildings are:

  - desks

  - tables

  - chairs and other seating

- domestic electrical or gas appliances (but not space or water heating appliances), carpets and carpeting materials (including underlay and carpet tiles), even when stuck to the floor

- other articles of a kind not ordinarily installed by builders as part of the construction work, eg all trees, shrubs, flowers; and articles which are not fixtures, for example free standing equipment

- any goods a company supplies for later use by a customer or for use by some other person supplying services to their customer

- goods supplied without construction services, eg by a builders' merchant

- goods bought for the business but which are later used for work on a person's own home or property, even if the work would have been zero-rated if another builder had done it for them. But if they use such goods to build a complete new house for themselves, special arrangements may apply.

Standard-rated work

Standard rating will apply in the following examples:

- the conversion, reconstruction, alteration or enlargement of any non-qualifying existing building

- any extension or annex which has internal access to the existing building

- any extension or annex to an existing building, the separate use, letting or disposal of which is prevented by the terms of any covenant, planning consent or similar permission.

More specific examples of standard-rated work are:

- where the outer walls of an existing building remain even without floor or roof, any building operations in or around that shell

- the reconstruction of any existing building where internal features are retained in addition to any part of the external wall structure.

11.5.12 LIABILITIES TO VAT IN RESPECT OF COMMERCIAL BUILDINGS

The principles of assessment

All liabilities to charge VAT or otherwise in connection with premises fall within one or other of the three stages defined at 11.5.4. above.

It is important to understand that land does not become 'development land' (as opposed to remaining 'non-development land' as considered below) merely on receiving the benefit of a planning permission for construction thereon. It only ceases to become non-development land when work is carried out to it to bring it within the second-stage category, ie land under development.

Similarly, buildings may be complete and ready for occupation, but they still classify as 'land under development' until they meet the trigger point criteria for 'land with mature development' as defined above. The reason for this complicated set of definitions is that land, and the buildings under construction or built on it, are treated as inseparable for the purposes of VAT legislation - and, indeed, under the law of property.

Equally the supply of services such as construction or consultancy will potentially incur a different VAT charge depending on the stage at which they are provided.

Liabilities in respect of the more common supplies

Fig. 11.5.C (over the page) lists the liability to VAT in respect of the more commonly occurring transactions involving premises.

Fig. 11.5.C
VAT liability for some commonly occurring premises transaction

Nature of supply	Status of land / tax rate		
	Non-development	Under development	With mature development
Parking facilities	S	S	S
Most licenses to occupy	E/o	E/o	E/o
Most leases	E/o	E/o	E/o
Most freeholds	E/o	E/o	E/o
Professional services on S-rated disposal	S	S	S
Premium on S-rated disposal	S	S	S
Surrender	S	S	S
New civil engineering work	-	S	S
Construction work	-	S	S
Design-and-build	-	S	S
Independent Professional services (construction)	-	S	S
Material supplies	-	S	S
Specialist services	-	S	S
Rent	-	-	E/o
Further rent	-	-	E/o*
Separate supply of facilities	-	-	S

Notes: S = Standard-rated

E/o = Exempt within the option to tax

* = the tax-rate for the supply will follow that of the rent

11.6 BUSINESS RATES AND COUNCIL TAX

Introduction

Almost all occupier of business premises, ie non-domestic property, are subject to the payment of business rates unless some exemption, relief or concession is available to remove or mitigate the burden.

England, Scotland and Wales have largely similar schemes for business rates. (In Northern Ireland, the amount paid is based on rateable values and a 'local' rate poundage. Also, many manufacturing properties are de-rated, ie there is no charge.)

The facilities manager may need to consider the impact of business property rates from time to time. In particular the following are likely to be important:

- liability to pay for business rates, having regard to any exemptions, reliefs and concessions

- rates on empty buildings, including buildings from which staff are being decanted (or vice versa)

- the impact of the five-yearly national revaluation

- any need to re-value a property between revaluations

- the availability of exemptions and reliefs, particularly for charities

- the application of transitional relief following a revaluation

- in general, various procedures in the rating system.

Briefly, liability to pay is calculated according to the formula:

Business Rates = Rateable Value (RV) x National Non-domestic Rating Multiplier (NNDRM)

However, the NNDRM is also known as the uniform business rate (UBR) and this expression will be used in this chapter. In 2001/2002 it was determined by national government at 43p and 42.6p in the pound in England and Wales respectively. For Scotland it was 45p for property with rateable values of £10,000 or more. UBR increases are limited by rates of inflation each year.

Rating is a specialist topic involving rating surveyors, plant and machinery valuers and, of course, lawyers. The treatment below is intended to give a flavour or feel of the areas where the facilities manager might ask pertinent questions of professional advisors.

It may be noted that the government has been - and is currently - consulting with various relevant bodies on a number of matters affecting the rating system. Changes are likely but details of any recommendations are not yet available in official form.

11.6.1 THE NATURE OF BUSINESS RATES

The evolution of the rating system

Prior to 1997 the rates levy on businesses, as a contribution towards locally-based public services, was calculated and administered by the local authority. The amount of the levy was the product of the 'notional' value of the premises occupied to which a 'rate in the pound' - known as 'poundage' was applied annually. The resulting amount was billed to the occupier of the premises who might or might not be the owner.

The system had its origins in the Poor Relief Act of 1601; 400 years of application and contest resulted in a well tried and tested system albeit that only a few specialists understood how the complex system of hypothetical tenancies, hereditaments and valuation lists actually worked.

During the 1980s, the business rates in Central London and many provincial cities started to make the overall level of occupancy costs, based on the very high passing rents, look excessive, leading to general discontent with the whole system, as well as its implementation. The Local Government Finance Act 1988 (LGFA), as substantially amended by the Local Government and Housing Act 1989, resulted in the demise of the old system. Together with a plethora of secondary legislation, they completely changed the basis of the levy in that:

- domestic rating was dropped completely out of the process, to be replaced (now) by Council Tax

- the level of rates "poundage" is now calculated by central as opposed to local government, ie the UBR

- the proceeds are collected locally but distributed to the local authorities by central government.

The principles of liability to rating and methods of valuation have remained, although with a revised terminology built upon, but slightly differing from, the original.

Before going into the detail of how the levy is computed, it is first necessary to determine when liability, if any, exists.

Liability to pay business rates

The tests of an organisation's liability to rates under the Uniform Business Rate (UBR) are that:

- the organisation is in occupation of the premises in question

- the premises constitute a 'relevant non-domestic or composite hereditament'

- the premises are not exempt, or partially exempt, from UBR.

Clearly the non-rating expert needs to understand the precise legal meaning of some of these terms; the facilities manager's interest will lie particularly in any liability to pay rates on occupied premises, empty premises, temporary premises held under licence and sub-leased premises or assigned premises. Also, when it is proposed that property is to be altered, partly or wholly demolished or redeveloped, the facilities manager may need to consider the business rates implications. For instance, it may be possible to propose a reduction in the assessment to the Valuation Office. If agreed directly or on appeal there is a reduction; backdating of the reduction may be available - subject to certain restrictions.

Occupation and ownership

The historic concept that the rates charge was on the occupier of the property - who was not necessarily the owner - has survived the new order. So, although the charge is calculated on the value of the property upon which it is levied, payment of the levy is the liability of whomsoever is in occupation for the period of the 'chargeable financial year' in question. The current occupier is not liable for any default of any predecessors or successors in occupation.

However, if the hereditament, ie premises (see below), is empty it will be the owner who is liable to pay the rate on the empty building - the 'empty rate'.

In the context of the UBR, as in the general law of real estate, the owner is the person who is entitled to possession; but whereas 'possession' in land law is determined by a person's right to receive rents and profits arising from it, possession under the uniform business rate is based upon the person's right to take physical possession of the property. The latter distinction is of particular significance where property is mortgaged and where leases are forfeited, surrendered or disclaimed.

Although a mortgagee (the one lending against the security) may be entitled to possession he or she will not be liable for the rates on a building while another party is in actual physical possession - even if the latter is in liquidation.

A landlord may become liable for rates on a building on exercising a right of forfeiture under a lease, or taking a surrender or if it is disclaimed by a liquidator. In all those circumstances the landlord will be entitled to physical possession and is thereby the owner for purposes of UBR; however, the liability for payments of rates does not arise until the building is 'empty'. The matter of 'empty rates' is discussed further below.

A non-domestic hereditament

The Local Government Finance Act 1988 defines the term hereditament by reference to the definition in the General Rate Act 1967. Although the 1988 Act fully repeals the latter, it is necessary to resort to the 1967 Act to understand what the term 'hereditament' means in its current context.

In order to qualify as a hereditament - which of itself does not automatically invoke a current liability to rating - a property, (or unit within it) is one which is, or would fall to be, shown as separate item in the rating list.

The rating list schedules all non-domestic (see below) properties, and units therein, which are liable to have a charge levied upon them, together with their respective rateable values, ie the amount upon which the charging authority (formerly the rating authority) levies its non-domestic rating multiplier (formerly poundage - see above!).

In order to attract uniform business rates premises have to classify as a relevant non-domestic hereditament. Although offices, manufacturing and mining premises clearly come into the category of non-domestic, the term can also include advertisement hoardings let out by the occupier or by the owner of otherwise empty land. What is non-domestic is established by reference to what the statutory instrument defines as domestic! To précis the position - which does seem fairly obvious in most cases - a hereditament is non-domestic if its principal use is as a place of business for persons who either do not live there, or whose principal place of residence is elsewhere.

Where people live and work in the same building but the business part is not self-contained, business rates can be levied on the latter part of a 'composite hereditament'. Such properties as offices with an overnight residential suite or caretaker's accommodation, or shops with an integral flat may come into this category.

The issue of 'composite hereditament' as it affects people working from home - 'home-workers' - where the business takes over the accommodation to the extent that structural alternations have to be made to facilitate it, or the owner moves out to another main residence, is obviously one which will need to be carefully watched by those companies pursuing this employment policy.

A non-domestic hereditament is relevant if it is rateable (to use the old parlance), which means that it will appear in the rating list.

11.6.2 EXEMPTIONS AND RELIEFS

The facilities managers of business property and non-commercial property, (eg churches), respectively should be alert to the opportunities to avoid rates altogether or at least mitigate the impact.

Exemptions from rating

Firstly, there are numerous classes of exempt property. Thus, Schedule 5 to the Local Government Finance Act 1988 exempts certain types of business premises from liability, notably:

- agricultural land and buildings, fish farms and fishing rights
- places of religious worship
- property of drainage authorities, and public sewers
- property used for the disabled
- property in Enterprise Zones
- parks
- air-raid protection works
- swinging moorings
- certain property of Trinity House
- road crossings over water courses.

Other exemptions include diplomatic immunities and the Crown. However, the Crown makes payments in lieu of rates

If, on a review of the property holdings, it seems that an exemption is available but has not hitherto been claimed, the facilities manager might find it necessary to consult the organisation's rating surveyor or lawyer.

Relief from rating

Charities: avoidance or mitigation of the rates burden may be available in other circumstances. Thus, the facilities manager acting for a charity may note that charities and certain other bodies concerned with "good" objects are eligible for relief. Charities have a mandatory 80% relief and may obtain 20% local authority discretionary relief. Discretionary relief at 20% is available to bodies with philanthropic, religious or recreational objects, ie non-profit making.

Hardship: also, relief may be given on the grounds of hardship.

Alterations and Vacation: a partial or complete reduction in rates may be obtained when building is wholly or partly demolished or there is a change of use which takes it out of the non-domestic class. Also, when a building is being vacated or has become vacant rates may be reduced to some extent. (However, see the next section on empty property.)

Separated/Joined property: sometimes, separate units of accommodation in one building may be capable of being joined together, perhaps after an acquisition. Similarly, where the organisation separately occupies buildings, perhaps after acquisition or a merger of companies, they may be capable for forming one site. In these circumstances, it may be prudent of the facilities manager to find out whether a reduction in rateable value is possible on valuation grounds.

Village shops: enjoy a 50% relief.

Transitional relief: in England between revaluations changes in rates payable are phased. Thus for large properties, initially no more than 12.5% of an increase or 2.5% of a decrease will be paid (before allowing for inflation). The relief takes a different form elsewhere.

11.6.3 RATES ON EMPTY BUILDINGS

Wholly-unoccupied property

The rates levy on unoccupied buildings is only 50% of the full rate, so both developers and occupiers need to have their wits about them to ensure that they get their proper entitlement to this relief.

Again, the Local Government Finance Act 1988 lays down the provisions as to when 'unoccupied rate' (empty rate) is payable. In order for a liability (or indeed a concession) to arise, the following principal conditions must apply:

- the property must attract liability as a 'relevant non-domestic hereditament'

- no part of it must be occupied on a particular day (rates are calculated on a daily basis - see below)

- the hereditament must not be exempted from unoccupied rating by the legislation, eg, certain defined industrial land and buildings, properties below a certain rateable value or properties prevented from occupation by some statutory or other official intervention

- an 'existing' hereditament has been wholly unoccupied for a continuous period in excess of three months (ignoring any periods or re-occupation of less than six weeks within the three month period).

- a new hereditament, including merely a part capable of separate occupation, has been wholly unoccupied for three months following either:

  - the date of service by the local authority of a completion notice on a building or part thereof which has already been completed, or

  - the date given in the Local Authority's completion notice (forecast not more than three months ahead) when the building or part thereof is expected to be complete.

Where the date of actual completion is within the three months forecast by the authority and is agreed by the developer (or the future rate-payer) then it must stand; however, if the rate-payers disagree and can prove completion was more than three months after the notices was served they can request service of a new notice.

Partly-occupied property

For general purposes of rating business premises a partly occupied hereditament is deemed to be wholly-occupied, but the charging authorities (formerly rating authorities) may, at their discretion, if the partial occupation is for a short period - as in gradual decanting - apportion the rateable liability as between the occupied and unoccupied parts enlisting the help of the Valuation Officer in making the calculation.

New properties filling up and existing premises decanting slowly over time or downsizing can all benefit from partial-occupation relief, but certain important procedures must be observed by the ratepayer in order to be reasonably sure of getting it. Absolutely critical is the establishment of a separate rating assessment for the unoccupied part. Among criteria the Valuation Office Agency of the Inland Revenue will take into account on receipt of an appeal in this respect are:

- whether the parts claimed to be unoccupied are completely empty - best not to leave any bits or pieces around in case they give rise to a suspicion of beneficial occupation

- the areas appealed should be clearly defined having independent direct access from the main core or direct from the street

- it must not be seen to be merely in a temporarily decanted state as part of a natural internal re-organisation

- there must be full compliance with statutory liabilities including health and safety and means of escape (in case of fire).

Where there are a number of buildings in a complex, care must be exercised to pick out discrete buildings which will qualify for 'empty rate' relief. Having done so, their complete separation from the complex must be maintained and not compromised by continuing to afford access to other parts or relying upon a common security regime.

11.6.4 RATEABLE VALUE

The basis of valuation

The definition in the Local Government Finance Act 1988 perpetuates, or fails to discount, the concept of a 'hypothetical lease', which has become the cornerstone of the rating surveyor's discipline and fee income for specialists in the legal profession over the years. Schedule 6 paragraph 2(1) provides "rateable value" as the basis of valuation.

This all boils down to something approaching the rack rental passing from year to year where a tenant is on a full repairing and insuring lease (see Chapter 3.2 - leasehold conditions). Although the definition implies a property to let with vacant possession the 'hypothetical tenant' can be the owner-occupier paying a notional rent (as often done in a 'notional rent' accounting convention). Although the hypothetical tenancy is from year to year this is probably only to keep the hypothetical rent at market level rather than to preclude the prospect of its continuance beyond the end of any one year.

Alterations to the rating list

There are about 1.7 million non-domestic properties which have been valued by the Valuation Office Agency for the Revaluation 2000 (Reval 2000). The date of Reval 2000 was 1 April 2000 and reflected values of 1 April 1998. The next revaluation is due to come in in 2005. (However, the government is consulting on possible changes to the rating system.)

Alteration to the list following Reval 2000

The list was published at the end of 1999 and ratepayers are likely to be considering the rateable value ascribed to their property. From 1 April 2000 any proposals to alter the entry were made to the Valuation Officer by 'interested' persons, eg the occupier, owner or the local authority. This needed to be done within six months in the manner prescribed. If the Valuation Officer accepts the proposal the list will be altered accordingly. If not the interested person may appeal.

Alterations to the list in other circumstances

A proposal to alter the rating list may arise in certain circumstances. Provided the proposal is lodged with the Valuation Officer within six months of the date when the effect on the value was first felt, ie the 'event'.

Such circumstances include:

- temporary falls in value due to disturbance from local building or civil engineering works

- permanent changes in status of the locality caused by external factors such as closure of a railway station or a by-pass encroaching on the previously green-field curtilage

- reductions to rateable values of similar properties in the vicinity or other comparable locations. In the latter case, if the changes sought follows the decision of a Valuation Tribunal, the right of appeal is automatic for a period of six months. On the other hand, if the base change decision emanates from agreement with the local Valuation Officer there is no such right of appeal: the Valuation Officer may - and should - take the necessary actions to correct the rateable values of comparable properties in the list.

Importantly, the charging authority may now make proposals to the Valuation Officer in respect of alterations to the rating list, eg as may any 'interested person'; this term includes not just the occupier but also any other person owning a legal estate or some reversionary right of possession as well as subsidiaries, co-members of a group, associated companies and the like having a 'qualifying' connection with the occupier.

Proposals may be served by e-mail, the VOA website, by fax or in writing, stating the extent of and reason for the alteration being sought and the date of the event causing the change in value.

The process of making proposals is a specialist area for the rating surveyors; in major issues the resources of legal specialists may be involved to ultimate advantage.

If negotiations fail the proposal may go to an appeal to the Valuation Tribunal involving yet more surveying and possible legal fees - and an almost certainly far better briefed VO!

11.6.5 METHODS OF VALUATION

Apart from hereditaments in the 'central non-domestic rating list', which have to be valued on a prescribed basis, the Valuation Officer may use absolute discretion in choosing the method of valuation.

The usual methods for rating involve:

- use of the rents actually paid
- comparison of rents
- extrapolation from cost using the contractor's basis
- extrapolation from open market capital value
- valuation by reference to profits
- statutory formula.

The general principles underlying all these methods and their components are discussed and illustrated in Chapter 3.4. For rating, the valuation date is given as 1 April 1998 for the recently completed revaluation. Other assumptions are concerned with the tenure (basically full repairing and insuring), the state of the premises and the nature of the locality (see Schedule 6 paragraph 2(7) to the 1988 Act and the Rating (Valuation) Act 1999).

In nearly all cases the comparative rent method will be adopted as the Valuation Officers have a vast network of comparable data which is must easier to use in the substantiation of values than the other more scientific, but relatively subjective, approaches. The latter may, however, be used for specialised property or as a check.

11.6.6 PLANT AND MACHINERY

The facilities manager may be surprised to note that certain types of plant and machinery are included in the property for rating purposes. They are prescribed by the Valuation for Rating (Plant and Machinery) Regulations 1994 and include the following classes:

- Class 1 Power Plant
- Class 2 Services
- Class 3 Conveyors and Pipelines
- Class 4 Certain structural plant.

Several alternative approaches are available to the valuer in valuing the plant and machinery in a property.

11.6.7 DOMESTIC PROPERTY: COUNCIL TAX

Council tax

Dwellings or domestic property are dealt with under a completely different regime of taxation called 'council tax' which is based upon capital values set in sets of bands for England, Scotland and Wales. The tax is administered by the local authority, eg district council, which sets the level of tax. It is subject to exemptions and reliefs.

Dwellings

Dwellings, as such, are valued to capital values as at 1 April 1991 and put within eight bands A to H for council tax purposes. The Local Government Finance Act 1992 and the Council Tax (Situation and Valuation of Dwellings) Regulations 1992 address this area of local taxation. A revaluation of dwellings has not been carried since the earlier 1990s.

"Composite Property"

Generally, the facilities manager will not be very much concerned with local taxation and domestic property. However, as far as business property is concerned some may be described as 'composite property', ie mixed property being part non-domestic (business) and part domestic (dwelling). The facilities manager may note that only the non-domestic or business part is valued for business rates purposes, reflecting in the value any effect the domestic part may have (paragraphs 1A and 1B to Schedule 6 of the 1988 Act cover this aspect of valuation).

Short-stay accommodation

Some 'dwellings' are used for the purposes of short-stay accommodation. Although few facilities managers are likely to be involved with such accommodation it may be pertinent to some. If short-stay accommodation is identified as non-domestic use a liability to business rates may arise. Obviously hotel accommodation is non-domestic, but some accommodation may not be, eg that used by staff or long-stay guests.

11.6.8 APPEALS

Following any negotiations on a proposal, an appeal against the Valuation Officer's decision may be made to the Valuation Tribunal. Further appeal to the Lands Tribunal may be made and hence, on a point of law, to the Court of Appeal and with leave to the House of Lords.

For the Reval 2000, appeals to the Valuation Tribunal have been and will be programmed locally as part of processing the proposals. Thus, where negotiations on a proposal do not result in an agreement, the appeal will be arranged by reference to a target date. Appeals on similar properties should, therefore, be heard at about the same time.

For the existing valuation list appeals must be made before 31 March 2005 but there are restrictions for certain circumstances.

PART F

The Facilities Audit

Section 12

Facilities Auditing Processes

12.1   THE FACILITIES MANAGEMENT AUDIT

Introduction

The modern-day facilities audit belies its title for the term 'audit' implies an arithmetical and procedural check of a company's financial position; the facilities audit goes a lot further than that.

A facilities management audit is an independent review of the efficiency and effectiveness of the process of providing and operating facilities, together with cost, performance levels, space use, management structures and systems.

Where appropriate the auditor will provide peer group benchmarks and indicate areas where improvements might be effected. This chapter traces the origins of the process and considers what the facilities management audit seeks to achieve and the circumstances in which it is likely to be beneficial.

Benchmarking is considered in greater depth in Chapter 12.2.

12.1.1 THE CONCEPT AND ITS DEVELOPMENT

The premises audit

The first facilities auditors were the new breed of space planners who came into the UK from the USA in the early 1970's. In the main, space planning as a discipline has since become related more to interior design than to facilities management audit. The appraisal and auditing of space use is considered in depth in Section 4 - Space Management.

In the same way that some accountants have used their auditing role as a platform for development of business management consultancy, some of the new breed of facilities management consultants can trace their roots directly back to the simple costs-benchmarking exercises arising out of space use analysis in the 1970's and 1980's.

The concept of a formal premises audit was developed in the early 1980's. Its broad recognition as a discipline came finally through the publication of 'Premises Audits'[1], first written as a series of articles for 'Facilities'[2] and then produced in 1986 as a book under the same title.

Although space use audits, pioneered by space planners in the UK from the early 1970's, had gained commercial acceptance by the time the series was written, interest in the operating costs of premises had remained firmly on an academic plane until then.

The activities of the space planners became the catalyst for development of the base data which was so essential to effective auditing of premises costs. The usual outcome of the space planners' work was the identification of the need for change. Premises were either too large or too small, the wrong configuration, in the wrong location or deficient in some other way.

Alternative solutions for space problems, involving comparison on economic as well as ergonomic bases, had to be evaluated; whatever the options - refurbishment, redevelopment or green/brown-field development and so on - the present and predicted operating costs had to be fed into the financial equation and this meant a lot of searching and investigation to get them out of the organisation's usually inadequate records.

---

[1] *Williams, B. (1986) 'Premises Audits' (Bulstrode Press - out of print)*

[2] *'Facilities' (originally Bulstrode Press, and now MCB University Press)*

Although the operating costs rarely influenced the outcome of premises investment options, the gathering of this data coincided with the ICT boom of the early 1980's and its significant impact on both capital and operating costs of buildings and space utilisation.

Mounting costs saw facilities managers under increasing pressure to defend budgets which were wholly inadequate for demands being placed upon the premises by the business function. In most cases the defence arguments presented against budget cuts were inadequate; this was partly due to inexperience of the facilities personnel, unable to appreciate the root cause of the problems, and partly due to the lack of any comparable cost data from their peer groups to give credence to their budget proposals.

Cost benchmarking

With the growing database of premises costs, carefully sifted into cost centres by reference to standard rules of classification, the premises audit procedures were expanded to include the cost 'benchmarking' (see Chapter 12.2.7) which was, and is, so critical to facilities managers. The more premises audits carried out, the greater the depth of knowledge which was gained, not only of comparative costs but also, and more importantly, of the underlying performance, ergonomic and management issues which generated the cost levels which were uncovered.

So with the passage of time the audit process has been extended way beyond just the operating costs to take in all the management issues.

The knowledge audit

As discussed in Chapter 2.6.2 knowledge is the key to meeting an organisation's primary business objectives.

The meaning of the term 'knowledge management' varies according to context but is essentially the effective utilisation of classified and processed information. In turn, the extent to which knowledge is effectively put to use in an organisation can be described as the intelligence of a business. Although some managers may feel they know instinctively how intelligent their enterprise is, a quantifiably assured answer is not easy to give. Enterprise intelligence, or intellectual capital, is vital to the future success of the business; auditing its management process is a vital activity for the whole organisation including its facilities management function.

Knowledge is effectively actionable information; it adds meaning and understanding. By undergoing a knowledge audit, an organisation can determine the value of its intellectual capital. Such an audit can also provide an overview of the strengths and weaknesses of the organisation, identify potential areas for improvement and opportunities to leverage knowledge.

The factors which reflect, augment, or adversely affect enterprise intelligence should be measured. A knowledge audit is a systematic examination, verification and evaluation of knowledge assets - effectively, an inventory of the knowledge base of the organisation. This will include both explicit knowledge, held in systems and documentation, and tacit knowledge held in the heads of employees.

The exercise will also include measurement and evaluation of the risks and opportunities faced by the organisation with respect to its corporate knowledge.

A knowledge audit provides a method of accounting for knowledge assets in terms of:

- identification - origin, nature, ownership, characteristics

- measurement - quantity, dimension, capacity

- evaluation - quality, value, significance.

The audit investigates existing processes for the capture, storage, use and sharing of knowledge, the level of awareness of existing and new knowledge sources, and any existing barriers to the growth and development of knowledge in the organisation. It will also examine the work culture and attitudes of employees and the extent to which the company's processes support knowledge sharing.

A knowledge audit is concerned with the structure of corporate knowledge rather than its detailed content. It is a structured process in which knowledge and its sources are labelled or categorised and it entails eliciting what teams, departments, knowledge workers and experts know, and need to know, together with the relationships between different knowledge entities, users and their needs.

The knowledge audit culminates in a report giving the diagnosis and prognosis for:

- knowledge risks & opportunities

- current 'knowledge health'

- corporate knowledge value.

A knowledge audit is not an information or computer/systems audit.

Matters coming within the scope of a knowledge audit include:

- how much is to be spent on the exercise?

- where are the known problem areas?

- what are the most vital business processes?

- in which area is key knowledge most vulnerable?

- to what extent is valuable knowledge contained and perhaps hidden in documents?

- how efficient are the organisation's knowledge management systems in storing and making knowledge available?

- is valuable customer knowledge being ignored or wasted?

- is knowledge being used and re-used effectively?

The audit may initially involve:

- a department (marketing, facilities management)

- a business process (document management, equipment maintenance)

- a team (intelligent client function, telephone enquiries, product delivery)

- a branch (head office, regional office, local office).

It must be manageable in terms of the ability to review and act on each specific area audited and is therefore best carried out incrementally rather than wholesale.

The main reason for carrying out a knowledge audit is to unearth hidden knowledge: business knowledge is a primary asset and must be accounted for. It is vital to establish what is known and what is not known in order to successfully implement a knowledge management programme.

The document output audit

Research by the Gartner Group shows that organisations spend 3% of their overall revenue on document output from copiers, printers and fax machines. Substantial economies are achievable by 'rightsizing' these fleets of output devices to match requirements. In order to do this it is necessary to undertake an output audit in order to identify the number of devices, quantify the output and assess how departmental and corporate needs are met.

If an enterprise output strategy is to be developed an output audit should encompass the organisation's overall print requirement including externally-sourced work: this would include the production of marketing materials, training and technical manuals, corporate brochures, invoices and statements, and stationery items such as letterheads and business forms. Expenditure in this broader area typically represents a further 3 to 5% of overall revenues. An enterprise document output audit may therefore examine expenditure amounting to 6 to 8% of revenue. The objective of a comprehensive analysis of an audit is to devise and effectively implement an enterprise output strategy.

Specific output audits

Specialist consultants may undertake a variety of audits of a client's output environment. Output audits include on-site information gathering and analysis, documentation of findings, and formal delivery of the audit's results with explanations. These audits include:

- an enterprise-wide output study (comprising a number of specific audits)
- conventional and electronic document management and storage
- centralised and distributed print environment
- local and remote print facilities
- output capacity planning
- output hardware and software evaluation
- externally-sourced print
- print and distribution environments (production mailing).

An all-embracing audit may embrace the entire life cycle of the document, from creation, through reproduction, to distribution, filing and archiving. This concerns all documents within the organisation, including computer output, internal and external communications, scanning, distribution and archiving of incoming correspondence and conventionally printed materials. Such an audit would normally be structured into several manageable units rather than be attempted as a single overall project.

The initial phase would involve a high level corporate study involving a review of the client organisation's business, management structure and the types of documents present within the corporate environment or to the level of corporate management seeking the study: for example a director may choose to have a document management audit performed for his department rather than enterprise-wide.

Having established relevant information on document output from an audit, a strategy can be developed. The outcome is likely to be a variation of the following:

- eliminate internal document output (accomplished by means of software solutions)
  - on-line report viewing
  - network fax/unified messaging
  - email and intranet
- improve external document processes (accomplished using specialist expertise)
  - integrate mail, central repro, data centre printing

- electronic forms management

- re-engineer mission critical documents

- change to print-on-demand model rather than print-and-stock 'distribute & print' vs. 'print and distribute'.

A comprehensive output audit will establish not only direct costs but also indirect and therefore opportunity costs. Indirect costs include waste, administration, time spent by employees on non-core functions, the management overhead of dealing with non-core functions and the cost of employee turnover and temporary staff in areas which may not be managed as efficiently as they should be. Opportunity costs include the effects of equipment downtime, missed deadlines, inferior quality, being over- or under-equipped, and low productivity.

The output audit provides the opportunity to examine an often neglected area of corporate activity yet it is potentially one of the largest in terms of scope for savings and efficiencies.

Containment of risk

A principal objective in auditing is to keep the risk of failure within acceptable bounds. To this end the auditor will concentrate most effort on functions and actions which may be expected have the most serious consequences in the event of failure.

Audit methodology developed for one large international company involves the identification of documents required at every stage of a project and giving them a 'risk rating'. The auditor then categorises each project according to the most important aspects, eg cost, quality, time and then selects for audit the documents which have the highest risk rating relevant to the risk category.

In this way, it is only necessary to 'dip into' parts of projects to keep an eye on the key issues and this, in turn, keeps the people involved in the projects on their toes. In particular, since they know how the system works, they will give special attention to getting the important activities right in case they are selected for audit.

Whereas an audit of accounts will be concerned with the accuracy of the figure the facilities audit is principally concerned with the quality and appropriateness of activities and the documents which normally evidence their completion.

12.1.2 STRATEGIC FACILITIES MANAGEMENT AUDIT CENTRES

The main strategic management areas in which most facilities management auditors can be expected to concentrate their attention are:

- the Intelligent Client Function (ICF)

- facilities policy and value management

- quality and risk management

- task, property, asset and project management

- financial management

- Information and Communication management.

Good management practice is inevitably subjective. So, unless the commission is merely to audit currently agreed procedures, the auditor will have to operate in the 'management consultancy mode'. This entails comparing existing activities with best practice in the consultant's own experience. Effectively this becomes a process review informed by 'best performance' benchmarks.

A case study on such a process is included in the book 'An Introduction to Benchmarking and Justifying the Investment in Facilities'[3] the findings of which are summarised in Fig. 12.1.A.

Fig. 12.1.A
Facilities management efficiency benchmarked to peer range (case study results)

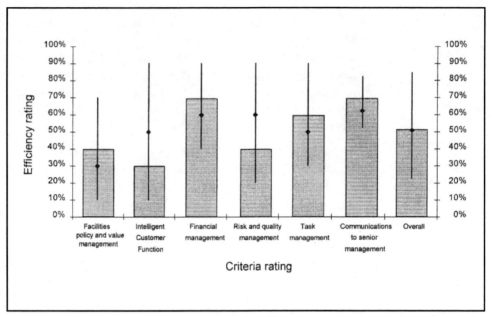

The convention used in this figure wherein client's performance is shown as a histogram and the range of performance is indicated by a vertical bar (with the median shown by the diamond) is used throughout the following chapter on benchmarking.

In this example the criteria were not given a weighting of importance; in practice, it would be difficult to differentiate between them in this respect since failure in any one of them would quickly spell disaster.

[3] Williams, B. (2000) An Introduction to Benchmarking and Justifying the Investment in Facilities, First Ed.,BEB Ltd, Bromley, Kent, UK (CD-Rom also available).

12.2 BENCHMARKING

Introduction

The term 'benchmarking', and it's practice, has been known to industry-at-large since the 1970's.

In Chapter 12.1.1 reference was made to the growing importance of benchmarking as a tool of facilities management consultancy.

This chapter explains what the process is for and different ways in which it can be carried out.

The subject is addressed in greater detail in the book 'An Introduction to Benchmarking Facilities'[1] by the same author.

12.2.1 THE MEANING OF BENCHMARKING

Benchmarking is defined here as 'the process of comparing a product, service, process - indeed any activity or object - with other samples from a peer group, with a view to identifying 'best buy' or 'best practice' and targeting oneself to emulate it'.

The key words here are:

- peer group

- best practice

- emulate.

The '**peer group**' refers to any organisation or unit that is carrying out an activity with similar characteristics or end product to the one to be benchmarked. There is a common fallacy (usually evoked by facilities managers fearful of being exposed by the process) that because no two organisations are similar, comparisons are thereby rendered meaningless. Nothing could be further from the truth; similarity of business function is not an essential factor in selection of a peer group, although organisations are naturally anxious to know where they stand in their own division of the league. This comparison is not, however, the main purpose of benchmarking, for 'best practice' will almost certainly be found in some other unrelated business sector.

Although it can be useful to benchmark to your closest peers - and internal benchmarking within different parts or organisations has a lot of merit - the possibility must always be acknowledged that someone, somewhere, in quite a different sphere may be doing the same sort of thing that you do - and better.

It is the continuing and relentless pursuit of '**best practice**' - 'best-of-breed' or 'best-in-class' as some call it - which is at the root of the benchmarker's philosophy. Having found it, the key to success is to set about '**emulating**' it whether in terms of cost, quality, speed or risk management - all of them if at all possible.

A case study highlighting the mistake of treating benchmarking as a one-off exercise instead of as part of a process of continued improvement within a value management regime is given at 12.2.4.

'Emulate' means 'try to equal or excel'[2] and, as long as the peer group best performer is a high-level achiever, just matching this performance will bring enormous benefits. Of course, the truly zealous will want to improve on the best performance once they have found it, and, indeed upon their own best performance as time goes on. It is

[1] Williams, B (2000) 'An Introduction to Benchmarking Facilities'. BEB Ltd, Bromley, Kent.

[2] The Oxford English Dictionary - (1996), Oxford University Press, Oxford.

much like top athletes who see race records as a benchmark for their progress but who then want to go on creating new records once they have become record holders.

12.2.2 THE SUBJECT AREAS

The whole spectrum of facilities as described in Chapter 1.1.1 - Fig. 1.1.A - can be tested including the facilities management itself (see Chapter 12.1.1) and any systems and processes used in the management.

Benchmarking is not just about costs, although that is a key area and can be the catalyst for a closer examination of performance and processes.

Processes are normally best considered in 'benchmarking clubs' (see 12.2.4) when methodologies can be explained and appraised at first hand. However, where best performance processes have been written up they can either be used for reference by individual organisations or introduced as part of the data considered in a 'benchmarking club' or 'data exchange group'.

It is important to recognise that other companies, or parts of one company, have different processes and regimes for dealing with similar business requirements.

For instance, Fig. 12.2.A examines the space use per capita in local authority departments in the context of the equivalent 'best-of-breed' in the cost-conscious corporate commercial sector.

Fig. 12.2.A
Space standards comparison - local authority and financial services company

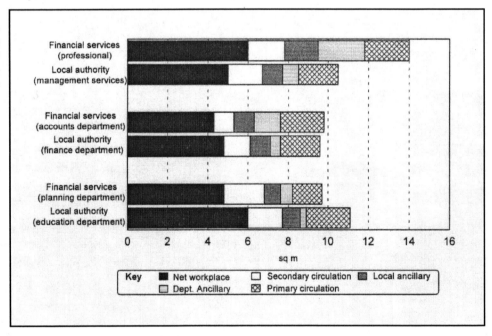

This is a good example of the advantages of looking outside the obvious peer group range, since an inter-authority space comparison might well have produced a high and inefficient common denominator. The way the space is distributed is as meaningful as the total used and should be noted. In the example, the commercial company's financial services (accounts) department uses a little more space than the local authority's finance department but has extra ancillary space, eg meeting rooms, gained mainly at the expense of wasteful secondary circulation. Nevertheless, both departments have more or less similar functional requirements.

Building costs and quality can be benchmarked by experts in the field and in the latter case, as we have seen in Chapter 1.2.4, there are a number of 'scoring' systems which give a definitive statement of quality expressed in numeric terms.

Office services such as stationery, reprographics and the like are usually benchmarked on a cost per capita per full time equivalent (FTE) and cost per item. However in the case of premises services such as cleaning and maintenance the unit of floor area is usually a more appropriate parameter. In all cases, the protocol for classification of the parameter, ie the unit of measurement, and the content of the cost centre, must be clearly stated, eg £ per sq m of gross internal area (GIA) and, (as in say, 'cleaning') to include/exclude pest control and window cleaning.

Then there is the helpdesk. You can, with benefit, benchmark the efficiency and cost of the helpdesk operation itself - some are a lot better than others - as well as analysing and benchmarking the data it produces on response times etc.

In fact the helpdesk data can be of use to contractors as well as users; in one slightly unusual case a firm of contractors recently commissioned an external benchmarking of their own response times and job costs (as calculated via the helpdesk) against the market competitors. In this case they were seeking to renew their contract without re-bidding; although some clients would prefer the 'safety' of re-tendering, good benchmarking to a sufficiently broad and competitive peer group is an excellent substitute for the expensive bidding round, and enables continuity of experience and relationships to be maintained within a market-tested price regime.

Of course, the words 'broad' and 'competitive' are crucial. How can you be sure that you really have found the 'best of breed' in your peer group? Well, that depends on whether the peer group is robust and has been drawn widely enough.

12.2.3 APPROACHES TO BENCHMARKING

As was implied in the definition above, the success of benchmarking depends largely on the ability to identify 'best-buy' or best practice from a peer group.

In practice this can be quite difficult to achieve in the fullest sense, for two main reasons:

- the absolute 'best-of-breed' is only likely to be found in a very large sample

- peers in competition are usually unwilling to divulge their confidential data.

Whatever the subject area - be it cost, quality, process etc - benchmarking may be carried out either to an internal or external peer group or, indeed, both. Whichever route is chosen there are three principal approaches to benchmarking:

- benchmarking clubs

- data exchange groups

- database comparison to proprietary data-base.

Benchmarking club: is an arrangement by which a number of organisations or departments within organisations, come together on a regular basis to compare data and processes with a view to improvement.

Data exchange group: is like a 'club' except that the data is normally circulated to the members without any first-hand exchange of views or information

Proprietary database: certain aspects of facilities management such as costs, service levels and user satisfaction, can be satisfactorily benchmarked to a 'database club' in which the owner of a proprietary data-base brings to the table a set of relevant but anonymous data, drawn from studies carried out on behalf of similar organisations with similar facilities. In selecting the peer group, the database providers use their knowledge of the organisation to be benchmarked to ensure that the peer group is fully represented in the data used for the comparison. Provided the database is large, robust and well-structured the peer group performance should be representative of normal industry standards.

A distinction needs to be drawn between **site-specific** benchmarking where the peer group data is selected for its relevance to the user's specific circumstances (e.g. building type, design, specification, age, size, condition, usage) and **non-specific** where it appears in the form of published results of questionnaires. The latter may only be used for a high level guide to general levels of cost - which is certainly not "benchmarking" in the context of the definition adopted in this text.

12.2.4 BENCHMARKING CLUBS

The pros and cons

Formally assembled 'benchmarking clubs' of an ad hoc or even carefully selected composition are really not much use in assessing best performance cost and quality: they serve mainly to introduce participants to the key issues and variables as a forerunner to a more in-depth and widespread search for the best performers.

In fact the process of accessing the data for benchmarking is usually difficult and, at times, frustrating which is one of the reasons why the benchmarking clubs have, on the whole, had only limited success. The other problems are, however, equally large and frequently insurmountable, some of the major obstacles being:

* small peer group

* inappropriate peer group

* no direct competitors in the peer group (for obvious reasons)

* difficulty of accessing data

* inconsistency of protocol

* matching diary dates

* keeping up enthusiasm

* low priority over other daily activities

* inexperience.

Intra-organisational benchmarking

A 'club' formed from different parts of one organisation may fare better, especially if it comes together in response to high-level pressure to increase efficiency. It is not uncommon in such cases for a relatively low cost 'first-strike' exercise to yield very significant cost savings.

The example at Fig. 12.2.B (over the page) is from an exercise carried out using internal cost data for comparison. The company saved 34% of its total premises operating costs using the simple follow-up technique of examining the operations in the upper and lower quartiles and applying the lessons learned across the whole estate.

Unfortunately the sting in the story is in the tail: the results shown here are actually what was found when a **further** benchmarking study was carried out four years after the first benchmarking study. The company's FM group had changed personnel and the lessons once learned were no longer common knowledge, leading to an insidious process of slipping back into the bad old ways. Once an organisation has been through the first benchmarking exercise the process should become a regular, automatic and integral part of the facilities value management process.

Fig. 12.2.B
Cleaning costs for 120 branches

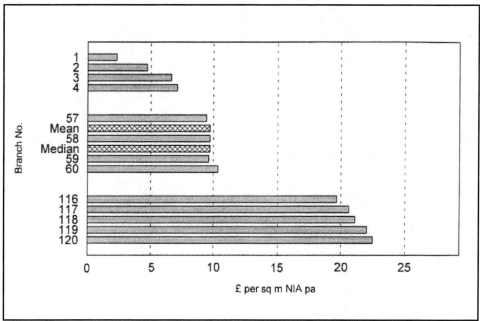

Facilitation

However, whether the peer group is internal, as in the above example, or external the process is unlikely to work unless it is managed by someone with the experience and personality to drive it along. If that person is also a benchmarking specialist then so much the better; failing that the club should have a specialist on the team to guide them through the muddy waters of data access, analysis, interpretation and comparison.

Finding best performance

Clubs, if they work, are an excellent vehicle for in-depth study and development of an understanding of what does, and does not, work. Given the right personalities, ideas can spin off from discussion and all members can find out the best approach by reference to examples of bad, as well as good, practice.

Although the world's best performer may not be found in the club itself, it should be possible to identify the 'cost and quality drivers' and point the participants in the right direction to find that highly sought after 'gold medal' of excellence.

Setting up and running a benchmarking club

Too often clubs are formulated from groups of friends who enjoy each others' company and know that setting up will be easy and the process enjoyable. Of course it should be enjoyable, but great care is needed to ensure that the peer group range is sufficiently diverse to guarantee that individual business sector conventions do not dictate the level of experience and wisdom brought to the table.

Involving a few direct competitors is desirable - and sometimes achievable where the competition is not too commercially fierce; sometimes friendly executives in rival companies exchange non-confidential data for the purposes of improving their own performance within their own organisations.

A good number for a club is seven or eight - the old military comparison is a platoon or squad of a size than can be managed by one person. However, in some cases large benchmarking groups supply data to a central source and then attend seminars and workshops to review findings and processes. As also discussed above the club co-ordinator may - and probably should - be a skilled facilitator with expertise in the subject area. For example, if it is an ICT benchmarking club, a good ICT specialist would be ideal. However, it may be desirable to ensure that such a specialist is independent of any organisations supplying services to any member of the group to avoid any conflict of interest arising; individual personalities and ability may, however, be taken into consideration before rigidly applying the 'independence criterion'.

The facilitator should help to put the club together using knowledge of the market to recommend suitable peers for club membership.

Obviously dates should be set well in advance and rigidly adhered to. Deputies should be nominated to stand by to take the place of the lead delegate from an organisation in the case of unavoidable absence.

It is also very important that those higher up the ladder buy into the process; if the managing director supports it, he or she is less inclined to call the delegate to his or her office for a half-hour meeting at lunchtime on the day the club is meeting in the next city. Such events can, of course, be unavoidable.

It is equally important that anyone else in the organisation who has to make a contribution in terms of providing data, viewing facilities, and so on, is given plenty of warning and briefed as to the following:

- purpose of the exercise

- benefits to the organisation (to the individual as well, if applicable)

- weight of authority behind the venture.

Data collection

In fact, most benchmarking clubs that rely upon the production of data - especially costs and service levels - quickly fall apart when members cannot meet their contribution commitments. Here again, a skilled facilitator should be able to overcome the problem of data-gathering by visiting the struggling companies and helping to get out the essential bulk of the information which (according to Pareto's principle) is contained in merely 20% of the items.

Some 'nearly good' data - appropriately labeled - is better than no 'perfect' data. Its availability should help to avoid would-be strugglers holding up the process and thereby risking loss of enthusiasm amongst those who have complied.

The 'oranges and apples' syndrome

Many people get concerned about the problems of the 'oranges-compared-with-apples' syndrome; this evidences itself both in the context of other organisations having different cultures and in respect of data not following a common protocol in terms of measurement and/or descriptions. An experienced facilitator can easily overcome the latter but the former may require more careful handling.

In practice, seemingly diverse operations may be adjusted to form a basis from which the others can be benchmarked. The very origin of the term 'benchmarking' comes from surveying where a datum point, such as sea level, is used as the plateau from which higher and lower points are accurately established. A point X on a kerb on the roadside may be benchmarked (as in Fig. 12.2.C over the page) and used as the basis for measuring the difference in height first between X and Y, and then between Y and sea level.

The principle to understand here is that, as long as the difference can be properly identified and explained, the relativity of one to the other can be used for comparison. Of course, if either of them is incorrectly measured - or if sea level (zero base) is misinterpreted - the results will be meaningless.

Fig. 12.2.C
The origin of the
term 'benchmarking'

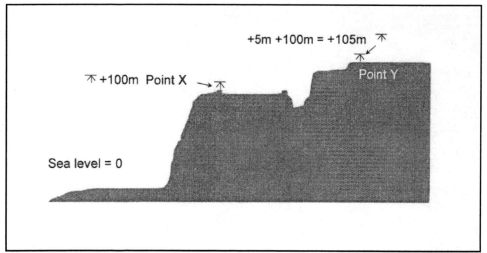

A benchmarking club in operation - a case study

Nowhere was this principle so important as in a club project recently completed in which a small but totally disparate group of organisations came together under a skilled facilitator to benchmark their support services. The nature of the group is shown in Fig.12.2.D.

Fig. 12.2.D
The benchmarking
club members

Organisation	Nature of business / premises
A	Regional headquarters - large heavy goods manufacturer
B	Medium size professional office
C	"Flagship" headquarters of multi-national industrial company
D	Large firm of accountants

The services reviewed were:

- document distribution services
- reprographics and printing
- stationery supplies
- catering
- fleet management
- ICT.

This list was selected by the group at its first meeting when it was also agreed that the best way of getting to grips with these issues was to carry out a 'first-strike' analysis of the costs in each category. Five half-day meetings were arranged with venues rotating between the members. The inaugural meeting was conducted by the facilitator who introduced each cost centre by illustrating the very considerable cost ranges found among data they had gathered from various sources in the course of their consultancy activities.

The group was then tasked to bring to the next meeting their most recent cost data in four of the subject areas, together with the approximate elemental analysis of the cost of each component of the figures and the headcount to which they applied.

No attempt was made to provide a protocol at that time, the reason for this being to make sure that everyone brought along **some** data with which they were familiar; this strategy was to counter the risk that some members might refuse to continue when faced with a seemingly insurmountable first hurdle.

Nevertheless, and not surprisingly, the data was wildly variable and the whole of the first meeting was spent trying to make sense of some apparently ridiculous anomalies. For example, Fig.12.2.E shows the first set of data from the four organisations in respect of the stationery budget.

Fig. 12.2.E
*First comparison
of raw data*

Organisation	Stationery cost (£ per capita)
A	110
B	290
C	365
D	1,095

How could organisation A spend only £110 per capita whilst D spend £1,095 ie nearly 10 times the amount? Much of the differential turned out to be explained by the inevitable mis-analysis or, rather, the term varying analysis is more appropriate: without a standard protocol, who is to say that paper for faxes or printed brochures should be analysed in 'electronic communications' and 'printing' respectively rather than in stationery? And should the headcount relate to seats, or the people sitting on them? Or the number of 'full-time equivalent' people occupying those seats on a job-sharing basis?

In the case of organisation A, the headcount given included 65% who were blue-collar workers who rarely, if ever, used any stationery.

Another key factor in the differentials was that organisation D's stationery costs were calculated simply by the addition of all the year's invoices from the stationery supplier. One of these suppliers also sold office furniture, and Organisation D frequently used that company (rather than their normal furniture supplier) for purchasing occasional special or non-standard items of furniture.

After the necessary adjustments were made between meetings, the figures presented next time still showed differences, but they had narrowed considerably. The next step was to brainstorm the issues to see what the causes of the differences might be and whether they might be justifiable. The cost drivers identified were:

• the business sector

• the success, or otherwise, of the service in each company

• quality of distributed documents

• proportion of non-standard materials

• response times for special items

• proportion of company-specific items, eg letterheads.

The group then set about considering how significant each of these factors might be in terms of their effect upon cost per capita, and then how relevant each was to each organisation. By a process of weighted evaluation they were able to see the relationship between the weighted scores and the cost per capita (see Fig. 12.2.F).

Fig. 12.2.F
*Raw benchmarking
cost data adjusted
for protocol
cost drivers*

Organisation	Stationery cost (£ per capita)	Weighted cost driver scoring
A	200	10
B	270	18
C	310	22
D	660	28

Therefore D's costs could be expected to be 2.8 times A's whereas they were in fact 3.3 times greater (660 ÷ 200).

Given the relatively crude method of assessing the weightings of the resource drivers none of the members could get absolute guidance as to best performance from the results. However, this simple process enabled each of the organisations to come to terms with the general level of their costs in all of the cost centres examined. This small, disparate group could not produce a best-of-breed but, in examining everyone's processes and procedures in great detail, all participants learned a lot more about office services, how to analyse their costs and how to run them effectively.

The process of seeking data without first establishing a protocol would not normally be recommended in this more advanced day and age. However, in this case study of a small group, given the pre-identified problems of data gathering, it worked well by enabling the club to get going and maintain its momentum.

Principal benefits

Benchmarking clubs can be interesting and enjoyable and are a frequent source of new-found and beneficial business relationships. They will never satisfactorily take the place of a good database club when it comes to assessing costs and service levels but, as a means of improving one's knowledge of facilities services and systems and how to delivery them more effectively, they can be a worthwhile investment, albeit of a considerable amount of time and money.

12.2.5 DATA EXCHANGE GROUPS

Purpose and operation

A Data Exchange Group (DEG) consists of a number of organisations that get together under a facilitator - normally an academic centre or specialist consultancy - to provide and receive benchmark data on costs and performance of facilities.

Information is provided to the facilitator by questionnaire (sometimes via the internet - see later). The facilitator processes the data and distributes the results by way of reports at agreed intervals.

The protocol by which the data is to be presented is given to each of the group members who do their best to comply. Normally the facilitator will carry out some audit checks on the validity of data, maybe using specialist knowledge or experience of facilities costs or performance to identify data which looks to be suspect.

Some DEGs organise workshops to review the findings and/or explore the data and the processes underlying the results. To this extent they act as benchmarking clubs, although the opportunities to verify the data in depth are limited by the size of the groups and the numbers and experience of the organiser's resource.

In their most basic form DEG's merely facilitate the exchange of un-audited, almost certainly unusable, data which should carry a business health warning - little or no better than similar data contained in most of the reference works available over the bookshop counter. However, at their best DEG's can help the assembly of realistic data on levels of cost and performance - albeit generally still lacking any adjustments or guidance in respect of **site-specific** resource drivers (see 12.2.3 above).

Accuracy of data

Data submitted on questionnaire is notoriously unreliable even where the protocol is quite clearly stated. So, unless the facilitator gathers the data direct - or audits extensively - the chances of it being even reasonably accurate are quite small. A recent case study on pan-European benchmarking within one organisation (pseudonym

'Pepco' here) showed the following disparities in area and costs measurement between the questionnaire returns and the expert facilitator's personally collated data. The disturbing results are given in Figs. 12.2.G and 12.2.H.

Fig. 12.2.G
Pepco floor areas - as submitted and actual

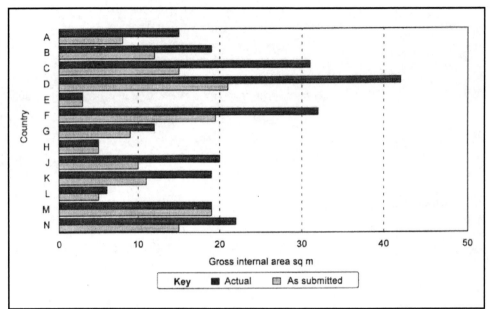

Fig. 12.2.H
Pepco occupancy costs - as submitted and actual

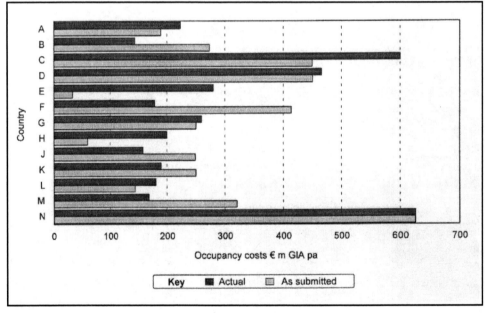

The Building Cost Information Service (BCIS) in the UK includes data on capital costs of a very large number of building types which is used extensively as a basis for cost planning new projects.

The BCIS is probably the world's most successful data-collection service, but the reason for its success lies in the fact that:

- the data is produced by specialist cost consultants, ie quantity surveyors rather than their clients

- the protocol is familiar to all quantity surveyors who use it daily in their role as cost consultants

- the costs at tender are analysed automatically and accurately into the protocol as part of the cost/control procurement procedures.

Compare this situation to that in facilities management where there is (as yet):

- no comparable professional facilities management cost discipline

- no generally accepted standard protocol

- very little attempt at sophisticated cost control of facilities within organisations.

Consequently good facilities data is not automatically available for distribution in clubs and groups and they often flounder due to lack of confidence in the results.

12.2.6 DATABASE BENCHMARKING

Composition of databases

Certain independent specialist companies offer the database approach utilising consistently analysed and 'cleansed' facilities data. Such databases, to be of any value, must include costs, service levels, user-satisfaction levels, space standards and management structures. Using a database, a specialist may form 'instant benchmarking clubs' for each service or facilities feature a client wishes to appraise.

The system relies on the specialist's knowledge of the database - and the facilities regimes of the organisations in it - because when comparative data is put on the table it is anonymous and the client has to trust the specialist to assemble appropriate comparables.

Good data has the considerable merit of having been unscrambled to conform with a classification and measurement protocol so that, not only are all the oranges compared with oranges, but the parameters - eg per capita, per sq m of net internal area - have all been professionally measured on a common basis before the data to which they have been applied gets into the database.

Using a database

The use of a specialist's proprietary database to form a peer group is a quite different concept from a physical benchmarking club in many respects, notably that in the former (given good practice):

- sources of data are completely anonymous

- all peer group data will have been professionally adapted to a set protocol

- all the subject company's data will be re-analysed to the same protocol

- the peer group can be widely drawn numerically and culturally

- the process is quick and thorough.

The problem facing the client is how to know that the proprietary database is valid and/or that the specialists really do know their business. So many firms have been jumping on this particular bandwagon - including management consultants, contractors and facilities consultants - that only by taking thorough references can the client be reasonably sure of making the right appointment.

A major obstacle to successful benchmarking is the 'skewing' of data in the direction of one particular sector or organisation or one service provider. Skewing is as likely to be a feature of a proprietary data-base as it is in an introspective benchmarking club or data exchange group so due diligence on sources of data provided by 'specialists' is strongly recommended.

Offers by contractors to benchmark without charge in the hope of being invited to bid to take over and improve the facilities management operation should be treated with great caution. They may only have their own managed facilities in the peer group and, in any case, may have a vested interest in showing up the user's data in a poor light. Many are trustworthy and know what they are about but the presence of a good number of less reliable operators makes selection difficult and risky.

The client should ask to inspect the peer group data, albeit anonymised, and reserve the right to ask for samples of specific data to be verified.

The use of a good proprietary database is the only way to get a large trawl of peer group data which is both reliable in terms of quality and integrity and relevant in terms of best performance. Nevertheless it does not immediately afford the opportunity to explore the processes underpinning best performance results; this is only possible where the consultant is able to use knowledge of the data to either describe the processes or introduce the client personally to the organisation(s) carrying out the best performance operations.

The proprietary database approach is particularly useful when it comes to benchmarking the costs and quality of facilities services and accommodation.

'First-strike' benchmarking

A simple illustration of the sort of information presented to a client using this conventional database benchmarking procedure is given at Fig. 12.2.J which compares the cost and comparable levels of user satisfaction of an organisation's reprographics service with a database peer group.

Fig. 12.2.J
First strike cost and performance benchmarking - reprographics service

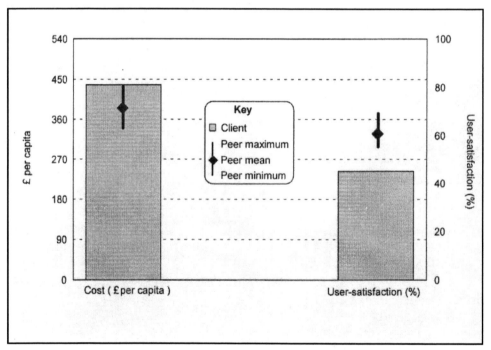

At this stage absolute accuracy, of course, is neither possible nor necessary; this 'high level' comparison is what is called a 'First Strike' benchmarking study, the purpose of which is merely to highlight any results which are abnormal and to see if anything needs a more careful and detailed study. Often these results do not surprise the clients - indeed they may already be vaguely aware of the causes and any special circumstances but lack the 'hard' information needed to enable positive steps to be taken.

In this case, the exercise shows clearly that the client is paying a high price for the service whilst, at the same time, the users do not think too highly of its quality. The comparison does depend heavily on the presenter's knowledge and expertise and, in practice, an experienced benchmarking specialist has the comparables fairly well established in his or her head - much like a professional cost consultant giving a building cost estimate in £ per sq m of gross floor area based on experience from extensive involvement in cost control of similar projects. But the existence of the database is a comfort, and the client can interrogate the presenter on the anonymised database and also be given details of the kinds of organisations in the peer group range.

Variable data-drivers

The variables surrounding the data in Fig.12.2.J and how the apple-cart could be upset (spilling all the oranges of course!) by tripping-up in the analysis should now be considered. Among the questions that need to be asked are:

- is the peer group truly comparable in terms of usage?

- do the actual costs include the photocopy paper (most usually found in the stationery bill)?

- is VAT included?

- are there any distribution costs from a reprographics centre?

- are there any external contracts?

- is any equipment owned? If so, is the depreciation included?

- what proportion of reproduction is carried out directly from computers?

- when does reprographics become short-run printing and is that an issue here?

- is the 'per capita' calculation based on full-time equivalent or payroll and does it include site-based contractors?

- are the survey questionnaires on which the client satisfaction levels are assessed on a comparable basis to those forming the peer group?

This is by no means an exhaustive list but it does serve to highlight the pitfalls and explain the nonsense results that can come out if there is even one misconception amongst all these issues.

Budget preparation

Database benchmarking like this has become an increasingly used tool in development of life-cycle budgets for single-point responsibility projects - as also in due diligence on the results. In this connection, however, the need for a more scientific approach to cost forecasting is apparent given the long-term nature of the commitments.

12.2.7 BENCHMARKING COSTS

Peer group comparables

It is important to recognise that, in drawing up peer group comparables, there is considerable dependence upon the need for a thorough knowledge of the quality achieved in each case, together with any particular features which drive the costs up or down. For example, a new or refurbished air-conditioning system should require less maintenance than one in mid-life crisis, and the maintenance strategy, eg planned preventative maintenance, condition-based, or 'emergency only' will also have a major impact on costs (and, of course, on performance and value as well). Again, buildings with a high window to floor area ratio will have window cleaning costs well above the norm when these are reduced to £ per sq m of floor area.

A good facilitator will quickly pick out any abnormal costs, many of which may be the result of the 'oranges and apples' syndrome, while others may be explained by special cost drivers. Where obviously and unexpectedly abnormal costs are highlighted in the course of the study, and antidotes recommended, it is quite normal for the relevant facilities manager to have the remedies up and running and the cure under way long before the final report lands on the chairman's desk. In spite of what the cynics say, it is actually most unusual for a facilities manager to be criticised for having found a better and more cost-effective way of carrying out a hitherto inefficient activity. More likely they will get a pat on the back and a good note on the staff record sheet.

Typical cost ranges

There are numerous examples of typical cost ranges throughout the text, in particular in Sections 5 to 8 dealing with costs of facilities services and projects. Such costs can, of course, only be used as very high level indicators of the ranges of costs applicable to a cost centre, and using them to benchmark costs (using the definition of benchmarking adopted throughout this text) for specific sites is not a worthwhile exercise - indeed it will probably be quite misleading.

Cost benchmarking models

One program available under licence[1] models a large database and, by use of carefully weighted resource driver factors, is able to predict, with a high level of reliability, the appropriate benchmarked market price for any given facilities service on any site in any given set of operating circumstances.

At the time of publication this model is being developed as an interactive web-site offering site-specific cost and quality benchmarks in all EU countries and N.America via the internet.

The importance of protocol

Databases which are reliably constructed usually derive from data compiled during one-to-one benchmarking studies or facilitated benchmarking clubs where there is the opportunity to challenge the validity of the data at first-hand.

It is absolutely critical for the benchmarker to compare like with like when considering an organisation's costs against peer group data. Sometimes an initial difference between the client's costs and the benchmark will show up an area for closer scrutiny; such scrutiny will often pick up mis-analysis as the source of the apparent problem.

An example of mis-analysis distorting the figures is shown at Fig. 12.2.K (over the page). Here the processes of upgrading and 'churn' (See Chapter 4.2), being carried out by an in-house building maintenance unit, were merged under the heading of maintenance. To make matters worse, in this example maintenance of the services was accounted for under 'engineers' so a further sizeable adjustment to the maintenance costs had to be made before proper benchmarking could begin.

Not only were the figures misleading to the benchmarker, they were also misleading to the business management who did not appreciate the obsolescence and 'churn rate' being concealed under the maintenance category nor the actual cost of the true maintenance overall. Of course, since the cost centre had not previously been benchmarked they were not aware that a problem even existed.

Space definitions

Equally, the measurement of space must be in accordance with known and accepted rules. The authors' definitions of space are given in Chapter 4.1.

Using the wrongly defined parameter or, worse still, committing the cardinal crime of not stating precisely the parameter being used, can cause very serious errors.

---

[1] The Frisque (Facilities Risk and Quality Evaluation) suite of programs. (BWA Facilities Consultancy).

Fig. 12.2.K
_Incorrect analysis -
upgrading and
'churn' disguised as
maintenance_

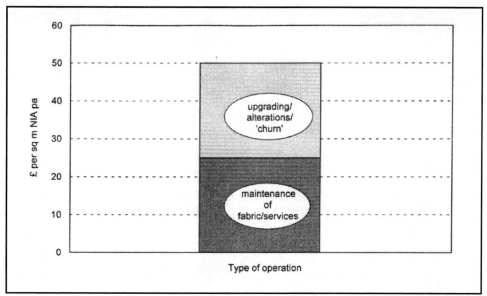

No-one, whether user, contractor or consultant, must ever use the term square metres (sq m) without qualifying it appropriately, eg gross internal area, net internal (lettable) area, net occupiable area. To see how misleading the misinterpretation of the data can be, refer to Fig. 12.2.L which shows how the cost of maintenance of services will vary per unit of area depending on the choice of parameter. It should also be note that, in this case, one of the figures includes VAT and the other does not - a further opportunity for mis-information to win the day.

Fig. 12.2.L
_Effect of parameters
on level of cost
expressed_

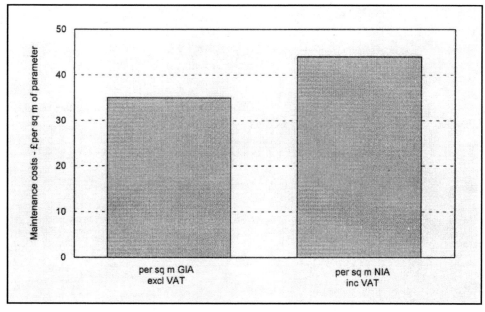

For most cost centres it does not particularly matter whether the gross or net internal area is used - so long as the user specifically states the denomination of sq m being used as the divisor.

Headcount

All facilities costs can be usefully apportioned to the number of people using them and in many cases that is the only meaningful parameter. However, there are two main pitfalls here:

- measuring the numbers

- assessing who uses what facilities.

In the former case it is important to know whether the headcount is:

- personnel directly employed
- FTE's, ie the number of full-time jobs including only relevant proportions of part-time or shift workers
- designed occupancy, ie workplaces
- whether contractors resident on site are included
- whether visitors are included.

Sometimes the numbers of people actually using a facility can be equally, if not more, useful as an indicator than the total headcount. So, for instance, the average number of people using the catering service may be the best parameter for expressing cost, with this number, in turn, being expressed as a ratio of diners: total headcount.

The possible range of headcount statistics on any one site depending upon the measurement protocol is enormous and, clearly, any failure to specify what 'per capita' means is as dangerous as giving sq m without saying that sort of sq m they are.

The cost per capita or per unit of area can be misinterpreted by up to 30% or so even in normal circumstances; if the recipient of the information makes the wrong assumption as to the inclusion or otherwise of VAT - not to mention the classification protocol itself - it is very clear how errors or differences of the magnitude of those shown in Figs 12.2.E, G, H, K and L might occur. It is a very good example of how benchmarking could be a very blunt and maybe damaging tool in inexperienced hands.

For this reason the practice of taking cross-references to costs per sq m or per capita either from published data, by anecdote or via exchange groups unsupported by specialists is to be avoided at all costs.

Using the comparators

Whatever parameters are chosen, the resulting benchmark still needs to be interpreted in the context of every factor bearing upon it.

The example at Fig. 12.2.M illustrates the simple fact that the operating costs per unit of floor area will rise as the density increases but that the cost per capita of the same cost centres will fall.

Fig. 12.2.M
Effect of varying density of space use on operating costs per capita and per unit of floor area

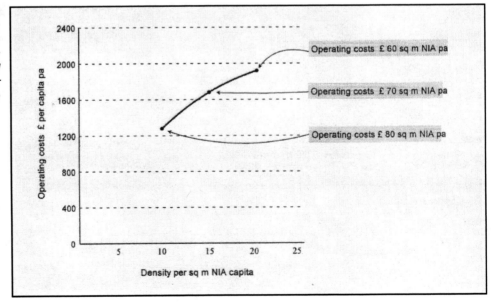

If the operating costs **alone** were being benchmarked on a per capita basis the point might well be missed that the improved space use would have a much more dramatic impact on the total premises costs per capita once the rent/taxes etc come into the equation - see Fig.12.2.N - and note that this is to a much smaller scale than Fig.12.2.M.

Fig. 12.2.N
Effect of density on premises costs per capita

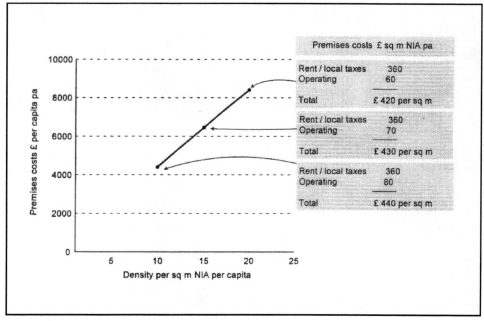

12.2.8 BENCHMARKING QUALITY

Overcoming subjectivity

Experienced facilities managers and consultants believe they have a reasonably good idea about what constitutes good, bad or indifferent quality in terms of buildings or service levels. On the other hand, the appropriateness - or otherwise - of one level or another in terms of benefit to the business is likely to be the source of major divergences of opinion. (Quality management is discussed in detail in Chapter 2.4.)

Generally speaking most people in facilities will try to incorporate the highest quality available within their budgets, and usually complain bitterly when financial constraints prevent them from achieving their total objectives.

One way of addressing this dilemma is by benchmarking quality. In the process it is necessary to recognise that, whereas costs are absolutely definitive, quality can be highly subjective.

As was explained earlier quality has many connotations, and methods of assessing it are also many and varied.

Input and Output

The key issue to consider is the relationship between input quality and output quality; in the context of facilities the input quality relates to service levels and the output quality relates to functional performance.

As previously discussed, benchmarking is a key ingredient in the process of value engineering, an important component of which (as has been defined in Chapter 2.2.3) is the 'elimination of redundant performance and attendant extra costs', ie avoidance of the provision of resources greater than required for the purpose.

The difficulty is in trying to determine what service level is appropriate to achieve a given output performance - or, indeed, what output performance is required in any given set of circumstances? Unless these questions can be answered satisfactorily the facilities manager can compare quality but not benchmark it to best performance and so cannot begin to value engineer solutions.

Measuring quality

To some extent quality, like beauty, is in the eye of the beholder - at least in respect of the usefulness of the end product where opinion varies significantly from one standpoint to another. So, how can facilities managers get back to some common denominator by which they can objectively assess and compare the performance of facilities? It is suggested that there are four ways of doing this, each of which is valid in its own right in the context in which it is applied - however, none of them is, of itself, a sole indicator by which to evaluate and compare results. The techniques are:

- user satisfaction surveys

- indexing output performance (a measure of the functional performance)

- indexing service levels (a measure of the specified input of resources)

- service level performance indicators (measures of service levels delivered).

Benchmarking user satisfaction

In facilities terms, the adage about the customer always being right is not totally applicable; however in some respects any user dissatisfaction at the quality of service, however misconceived in terms of the business requirement, may yet cause a loss of enthusiasm for the job and/or for the employing organisation resulting in losses in productivity.

Most organisations carry out user-satisfaction surveys in one form or another and the results are usually beneficial, if only as an internal guide to where things need to be improved. Once carried out, surveys should be repeated at regular intervals in the same format so as to enable tracking of changes in the users' views - often in response to changed levels of quality of services provided.

To be successful external benchmarking is dependent upon everyone's questions being the same, eg 'Are you satisfied with the catering facilities?' is a lot different from 'how satisfied are you with the catering facilities?' Both questions need to be read in the context of the level of importance attached to the services across and between the peer group.

The FacQual program[2] is based on a simple format of standard questions, see Fig. 12.2.P (over the page), the answers to which respondents select from a choice of cartoon-like facial expressions indicating varying degrees of satisfaction with each service. They also state how important each of the services is to them personally on a scale of 0 to 5.

The size and distribution of the sample is obviously important, and the FacQual program follows strict guidelines in terms of these factors. Interestingly, however, results from a very large number of surveys in many and varied organisations suggest that a small sample, carefully distributed, will always mirror very accurately the views of the whole organisation. Furthermore, the consensus view of relative importance is surprisingly consistent, the odd anomaly being caused by local issues, eg car-parking facilities being more important in out-of-town locations.

Fig. 12.2.Q (over the page) shows how the levels of user-satisfaction and cost for one service can be compared across an estate.

---

[2] Facilities and Quality Evaluation Program, BWA Facilities Consultancy.

Fig. 12.2.P
*Extract from user -
satisfaction survey*

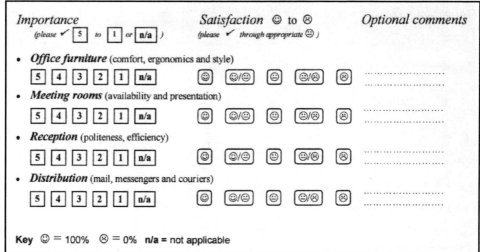

Fig. 12.2.Q
*Comparison
between
expenditure and
user-satisfaction*

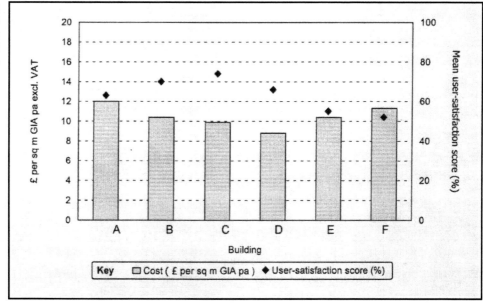

Figure 12.2.R shows how such data (with each service weighted according to the average of the levels of importance recorded in each centre) can be converted into a peer group index of overall weighted customer satisfaction. Building B produced the best figures and, on analysis, was found to be costing the least!

Fig. 12.2.R
*Summary of overall
weighted
satisfaction scores*

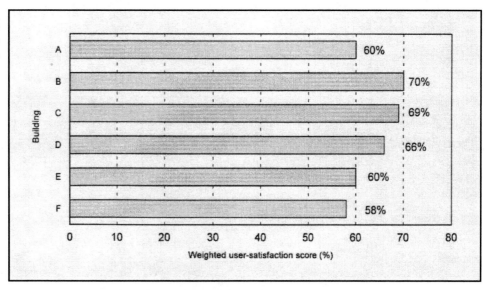

Such an internal 'best-of-breed' result can be a good benchmark to assist in the 'improvement' process but is still short of the benefits of an external benchmarking assessment which should provide best performance targets from a wide peer-group range. An example of this process from FacQual at Fig.12.2.S shows the external peer group comparison of user satisfaction.

Fig. 12.2.S
External peer group comparison of user-satisfaction

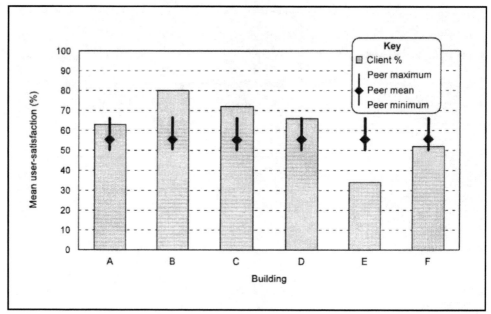

Methods of benchmarking building quality have been discussed in Chapters 1.2.4, 2.4.2 and 9.1.3.

12.2.9 BENCHMARKING CONTRACTOR PERFORMANCE

Benchmarking can be used at any stage of facilities management and by any one of the contributors. Reference was made earlier to a case study involving benchmarking the whole function of the internal facilities management team.

Fig. 12.2.T
Benchmarking cost of 'small' maintenance works

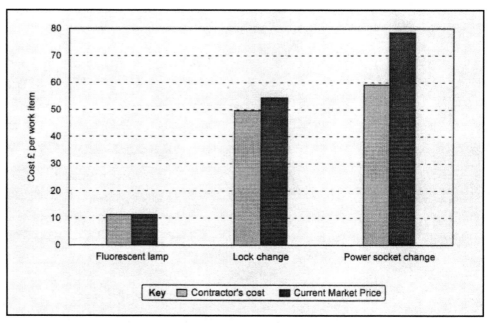

In another case study a contractor, seeking to re-negotiate an outsourced contract rather than have to re-bid (an unsatisfactory option for the client if the contractor is doing a good job), went to the trouble of having the task operations benchmarked by an external consultant.

'Response-and-fix' times for maintenance work for example were laid down and 'actual' versus 'target' regularly monitored to ensure that the high level strategy was protected. The helpdesk system made this monitoring process much easier by providing full details of facilities operations. Fig. 12.2.T shows that the average cost of carrying-out a sample of standard operations was at, or below, the norm. This was one of a number of benchmarking tests which gave the contractor the information needed for what was to be a successful request to the client to negotiate a contract extension.

12.2.10 THE FUTURE FOR BENCHMARKING FACILITIES

Benchmarking has been described as a 'key tool of value management' and, as such, it will not disappear from use however sophisticated facilities management may become in future years.

However, as was indicated in 12.2.7 and 12.2.8 the tools with which to develop and analyse peer group data in respect of cost and performance are themselves becoming more and more sophisticated.

The benchmarking will be better - and so will the value of the facilities. And that, in essence, is what facilities economics is all about.

PART G

Appendices

Appendix 1 Professional Associations and Educational and Research Institutions

International bodies

EuroFM   The EuroFM network embraces a large number of research and educational establishments in the EU member states and elsewhere in Europe.

IFMA   The International Facilities Management Association (IFMA) is well established in the USA and now has several chapters operating in the EU member states.

Facilities management - national associations

British Institute for Facilities Management (BIFM)

Institute of Value Management (IVM)

Royal Institution of Chartered Surveyors (RICS)

Facilities management - educational institutions

Anglia Polytechnic University, Chelmsford

Bell College of Technology, Hamilton

Bournemouth University

College of Estate Management, Reading

Heriot-Watt University, Edinburgh

Highbury College, Portsmouth

Institute of Administrative Management, Orpington

Leeds College of Building

Leeds Metropolitan University

Middlesex University and the College of North East London

Napier University

Nescot, Epsom

Newham College of Further Education, London

Nottingham Trent University

Sheffield Hallam University, Sheffield

South Bank University, London

Staffordshire University, Stoke-on-Trent

The City University, London

University College London (UCL)

University College, Scarborough

University of Central England, Birmingham

University of Greenwich, London

University of Humberside, Hull

Universtiy of Luton

University of Reading

University of the West of England, Bristol

University of Westminster, London

Facilities management - research institutions

Centre for Facilities Management

Building Research Establishment

Building Services Research and Information Association

Construction Industry Research and Information Association

Economic and Social Research Council

RICS Research Foundation

Appendix 2 Tables of Enactments and of Standards and Guidelines

Tables of Enactments

Appendix 3 Table of Figures

Appendix 4 Abbreviations

AE   annual equivalent
AIM   Alternative Investment Market
approx   approximately
ASF   anti-shatter film
Aug   August

B2B   business to business
BALI   British Association of Landscape
            Industries
BBRI   Belgian Building Research Institute
BCIS   Building Costs Information Service
BEMS   building energy management systems
Bn   billion
BOD   biochemical oxygen demand
BPEO   Best Practical Environmental Option
BQA   building quality assessment
BS   British Standard
BSC   balanced scorecard
BSI   British Standards Institute
BQA   building quality assessment

CABS   Centre for Ageing and Biographical
            Studies
CAD   computer aided drafting or design
CAFIM   computer aided facilities information
            management systems
CAFMS   computer aided facilities management
            systems
CAFOM   computer aided facilities operational
            management systems
CAT5   computer cable (colloquiallism)
CBI   Confederate of British Industry, The
CDROM   compact disk read only memory
CEN   European Committee for Standardisation,
CFI   Court of First Instance
CHD   coronary heart disease
CHP   combined heat and power
CIBA   Continental Intelligent Buildings
            Association
CITC   community investment tax credit
CLI   calling line identification
CMS   content management system
COD   chemical oxygen demand
COM   computer output microfilm
CPA   critical path analysis
CPM   critical path method
CRD   central reprographic department
CRT   cathode ray tube
CSF   Critical Success Factors

DCF   discounted cash flow
DDI   direct dial in
DEBS   Design Economics for Building Services in
            Offices
Dec   December
DECT   digital enhanced cordless telephone
DEFRA   Department of Environment, Food and
            Rural Affairs
DEG   Data Exchange Group
DIN   Deutsches Institut für Normung e.V.
DIP   document image processing
DQI   design quality index
DRC   Depreciated Replacement Cost
DVDROM   digital versatile disk read only memory
dwg   drawing

€   euro/euros
eFIG   European Federation of Interior Landscape
            Groups
E-FM   the Internet and facilities management
EBRD   European Bank of Reconstruction and
            Development
EC   1. European Commission
            2. European Community
ECB   European Central Bank
ECDG   European Commission Directorate
            General
ECJ   European Court of Justice
EDI   electronic data interchange
EDM   electronic data/document management
EEC   European Economic Community
EFMA   European Facilities Management
            Association
eg   for example
EIB   European Investment Bank
EIBG   European Intelligent Buildings Group
EIIM   electronic information and image
            management
ELI   employer liability insurance
ELV   end of life vehicle
EMLV   European Mortgage Lending Value
EMS   environmental management system
EN   European Normalisation
EPA90   Environmental Protection Act 1990
EQF   element quantity ratio factor
EU   European Union
EUR   element unit rate
EVS   European Valuation Standards

EU	European Union	ISO	International Organisation for Standardisation
excl	exclusive		
EZ	enterprise zone	ISP	internet service provider
		IT	information technology
FacQual	Facilities quality benchmarking program	IVM	Institute of Value Management
FAST	Functional Analysis System Technique	IVSC	International Valuation Standards Committee
FFI	Fitness for Industry		
FIMS	Facilities Information Management System		
FM	facilities management	K/k	thousands
FTE	full time equivalent	Kbps	Kilobytes per second
		KC	Knight Cornell factor
GDP	gross domestic product	KPI	key performance indicator
GEA	gross external area	KVA	Kilovolts per annum
GIA	gross internal area	kWh	kiloWatt hours
GIFA	gross internal floor area		
GN	Guidance Note	LAN	local area network
GOA	gross outside area	LCA	life cycle analysis
GPRS	general packet radio service	LCR	land condition report
GPT	green transport plan	LDl	low density liptoprotein
gsm	grams per square meter	LGFA	Local Government Finance Act
		Ltd	Limited
HAPM	Housing Association Property Mutual/Manual		
		m	metres
HAZOP	hazard and operability study	M	million
HDD	hard disk drive	Mb	Megabytes
HDL	high density liptoprotein	Mbs	Megabytes per second
HMC&E	Her Majesty's Customs and Excise	MEP	Member of the European Parliament
HPD	hearing protection device	MFD	multi-functional devices
HQ	headquarters	Mhz	Megahertz
HVAC	heating ventilation and air conitioning	MLV	mortgage lending value
		MMI	man-machine interface
i	Interest earned by □1 in one year at a given rate of interest percent (R)	NAIR	national arrangements for incidents involving radioactivity
IBMS	integrated building management system		
ICF	informed/intelligent client function	NATO	North Atlantic Treaty Organisation
ICT	information and communication technology	NEN	Norm (or standards) (The Netherlands)
		nga	net grant-equivalent
ie	that is	NIA	net internal area
IED	improvised explosive device	NLA	net lettable area
IEMA	Institute of Environmental Managers and Assessors	NNDRM	national non-domestic rating multiplier
		Nov	November
IFMA	International Facilities Management Association	NOA	net occupiable area
		NPV	net present value
IHT	inheritance tax	NRA	net rental area
inc	inclusive	NUS	net useable area
IOS	International Organisation for Standardisation		
		OECD	Organisation for Economic Co-operation and Development
IP	internet protocol		
IRR	internal rate of return	OH and P	overheads and profit
ISDN	Integrated Services Digital Network	OIS	optical information system

OJ	Official Journal		SMDS	switched multi-rate data service
OJEC	(Supplement to) the Official Journal of the European Communities		SMM	Standard Method of Measurement
			SOR	statement of requirements
			sq	square
pa	per annum		SSAP	Statement of Standard Accounting Practice
PABX	private automatic branch exchange			
pc	personal computer		TEGoVA	European Group of Valuers' Associations
PC	prime cost		TFT	thin film transistor
PDA	personal digital assistant		TQM	total quality management
Perp	perpetuity		TUPE	Transfer of Undertakings (Protection of Employment) (Regulations 1981)
PERT	program evaluation review technique			
PFI	Private Finance Initiative		TV	television
PI's	performance indicators			
PII	professional indemnity insurance		UBR	uniform business rate
PLI	public liability insurance		UK	United Kingdom
PPE	personal protective equipment		.uk	domain name "suffix" for the United Kingdom
PPG	planning policy guidance			
PPM	planned preventive management		UMTS	universal mobile telephone service
PPP	1. Purchasing Power Parity		UNCTAD	United Nations Conference on Trade and Development
	2. Public Private Partnership			
PR	public relations		UPS	uninterrupted power supply
PSTN	public switched telephone network		USA	United States of America
PTPT	point-to-point-tunnelling (protocol)		UWWTD	Urban Waste Water Treatment Directive
QA	quality assurance		VAT	Value Added Tax
QMF	quality managed facilities		VAV	variable air volume
			VDU	visual display unit
R	rate of interest, being amount earned by £100 in one year		VM	value management
			VOIP	voice over internet protocol
R&D	research and development		VPN	virtual private network
RDA	regional development agency			
reg	Regulations		WAN	wide area network
Reval	revaluation		WAP	wireless application protocol
RICS	Royal Institution of Chartered Surveyors		WBS	work breakdown structure
RoI	return on investment		WORM	write once read many
RSA	regional selective assistance		WPL	workplace parking levy
RV	rateable value		WC/wc	water closet
			WDV	written down value
SAP	Standard Accounting Practice			
SBS	sick building syndrome		YP	years purchase
SDRT	stamp duty reserve tax			
SECO	Synthetic Environment and Modelling and Simulation (UK MoD Co-ordination office)		%	percent/percentage
SEPA	Scottish Environmental Protection Agency			
Sept	September			
SIA	Security Industry Authority			
SKr	Swedish Krona			
SLA	service level agreement			
SLC	service level commitment			

PART H

Indexes

Amplified Contents Index

PART C SUPPORT SERVICES

taxation, Consumption taxation, Environmental taxation.

11.1.5 CONFIGURATION OF ORGANISATION FOR TAXES

11.1.6 EXPENDITURE ON PROPERTY

11.1.7 MANAGEMENT OF TAXATION: Government, Executive, Court action and appeals, Tax year.

CHAPTER 11.2   CORPORATION TAX AND INCOME TAX: Introduction.

11.2.1 SOURCES OF INCOME: Schedules of income taxation assessment, Taxpayers.

11.2.2 RATES OF INCOME TAXATION

11.2.3 EXEMPTIONS AND RELIEFS

11.2.4 DEDUCTIONS IN RESPECT OF REVENUE EXPENDITURE

11.2.5 CAPITAL ALLOWANCES: Government policy, Nature and amounts of capital allowances, Corporation tax planning, Disposals.

CHAPTER 11.3   CAPITAL TAXES: Introduction.

11.3.1 CAPITAL GAINS TAX: Brief History, Taxpayers and non-taxpayers, Disposals, Date of disposal, Exemptions and reliefs, Computations, Taxes interaction.

11.3.2 INHERTITANCE TAX (IHT): Brief History, Facilities manager and IHT, Taxable estate, Exemptions and reliefs, Tax planning.

11.3.3 STAMP DUTY: Shares, Land and Buildings, Leases, Exemptions, reliefs and tax mitigation, Stamp Duty Reserve Tax (SDRT), New proposals.

CHAPTER 11.4   ENVIRONMENTAL TAXATION: Introduction.

11.4.1 ENERGY TAXATION: Fuel taxation.

11.4.2 HEALTH TAXATION

11.4.3 POLLUTION TAXATION

11.4.4 TRANSPORTATION TAXATION

11.4.5 DISADVANTAGED AREAS

CHAPTER 11.5   VALUE ADDED TAX (VAT): Introduction.

11.5.1 VAT AND THE FACILITIES MANAGER

11.5.2 GENERAL PRINCIPLES OF VAT: Taxable persons, Input tax and output tax, VAT returns and payments, Recovery of VAT, Kinds of rates and exemption, Listed buildings and monuments etc, Exempt supplies, Lower rate, Treatment in account and in taxation, Taxes interaction, Recovery of overpaid VAT, Incorrect certificates as to zero rating etc, 'Capital goods' scheme.

11.5.3 RELEVANT SUPPLIES: Disposal of interests in land and buildings,

Key Words Index

A

C

D

E

F

G

H

I

O

P

Q

S

T

U

V

W

Z

Y